ENCYCLOPEDIA OF
NEW VENTURE
MANAGEMENT

Contents

List of Entries

Reader's Guide

Corporate Entrepreneurship

Championing Corporate Ventures
Change Management: Corporate
Corporate Entrepreneurship and Innovation
Corporate Venturing
Crisis Management: Corporate
New Product Development

Entrepreneurial Characteristics and Skills

Accounting
Agility and Rapid Response
Business Plans
Championing New Ventures
Cognition
Commitment and Persistence
Competitive Intelligence
Creativity
Credentials
Entrepreneurial Orientation
Knowledge
Learning
Negotiating Strategies
Networks
Obstacle Identification
Passion
Risk Management
Selling Products and Services
Time Management

Entrepreneurial Decision Making

Business Failure
Change
Cognition in Experts and Novices
Communication Styles
Discovery and Exploitation
Emotions

Intentions
Locus of Control
Overconfidence
Planning Fallacy
Tolerance for Failure

Entrepreneurial Leadership and Human Resources

Goal Setting
Human Resource Strategy
Labor Costs
Labor-Management Relations in Start-Ups
Leadership
Leadership: Training and Development
Leadership: Transformational
Managing Human and Social Capital
Team Composition
Women's Entrepreneurship
Work-Life Balance

Entrepreneurial Marketing

Advertising
Business-to-Business Marketing
Competition
Contextual Marketing
Customer Orientation
E-Commerce
Entrepreneurial Marketing
Focus Groups
Licensing
Market Evaluation
Market Orientation
Positioning a New Product or Service
Retailing
Target Markets
Test Markets
Wholesale Markets

Entrepreneurial Opportunity and Education

Creativity and Opportunities
Entrepreneurship Education: Graduate
    Programs
Entrepreneurship Education: High School
Entrepreneurship Education: Undergraduate
    Programs
Entrepreneurship Pedagogy
Ethics
Master of Business Administration
Opportunity Development
Opportunity Identification and Structural
    Alignment
Opportunity Recognition
Opportunity Sources
Search-Based Discovery
Start-Up Teams
Systematic Search

Entrepreneurs: Biographies and Case Studies

Entrepreneurs in Consumer Products
Entrepreneurs in Energy
Entrepreneurs in Entertainment
Entrepreneurs in Finance and Banking
Entrepreneurs in Food
Entrepreneurs in History
Entrepreneurs in Media
Entrepreneurs in Real Estate
Entrepreneurs in Technology
Entrepreneurs in Transportation

Entrepreneurship Financing and Economic Development

Bankruptcy
Barriers to Entry
Barter
Business Angels
Business Models
Capitalism
Cash Flow
Community/Government Buy-Ins
Credit
Debt
Debt-Based Financing
Entrepreneurial Support Systems
Entrepreneurial Training
Equity- and Debt-Based Financing
Exit Strategies
Feasibility Studies

Geographic Location
Growth
Information
Initial Public Offering
Job Creation
Public Policy: Government Stimulation of
    Start-Ups
Research and Development
Revenue: Current Versus Deferred
Selling Successful Businesses
Strategy
Venture Capital
Venture Management Firms
Venture Valuation

Franchising

Entrepreneurs in Franchising
Franchisee and Franchisor
Franchises: Legal Aspects
Franchises: Starting
Territorial Strategy and Regions

Gender and Minority Entrepreneurship

African Americans and Entrepreneurship
Gender and Acquiring Resources
Gender and Industry Preferences
Gender and Performance
Hispanics and Entrepreneurship
Minorities in New Business Ventures
Motivation and Gender
Women's Entrepreneurship: Best Practices

Innovation

Geography of Innovation
Innovation Advantage
Innovation Diffusion
Innovation in Low-Tech Industries
Innovation Management
Innovation Management: Corporate
Innovation Measurement
Innovation Processes
Product Innovation
Radical and Incremental Innovation
Service Innovation

International Entrepreneurship

Culture and Entrepreneurship
Globalization

About the Editor

Matthew R. Marvel, Ph.D., is an associate professor and Vitale research fellow at the Gordon Ford College of Business at Western Kentucky University. He earned his Ph.D. at the University of Illinois, Urbana-Champaign, and received a Kauffman Dissertation Fellowship. Marvel's research focuses on how individual knowledge, motivation, and learning promote entrepreneurial outcomes like opportunity identification, innovation, and job creation. Most of his research uses the high-tech context to examine how individuals leverage different aspects of knowledge to create breakthroughs—or radical innovations. Matt's research has been published in *Entrepreneurship Theory and Practice*, *Journal of Management Studies*, and *Journal of Small Business Management*. Current research interests involve multidimensional views of knowledge, human capital, and exploring how individuals effectively exploit varying sources of opportunity. Marvel earned his Bachelor of Science in marketing from Southern Illinois University and went on to complete an M.B.A. at Eastern Illinois University. He has worked in a variety of consulting and sales roles focused on technical training and software development.

List of Contributors

Leona Achtenhagen
Jönköping International Business School

Alejandro Amezcua
Syracuse University

Kenneth Anderson
Gonzaga University

Joseph H. Astrachan
Kennesaw State University

Preeta M. Banerjee
Brandeis University

Henrique Barreto
Kaplan University

R. Greg Bell
University of Dallas

Michael M. Beyerlein
Purdue University

Magdalena Bielenia-Grajewska
University of Gdansk, Institute of English

Adam J. Bock
University of Edinburgh

Sarah E. Boslaugh
Kennesaw State University

Joe Anthony Bradley Sr.
Applied Research Associates, Inc.

Nigel Bradly
SUBSEN

Peter T. Bryant
IE Business School, Madrid

Paul Buller
Gonzaga University

Rachel C. Callan
Old Dominion University

Benjamin A. Campbell
The Ohio State University

Diane A. Carlin
Business Librarian and Development Research Consultant

Wm. Camron Casper
Oklahoma State University

Farzana Chowdhury
Indiana University

Cristina E. Ciocirlan
Elizabethtown College

Andrew Corbett
Babson College

Jon Cordas
Purdue University

Dana Cosby-Simmons
Western Kentucky University

Alexander W. Crispo
Purdue University

Anthony D. Daniel
Ashford University

Ariane David
California Lutheran University

Amy E. Davis
College of Charleston

Justin L. Davis
Ohio University

Jonathan H. Deacon
University of Wales, Newport

Dominic DePersis
Broome Community College

Scott Droege
Western Kentucky University

Devkamal Dutta
University of New Hampshire

Kimberly Eddleston
Northeastern University

John Oselenbalu Ekore
University of Ibadan

Sarah E. Fancher
Saint Louis University

Andrew Fodor
Ohio University

Rebecca J. Franklin
Oklahoma State University

Sue Freedman
University of Texas, Dallas

Ina Freeman
Jones International University

Sascha Fuerst
Universidad EAFIT

Carolyn Popp Garrity
Louisiana State University

Hans Georg Gemünden
Technical University of Berlin

Michael M. Gielnik
Leuphana University of Lüneburg

Brian Glassman
International Journal of Innovation Science

Samuel Gómez-Haro
University of Granada

Josie Graham
Canadian Innovation Centre

David Gras
Syracuse University

Tracy L. Green
University of California, Los Angeles

Denis A. Grégoire
Syracuse University

Terje Grønning
University of Oslo

Maribel Guerrero
Basque Institute of Competitiveness, Deusto Business School

Monica J. Hagan
University of California, Los Angeles

George T. Haley
University of New Haven

Usha C. V. Haley
Massey University

Carol Hancock
Kaplan University

David J. Hansen
College of Charleston

Amir Hasnaoui
Groupe Sup de Co La Rochelle and Centre de Recherche Télécom École de Management

Steven John Henderson
Southampton Solent University

Mike Henry
Grant MacEwan University

Daniel T. Holt
Mississippi State University

Claes M. Hultman
Swedish Business School at Örebro University

Katherine Hyatt
Reinhardt University

Dinesh N. Iyer
Ohio University

Maura Kessel
Technical University of Berlin

Dan Kipley
Azusa Pacific University

Nicola B. Klaus
University BW Munich

Dean A. Koutroumanis
University of Tampa

Phyllis R. Kramer
New Venture Management

Jan Kratzer
Technical University of Berlin

Bill Kte'pi
Independent Scholar

Graciela Kuechle
Basque Institute of Competitiveness, Deusto Business School

Richard N. Landers
Old Dominion University

Djamel Eddine Laouisset
Alhosn University, Abu Dhabi

In Hyeock "Ian" Lee
Western Kentucky University

Alfred Lewis
Hamline University

Amy C. Lewis
Drury University

Eric W. Liguori
California State University, Fresno

Loykie L. Lominé
University of Winchester

Terri Lonier
Columbia College, Chicago

G. T. Lumpkin
Syracuse University

Matthew R. Marvel
Western Kentucky University

Andrew Lewis Maxwell
Canadian Innovation Centre

Tom D. McFarland
Tusculum College

Jake Messersmith
University of Nebraska, Kearney

Javier Monllor
DePaul University

Robert J. Moreland
Columbia College, Chicago

John M. Mueller
University of Louisville

Jeffrey Muldoon
Louisiana State University

Maria L. Nathan
Lynchburg College

Lukas Neville
Queen's University

Vias C. Nicolaides
George Mason University

Enrique Nuñez
Ramapo College of New Jersey

Chris Peace
Massey University

Martin Perry
Massey University

Torsten M. Pieper
Kennesaw State University

Craig M. Reddock
Old Dominion University

Maija Renko
University of Illinois, Chicago

Lisa Rosh
Yeshiva University

Matthew W. Rutherford
Virginia Commonwealth University

Sonja A. Sackmann
University BW Munich

Angel J. Salazar
Manchester Metropolitan University

Manjula S. Salimath
University of North Texas

Darrel L. Sandall
Purdue University

Tom J. Sanders
University of Montevallo

Shruti Sardeshmukh
University of South Australia

Janet Grace Sayers
Massey University

Katharina Schuster
University BW Munich

Leslie E. Sekerka
Menlo College

Luigi Serio
Catholic University of the Sacred Heart, Milan

Ronda M. Smith-Nelson
University of Georgia

Danny Soetanto
Lancaster University

George T. Solomon
George Washington University

Jason Stoner
Ohio University

Diane McMeekin Sullivan
University of Dayton

François Therin
University College of Media Arts and Sciences

Neil Tocher
Idaho State University

Kim O. Tokarski
Bern University of Applied Sciences

Marcello Tonelli
Australian Centre for Entrepreneurship Research

Asli Tuncay-Celikel
Isik University and University of Sussex

Dale B. Tuttle
University of Michigan, Flint

David Urbano
Autonomous University of Barcelona

Christine K. Volkmann
University of Wuppertal

Abram Walton
Purdue University

David W. Williams
University of Tennessee

Hannes Zacher
The University of Queensland

Shuyi Zhang
Shanghai Finance University

Roxanne Zolin
Queensland University of Technology

Introduction

What is more important to our society and economy than new and small businesses? Entrepreneurship and small businesses have been designated the engines of growth because they create new jobs, generate wealth, improve society, and have an enormous economic impact. Not only are small businesses responsible for the vast majority of new jobs; they also impact society through innovation. History shows us that entrepreneurs create the bulk of innovations as well as the majority of the breakthroughs that are the catalysts for major structural changes in the economy. Small businesses are critical and many individuals become entrepreneurs to pursue wealth creation, independence, personal fulfillment, or even escape a bad situation. Vast numbers of individuals around the globe engage in entrepreneurial activity, and estimates from the Global Entrepreneurship Monitor at Babson College indicate that more than 8 percent of the U.S. population is engaged in entrepreneurial activity. These aspects of entrepreneurship make it a fascinating topic, but many argue that we have only begun to scratch the surface of understanding. Indeed, new venture management is an important and popular topic, but what do we truly know?

Surging Interest

Entrepreneurs and exciting new businesses have become the center of attention, spurring our imagination and the thought of what can be possible. Increasingly, ambitious risk-taking young men and women dream of starting a new venture rather than rising through the seemingly ruthless corporate ranks. Many individuals think of business ownership as putting their fate in their own hands, and it appears much more attractive than placing their career in the hands of the established firm—known for disloyalty and downsizing. The degree of interest in entrepreneurship among high school and college students alike is surging. Almost every university has a growing number of new venture management courses and accompanying business plan competitions in efforts to match theory and practice. Courses, majors, and doctorate programs have gained great popularity as increasing numbers of students want to participate in and understand entrepreneurship and how to effectively manage new ventures in today's dynamic environment.

How to think and act entrepreneurially is of paramount interest to the established organization, too. As new technology allows for new possibilities and customer preferences change, large firms have come to the realization that today's competitive advantage is not a long-term guarantee for success. The ability to be proactive, creative, and think and act entrepreneurially is almost a requirement for the modern-day organization. The primary instrument of competition for many firms is innovation, and to increase this capability, the origination must tap into a profound force—the creative power of its members. The goal in many leading organizations is continuous innovation in terms of new products, processes, or services, and the evidence suggests that there is much to learn from the study of entrepreneurship.

This interest has generated significant demand for systematic knowledge about the distinctive features and promises of new venture management. Unfortunately, the supply of knowledge about new businesses and how to manage them effectively has not kept up with the increased demand. Unlike many other academic areas, entrepreneurship is a relatively young academic field of study. Much of what is known is fragmented, and our collective knowledge about opportunities, the resources and strategies used to exploit them, and the outcomes of the process is limited. What we do know is that new venture management is one of the most important topics for today's global economy and one approach does not fit all. Strategies that work in the early stages of venture development often do not produce the same results when the venture encounters new challenges and the need for reinvention. Despite the fact that many questions remain, the study of new venture management has come a long and fruitful way. The following paragraphs highlight the development of the field and where we find ourselves today.

Synopsis of the Study of Entrepreneurship

The study of entrepreneurship is multidisciplinary and has emerged from literature spanning economics, education, management, psychology, sociology, and other fields. Joseph Schumpeter is widely accepted as the founding father of entrepreneurship theory. He emphasized entrepreneurship as a process of driving out innovation through new combinations. The bulk of early entrepreneurship research focused on whether entrepreneurs were unique from the general population. This research, grounded in psychology, regarded entrepreneurship as a function of stable characteristics possessed by some people and not others. A number of studies seemed to offer some justification for this view, as motivation, higher needs for achievement, and a high tolerance for risk taking were found to differentiate entrepreneurs from nonentrepreneurs.

However, not all of these studies found entrepreneurs to be distinctive. This research stream on how entrepreneurs are unique and different from the general population, termed *trait research*, came under harsh criticism. A premise of this personality perspective is the notion that certain individuals have a unique set of inherent, stable, and enduring personality characteristics that predispose them to entrepreneurial activity. William Gartner's 1985 article "'Who Is an Entrepreneur?' Is the Wrong Question" marked a turning point and led to a paradigm shift and the integration of a behavioral perspective. From the behavioral perspective, entrepreneurship is a set of activities involved in organization creation, whereas in trait approaches the focus is the entrepreneur as a set of personality characteristics. The behavioral approach concentrates on what entrepreneurs do rather than who they are and considers the evolutionary process of venture creation. Today the process nature of entrepreneurship is well recognized. Alert individuals, called entrepreneurs, identify opportunities and develop ideas for how to exploit them by developing new products or services. Therefore, venture creation may be viewed as a process beginning with opportunity identification, then exploitation, and finally venture outcomes: innovation, job creation, or less attractive outcomes such as bankruptcy.

Scott Shane, of Case Western University, has contributed heavily to the field of entrepreneurship and points out that a pure individual process orientation will not lead to a comprehensive understanding either. People engage in entrepreneurial activity at particular points in time and in response to specific situations, making it impossible to account for entrepreneurship by examining the individual alone, and contextual aspects should not be overlooked. For example, some scholars have approached the study of entrepreneurship by focusing on the environment. This school of thought has explored what environmental aspect explains entrepreneurial activity in terms of new firm formation, technology change, and industry dynamics. While valuable, much of this research ignores the human agent.

Without doubt, entrepreneurship is a self-directed activity and cannot occur spontaneously through technology or social change alone. Both the environment-centric and individual-centric approaches are valuable, and each contributes to the academic field of entrepreneurship, although little research is available integrating both approaches. The field will benefit from comprehensive approaches that integrate individual and environmental effects. Future research endeavors will undoubtedly combine these perspectives as we continue to develop our knowledge of new venture management.

Growth of the Academic Field

The academic field of entrepreneurship is now well established and continues to grow. Jerome Katz of St. Louis University examined the development of the field in terms of peer-reviewed journals, endowed professorships, and academic programs. In less than a decade, the number of entrepreneurship journals listed on the Social Sciences Citation Index (SSCI), a database that covers the world's leading journals across many disciplines, has grown from four journals to eleven. The fact that SSCI and the other major indexing services include a growing number of entrepreneurship journals shows the growth in acceptance of entrepreneurship as a field of study. Endowed professors in entrepreneurship have also increased in number. Endowed professors, as the name implies, are the top performers in their field and represent outstanding leaders in the academic discipline. In just about 10 years' time, the number of endowed chairs in entrepreneurship or small business management at U.S. colleges grew by more than 300 percent, to 406 positions in 2004.

The pattern of growth in terms of journals and professorships, however, may not match the extent of growth in academic programs. Almost every university offers entrepreneurship and small business management programs at the undergraduate level, as the demand is immense. Today, more than twelve universities offer organized doctorate programs specific to entrepreneurship, and more are needed as the need for entrepreneurship faculty grows.

The Encyclopedia

The purpose of this text is to offer a comprehensive set of articles on the body of knowledge in the field of new venture management—or entrepreneurship. While much progress has been made and we continue to increase our understanding of entrepreneurship, the reality is that much of this knowledge is fragmented. What we know about entrepreneurial opportunities, the people who pursue them, the skills and strategies used to exploit them, the environmental conditions that affect this activity, and how to promote the positive outcomes of entrepreneurship and small business is difficult to find in any one text.

The *Encyclopedia of New Venture Management* is an effort to bring together an important collection of articles and increase understanding for scholars, practitioners, educators, and students alike. This volume contains more than 190 carefully selected contributions, and each entry focuses on a specific aspect of new venture management. The authors are leading academic experts on their specific topics and from a diversity of fields. The rapidly increasing literature surrounding new venture management is characterized by a multitude of perspectives that cut across specializations and disciplines. It is essential to bring these diverse concepts, theories, and approaches to new venture management together in one place. While numerous questions remain and the importance of continued research cannot be overemphasized, this volume summarizes what is currently known about entrepreneurship and new venture management.

Few fields are as important or capture the attention of society like entrepreneurship. I hope that the *Encyclopedia of New Venture Management* helps map out, explain, and challenge our collective thinking as the field continues to grow.

Matthew R. Marvel
Editor

Chronology

1790

The U.S. Congress passes the Patent Act, creating the modern patent system by providing inventors with the sole right to make and sell patented inventions (which originally applied for 14 years following grant of the patent).

1883

The Paris Convention for the Protection of Industrial Property is signed by 11 countries (currently 173 countries are parties to the convention), signifying that patents granted in one of the signatories will be honored by the others.

1900

Booker T. Washington, with the support of Andrew Carnegie, founds the National Negro Business League in Boston, Massachusetts. The league's founding coincides with a "buy black" movement, and the number of African American enterprises in the United States approximately doubles between 1900 and 1910.

1908

The first master of business administration (MBA) program in the United States is founded at Harvard University.

1913

The Federal Reserve system is established in the United States, creating the modern central banking system.

1919

Alex Faickney Osborn founds the U.S. advertising agency BBDO, where he will develop the technique of brainstorming, which is popularized through several Osborn publications in the late 1940s and 1950s.

1933

In the wake of the stock market crash, the U.S. government passes the Securities Act of 1933, which is the first federal effort to regulate the securities trade, a matter previously left primarily to state laws. The law's main reforms are that potential investors must receive significant information about securities offered for public sale and that fraud and misrepresentation are prohibited in such sales.

The U.S. Congress passes the Glass-Steagall Act, also known as the Banking Act of 1933, which establishes the Federal Deposit Insurance Corporation (FDIC), allows Federal Reserve interest rates on savings accounts, and establishes a separation between depository and investment banks.

1937

The Radio Research Project, a research organization funded by the Rockefeller Foundation to look at the societal effects of the mass media, is created at Princeton University. In 1939 it moves to Columbia University and in 1944 is renamed the Bureau of Applied Social Research. Among his many accomplishments, Robert K. Merton develops the use of focus groups for research while serving as head of the bureau.

1939

Hewlett-Packard, created by two electrical engineers (Bill Hewlett and Dave Packard) from Stanford University, is founded in Palo Alto, California.

1940

The University of Chicago establishes the first master of business administration (MBA) program for working professionals, often dubbed the "executive MBA."

1944

The World Bank and International Monetary Fund are established during the Bretton Woods Conference, a gathering of representatives from Allied nations seeking to establish economic order after World War II.

1946

The first venture capital firms in the United States are founded: J. H. Whitney & Company and American Research and Development Corporation.

1947

Professor Myles Mace delivers his first lecture on entrepreneurship at Harvard University.

Texas Instruments is founded by Cecil Green, J. Erik Johnsson, Patrick Haggerty, and Eugene McDermott to manufacture transistors (recently discovered at Bell Labs).

1949

The General Agreement on Tariffs and Trade (GATT) is formed to regulate international trade and to facilitate tariff reduction.

1951

The Stanford Industrial Park, now known as the Stanford Research Park, is built on land owned by Stanford University and becomes the first university-owned industrial park (and perhaps the first technology-focused office park as well). It is home to companies including Lockheed and General Electric and plays a key role in the development of Silicon Valley.

1953

The Small Business Administration (SBA), an agency of the federal government, is founded to provide support for small business in the United States.

1954

The Creative Education Foundation is founded by Alex Faickney Osborn (who also founded the advertising agency BBDO) with the goal of teaching children and adults to be more creative. The first Creative Problem Solving Institute (CPSI) is held the same year and has been held annually since.

1956

William Shockley founds the Shockley Semiconductor Laboratory to develop silicon transistors.

1957

Toyota enters the American car market. The company's first U.S. model, the Toyotapet, is not popular, but the gas crisis of the early 1970s creates consumer interest in the more fuel-efficient cars produced by Toyota and other Japanese manufacturers.

INSEAD, a graduate school with campuses in Europe, Asia, and the Middle East, is founded and offers the first master of business administration (MBA) program in Europe.

1961

The Area Redevelopment Act, which offers low-interest business loans intended to foster job creation in declining communities in the United States, is signed by President John F. Kennedy; the program is shut down two years later.

1962

The sociologist E. M. Rogers publishes *Diffusion of Innovations*, a seminal work in the field. In it, he identifies four elements that influence the spread of a novel idea: the innovation itself, communication channels, time, and the social system in place.

1964

As part of the Equal Opportunity Act intended to fight poverty in the United States, the Community Action Plan (CAP) fosters the creation of community action agencies (CAAs), which provide programs intended to empower poor Americans, including job training and administration of Head Start preschool programs.

Economist Gary S. Becker publishes *Human Capital*, which popularizes the concept that one can invest in human capital (through education and training, for example) and that the investment can yield returns through increased productivity.

1969

The first message is sent over the Advanced Research Projects Agency Network (ARPANET), a precursor to the Internet.

1971

A series of newspaper articles uses the term "Silicon Valley" to describe the Santa Clara Valley and surrounding area as the home of many semiconductor and computer companies.

Southwest Airlines begins operation as Air Southwest under a business model that is novel for airlines; it includes providing service to limited areas, using mainly secondary airports, and using only a single type of aircraft, the Boeing 737. Southwest also introduces other innovations, including unreserved seating, lack of in-flight entertainment, and limited food and beverage service.

Intel introduces the first single-chip microprocessor, the Intel 4004.

1972

The venture capital firm Sequoia Capital is founded; among the companies funded by Sequoia are Atari, Apple, Google, Cisco, Yahoo! and PayPal.

1973

The National Venture Capital Association (NVCA), a trade group representing the interests of the venture capital industry, is founded in the United States.

An oil embargo by Arab members of the Organization of Petroleum Exporting Countries (OPEC) plus Egypt, Syria, and Tunisia sparks a gas shortage in the United States and creates an interest in more fuel-efficient vehicles.

1975

The National Association of Women Business Owners (NAWBO) is founded in Washington, D.C., to further the interests of women business owners. Participation in NAWBO grows to more than 80 chapters and 7,000 members by 2010.

Microsoft Corporation is founded by Bill Gates and Paul Allen.

1976

Muhammad Yunus founds the Grameen Bank in Bangladesh to provide microcredit (very small loans) to the poor.

Apple Computer Inc. (now Apple Inc.) is founded in Cupertino, California, by Steve Jobs, Steve Wozniak, and Ronald Wayne.

1978

The U.S. labor department modifies the Employee Retirement Income Security Act (ERISA) to allow corporate pension funds to invest in riskier ventures, freeing up a great deal of money for venture capital investment.

1979

Sony introduces the Walkman, a portable media player that enables people to listen to cassette tapes through headphones.

Daniel Kahneman and Amos Tversky publish "Prospect Theory: An Analysis of Decision Under Risk," which applies knowledge from cognitive psychology to explain why observed economic behavior often diverges from that predicted by assumptions of rationality. Kahneman will be awarded the Nobel Prize in 2002 for his work in this field (Tversky died in 1996 and was thus not eligible for the award).

VisiCalc, the first spreadsheet application for personal computers, is released and proves to be a "killer app" (an application that is so popular people will buy hardware to enable them to use it). It is believed to greatly increase the sales of Apple computers.

1980s

In the United States, 35 states adopt enterprise zones, which provide tax breaks to businesses that are willing to locate in poor communities.

1981

The scanning tunneling microscope (SCM), an early application of nanotechnology, is created. Physicists Gerd Binnig and Heinrich Rohrer will be awarded the Nobel Prize in 1986 for their contributions to this effort.

The Economic Recovery Act of 1981 is signed into law by U.S. President Ronald Reagan; meant to encourage economic growth, it reduces marginal income taxes, estate taxes, and capital gains taxes; expands provisions for employee stock ownership plans; and increases the number of people eligible to establish individual retirement accounts.

Psychologist Albert Bandura performs the Bobo doll experiment, which establishes that children are more likely to behave aggressively if they are exposed to a model who behaves aggressively, particularly if the model is of the same gender. This lends support to Bandura's social learning theory, which states that people can learn behavior by observing it in their environment.

IBM introduces the personal computer, or PC, which uses many off-the-shelf components to reduce costs and a copyrighted operating system intended to prevent competitors from building compatible computers.

1982

The first compact disc (CD) is released in Japan. The discs, as well as CD players, are released in the United States in 1983.

1984

Apple Computer launches the Macintosh computer, in part through a famous commercial aired during the Super Bowl that posits Apple as a force of freedom in an otherwise dystopian future.

The Jeep Cherokee, the first modern sports utility vehicle (SUV), is introduced to the U.S. market. This type of vehicle proves to be hugely popular with customers and profitable for auto manufacturers until the late years of the first decade of the 21st century, when rising fuel prices and the economic crisis make SUVs less attractive to consumers and damage sales.

1985

Microsoft releases Microsoft Windows, a computer operating system with graphical access, which will come to dominate the market.

1986

Robert G. Cooper publishes *Winning at New Products*, a book that describes the stage-gate process of product development.

1989

Hummer Winblad Venture Partners, the first venture capital fund, is founded; it invests exclusively in software companies.

1994

In the United States, the Reigle Community Development and Regulatory Improvement Act establishes the concept of community development financial institutions (CDFIs) to provide credit and other financial services to populations otherwise underserved, and also provides federal funding for CDFI programs.

The online retailer Amazon is founded by Jeff Bezos in Seattle, originally as an online bookstore.

1995

The World Trade Organization (WTO) is founded; it provides a framework for international trade agreements and hears disputes between participating countries.

Pierre Omidyar founds the online auction Website eBay, which facilitates buying and selling, sometimes of quite obscure items (reportedly one of the first items sold was a broken laser pointer); transactions occur among individuals who do not necessarily know each other and who may be in far-removed geographic locations.

1996

Google begins as a research product by two students at Stanford University, Larry Page and Sergey Brin, to create a search engine that ranks results based on the relevance or importance of each Website. The company is incorporated in 1998 and has its initial public offering in 2004.

1997

Toyota introduces the Prius in Japan, making it the first mass-produced hybrid electric automobile on the market. The Prius is introduced worldwide in 2001; its largest current market is the United States.

1998

PayPal, a company that developed a system allowing money to be exchanged over the Internet, greatly facilitates the growth of online commerce. In 2002, PayPal becomes a wholly owned subsidiary of eBay.

1999

The Gramm-Leach-Bailey Act repeals some provisions of the Glass-Steagall Act of 1933, including removing the legal separation between depository banks and investment banks.

Shawn Fanning creates the peer-to-peer file-sharing program Napster. Although it remains in operation for only three years (due to copyright violations), Napster establishes the feasibility of distributing music electronically.

The Global Entrepreneurship Monitor (GEM) is established as a partnership between Babson and London Business School to study entrepreneurship at the national level.

2001

Apple Computer introduces the iPod, a portable media player.

2002

The social networking service Friendster is founded in California by Jonathan Abrams, Peter Chin, and Dave Lee. Friendster is among the first services to allow users to browse user profiles and thus increase their circle of acquaintances; predating Myspace and Facebook, Friendster enjoys wide initial success. Although it is later surpassed in the United States by Facebook, it retains a strong presence in Asia.

Richard Florida publishes *The Rise of the Creative Class*, which argues that economic development in urban areas is best accomplished not by large, single projects such as sports stadiums but by cultivating the presence of creative individuals, including artists, musicians, and high-tech workers, who will attract businesses and capital investment as well as other creative people.

2003

Myspace, a social networking service, is created in California partly in imitation of Friendster. It becomes the most popular social networking service until later surpassed by Facebook.

2004

Mark Zuckerberg and colleagues found Facebook, a social networking service and Website that, as of 2009, will become the most widely used social network in the world.

2005

The video-sharing Website YouTube is created by Chad Hurley, Steve Chen, and Jawed Karim in San Mateo, California, with financing from Sequoia Capital.

2006

Chris Anderson publishes *The Long Tail: Why the Future of Business Is Selling Less of More*, which elaborates on ideas he put forth in a 2004 *Wired* magazine article. Anderson argues that the future lies in selling relatively small numbers of items for people with highly specialized tastes, a process facilitated by the availability of the Internet and other means of electronic communications.

2008

Groupon, a Website offering discounted gift certificates, is founded in November in Chicago; by 2010 it has expanded to over 200 cities worldwide.

Lehman Brothers, a financial services firm headquartered in New York City, declares bankruptcy.

Kickstarter, a Website that facilitates crowd funding of creative projects and small business projects, is founded.

Apple Computer opens the online App Store to sell and distribute applications for Apple products, including the iPhone, iPod, and iPad. In January 2011, the 10 billionth application is downloaded.

2010

Inside Job, a film about the U.S. financial crisis directed by Charles Ferguson, wins the Academy Award for Best Documentary.

Michael Lewis's book *The Big Short*, which analyzes the U.S. financial crisis, is a *New York Times* bestseller.

2011

The professional and social networking site LinkedIn goes public in May.

Angie's List, an online consumer recommendations site, goes public in November.

2012

The National Venture Capital Association and PricewaterhouseCoopers report that venture capital investments in New York rose 64.3 percent since 2010, much faster than California's 24.4 percent.

Sarah E. Boslaugh
Kennesaw State University

ACCOUNTING

The accounting function is acknowledged as a core component of any business. Above all, it allows tracking of the venture's profitability and determination of the underlying trends integral to daily management responsibilities. It also facilitates the company, providing complete and accurate financial information to management and investors. Additionally, it is necessary for preparation of any and all tax returns.

The most common outputs of accounting activities are the income statement, the balance sheet, and the cash flow statement. Cash budgeting and management and the establishment of accounting information systems are also central management responsibilities. Financial ratios, which can be calculated once the financial statements are compiled, provide important analytical information to support managerial decision making. To that point, current accounting software packages can generate financial reports in a reliable, automated manner, providing the new venture manager with the best possible financial information and enhancing prospects for business success.

Financial Statements

Income statements are often the first financial statement a business owner or investor focuses on. In many respects the same mind-sets and management concerns are present in both profit and not-for-profit business settings. The income statement begins with an articulation of the sales or revenues generated by a business. (Sales typically are used to denote a business selling a product, whereas revenues are more commonly associated with a service-oriented business.) The statement culminates with a net figure, indicating whether a profit or loss was made by the business during the specific time frame. Whereas novice business owners likely focus on the profit or loss figure, more experienced business professionals pay close attention to the areas between the sales/revenue numbers and the net profit/loss calculations—the areas where the financial implications of business operations are often revealed.

The income statement is created in a stepwise manner, often in three distinct breakout areas. First, costs directly attributable to the products or services sold are enumerated. Then, the general corporate and overhead expenses are specified. Finally, expenses associated with how the company obtained financing (above and beyond that provided by the entrepreneur and other equity investors) are presented. Each breakout allows the new venture manager to gauge whether the business is operating efficiently, both on an absolute basis and relative to standards that could include comparisons to others in the industry.

The first cost segment, often characterized as cost of goods sold (COGS), reflects the cost of the items directly attributed to the production of the good or service being sold. Managers often calculate what portion these costs are relative to the overall sales/revenues and, after subtracting from 1, refer to this as the gross margin (where the term *margin* is understood to be a percentage figure). Given that the format and sequence for building income statements are largely universal, this allows new venture managers to assess their own company's profit-making potential relative to others in the same line of business. Since all publicly traded companies are required to make their financial statements publicly available, data for comparisons are abundant.

The second major category of expenses deducted from revenues is colloquially termed *overhead*. These typically include costs broadly associated with the business, including office space as well as salaries of the officers and top-level management. Expenses linked to selling products (or services) of the firm are included in this category. The aim of this expense step is to be able to tally all of the operating expenses of the business, which would include the direct expenses above, plus these indirect expenses. With this figure in hand, an operating margin can be calculated and compared to the original business plan, and to entities similar to the business in question. It is important to note that early in a venture's life, overhead expenses may be a disproportionate component of total expenses. This is a result of the fact that many of these expenses are "lumpy," meaning that a business must incur one or more of these expenses as a large outlay, even if the business needs are not yet of the requisite scale. For example, a firm may be forced to hire a chief financial officer on a full-time basis or outfit a production facility not yet required to run at

It is essential for organizations to produce at minimum an income statement, a balance sheet, and a statement of cash flow. Financial ratios can be calculated once the financial statements are compiled and provide analytical information as needed for managerial decision making. (Photos.com)

maximum capacity, before the business has secured its financial footing.

The third and final breakout area presents expenses associated with financing costs, such as interest expenses. Also in this area are gains or losses from sales of existing assets, known as disinvestments. The resulting figure is the company's earnings before taxes. This step has a far greater impact on net income if the company in question is heavily financed by debt; conversely, new ventures with little borrowing ability will not be affected by such costs.

Assuming the new venture is itself taxable, the deduction of taxes leaves the net income figure. Positive net income is often termed *making money*, but as addressed below, making money and having money can be two different things, and this constitutes an important distinction in the ongoing viability of a new venture. The significance of the income statement is that it indicates the profitability of the venture at a specific point in time, and these profits can be used to finance the continued growth of the new venture. Without profits, the business must look elsewhere for funds and, particularly for new ventures, there may be few places to turn.

The balance sheet, another important financial statement, presents a tabulation of the items the business owns or controls (assets) and how these assets were paid for (liabilities and the owner's equity). By definition, the totals of these two categories must always equal each other. Thus, true to its name, this statement always balances, reflected in the basic accounting equation: assets = liabilities + owners' equity. As with the income statement, the structure of the balance sheet can give the new venture owner insights into what is possible with the business and where difficulties may lie.

Both assets and liabilities are typically broken into two components: short-term and long-term. Any asset labeled as short-term (such as inventories or accounts receivable) is expected to transition through the normal cycle of the business and be exchanged for cash within a year. Similarly, any liability (bills or debts) labeled short-term is expected to be paid within a year's time. To experienced eyes, the balance sheet can give clues to whether a business is going to need a cash infusion or might be expecting larger cash balances in the near future.

Long-term assets and liabilities are those that have longer useful lives. This includes any equity in a business, since the business has no legal obligation ever to pay the equity holders anything. Significant long-term assets are not typically found in new ventures prior to the proving of the basic business premise. Similarly, prior to the proving of a business plan, few creditors will be willing to accept the risk of being paid back in the distant future, when the near-term prospects of a firm are still murky. Hence, most new ventures typically find the majority of their assets and liabilities concentrated in the short-term category; this, too, points to a greater need in new ventures to be highly mindful of issues relating to day-to-day management tasks.

The cash flow statement is considered the last of the three essential financial reports and arguably the most important statement for new ventures. This statement summarizes where cash comes from in the operations of a business, and where it was used. Successful companies generate most of their cash from operational activities (like making a profit), but interestingly, a profitable business can show zero or even negative cash flow. For example, if the company is investing heavily in items that cannot be immediately expensed, such as inventories or fixed assets, then the long-term prospects of the firm can be bright, while in the near term cash could be scarce. Similarly, profits could be used to pay debts of the firm, in which case the future expenses of the firm would be lowered while, again, near-term cash could be reduced dramatically. Many new ventures overlook the value of monitoring cash flow, focusing instead on sales or expenses. However, without adequate cash, a new venture can face a serious threat to its ongoing operations.

Cash Budgeting

Each of the three financial statements mentioned can provide significant insights into how a new venture is performing and the risks it is facing. However, these statements tend to be generated intermittently, often on a quarterly and annual reporting cycle. This frequency, and the detail of the information, is often not sufficient for true day-to-day management of a new enterprise. Another internal document—a cash budget—is an important complement to the three core financial statements and can serve the new venture in important ways.

Cash budgeting includes forecasting precisely the sources and uses (and timing thereof) of this commonly scarce resource in new ventures. Cash budgeting is not an activity that exists in its own universe; rather, it is inextricably intertwined with more traditional accounting activities. Since all financial aspects of a business ultimately tie together, a cash budget that is integrated with a firm's balance sheet and income statement allows the entrepreneur to better gauge the amount of capital needed at business inception. It is this initial infusion of cash that funds asset acquisition and pays all necessary expenses prior to the generation of free cash flow from operations.

Cash budgeting is not the same as the statement of cash flows. The latter is, like its income statement and balance sheet brethren, more of an examination of history than it is a forecasting effort. A cash budget, in its truest form, articulates when cash is expected from each source and how much and when cash will be used (spent). In many businesses, this is a daily management task, not a quarterly or annual reporting function. A business generating more cash than it spends is deemed to be generating free cash flow. This has the positive implication that these monies could be paid to the firm's owners as a component of their total return on investment or applied to activities that support the continued growth of the firm. Free cash flow is specifically defined as the amount above and beyond additional day-to-day working capital requirements and incremental long-term investment needs. Entrepreneurs must consider whether the profits and the free cash flow are large enough to justify pursuing the business idea, before undertaking any new business venture.

Relationship of Financial Statements to the Cash Budget

As an example of how the three primary financial statements and a cash budget are all interrelated, let us walk through an example where, at the outset, start-up capital is invested by the business owner. It is assumed that the entrepreneur has a limited amount of capital (cash) to invest, has an eye toward risk management (not losing his/her investment), and seeks to maximize the return on invested capital. Therefore, the project at hand is determining how to leverage the initial investment into a greater pool of resources in a cost-effective manner. Monitoring all of the interaction effects requires, by its nature, that the entrepreneur will have to be mindful of impacts on each financial statement when any decision is made.

With the initial capital contribution in hand and the firm's first assets purchased (using those monies), the new venture owner will want to consider if those initial assets can be used to garner additional assets, possibly by using them as collateral to obtain debt financing. Debt providers may well be wary of a small new firm, but if assets of marketable value are specifically pledged to guarantee a loan, the asset base of the company could thereby be increased. Such an activity, however, will ripple through all three key financial statements. For example, the inclusion of interest-bearing debt into the firm's financing mix adds principal and interest payments into the cash budget, because the aforementioned liability will be added to the balance sheet. An expense line (interest expense) also is added to the income statement. The accounting-related management task embedded in this decision is making sure that all of the side effects of each decision are understood.

The next step in our example considers another source of capital to the new venture, so-called spontaneous financing. Many businesses acquire goods and services utilizing trade credit, and for many this is a critical method of financing the ongoing business. This form of financing often comes with no explicit (cash payment) required. As the term *spontaneous* implies, it usually appears in the normal course of business; in effect, the business has been able to expand its asset base without spending its own cash up front. The fact that these short-term credits will need to be paid clearly impacts the cash budget. If a new business is able to obtain trade credit, its reliance on owner-supplied capital can be reduced, and the capital provided by that owner can be used elsewhere. Similarly, businesses that pre-sell their goods and services have the ability to obtain cash up front prior to the delivery (and expenditure on) products and services to be delivered. This advance of cash, however, appears in the balance sheet as a liability, since the new venture now "owes" the buyer the product or service. Any expenses that need to be incurred to satisfy that buyer will subsequently appear in the income statement as well as the cash budget forecast.

While it appears appealing to use someone else's money to run a business, there is a double edge to this spontaneous financing sword. If the clients of the new enterprise also require trade credit from this new venture, then the new venture's cash will be tied up when the customers agree to purchase the products or services, but do not pay for them on the spot. In effect, the new venture's cash is being used to finance clients rather than the business itself. Whereas sales have gone up and the income statement appears strong, cash has become scarcer and the balance sheet appears less attractive. Hence, before granting clients trade credit, management of the cash-limited new enterprise should be consciously evaluating each such decision in order to determine if the profits from those sales justify the full cost of goods/services sold.

Financial Ratios

Additional indicators of a venture's performance and financial situation can be found in financial ratios. Most are calculated from information obtained from the three key financial statements. The current ratio (also known as the working capital ratio) is expressed by the formula: current assets/current liabilities. Standard values for current ratios differ by industry and individual firm; however, in a traditional interpretation, if current assets (those likely to be transformed into cash through normal business activity in the near term) exceed current liabilities (those bills or claims that will need to be paid in the near term), then the firm, with a current ratio greater than one, is likely to remain solvent and continue as an ongoing concern.

The quick ratio is another indicator of a firm's financial condition, particularly its liquidity and ability to pay short-term liabilities. It is calculated using only the most liquid of the current assets—typically cash and marketable securities—and thereby typically excludes inventories. It compares these most liquid assets to current liabilities, in order to determine if the firm could pay near-term claims immediately, if it needed to do so. As with the current ratio, a firm is deemed to have less risk of insolvency if that ratio is close to, or greater than, one. With both the current and quick ratio, a higher ratio figure is more appealing to creditors, since it indicates a greater chance of the firm being able to pay. In contrast, business owners often prefer a lower figure, as it means more of the venture's assets are being used to grow the firm and generate profits.

The cash conversion cycle is a compendium of accounting ratios that business managers employ in the evaluation and fine-tuning of their businesses. Activity ratios include accounts receivable turnover (credit sales/average accounts receivable) and inventory turnover (cost of goods sold/average inventory). Greater turnovers are typically indicative of a company that has less money tied up in the day-to-day operations of the firm, a positive indicator of performance. Taking the inverse of each of these figures and multiplying by the number of days in a year reveals the average day's balance in each account, or how much cash is invested in day-to-day operations (working capital) of the business.

Another important financial ratio for the new venture manager is the net profit margin. This is found by dividing net profit by total sales or revenues. The goal of every firm is to maximize this figure over the long term. Similarly, the return-on-equity ratio is of interest to investors in the new venture, since it indicates the rate of return being earned on their investment in the company. It is calculated based on information from two different financial statements: dividing net income by the equity invested in the business. As is true with all profit margins, a larger percentage is preferred to a smaller (or worse, negative) percentage.

The debt-to-equity ratio is a key risk measure. Its financial calculation is: debt taken on by the firm/ equity of the firm. More debt means greater risk of not being able to repay it. However, if the firm can use this debt to make more profit than the debt cost the firm, the shareholders of the firm reap those rewards. Also, more debt puts greater strain on the cash budget, because of interest payment commitments to debt providers. Creditors prefer to see small debt-to-equity ratios, while business managers worry that they can make the required cash payments to those creditors. A ratio that usually is considered by both parties is termed the times-interest-earned ratio. This ratio literally computes whether the business is generating enough pretax profit to pay the current interest expense. (The reader may refer to the foregoing discussion of the income statement's construction to review where this falls in the stepwise process.) Earnings before interest and taxes are compared to the interest expense figure, and if the ratio of these two is greater than one, this firm can afford/pay the interest expense.

As these financial statements and ratios illustrate, there is a wealth of accounting information available to new venture managers. Developing the skill to assess multiple and intertwined situations simultaneously, however, is where the art of management truly becomes apparent. How can new venture management teams coordinate the multitude of financial information in some orderly, usable way? In many respects these tasks can be reasonably accomplished with accounting software packages (assuming accurate data entry and a relatively small business). New business owners justifiably are concerned with maintaining their focus on growing and managing their business, and they often delegate accounting activity to a trained accountant with the hope of satisfying the forthcoming tax filings and payments without any missteps. It is crucial, however, for all new venture managers to have a solid understanding of the financial aspects of the firm. As the firm grows and financial tasks are delegated, it remains imperative for the venture's key decision makers to remain vigilant regarding financial matters.

Above and beyond accounting software packages that focus almost entirely on producing the three basic accounting statements, there is a burgeoning area termed accounting information systems (AIS). These systems collect and store accounting data and then process those data into information to be used by business managers and owners/investors. Without appropriate, timely information, the management of a firm cannot make adjustments to operations and business practices—decisions that ultimately lead to optimal utilization of company resources. The AIS discipline is a hybrid, linking traditional accounting methods and controls with information technology that increasingly finds its way into all aspects of business management.

The overriding objective in the AIS effort is to automate and streamline reporting and analysis functions in order for managers to be able to quickly detect where variances from proposed plans are occurring. Of key importance to new ventures is that cash budgeting, the most operationally oriented of the accounting functions, can be efficiently integrated into the overall financial plan and AIS of an organization. Returning full circle, this information can all be linked to the generation of the key periodic financial reports such as income statements and balance sheets that are required by investors, creditors, and new venture owners.

Robert J. Moreland
Terri Lonier
Columbia College, Chicago

See also Cash Flow; Debt; Equity- and Debt-Based Financing; Risk Management

Further Readings

Keown, Arthur J., John D. Martin, and J. William Petty. *Foundations of Finance: The Logic and Practice of Financial Management*, 7th ed. Boston: Pearson, 2010.

Kimmel, Paul D., Jerry J. Weygandt, and Donald E. Keiso. *Accounting: Tools for Decision Making*. New York: Wiley, 2008.

Ogden, William A., Michael D. Wilson, and Srinivasan Sundaram. "An Accounting System Approach to Estimating Capital Requirements for New Ventures." *Journal of Business and Entrepreneurship* (March 2001).

ADAPTATION

Adaptation is a concept borrowed from biological sciences and applied to firm behavior and learning. This perspective, found primarily in evolutionary economics and organizational learning theory, states that firms can adjust so as to become better suited for survival to changing environments. As change occurs constantly in the economy, some kind of evolutionary process must be in effect, and there has been a proposal that this process is Darwinian in nature. Both perspectives treat firms, including new ventures, as biological organisms that actively adapt to their environments.

Evolutionary economics emerged in the early 1980s with the publication of *An Evolutionary Theory of Economic Change*, a seminal work by Richard Nelson and Sidney Winter. It builds on earlier work from the 1940s and 1950s by distinguished economists including Joseph Schumpeter, Herbert Simon, and Edith Penrose. Evolutionary economics started mainly as a critique of mainstream economics, which explains economic phenomena as outgrowths of the rational choices of profit-maximizing firms and utility-maximizing agents. Evolutionary economists argue instead that most decisions of firms and consumers are taken in a habitual manner because their rationality is bounded. It has been proposed that markets act as the major selection vehicles. As firms compete, unsuccessful rivals fail to capture an appropriate market share, go bankrupt, and have to exit. The variety of competing firms is in both products and practices. Both products and practices are determined by routines that firms use: standardized patterns of actions implemented constantly. By imitating these routines, firms propagate them and thus establish inheritance of successful practices. That is to say, routines are the mechanisms that provide selection, generate variation, and establish self-replication, akin to biological genes. Firms with low-productivity routines will lose market share and will eventually exit the market, while firms with high-productivity routines will gain market share and prosper.

Evolutionary economics is complemented by organizational learning theory. Organizational learning theory states that, in order to be competitive in a changing environment, organizations must change their goals and actions to reach those goals. Learning is a characteristic of an adaptive organization, as organizations need to sense changes in signals from the environment, both internal and external, and adapt accordingly. There are studies, models, and theories about the way an organization learns and adapts. In order for learning to occur, however, the firm must make a conscious decision to change actions in response to a change in circumstances, must consciously link action to outcome, and must remember the outcome. Firms are said to employ experimental processes where successful behaviors are repeated and unsuccessful behaviors discarded. The key to an organization's survival is whether it can adapt when change is happening faster than its people can learn. Thus, effective entrepreneurs are considered to be exceptional learners. Organizational learning has many similarities to psychology and cognitive research, because the initial learning takes place at the individual level; however, it does not become organizational learning until the information is shared, stored in organizational memory in such a way that it may be transmitted and accessed, and used collectively for organizational goals.

There are three components of organizational learning. First, a firm acquires a memory of valid action-outcome links, the environmental conditions under which they are valid, the probabilities of the outcomes, and the uncertainty around that probability (data acquisition). Second, an organization continually compares actual to expected results to update or add to organizational memory (interpretation). Third, the organization takes the interpreted knowledge and uses it to select new action-outcome links appropriate to the new environmental conditions (actual adaptation). The environment is also important in organizational theory, where organizations whose structures are not fitted to the environment (which includes other organizations, communities, customers, governments, and so forth) will not perform well and will fail. Most new organizations fail within the first few years. This is called the liability of newness. If the environment is stable, this selection process will lead most organizations to being well adapted to the environment, not because they all changed but because those that were not well adapted will have died off.

Thus, adaptation links to the theory of firm growth. Larry Greiner notes that the typical process of small firm growth is marked by periods of evolution and revolution. He defines five successive phases, each of which can be traversed only by dealing with a particular crisis. The first phase is growth through creativity, or developing from the birth stage of an organization. In this phase, the founders are usually technically or entrepreneurially oriented; communication is frequent and informal; long hours of work are rewarded with modest salaries and the promise of ownership benefits; and decisions and motivations are highly sensitive to market feedback. Eventually, the firm encounters a crisis of leadership where informal communication becomes infeasible, additional functions must be implemented, and the first critical decision in an organization's development is to locate and install a strong business manager.

The second phase is growth through direction. In this phase, different departments are designed; formal communication results as hierarchy and employees increase; systems are set up for inventory control, accounting, and order processing; and efficiency increases. However, the firm soon faces a crisis of autonomy. In an autonomy crisis, the firm becomes torn as lower-level employees often possess more knowledge about markets and machinery than management. The next decision for management is decentralization.

The third phase is growth through delegation. In this phase, typified by greater empowerment of managers and diversification of products, the firm often encounters a crisis of control. Lower-level managers begin running their own show without coordinating with the rest of the organization and management must again focus on control.

The fourth phase is growth through coordination, characterized by the formation of product groups called strategic business units. In this phase, the firm must overcome a crisis of red tape. Procedures take precedence over problem solving such as formal planning procedures. Steps must be taken to manage the company's size and complexity.

The final phase of firm evolution and revolution is growth through collaboration. At this point, the organization should be able to handle the right teams for the right problems, where social control and self-discipline replace formal control.

Preeta M. Banerjee
Brandeis University

See also Agility and Rapid Response; Change; Change Management: Corporate; Growth; Learning Theory; Market Evaluation; Obstacle Identification

Further Readings

Aldrich, H. E. *Organizations Evolving*. London: Sage, 1999.

Cyert, R. M. and J. G. March. *A Behavioral Theory of the Firm*. Upper Saddle River, NJ: Prentice-Hall, 1963.

Greiner, Larry E. "Evolution and Revolution as Organizations Grow." *Harvard Business Review*, v.50/4 (1972).

Levinthal, D. and G. Gavetti. "Looking Forward and Looking Backward: Cognitive and Experiential Search." *Administrative Science Quarterly*, v.45 (2000).

Nelson, R. R. and S. G. Winter. *An Evolutionary Theory of Economic Change*. Cambridge, MA: Harvard University Press, 1982.

Penrose, Edith T. *The Theory of the Growth of the Firm*. Oxford, UK: Basil Blackwell, 1959.

Schumpeter, J. A. *Capitalism, Socialism, and Democracy*. New York: Harper and Brothers, 1942.

Simon, Herbert A. *Models of Man*. New York: John Wiley and Sons, 1957.

ADVERTISING

Advertising, as well as similar domains such as branding, marketing, and public relations, plays an important role not only in venture management but also in other spheres of contemporary life. Since everyone is exposed daily to thousands of ads and commercials that deal with all aspects of human existence, advertising serves many functions in modern reality. Its multifunctionality leads to the number and variety of scientists interested in advertising, representing, among others, such domains as sociology, economics, psychology, and linguistics. All of them stress another aspect of advertising; thus it is a concept that escapes easy categorization.

Although the definition of advertising varies across different disciplines, certain factors define modern advertising. First, it is a form of paid communication, since companies have to remunerate, for example, publishers and broadcasters for time, costs, and people if they want to publicize their offer to attract regular and potential customers. Moreover, it is a public mode of communication. In most cases, advertising aims at communicating a message to a relatively wide spectrum of people. The third aspect is its persuasive nature. Advertising aims at convincing people to opt for promoted products or services. The fourth feature is the variety of entities that can be advertised, including products, services, ideas, thoughts, people, and even countries. The fifth facet is its impersonality, since advertising is mainly monologic. Dialogism can be traced in the positive reaction toward the presented commodity or idea when customers make their choices. An exception occurs in direct response advertising, which engages clientele in active communication—for example, having them respond to an offer by e-mail or telephone.

Moreover, advertising does not exist in a vacuum since it reflects cultural, legal, political, and economic reality. As far as the legal sphere is concerned, there are certain limitations related to the timing and methods used to advertise certain types of products. Most of these restrictions concern cigarettes and alcohol, which must be accompanied by a notice about harmful effects. There are also certain rules concerning products for children and their advertising. As far as this aspect is concerned, the Children's Advertising Review Unit (CARU) is the organization that pays attention to the issues presented in the advertisements directed at children. To stay within the legal and ethical sphere of promotion, deceptive advertising should be avoided; deceptive advertising includes bait-and-switch advertising, which draws the attention of potential customers by offering low-priced products with the real aim of attracting customers to more expensive offers.

Approaches to Advertising

There are two views on advertising. One treats advertising as an effective tool of marketing. Advertising is understood as the sum of the activities related to promoting individuals, products, services, and ideas in order to make people choose the particular product, service, or idea among other competitive offers. According to the second perspective, advertising is a sociocultural instrument of educating and socializing members of society.

As far as the first aspect is concerned, advertising informs about available products and services and may promote healthy or socially demanded behaviors. Taking into account the economic sphere of advertising, some scientists state that advertising speeds up economic growth and determines the number of employment possibilities. On the other hand, some postulate that advertising may result in a loss of jobs, since some products may attract fewer customers after the launch of advertising campaigns. Apart from the above-mentioned economic and social benefits related to the advertised products, customers want the available commodities to meet their emotional needs. Thus, the social sphere of advertising is understood in the broad sense, encompassing both sociological and psychological dimensions of individuals and organizations.

History of Advertising

Although advertising is a part of modern venture management, its origins can be traced back to the ancient times, because people have always wanted to communicate and exchange goods. For example, in ancient Greece signboards and billboards were popular among shopkeepers for advertising their goods. In Egypt, professional criers were used to inform people about incoming trading ships. The first forms of ancient advertising as well as the methods used in the Middle Ages relied heavily on the spoken mode of communication. The first printed advertisement for a prayer book was published in England in 1477. The year 1625 marked the introduction of newspaper advertisements.

The 19th century brought some changes in the methods of advertising. For example, the inn sign or the apothecary's container with some colorful liquid belonged to the visual sphere of advertising at the beginning of the 19th century. Mid-19th-century advertising made use of movable promotion, including wooden vehicles with posters that could be pulled by horses and sandwich boards that were strapped to people's bodies. Printed media were very important in advertising in the 19th century. The

20th century relied heavily on radio and later on television. The 21st century, apart from the already mentioned channels, saw the addition of many online modes of communication. The growth of advertising throughout history is related to increases in population, the size of settlement or market at which the advertising is aimed, the role of mass production, the development of infrastructure, and the proliferation of mass media. However, although the methods and tools have changed considerably over the last centuries—from very simple to very sophisticated ones—the core idea remains the same: to attract the potential customers.

The reasons for advertising are primarily connected with modern times. More and more companies have produced similar products, with supply far exceeding demand. Thus, advertising is needed to make a person pay attention to one product and select it at the expense of competitive commodities. This is connected with the first function of advertising, namely, to communicate with regular and potential customers. What is more, advertising speeds up the process of commercial exchange, since it determines the flow of products and services from producers to customers. Other functions of advertising depend on the type of advertising.

Types of Advertising

Advertising can be classified in a number of ways. Advertising can be divided by taking into account the type of response it should elicit. As far as the reply is concerned, advertisements can be divided into those resulting in direct and indirect actions. Taking the focus of elicited response into account, advertising can be primary and secondary. Primary advertising, also called generic advertising, focuses on generating the demand for a product, not for a particular brand. This type of promotion is used especially in the case of social advertising, with the aim of introducing or maintaining some required habits within the society. A similar approach is shared by idea advertising, which is nonproduct advertising related to, for example, environmental or health problems. On the other hand, secondary or selective advertising aims at choosing a particular brand.

Advertising can also be divided by taking the aim into consideration. Product advertising concentrates on a particular product or products. Consumer advertising, also sometimes called retail advertising, is directed at the general public to attract attention to the company. Sometimes the aim of advertising is not to persuade anyone to buy products or services. In the case of institutional advertising, the efforts are directed at creating the corporate image, with no specific product being advertised. Thus, the aim is to show the potential users as well as the established clientele all the corporation's positive features. This approach comprises both short- and long-term strategies that aim at strengthening brand awareness.

Business-to-business advertising (industrial advertising) is directed at other companies, at selected markets. In the past it was called trade-and-technical advertising. Financial advertising is related to publishing financial results in the press, which strengthens the corporate image and its position on the market. Recruitment advertising is used in finding new staff. Depending on the types of specialists needed, different channels and strategies are employed. It can be divided into recruitment advertising performed by employees and recruitment advertising performed by employers.

Advertising can also be discussed by taking into account the tools used: national newspapers, technical journals, regional press, and free newspapers can be distinguished. Effects can also be used to categorize advertising: Instantaneous effects are related to the customers' immediate reactions to the ad; carryover effects, on the other hand, are those that do not take place immediately after the customers see the ad. Advertising also can be discussed through the geographic prism: local, regional, national, and global advertising. As far as its aim is concerned, advertising can be divided into informative, persuasive, and reminder-oriented. Informative advertising focuses on raising the awareness of customers, whereas persuasive advertising deals with those techniques and methods that persuade customers to opt for the offered products. Reminder-oriented advertising aims at refreshing customers' memories of corporate offers. As far as the number of sponsors is concerned, advertising can be divided into single advertising and cooperative advertising, with horizontal or vertical sponsors. Advertising can also be branched into above-the-line advertising and below-the-line advertising; the former encompasses advertising conducted by hired agencies to act on behalf of the companies that want to sell products and services, whereas the latter deals with advertising activities conducted by the companies themselves (leaflets, letters, brochures, and so on), with the aim of increasing the number of customers.

Advertising also depends on the type of products advertised. Thus, different techniques are used for consumer goods advertising (commodities purchased on a regular basis, connected with everyday existence, such as fast-moving consumer goods) and others for consumer durables advertising (rarely bought goods and luxury products). Advertising can be discussed by taking the mode of expression into consideration; thus, the sense on which it relies (such as verbal, non-verbal, organoleptic, or sonic) can be treated as the distinguishing element. Verbal advertising is strictly related to linguistic repertoires, whereas nonverbal advertising includes the subbranches of visual, organoleptic, and sonic advertising. Two types of subconscious advertising can also belong to this type of advertising. Ambient advertising, including logos and other promotional elements, is embedded in everyday reality. The place in which the advertising signs are present reflects the needs addressed by them. Subliminal advertising is related to using images or words that are not directly perceived by customers.

Sometimes a mixture of the methods mentioned is used to strengthen the power of advertising. Advertising can make use of these sources simultaneously, since hybrid advertising offers broad coverage and may result in more customers and an improved corporate image. Advertising can also be divided by taking into account the type of medium: television, radio, magazines, and newspapers. Moreover, new media may involve interactive advertising, which has become popular with the rise of e-commerce, taking advantage of people spending a considerable amount of time in front of their computers. Affiliate marketing occurs when one Website advertises other online offers. The e-zine, comprising online magazines and newsletters, belongs to the more monologic forms of online advertising. Taking the location into account, place advertising, with such items as billboards, posters, transit ads, and cinema advertising, can be discussed.

Outdoor advertising covers all the types of advertising used in the open air. This form of advertising uses such tools as adshels (popular at bus stops and railway stations), billboards, aerial advertising (banners dragged by airplanes), banners moved by cars, vehicle wraps, and information placed on taxi cabs. Such forms are sometimes called transport advertising.

Advertising can also be performed in the shop. To the so-called point-of-purchase category belong various store signs, shopping cart ads, and in-store television and radio announcements designed to promote products available on display in the store. Advertising has to take into account the type of users: loyal users, light users, and those aware of the product but not users. Each of them requires different strategies and methods to be persuaded to expand use of the product or buy it for the first time. Other aspects are related to the attitude of customers toward the ad. Wearing advertising describes the interest of the public in the advertising, whereas wear out advertising suggests the decline of customers' interest. Other types of advertising include advocacy or issue advertising, when the company offers an opinion on controversial topics as well as supporting its position at the same time, and comparative advertising, when the product is compared directly or indirectly to a competitive one and pictured as the superior one. In some countries, this method of advertising is illegal.

Advertising can also be analyzed through the cost perspective. Cooperative advertising belongs to retail advertising and can be realized in various ways, including common logotypes or shared costs. Advertising can also be discussed by taking into account the scope of its activities. Mass advertising is directed at the mass audience, whereas personal advertising aims at the individual. In the case of mass advertising, the methods used have the potential to involve the attention of many people and include television, the press, and outdoor tools. Other methods include inserts, such as the catalogs in magazines, or cross-ruffs, coupons placed with the product offering discounts for other products from the same company.

Elements of Advertising

The most important elements of advertising are advertising strategies and advertising appeals. Advertising strategies are all the actions taken to persuade and inform customers. The adapted strategy depends on the product and the type of target user. As far as the target consumer is concerned, there are two consumer insights determining advertising: related to the target and connected with the brand position. The choice of appeals depends on the type of product or service being advertised as well as the target users. For example, fear is used in advertising cars, health issues, or insurance. On the other hand, humor is used to strengthen the corporate image and to make the brand more memorable. The last has to be used cautiously, taking into consideration various cultural factors, such as the gender and age of the consumer.

Magdalena Bielenia-Grajewska
University of Gdansk, Institute of English

See also Business-to-Business Marketing; Competition; Customer Orientation; E-Commerce; Entrepreneurial Marketing; Focus Groups; International Markets; Market Evaluation; Social Networks; Target Markets; Test Markets

Further Readings

Boone, L. E., D. L. Kurtz, H. F. MacKenzie, and K. Snow. *Contemporary Marketing.* Scarborough, ON: Nelson Education, 2010.

Chauhan, M. R. *Advertising: The Social Ad Challenge.* New Delhi, India: Anmol Publications, 2001.

Jefkins, F. and D. Yadin. *Advertising.* Saddle River, NJ: Pearson Education, 2000.

MacRury, I. *Advertising.* Abingdon, UK: Routledge, 2009.

Petley, J. *Advertising.* North Mankato, MN: Smart Apple Media, 2004.

Shimp, T. A. *Advertising Promotion and Other Aspects of Integrated Marketing Communications.* Mason, OH: South-Western Cengage Learning, 2008.

Sinclair, J. *Images Incorporated: Advertising as Industry and Ideology.* London: Routledge, 1987.

Tellis, G. J. *Effective Advertising: Understanding When, How, and Why Advertising Works.* Thousand Oaks, CA: Sage, 2004.

Yadin, D. L. *The International Dictionary of Marketing: Over 2,000 Professional Terms and Techniques.* London: Kogan Page, 2002.

AFRICAN AMERICANS AND ENTREPRENEURSHIP

Prior to Emancipation, slave and free African Americans (AAs) started and ran successful businesses. Events of the last century, such as the Great Migration north and the modernization of the American industry, created traditionally lower AA participation in entrepreneurship, and much of the history of successful AA entrepreneurs has been lost.

Only now is AA participation in entrepreneurship returning to previously high levels.

In this entry we review current literature on AA entrepreneurship and attempt to answer questions like "What is the history of AA entrepreneurship?" "What are the barriers?" "What interventions were attempted?" "What are the individual and collective AA success stories?" and "What is the future of AA entrepreneurship?"

Entrepreneurship, Entrepreneurs, and Black-Owned Businesses

Before discussing AA entrepreneurship, it is important to get a clear idea of what we mean by *entrepreneurship* and *entrepreneur.* Researchers have defined an entrepreneur as a person who can perceive an opportunity and creates an organization to pursue it. There is some discussion about the definition of entrepreneur, with some proposing that only those who start a new enterprise can be defined as entrepreneurs. For the purpose of this article, we choose to use the more general definition of entrepreneur as anyone self-employed in business, including anyone who has bought or inherited a business. The 2007 *Survey of Business Owners* (SBO) defines black-owned businesses as firms in which AAs own 51 percent or more of the stock or equity of the business.

Participation of AAs in Entrepreneurship

While research is showing that groups such as immigrants and women who are disadvantaged in employment often turn to enterprise, this does not appear to be the case with AAs. AAs owned 1.9 million nonfarm U.S. businesses in 2007, an increase of 60.5 percent from 2002, at a time when all U.S. firms increased only 18 percent, according to the U.S. Census Bureau. In 2007, black-owned firms accounted for 7.1 percent of all non-farm businesses in the United States, 0.8 percent of total employment and 0.5 percent of total receipts.

The participation of AAs in enterprise has been estimated at about one third of white Americans (WAs) for nearly a century, although one researcher has found that in 1910 AAs were more likely than WAs to be employers (13.91 percent compared to 12.52 percent) and almost as likely as WAs to be self-employed (12.88 compared to 16.30 percent). By 1996, only 4.4 percent of AA men were self-employed compared to 12 percent of WA men. The participation rate is even lower for AA women; only 2 percent of employed AA women are self-employed.

AA participation in entrepreneurship is affected by interest in entrepreneurship as a career, attempting to start a business, successful business start-ups, and years in business. Indications are that AAs are interested in business and start businesses at a higher rate than WAs, but they face greater barriers, which in turn leads to less success and higher failure rates, although successful AAs stay in business longer than other minorities. Fairlie found that the entry gap between AAs and WAs was partly explained by lower asset levels and lower probability of having a self-employed father, but those factors did not explain the exit gap.

A Brief History of AAE

AA participation in entrepreneurship can be divided into three major eras: the era of slavery and the Civil War (before 1865), the era of emancipation and Jim Crow segregation (1865–1915), and the era of entry into urban-industrial society (after 1915).

Before emancipation, both slave and free AAs participated in entrepreneurship. Butler notes that free AAs dominated the restaurant and service industries in the North before the Civil War. Southern craftsmen applied for and received dozens of federal patents, and some successfully marketed their inventions. Slaves and former slaves dominated the crafts industries in the South until laws were passed forbidding people to own the tools of their trade and restrictive unions organized crafts workers to include only white men of good character.

The Emancipation Proclamation by Abraham Lincoln on January 1, 1863, proclaimed the freedom of 3.1 million of the United States' 4 million slaves, and the Thirteenth Amendment to the U.S. Constitution, which officially abolished and continues to prohibit slavery and involuntary servitude, was adopted on December 6, 1865. A number of significant events followed that impacted AA entrepreneurship.

While for WAs the watershed of the 1890s was characterized by advances in industry, technology, migration to the cities, immigration, increased material consumption, and a rags-to-riches mentality, for AAs it was also an age of lynching, restricted citizenship, segregation, and Jim Crow politics. Jim Crow came from a song sung in the 1930s tradition of white minstrels, who applied black cork to their faces and performed songs and dances in imitation of African American slaves.

The period introduced a segregated system that locked AAs out of mainstream politics, economy, and culture but was countered by the development of strong local AA communities. However, segregation, which confined AAs to ethnic enclaves, could have encouraged AA enterprises. In 1863 the U.S. Census Bureau reported 2000 AA-owned businesses. By 1913, that number had increased to 40,000.

The National Negro Business League (NNBL) was founded in Boston, Massachusetts, in 1900 by Booker T. Washington, with the support of Andrew Carnegie. The mission and main goal of the NNBL was to promote ". . . the commercial and financial development of the Negro." The NNBL coincided with a "buy black" movement, which supported AA entrepreneurship. During this time, the number of AA enterprises appears to have increased from approximately 9838 in 1900 to 19,000 in 1910. Typical AA enterprises included funeral parlors, barber shops, beauty salons, cafés, and convenience stores. At about the same time, W. E. B. Du Bois promoted higher education for AAs as a major priority and necessity for successful entry into business.

Booker T. Washington founded the National Negro Business League in 1900 with the help of Andrew Carnegie. The mission of the National Negro Business League was to promote "educational, and industrial advancement . . . and the commercial and financial development of the Negro." (Library of Congress)

Starting in the late 19th century through the Great Migration of southern AAs to northern cities following World War I, ethnic enclaves provided AA enterprises with sizable, geographically concentrated AA markets. By 1914, nearly 1.5 million AA southerners had migrated north. Boyd shows that the residential segregation of AAs was positively associated with AAs' shopkeeping ratio, indicating that racial segregation bolstered AA business ownership opportunities, particularly in the areas of barbering and retail.

By 1950, more than 9 million AAs lived in urban areas, making it the first decade that more AAs lived in cities than in rural areas. The influx of AAs into the cities was accompanied by a flight of WAs to the suburbs, creating "pockets of poverty" requiring "urban renewal" through the federal government's Housing Act of 1949. Urban renewal became known as "Negro removal," and AA businesses removed rarely survived.

Before the civil rights movement of the 1960s, U.S. AAs and WAs were segregated throughout most of the southern United States through separate restaurants, hotels, schools, and hospitals. Ironically, success in integrating housing, education, and workplaces contributed to the demise of AA enterprises, as WA enterprises were forced to serve AA patrons and local AA enterprises found that they could not compete with large chains.

Community Interventions and Impacts on AA Enterprise

The 1960s were known for the civil rights riots in many major cities, which often left AA communities in a state of further damage and despair. AA-owned retail and service shops were often replaced by liquor stores and check-cashing shops. President John F. Kennedy initiated the Area Redevelopment Act of 1961, which was designed to subsidize new job opportunities in declining communities by offering low-interest business loans. After two years on a reduced budget the program shut down. However, it was praised because it discussed and addressed economic change and structural unemployment as sources of community decline. President Lyndon B. Johnson initiated the Community Action Program (CAP) to allow the poor to assume a direct role in designing and implementing antipoverty programs and to provide jobs for the poor. The program was poorly administered,

and by the 1970s CAP had lost its government support.

In the mid- to late 1960s, Johnson initiated the Model Cities Program, which was canceled as a result of insufficient funding. The following Special Impact Program was designed to revitalize neighborhoods characterized by high poverty and chronic unemployment by providing block grants to community-based organizations to design and administer their own development strategies. In 1972, the Small Business Investment Companies program was expanded to create private Minority Enterprise Small Business Investment companies to provide equity capital and long-term debt financing to minority entrepreneurs. This was not particularly successful in attracting private investment, and the Small Business Administration (SBA) stopped funding in 1993.

The community development block grants created by the Housing and Community Development Act of 1974 replaced specialty grant programs and gave localities discretion in allocating funds to urban development. Community development corporations (CDCs) linked business development, housing, and commercial development in novel training, compensation, and ownership arrangements, but high-poverty neighborhoods increased in number and size through the 1970s and 1980s. The New Markets Tax Credit program offered tax credits for community investments. In the 1980s, 35 states adopted enterprise zones to provide tax breaks to businesses as an incentive to locate in poor communities. In 1993, the Empowerment Zone/Enterprise Community program was adopted, which had larger grants for social services and economic development, regulatory waivers, and tax breaks for employing within the zone. Eleven cities received Empowerment Zone designations, making them eligible for grants and tax breaks up to $100 million, and 95 smaller Enterprise Communities received smaller grants and business incentives. In 2000, the Community Renewal Tax Relief Act provided $25 billion in tax incentives for renewal communities, new markets tax credits, expansions of the empowerment zones, low income housing tax credits, and private activity bonds. Administered by the Community Development Financial Institutions Fund (CDFI), the New Markets Program encourages participation of public and private for-profit entities such as community development entities (CDEs), investors, qualified low-income community investments, and qualified low-income community businesses. CDFI evaluates business strategies, capitalization strategies, management capacity, and community impact to provide grants, loans, equity capital, and technical assistance to community development financial institutions with the mission of advancing social responsibility and economic profit. In 2006, the program was extended, and as of 2007, 233 awards were made. While the program has revitalized poor communities with projects, such as new shopping centers, only 6 percent of the transactions involved minority-owned businesses, which received only 3 percent of the funding. While this reflects the percentage of AA businesses, it does not reflect the percentage of AAs in the population. Jackson proposes that the program is misdirected and should focus investments in minority-owned enterprises, which are more likely to employ minorities and local residents, to successfully revitalize urban minority communities.

Nongovernment programs also focused on strengthening AA entrepreneurship. Since 1989, Nissan North has helped enrich the business school faculty and curriculum of historically black colleges and universities (HBCUs) by sponsoring the Nissan-HBCU Summer Institute. Some HBCUs, including Howard University, Clark Atlanta, Florida A&M, and Norfolk State University, have business centers.

Barriers to AA Participation in Entrepreneurship

Differences between WA and AA enterprise participation rates can be explained by historic, economic, and demographic differences between the two groups, which typically create barriers to AA enterprise participation. Differences in the opportunity recognition processes of AA and WA nascent entrepreneurs may also play a part. To some extent, the challenges AAs face in business are the same as those faced by WA entrepreneurs. A study of the critical challenges facing rural small businesses that consult the SBA categorized the challenges as administrative, operating, and strategic and found that these challenges differed more by stage of the business life cycle than by race. However, barriers can reduce the percentage of AAs that enter business and increase the AA business failure rate. Researchers have found that AAs were more optimistic and almost twice as likely to attempt starting a business compared to WAs, suggesting that underrepresentation is not due

to a lack of trying but instead to barriers to entry and higher failure rates. In the construction industries, racial discrimination has been found to occur in unions, in white general contractors' contracting and bidding processes, in construction project conditions, and in the bonding, lending, and supplier networks critical to a successful construction business.

Historic Differences

Levenstein proposes three historic differences in AA entrepreneurship, which could lead to lower AA participation. First, at the turn of the century AAs were more highly concentrated in agriculture than were WAs. Second, AA women were more entrepreneurial than WA women and represented a higher percentage of the AA workforce. Third, a larger proportion of AA men in agriculture were employers and a large proportion of AA women were self-employed in agriculture and personal services. Levenstein speculates that as the agriculture industry declined, so too did AA entrepreneurship.

Levenstein found evidence that, like other immigrant entrepreneurs who congregated in ethnic enclaves, AA entrepreneurs were more likely to be located in counties with a higher percentage of AA population. The reducing wealth of the AA community would also erode the success and profitability of AA enterprises. In a national comparison of business performance among AA entrepreneurs located in cities and suburbs, AAs located outside their ethnic enclave were found to perform consistently better than those doing business within it.

Economic Differences

Researchers have found that the earnings of AA males are consistently below those of WA males throughout their lifetimes. AAs are most often the first fired but not typically the last hired during an economic downturn. AAs have levels of wealth one-eleventh those of WAs. Starting with this disparity, researchers found AAs to be much less likely to start businesses than WAs, which has resulted in a substantially lower rate of business ownership. Even for those AA entrepreneurs who are successful in starting businesses, Robb and Fairlie find that on average they invest much less capital at start-up than WA entrepreneurs. Lower levels of start-up capital among AA businesses appear to also limit their ability to grow and succeed. Racial disparities in start-up capital contributed to higher failure rates, lower sales and profits, less employment among AA-owned businesses, and less survivability of the business.

Economic disadvantage translates into disadvantage in all types of resources, from computer and Internet to education and access to capital. While it has been found that a "digital divide" exists between AAs and WAs, this divide has been larger for children than for adults. These differences were only partly explained by differences in education and income, but luckily the digital divide seems to be disappearing at a rapid rate.

Disadvantages in Accessing Finance

In 1998, a telephone survey by researchers on bank financing of AA and WA small businesses owners concluded that AAs are discriminated against, even when they are as creditworthy as WAs. A smaller percentage of AAs received loans, more AAs received less than the amount requested, AAs started their business with a smaller percentage of borrowed capital, and more AA business owners had completed a college education.

In 2005, a study of small business credit sources found that AA owners are more dependent on loans from nonbank sources than are WA owners, and they also were more likely to be rejected for trade credit.

Education Differences

Education is significantly related to entering and succeeding in business. While researchers have found that AAs in business have educational levels similar to those of WAs, as a group AAs do not have the same education levels, which can explain lower AA participation in entrepreneurship.

A study of AAs attending a historically AA university in the southeastern United States found that AA males had a more positive attitude toward entrepreneurship and education than did AA females, although not statistically significant. They also found that as age and grade point average increased, so did positive attitudes toward entrepreneurship and education. Similar to what has been found in other studies, AA students with entrepreneurial parents had more favorable attitudes toward entrepreneurship and education. Possibly as a result of less formal education and business experience, AA women value business training more than their WA counterparts.

Differences in Opportunity Recognition

Studies show that the opportunity recognition processes of AAs differs from those of WA entrepreneurs. One study proposed that opportunity recognition could be externally stimulated (that is, the decision to start a venture precedes opportunity recognition) or internally stimulated (the opportunity is identified and the decision to create a venture follows). Nascent entrepreneurs pursuing internally stimulated opportunities were found to have greater education and financial resources. AA nascent entrepreneurs pursue externally stimulated opportunities with lower expected revenues than did WA nascent entrepreneurs.

Black Enterprise 100

To get a bigger picture of AA entrepreneurs, a 2007 longitudinal study (covering the period from 1975 to 2004) was based upon *Black Enterprise* magazine's Black Enterprise (BE) 100, a listing of America's 100 largest businesses with more than 50 percent of the company's voting stock owned by AAs. The analysis showed that AA-owned companies grew significantly, with an increase of almost 2,800 percent from 1974 to 2002. Nevertheless, the BE 100's largest firm in 2004 was $1.4 billion, compared to the largest Fortune 500 firm, with $291 billion. The BE 100 also had low survival rates; only 21 of the 1974 firms continued onto the 1984 listing, only five making it to the 1994 listing, and only two surviving to the 2004 listing. This is at least partly because some of the most successful BE 100 firms were acquired by mainstream majority-owned companies and lost their AA-owned status following a period of mergers and acquisitions in the U.S. economy and recognition of the value of black buying power. During this time, AA-owned auto dealerships grew significantly in the BE listings, but the construction/contracting and energy sectors declined, possibly because of the changing nature of government set-aside procurement and contract programs.

The food and beverage wholesale/retail sector also declined, because of a move toward multiple franchise arrangements. The technology sector appeared on the BE 100 and grew with government set-aside purchases of information technology. Corporate minority procurement and government set-aside programs have helped start AA businesses, but they typically account for less than 5 percent of expenditures and may benefit somewhat while hurting other AA and minority-owned businesses. While most minority businesses may start or grow with the assistance of set-aside contracts, they are often unable to "graduate" from the program or maintain profitable sales in the long run.

Conclusion

Despite enormous barriers, African Americans have made significant contributions to U.S. entrepreneurship in industries such as agriculture, skilled crafts, services, and retail. In the 19th century, changes in traditional AA industries, lack of education, less wealth, lack of access to financing, and lack of parental entrepreneurship role models contributed to lower AA entrepreneurship participation rates. Today, AA entrepreneurship is growing at three times the rate of WA ventures, indicating a potential resurgence of AA entrepreneurship in the United States.

Roxanne Zolin
Queensland University of Technology

See also Hispanics and Entrepreneurship; Minorities in New Business Ventures

Further Readings

Conrad, Cecilia A. et al. *African Americans in the U.S. Economy.* Lanham, MD: Rowman and Littlefield, 2005.

Haskins, James. *African American Entrepreneurs.* New York: John Wiley & Sons, 1998.

Lee, Dante. *Business Secrets: 500 Tips, Strategies, and Resources for the African American Entrepreneur.* Carson, CA: Smiley's Books, 2010.

Walker, J. *Encyclopedia of African American Business History.* Westport, CT: Greenwood Press, 1999.

Walker, J. *The History of Black Business in America: Capitalism, Race, Entrepreneurship.* New York: Macmillan, 1998.

AGENCY THEORY

An economic term, *agency theory* is one of the main concepts of the contract theory of institutional economics. It focuses on the agency relationship that arises whenever one or more individuals, called principals, hire one or more other individuals, called agents, to perform some service and then delegate decision-making authority to the agents and reward the service based on the quality and quantity provided by the agents.

Agency theory is based on asymmetric informative game theory, where the asymmetric information refers to the fact that some participants have information that other participants do not have. It is often seen in start-ups, when the entrepreneur employs a manager to conduct the business on his or her behalf, or if there are conflicts between the owner and managers, as well as between the manager and outside shareholders. If agency occurs, it also tends to give rise to agency costs, which are expenses incurred in order to sustain an effective agency relationship. For instance, the entrepreneur may offer managers performance bonuses to encourage managers to act in the interests of entrepreneur and shareholders alike. Accordingly, agency theory has emerged as a dominant model in management and is widely discussed in the context of business ethics as well.

Agency theory in a formal sense originated in the early 1970s, but the concepts behind it have a long and varied history originating from "specialization," which is the result of productivity development and mass production. On one hand, because of limited knowledge, capabilities, and energy, the principal cannot exercise the power; the agent, who has professional knowledge and energy, performs the rights efficiently because of the division of labor. Usually the principal pursues more wealth while the agent aims to maximize his or her wages, allowance, luxurious consumption, and leisure. This gives rise to an inevitable conflict if there is no efficient institutional arrangement. Therefore, both parties hope to work out an optimal contract concerning the managerial compensation to increase the manager's incentive to maximize the entrepreneur's value. The effect of the contract on the actions of managers should reflect better aligned incentives, resulting in greater managerial effort, lower consumption of perquisites, and thus increased firm performance.

On the other hand, the agent's action is observable; the principal could reward the agent based on the observed action; the Pareto risk share and Pareto optimal effort could be fulfilled. As for the new business, because of the asymmetric information the entrepreneur can observe only the related variables and not the manager's behavior; the variables are codetermined by the manager's behavior and other exogenous random factors. Agency theory is dedicated to designing an optimal contract to motivate the agent, the manager, on account of asymmetric information and agency conflicts.

Agency theory has analyzed internal and external mandate relationships using the model method during the last two decades. Three methods are most attractive. The first one is the state space formulation, which manifests the technical relationship naturally but fails to get the informative solution; the second one is the parameterized distribution formulation, which is now the standard method; the third one is called the general distribution formulation and is the most abstract one that has the concise general model.

Usually, agency theory can be studied statically or dynamically and applied to entrepreneurial issues. The former deals with the situation in which the principal motivates the agent to choose the expected action and rewards or punishes the agent according to the observable results. The latter takes the following approach: The repeated theoretical game theory explains that if the principal established a longtime relationship with the agent and both of them are patient, Pareto first-order risk sharing and motivation can be fulfilled. This can also be explained by the reputation model, which states that if the manager's behavior is hard to observe, the long-term agent contract has its advantage, and the manager will have a strong desire to polish his reputation so as to get more revenue in the future; this may cause the risk of a ratchet effect, with the entrepreneur taking the previous performance as the reference to decide the annual target. The harder the manager works, the higher the target is. That is not the desire of the manager; the manager may slow down and do less until retirement. This problem can be resolved using seniority pay that could curb laziness in the long run. During the manager's early career, when the agent salary is lower than the marginal productivity, the gap is the security deposit (for instance, the stock option); when laziness is found, the manager is fired without exercising the option. As time moves on, the manager's salary is bigger than the marginal productivity, and of course no one volunteers to retire; hence, retirement is a must for those who exceed the retirement age.

In the simple agent model, only one principal has been considered. In fact, there can be many principals at the same time. Many economists have studied the case of multiagency—the team, for instance, whose marginal contribution depends on every member's effort level, which is not observable independently. The individual's salary is determined by his performance, while the team depends more on the others. The important factors that determine the teamwork, whether optimal or not, are strategic interdependency, complementation or substitution, and attitude toward work.

Shuyi Zhang
Shanghai Finance University

See also Advertising; Branding; Contextual Marketing

Further Readings

Bitler, Marianne P., Tobias J. Moskowitz, and Annette Vissing-Jørgensen. "Testing Agency Theory With Entrepreneur Effort and Wealth." *Journal of Finance*, v.60/2 (2005).

Eisenhardt, K. "Agency Theory: An Assessment and Review." *Academy of Management Review*, v.14/1 (1989).

Fama, Eugene and Michael Jensen. "Agency Problems and Residual Claims." *Journal of Law and Economics*, v.26 (1983).

Jensen, Michael C. and William H. Meckling. "Theory of the Firm, Managerial Behavior, Agency Costs, and Ownership Structure." *Journal of Financial Economics*, v.3 (1976).

Sappington, David E. M. "Incentives in Principal-Agent Relationships." *Journal of Economic Perspectives*, v.5/2 (1991).

AGILITY AND RAPID RESPONSE

In a business context, agility is a business's capacity for flexibility, coordination, and rapid, effective, cost-efficient response to changes in the business environment. *Agility*, a term usually referring to the physical abilities of the body, is a concept that covers more than just speed of response. It incorporates notions of balance, flexibility, thinking on one's feet, coordinating multiple systems, adaptability, and situational awareness, especially the idea of the business responding as one organism. An agile business not only responds quickly but also does so in such a way that it remains productive and cost-efficient even amid changes to the circumstances affecting its operations.

This idea of agility is one that has been heavily influenced by the study of complexity and complex adaptive systems in the late 20th and 21st centuries. The behavior of complex systems—systems in which the parts are networked and interrelated, not simply a collection of static entities—has been of particular interest to biology and physics, among other hard sciences, and by extension to the mathematicians and computer scientists who have addressed the challenge of modeling such systems. In a complex system, relationships and interactions between parts of the system give rise to the collective behaviors of that system. The system in question may be a local pond and all the forms of life that dwell in it, on it, and at its edge, or that rely upon it for drinking water; it may be the behavior of falling raindrops on the surface of that pond, and the mechanics of how those forces are distributed across the body of water and the things floating in or upon it; it may be the economy of the community where the pond is located and its value as a source of clean water. The study of complex systems often focuses on non-linearity and on the phenomena that emerge from a complex system. Classical political economics, for instance, states that the order of a market system emerges from human behavior but is not the product of human design—the market is orderly, but not because anyone tried to bring order to it. Modern complexity theory is grounded in chaos theory, which views chaos as deterministic—that is, not as completely random phenomena, but phenomena emerging from a system so deeply complicated and interconnected that cause-and-effect relationships are difficult to establish and will not appear to exist without deep study.

Complex adaptive systems are a special class of complex systems in which the behavior of the system, and of its individual constituent parts, changes in response to experience. The brain is a complex adaptive system, the immune system is a complex adaptive system, but so is the stock market or a political party. As circumstances change and as the system experiences different conditions, it and its constituent parts adapt agilely. Like any social endeavor, a business or an entire industry can be seen as a complex adaptive system. Complex adaptive systems must have a number of elements sufficiently large that simply listing them provides no real understanding of the system; the interactions among elements must be rich, meaning that all elements can be affected by and can affect other elements; many interactions are nonlinear, meaning

that minor changes can have significant results; and the system operates with a constant flow of energy to maintain its organization—in other words, it does not achieve equilibrium. It is also generally said that the elements in the system respond only to what is going on within their immediate location—that the elements are ignorant of the system's behavior and act without knowledge of it. This is a murky statement when discussing human social systems, where the players in a system are so often engaged in discussion and analysis of the system.

That lack of equilibrium means that change is constant. For an agile business, change is routine. Change is part of the organization's life. Treating change as a routine phenomenon helps the business avoid the paralysis and hideous missteps that many businesses make in response to environmental changes or the creation of new markets. Coaching businesses and managers on thinking and acting in agile ways and perceiving the business environment accordingly has become a cottage industry among management consultants, and recent history—such as the advent of e-commerce, the housing boom, the derivatives market and subsequent financial crisis, and the growth of new markets in or enabled by the telecommunications sector—has provided ample examples of businesses that thrived or suffered according to their agility in a changing landscape.

However, sometimes, for a business to be agile, it requires more than just agile-minded managers. A business's structure can be designed to let it better respond to changes in circumstance. A nonhierarchical organization without centralized control can sometimes respond more quickly, even in a way that could be called instinctively. A common metaphor for this type of agility refers to the way the body responds to temperature changes: Not only does the autonomic nervous system control temperature-regulating functions such as perspiration below the level of consciousness, but a hand that brushes against a hot oven will instinctively flinch away from it. Flinching is an extraordinary advantage over conscious decision making—the brain is never asked to evaluate the circumstance and determine whether burning is occurring, while the flesh takes more and more damage. The flinch happens so quickly that the response and the catalyst are consciously registered at the same time. Such fast, instinctive responses on the part of complex systems save lives—literally in the case of the body, figuratively in the business world.

What does it mean for a business to be "nonhierarchical," though? It means individuals within the business function with a significant degree of autonomy, interacting with one another—not necessarily as a group—to identify the work that needs to be done and then assuming the roles and responsibilities that best accomplish that work. It may be difficult to picture this behavior in a business setting, yet we see such self-organizing with minimal discussion happen all the time among, for instance, families at airports, where parents and older children instinctively assume the responsibilities for themselves and for the younger children in order to go through the process of check-in. Sometimes this family behavior may depend on established roles—one parent may be carrying the wallet, another parent may hold the tickets, and an older sibling may have been told to keep an eye on his younger siblings. However, it can arise simply from situational awareness, awareness of the circumstance surrounding the complex system of the family and awareness among the members of that system of each member's needs and abilities.

Decisions in an organization without central control are made on the fly and collaboratively, and knowledge and responsibility must thus be distributed throughout the organization. This is in contrast not only to the hierarchical organization with a centralized concentration of authority but also to the traditional notion of planning. Agility does not rely on a list of predetermined possible occurrences with predetermined responses, any more than a gorilla swings through the jungle by mapping the trees out in advance. Planning, at its extreme, requires certainty. It requires a finite set of circumstances and responses. Agility is not impaired by uncertain foreknowledge. A common approach to business agility is to combine planning with self-organizing, letting the complex system that makes up the business adjust to changing circumstances and search for the ideal distribution of resources.

One reason agility is so important is that the market is competitive. Often not every business can survive—certainly all businesses cannot thrive equally. When circumstances change, the ability to respond instantly to them helps prevent prosperity from being simply a matter of luck. Agility is key to the sustainability of a business, allowing it to continue to exist and thrive through fads, economic changes, changes to the industry, the opening and closing of markets, changes to the regulatory environment, and changes to the customer base. Consider the changes experienced in the last few decades by phone companies—which not long ago competed for long-distance and collect-calling customers—or by the tobacco industry. One industry has seen an explosion, at times confusing, of new opportunities and new customers; the other industry has dealt with increased antismoking regulations and the threat of class-action lawsuits. Both industries thrive, but not every company in them adapted equally well to the changes. Consider, for that matter, the railroads, which were once the most important and profitable companies in the country; while railroads remain critical, the market does not have room for as many companies as it would have if not for the advent of automobiles and airplanes, and many companies were left behind in the transition to the present.

Agility is not simply the ability to recognize an opportunity as circumstances change. During the dot-com boom, eBay, Pets.com, and America Online all took advantage of the interest in e-commerce, with major success in the short-term but significantly different results in the long term. eBay, selling an auction service that presented it with no need for warehousing, shipping, or some of the other logistics that cut into the cash flow of online retailers, remains prosperous. As time went on, it acquired PayPal. Pets.com was one of the highest-profile busts when the bubble burst, spending exorbitantly on advertising but unable to provide a profitable service because of the expensive cost of shipping cat litter and bulk pet food, making them unable to compete with brick-and-mortar stores. America Online pioneered dial-up Internet access and became wealthy enough to acquire Time Warner but soon found its brand synonymous with obsolescence as cable and phone companies assumed most of the burden of providing high-speed Internet access and news reports revealed that the bulk of AOL profits came from subscribers unaware that they were paying for a service they did not use.

Agility is key not only to new ventures as they establish themselves or to established companies weathering changes in circumstances but also to entrepreneurs in creating new ventures. Very often there is a brief window of opportunity during which a new venture may be launched, whether because of time-limited circumstances, the need to use resources while they are available, or the need to launch a venture before the marketplace becomes crowded and somebody else occupies the niche. Being first is not all that matters, but it helps, and competing for business when there is not yet an established market leader is an easier proposition for a small business. Entrepreneurship is really the ability to identify opportunities, quickly assess the situation and the resources needed to capitalize on those opportunities, and move forward with a rapid response.

Bill Kte'pi
Independent Scholar

See also Adaptation; Cash Flow; Change; Change Management: Corporate; Crisis Management: Corporate; Innovation Processes; Learning; Planning Fallacy

Further Readings

Bennet, A. and D. Bennet. *Organizational Survival in the New World: The Intelligent Complex Adaptive System.* New York: Elsevier, 2004.

Godin, Seth. *Purple Cow*. New York: Portfolio, 2009.

Richardson, K., ed. *Managing Organizational Complexity: Philosophy, Theory, and Application.* Greenwich, CT: Information Edge Press, 2005.

B

BANKRUPTCY

To be bankrupt is the state or condition of a person, whether individual, partnership, corporation, or municipality that is unable to pay its debts. Formally, bankruptcy laws provide a debtor with the means to make use of the federal and/or state bankruptcy code for protection from creditors. Under the federal law of the United States, 11 United States Code Annotated codifies the rights of creditors and debtors when debtors are unable to pay their debts.

Numerous studies have looked at small-business failure rates over the past 30 years. According to the National Federation of Independent Business Education Foundation, 2.9 million businesses were launched in 1997, involving nearly 4 million people. Another 1 million people purchased 700,000 existing businesses that year.

The data showed that most new businesses are very small. More than two-thirds start in the owner's home, and only 21 percent initially employ someone besides the owner. According to the Bureau of Labor Statistics, of the two-thirds that survive past two years, only about 40 percent last as long as four years. One of the biggest reasons for new-business failure is inadequate financing. Far too many businesses have been launched with insufficient working capital, without enough money to cover all expenses plus allow for contingencies until a reliable income stream can be generated.

New ventures are particularly vulnerable to failure due to several reasons that include unfavorable economic conditions, ineffective marketing of the business, incompetence of owner(s), and financial vulnerability. The failure rate of new ventures particularly as related to debt is high during the first five to 10 years.

The data collected for small business for example in the United States is composed of majority nonemployer firms. As of 2006, it was estimated that there were about 25 million nonemployer businesses, which include contractors, freelancers, and others who choose to work alone. The average earnings from these firms were about $47,000. It is also noted that nonemployer firms are more susceptible to failure than any other type of small-business venture. Business failure is captured through disappearance from the tax records signifying demise. This measure is somewhat misleading given that a name change or conversion from a nonemployee to an employer status may be counted as a failure of the previous business type.

In 2006, for example, the U.S. Small Business Administration (SBA) reported 671,800 new businesses and 544,800 business closures in the same year. A footnote however noted that the figures did not mean that all closures were a result of bankruptcy.

Petition for Bankruptcy

A case of voluntary petition for bankruptcy relief is initiated by the debtor. A case of involuntary petition for bankruptcy relief is made by the creditor. In both scenarios the assets of the debtor can be marshaled and managed by a trustee. A trustee is a position appointed by the bankruptcy court to take charge of the debtor's estate, to collect assets, to bring suit on debtor's claims, to defend actions against it, and otherwise administer the debtor's estate. Creditors wish to be paid all or at least a portion of what they are owed from the assets of the debtor once those assets are liquidated. Creditors are almost always paid in order of their priority. This means that the first to become a creditor of the debtor, or more importantly, the first to document that they are a creditor of the debtor in a way that allows the public to know of their status as creditor, will be the first to be paid from the liquidated assets of the debtor's estate.

There is both secured and unsecured debt. Unsecured debt is money lent to a debtor or credit extended where nothing is pledged as collateral. A credit card is a type of unsecured debt. The credit card company provides a line of credit to the consumer of such service. The consumer uses the card to charge a purchase and intends to pay at a later time. For instance, a consumer may charge a sweater at a store for $40.00. The bill will come later and if the debtor is unable to pay the $40.00 plus interest to the creditor, the creditor may later attempt to collect the debt. This is a form of unsecured credit because the sweater itself was not pledged as collateral for the credit. No one will come to the debtor and take the sweater away. Thus, when the assets of the debtor are marshaled in a bankruptcy case the unsecured creditor will collect cash or some of the cash that it is entitled to only after the secured creditor has taken the collateral, which it helped the debtor obtain.

An example of secured credit is a purchase money mortgage for a home. In this instance the collateral is the home. The creditor's money has been advanced specifically for the purchase of the listed collateral, the home. When the debtor cannot pay its bills and files for bankruptcy, the creditor will have a first lien and first right to collect the collateral pledged, which is the home in this instance. Thus, this collateral will come out of the pool of assets that other creditors can liquidate in order to be repaid the credit that they extended.

In some instances, bankruptcy can be used to reorganize. When a debtor realizes that it cannot or will soon be unable to pay its debts as they become due, a petition can be filed in the bankruptcy court to allow for reorganization. The debtor continues its business, but with the oversight of the bankruptcy court, it organizes its debt, liquidates property, enters realistic repayment plans with creditors, and is thus allowed an agreed-upon time to repay/settle its obligations.

Business reorganization is a Chapter 11 Bankruptcy, Straight Bankruptcy is a Chapter 7 Bankruptcy, Family Farmer Bankruptcy is a Chapter 12 Bankruptcy, and Chapter 13 is a Wage Earner's Bankruptcy. The States of the United States also have provisions allowing bankruptcy. Texas is considered one of the most liberal and favorable to the debtor.

The Bankruptcy Code states, "Notwithstanding any other provision of this section, only a person that resides or has a domicile, a place of business, or property in the United States, or a municipality, may be a debtor under this title." It also stipulates that "an involuntary case may be commenced only under chapter 7 or 11 of this title, and only against a person, except a farmer, family farmer, or a corporation that is not a moneyed, business, or commercial corporation, that may be a debtor under the chapter under which such case is commenced."

Once a bankruptcy petition is filed, an automatic stay can operate as a hold prohibiting the commencement or continuation of any judicial, administrative, or other action or proceeding against the debtor that was or could have been commenced before the commencement of the case under this title, or to recover a claim against the debtor that arose before the commencement of the case under this title.

There is certain property that is exempted from taking by a creditor in a bankruptcy case. The federal statute is designed to allow the debtor to continue life, regain financial footing, and recover. With certain exceptions the debtor's residence is exempt, motor vehicle, household furnishings, life insurance, health aids, social security benefits, alimony, support, and the like.

A judicial discharge of debt by a bankruptcy court voids any judgment at any time obtained, to the extent that such judgment is a determination of the personal liability of the debtor with respect to any debt under a particular section of the Bankruptcy Code. Also, the discharge operates as an injunction against the commencement or continuation of an action, the employment of process, or any act, to collect, recover, or offset any such debt as a personal liability of the debtor, whether or not discharge of such debt is waived.

While it is difficult to consistently predict the direction of the overall economy, understanding the drivers (interest rates, inflation, unemployment, consumer indebtedness, and currency values) goes a long way toward making sound decisions about how to manage a business especially at the early stages. Some specific risks faced by small business include: credit, legal, and regulatory risks. As a result of credit risk it is typically difficult for small business and new ventures to secure financing. On the legal risk dimension, there is a risk of being sued for compromised data, faulty products, or hazardous working conditions. In 2008, data breaches were up 69 percent over the prior year, according to the Identity Theft Resource Center. There is also the regulatory risk of keeping pace with government mandates.

The Internal Revenue Service (IRS) *Publication 908: Bankruptcy Tax Guide* outlines the tax consequences of bankruptcy. Debtors must continue to file appropriate tax forms and deposit payroll taxes withheld for employees. The IRS holds business owners personally liable for unpaid payroll taxes. Payroll taxes include withheld state and federal income taxes, Medicare and Social Security taxes, and unemployment insurance taxes. When a business declares bankruptcy, the IRS can take personal assets to satisfy these debts. The IRS provides a few options for settling unpaid taxes that are particularly appropriate in bankruptcy cases. In most cases, they set up an installment payment plan. In rare cases, the IRS will accept an offer for less than the total amount due.

Dominic DePersis
Broome Community College
Alfred Lewis
Hamline University

See also Accounting; Barriers to Entry; Business Failure; Cash Flow; Credit; Debt

Further Readings

Black's Law Dictionary, 6th ed. Eagan, MN: West Publishing Co., 1990.
Hansen, Bradley and Mary Hansen. "Legal Rules and Bankruptcy Rates: Historical Evidence From the States." Social Science Research Network. http://papers.ssrn.com/sol3/papers.cfm?abstract_id=954393 (Accessed August 2011).
Kehoe, Timothy J. and David K. Levine. "Bankruptcy and Collateral in Debt Constrained Markets." Social Science Research Network. http://papers.ssrn.com/sol3/papers.cfm?abstract_id=940605 (Accessed August 2011).
Korteweg, Arthur G. "The Costs of Financial Distress Across Industries." Social Science Research Network. http://papers.ssrn.com/sol3/papers.cfm?abstract_id=945425 (Accessed August 2011).
Lawless, Robert M. "The Relationship Between Nonbusiness Bankruptcy Filings and Various Measure of Consumer Debt." Social Science Research Network. http://papers.ssrn.com/sol3/papers.cfm?abstract_id=934798 (Accessed August 2011).
Lawless, Robert M. and Elizabeth Warren. "Shrinking the Safety Net: The 2005 Changes in U.S. Bankruptcy Law." Social Science Research Network. http://papers.ssrn.com/sol3/papers.cfm?abstract_id=949629 (Accessed August 2011).
Lyandres, Evgeny and Alexei Zhdanov. "Investment Opportunities and Bankruptcy Prediction." Social Science Research Network. http://papers.ssrn.com/sol3/papers.cfm?abstract_id=946240 (Accessed August 2011).
National Federation of Independent Business. http://www.nfib.com (Accessed August 2011).
Sutton, Chavon and Brett Nelson. "The Biggest Risks to Your Business." http://www.forbes.com/2009/04/15/biggest-business-risks-entrepreneurs-management-risk.html (Accessed August 2011).
U.S. Internal Revenue Service. http://www.irs.gov (Accessed August 2011).
U.S. Small Business Administration. http://www.sba.gov (Accessed August 2011).

BARRIERS TO ENTRY

An economics and business term, *barriers to entry* is based on the theory of competition in which the tendency of competitors in the market is to limit competition in an effort to raise profits to a maximum. The first thorough study of the nature and extent of barriers to entry was conducted by Joe S. Bain in his 1956 book titled *Barriers to New Competition*, in which he defined an entry barrier as the set of technology or product conditions that allows incumbent firms to earn economic profits in the long run. Bain identifies three sets of conditions in which barriers to entry are evident: economies of scale, product differentiation, and absolute cost advantages. Since Bain's 1956 definition, barriers to entry have been further expanded to include those procedural, regulatory, economic, and technological factors that obstruct or restrict new competitors from easily entering an industry or area of business even when incumbent firms are earning excess profits.

There are two broad classes of barriers: structural and strategic. Structural barriers (also known as exogenous barriers) are those entry conditions that are naturally occurring barriers, such as technology, patents, economies of scale, a strong brand identity, strong customer loyalty, high start-up costs, cultural differences, unstable economic conditions, or high customer switching costs. Strategic barriers include building market leadership, developing consumer loyalty, establishing product branding, forming strategic alliances, exclusive resource ownership, controlling the distribution network, and protecting intellectual property rights; they may also include predatory pricing policies that result from lowering prices to a level that would force any new entrants to operate at a loss.

Barriers to entry can also exist as a result of governmental intervention, making entry more difficult or impossible through industry regulations, legislative limitations on new firms, special tax benefits to existing firms, or requirements for licenses and permits. In extreme cases, government regulations may make competition illegal and, as a result, establish a statutory monopoly. One of the key points in discussions between governments via the World Trade Organization is the infant industry protection argument used by governments to defend artificial barriers that reduce international competition via the imposition of tariffs and nontariff barriers imposed to increase the final cost of foreign competitors.

Entrance into a new market carries the barriers of convincing existing customers to buy the new product and finding distribution channels to carry the goods. Barriers to entry protect existing firms by reducing the level of competition. (Photos.com)

Barriers to entry protect incumbent firms from new competition by reducing the level of competition and as such provide the firm with the ability to raise prices and protect profits without losing market share. As such, barriers to entry are a central subject of contention in antitrust lawsuits, when within industry; those incumbents permanently reduce competition from new entrant firms.

Barriers to entry are always present to a new entrant as the very nature of the rules of the game: investment is always required, however minimal it may be. Entrance into a new market will require convincing the existing customers to buy and distribution channels to carry the goods. There are also barriers to exit that can prevent a new company from entering the market. If a company is inhibited in its ability to leave the market, it increases rivalry because in order to stay in the market the company has to compete. Barriers to exiting an industry have several associated costs:

1. *Write-down of assets:* the expense associated with writing off plant and machinery and stocks.

2. *Harvesting costs:* typically considered closure costs, including exiting a contract with a supplier as well as the penalty costs from premature exiting leasing arrangements for property and machinery.

3. *Loss of goodwill and reputation among customers:* exiting a market can have deleterious effects on the goodwill among customers, not least those who have bought a product that is then withdrawn and for which replacement parts become difficult or impossible to obtain.

4. *Sunk costs:* capital input that is specific to a particular market and that has little or no resale value if a business decides to exit the industry; typically sunk costs include monies spent on advertising, marketing, and research that cannot be carried forward into another market or industry.

In Michael Porter's seminal 1979 article "How Competitive Forces Shape Strategy," he classifies barriers to entry and exit into four general cases:

1. High barrier to entry and high exit barrier (as in the case of pharmaceuticals or aircraft)

2. High barrier to entry and low exit barrier (education, consulting)

3. Low barrier to entry and high exit barrier (hotels, ironworks)

4. Low barrier to entry and low barrier to exit (retail, e-retailing)

Furthermore, Porter states that markets with high entry barriers have fewer competitors and thus higher profit margins. Markets with low entry barriers typically have multiple competitors and, therefore, lower profit margins. Extending his classification of barriers, Porter states that markets with high exit barriers are unstable and not self-regulated; thus, the profit margins tend to fluctuate over time. On the other hand, markets with low exit barriers are stable and are self-regulated; hence, the profit margins remain stable over time. Finally, barriers to entry constitute the key characteristic that separates oligopoly from monopolistic competition on the continuum of market structure. Porter states that the higher the barriers to entry and exit, the more prone a market tends to be a natural monopoly, and the lower the barriers, the more likely the market is to become a perfect competition.

The concept of entry deterrence is not without opponents who feel that entry barriers are rather ineffectual in preventing competitive entry. In 1982, George S. Yip published a book entitled *Barriers to Entry: A Corporate Perspective* in which incumbents look to barriers to entry as a secure, protective covering against threats and subsequently build an overdependence on these structures, creating a false sense of security and unwillingness or inability to engage in innovations. Yip supports his claim by discussing the ever-increasing late entrants into the marketplace leapfrogging into leadership positions on the strength of their successful innovations, substantiating his claim regarding the ineffectiveness of the barriers to entry and that they appear to provide little or no protection for incumbents.

Dominic DePersis
Broome Community College
Alfred Lewis
Hamline University

See also Business Angels; Business Models; Cash Flow; Community/Government Buy-Ins; Credit; Debt; Feasibility Studies; Public Policy: Government

Stimulation of Start-Ups; Strategy; Venture Capital; Venture Management Firms; Venture Valuation

Further Readings

Bain, Joe S. *Barriers to New Competition.* Cambridge, MA: Harvard University Press, 1956.
Porter, Michael. "How Competitive Forces Shape Strategy." *Harvard Business Review* (March/April 1979).
Yip, George S. *Barriers to Entry: A Corporate Perspective.* Lexington, MA: Lexington Books, 1982.

BARTER

To barter is to trade or exchange goods, services, or things of value for other goods, services, or things of value without using money as the medium. There are hundreds of formal barter exchanges located around the world in both developed and developing countries and likely thousands of informal systems of barter. The International Reciprocal Trade Association (IRTA) is a nonprofit organization with the stated mission of being committed to promoting just and equitable standards of practice and operation within the modern trade and barter and alternative capital systems industry, and raising awareness regarding the value of these processes. The barter system of exchange of goods and services dates back centuries. Bartering was used before money was created. People who had specific items or services would exchange them with others for the things they needed. Barter tended to fade in popularity and eventually became subordinate to the use of money in thriving economies, but with today's decline in the economy and high unemployment, barter has regained favor. In years past, barter would have occurred only in local exchanges because of the lack of contact with those located geographically far away. Today, however, individuals can easily barter on a global level: Websites on the Internet are filled with proposals for barter.

For those starting new businesses, the expense can be great and can pose a major barrier of entry into a new market. Many entrepreneurs are bartering with other entrepreneurs for goods and services needed for their new businesses, each offering their strengths in exchange for those of another. The *Wall Street Journal* has highlighted the benefits of barter in an article showcasing entrepreneurs who are

Bartering at the local market in Pátzcuaro, Michoacán, Mexico. Barter exchanges take place around the world in both developed and developing countries and date back centuries. (Wikimedia)

keeping overhead low by sharing office space, trading on photographs and artwork, modeling work, and sharing public-relations expertise. Barter is common for small start-up companies and is also widely used by Fortune 500 companies. Professionals are also utilizing bartering as a means of exchange. The North Carolina Bar Association, for example, formally adopted an Ethics Committee Opinion that allows lawyers in North Carolina to participate in barter exchanges.

Today, advances in technology have made it possible to use the barter system in a much more sophisticated way than was previously possible. The basis of barter, however, remains as rudimentary as ever: the need for something that one does not have and someone else does in exchange for something one possesses in excess or a skill or knowledge that one can offer in trade. The barter system allows one to negotiate the worth of an item, service, skill, or ability in relation to products or services that are needed without money being an obstacle.

As in any business transaction, negotiation is the key to making good barter contracts. Many people and businesses as well as not-for-profit entities have acquired as well as disposed of goods and services by means of technology. Businesses, including new ventures, can now take advantage of expertise,

goods, services, and other resources located in another industry, another stage of development, or another geographic location to move their enterprise forward. Barter may even be preferable to money in some instances. Money varies in its use and its value, which can fluctuate in unpredictable and sporadic ways. Barter exchanges may prove steadier and more representative of true value between two parties executing a trade.

In the economic environment of the early 2010s, with the aid of cheap and readily available technology, creative individuals and ventures can increase their wealth as well as fulfill their basic needs through barter. Laid-off workers with a computer can begin to sustain their homes and families through barter. The barter system can be referred to as an economic matchmaking process. Companies have been established to serve as clearinghouses for barter. The clearinghouses typically charge an annual membership fee and a percentage in real dollars for each transaction. In exchange, they provide a place for those interested in the exchange of goods and services to meet without having to seek each other out on a case-by-case basis. These clearinghouses provide another efficiency of the modern economy: an alternative mode of financing transactions in the interconnected global economy.

One may barter on a housing arrangement, tutoring services, manual labor, a skill, goods, and know-how. Finding the right match is the first step, followed by negotiating what both parties feel is a fair trade. A successful barter transaction can also provide a networking opportunity for future barter as word travels about one's offerings. Barter may exist on a onetime basis, a trade that develops because a party possesses a specific good or item another enterprise or individual needs, or barter may involve the exchange of a service that others cannot afford to pay money for in a particular community or at a particular time. Barter may be a method of paying debt, in that a creditor may agree to accept a good or service in exchange for a cash payment due.

Parties to a barter transaction should be aware of and careful to consider all relevant laws for contract, capacity to contract, jurisdiction, and taxation, among other issues in any given transaction. In the United States, barter exchanges are defined as third-party record keepers under the Tax Equity and Fiscal Responsibility Act of 1982 (TEFRA) and as such are subject to Internal Revenue Service (IRS) reporting for the annual gross barter sales of the barter exchange's members. As a result, barter exchanges are also subject to IRS-imposed civil penalties for nonmatching tax identification numbers (TINs) and therefore must comply with solicitation requirements where nonmatching tax identification numbers have been identified.

Dominic DePersis
Broome Community College
Alfred Lewis
Hamline University

See also Credit; Debt; Entrepreneurial Training; Equity- and Debt-Based Financing; Job Creation; Sales; Selling Products and Services; Strategy

Further Readings

Gigafree Network. "Barter Exchanges." http://www .gigafree.com/barter.html (Accessed February 2011).

Glenn, Pam. *Barter World*. Portland, OR: Class Action Ink, 2009.

Hoffman, Karen S. and Shera D. Dalin. *The Art of Barter: How to Trade for Almost Anything*. New York: Skyhorse, 2010.

Internal Revenue Service. "Tax Responsibilities of Bartering Participants." http://www.irs.gov/businesses/small (Accessed February 2011).

International Reciprocal Trade Association. http://www.irta .com (Accessed February 2011).

Richmond, R. "Starting on a Shoestring." *Wall Street Journal* (July 13, 2009).

Sadoff, Ira. *Barter*. Urbana: University of Illinois Press, 2003.

Youn, Monica. *Barter*. Saint Paul, MN: Graywolf Press, 2003.

BOARDS OF DIRECTORS

A board of directors (BOD) is a group appointed at the inception of an organization or elected to provide oversight in terms of the operations of an organization or corporation. In certain instances, especially in not-for-profit organizations (NFPs), the BOD is referred to as board of governors, board of trustees, or governing board. The task of the BOD is typically delineated in the articles of incorporation and bylaws or conferred by an external authority or body. The bylaws will typically specify the maximum number of board members, selection criteria, terms of service, and required meetings. In a publicly traded corporation, the BOD is elected by the common stockholders, who are the legal owners of the enterprise, given their capital investment. In other instances, such as foundations and some NFPs, the BOD is the ultimate governing instrument of the organization.

The role of the director is that of corporate stewardship. Qualifications to be a director are few. In New York, like most jurisdictions, directors simply need to be at least 18 years of age. Most statutes state that the certificate of incorporation or the bylaws may prescribe other qualifications for directors. The law itself, however, does not prescribe any experience or training or knowledge in the business of the corporation or in business in general. Most corporations seek to have a balanced board, meaning that they want some inside and some outside members. Inside members are those who are full-time employees of the corporation and members of the management team. An outside director is one whose full-time employment is something other than the corporation of which he or she is a director.

There is much published about the makeup of a board: the strategy, the psychology, rotation of members, and optimal use of members. All corporations need directors. The board consists of one or more members. When a business is young and just beginning, it may in fact have only one member. That one member may be the owner of the business, who is doing all of the functions. On the other end of the spectrum, where there are businesses that have been in existence and are successful and known, then directors may be detached and aloof from the operation of the business. The director may be chosen for reasons such as his or her ability to attract business to the corporation or to enhance the corporation's prestige as a result of the director's own reputation.

The existence of the corporation begins upon the filing of the certificate of incorporation with the department of state. After the corporate existence has begun, an organizational meeting of the incorporator or incorporators must be held for the purpose of adopting bylaws, electing directors, and transacting business. The initial bylaws of a corporation are adopted by its incorporator or incorporators at the organization meeting. Thereafter, directors take on the role of amending or enhancing the bylaws under which the corporation operates.

The corporation is required to keep correct and complete books and records of account and must keep minutes of the proceedings of its shareholders, as well as any meetings of the BOD or executive committee. The corporation must also keep a record containing the names and addresses of all shareholders, the number and class of shares held by each, and the dates when they respectively became the owners of record. In addition, a meeting of shareholders must be held annually for the election of directors and the transaction of other business on a date fixed by or under the bylaws. The department of state does not require or maintain information regarding the names and addresses of officers or directors of corporations, the members or managers of a limited liability company, the limited partners of a limited partnership, or the partners in a limited liability partnership. These records are internal records maintained by the corporation, limited liability company, limited partnership, or limited liability partnership.

Organizations such as the National Association of Corporate Directors (NACD) exist to (in the words of NACD's mission statement) "aid in helping boards and directors do their jobs better, faster, and more efficiently. Members remain ahead of their profession and benefit from value that no great book, onetime course, or single consultant can offer. The training allows a board to reinforce its strengths

with services, education, resources, and connections." The Corporate Board Member, an NYSE Euronext company, "provides information resources for senior officers and directors of publicly traded corporations. The quarterly publication, *Corporate Board Member* magazine, provides readers with decision-making tools to deal with the strategic and corporate governance challenges confronting their boards."

There are a variety of views about the roles and responsibilities of a BOD. The directors are legally charged with the responsibility to govern a corporation. In a for-profit corporation, the BOD is responsible to the stockholders. In a nonprofit corporation, the board reports to stakeholders, particularly the local communities that the nonprofit serves and/or the parent organization that chartered it. Unless they are inside-directors, the directors do not concern themselves with the daily operations of the corporation or interact with employees or customers. The directors do supervise and provide guidance to executives. They can do this only with accurate and complete information. Directors have a duty to exercise due diligence to seek information and knowledge that will allow them to exercise educated judgment. The corporation's financial condition is of utmost importance, and the directors must be apprised of the company's financial status and must seek out information and ask tough questions about the reports that they are handed. The directors hire and fire the executive officers who report to them, and their relationship with these individuals should be good and information complete, accurate, and freely forthcoming.

Scholars such as Dr. Toby Stuart have recently studied interlocking boards and the experience and prestige of directors and their influence in change-of-control transactions.

The board chairman and board secretary play pivotal roles. The secretary plays a key role in soliciting and assembling the information on which the other directors rely. Also, the secretary records accurate minutes of what transpires during board meetings and advises members of the meetings in the hope that a quorum will be present to conduct the corporation's affairs. The secretary prepares an agenda and distributes it. Meetings by the board may be held at any place within or without the state, unless otherwise provided by the certificate of incorporation or the bylaws. The time and place for holding meetings of the board may be fixed by or under the bylaws or, if not so fixed, by the board. Business of the board can be conducted when a quorum is present. Unless a greater or lesser proportion is required by the certificate of incorporation, a majority of the entire board constitutes a quorum.

Statutory law in each state provides rules on the addition, subtraction, and replacement of board members to help ensure that the board is not manipulated for purposes not in line with the best interests of the entity and its stockholders. Directors especially have a responsibility to act in the best interest of the corporation. Directors can be legally liable for their acts and failures to act. Moreover, a director who is present at a meeting where an action in contravention of good-faith execution of duties takes place is presumed to have concurred in the action unless his or her dissent was entered into the minutes of the meeting. Thus, being a director requires a strong personality and leadership skills. A director who is absent at a meeting has a responsibility to read the minutes of the meeting and object in writing to any wrongdoing by the other directors.

Dominic DePersis
Broome Community College
Alfred Lewis
Hamline University

See also Family Business; Stakeholders; Succession Planning

Further Readings

Dornstein, Miriam. *Boards of Directors Under Public Ownership: A Comparative Perspective.* Berlin, Germany: W. de Gruyter, 1988.

Lee, Chang Min. *Three Essays on Boards of Directors.* Bloomington: Indiana University, 2008.

Lipton, Martin. *Deconstructing American Business II and Some Thoughts on Boards of Directors in 2007.* Washington, DC: National Legal Center for the Public Interest, 2006.

National Association of Corporate Directors. http://www .nacdonline.org (Accessed February 2011).

Stuart, Toby E. and Soojin Yim. "Board Interlocks and the Propensity to Be Targeted in Private Equity Transactions." *Journal of Financial Economics*, v.97/1 (July 2010).

Vinnicombe, Susan et al. *Women on Corporate Boards of Directors: International Research and Practice.* Northampton, MA: Edward Elgar, 2008.

BRANDING

Branding can be described as all the actions related to introducing new products or services to the market. Taking the wide spectrum of branding activities into account, it encompasses both individuals and organizations. Thus, it is important for customers, since everyday activities are accompanied by the existence of different brands and branding determines regular product or service choices. Branding is also crucial for managers, because it is an important part of new venture management—it makes more stakeholders interested in the offer, maintains the desired level of satisfaction among regular users, determines the complete life cycle of products and services, and also responds to the accumulated experience of their users, adapting to the changing circumstances of the environment.

The increasing role of technology and media in modern reality belongs to these changing conditions. For example, social networking, blogging, and Websites determine branding, with printed media being less important than in the past. Technology is also related to branding and different products' life spans through the creation of online brands.

As far as the phases of brands are concerned, two types of branding can be distinguished. The first one, branding itself, encompasses all the activities related to introducing a new product or service to the market, as previously mentioned. The second type, rebranding, deals with adapting the brand to the new conditions of its environment.

Branding can be discussed by taking different notions into consideration. The first perspective encompasses brand constituents. A brand is constituted by both tangible and intangible elements that distinguish its products from other competitive products or services. Its material representation is visible in logos, names, colors, and designs. Although all these elements are important, the name comes first when one thinks about a brand. Thus, branding will encompass all the activities related to the process of naming or renaming the brand. Given the importance of the brand name in every customer's mind, it is one of the first elements to be considered when a new venture is established and also one of the last elements to be changed when any reorganization takes place. Sometimes the name of the brand is altered, especially when it has become associated with negative issues or is offensive in itself in the target culture of the brand. The name can be an acronym, a regular word, the founder's surname, or a coined word (such as a conglomerate of parts coming from other words, names, or surnames). In addition to its name, the brand is often built by special wording that accompanies the name. At the verbal level of branding, the following words are among the most popular: "the best," "number one," "top class," and "leading." Given the complexities of naming strategies, effective linguistic branding is key in international marketing and management.

A second consideration in the process of branding is to take into account the scope of branding strategies. Consequently, this marketing tool can be divided into different types of branding: individual branding, family branding, corporate branding, and global branding. Individual branding, or product branding, is the use of different brands for different products. Thus, products manufactured by the same company have different names. This strategy proves to be very useful in any crisis situation, since the bad image of one product need not affect other commodities produced by the company. However, at the same time, each product's brand must work well independently for its success, and thus poor branding of one of the company's products can negatively impact the overall bottom line. Family branding (also called umbrella or validated identity branding), on the other hand, is related to using the same name for various products. The same brand name can reduce the overall cost of marketing related to gaining and maintaining a good market position for various products or services. Family branding can also make it easier to introduce new products. However, when one product loses market position, its bad situation will negatively influence the other products' market positions. Corporate branding ties the identity and brand of the entire corporation to all of its products. This strategy carries the same cost-saving advantages as does family branding but also threatens the same potentially negative chain reaction should the corporation lose the market position of one of the products. Global branding is connected with creating a product that is globally recognized. However, it does not necessarily have to be associated with exactly the same commodity in every country in which the company is present. Sometimes the global brand carries different names in various cultures.

There are various ways of making a brand a global one. One of them is to internationalize local brands, with certain changes being applied in order to tailor the brand's appeal to customers in different cultures. The other way is to connect local values to one global brand in order to enlarge the spectrum of its users. In the case when no local product can be adapted to meet the needs of a modern diversified market, a new global brand is created. This method is popular in industries involved in information technology and the production of technological devices. Another method for creating global brands is related to mergers and acquisitions, when a local brand is purchased to expand the power of a global brand. The other option is to use the name of the existing brand for new products, thereby incorporating new product categories into the existing one.

Branding can also be divided into different types: nation branding, place branding, destination branding, and sport branding. Branding also encompasses nonprofit and commercial branding. Nonprofit branding entails branding of such organizations as charities and foundations. As far as personal branding is concerned, people—from famous sports figures to cooks, celebrities, politicians—can become brands.

Taking the visual aspect of brands into account, it should be stressed that branding encompasses creating logos and packaging. Consequently, branding is a multidimensional process. The brand idea is what the brand represents. The brand personality encompasses the attitude it mirrors. The verbal identity is related to the name of the brand and the narrative associated with it. The visual identity is connected to the way it looks. The sensory identity is related to its sensual dimensions, such as sounds and the feelings the brand evokes. Sonic branding, for example, entails using music and other sounds to communicate brands. Scent branding is related to linking smells with particular brands. This does not necessarily have to entail food products, since other products are associated with certain smells as well. Scent branding is connected with the real smell of the product and the fragrance used by workers or sprayed in corporate interiors.

Branding should also take into account different roles that are carried by the brands themselves. Sometimes people choose specific brands to show their status, to display their identity, to influence others. One aspect of branding is, consequently, brand positioning, which is creating the perception of a brand in users' minds. Because of brand positioning, the customer knows why the brand is superior to other ones and why it is worth choosing. In order to position the brand efficiently, certain aspects have to be taken into account. As far as brand positioning is concerned, there are mainly two ways of applying these methods. In single major brand positioning, the producer chooses one important notion. However, since existing in different markets is connected with adapting to various needs, sometimes a company opts for second-benefit positioning to meet the needs and expectations of the local users. There are different ways of choosing the right positioning. In attribute positioning, the company concentrates its efforts on one important feature and the outstanding attribute becomes the key element of the product. In benefit positioning, the advantages connected with using the product are stressed, such as effectiveness and safety. In use or application positioning, the best commodity's utility is highlighted. User positioning stresses the best potential user group for the products. In competitor positioning, the comparison to competing products is involved. In category position, the leading position of the producer and its products within the category is stressed. Quality and price positioning stresses the quality or price of the positioned products.

Certain elements must be avoided in brand positioning. Underpositioning occurs when the product is not known by customers and, consequently, not purchased by them. On the other hand, overpositioning happens when the brand is too specialized and not required on an everyday basis. Confused positioning occurs when the brand is connected with too many, often contradictory, positions or actions. Irrelevant positioning occurs when the brand is connected to a product that interests a very narrow group or very few customers. Doubtful positioning results when people do not believe that the product has special qualities. It can be expected that, with the further development of new venture management, new forms and types of branding will appear.

Magdalena Bielenia-Grajewska
University of Gdansk, Institute of English

See also Advertising; Change; Franchises: Starting; Patent Protection; Positioning a New Product or Service; Retailing; Trademarks

Further Readings

Bennett, G. *The Big Book of Marketing*. New York: McGraw-Hill, 2010.

De Mooij, M. *Global Marketing and Advertising: Understanding Cultural Paradoxes*. Thousand Oaks, CA: Sage, 2009.

Holt, D. B. *How Brands Become Icons: The Principles of Cultural Branding*. Boston: Harvard Business School Press, 2004.

Kapferer, J. N. *The New Strategic Brand Management: Creating and Sustaining Brand Equity*. London: Kogan Page, 2008.

Kotler, P. *Kotler on Marketing: How to Create, Win and Dominate Markets*. New York: The Free Press, 1999.

Tybout, A. and G. S. Carpenter. "Creating and Managing Brands." In *Kellogg on Marketing*, A. J. Tybout and B. J. Calder, eds. Hoboken, NJ: John Wiley and Sons, 2010.

Tybout, A. and B. Sterntha. "Brand Positioning." In *Kellogg on Branding*, A. M. Tybout and T. Calkins, eds. Hoboken, NJ: John Wiley and Sons, 2005.

BUSINESS ANGELS

Business angels are an important source of capital to early-stage ventures. They invest in high-potential companies and entrepreneurs who are unlikely to be able to raise more debt or to attract financing elsewhere. Business angels invest at the early stage of the venture creation process, when the venture is not likely to be viable without the direct participation of the entrepreneur. In most cases, business angels believe that their direct involvement in the company after investing significantly will increase the likelihood that the venture will be successful. Business angels are important not only to entrepreneurs and new ventures but also to the local economy, and their importance in stimulating new technological ventures is increasing.

Who Are Business Angels?

Entrepreneurs starting businesses need to invest money ahead of revenues. This money may fund inventory, product development, or simply overheads and payables. In most cases, entrepreneurs' initial source of this money is from their own pockets. Once they have exhausted their own savings and other assets, they often take on personal debt, either through personal credit cards or through guaranteed loans. In some cases, once these sources are exhausted, the entrepreneur may be able to borrow money from family and friends; however, such investment is hardly at arm's length, and most invest as a favor, with limited expectations of a return.

While banks are often cited as an important source of financing for early-stage ventures, they are useful to the early-stage entrepreneur only if she or he can provide some level of business security (such as receivables or inventory) or a further personal guarantee. This is often not that useful or even feasibly for the early-stage entrepreneur, and limited access to sources of cash constrains the growth activities of most early-stage entrepreneurs. High-growth businesses, even if extremely profitable, are also likely to need additional cash, above and beyond that generated from the profitable growth of the enterprise.

For high-potential businesses, there is another option: The entrepreneur can share the risk in the company (and the return) by attracting third-party investors to provide cash in return for equity. These investors, who have no direct relationship to the entrepreneur, are known as business angels. The term *business angel* derives from the tradition of angel investors who financed very risky theatrical productions on Broadway in the early part of the 20th century. In part the risk of investment was based on information asymmetry between the entrepreneur and the investor: The investor could not determine important factors about the entrepreneur because of a lack of information about both the product and its track record. The business angel invests money, usually in return for a significant equity share, with the hope that in the future a sale of equity can provide a satisfactory return on investment.

Business angels are financially secure individuals (often termed to be accredited investors based on their personal net worth, such that governments allow direct investment to take place in the entrepreneur's business without the onerous requirements of a public listing) who invest their own money. In addition, business angels usually see the provision of direct assistance to the entrepreneur running the venture as a way of increasing the likelihood of the long-term success of the venture. Many of the more successful angel investors have previous entrepreneurial or industry experience and tend to invest in technologies or markets with which they

are familiar, which enables them to provide some relevant guidance to the entrepreneur and often gives them credibility in the eyes of the entrepreneur. This "smart money" enhances the likelihood that a funded venture will be successful and reduces the business angel's perception of the investment risk.

A good example of a successful business angel, whose previous entrepreneurial and industry experience enabled him to contribute to the success of an invested company, is Mike Markulla. Markulla made his fortune in two successful Silicon Valley technology companies, Fairchild and Intel. After taking early retirement, he was then introduced to Steve Jobs and Steve Wozniak and became their first investor. Once at Apple computer, he helped them to write a business plan and, through his direct involvement, enabled them to obtain subsequent rounds of venture capital financing. (Business angel and venture capital investing is usually done in rounds, with the company's valuation increasing between each round, meaning that less equity is surrendered for the same amount of investment at subsequent rounds of financing.) Markulla also hired the company's first president and subsequently took on that role himself.

While most business angels invest small amounts of money in less than five companies, a limited number of business "super angels" invest larger amounts, sometimes in several ventures simultaneously. Furthermore, a growing number of business angels invest in syndication with other business angels, either to reduce their financial risk or to access the expertise or opportunities of a coinvestor.

Why Are Business Angels Important?

Business angels are a very important source of equity finance in regional economies, as they provide much-needed financing to entrepreneurs who otherwise would be unable to grow their businesses. For example, Bell Telephone (in 1874), Ford Motor Company (in 1903), and Apple Computer (in 1977) were all funded by business angels. Business angels typically invest at the early stage of the venture creation process and in lower amounts than the better-known venture capitalists, who are professional investors who invest other people's money. Unlike venture capital investors, business angels invest only in businesses where they believe they can develop a long-term relationship with the entrepreneur as well as the business. Although venture capitalists often invest with the idea that if an entrepreneur does not perform, he or she can be removed, removing the entrepreneur is rarely an option for business angels who invest in early-stage ventures.

More important, business angels, who invested $26 billion in 2007, fund as many as 30 times as many start-ups as do venture capitalists, and in most cases business angel investment is a prerequisite for future rounds of venture capital. (Venture capitalists invest a similar amount, but in larger individual investments.) Venture capitalists use both the endorsement by the business angel and the experience of the business angel in working with the entrepreneur as indicators of future success. According to the Center for Venture Research, in 2007 there were more than 258,000 business angels in the United States, and business angels were important sources of finance in most developed countries (including Canada, the United Kingdom, Germany, and Japan) and developing countries (such as China, Singapore, and nations in South America). However, because business angels are individuals, with different backgrounds, experiences, and motivations, it is not easy to come to conclusions about business angels; their roles and influence vary by region.

Business angels, who provide more venture financing than venture capitalists, typically look for an investment return of between 25 and 35 percent per annum and expect to be involved in the business for between five and seven years, before a suitable exit is identified. Most business angels are male, between ages 45 and 65, and fund local opportunities where they can both make a direct contribution to the venture's success and play a mentorship role for the entrepreneur and management team. Business angels not only are motivated by money but also often have a personal motivation beyond the potential financial rewards of their investment. This can include a desire to give back something to the community, to create an environment that fosters the next generation of entrepreneurs, or to become a role model.

How Do Business Angels Make Investment Decisions?

Entrepreneurs interested in obtaining investment from business angels may be hard pressed to understand exactly how a business angel makes such a decision. Unlike venture capitalists, who try to explain their investment decisions when they justify their investment decisions to funders, business angels each have their own investment criteria. Business angels often go with their "gut feeling" and make their decisions quite quickly, often with limited initial due diligence (the review of all pertinent information—such as market, technical, and financial—about the company, in order to confirm entrepreneur representations). Given the long-term personal relationships likely to develop between the business angel and the entrepreneur over the lengthy investment period, business angels often focus more attention on the entrepreneur than the opportunity and use heuristics to identify the critical factors that help them to make rapid investment decisions.

Given the large number of individuals involved in making investment decisions, it is challenging to explain how most are made. This is further complicated because most investment decisions are undertaken in private, as there is a concern by both parties that disclosing too much information could damage both the negotiation and the viability of the business. In addition, the business angel will often rely heavily on information about the entrepreneur implied by his or her previous work experience, academic background, and referral source. Our lack of understanding of how business angels make their investment assessment and the influence of their own experience makes it difficult for entrepreneurs to know which business angels to approach and what they are seeking.

Fortunately, there is a growing body of research into business angels' decision making and their investment process due to an increasing recognition of the importance of business angels in providing smart money to early-stage technology companies. In addition, media coverage and the development of an international television show, *Dragons' Den* (*Shark Tank* in the United States), now filmed in more than 20 countries, have created an increasing interest in both the role of business angels and how they make decisions. This research suggests that investors are concerned primarily with whether the company will increase in value sufficiently to provide the angel's required level of financial return. The calculation of the return on investment is based on the venture valuation at the time of investment and the likely company value at the point where the business angel is able to sell his or her equity position. This highlights the importance to the business angel of negotiating sufficient initial equity share and identifying exit strategies that maximize the future venture valuation. Entrepreneurs conscious of this can better approach the negotiation of initial equity valuation and provide evidence of likely future interested acquirers and valuations to a potential investor.

Investors also consider the investment risk, which consists of both the performance and the relationship risks. Performance risk is the likelihood that the venture will not achieve its potential valuation, while the relationship risk is the likelihood that the entrepreneur will not act in the best interests of the investor. The business angel often reduces the former by identifying resources that can help reduce this risk and reduces the latter by becoming directly involved in operating the business.

It would seem that business angels follow a staged decision-making process, where they first investigate venture factors and future valuation potential before determining investment risk. The business angel is also concerned with building a trusting long-term relationship with the entrepreneur, as replacing the entrepreneur is unlikely. The investor's assessment of each of these venture and risk factors is also influenced by their prior experience, their industry knowledge, and their own personality characteristics (particularly if they have been an entrepreneur themselves). During an investment interaction, when the entrepreneur is pitching to the investor, the investor's confidence in whether he or she can work with the entrepreneur over the long term is based primarily on the entrepreneur's displays or recollections of previous or actual behaviors.

The Future Role of Business Angels

It is increasingly challenging for existing companies to develop disruptive technologies, as their existing business structures are more suited to increasing sales of existing products. As a result, disruptive technologies are often better commercialized through the creation of new ventures that can take rapid advantage of new opportunities and react more quickly to technology and market trends. However, these new companies are cash constrained and unable to acquire debt; they often need to raise equity. Unfortunately, traditional investment sources are not that good at assessing radical new opportunities and have a limited inclination to provide guidance to early-stage entrepreneurs. Furthermore, most of these sources like to invest in large chunks and spend a disproportionately large amount of money and time on due diligence, making smaller, high-risk, early-stage opportunities unattractive. Because of these factors, business angels, especially those with direct entrepreneurial experience, are increasingly important to the development of new high-growth businesses. The direct involvement of business angels in these ventures probably contributes to the fact the companies funded by business angels are less likely to fail and more likely to attract venture capital than those without business angel investment.

Governments are increasingly aware of the importance of business angels and are taking steps to encourage business angel investment. They are creating tax breaks and incentives for business angels, providing additional resources to increase the likelihood that the companies in which they invest succeed and to catalyze business angel groups (or networks). Business angel groups can often have a positive impact on regional funding by sharing the risk of individual investment, the cost of due diligence, and the knowledge of coinvestors. In addition, business angels often take a low profile within a community, as an individual business angel may not wish to receive unwanted investment solicitations. In contrast, business angels working in groups can be exposed to more investment opportunities that may be aggregated and presented to many investors at the same time, increasing the number and quality of the deal flow (number of investable opportunities presented) and minimizing the time the business angel has to spend looking at each. The more sophisticated business angel groups often have full-time staff, a formal evaluation process, and sometimes access to coinvestment funds.

Current and Future Business Angel Research

Given the potential impact of business angels, there are two streams of concurrent research under way to minimize business angels' ignorance. The first stream looks at business angels from the perspective of regional economies and tries to identify the number of business angels who operate, the different types of business angels, and how they work together to identify and consummate investment opportunities.

Some initial research in this area breaks down business angels into types based on sociological classifications or how personal wealth was acquired. Understanding these different types of business angels provides insights into how to stimulate business angel investment activities and how the overall level of success of business angel investments can be increased. Two interesting observations include the identification of virgin business angel investors who have the ability and motivation to invest but have yet to make a single investment, and the nature of how prior experience influences future decisions.

The second research stream examines the investment decision-making process in detail, looking at recordings of actual interactions of real investment decisions. Whereas this research reinforces the relative importance of specific business factors, it allows the personalities of both business angel and entrepreneur to be examined during the interaction, in the context of decision making under conditions of real risk. In the investment decision-making process, it would seem that while initial assessments are made about specific technology and market factors and their contribution to the likely investment return, more attention has been focused on the behaviors and social skills of the entrepreneur during the interaction and how this influences the investment outcome. Particular importance has recently focused on how manifestations of trust behaviors influence the likelihood of the business angel's making a positive decision to enter a long-term relationship with the entrepreneur.

Andrew Lewis Maxwell
Canadian Innovation Centre

See also African Americans and Entrepreneurship; Debt; Equity- and Debt-Based Financing; Venture Capital; Venture Valuation

Further Readings

Angel Capital Education Foundation. http://www .angelcapitaleducation.org (Accessed February 2011).

Benjamin, Gerald and Joel Margulis. *Angel Capital: How to Raise Early-Stage Private Equity Financing*. New York: Wiley and Sons, 2005.

Bygrave, William D. and Andrew Zacharakis. *Entrepreneurship*, 2nd ed. New York: Wiley and Sons, 2010.

Canadian Innovation Centre. "Seducing Business Angels." http://www.innovationcentre.ca/files/upload/Seducing_Business_Angels1.pdf (Accessed February 2011).

Landström, Hans. *Handbook of Research on Venture Capital*. Northampton, MA: Edward Elgar, 2007.

Shane, Scott. *Fool's Gold? The Truth Behind Angel Investing in America*. New York: Oxford University Press, 2007. University of New Hampshire, Centre for Venture Research. http://www.wsbe.unh.edu/Centers_CVR/news.Cfm (Accessed February 2011).

Van Osnabrugge, Mark and Robert J. Robinson. *Angel Investing: Matching Startup Funds With Startup Companies—the Guide for Entrepreneurs, Individual Investors, and Venture Capitalists*. San Francisco: Jossey-Bass, 2000.

World Business Angel Association. http://www.wbaa.biz (Accessed February 2011).

BUSINESS FAILURE

I was further out than you thought,

And not waving but drowning

—Stevie Smith

New ventures are invariably founded with a sense of optimism for the future, whether justified by preliminary research or not. Although most of our management thinking concerns success, it is equally important to consider the consequences of the statistically likely outcome that the venture will not be successful or that the founders will not necessarily share in the firm's successes.

Definitions of failure usually identify discontinuance and financial loss as prime aspects, frequently identified as bankruptcy or insolvency depending upon the firm's legal status. In many ways the term *failure* is unnecessarily pejorative, because it is economically sensible to close a business once its distinctive skills and competencies do not best serve a changing environment. However, it is relatively rare to find businesses ending with a rational exit strategy, as management teams and entrepreneurs generally struggle to save their businesses regardless of failure to meet performance thresholds. For entrepreneurs the costs of failure can be high not only in legal and financial terms but also in terms of psychological trauma, stress to close relationships, and social stigma.

Failure and its consequences differ according to the stage of the business at the time it failed. Failure rates are high for new ventures in the first months and years. For an experienced or serial entrepreneur, failure may be regarded as part of doing business and care is taken to avoid supporting a frail enterprise with personal assets. Hence, failure is regarded as an unfortunate turn in a generally positive sequence of ventures. However, for an inexperienced entrepreneur, the effects of failure can be devastating. Even though incorporation may separate business and person legally, wily lenders will require security that most start-ups do not have, and the founder is required to pledge assets. At worst, bankrupt entrepreneurs may face credit restrictions, exclusion from participating in some professions, and possibly the loss of hearth and home.

The experience of business failure at this stage can affect the future intentions of entrepreneurs, possibly leaving them so traumatized by their experience that they may never again attempt to initiate another venture or, if subsequently employed, attain a position that reflects their true abilities and experience. On a more positive note, the learning experience gained during the process that results in business failure may help the entrepreneur to perform better

Closing a business should not always be referred to as a "failure" since at times it is the most economically sensible course of action after the business's skills and services do not fit the current customer and environment. (Photos.com)

if they are willing to accept further entrepreneurial challenges. Many successful, high-profile entrepreneurs are happy to admit to their early disasters.

Failure is not limited to those ventures that may have been inadequately prepared or based on a misreading of the market. New ventures may perform substantially better than anticipated, and the temptation is to expand beyond an adequate asset base—particularly working capital. Such high-flying firms have a short but spectacular life cycle and indicate the size and scope of the potential market to other entrepreneurs. On other occasions, founders are able to secure additional capital, although this may involve ceding some degree of ownership to new investors or increasing leverage.

A second end-point cessation, based on good performance, may arise surprisingly quickly in the life of a firm. Spectacular performance in the early years may attract the attention of a buyer willing to pay for the potential of the business; indeed, some entrepreneurs may specialize in such ventures, particularly in high-tech sectors. Similarly, if the firm is backed by venture capital it is likely that investors will wish to sell their interests earlier rather than later. A founder who sells at this point is likely to make capital gains and have the wherewithal to start another business. Hanging on may lead to a long-term income stream, but if organic funds are not sufficient to support further growth, the firm may run into difficulties through excessive leverage and poor liquidity.

Survival through the early years is no guide to continued performance; a business can still fail within 12 months of a record year of growth. Moreover, second- or third-generation family firms are not immune to the risk of failure. After 10 years, only 5 percent of new ventures exist in a recognizable form. The failure process often commences with a period where performance is poor compared to that of peers—even if this level of performance is satisfactory or good by the firm's own reckoning. A high-cost base, often the result of high research and development costs or investment as much as slack financial management, and changing environment are prime culprits of the poor performance, particularly dangerous for a risky venture in a technological sector. Grinyer et al. describe the restoration of profitability and growth as a "sharpbend" and hold that there are several chances for a sharpbend during the life cycle of a business. Major changes in management, an impatient external stakeholder, and a slight improvement in trading conditions usually herald the beginning of the sharpbend; entrepreneurs might find it easier, at this point, to exit and realize a return on their investment and start another business. The last chance to recover a struggling business is referred to as a turnaround.

A turnaround is a more extreme and desperate version of sharpbend—when the survival of the firm is in question (indeed, it may have already failed and new owners are attempting to recover the firm). Recovery is achieved through restructuring and is one of the most difficult business activities to undertake. Usually, this action is "brutal," with no part of a business escaping scrutiny and reorganization. Every aspect of management, staff, and procedures, including ownership, may be thought to be in need of change. This activity could result in, for example, loss of shareholder value, changes in employment levels and practices, changes in suppliers of goods and services, and proactively entering new markets or exporting. Almost inevitably, the result is a smaller, if fitter, firm, with obvious implications for stock values in the medium term. Existing management teams rarely survive the restructuring. It must be said that most turnarounds do not succeed in spite of the pain.

In many respects the worst outcome of a turnaround is a partial success, where the firm is not in imminent danger of failing but nonetheless does not have the strength to perform well in future. Investors will always be disappointed, and the most able, ambitious managers are likely to move on. Slatter describes this as a mean existence, which ties up labor and capital that could be more effectively deployed elsewhere in an economy.

At a late stage in the failure process, it may be in the interests of all concerned to ignore the firm's poor position. An owner in danger of losing personal assets is unlikely to bring the matter to the attention of financial stakeholders and may use a variety of expensive lines of credit to conceal matters, since the prospect of losing everything cannot be made worse by borrowing more. What is more, many owners find that their loyalty to staff prevents them taking the obvious steps of closing the business. Similarly, some financial stakeholders may prefer to keep the firm alive, since the firm's debts appear as assets on their balance sheet, whereas acknowledging failure creates an immediate loss through their profit-and-loss account. Thus, the firm continues to trade deplorably.

Although not inevitable, bankruptcy or insolvency is the final stage in the failure process, and it is rarely the decision of an entrepreneur or management team. It is often a priority creditor, such as a tax agency, that forces the issue. The effect on an entrepreneur's personal wealth and ability to start and manage another business will depend on the legal status of the business, the size of the shareholding, and whether personal guarantees have been given to secure financial support. With limited-liability incorporation, the legal responsibility for losses is limited to the outstanding, if any, sums owed on shares owned in a business. Other business forms and their owners carry varying amounts of liability for losses, from unlimited to restricted liability. No legal status affords complete protection from penalties if shareholders and other managing stakeholders have committed fraudulent acts to protect the business.

Steven John Henderson
Southampton Solent University
Nigel Bradly
SUBSEN

See also Change; Emotions; Intentions; Overconfidence; Planning Fallacy; Tolerance for Failure

Further Readings

Cochran, A. B. "Small Business Mortality Rates: A Review of the Literature." *Journal of Small Business Management*, v.19/4 (1981).

Dun and Bradstreet. *The Business Failure Record*. New York: Author, 1979.

Fredland, E. J. and C. E. Morris. "A Cross Section Analysis of Small Business Failure." *American Journal of Small Business*, v.1 (July 1976).

Grinyer, P. H., D. G. Mayes, and P. McKiernan. *Sharpbender: The Secrets of Unleashing Corporate Potential*. Oxford, UK: Blackwell, 1988.

Rajak, H. *Insolvency Law: Theory and Practice*. London: Sweet and Maxwell, 1993.

Slatter, S. *Corporate Recovery: A Guide to Turnaround Management*. Harmondsworth, UK: Penguin, 1987.

Ulmer, M. J. and A. Nielsen. "Business Turn-Over and Causes of Failure." *Survey of Current Business*, v.27/4 (1947).

BUSINESS MODELS

A business model represents how a business will make money and remain profitable across time. The choice, by managers and entrepreneurs of different business models, represents the most fundamental strategic question that a business needs to answer. Specifically, the business model defines how the company creates value for customers and what role the company plays in the overall supply chain. Entrepreneurs are most interested in developing a business model because it is critical to their business and an essential part of both attracting customers and developing a business plan. Interestingly, for existing companies, Boston Consulting Groups identifies business model innovation as the innovation opportunity most likely to enhance company profitability—even more important than product, process, or service innovation. H. Chesbrough's six different functions of a business model explain the concept well. It is also important to address why some technology innovations require the development of a new business model while others do not, as well as the difference between a business model and a business plan.

Definition

The definition of a business model provided by Chesbrough (2003) includes a statement or document that

- articulates the value proposition,
- identifies a market segment,
- defines the structure of the firm's value chain,
- specifies the revenue generation mechanisms,
- describes the position of the firm within the value network, and
- formulates the competitive strategy.

The traditional business model envisages a "craft" view of the world, where an individual creates a value-added product (or service), which she or he then sells to the customer at a profit, such that the cost of materials and labor is less than the selling price. This basic business model has been expanded over the years, through the creation of supply chains and organizations. Organizations replace individual activities with team-based activities within a company that perform the value creation function. Supply chains remove certain functions from the direct control of the company; for example, component manufacture is often outsourced to a reliable partner, whereas the end user of the product or service may have no direct contact with the manufacturer but may instead purchase from a retail source.

This traditional view of the business model has dominated the free-market economy for the past 200 years and has encouraged the development of the industrial society. This approach to value creation and supply-chain management encourages individuals within the organization and those within supply chains to clarify their roles and optimize performance efficiency. Inside the organization, productivity enhancements can be fostered by improved process innovation or through the deployment of technological innovation in the process. Supply-chain innovation can be stimulated, either by collaborating with the supplier to identify product improvement opportunities or by switching suppliers to one who is more productive or innovative.

Understanding the current business model is critical to the success of a business, an essential step in the process of identifying opportunities for business model improvement. It has been noted that most executives cannot articulate their business models; therefore, it is important that identifying opportunities to improve the business model starts with an understanding of how a business creates value for current customers and the role the business fills in the supply chain. Given that the definition of a business model must start with an understanding of the value offered to customers (and how they will pay for it), a business model starts by identifying both the value proposition and the evidence of what customers will pay for that value. Starting at this point and perhaps making some assumptions about volumes, the company can begin to calculate costs and therefore profits. Once the basic profitability of the business is determined, the company can review the functions it performs and the functions it will outsource. Rather than perform all functions inside the company, management or entrepreneurs can identify possible outsourcing opportunities, where the use of a subcontractor reduces costs, improves volume, or allows the company to optimize deployment of its limited resources.

Changing the Business Model

Since the early part of the 20th century, this traditional business model has seen fundamental changes, which have led to both a variety of different business revenue models and global supply-chain options. Although the traditional business model of providing a product or service for sale is still the dominant business model, there have been a number of changes to even this basic business model. The three most evident adaptations of the business model include market segmentation, embedding service, and outsource manufacturing. Market segmentation is often introduced based on price—for example, by adopting a premium pricing strategy that segments the market based on perceived customer value (Apple is an example). This strategy contrasts with a cost-based pricing strategy, where the company targets volume at the expense of unit price and unit profitability.

The choice of which strategy is the most appropriate for a specific company depends on five key factors: its current brand and customer position; the competitive nature of the marketplace; its cost structure; availability of complementary products, services, and channels; and the long-term business strategy. For example, it is not appropriate for a company to enter a market based on low price if it does not have an inherent advantage in its cost base. It is important to note that the risks of a low-price strategy are associated with maintaining a low-cost advantage, which may be influenced by factors, such as exchange rates, other than simple manufacturing productivity.

Embedding service is a common business model enhancement that increases both bottom-line profitability and customer satisfaction. At the time of selling a product, the customer is offered some type of optional service plan, which promises to cover any of the costs associated with repair, once any warranty has expired. Whereas there are some benefits of this type of service to the consumer, the retailer benefits both by removing a potential cause of discontent from the relationship and by selling a service that may never have an associated cost. In many cases, retailers make more profit from this type of business than from selling products.

Outsourcing can be used to give a smaller company scale economies by allowing it to share its factory and overhead costs with other organizations and operate both at a lower unit cost and with lower overheads. However, such a strategy may not be appropriate if existing large competitors are already sourcing from the same factory or the company becomes concerned that the factory might become a direct competitor.

In recent years, this traditional business model has been frequently augmented by the adoption of alternate business models, which utilize a better understanding of customer behaviors, the development of a new technology, or the combination of the two. Furthermore, the development of a new business model often allows new businesses to enter a marketplace, proving to be of particular interest to new ventures trying to enter a market. Among the top seven new business models are the following:

1. Give away the product conditional on the customer signing up for an associated service for a defined period (example: cell phone plans).

2. Rather than sell a product, provide it as a monthly service (example: software as a service).

3. Create new intellectual property and license its use to third parties for inclusion in their own products (example: encryption technology used in wireless devices).

4. Provide a free service to create a community of users and charge others for access to that community (example: advertising to users of search engines).

5. Create an open community where knowledge is shared and used by the community, creating value for all participants (example: open-source software).

6. Create a new and distinct marketplace that facilitates transactions between previously unknown buyers and sellers and embeds both ease of transaction and performance feedback (example: online marketplace).

7. Add an embedded service component to the provision of a traditional product (example: service plans when buying consumer electronics).

Each of these new business models provides some ideas to existing businesses and entrepreneurs to enhance their profitability. Managers embedded in their current business models can adopt new business models to expand their businesses by driving revenue growth and profitability improvement. Entrepreneurs exploring new business models can address adoption concerns and rapidly prove their value propositions. In addition, exploring new business models, which address both profitability and adoption objectives, encourages companies to examine their current value proposition and identify ways in which they can better serve their existing or potential markets. As Peter Drucker observed, "The customer rarely buys what the company thinks it is selling him," noting the classic that a customer needs to make a one-inch hole, not necessarily to own a one-inch drill.

The challenge with adopting new business models is that it can be difficult for existing companies to take full advantage of them, or even to come up with a viable defensive strategy, when a new entrant deploys an alternate business model. This can be because the company needs to protect its existing customer relationships or because the resources necessary to be successful with the new business model are not available in the existing organization. These are other reasons that business model innovation provides an opportunity for new market entrants.

The Role of Supply Chains in Developing Business Models

While the basic business model assesses how you get paid for creating value for customers, the importance of the supply chain in influencing this value proposition has already been identified. Initial constraints on the strategies able to be adopted by companies have been reduced by fundamental changes in the opportunities for improvements in the supply chain. Three trends have combined to create an increasing number of supply-chain options for companies (and customers):

1. The emerging economies of China, India, and other nations have created sophisticated socioeconomic systems that can produce high-quality products and services in a timely fashion, at a significant cost advantage over traditional factories.

2. Increasingly sophisticated technology is becoming ubiquitous in many product areas, thus stimulating the development of sophisticated suppliers who both develop and produce increasingly powerful components. These components can subsequently be used to create a competitive advantage in the marketplace for original equipment manufacturers that would not have been able to develop or produce either the individual component themselves or the wide range of innovative technologies that might be required in a new high-technology item.

3. Increasing development of reliable electronic communications, with high bandwidth, enables rapid communication between distributed design, prototyping, and manufacturing facilities, without the delays and rework that previously hampered the development of such relationships. This is supported by the development of sophisticated global supply-chain infrastructure.

Changes in the supply chain can be seen in every industry. For example, while initially Ford exemplified a "vertically integrated" company, which owned not only the final assembly plants and the engine shops but also the steel mills and the coal mines, the benefits of vertical integration have now been challenged by an increasing reliance on strategic partnerships. There has been a growing trend for automobile manufacturers to outsource both design and component manufacture to strategic suppliers. For example, an agreement between the automobile parts company Magna and the automobile company BMW to outsource complete vehicle manufacture has just ended (2010).

The trend toward outsourcing can be extremely attractive, allowing a company to become more flexible and to adapt more rapidly to changes in technology and the marketplace. This approach has brought major benefits to companies such as Dell and Walmart, which work closely with their suppliers throughout the supply chain. Each partner has visibility of current sales volumes and measures deliveries in terms of hours, not weeks. However, there are some challenges in outsourcing. First, dependence on external partners can increase the risk in the business caused by reliance on others and exposure to their actions. Second, the management of relationships with a large number of external suppliers requires the development of nontraditional relationships, which may not suit the current organization or enable the company to manage its business using existing tools and processes.

There are three key benefits and three key risks to which a business can be exposed if outsourcing. Both the benefits and the risks of outsourcing need to be considered by the management of the company and other business partners. The benefits of outsourcing are that it allows increased flexibility and access to new technologies; leverages partners' economies of scale; and allows the company to focus limited resources of key areas of the supply chain that it controls. The risks are that outsourcing will make the company dependent on a third party, increasing supply-chain uncertainty; allow partners to control critical elements of the supply chain, increasing vulnerability; and create potential competitors, in the form of either the subcontractor or other companies that can access the same subcontractor.

To make a decision about the supply chain, the business must evaluate each function in the supply chain and the benefits and risks associated with outsourcing each, in order to decide which functions to keep in house and which to outsource. Companies must pay particular attention to ownership of intellectual property (which can become complicated in partnerships) and the ability and resources to manage such relationships (where performance is achieved by mutual consent, not by control).

Why Some Technology Innovations Require a New Business Model and Others Do Not

Technology innovations that disrupt the marketplace create a new value for customers. However, rather than replacing an existing supplier, disruptive technologies often create demand for a new product or service. Unfortunately, convincing customers of the need for (or benefits of) this innovative product or service can be challenging, especially at the early stage of an innovative technology's life cycle. As a result, in some cases the technology innovator must develop a new business model to encourage early adoption. For example, when Chester Carlson was launching Xerography, it became evident that offices would not pay the capital cost for his large, expensive photocopying machines. His understanding of both the demand for the technology and the behavior of users allowed him to negotiate a much lower rental cost, with a per-copy "click" charge. This strategy reduced the risk to the companies acquiring the units, as they knew that there would be a cost only when the machine was used. In practice, most of the units installed became so heavily used that the click charge and the rental charge together were greater, creating more revenue for Xerox than would have been generated if he had relied solely on the initial capital cost. However, changing the cost perceived by the customer from fixed to variable overcame the reluctance to adopt the new technology that the customer company faced when

making an initial decision to acquire the machine. This "pay per use" business model is now applied in many industries to overcome the barriers of high capital costs.

For incremental innovations, there is little need to change the business model. Incremental innovations tend to replace an existing technology with a new and improved version of the same technology or a new technology that performs the same function as the technology it is replacing. The customer is then familiar with the technology application and is already accustomed to paying for it. It is relatively simple, then, to persuade him or her to pay a similar, or sometimes reduced, price for the improved version, as the benefits are clear and the enhanced value self-evident.

Business Models Versus Business Plans

Our definition of a business model makes it clear that it explains the value proposition, how the company makes money and where in the supply chain it operates. In contrast, a business plan is a detailed document that builds on the assumptions in the business model. The business plan explains how the implementation of the business model will be achieved and the associated financial projections, including cash flow, profit and loss, and pro forma balance sheets. The business plan provides guidance to people within the company on implementation of the business strategy and the financial consequences. If the company wants to borrow money or raise external equity, the business plan shows how the loan can be repaid or the required return on investment achieved.

Andrew Lewis Maxwell
Canadian Innovation Centre

See also Business-to-Business Marketing; Competition; Customer Orientation; E-Commerce; Entrepreneurial Marketing; International Markets; Market Evaluation; Positioning a New Product or Service; Retailing

Further Readings

Afuah, A. and C. Tucci. *Internet Business Models and Strategies*. New York: McGraw-Hill Irwin, 2000.
Canadian Innovation Centre. "Building a Better Business Model." http://www.innovationcentre.ca/downloads/ Building%20a%20Better%20Business%20Model%20 Season%201.Pdf (Accessed February 2011).

Chesbrough, H. *Open Innovation: The New Imperative for Creating and Profiting From Technology.* Boston: Harvard Business School Press, 2003.

Chesbrough, H. and R. S. Rosenbloom. "The Role of the Business Model in Capturing Value From Innovation: Evidence From Xerox Corporation's Technology Spin-Off Companies." *Industrial and Corporate Change*, v.11/3 (2002).

Hedman, J. and K. Kalling. "The Business Model Concept: Theoretical Underpinnings and Empirical Illustrations." *European Journal of Information Systems*, v.12 (2003).

Linder, J. C. and S. Cantrell. "Changing Business Models: Surveying the Landscape." White Paper, Institute for Strategic Change, Accenture, 2000.

Business Plans

Before any new venture is launched, it is imperative that a sound business plan be developed. Even those who have been in business for a while can benefit from business plan development. Business plans allow entrepreneurs to set forth the details of the business, communicate with executives and staff, and ultimately save time and money. This guideline for how to operate and market a business, which includes the projected financials, is often required by investors or creditors when the entrepreneur, including the new venture owner, seeks capital for the business. In developing a business plan, it is important to consider the type of funding being requested in order to guide the venture's development. Other purposes served by business plans are to determine the resources needed, determine the actions to be taken, identify issues not previously considered, and lay out a pathway to improved performance and success.

There are several different types of business plans, including the concept plan, the bank loan plan, the Internet plan, the retail plan, and the "angel investor" plan. A concept plan discusses the concept, research needed, ways to approach it, and other potential options. The bank loan plan is for starting a business or growing a preexisting small business that is seeking financing; it is typically modeled for a sole proprietor. Retail plans are designed for retail locations with a storefront and involve a detailed marketing and operations plan. The retail plan involves analyzing customers and competitors and typically is prepared for enterprises with more than one employee. The retail plan also includes a financial plan. The Internet plan discusses starting a business mostly online. An angel investor plan is designed to allow the new venture entrepreneur to present his or her idea to someone who might invest in it.

Before starting a business, the new venture entrepreneur must determine a name for the business and how it will reflect what it is that the business does. A business plan typically begins with a cover page. The cover page should list the name of the business, the names of the owners, and their contact information. A statement of confidentiality may also be included on the cover page. The cover page is often followed by the table of contents, which lists all the different sections of the plan as well as the page on which each section begins. Readers can then turn to a specific page and begin reading that section of the plan.

Executive Summary

The business plan usually begins with an executive summary (which can be written last). It encapsulates the business and is often read first. It may contain a shorter version of each of the main sections of the plan. The executive summary contains the most important points of the business plan and is often one to three pages in length. It is frequently considered the "sales pitch" to investors and creditors. The executive summary should gain and keep the reader's attention to ensure that he or she will read the entire plan. Many busy executives may not have time or want to read the entire plan, so they turn to the executive summary or look at the table of contents to locate sections of greatest importance.

Often a business plan is broken into four main sections: general information about the organization, marketing, operations, and financing. Each of these sections contains subheadings followed by detailed information.

General Information

The first main section of the business plan offers an introduction to and general information about the business. It should be followed by a mission and vision statement. A mission statement articulates the purpose for being in business beyond making money. The vision statement identifies the goal that the business will strive to achieve and the focus or direction of the organization—the "dream" of the organization. In writing these statements, the entrepreneur should consider his or her customers, products, services, market, technology, and employees, to name a few areas. The mission and vision should be followed by the goals and objectives of the organization. Goals should be specific, measurable, attainable, realistic, and time based. Objectives are the steps that will be taken to reach those goals.

General information also covers who the customers or clients will be, describes products and services, and places these within the overall industry. Target markets are described; for example, if there is a particular niche market the business seeks to serve, it should also be detailed here, along with plans for how to reach that market. Products and services should be covered in some depth. Fees and pricing structures should be identified. Entrepreneurs should also describe their own strengths, experience, and core competencies (what they do best) and how those skills will set them apart from competitors.

The form of the organization is also identified here: sole proprietorship, partnership, corporation, or a limited liability corporation (LLC). Each of these business forms has different advantages and disadvantages with regard to taxes, liability, management control, and the ability to raise capital, so the reasons for the choice of business form should be justified in a way that makes sense to potential investors.

Entrepreneurs should analyze the organization's SWOT: strengths, weaknesses, opportunities, and threats. Potential problems and how they will be overcome are addressed here. Part of this analysis will consider competitors and their strengths and weaknesses, locations, customers, and strategies. Changing environmental "PEST" factors may be important to discuss: political, economic, social, and technological (as well as environmental and other concerns, depending on the business).

Marketing Plan

In order to address the areas identified in the business plan's general information, an entrepreneur needs to create a marketing plan as part of his or her business plan. The four *P*s of marketing that must be addressed in the plan are product, price, promotion, and place of distribution. The market plan involves market research, including primary and secondary data. Secondary data may come from trade publications, government reports, or industry and company profiles. Primary research involves doing original research to gather new data—whether through observation, surveys, or interviews—that are related specifically to the new business and market served. For both types of data, the marketing plan should cite statistics and sources.

First it is important to discuss the industry, which entails an overview of not only the broader sector of products and services but also the size of the market, market share, demand, trends, potential for growth, barriers to entry, and how the business will surmount those barriers and other environmental factors. Barriers to entry might include high costs, consumers' lack of brand recognition, unions and labor laws, technological issues, and staff training and skills.

From a customer perspective, products and services should be covered: important features, benefits, and anything else that customers will find particularly compelling. The customer in the target market should be fully detailed based on research: age, gender, location, education, income level, occupation, and other characteristics. Identifying methods for delivering customer service matched to this customer profile is another key ingredient of the marketing plan.

The entrepreneur must also describe competitors, starting with their names and contact information. Each competitor needs to be fully described in relation to how the new venture will compare in terms of products and services. Next, a description of the marketing strategy should be included; it should outline the promotional mix: fliers, newspaper ads, bulletin boards, Websites, social networking tools, direct mail, logos, letters, and all other means of communicating with potential customers. Ways of identifying repeat customers must be included. Then the marketing budget and how it will be allocated to serve the strategy should be detailed. It is important to think about what forms of advertising will be used, the costs of each, the target market preferences in terms of advertising, and the number of people who will be reached.

The prices of the business's products and services should also be addressed: Will the business be a low-cost leader, in the middle, or at the highest price point for the product or service (that is, will price be a competitive factor)? What type of markup will there be? What is the rationale for choosing this strategy? Will the business sell to customers on credit?

Next, proposed location is covered. Will the business occupy a warehouse and/or a retail space? Should it begin as a home-based business or online? Does it need to be highly visible, open to foot traffic, so that people on the street are likely to stop and enter the location? What is important in real estate is equally important for many businesses: location, location, location. A good location is accessible to customers, to the location of a competitor, and to available resources. The costs to make the site feasible should be covered, such as rent, leasing, or purchasing, as well as utilities and other fees. The hours of operation are also critical to success, both in a particular location and for the type of business and customers served. Equipment and other fixed assets, from furniture to buildings, should be listed and their costs identified.

The distribution chain is key: Will the business maintain a Website or support direct-mail distribution? Will warehousing, retail space, a sales team, or independent field representatives be needed? What will it cost to ship products or deliver services to the customer? It is important to consider holding costs, inventory costs, and all other expenses associated with the business's location and distribution. These numbers need to be taken into account in sales forecasts and financial statements.

Operations Plan

Certainly an area that bankers, creditors, investors, and suppliers will be interested in is the operations plan. In this section of the business plan, the entrepreneur must consider the who, what, how, and when of operating the business. How many employees will be needed, and of what type (skills, experience, education)? Will they require on-the-job training? How will they be located (advertising costs) and hired (time costs), how will they be paid (payroll), and will the business need to offer benefits such as medical insurance, paid vacation, and sick leave? Who will perform what tasks? Will employees be full-time, hourly, independent contractors, or a combination of these? The operations plan may well include job descriptions for the personnel who will need to be hired, policies and procedures, and even schedules.

Entrepreneurs may wish to consider (and address in the business plan) the need to solicit professional services to accomplish these tasks, whether from lawyers, accountants, other professionals, or an advisory board or board of directors that includes such individuals. A network of these individuals may be needed to accomplish such tasks as tax return preparation, corporate filings, and other paperwork. It is important to locate an insurance agent, a bank, and possibly consultants who can help with the organization when needed. The operations plan will include a detailed description of the management team: their expertise and what they will contribute to the business. This discussion will emphasize the qualifications of the management team but also identify potential weaknesses, so that the entrepreneur can demonstrate readiness to recruit competent advisers and avoid incompetent ones. The operations plan may even include biographical sketches and resumes of key individuals who have already been identified.

Inventory is another important consideration in the operations plan. Will the business stockpile or warehouse raw materials, supplies, or finished products in its location? How many or how much? Items to consider include the costs to hold raw materials and inventory, and at what price these will be sold. Also, will some seasons be busier than others, and how will that affect inventory and attendant costs?

Suppliers should also be determined on the basis of sound research into their credit, delivery, and payment policies. Names, addresses, and other pertinent information about these suppliers should be listed, including history, return policies, and reliability. Backup suppliers should also be identified here.

The operations plan is also the place to describe the policies of the business and what will need to be done when selling to someone else, especially on credit. What terms will be offered and will there be discounts? Will a customer need to meet any qualifications in order to obtain credit with the organization? The amount and length of credit terms that will be offered may influence the accounts receivable balance. In terms of customer service, the operations plan should identify how, where, and when the business will sell its products or services to customers.

In addition to staffing, it is necessary to consider technology and customer service in this section of the plan, including any hardware and software needed to run the business, as well as their ongoing maintenance and projected updating or replacement.

Facilities are a large part of the operations plan. The operations plan should address the building or plant, land, location, distribution costs, risk, insurance, supply cost and availability, employees, and any special permits that might need to be obtained. Laws, regulations, and government guidelines—such as those arising from labor law or those that affect whether the business can obtain government assistance—are addressed in the operations plan.

Financial Plan

Investors and creditors will pay close attention to finance statements as set forth in the financial plan. They will want a detailed list of start-up expenses, a projected income statement, a balance sheet, and a statement of cash flows. An income statement shows expenses and revenues. A balance sheet shows assets, liabilities, and stockholders' equity. A statement of cash flows shows the amount of cash flow into and out of a business. Even if the business shows a profit, the business can fail if it does not have a sufficient positive cash inflow greater than cash outflow. The financial plan should show when the enterprise will break even and when it will begin earning a profit. Investors and creditors will judge these numbers to see if they seem realistic and may ask many questions about this portion of the business plan. They will want to know that the entrepreneur/owner has handled his or her personal money well and has a particular net worth, in addition to a good education, solid experience, and superior skills; such qualifications are needed to prove that the entrepreneur can manage the organization's finances well. These qualifications signal an enterprise worthy of lending and investment. The projections of the financial plan should be as realistic as possible and therefore require significant research and the ability to explain why the numbers are reasonable and trustworthy.

Along with the financial statements, this portion of the business plan may include a budget that takes into account different scenarios—such as "best," "worst," and "expected" performance—as well as potential outlays for operating and maintaining the business. These plans and projections should be conservative but realistic. Often the expectation is that they will be presented in a well-constructed spreadsheet produced by standard software such as Microsoft Excel.

Other Information and Uses

Finally, the business plan will often contain appendices in which copies of relevant documents are presented: sample marketing materials, location information, contracts, estimates, letters from potential suppliers, customer lists, market research data, and anything else that supports the business plan.

Once the basic plan has been created, it can be refined to meet different purposes. If it is being used to get a loan from a bank, then it needs to state the amount of the loan or the credit for which the business is applying, how those funds will be allocated, the collateral that will be used to secure the loan, and precisely how and when the loan will be paid back. If the business plan is being used to present to potential investors, then the entrepreneur must be able to show them that their investment will see returns quickly and demonstrate exactly how the profits will be shared. Investors expect a statement that identifies the amount of short-term funds requested, the estimated return on investment, the exit strategy, ownership status, and how the funds will be used.

Different types of business plans may require different components. For example, a manufacturing business will need to consider manufacturing levels, costs (both direct and indirect), prices, profit margins, the production facility's capacity, and the capacity of each machine. Such a plan will also need to identify purchasing and inventory management procedures. A service business needs to consider prices, competitive factors, costs, payment policies, customers, and marketing. Some organizations, such as high-tech enterprises, may depend on the economic outlook for the industry, research and development, property rights, staying current with technology, keeping valued employees, and having enough funds to invest in this type of business. Such businesses may even go a long time before becoming profitable. Entrepreneurs starting an Internet business as opposed to a storefront need to take these additional considerations into account. Buying a franchise, family business, or going international also entail special considerations.

Regardless of the type of business, the entrepreneur must also have an exit strategy: a plan to enable the owner to leave or sell the business. The exit strategy may involve reducing the product or service lines, giving or selling the business to a family member, closing it, or selling it to investors, another person, or another business.

Many different groups can help create a business plan, including SCORE and various business development centers that are affiliated with the U.S. Small Business Administration (SBA). These groups can also review areas entrepreneurs must master before presenting their business plans to bankers and potential investors. Inexperienced entrepreneurs may even want to take business courses that cover business plans and related considerations. Those considerations are numerous for anyone wanting to start a small business, and the business plan is the place where they are identified, collected, and addressed.

Katherine Hyatt
Reinhardt University

See also Accounting; Business Models; Competition; Customer Orientation; Entrepreneurial Marketing; Goal Setting; Incorporation; Insurance; Taxes; Venture Capital

Further Readings

Delmar, F. and S. Shane. "Does Business Planning Facilitate the Development of New Ventures?" *Strategic Management Journal*, v.24 (2003).

Franklin, Burke and Jill E. Kapron. *BizPlan Builder Express: A Guide to Creating a Business Plan With BizPlanBuilder10*, 3rd ed. Mason, OH: Thomson South-Western, 2007.

Henricks, Mark and John Riddle. *Business Plans Made Easy*. Irvine, CA: Entrepreneur Press, 2002.

Longnecker, Justin, Carlos Moore, J. William Petty, and Leslie Palich. *Small Business Management: Launching and Growing Entrepreneurial Ventures*, 14th ed. Mason, OH: Thomson South-Western, 2008.

Microsoft Word. "Microsoft Office Business Plan Template." http://office.microsoft.com/en-us/templates/business-plan-for-startup-business-TC001017520.aspx (Accessed February 2011).

U.S. Small Business Administration. "Manage Your Business From Start to Finish." http://www.sba.gov/smallbusinessplanner/index.html (Accessed November 2010).

Business-to-Business Marketing

Marketing to businesses, governments, and non-profit organizations is termed business-to-business (B2B) marketing. Understanding the concepts and principles of B2B marketing is crucial for all entrepreneurs. Although some entrepreneurs may deal with consumer markets, all participate in B2B markets, either as vendors or as purchasers, and generally both. Additionally, the B2B market is larger than the consumer market (B2C) and has more points of entry to participation. Although the underlying philosophy of B2B and B2C is the same—to earn profits through satisfying the needs and wants of the customer—there are substantial differences between B2B and B2C. Traditional marketing classes, focusing almost exclusively on B2C, rarely discuss these differences.

First among those differences is that the underlying basis for consumer decision making is the psychology of the individual. In B2B, the underlying basis is more varied. For sales to small companies and for insubstantial sales to larger companies, individuals are generally the decision makers and the psychology of the individual dominates. For substantial sales to larger companies, a small number of company executives generally make joint purchase decisions. Thus, small group psychology is the underlying decision-making basis for B2B purchaser's larger, more important purchases. In making sales presentations, vendors have to consider the potential decision-making influences of individuals they may never meet and who have varying interests that need to be addressed in the sales presentation. For example, in considering alternative product offerings, manufacturing executives will place greater emphasis on product characteristics that maximize the efficiency of manufacturing operations, finance executives will emphasize product characteristics that maximize estimated financial returns, and marketing executives will emphasize product characteristics that help them maximize their ability to satisfy varying customer needs. Vendors have to address these different interests in making their sales presentations and in preparing promotional materials. They must also account for the effects of the give and take of a group decision-making process.

Although B2B relationships are more complex than consumer relationships, they are also generally stronger. Both vendors and purchasers maximize profits through repeat purchases; thus they generally work hard to build strong relationships. The buy-grid model offers a good way to understand why strong, continuing relationships between vendors and purchasers are a source of greater profitability. The steps necessary for each purchase situation are checked off. The model shows the relative complexity of each purchase situation, and the more complex the situation is, the more time-consuming and costly it is. Repeat purchases, termed straight re-buy situations, are the least complex of the three purchase situations. The other two are the modified re-buy and the new purchase. In the modified re-buy situation, column 1 represents a purchaser unhappy with the product purchased but happy with the vendor; column 2 represents a purchaser happy with the product purchased but unhappy with the vendor. Straight re-buy situations occur when a purchaser is satisfied with both the product purchased and the product's supplier. Inventory trigger points are frequently the basis for purchase decisions. Often made without human intervention, the straight re-buy is very low-cost for both the purchaser and the vendor. In a modified re-buy, the purchaser is dissatisfied with either the product or the vendor and has to conduct research to try to rectify the situation either by changing suppliers or by changing product specifications. In the new purchase, the purchaser is making a major purchase for the first time or is dissatisfied with both the product and vendor and must research all aspects of the purchase situation to determine the best possible supplier and product specifications.

The need for strong relationships together with the generally larger sales quantities of B2B transactions creates shorter distribution channels. The shorter distribution channels make for far greater numbers of direct manufacturer to end-user sales situations in B2B than are found in B2C. Far greater emphasis on personal selling in promoting a product is a second effect of these characteristics. Personal selling is both the most effective and the most expensive form of promotion on a per-communication basis.

The tendency toward industry concentration also facilitates personal selling. B2B markets are geographically concentrated when compared to consumer markets. Although one finds small companies in virtually all industries dispersed geographically, the tendency is for most industries to cluster in relatively small geographic regions. Thus, historically Detroit has been synonymous with the auto industry, Toledo with the tire industry, and Pittsburgh with the steel industry. This concentration permits a supplier to use a relatively small number of trained sales personnel to reach a very significant share of their potential market. Industries can migrate. For instance, the textile industry in the United States was concentrated in the New England states, migrated to the American South, and is presently migrating out of the United States to other countries that possess greater competitive advantages in the textile industry.

The Buy-Grid Model

Purchase Steps	Straight Re-Buy	Modified Re-Buy 1	Modified Re-Buy 2	New Purchase
Need recognition	✓	✓	✓	✓
Product definition		✓		✓
Product specification		✓		✓
Supplier search			✓	✓
Acquisition/evaluation of proposals			✓	✓
Negotiation			✓	✓
Purchase	✓	✓	✓	✓
Post-purchase evaluation	✓	✓	✓	✓

Source: Adapted from the original model developed by Patrick J. Robinson, Charles W. Faris, and Yoram Wind, *Industrial Buying and Creative Marketing* (Boston: Allyn and Bacon, 1967).

Although the B2B market is larger than the consumer market, B2B markets are largely dependent on consumer markets. The basic reason for this dependence is that the demand for consumer products is the source of the demand for most B2B products. To understand this characteristic, termed derived demand, consider a consumer product—for example a shoe. The retailer's sale of the shoe to the consumer represents a consumer sale; the manufacturer's sale of that same shoe to the retailer represents a B2B sale. The sale to the manufacturer of the various components of that shoe—leather, rubber, string, metal, and glue—represent B2B sales. However, if there is no consumer demand for shoes to begin with, the retailer will not purchase shoes from the manufacturer, and the manufacturer will have no need to purchase the different shoe components. Hence, B2B demand is derived from consumer demand.

A second kind of demand that greatly influences B2B demand is joint demand. Joint demand reflects the fact that most products require all their basic components in order to achieve utility. If for any reason the manufacturer is unable to find any necessary component of its product or an acceptable substitute, it cannot make its product. Hence, it will have no need to purchase any other component of its product. If the shoe manufacturer cannot acquire rubber for the shoe's heel and cannot acquire additional leather to serve as a substitute material, it has no need to acquire the shoe leather or any of the other component materials. Thus, demand for one component of a product is conjoint with the availability of all other necessary product components.

Relatively inelastic demand for B2B products is an important result of derived demand. B2B customers will purchase only as much product as is necessary for them to satisfy the demand of their own customers. As consumer demand is the source of demand for B2B products and companies will purchase quantities sufficient to satisfy their customers' projected demand, they tend to possess inelastic demand curves. This has a substantial effect on pricing strategy.

When considering a price reduction strategy, it is important to determine the relative transparency of the market. A transparent market is one in which competitors readily learn about one another's prices and any pricing changes that occur. Thus, lowering price will not increase demand for a product, because competitors will quickly learn of the pricing change and match it. In transparent markets, a price reduction strategy will do little more than reduce all suppliers' margins and reward only the lowest-cost suppliers. In relatively opaque markets, a price reduction strategy will have a greater likelihood of success.

A further difference between B2B marketing and B2C occurs in market research. Traditional marketing research is consumer oriented and emphasizes randomized sampling to ensure the generalizability of results. Most B2B markets do not meet a basic assumption for valid randomization. Random sampling, to be valid, requires that all sample population members have relatively equal influence on results and that that influence should approach zero. This situation does not exist in most business markets; hence the preferred sampling methodology is the judgment sample. Most business markets have dominant members. For example, there are more than one thousand computer companies in the United States alone, yet a handful of companies—IBM, Acer, Apple, Dell, Fujitsu, Hewlett Packard, Lenovo, Sony, and Toshiba—dominate the world computer industry. Market research that does not focus on the needs and interests of these dominant companies is virtually useless, and nine companies are too small a population to bother with sampling. Most major industries have similar structures, with a few major companies determining the needs and direction of the entire industry.

There is little theory development and limited research on marketing and entrepreneurial/small business, and even less on B2B marketing and entrepreneurial/small business. Wai-Sum Siu and David Kirby, in their 1998 review article on the field, concluded that empirical investigation into marketing in small businesses has been ad hoc and has failed to generate sufficient knowledge of marketing in small business. Subsequent researchers have confirmed these conclusions. The field is ripe for further research and is arguably the most neglected research area in B2B.

Finally, new venture entrepreneurs should consider B2B markets, as many large companies have support programs for small businesses. These programs, offered to small suppliers and minority enterprises in an effort to support local communities, can represent substantial assistance toward success.

George T. Haley
University of New Haven

See also Advertising; Business Models; Competition; Contextual Marketing; Distribution; E-Commerce; Licensing; Market Evaluation; Sales; Selling Products and Services; Social Networks; Wholesale Markets

Further Readings

Anderson, James C., James A. Narus, and Das Narayandas. *Business Market Management: Understanding, Delivering, and Creating Value*, 3rd ed. Upper Saddle River, NJ: Prentice-Hall, 2008.

Bingham, Frank G., Roger Gomes, and Patricia A. Knowles. *Business Marketing*, 3rd ed. New York: McGraw-Hill Irwin, 2005.

Dwyer, F. Robert and John F. Tanner. *Business Marketing: Connecting Strategy, Relationships, and Learning*, 4th ed. New York: McGraw-Hill Irwin, 2009.

Hills, Gerald E. and Claes E. Hultman. "Academic Roots: The Past and Present of Entrepreneurial Marketing." *Journal of Small Business and Entrepreneurship*, v.23/1 (2011).

Hutt, Michael D. and Thomas W. Speh. *Business Marketing Management: B2B*, 10th ed. Cincinnati, OH: South-Western College, 2009.

Jain, Subhash C. and George T. Haley. *Marketing: Planning and Strategy*, 8th ed. Mason, OH: Cengage Learning, 2009.

Robinson, Patrick J., Charles W. Faris, and Yoram Wind. *Industrial Buying and Creative Marketing*. Boston: Allyn and Bacon, 1967.

Siu, Wai-Sum and David A. Kirby. "Approaches to Small Firm Marketing: A Critique." *European Journal of Marketing*, v.32/1–2 (1998).

CAPITALISM

Capitalism as an economic system is based on individual ownership of the means and distribution of production as well as individual purchasing decisions in the marketplace, which, in turn, drive producer decisions. Its reach and impact on society are spread far beyond the economic realm as it is an interacting cultural factor, is the foundation for political and legal systems, and can be a driving force behind technological innovations and change. Joseph Schumpeter defined entrepreneurs as individuals who focus on innovation in developing new products or services; hence, entrepreneurship is particularly attuned to a capitalistic economy. Because of its complexity, no universal definition of capitalism exists.

Economic systems must answer the basic questions about goods and services: what goods and services are to be produced, how they are to be produced, and for whom they are to be produced. Entrepreneurial firms attempt to provide answers. As an interacting factor with a society's culture, the economic system shapes the way people live through the way that they work by influencing the values, beliefs, expectations, feelings, and assumptions held by the society. Conversely, the way people work is shaped by the way they live; one view is that the economy and the culture are two sides of the same coin. The political system, in a simplified manner, is the management structure for a society's culture and economy. Capitalism flourishes when the political and legal system acts as a disinterested umpire ensuring common rules and the fair enforcement of those rules. Indeed, the alternative economic system, socialism, is based on political control of production and distribution of goods and services.

The government's role in the economy is fundamental to the establishment of political institutions and legal systems. Stripping technology to its most basic form of applied knowledge, society's views on basic research and education determine the level of technology available to its culture and economy. The tools, equipment, methods, procedures, and practices that shape the lives and work of a society incorporate the knowledge that the society has developed or has adopted. Whether knowledge is created, applied, and/or owned by individuals or by political institutions has a profound impact on the rate and nature of technological development. It is clear that one cannot understand an economic system without understanding the society of which it is an integral part.

In pure capitalism, the means of production (factories, farms, shops, equipment) and distribution (railways, trucks, warehouses, stores, the Internet) are privately owned with the profit motive. Signals from the market (quantity, quality, timing of demand) impact private decision makers, affecting price, supply, distribution, and investment and resulting in capital goods that are utilized in the production of consumer goods. Investors that misread or improperly react to these market signals suffer loss or bankruptcy. Those who accurately respond are rewarded with profits, which over time create wealth. Accepting the risk of failure is a key aspect of new ventures, and the process of incrementally creating wealth is at the heart of entrepreneurship.

Profits do not accrue only to investors in the capitalistic economy, for incentives exist to share profits with customers (lower prices), workers (increase quality of work life), and suppliers (establish longer and more profitable relationships). Profits can be used strategically with all stakeholders in the system; the distribution of profits is a matter for the private owners. Under socialism, profits must still be created, but their ownership and distribution are a matter of political calculation.

Private property rights are essential to the functioning of capitalism. These rights are vested in the labor, capital, knowledge, and land (resources) necessary for production. Labor may be manual or mental; knowledge may be basic or applied; and resources include both natural and man-made (knowledge interacting with nature). Property rights are both an incentive to produce and a reward for production. Private property rights bestow the right to control property, including its use and by whom, the ownership of revenue generated by the property, and terms and conditions of rental or sale. Property rights apply to both real and personal property but do not comprise unlimited rights, as legal limits have been established. Capitalism, typically, refers to the ownership of capital goods, resources, and intellectual property. Entrepreneurial labor may be capital, but labor is generally considered an input factor to be purchased in labor markets.

Another critical dimension of capitalism is freedom of choice and enterprise. With minimal government involvement, producers are free to determine how, at what, for whom, and at what price they will work, and consumers are free to purchase whatever goods or services they can afford. Consumer freedom is the most profound force in the system. The satisfaction of individual wants is the independent factor that dictates what producers and suppliers offer and at what price. The consumer is sovereign, within legal limits. Voluntary buying and selling in the market are guided, as Adam Smith labeled it, by an "invisible hand." This unseen force couples self-interest with the most profitable use of scarce resources, which, in turn, promotes the general welfare. Whereas capitalism encourages economic growth, it results in the unequal distribution of benefits. Winston Churchill is said to have observed that "the inherent vice of capitalism is the unequal sharing of blessings; the inherent virtue of socialism is the equal sharing of miseries."

Self-interest, not selfishness, is a defining characteristic of capitalism. Individualism is at its core; however, self-interest is served best over the long term with honesty, integrity, fairness, and judgment as moral imperatives. Producers seek the maximum ethical rent or profits, whereas consumers pursue their perceived greatest value (price and functionality). Unethical and illegal behavior takes away freedom and destroys reputations and wealth—certainly not in one's self-interest.

Competition among producers for the consumer's choice and competition among consumers for the producer's output create an economic supply-and-demand relationship. Capitalism assumes that a large number of independently acting producers and consumers exist for specific products or resources and that they are free to join or exit the particular markets. Large numbers diffuse the economic power of any individual producer or consumer; scarcity in supply leads to higher prices, scarcity in demand to lower prices. In a large market, an individual producer or consumer has an inconsequential impact. Freedom to expand or exit provides the flexibility and efficiency needed to adjust to changes in consumer demand, resource availability, technological developments, and political and legal changes. Schumpeter's "creative destruction" reflects the role of risk-taking entrepreneurs in the economy.

Prices act as the coordinating mechanism to match supply with demand. Preferences are expressed by decisions to consume or produce; prices provide guides to consumers, producers, and resource owners to make and revise decisions furthering their self-interests. These decisions are made and executed in the market system, which is a complex communication network that facilitates innumerable consumer and producer choices that are recorded and balanced. Competition provides control for the system, and the market provides the means and methods to coordinate and communicate the allocation of resources and the distribution of outputs for society.

Thus, a competitive, market-based capitalist economy is assumed to support a highly efficient use of resources that requires only limited governmental intervention and then only with broad legal limits. Pure capitalism, as a concept, predicates a self-regulating and self-adjusting economic system; however, capitalism does have undesirable consequences and limitations.

Issues with capitalism include power relations, wage levels, economic stratification, and market deficiencies. Within the market itself, there are no means to protect property rights or enforce contracts; markets may be monopolized if competition can be eliminated; third parties not involved in a market transaction may be affected by the side effects of the production or consumption of goods or services; individuals without resources are excluded from the market; and public goods that cannot be owned or sold lack incentives for private production. These issues are used to justify political intervention to protect both the market system and society, and they are often cited to support partial or full governmental control of the economic system. Governments create legal systems to protect property rights, enforce contracts, and impose social constraints; to fight monopolies and engage in antitrust actions; to provide means for third parties to seek justice and protection; to influence the allocation of resources and stabilize the economy; to redistribute wealth to those excluded from the market; and to produce those public goods that cannot be served through markets. Exploitation, inequality, inefficiency, market failure and instability, unemployment, and sustainability are key words for those who criticize capitalism.

Capitalism has been modified into many different forms: free market, corporate, social market, state, autocratic, distributed, and laissez-faire, as well as others. Different economic systems include mercantilism, socialism, and communism. Most economic systems today are mixed with the dominant systems—capitalism or socialism—and the names of those two dominant forms are used to characterize the balance among political, cultural, economic, and technological forces.

Authoritarian capitalism, or fascism, is an economic system with private ownership of property but a high degree of governmental control and intervention in the means and distribution of production as well as the regulation of consumption. This permits the government to effectively direct the economy without the responsibility of ownership.

Communism was Karl Marx's ideal system of a stateless, classless economy, requiring each worker to contribute according to his or her ability and receive according to his or her needs. In Marx's ideal system, there would be no need for a central authority to pursue the public interest, and without private property self-interest would be discouraged. Altruism and equality of outcomes would encourage cooperation; profits are seen as unjust payments and Marx believed that markets would destroy themselves through relentless greed. His vision was that private ownership and exploitation would create a class struggle that would lead to a command-and-control economic system in the public interest. He saw socialism as an intermediate stage between capitalism and communism.

Corporate capitalism describes a market system dominated by large corporations with mutual benefits flowing between the government and these corporations. Corporations exercise influence over government policy and their regulatory agencies such that the state is used to limit competition and promote the interests of favored corporations while the state benefits from numerous political and social actions of the established corporations.

Karl Marx was a 19th-century philosopher, social scientist, historian, and revolutionary who believed that altruism and an equality of outcomes would encourage cooperation. In his work *Capital,* Marx elaborated on his concept that surplus value and exploitation would ultimately lead to falling profits and the collapse of industrial capitalism. (Library of Congress)

Crony capitalism exists when businesses and political interests intertwine to create self-serving relationships. This leads to favoritism in governmental decisions and actions such as issuing permits, letting contracts, creating tax breaks, and providing government grants. The government creates a labyrinth of rules and regulations that are intentionally confusing and require interpretation by officials. Personal ties and exchange of favors become the norm as laws are applied inconsistently. This places businesses in a dependent relationship and fosters collusion and anticompetitive practices. Crony capitalism may permeate an entire government or be limited to certain agencies and regulated industries.

Distributed capitalism is an economy based on individualized consumption through relationships and tools instead of products and services. This relies on distributed assets, distributed information, and distributed social and management systems made possible through information and communication technologies.

Free-market capitalism emphasizes that equilibrium of supply and demand is determined by free prices without government interference. The state is restricted to protecting property rights.

Laissez-faire capitalism (pure or industrial capitalism) permits virtually no role for government involvement in the economy, as all resource allocation decisions are made by individuals through the market system. Characteristics of this early form of capitalism include the specialization of labor, routine work in factories, and the capitalist replacing the merchant in the foremost economic role.

Merchant capitalism (mercantilism) is an economic system in which basic economic decisions are made through monopolies granted by the government: "the invisible foot." This system was an outgrowth of medieval feudalism; as markets expanded, governments (kings) become politically involved in both encouraging growth in investments in a variety of ventures and limiting growth to protect those ventures. A central tenet is that a positive balance of trade increases national wealth.

Social market economies are supported by considerable state involvement in social benefits—retirement, unemployment, medical and labor rights—with limited government interference with prices and property rights. This form of capitalism is distinctly not socialism.

Socialism is an economic system based on government ownership and central planning of the means, distribution, and allocation of production. Central planners determine what is to be produced, how that is to be produced, and for whom it is to be produced using criteria they believe to be socially beneficial. A market socialist economy features government ownership with decentralized planning allocation of production through reliance on markets. Social democrats believe the flaws of capitalism can be overcome through political reforms and structural changes. Revolutionary socialism holds that a revolution is necessary to displace capitalism.

State monopoly capitalism is explained by Marxian theory as the merging of monopolistic businesses with the government. This system works to support highly effective, mammoth corporations that integrate labor and unions into a triad.

State capitalism (welfare capitalism) mixes public and private ownership of resources with state intervention in markets to alter price signals; this system is typical in western Europe. The state may own profit-seeking companies as well as nationalized industries that are operated by a state authority directly responsible to the government. In this system, the extent of government intervention is substantial, through comprehensive national planning and protection of specific companies and industries. The term is used across the political spectrum to describe a range of government intervention in both scale and scope.

These distinctions are not strong or always clear-cut; furthermore, this list is indicative rather than comprehensive. As noted above, there is not a universally accepted definition of capitalism. U.S. capitalism has, historically, been the closest to pure capitalism of the many varieties. Decisions regarding resource ownership and allocation have been made by individuals with limited governmental intervention. However, the role and nature of government involvement in the economy have been consistently expanding over the past several decades.

Entrepreneurial firms can exist in any economic system, but the benefits to the individual and society decrease as the role of government in the economy increases.

Tom D. McFarland
Tusculum College

See also Barriers to Entry; Competition; Culture and Entrepreneurship; Entrepreneurial Orientation; Growth; Political Economy and Entrepreneurship; Venture Capital

Further Readings

Friedman, M. *Capitalism and Freedom.* Chicago: University of Chicago Press, 1962.

Hayek, F. A. *The Road to Serfdom.* Chicago: University of Chicago Press, 1944.

Heilbroner, R. L. *Between Capitalism and Socialism.* New York: Vintage, 1970.

Lewis, M. *The Real Price of Everything: Rediscovering the Six Classics of Economics.* New York: Sterling, 2007.

Marx, Karl. *Das Kapital.* 1867. Reprint, Washington, DC: Regnery, 2000.

Rand, Ayn. *Capitalism: The Unknown Ideal.* New York: Signet, 1967.

Reich, R. B. *The Work of Nations: Preparing Ourselves for 21st Century Capitalism.* New York: Alfred A. Knopf, 1991.

Romano, R. and M. Leiman. *Views on Capitalism,* 2nd ed. Beverly Hills, CA: Glencoe, 1975.

Schumpeter, J. A. *Capitalism, Socialism, and Democracy.* New York: Harper and Brothers, 1942.

Thurow, L. C. *The Future of Capitalism: How Today's Economic Forces Shape Tomorrow's World.* New York: William Morrow, 1996.

Von Mises, L. *The Anti-Capitalist Mentality.* Princeton, NJ: D. Van Nostrand, 1956.

Weber, M. *The Protestant Ethic and the Spirit of Capitalism.* New York: Scribner, 1930.

Zuboff, S. and J. Maxmin. *The Support Economy.* New York: Viking Penguin, 2002.

CASH FLOW

Cash flow, not profit, is the key to a healthy business. The "cash" here refers simply to money, not to hard currency. Cash flow is the movement of money in and out of the business: the money received or otherwise generated by the business, minus the money

Net income (the sum remaining after all expenses have been met or deducted) is usually used to determine a business's profitability; however, it can become artificially deflated by noncash expenses like the depreciation of fixed assets. (Photos.com)

used to pay for its expenses, over a finite period of time. A positive cash flow, in which received cash consistently exceeds the amount of cash payments, is the central goal of any business.

Even a profitable business can fail or experience serious problems because of a cash shortage. Tracking the cash flow of a business keeps tabs on the business's liquidity: its ability to pay debts as they become due. The operating cash flow ratio of a business is the operating cash flow divided by current liabilities, an easy measure of liquidity. Operating cash flow is the total amount of cash from a company's revenues minus the company's costs. Whereas net income is usually used to determine a business's profitability, it becomes artificially deflated by noncash expenses like the depreciation of fixed assets (which become less valuable as they become older, but which in so doing do not actually represent a loss that impairs the business's ability to pay its debts).

Many investors or potential investors in a business prefer to look at a business's cash flow statement rather than its income statement, because its preparation gives management less discretion, and therefore the cash flow statement tends to be seen as the truer picture of the business. The cash flow statement lays out the business's operating activities, investing, and financing, focusing on current liquidity and the company's ability to adjust cash flows in the future. Noncash activity, such as the exchange of assets for other assets, the issuance of shares for assets, and the conversion of debt to equity, is still disclosed on the cash flow statement, in the form of footnotes. Because the Generally Accepted Accounting Principles (GAAP), the standard followed throughout the United States in the preparation of financial statements, leaves so little leeway or room for variation in its prescription for cash flow statements, a cash flow statement is one of the easiest ways to compare the performance of two or more companies.

Cash flow is generally calculated for a finite period of time, but just as it can be calculated to reflect the business's current state of affairs or a particular point in the past, so too can it be prepared as a projection, to show the expected cash flow in and out of the business in the near future based on the information available. Revenue projections may be based on upcoming events, which may be known with a great degree of certainty—such as a landlord projecting that the rent he collects six months from now will be reasonably equivalent to the rent he collected this month—or may be based on more speculative sales projections derived from past performance modified by the changes expected to occur in the future. A cash flow projection may be calculated in order to show the likely results of a proposed change, for instance, or for that matter the results of continuing the present course. Such projections are valuable to shareholders and potential investors, as well as to potential backers of young enterprises, but by its nature a projection cannot be expected to be as reliable as a statement about the present. Cash flow projections are an important part of a business plan, detailing cash revenues from projected sales and other sources, cash disbursements, and reconciliations with previous periods. Typically, sales projections are based on past performance, when possible, and on the performance of analogous businesses when there is insufficient past performance on which to draw: For instance, a bookstore opening on a major thoroughfare in a city of 300,000 would base its projections on the performance of bookstores of similar size, location, and local demographics.

Cash flow can also be tracked for a specific project within a business, such as a new product launch, a marketing campaign, or a division within the company. This can be especially useful when keeping an eye on a particular spending limit or when generating profits is either inapplicable or not a major part of the project's goal. For instance, a company running a social game on Facebook puts a lot of capital into the development and running of the game, which customers access for free. Revenue is generated not by charging for access to the game but by selling premium game items to dedicated players who have become invested in their performance or by acting as a broker for transactions with promotional partners (giving in-game benefits to players who sign up for trial magazine subscriptions, for example, generating revenue for the game company in the form of a commission). Cash flow statements can be prepared for the various ways the game generates revenue, in order to reveal which are the most profitable, and for the ongoing costs of the game.

More than large corporations, new ventures and small businesses find themselves in short-term cash flow crunches, as they lack the capital buffer of those corporations and the sheer amount of assets that can be leveraged for cash-poor times. One remedy is to offer repeat customers, if relevant to the firm, a discount if they prepay for services. This is common with business-to-business transactions, for instance. There may also be a problem with the balance of the venture's spending—not enough may be spent on generating revenue and too much on brand building, particularly if there is an ongoing attempt to capture a particular niche. This was a recurring problem in the bust of the dot-com bubble, in which many start-up Internet businesses prioritized brand identity in order to become the brand most associated with a particular type of online business, and invested money in those efforts entirely disproportionate to their actual revenue-generating capabilities. Even healthy activities, though—such as growing the business and expanding to new markets or adding to the product line—consume cash flow and may need to be reined in.

Keeping track of the cash flow in and out of the petty cash fund (discretionary cash in small amounts, usually around $100, for office supplies and incidental cash expenses) helps to elucidate whether an incidental expense has become a recurring expense, as well as to track the usage of various goods and services. When the business is a retail store, "petty cash" may in fact be one or more of the cash registers, in which managers will leave vouchers or receipts for cash removed for expenses—and it is helpful to track this too.

The importance of cash flow can impact management decisions. For instance, keeping an eye on maintaining a positive cash flow may encourage a business's operators to keep inventory at low levels—avoiding running out of stock, but without hoarding inventory at the expense of liquidity. It also encourages managers to delay their payments to suppliers, contractors, and others to the far end of the accepted norm for the industry, retaining cash on hand for as long as possible. In some cases receivables can be converted to cash through sale to a commercial finance firm—the appeal and practicality of this will vary according to the size and nature of the business, but the practice of rich corporations selling their buildings only to lease them back is one that favors being cash-rich over being asset-rich, for instance.

Bill Kte'pi
Independent Scholar

See also Accounting; Agility and Rapid Response

Further Readings

Mulford, Charles W. and Eugene E. Comiskey. *Creative Cash Flow Reporting.* Hoboken, NJ: Wiley, 2005.

O'Berry, Denise. *Small Business Cash Flow.* Hoboken, NJ: Wiley, 2006.

Pinson, Linda. *Keeping the Books.* New York: Kaplan Business, 2007.

CHAMPIONING CORPORATE VENTURES

While some new ventures will constitute new small businesses, perhaps with only one employee, other ventures originate in a corporate environment, where there is already an established business plan and accepted set of procedures and expectations. There are various reasons that the new venture may originate in, and be best suited for, this environment: It may be a natural extension of the firm's activities

into a new area (even if it does not immediately appear to be so), it may capitalize on the firm's existing resources, or it may simply originate as work product by an employee. A new corporate venture may begin in businesses of any scale, from a small company, to a joint venture among multiple organizations, to a diversified multinational corporation. In any of these situations, a champion—an individual in the organization who emerges as the venture's unofficial "sponsor"—is critical to the venture's success. The champion may find himself swimming against the tide, his enthusiasm for the idea keeping it alive despite the inertia of existing practices and existing uses of resources. It is the corporate champion whose relationship to the idea helps identify its best implementation and rallies support and resources, and who is best suited to identifying whether a proposed business plan is compatible with the idea.

A new venture will usually take at least two years to develop momentum and generate profit, often twice as long. This is one reason the champion role is necessary. Someone involved with the venture simply must possess sufficient enthusiasm and faith to stick with the venture and continue to promote it and see it through, rather than simply releasing it and hoping for the best. One of the keys to long-term corporate success is the ability to respond to changing business circumstances. Those changes may transpire in the industry in the regulatory or technological environment or as a result of new markets opening or new competitors entering the field. They may transpire at larger or smaller scales, as a result of economic changes or changes within the company. The one constant is change itself and the need to treat it as noncalamitous and be able to adapt.

Entrepreneurial individuals working within a corporation are sometimes called intrapreneurs, promoting new ventures for the corporation to take on and actively encouraging or pursuing business development—the creation of new products and markets. The advantage intrapreneurs have over entrepreneurs is that they are not limited to their personal resources and skill sets in developing an idea; they may recognize that a particular competency is required, which they lack but that someone elsewhere in the organization possesses, someone who can be recruited and persuaded of the venture's worth. Intrapreneurship thus requires an understanding of other people's skills and the ability to pick the right people, the people the venture really needs. Whereas intrapreneurs originate ideas and innovations, champions need not necessarily be the originators of the ideas behind the ventures they champion. The role is an unofficial one.

Often, corporate champions are those who take advantage of change. When sound technology became available for films, many movie studios believed "talkies" would add little of value except as the occasional novelty feature—Jack Warner, founder of Warner Bros., pointed out that the success of film relied on its international language; the lack of dialogue stimulated the imagination so that audiences all over the world could fill in the blanks for themselves regardless of what language they spoke. In this he was not entirely wrong, but in time sound pictures did even better business than silent films had. Those actors and studios that best capitalized on this early thrived. Those who waited until the technology had proven to be a permanent change and not a fad looked foolish and old-fashioned.

About 30 years later, another new technology was introduced to film: 3-D. Once again there was debate in the industry about what this innovation brought to the table. Warner, still running Warner Bros., may have thought he had learned his lesson; after the success of the 3-D film *Bwana Devil* (from United Artists), he agreed to enter the 3-D arena, with Warner Bros.' very successful thriller *House of Wax*. However, he misjudged the success, declared his belief that in the near future all films would be shot in 3-D, and shut down the animation studio responsible for Looney Tunes and Merrie Melodies (cartoons still being hand-drawn at the time, so transferring them to the 3-D process would be impractical). In time, this decision was reversed, and by the end of the 1950s, 3-D movies were considered just another of that fad-obsessed decade's brief obsessions.

Warner was a more than competent studio executive, as the long legacy of Warner Bros. and his considerable tenure there show. However, he misjudged two significant changes in the industry, in opposite ways. Had he acted more impulsively and had Warner Bros. been a smaller studio with less room for error, he could have ruined the studio in an attempt to convert to an all–3-D operation. Therefore, it is not enough simply to capitalize on the opportunities that change presents; it is not enough simply to change operations or methodologies because circumstances have changed. Rather, it is necessary to understand how to respond, when to respond, and the nature of the change that is occurring.

Ideally, new corporate ventures are championed when they make the most of the firm's resources and competencies, by someone who understands the customer base and the market. That was Warner's error, misjudging the market. 3-D turned out to be a short-lived phase, but it would not have survived at all without champions like him. Champions are like forces of Darwinian natural selection, selecting the fittest of available changes and ventures, the ventures best adapted to available resources and competencies, to a particular niche. They may champion a particular kind of opportunistic behavior, perceiving the opening of a niche and encouraging their business to act to fill it.

A corporate venture may involve multiple champions in various roles. Championing an idea in a corporation is a political process, involving coalitions within the company both supporting and opposing the venture. The disruption of routine, of established procedures, must be justified. The individuals who promote the venture to people responsible for the necessary resources—whether they are within the corporation or outside investors—are sometimes called resource champions, while those who intercede to smooth the way for the venture to be incorporated into the culture of the rest of the corporation are incorporation champions, ensuring consistency of values and business practices.

Bill Kte'pi
Independent Scholar

See also Agility and Rapid Response; Championing New Ventures; Entrepreneurs in History

Further Readings

Calish, Irving G. and R. Donald Gamache. "Wizards and Champions: The Kingdom of New Venture Management." *Journal of Product Innovation Management*, v.1/4 (December 1984).

Fiol, C. Marlene. "Consensus, Diversity, and Learning in Organizations." *Organization Science*, v.5/3 (August 1994).

Godin, Seth. *Tribes*. New York: Portfolio, 2008.

Gupta, Samir, Jack Cadeaux, and Chris Dubellar. "Uncovering Multiple Champion Roles in Implementing New Technology Ventures." *Journal of Business Research*, v.59/5 (May 2006).

Jantsch, John. *Duct-Tape Marketing*. Nashville, TN: Thomas Nelson, 2008.

CHAMPIONING NEW VENTURES

Creating a new corporate venture occurs in a number of contexts, but in all of them it needs a champion—that is, an advocate, someone who will fight for it and push forward to continue to promote its potential while the market and its possibilities are explored. New ventures do not happen by accident, and even the most brilliant ideas will not be adopted effortlessly. Championing a new venture often requires taking on a leadership role even when one is not the organization's leader. At the same time it is not the same role as that of the traditional manager, whose role is defined more by overseeing the performance of established business processes than by exploring and discovering the best expression and implementation of a new idea. The unique skill of the entrepreneur is to blend the managerial and the creative.

In the technology sector especially, knowledge plays a key role in opportunity recognition. Fast-moving fields can include opportunities for new ventures that are not immediately apparent except to those well versed in the industry, which is why venture capitalists, for instance, tend to specialize in a particular industry, so that they can better evaluate the potential of start-up firms. Market research can help to gather relevant knowledge on the venture's competitors, potential customers, and industrial environment.

Championing a new venture requires that the champion understand the customer, the needs or desires that the venture will meet, and how customers can be courted and retained. Seemingly minor factors can make the product or service unappealing or work against the interest of potential customers. The venture champion must believe in the idea but also understand the customers who will be served by it, in order to develop its best implementation. It is critical to understand how the customer will see the product or service—whether it fills a perennial need, whether it competes with some other solution, what customers appreciate or resent about competing solutions, and whether potential customers of the new venture are by definition also customers of some other product. For instance, a venture developing a new smart-phone application (app) should understand the customer bases of the various smart-phone brands; the product may turn out to be more appealing to owners of one smart phone than another or may complement or compete with apps for a particular smart phone. New ventures are as often as not niche ventures, and niche customers can be easily alienated.

It is also necessary to know the business and its capabilities; Taco Bell can no more make the most of a television series concept than Coca-Cola can capitalize on a taco delivery system. Knowing a business's capabilities is important even for a new firm that is being created specifically for the venture being championed, because while it will not have the problem of having its resources committed to a course of action incompatible with the new venture, it will be finite in resources, capital, and territory. When Netflix was starting up, it had to understand its limitations in order to proceed with committing resources and setting prices: namely, that in the face of the sheer impracticality of employing a dedicated DVD delivery fleet, it would be bound by existing modes of delivery. This would impact not only its costs but also its customer base and availability: while FedEx, UPS, and other carriers might be able to offer faster or even more reliable DVD delivery, Netflix chose to rely on the U.S. postal service, which is frequently cheaper and which, more important, is required as a government agency to deliver to all American addresses. Rural and remote customers might have been excluded from Netflix's potential customers otherwise. The choice of carrier also impacts the range of potential turnaround times, from sending a DVD out to receiving it back from the customer—which impacts the customer's happiness with the service and Netflix's inventory needs.

Furthermore, a new venture can often take three to five years to begin generating profit. The entrepreneur must be sure that this wait is acceptable. One reason for the high fatality rate among new ventures is the overconfidence or naïveté that assumes a venture will begin turning a profit in its first or second year and that thus moves forward from a position requiring that profit and lacking the resources to continue operations without it. Depending on the product or service and the start-up costs, loan terms, and other conditions, some ventures—even assuming equal "success"—may take longer to show a profit than others, and it is critical to venture survival that the entrepreneur understand where on the spectrum they lie.

Understanding the venture's resources includes an understanding of the skill and knowledge base. The aforementioned example of the app developer need not achieve the same level of success as *Angry Birds*. The key is that goals should be commensurate with resources. There is nothing wrong with third place—or eleventh place—provided expenditures are proportionate so that profit is still earned. A venture's success is defined not solely by its position in the marketplace. Ambition can be scaled to skill levels. Social capital is important too; the new venture needs to have ties to the community of customers it wishes to serve.

In many cases, the new venture may have no direct competitors. Whereas Netflix dominates the DVD-by-mail market, there are niches it does not serve or serves poorly, such as foreign-language DVDs, educational DVDs (such as for school or home schooling use), X-rated DVDs, and DVDs from other regions. Some niches may be more easily served than others, and the niche may suggest changes to the approach to business. For instance, a Vietnamese-language DVD delivery service might have limited success on a nationwide scale with a Netflix-like online interface, but a service delivering DVDs by hand (like the milkman of old) in a city's Little Vietnam neighborhood may be appropriately scaled to turn a profit. Such a service might even be a viable franchise model, licensing the franchise to operators in other cities. A DVD rental service for home-schooling parents may find it useful to be more flexible about the number of DVDs rented at a time or to include other materials with the DVDs.

Changes to the marketplace, such as the rise in outsourcing, may create opportunities as well. One new venture may be predicated on streamlining its operations by outsourcing some of its processes. Another new venture may be the firm to which processes are outsourced. Changes to the regulatory environment can create an opportunity for new ventures that advise existing firms on compliance issues, just as new technologies create new opportunities, as with the DVD delivery and smart-phone app examples. The fundamental questions are always how value is created for the customer and how the venture's resources are applied to generating an eventual profit. It is key, for instance, to know whether or not repeat business is possible: Customers may rent DVDs regularly but buy a particular app only once, and after a certain number of sales, the app is not likely to sell further. A finite venture can still be a profitable one, but it needs to be understood as such.

Ultimately, what leads to the success of new ventures is a champion pursuing that success, someone who emerges from the company as the person who really understands the idea, who resonates with it, and thus who promotes it and generates enthusiasm for it while also being sufficiently in tune with what makes the idea work to be able to gauge if it is being implemented appropriately. The champion may not even be the person who originated the idea but one who, in the champion role, helps overcome skepticism and resistance to change, which are natural dampers on a firm's ability to capitalize on a recognized opportunity. Put another way, an idea without a champion will simply wither.

Champions create mechanisms for making consensus decisions about the new venture. They persuade, usually informally and sometimes simply through their enthusiasm, other people to support the venture, whether other members of the company, potential business partners, investors, or customers. They safeguard innovation from the interfering effects of organizational hierarchies, sometimes from the managers themselves. They maximize the creative use of the organization's resources related to the new venture, and they provide autonomy from existing procedures and systems.

Bill Kte'pi
Independent Scholar

See also Championing Corporate Ventures; Entrepreneurial Marketing

Further Readings

Day, Diana L. "Raising Radicals: Different Processes for Championing Innovative Corporate Ventures." *Organization Science*, v.5/2 (May 1994).
Godin, Seth. *Tribes*. New York: Portfolio, 2008.
Stack, Jack. *The Great Game of Business*. New York: Doubleday, 1994.

CHANGE

Since the mid-1980s, organizations have scrambled to compete with a changing global environment that has demanded the development of new operating strategies. The picture of business in the 1950s showed little need for change. However, that picture in the 2000s is dramatically different. Had someone told a group of managers that organizations in the 21st century would be seeking ways over a period of 18 to 36 months to increase productivity by 20 percent to 50 percent, improve quality by 30 percent to 100 percent, while increasing new-product development by 30 percent to 80 percent, they would have scorned the informant.

Changes in technology and communications, such as Internet capabilities, have expanded the operations of business globally, and organizations have had to adapt through changes in structure, culture, and strategy that provide little stability. Major change efforts have helped some organizations adapt significantly to shifting conditions, have improved the competitive standing of others, and have positioned a few for a far better future. Demands on leaner budgets have resulted in the reengineering of processes and implementation of services. Most of these organizations, in order to survive, have been pushed toward transformational change. The instability in today's fast-moving, global environment demands that organizations be skillful at changing direction, mission, vision, structures, processes, technological innovation, and marketing.

Although globalization has created difficult circumstances for well-established businesses, such environments have become crucially important for new businesses. The diversity of the business community has created an increased awareness of an eclectic approach to the creation and operation of business. For example, a new business that wishes to use Internet sales as an outlet must contend with global ramifications. Established organizations have had the luxury of experiencing the transition of such diverse populations. However, the new organization must learn strategies that are outside the norm for business operations, especially in entrepreneurial businesses. On the other hand, long-term existence can be a hindrance to opportunity, which the new business will not experience. Entrenched paradigms, structures, beliefs, and norms become difficult to unfreeze. New businesses are not required to experience these difficulties, since these operating structures can be formulated on current environmental foundations.

One major advantage that new entrepreneurs experience is the global resource of electronic learning formats. Advancements in this area have caused businesses, governments, and institutions of higher education to rethink learning and development. Countless online resources are available to new business owners that help create a learning environment of sustainability. Almost every business, both large and small, utilizes the Internet as a means of advertisement and business. Those seeking to start new businesses can call on this resource to gain insight into competitors' strategies, market shares, strengths, weaknesses, and operations. The major difference in today's society is that information, which used to be available only through traditional settings, is now available by the click of a mouse, much more quickly and in larger quantities. This has proven to be very effective for the entrepreneur, who can now find information and locate hands-on training for just about any subject that a business may need. The Internet has also created avenues for collaborative learning on topics of business strategy, strategic planning, marketing, business plans, human resource allocation, and performance management. Governments have incorporated electronic learning formats as a resource for business owners to help in different aspects of governmental compliance. Such education is readily available to entrepreneurs to assist them as they begin and operate their businesses.

Individuals have the opportunity to attend college and receive viable degrees from online universities

Internet capabilities and other advancements in technology and communications have expanded the scope of global business operations. Organizations have had to adapt. This process has improved the competitive standing of some and left others struggling to survive. (Photos.com)

that maintain a high ranking in academia. This, combined with the rise of traditional universities' online presence, has created more avenues to higher education for nontraditional students. The result has been an increase in those obtaining higher degrees. Many of these individuals have been entrepreneurs who needed higher education to help their businesses run more efficiently.

Since the early 1980s, and especially since 2001, many economic and social forces have driven the need for transformational change. Such forces include technology, faster and improved communication (e-mail, fax, webinars), international economic integration, global trade agreements, increased deregulation, and the transition of communist and socialist countries to capitalist systems. There are also internal forces, including culture, learning mechanisms, structuring for efficiencies, and leadership development, that are now more closely monitored.

New businesses must come to the realization that these factors are at the forefront of business operations and must create strategies to integrate them. It is imperative that a new business in the 21st century have structures and processes in place that deal with cultural awareness, identification and dynamics of various cultures, behavioral practices affecting business, and strategies that deal with cultural differences. Such businesses, in order to compete, must create strategies that have global implications. Businesses that recognize the need for change create environments that remain open to new opportunities and view change as offering the potential for growth instead of a negative threat to survival. Instilling this perception in the mechanisms of the business positions an organization to move ahead as a system instead of being divided. Changing external environments result in internal changes that produce changes in vision, mission, structure, and strategy. The new business venture can thereby balance the internal and external environments more efficiently. Businesses that are open to diversity and possess the capacity to adapt will set themselves apart, becoming creative and innovative in solving problems in the changing global environment.

Since 2000, the labor market has become very tight, which has resulted in human resource departments recruiting from a wider, more diverse pool of candidates. Organizations used to try to identify and assimilate cultural differences. However, organizations today, especially new businesses, must concentrate on accepting cultural differences and finding ways to bring members of their workforce together to benefit the organization.

Since 2009, changes in world environments have created opportunities for new business. Cultures that once were tightly controlled and steered away from entrepreneurial ventures have been opened. Events throughout the world have created a global environment that is conducive to new business. In the wake of the global recession, policy makers and entrepreneurs have become interactive in attempting to create political policies that help facilitate business.

Changes in the political climate since 2008 have initiated a friendly environment for new business growth. Realizing that small business and the entrepreneurial spirit are driving growth, political organizations, including policy makers, have attempted to create laws that facilitate new business creation. Incentives have been implemented to help level the playing field for new business ventures. One major problem, however, is the impact of the global financial crisis. In this environment, changes in policy designed to create incentives do not necessarily facilitate growth. They can result in stagnation and decline. Therefore, it is imperative that the key actors for policy leveraged toward new business continue to reduce risk and transaction costs, including social, economic, and environmental costs. Researchers indicate that the timing for new business ventures is exceptional. A weeding-out process that has occurred since 2009 has created opportunities for new business. Entrepreneurs who balance operational strategies with economic factors such as debt control and growth have a much better opportunity for success.

The foundation of organizational learning is in the discovery, invention, production, and generalization of new information and behaviors. These are applied to organizations' structures, information systems, human resource practices, cultures, and leaders. Knowledge is basically acquired by members imitating a role model through implementation of trial and error to determine what works and what does not. This acquired knowledge can then be applied to the competitive strategies of the organization. Research indicates that one of the major drivers of new business growth has been the creation and expansion of social media, which create an avenue for networking in global industry. Social media, in turn, have accelerated the need to learn new technology and marketing techniques. Established organizations have had difficulty adapting to this societal change. However, new business start-ups incorporate social media regularly in their operational strategies. Businesses must be savvy in creating social media that will be attractive to the public and tell the story of the business in a limited space. This type of marketing is not just for the younger generation. Research indicates that users of social media come from a variety of age groups. Adapting social media marketing to a particular group for a certain product is a unique yet necessary objective for the new business.

Since the mid-2000s, organizations have become more dependent on teams to execute strategies. Once an individual-driven field, business is increasingly becoming a team-driven project. Leaders and managers have realized the importance of teams in strategies of execution, and the creation of new businesses demands a strong commitment from a coalition of teams.

Not only has there been a change in how the public views business; many business organizations have turned their perspective inward to gain a deeper understanding of why and how they exist. These businesses have revised their branding to make it more customer friendly and team oriented. Organizations have reviewed their vision and mission statements to ensure that processes and structures for congruency are in place. Many have restructured lines of communication to make the organization friendlier to employees as well. This is a drastic change from years past, when the focus was solely on the bottom line, and suggests recognizing that more sophisticated methods of human resource management are now contributing to that bottom line.

Such changes have created a paradigm shift in business and organizational behavior. Successful entrepreneurs and other new business ventures have established processes and structures to help identify operational weaknesses and well-defined strategies that are targeted at such weaknesses. This enables leaders to address operational issues proactively and enhance organizational efficiencies and effectiveness.

Empowering members in the process is a powerful tool to gain support during the effort. Past generational workers were more stable in employment decisions and rarely changed jobs or careers. However, since the 1980s, workers have been much more transient and have moved from one organization to another for minor reasons. Organizations today have begun to develop unique strategies to motivate employees, which has been shown to maintain high retention rates. Scholars agree that organizations that empower their employees experience higher productivity, retention, and effectiveness. Doing so helps remove structural barriers, increases buy-in, provides training, and helps stimulate motivation for increased job performance. Leaders must recognize that empowering their employees taps an enormous source of power. Realizing and embracing this change in the workforce is crucial to new businesses as well as existing organizations. In order for new businesses to survive and grow, they must create motivation and empowerment programs that will increase retention.

In sum, modern organizations must be adaptive to change and learn to implement strategic actions that help facilitate change efforts. Moreover, entrepreneurs looking for new business ventures can learn from these changes to facilitate strong structures and processes that will ensure sustainability and strength in both good and hard economic times. The business community's identity is changing at an astounding rate. Those organizations that fail to adapt will cease to exist in today's market.

Anthony D. Daniel
Ashford University

See also African Americans and Entrepreneurship; Change Management: Corporate; Culture and Entrepreneurship; Learning

Further Readings

Cummings, T. G. and C. G. Worley. *Organizational Development and Change*, 3rd ed. Mason, OH: South-Western, 2005.

Daft, R. L. *The Leadership Experience*, 2nd ed. Mason, OH: Thompson/South-Western, 2002.

Daniels, J. D., L. H. Radebaugh, and D. P. Sullivan. *International Business: Environments and Operations*, 13th ed. New York: Prentice Hall, 2001.

Dennis, W. J., Jr. "Entrepreneurship, Small Business, and Public Policy Levers." *Journal of Small Business Management*, v.49/1 (2011).

Faminow, M. D., S. E. Carter, and M. Lundy. "Social Entrepreneurship and Learning: The Case of the Central America Learning Alliance." *Journal of Developmental Entrepreneurship*, v.14/4 (2009).

Kirschner, P. A. "Design, Development, and Implementation of Electronic Learning Environments for Collaborative Learning." *Educational Technology Research and Development*, v.52/3 (2004).

Kotter, J. P. *Leading Change.* Boston: Harvard Business School Press, 1996.

Kotter, J. P. and D. S. Cohen. *The Heart of Change: Real-Life Stories of How People Change Their Organizations.* Boston: Harvard Business School Press, 2002.

Schein, E. H. *Organizational Culture and Leadership*, 3rd ed. San Francisco: Jossey Bass, 2004.

Senge, P. M. *The Fifth Discipline: The Art and Practice of the Learning Organization.* New York: Currency-Doubleday, 1990.

CHANGE MANAGEMENT: CORPORATE

Corporate change management is the ability to implement change and significantly modify the direction or culture of a company to keep it competitive in today's fast-paced global marketplace. Changing markets and technologies are only two of the examples of changes that can quickly make a business obsolete. Companies that cannot innovate and continuously change and improve will not survive. Good change management skills give organizations the agility to move quickly in and out of new markets and stay competitive.

Starting a new venture or making an intervention to renew an aging business means bringing about change. In some cases it is necessary to abandon past practices altogether and start over. Research would suggest that change is difficult and that most people equate change with a loss or a negative consequence. If asked, most people would define their feelings, when faced with change, using language that suggests a deficit. In fact, about 75 percent of the words used to describe change are negative. Entrepreneurs and employees alike want to see their organizations succeed, but they also want to know what is in it for them. Change managers therefore need to put a positive spin on corporate change initiatives.

First, the organization needs to understand that even if the change makes great business sense, it might not be recognized as necessary by all stakeholders. Most members of any organization are in a constant struggle to protect the status quo and can find change threatening. With changes coming fast and furious in today's business environment, organizations need to master the skills necessary to implement change. Many experts write about their best ideas to facilitate change, but in reality each case needs to be handled on an individual basis. Reading many books, cases, and articles on the subject is a good place to start, but a change methodology that fits the specific organizational needs must be designed by the change leader.

Second, leaders need to understand that it does not take a degree in psychology to manage corporate change. What is really needed is an understanding and mastery of soft, or interpersonal, skills. Leaders need to win the hearts and minds of their employees if they want people to follow. Employees need to be convinced that the change is beneficial, not only to the organization but also to the employees. A leader wins the hearts and minds of employees by approaching change initiatives with open and honest communication. It might be painful for both leader and employee, but communicating what will and what will not change, as a result of the initiative, is imperative.

Employees need to know how the organization will benefit from the initiative. Leaders also need to explain the situation clearly and why or how this change initiative will be approached realistically. Without truthful and sufficient explanations, rumors will fill the void; those affected will create the reasons for change and possibly start a resistance movement that may be difficult to bring back under control. Resistance to change is a natural reaction. Many organizations look at resistors as people who block needed change and react toward them with punitive measures. It should be understood that resistance is natural, and those resisting probably have their own survival and the survival of the organization at heart. Resistance should be viewed as an asset and not a negative reaction. Leaders can learn from the resistance if it is treated appropriately.

The reason or purpose for any change needs to be explored with as many stakeholders as is reasonably possible, so that when the change is finally initiated it has meaning and there is a widespread sense that the change is actually necessary. Employees need to be convinced that the change represents a valid solution. Once individuals understand the benefits of the proposed change, it is important to get them involved. If people are not fully invested in the change they will have idle time on their hands and resulting rumors could ultimately sabotage the process. To ensure a fast and successful transition, the best people—team players, self-starters, and those with strong positive attitudes—should be involved.

As individuals begin to let go of past practices and become comfortable with the change, it behooves management to look at creative systems and processes. Employees in the neutral zone, between old and new, are malleable and thirst for new and creative ways to normalize this emotional part of any transition. This is also a prime time to involve employees in brainstorming new ideas and to offer new skills training aimed at supporting and further communicating the change. The importance of good communication cannot be overemphasized. Managers must communicate in as many different media formats as possible and as often as possible, and it is important to remember that face-to-face communication is still the most effective form. Managers must, moreover, be consistent in their messaging and actions; any inconsistency will be viewed by the change targets as poor leadership.

As the change initiative starts to become solidified, it is time to start looking at a way to symbolize the new initiative. That might involve signage, logos, or a new lunch room. Managers will want to do something to indicate to all that a new atmosphere, culture, or business climate is emerging. Some of the most successful change initiatives are celebrated with gala events to thank those involved for the success of the transition.

Alexander W. Crispo
Purdue University

See also Change; Innovation Management; Leadership; Leadership: Transformational

Further Readings

Bridges, W. *Managing Transitions: Making the Most of Change.* Cambridge, MA: Perseus, 2009.

Karp, H. *The Change Leader: Using a Gestalt Approach With Work Groups.* San Diego, CA: Pfeiffer, 1996.

Kleiner, A. *The Age of Heretics: Heroes, Outlaws, and the Forerunners of Corporate Change.* New York: Bantam Doubleday Dell, 1996.

Kotter, J. and D. Cohn. *The Heart of Change: Real-Life Stories of How People Change Their Organizations.* Boston: Harvard Business School Press, 2002.

Palmer, I., R. Dunford, and G. Akin. *Managing Organizational Change: A Multiple Perspectives Approach.* New York: Irwin McGraw-Hill, 2009.

COGNITION

Who becomes an entrepreneur? Researchers have found that people from a wide variety of groups—from young to old, with minimal education to higher education, male and female, and from all ethnic groups—have attempted to launch their own business ideas. With such variety, researchers have looked for what those people have in common. A major commonality has been how they think: cognition. Their motivations may also differ, from desire to be wealthy or famous to fixing a social problem, from being one's own boss to being a boss over others, from living up to expectations of others to carving out a specific kind of identity, from job satisfaction to simply having a job with an income.

Entrepreneurs must be able to recognize, discover, and create business opportunities and then develop a business model that will turn them into a commercial concern with potential customers. That means entrepreneurs do a lot of thinking, learning, assessing, judging, and deciding. Cognition involves all those mental activities; developing a new business opportunity is like identifying a problem and searching for solutions.

Thinking like an entrepreneur involves several steps that may seem to be in a sequence but usually swing back and forth. The steps include spotting a problem, need, or opportunity (a problem some group of people are experiencing), learning about the problem or the people's need, inventing a solution to the problem, finding resources for solving the problem, assessing risks, scanning the market situation for trends and needs, creating a distribution system (new business or partnership), and growing the business. All these steps involve thinking, learning, and deciding, which are core cognitive skills. Skills can be improved through learning, including practice and coaching.

Entrepreneurs seem to think differently from most other people in two ways: They choose to look for opportunities and they choose to see themselves as entrepreneurs. Noticing a problem, a trend, or an idea in need of invention results from looking for them; hence, entrepreneurs have a way of seeing situations that can result in new products, services, or ways of organizing. Everything people do and all the things they use to accomplish what they do have emerged from someone seeing a way to improve on those processes with something that would add value, along with enough others appreciating that value to adopt the idea. Business opportunities exist all around us as potential new products and services that customers will buy for more than it costs to produce them. The first role of cognition in the entrepreneurial process, therefore, is spotting opportunities: product or service needs, potential customer groups or markets, or new ways of organizing, so delivery is more competitive. Michael Dell did not invent the personal computer; he invented a new way of delivering it to customers—tailored mass production.

Edward Lazear says, "Entrepreneurs are business innovators" rather than technology innovators. Consider the good chef who wants to start a new restaurant. Cooking is only a part of a much larger package of activities that would include finding funds and a location, hiring staff, keeping the books, and so forth. These kinds of activities are interdependent—a change in one, such as how staff are chosen, impacts others, such as how customers are cared for, so a considerable amount of expertise is required. The entrepreneur has three choices: learn the knowledge and skill for business, perhaps through working as an assistant manager; hire someone to run the new business; or fail (95 percent of new businesses fail within the first five years). Effective entrepreneurs are constantly learning, constantly looking for opportunities, and frequently making decisions about developing their ideas. The following sequence shows the development of expertise in each of the knowledge areas: novice, beginner, competent, proficient, and expert. A lot of learning must occur to move up one level in developing know-what, know-how, and know-why.

Many people have ideas about how to improve on a product, service, or process, but few develop their ideas to the point where they are marketed to a larger population. Factors such as expertise, connection to a network of relevant people, confidence, perceptions of value, perceptions of feasibility, and motivation work together to separate the entrepreneur from others with ideas. A key part of the mental framework the entrepreneur brings to the situation is optimism. It translates into persistence when the going gets tough. An entrepreneur invests a lot of time and energy, also known as sweat equity, in the development of the idea into a marketable output. The optimism can be a chosen point of view or a learned one that provides resilience when the challenges seem overwhelming. Optimism helps when fear starts to interfere with hope. Fear can result from worry that the product will get to market too late or cash reserves will be exhausted before income is generated or someone will steal the valued intellectual property and become a competitor. People think about negative information, such as fear-invoking news, differently from the way they think about positive information. Optimists focus on the positive first and the negative second, so they can persist with the work. Pessimists focus on the negative first and struggle to persist. When either the optimist or the pessimist assesses the desirability of the entrepreneurial project and the feasibility and then assesses the level of risk, he or she may choose to move ahead or back off on the work. The difference in their decision making depends on how their assessment is biased by their attitudes, as well as by their decision errors.

The following sequence shows the major decision points in the entrepreneurial process: seeing an opportunity, choosing to create, beginning to build an organization, launching the organization, and managing the launched organization. Decision making with both simple and complex issues occurs at each of these five stages of enterprise development for the entrepreneur. Everyone commits the same kinds of errors around decisions. Researchers have discovered dozens of error patterns that are called cognitive bias—patterns of decision making that take shortcuts around full rational analysis. Some of the errors result from information overload or inadequate information that impacts speed of decision making, some from discomfort with negative or contradictory information that blinds the entrepreneur to risk.

For the entrepreneur who builds a business around one idea, building a team that can generate additional ideas is an essential step in sustaining the business long term. Such a business needs an environment that stimulates entrepreneurial thinking, a cognitive infrastructure that supports invention and innovation of products, services, and processes.

Michael M. Beyerlein
Purdue University

See also Cognition in Experts and Novices; Cognition Theory; Discovery and Exploitation; Emotions; Knowledge; Learning; Opportunity Identification and Structural Alignment; Opportunity Recognition

Further Readings

Krueger, Norris F., Jr. "The Cognitive Psychology of Entrepreneurship." In *Handbook of Entrepreneurship Research*, Z. J. Acs and D. B. Audretsch, eds. Boston: Kluwer Law International, 2003.

Lazear, Edward. "Balanced Skills for Entrepreneurship." *American Economic Review*, v.94/2 (2004).

Leiblein, Michael J. and Jeffrey T. Macher. "The Problem Solving Perspective: A Strategic Approach to Understanding New Business Opportunities and Business Models." In *Economic Institutions of Strategy*, Jackson A. Nickerson and Brian S. Silverman, eds. Bingley, UK: Emerald/JAI, 2009.

COGNITION IN EXPERTS AND NOVICES

A number of studies suggest that entrepreneurial experts and novices differ in the way they think and reason—their cognition. Generally, experts are individuals with expertise in a specific domain, while novices, by contrast, lack such expertise and experience. Hence, to develop into a successful entrepreneur, knowing about these differences is critical. What are the characteristics of experts' cognitive styles—the ways they perceive, combine, and assess information—that ultimately result in judgment and decisions that lead to a new product, service, or venture?

Experts and Expertise

Being an expert is frequently associated with a brilliant scientist conducting groundbreaking research, a chess master beating a computer, or a virtuoso flawlessly performing a complex piano sonata. Such ideals have inspired researchers to investigate the differences between experts and novices from many different perspectives and in a variety of contexts. Ronald Mitchell and his colleagues define an expert generally as an individual having expertise in a given domain. Expertise is based on a combination of appropriate knowledge, skills, and experience that is suitable in a given situation. A novice, in contrast, is a beginner in a given field, a person who lacks the relevant combination of knowledge, skills, and experience in that field. Expertise implies an individual's ability to perform a task in a specific domain with clearly above-average or excellent performance as a result of years of accumulated practice and experience. William Chase and Herbert Simon observed in their early investigation of expert chess players that, in addition to intelligence, other factors contribute to expertise, such as how people store information, their perception and framing of problems, and how they generate solutions. Becoming an expert implies years of devoted practice, learning by doing, and continuous improvement based on the critical reflection. The cognitive structures associated with developing expertise in and mastery of a specific area become increasingly refined, differentiated, and interconnected. Expert entrepreneurs have developed their expertise in the field of entrepreneurship: creating or developing new ventures.

How Entrepreneurs Think and Make Decisions

Theories in the area of social cognition, information processing, and expertise provide general explanations for the understanding of cognition that can be applied to entrepreneurs. Entrepreneurial heuristics theory, entrepreneurial alertness theory, entrepreneurial expertise and script theory (explaining entrepreneurial information processing and decision-making processes), and effectuation theory are more recent approaches to the study of entrepreneurial cognition. Although research in entrepreneurial cognition is still at an early stage of development, a substantial body of knowledge exists in regard to thinking and decision making, especially concerning cognitions relating to entrepreneurial decision making. According to Mitchell and his colleagues,

> Entrepreneurial cognitions [mental models] are the knowledge structures that people use to make assessments, judgments, or decisions involving opportunity evaluation, venture creation, and growth. In other words, research in entrepreneurial cognition is about understanding how entrepreneurs use simplifying mental models to piece together previously unconnected information that helps them to identify and invent new products or services, and to assemble the necessary resources to start and grow businesses.

The terms *cognitions, knowledge,* and *cognitive structures and scripts* are often used synonymously and refer to information intake and processing, its combination with existing knowledge, its storage, and its application in assessment and judgment. *Expert scripts* refers to a specific field or domain of expertise. The knowledge and experience acquired in that domain in many years of practice are highly developed, differentiated as well as integrated and interconnected, and include knowledge about sequences of appropriate action in certain situations of that domain. Roger Schank and Robert Abelson define a script as a generally accepted sequence of events permitting experts a prompt comprehension of expertise-specific information. As stated in their definition given above, Mitchell and his colleagues consider the key elements of entrepreneurial cognitions those knowledge structures (heuristical or scripted) and decision-making processes (including assessment and judgment) that are set within the larger context of the distinctive and inclusive domain of entrepreneurship, consisting of opportunity evaluation, venture creation, and growth of the venture.

Cognitions in Experts and Novices in the Domain of Entrepreneurship

John Leddo and Robert Abelson identify two key points in expertise-specific situations by which experts and novices can be distinguished when the attempt to utilize, that is perform, an expert script might fail. The differentiating moments are the time of *script entry* and *script doing*. Whereas script entry depends on the availability of the necessary expert knowledge and experience, script doing depends on a combination of ability and willingness and implies that the actions that are appropriate in the specific domain can (expert) or cannot (novice) be performed.

Expert information-processing theory allows further insights into the differences between experts' and novices' cognitions by explaining how experts apply specialized scripts to outperform novices in the domain-specific tasks of entrepreneurship. Both differ in their ability to recognize a context-relevant cue from other information. When confronted with a complex problem, these context-relevant cues allow experts to infer and actualize additional and broader knowledge and information about the particular situation. Expert information-processing theory suggests that the repeated use of an expert script results in additional expertise. An example is that of a fire brigade entering the kitchen full of smoke but not seeing any open fire. All of a sudden, the chief orders his men to leave the house immediately— only seconds before the wooden floor breaks from the flames, since the fire had started in the basement underneath the kitchen. In a few seconds, the expert combined different kinds of pieces of information and immediately made a decision that saved lives.

On the basis of these arguments, the decision to create a new venture, a venture creation decision (VCD), has been conceptualized as a consequence of three different expert scripts: venture arrangement scripts, venture willingness scripts, and venture ability scripts. These scripts are influenced by cultural values and in turn are shaped by venturing outcomes in an iterative but not directly recursive process of reinforcement. Cultural values also moderate the relationship between the three expert scripts and VCD. Venture arrangement scripts are the individual's knowledge structures or cognitions about the specific arrangements necessary for an entrepreneurial engagement such as knowledge about needed, helpful, and relevant contacts, relationships, resources, and assets. These knowledge structures/cognitions include idea protection, venture networks, resource access, and venture-specific skills. Venture willingness scripts refer to the entrepreneurs' commitment to venturing and their receptivity to the idea of starting a venture. Venture willingness scripts contain cognitions regarding opportunity seeking, commitment tolerance, and venture opportunity pursuit. They clarify the understanding for the true nature of the VCD and its related risks. Venture ability scripts refer to the capabilities, skills, knowledge, norms, and attitudes necessary to create a new venture, such as scripts for venture diagnostics and assessment, situational knowledge, and ability-opportunity fit. These scripts include the capability to assess a venture's condition and potential, to draw on and apply lessons learned in a different venture, and to see the need for and deliver out value creation by matching capability and opportunity resulting in self-efficacy in making VCDs. Moreover, according to the results of Dominic Lim and his colleagues, the institutional environment, such as legal and financial systems, influences both venture arrangements and venture willingness scripts.

The Difference Between Expert and Novice Entrepreneurs

How do entrepreneurial experts and novices differ in their cognitions? Generally, novice entrepreneurs have not yet developed the expert scripts that characterize experts, because they lack the practice and experience that experts have accumulated over years in using their cognitions and applying developed scripts that become increasingly differentiated over time. More specifically, the acquired VCD scripts enable entrepreneurial experts to recognize relevant information cues and use that information for their new venture creation significantly better and also earlier than entrepreneurial novices. Because of their acquired and differentiated VCD scripts, entrepreneurial experts can see new venture opportunities in situations that appear to entrepreneurial novices only as a vast amount of undifferentiated information. Hence, entrepreneurial experts differ from novices in the ways they transform, store, recover, and use information, as well as in how they perform appropriate decisions and actions regarding venture creations.

Stuart Read and his colleagues suggest that differences exist in the ways expert entrepreneurs perceive, process, and use information that are parallel to the general expert-novice literature. First, entrepreneurial experts see the prognostic character of information based on market research and reject the use of predictive information. Even though they notice the predictive nature of key pieces of market research information, they reject the use of such predictive pieces as irrelevant. Second, they model the new venture creation problem as a Marchian-Knightian-Weickian space and argue effectually rather than causally when solving problems in that space. According to Frank Knight, problem spaces in an entrepreneurial context are characterized by uncertainty; they consist of goal ambiguity, according to James March, and they need enactment according to Karl Weick; that is, decisions need to be made under conditions of an unpredictable future and unclear goals in an environment that cannot serve as the ultimate selection mechanism. Third, failure emerges earlier and at lower levels of investment because expert entrepreneurs, in contrast to novices, use techniques such as affordable loss and commitments from partners.

In addition, research by Nicholas Dew and his colleagues reveals that expert entrepreneurs and novices frame problems in very different ways. Experts identify more distinct potential markets than novices, focus more on building the venture as a whole, discount or ignore predictive information, worry more about affordable losses than expected returns, and emphasize the creation of networks of partnerships. In contrast, novices use a "predictive frame" and tend to "go by the textbook." Miriam Sanchez-Manzanares and her colleagues also found that experts and novices differ in their problem-solving strategies, their time spent on problem representation, and the justifications and difficulties expressed in the course of the design process. Moreover, expertise influences the organizational design. Whereas novices and experts create organizations consistent with organic structures, novices tend to use mechanistic structures.

To summarize, cognitions differ between entrepreneurial experts and novices, including the perception of information, its processing, its storage, its retrieval, and related actions. Existing research and knowledge in this area suggest that the only shortcut on the path from novice to expert entrepreneur is through increasing the amount of repeated and reflexive practice, which in turn develops an increasing amount of differentiated and interconnected knowledge, skills, and experience.

Sonja A. Sackmann
Katharina Schuster
University BW Munich

See also Cognition; Cognition Theory; Learning Theory

Further Readings

Carsrud, Alan and Malin Brännback, eds. *Understanding the Entrepreneurial Mind: Opening the Black Box*. New York: Springer-Verlag, 2009.

Cohen, Michael D. and James G. March. *Leadership and Ambiguity*, 2nd ed. Cambridge, MA: Harvard Business School Press, 1986.

Dew, Nicholas, Saras D. Sarasvathy, Stuart Read, and Robert Wiltbank. "Immortal Firms in Mortal Markets? An Entrepreneurial Perspective on the 'Innovator's Dilemma.'" *European Journal of Innovation Management*, v.11/3 (2009).

Knight, Frank. *Risk, Uncertainty, and Profit*. Boston: Houghton Mifflin, 1921.

Leddo, J. and R. P. Abelson. "The Nature of Explanations." In *Knowledge Structures*, J. A. Galambos et al., eds. Hillsdale, NJ: Erlbaum, 1986.

Mitchell, Ronald et al. "Cross-Cultural Cognitions and the Venture Creation Decision." *Academy of Management Journal*, v.43/5 (2000).

Mitchell, Ronald et al. "Toward a Theory of Entrepreneurial Cognition: Rethinking the People Side of Entrepreneurship Research." *Entrepreneurship Theory and Practice*, v.27/2 (2002).

Read, Stuart, Robert Wiltbank, Saras Sarasvathy, and Robert Smith. *What Do Entrepreneurs Really Learn From Experience: The Differences Between Experts and Novice Entrepreneurs.* Babson Park, MA: Babson College, 2004. http://www.babson.edu/entrep/fer/BABSON2003/VII/VII-P4/VII-P4.html (Accessed February 2011).

Sanchez-Manzanar, Miriam, with Ramón Rico and Francisco Gil. "Designing Organizations: Does Expertise Matter?" *Journal of Business and Psychology,* v.23/4 (2008).

Schank, Robert and Robert Abelson. *Scripts, Plans, Goals and Understanding.* Hillsdale, NJ: Erlbaum, 1977.

Weick, Karl. *Sensemaking in Organizations.* Thousand Oaks, CA: Sage, 1995.

COGNITION THEORY

Cognition theory explains the general mechanisms and processes of human thinking. Cognition theories are grounded in the observation that everything people think, say, and do is influenced by mental processes, that is, by the cognitive mechanisms by which humans perceive the world, acquire information, and then process that information to accomplish a wide range of tasks.

Cognition theory blossomed in the second half of the 20th century, inspired by advances in cognitive psychology, linguistics, and information technologies. Different streams of theory emerged, reflecting alternative perspectives on the underlying realities of mental phenomena. One stream is mentalism, which studies the mental representations of the self, others, and the world. Another stream of cognition theory focuses on processes of human thinking, such as reasoning and decision making. A third stream integrates cognition across different levels of analysis, including neurological, personal, and social levels.

Cognition theory is widely recognized as relevant for the management of new ventures because these contexts are cognitively demanding. They require managers to perceive and process novel and often complex information, then use such information in making decisions in risky, uncertain, dynamic environments. Scholars therefore use theories of cognition to address a number of major questions about the founding and management of new ventures. First, which cognitive skills are required for the effective management of new ventures? Second,

to what extent are these skills unique to new venture situations, or are they broadly similar to the skills required in any dynamic, uncertain environment? Third, why do some people exhibit stronger skills in this regard? Are people born with these cognitive characteristics, or can they be developed through education and experience?

With respect to the first question just posed—which cognitive skills are required for managing new ventures—mentalist theories of cognition propose that some people possess mental representations of the self and the world that are more supportive of innovation and risk taking. For example, if a manager possesses a mental image of herself as an exploratory, innovative person, then she may be more effective in sensing and seizing new venture opportunities. Process theories, in contrast, suggest that some people perceive and transform information in a more effective manner. For example, one person may process environmental uncertainty and perceive a negative risk of failure, while another person will process the same information and perceive a positive risk of gain. Clearly, the latter style of cognitive processing is often required when managing new ventures. Cognition theory also illuminates the different levels of thinking that are required when managing new ventures. For example, when making decisions as the manager of a new venture, a person must be able rapidly to integrate individual perceptions and beliefs, socially derived motivations and goals, and environmental uncertainty.

Cognition theory also helps to answer whether the cognitive skills required for managing new ventures are unique to these situations. In other words, are the managers of new ventures different from other managers, in terms of their cognitive skills? During the 1980s especially, many scholars of entrepreneurship and new ventures sought to answer this question. They investigated a wide range of topics, including motivation, risk perception and propensity, and decision-making biases such as overconfidence. However, the consensus that emerged from this research was that the managers of new ventures are not unique in these respects. Other types of managers who operate in dynamic, uncertain environments possess very similar mental representations and cognitive capabilities. This finding does not diminish the relevance of cognition theory for the management of new ventures, but it does suggest that the requisite cognitive characteristics have more general relevance for management.

Scholars also draw on cognition theory to investigate why some people possess stronger cognitive skills and therefore are better equipped to manage new ventures. They inquire as to the extent these cognitive capabilities are the result of nature or nurture. Are they a genetic inheritance or the result of learning and experience? In fact, these are critical questions for cognition theory generally. Moreover, the debate is historic. In the 17th century, for example, John Locke argued that the mind of a newborn child is like a blank sheet of paper waiting for information. His argument was often challenged, recently by Noam Chomsky, who argued that children are born with the fundamentals of linguistic grammar imprinted in their brains. This debate continues. With respect to the management of new ventures, the consensus is that to some degree, managers' cognitive skills and capabilities are the result of inheritance, but these skills and capabilities are also significantly influenced by experience and learning.

Two innovative trends in cognition theory may further illuminate the management of new ventures. These trends are neurological research and theories of complex adaptive systems. Cognitive neurologists investigate how the physical and mental characteristics of persons develop and interact. These studies may help to explain why some individuals possess particular patterns of mental representation and information processing, with potential implications for thought within dynamic, uncertain environments. Similarly, if human cognition is viewed as a complex adaptive system, its processes and interactions can be systematically explored in relation to human personality and social factors. Future research on these topics may also help to explain the significant cognitive features of new venture management.

Cognition plays an important role in the new venture process, from founding to managing growth and organizational maturity. Cognition theory has already shed much light on these topics. As it continues to develop and deepen, cognition theory promises to remain an important source of insight for the management of new ventures.

Peter T. Bryant
IE Business School, Madrid

See also Cognition; Cognition in Experts and Novices; Creativity; Learning Theory

Further Readings

Baron, R. A. and T. B. Ward. "Expanding Entrepreneurial Cognition's Toolbox: Potential Contributions From the Field of Cognitive Science." *Entrepreneurship Theory and Practice*, v.28/6 (2004).

Eden, Colin, and J.-C. Spender. *Managerial and Organizational Cognition: Theory, Methods, and Research*. Thousand Oaks, CA: Sage, 1998.

Reed, Stephen K. *Cognition: Theory and Applications*, 7th ed. Belmont, CA: Thomson Wadsworth, 2007.

Sadler-Smith, E. "Cognitive Style and the Management of Small and Medium-Sized Enterprises." *Organization Studies*, v.25/2 (2004).

John Locke (1632–1704) was an English philosopher and considered the first of the British empiricists, but he was equally important to social contract theory. Locke argued that the mind of a newborn child is like a blank sheet of paper waiting for information. (Public Domain via Wikimedia)

COGNITIVE SCHEMAS AND SCRIPTS

All individuals do not think in the same manner. This fact is not surprising and is perhaps interesting. Of more interest, however, is that each individual does not always think in the same manner and that part of this intraindividual difference results from the various contexts in which one might find oneself. These primary concepts—borrowed from the field of psychology and social cognitive theory—have provided numerous insights into the field of entrepreneurship and new venture management over the past few decades. Cognition, the act and process of knowing, has been an important part of research in the field of entrepreneurship for more than three decades.

Research in entrepreneurship has shown that developing and/or managing a new venture successfully is linked to how individuals think and execute in their roles as entrepreneurs. At the foundation of this research into entrepreneurship and cognition are the concepts of schemas and scripts. Schemas are cognitive structures or mental models that represent knowledge about a particular concept—in this case the "mental models" of what it takes to start and run a new venture. Schemas are related to how one organizes prior knowledge. Scripts are related cognitive devices. Also known as event schemas, scripts describe sequences of events in commonly recognized situations.

Scholars in psychology and information processing have found that in order to execute a given action properly an individual must have the three elemental cognitive scripts. Individuals first must have a mental model about the arrangements—that is, the resources, tools, and materials necessary to complete a task. Later in the sequence, an individual must have a willingness script and the ability to enact the script. Within the field of entrepreneurship, researchers have isolated some of the broad scripts required to create and manage a new venture. Ron Mitchell and his colleagues have shown that these three cognitions—arrangements, willingness, and ability—appear to be at the core of the mental model of entrepreneurs. Similarly, a long line of research by Robert Baron suggests that successful entrepreneurs enact deliberate practices, following scripts such as these, in order to move themselves toward expert performance.

Creating or managing a new venture requires that an individual develop entrepreneurial arrangement scripts, which are knowledge structures about the specific use of concepts such as idea protection, personal and professional networks, access to business resources, and venture-specific skills. Entrepreneurial willingness scripts are also required. These knowledge structures are actionable thoughts about opportunity seeking, commitment tolerance, and pursuing opportunities. Finally, individuals must cultivate ability scripts: knowledge structure surrounding how to assess certain ventures, how to use prior knowledge in new and specific opportunities, and how to create value by matching resources such as people, materials, and products. Together, these three types of knowledge structures provide something of an expert script for new venture creation. Entrepreneurs think about these specific arrangements, willingness, and abilities as a script that can lead to venture formation. Perhaps most interesting, this model appears to hold across the globe. Regardless of culture or nationality, entrepreneurs tend to have very similar scripts regarding what it takes to create a new venture.

It may therefore appear that research in this area has found a place of finality, but that is untrue. In fact, a study examining the intersection of cognition and entrepreneurship has found that we have only just begun to mine the understanding that can come from applying a lens of cognition to entrepreneurship and new ventures. The current corpus of work in entrepreneurship cognition tends to focus narrowly on the results of individual entrepreneurs having certain cognitions (that is, individuals with a certain heuristic or mental model are more or less likely to be successful as an entrepreneur) in certain contexts (the "typical" independent start-up entrepreneur). This narrowness of research in the broader domain of entrepreneurship cognition also holds for the specific constructs of schemas and scripts. However, by reflecting on the existing predominance of a few areas within the extant research, we can see some opportunities for greater understanding. We can do this by simply expanding the parameters of the current focus.

We can move beyond a concentration on the outcomes of certain scripts or schemas and attempt to understand how and why these schemas develop. In other words, in addition to looking at the consequences of these cognitions, we need to examine their antecedents. Additionally, while examining the schemas of individuals has proven fruitful, it may be just as important to understand the collective schemas at other levels of analysis. New venture management shows that individuals rarely start their businesses on their own but instead flourish in teams. Research also shows that teams do indeed develop "team cognitions." The opportunities are ripe to investigate founding team schemas and founding team scripts.

Finally, perhaps the area that is ripest for research on scripts and schemas lies at the intersection of entrepreneurship, new venture management, and context. As noted, most research on scripts and schemas of entrepreneurs has been focused on individual, independent entrepreneurs. To date, little research has examined the importance of context to entrepreneurial scripts and schemas. The one exception is corporate entrepreneurship. Using social cognitive theory, researchers have demonstrated that the context of a new venture—that is, whether it is a nascent operation with little or no existing infrastructure, resources, and organization, as opposed to an existing firm with stable infrastructure, relatively munificent resources, and a fixed organization—has profound effects on the cognitions of "would-be" corporate entrepreneurs.

Research into new forms and contexts for entrepreneurship holds great promise for understanding the scripts and schemas of new venture development. For instance, future researchers can examine the development of ventures with a social mission, ventures in social media, and ventures in the environmental or green space, as well as more traditional contexts such as family businesses or high-technology ventures.

For example, a social entrepreneur is likely to have a different perspective on why someone should start a venture and how he or she should go about doing it. As a result, social entrepreneurs are likely to develop scripts and schemas that are different from those of traditional "for-profit-only" entrepreneurs. The same can be said for green entrepreneurs and entrepreneurs in social media and family businesses. Therefore, understanding how scripts and schemas develop and unfold for individuals within one of these particular fields is important for new venture management research. It is clear that there is still much to learn about entrepreneurial schemas and scripts. The development of these new insights will be beneficial for scholars, educators, and practitioners as well.

Andrew Corbett
Babson College

See also Cognition; Cognition in Experts and Novices; Cognition Theory; Learning Theory

Further Readings

Bandura, A. *Social Foundations of Thought and Action: A Social Cognitive Theory.* Englewood Cliffs, NJ: Prentice-Hall, 1986.

Baron, Robert and R. A. Henry. "How Entrepreneurs Acquire the Capacity to Excel: Insights From Basic Research on Expert Performance." *Strategic Entrepreneurship Journal*, v.4 (2010).

Corbett, A. C. and K. M. Hmieleski. "The Conflicting Cognitions of Corporate Entrepreneurs." *Entrepreneurship Theory and Practice*, v.31/1 (2007).

Grégoire, D. A., A. C. Corbett, and J. S. McMullen. "The Cognitive Perspective in Entrepreneurship: An Agenda for Future Research." *Journal of Management Studies*, v.48/6 (2011).

Krueger, N. F. "The Cognitive Infrastructure of Opportunity Recognition." *Entrepreneurship Theory and Practice*, v.24/3 (2000).

Krueger, N. F. "What Lies Beneath? The Experiential Essence of Entrepreneurial Thinking." *Entrepreneurship Theory and Practice*, v.31/1 (2007).

Leddo, J. and R. P. Abelson. "The Nature of Explanations." In *Knowledge Structures*, J. A. Galambos, R. P. Abelson, and J. A. Black, eds. Hillsdale, NJ: Erlbaum, 1986.

Mitchell, R. K. et al. "Are Entrepreneurial Cognitions Universal? Assessing Entrepreneurial Cognitions Across Cultures." *Entrepreneurship Theory and Practice*, v.27/2 (2002).

Mitchell, R. K. et al. "Toward a Theory of Entrepreneurial Cognition: Rethinking the People Side of Entrepreneurship Research." *Entrepreneurship Theory and Practice*, v.27/2 (2002).

Shepherd, D. A. and N. F. Krueger. "An Intentions-Based Model of Entrepreneurial Teams' Social Cognition." *Entrepreneurship Theory and Practice* (Winter 2002).

West, G. P. "Collective Cognition: When Entrepreneurial Teams, Not Individuals, Make Decisions." *Entrepreneurship Theory and Practice*, v.31/1 (2007).

Wood, R. and A. Bandura. "Social Cognitive Theory of Organizational Management." *Academy of Management Review*, v.14/3 (1989).

COMMITMENT AND PERSISTENCE

Commitment involves the willingness to persist toward a goal. It is an internal force that helps us persist in completing a task and is often demonstrated in the form of identification and loyalty. Commitment is often shown to be related to motivation and performance. Persistence goes one step further. It involves staying steadfast and continuing a course of action even through adversity or difficulties over a period of time. Entrepreneurs must be committed and persistent in order to be successful.

Entrepreneurial commitment may be described as affective commitment, behavioral commitment, and continuance. Affective commitment is the drive to start a business. Behavioral commitment is the willingness to put forth the effort required. Continuance refers to the entrepreneur's intention to persevere through difficult times. This theory can be expanded to organizational commitment. Three things go into this form of commitment: identification with the organization, the willingness to put forth the effort, and the desire to stay with that organization. Entrepreneurs often identify with the organization, are willing to put forth effort, and have the desire to persist. Entrepreneurs have the desire to see the business succeed, and they may have a commitment to developing their careers. They focus on their goals and behave in ways to reach them. In doing so, they often exhibit enthusiasm and excitement.

Three component models of organizational commitment, developed by John Meyer and Natalie Allen in the 1990s, suggest that commitment is a psychological bond: affective (attachment to a goal), continuance (considering the cost or consequences and benefits of continued effort and participation), and normative (based on obligations to meet a goal). Organizational commitment is the extent to which an employee identifies with the organization and is involved in it. Employees with high organizational commitment are more likely to be satisfied, change jobs (or organizations) less frequently, and perform at a higher level of productivity. Many things can influence commitment: leadership style, training, teams, decision making, autonomy, and feedback.

Expectancy theory can also help explain the entrepreneur's commitment in that entrepreneurs expect that their effort will lead to performance and that their performance will lead to a desired reward. Those who believe in their ability to affect the desired outcome through performance will often commit and persevere even through difficulties.

Certainly, starting a new business requires perseverance. Often people stay in business because of an ability to persevere and because of a commitment to the venture. Not everyone in the organization will have the same level of commitment and not all employees can be expected to feel the same way about the organization as the entrepreneur does.

Work persistence influences actions: what endeavors are undertaken and how one deals with success or failure. It involves exerting a high level of effort and "doing whatever it takes" to make something happen. Persistence and maintaining a positive attitude help people overcome difficult situations and attain success in their business.

A person with high self-efficacy (self-confidence) is more likely to exert effort for a longer period of time, have higher goals, overcome obstacles, and develop adequate plans to accomplish a goal. Such individuals are likely to succeed over time. Also, people with a high need for achievement tend to be committed to their goals and persevere through adversity. This achievement theory can explain entrepreneurial persistence. People with an achievement need think that they can control situations even in adversity and gain feedback on their progress. Starting and running a business can involve difficulties and uncertainty. People differ in their needs and their level of drive to do something. They have different values and will engage in those activities that satisfy these needs. This theory is known as the "need motive value theory."

Goals set by employees and managers lead to self-efficacy, which leads to motivation and commitment, which then leads to persistence. Successful people are goal oriented even in difficult times. Goals can motivate people to persist and overcome obstacles if those goals are seen as attainable and desirable by employees. However, goals should not be too difficult; otherwise people may become overconfident and fail. Entrepreneurs must believe that they can succeed and have confidence in themselves in order to commit and persist.

Attribution theory may also explain why some people are successful entrepreneurs. According to this theory one must have an intention, exert effort, and also have the ability to persist in difficult times. Often this involves having an internal locus of control, a sense that one has control over the situation and that one can succeed. Entrepreneurs who attribute their situation to internal factors feel they can persist and succeed in difficult times. However, if they attribute their success or failure to external (uncontrollable) causes, such as the economy, they may not commit or persist. Entrepreneurs who have a self-serving bias that things happen because of their internal characteristics tend to persist. Internal characteristics may lead people to believe that an opportunity is possible and can be controlled, so they see starting a business as positive.

Concomitantly, a high rate of failure is usually due to lack of persistence during times of adversity over the long term. Entrepreneurs may have good ideas, but it takes commitment to help them see these ideas succeed. They must think that these ideas are worth going after in order to commit to them.

Katherine Hyatt
Reinhardt University

See also Gender and Performance; Goal Setting; Intentions; Locus of Control; Motivation and Gender; Performance and Legitimacy

Further Readings

Bandura, A. *Self-Efficacy: The Exercise of Control*. New York: Freeman, 1997.

Eisenberger, R. and J. M. Leonard. "Effects of Conceptual Task Difficulty on Generalized Persistence." *American Journal of Psychology*, v.93 (1980).

Meyer, John P. and Natalie J. Allen. *Commitment in the Workplace; Theory, Research, and Application*. Thousand Oaks, CA: Sage, 1997.

Mowday, R. T., R. M. Steers, and L. W. Porter. "The Measurement of Organizational Commitment." *Journal of Vocational Behavior*, v.14/2 (1979).

Shaver, K. G. and L. R. Scott. "Person, Process, Choice: The Psychology of New Venture Creation." *Entrepreneurship Theory and Practice*, v.16/2 (1991).

Sibin Wu, Matthews and Grace K. Dagher. "Need for Achievement, Business Goals, and Entrepreneurial Persistence." *Management Research News*, v.30/12 (2007).

COMMUNICATION STYLES

Communication involves sending, receiving, and interpreting information. At all times, people are communicating with others, whether verbally or nonverbally. The verbal or nonverbal interaction with others shows how our communication should be received, filtered, and understood. This is known as our communication style, as suggested by R. W. Norton in 1978. Communication styles have been linked to self-esteem, confidence, and feelings of control. Communication styles connect people—in the new venture context, customers, employees, or other organizational stakeholders. Everyone typically has a dominant or primary style, a style that is observed by others, and the ability to adapt that style. Some people are more direct in their communication, whereas others are more indirect. Some people may be open, while others may be reserved. In all cases, however, good communication involves listening and not just hearing.

Communication styles can be influenced by gender. Men tend to use a more authoritarian style and tend to be more goal oriented and decisive in their communication styles. These styles can influence how managers or leaders are perceived in the organization as well. Women entrepreneurs tend to have a better understanding of good communication than men. Women tend to take the time to make sure their communication is effective. They focus on listening, group orientation, open communication channels, and good interpersonal relationships. Women tend to focus more on two-way communication and helping employees. Often communication channels are more open and informal when entrepreneurs start an organization. Also, women entrepreneurs are often more focused on communicating to promote relationships with their constituents.

Communication can also be influenced by the stage of an organization's growth or development. Early within a new venture, an organization tends to communicate with constituent groups more often. Communication channels are often direct and informal, usually face to face, by phone, or via e-mail. As the organization grows, it is important for the members to understand their roles and the roles of the persons with whom they are communicating,

Men tend to use an authoritarian communication style and are often more goal oriented and decisive in their expression. Women tend to focus on effective communication and will take the time to attempt to be clear while speaking. (Photos.com)

which determines how communication styles should be adapted in order to be effective both verbally and nonverbally.

Theories of Communication Style

Numerous theories about different communication styles have been developed, and often these systems or models find cognates among the other models.

Norton suggested that there are nine areas that relate to our communication styles: dominant, dramatic, contentious, animated, impression-leaving, relaxed, attentive, open, and friendly. A dominant person takes charge. Dramatic and animated people are expressive. Contentious people are argumentative. Open people are to the point. Attentive and friendly people make sure those with whom they communicate feel they are being listened to and focus on relationships. Many of these areas are derived from entrepreneurial characteristics, such as achievement motivation, commitment, perseverance, taking initiative, internal locus of control, risk tolerance, and work satisfaction. Being attentive, friendly, and relaxed is known as an attractive style. Entrepreneurs are often dominant and open in their communication styles. Based on these areas, other theories of communication styles have been developed.

Psychologist Carl Jung suggested that people have four communication styles, depending on whether they are task oriented or people oriented, relaxed or assertive. Differences in the types of organizations that entrepreneurs choose to start can also dictate their communication styles; four such types have been identified: analyzers, collaborators, controllers, and socializers.

Analyzers are detail-oriented people who try to be logical in analyzing solutions individually before making a decision and taking action. Such people are cautious in what they say, have limited facial expressions and gestures, and are often very soft-spoken, even monotonic. Individuals with this style are often accountants or analysts. They like to see the "whole picture" and process details in a linear fashion. They are reflective and analytical. Analyzers want as much information and data as possible. They need time to make decisions, can be technical, and like structure. They want to be recognized for their activities and results. In communicating with analyzers, it is important to be prepared,

ready to answer questions, and provide supporting details. Analyzers cannot be rushed; they must fully understand, for example, why change is important. Supervisors of analyzers should ask them to share their thoughts. Analyzers dislike conflict and will avoid it. As entrepreneurs, analyzers may start accounting or technical firms.

Collaborators focus on relationships and try to work with others in a relaxed manner. They are emotional and have lively expressions and gestures. They want everyone to be happy and often choose careers in human resources or in a service industry. They are supportive of others and relate well to others. They value friendship and do not want to be rejected. Collaborators respond well to communication that is enthusiastic, expressive, and full of examples. In working with collaborators, it is best not be too aggressive and to show them why a change is needed. Women entrepreneurs tend to focus more on collaboration and building relationships. They are often democratic, open, and group oriented. As entrepreneurs, collaborators may tend to open service-oriented organizations.

Controllers are assertive and focused on tasks. They are direct and instill urgency without emotional expression. They want just the facts and they often guard their time. They like to be in charge and take control of a situation. They like to direct others and are the drivers in the organization. This form of communication is often one-way. They like to do things in their own way, make the decisions quickly, enjoy challenges, seek results, and want to be recognized for their efforts. They like direct, to-the-point communication that is formal and focused on the task. They may even seem forceful to other people. When communicating with a controller, one should be direct, give facts, and focus on results. Controllers want to get to the point of what someone is trying to say immediately. As organizations grow and take on a formal organizational structure, communication tends to relate more to the controller style.

Socializers are outgoing, outspoken, assertive, expressive, excited, and quick to make decisions. They like to talk to people, and they also like change. They are creative, are easily bored, and see the big picture. Often one finds these individuals in advertising. They often try to sell people on their ideas. Socializers respond well to communicators who listen, provide support, empathize, and reassure them. In communicating with socializers, one must keep up with their pace and be patient when they get off track. As entrepreneurs, individuals who are socializers tend to start advertising, public relations, or marketing firms.

To communicate with each of these types of people, it is important to focus on their preferences and their communication styles. Therefore, it is best to communicate in a manner that appeals to them. Employers, managers, and customers can all adapt their styles to reflect the behavior of the person with whom they are communicating. Some people feel that communication styles and management styles are related. Some management styles of entrepreneurs can include being single-minded and focused, tending toward micromanagement, or relaxed, tending toward the informal. However, as their businesses grow and change in structure and culture, entrepreneurs should be alert to the need to adapt their styles to these changes and to the styles of the key players within the organization.

Other communication styles are based on four areas: tells, sells, consults, and joins. People who tell make decisions and want people to implement them, which relates to the controlling style. People who sell try to influence management and owners. The consult communication style involves asking for input but then making the final decision. The joins style allows the group to make decisions.

P. P. Mok suggested four other communication styles: sensor, thinker, intuitor, and feeler. The sensor style involves taking quick action and relates to the controlling style. The thinker tries to find logical solutions and relates to the analyzing style. The intuitor focuses on ideas and possibilities and relates to the collaborative style. The feeler focuses on relationships with others and their own emotions; feelers are related to socializers.

Communication styles may also involve blaming, directing, persuading, and problem solving. A person with a blaming style tries to place blame on other people. Those with directing styles try to tell others what to do and how with one-way communication. The persuasive style involves trying to get someone to do something, such as implement a process or complete a goal, by showing them the benefits of choosing to do so. The problem-solving style utilizes two-way communication to try to find a win-win solution to a problem and is similar to the collaborative style. None of these styles is considered necessarily bad, but the implied negatives of some of these styles may

allow entrepreneurs and managers to identify their primary styles in a way that can highlight the need to modify communication style where necessary. Some styles, for example, can conflict. Moreover, a new venture may have problem-solving focus at the outset, but as the organization grows the overall style may change to one of the other three.

Communication for New Ventures

Being able to communicate effectively is a critical skill for entrepreneurs in new ventures. Poor communication can damage an entrepreneur and the organization. When communicating with others, it is important to take several steps. First, one must ask oneself what one's primary style is. Next, it is important to identify the styles of the individuals with whom one is communicating. Finally, it is important to determine how to adapt one's style to those of others in order to elicit the best communication to advance the enterprise.

When new ventures start up, communication is often fluid, informal, and spontaneous, but as an organization grows the communication structure tends to be more formal. Informal communication structures allow for more open communication but can also lead to information overload. By contrast, as the business grows the entrepreneur may be subject to information blocks or filtering as channels and loops become more formalized, making it necessary for entrepreneurs to make decisions about where and how to involve themselves. Communication may evolve from a two–way style to a top-down, one-way structure as the organization grows.

Communication is especially critical to entrepreneurial success in internal corporate communications. Communication is an important part of leadership and management. How leaders or managers choose to communicate with others can influence whether or not work gets done, whether change happens, and whether emotions, motivations, and conflict are appropriately addressed. Also, the ways employees communicate to managers can influence the manager's communication style. Communication must be clear, consistent, and dynamic. It is important that entrepreneurs be able to communicate their vision to others. For example, some people are very direct and assertive; others are even more aggressive at communicating to others what they need and may even manipulate people to get what they want. Some people may be passive or devoid of emotion in talking with others and may never reveal to others, including management, what they want; these individuals' style avoids conflict and confrontation. Sometimes people are passive-aggressive, avoiding confrontation but still trying to manipulate others. Each type of communication style needs to be identified and addressed if detrimental to the new business venture.

Outside the organization, entrepreneurs must communicate effectively with customers, investors, and other stakeholders. They must be able to communicate their vision, values, and strategy for the organization. They also must inspire others through their communication. Often successful entrepreneurs will try to collaborate with others to find win-win solutions.

Communication styles are therefore key to the performance of a new venture. They shape the interaction between members of the organization as well as outside stakeholders, and thereby shape the organization itself. Communication also influences satisfaction within the organization and how well people work together as a team. Communication styles influence credibility and help to clarify roles within an organization. For all these reasons, it is essential to establish clear, effective, and positive communication styles and to monitor and appropriately modify them as the new venture evolves.

Katherine Hyatt
Reinhardt University

See also Change Management: Corporate; Information; Leadership; Learning Theory; Negotiating Strategies; Social Networks

Further Readings

Downs, Cal W. et al. "An Analysis of Communication Style Instruments." *Management Communication Quarterly*, v.1/4 (May 1998).

Freeman, S. and R. J. Varey. "The Effects of Entrepreneur Characteristics and Gender-Based Management and Communication Styles From an Internal Marketing Perspective Within Both a Small and Large Business Environment." *Marketing Education Review*, v.7/3 (1997).

Kumar, R. "Doing Business in India: Caveat Venditor." *Ivey Business Journal*, v.71/5 (2007).

Mok, P. P. *Interpretation Manual for Communicating Styles and Technology.* Richardson, TX: Training Associates Press, 1975.

Norton, R. W. "Foundation of a Communicator Style Construct." *Human Communication Research*, v.4 (1978).

Saini, S. and K. Plowman. "Effective Communications in Growing Pre-IPO Start-Ups." *Journal of Promotion Management*, v.13/3–4 (2007).

Smith, S. S. "You Got Personality." *Entrepreneur*, v.27/9 (1999).

COMMUNITY/GOVERNMENT BUY-INS

The velocity of technological change is quicker than ever before in today's global economy, and competitive advanced technologies are decisive in national economic growth. Private-sector investments in research and development are focused mainly on incremental improvements to capture faster returns for companies and their shareholders. Few financial institutions, venture capitalists, and angel investors fund unconfirmed, early-stage technologies. This approach, however, erodes the foundation for significant advances that are crucial to creating new capabilities, improving productivity, and ensuring growth. As a result, it is important to cultivate community and government buy-ins.

Community and government buy-ins help industry invest in long-term, high-risk research with payoffs far beyond private profit. Communities and governments can fund new ventures' high-risk research and accelerate the development of new-to-the-world technologies by sharing the cost and the risk with companies when research risks are too high for the new ventures to bear alone. By sharing the cost with companies, communities and governments can accelerate the development of early-stage, innovative technologies, helping industry raise its competitive potential while providing national populations with a higher standard of living in the form of higher-paying jobs, better consumer products, improved health, greater energy efficiency, and a cleaner environment.

Community and government can also conduct peer review for a merit-based, rigorous selection process that ensures high quality, objectivity, and fairness. Community and government can also encourage new ventures' partnerships and catalyze companies, universities, research organizations, and state and local entities to partner creatively to develop innovative technologies. Finally, community and government can encourage diffusion of knowledge, facilitating new ventures in publishing and sharing their results and pursuing patents and licensing to give others a chance to benefit from the new knowledge created during the venturing process.

In her article "The Role of Networks in the Entrepreneurial Process," Sue Birley, of the Cranfield School of Management, notes that during the process of starting a new firm, entrepreneurs seek not only financial resources but also advice, information, and reassurance. As a result, the aid and assistance received from both government networks and community networks will influence the nature of the firm considerably.

The need for community government to buy in to advanced technology development is fully acknowledged without ignoring the equally important role of social entrepreneurship and social change perspective. In development circles, there is now widespread consensus that social entrepreneurs represent a far better mechanism to respond to needs than we have ever had before—a decentralized and emergent force that remains our best hope for solutions that can keep pace with our problems and create a more peaceful world. Hence, the new strategy should be to increase new ventures' understanding of existing community and government resources. Even more than national leaders and political change agents, entrepreneurs need to have a deep understanding of the socioeconomic environment of which they are a part.

Government intervention in invigorating the diffusion of entrepreneurship is legitimized by the role new companies play in job and wealth creation and the dissemination of innovation within a territory. This has implications for public policies; Instead of incentive policies applied on a wide basis, policies tailored on a local basis may be more effective in inspiring new venture creation. Policy makers and providers of external resources are more interested in interacting with rapid-growth firms. Rapid-growth firms are also more interested in obtaining guidance from government sources and external resource providers—that is, the "entrepreneurial environment," which is a combination of factors that take part in the development of entrepreneurship. First, this environment refers to the overall economic, sociocultural, and sociopolitical factors that influence people's willingness and ability to undertake entrepreneurial activities. Second, it refers to the availability of assistance and support services that facilitate the start-up process.

Additionally, factors such as the accessibility of financial resources, large cities, and research universities are very important in enhancing the rate of new venture creation. As a matter of fact, because entrepreneurs face numerous obstacles—from lack of financial assistance to lack of information on different aspects of business, excessive taxation, and high rates of inflation—there is a need for policy initiatives to develop entrepreneurship. These much-needed strategic policy initiatives could include provision of venture capital funds, tax-based incentives, government procurement programs, and protection of proprietary ideas and innovations.

Djamel Eddine Laouisset
Alhosn University, Abu Dhabi

See also Entrepreneurial Support Systems; Leadership; Partnerships; University Start-Ups

Further Readings

Aucoin, Peter. "New Public Management and the Quality of Government: Coping With the New Political Governance in Canada." Conference on New Public Management and the Quality of Government. Structure and Organisation of Government and the Quality of Government Institute, University of Gothenburg, Sweden, November 13–15, 2008.

Birley, Sue. "The Role of Networks in the Entrepreneurial Process." *Journal of Business Venturing*, v.1 (1985).

Bornstein, David and Susan Davis. *Social Entrepreneurship: What Everyone Needs to Know.* New York: Oxford University Press, 2010.

Denhardt, Robert. *Public Administration: An Action Orientation.* Belmont, CA: Thomson Wadsworth, 2009.

Denhardt, Robert and Janet Denhardt. "The New Public Service: Serving Rather Than Steering." *Public Administration Review*, v.60/6 (2000).

Kettl, Donald and James Fessler. *The Politics of the Administrative Process.* Washington, DC: CQ Press, 2009.

Khan, Haroon. *Introduction to Public Administration.* Lanham, MD: University Press of America, 2008.

McKinney, Jerome and Lawrence Howard. *Public Administration: Balancing Power and Accountability.* Westport, CT: Praeger, 1998.

Stone, Diane. "Global Public Policy, Transnational Policy Communities and Their Networks." *Journal of Policy Sciences*, v.36/1 (2008).

COMPETITION

Since Adam Smith set forth the theory of economic competition in *An Inquiry Into the Nature and Causes of the Wealth of Nations*, the assumption that firms are free to set prices and can choose to do so as a way to compete against rivals has been widely accepted. For Smith and later economists, efficiently allocating productive resources to their most highly valued uses was a major activity for successful competition. Later economic theorists concluded that no system of resource allocation is more efficient than perfect competition. However, a continuing debate in the history of (micro)economics concerns whether or not monopolistic competition is distinctly different from and possibly more efficient at creating and sustaining markets than perfect competition and monopoly. Many distinguished scholars have demonstrated that monopolistic competition has a distinct structure and process. Monopolistic competition is often regarded as the typical intermediate case, whereas monopoly and perfect competition are extreme cases.

Three basic assumptions of monopolistic competition are important here: first, a large number of firms, in contrast to an infinite number of firms in perfect competition and one single dominant in monopoly (a variant of the latter is oligopoly, with a few firms with strong market power or the ability to command favorable conditions, such as premium prices); second, the assumption of free entry (although presumably with imperfect knowledge), in contrast to perfect competition, where perfect knowledge is assumed, and monopoly (and oligopoly), with strong barriers to entry imposed by the dominant firm(s); third, product differentiation, as a way to prevent (or encourage) product substitution, which has been the customary rationale for monopolistic competition. Product differentiation is used by firms confronting negatively sloped demand curves and (relatively) free entry. Sources of differentiation can range from trademarks, copyrights, and patents to new features enhancing the functionality and consumer appeal. More important, product innovation has increasingly become associated with product differentiation.

The mathematical analysis of competition is another aspect of competition but is beyond the present discussion. Readers wanting an elaboration of this should review Edward Hastings Chamberlin's *Theory of Monopolistic Competition* (1933), Joan Robinson's *Economics of Imperfect Competition* (1933), and the original works of Antoine Augustin Cournot on the analysis of equilibrium under the assumptions of perfect competition. It is worth noting that, while Cournot sees the transition to perfect competition taking place only on a scale of numbers of competitors, Chamberlin sees it as taking place also on the scale of substitution and differentiation of products. Likewise, Robinson considers monopoly merely as the opposite of competition and states that each seller has a monopoly on his own product, just as one of many conditions that in varying degrees make actual competition imperfect. Robinson's approach is based on that of Alfred Marshall, and readers interested to delve into partial equilibrium analysis should see Marshall's works.

The insights provided by these notorious economists still guide contemporary analysis, although many of the assumptions are being constantly challenged. In the 21st century, real-world economic and business problems impose new challenges to the basic notions of competition (as well as innovation and entrepreneurship, among other areas) and the underlying assumptions about what constitutes rational behavior of firms and consumers. In summary, analyses adopting explicit deviations from the perfect competition assumptions (such as industry structure, entry, and product differentiation) can provide useful insights into the behavior of firms under such conditions of imperfect competition—monopolistic competition being a form of this.

Not surprisingly, the old debate about whether or not monopolistic and oligopolistic competition are possibly more efficient at promoting innovation and economic growth than perfect competition and/or monopoly has been rekindled. For a recent discussion on these topics, see William Baumol's *The Free-Market Innovation Machine* (2002). More recently, John Mathews, drawing on Joseph Schumpeter's ideas, has advocated a radical departure from equilibrium analysis toward strategizing under disequilibrium.

As globalization is increasing competitive pressures on innovation efforts, how, from a pragmatic stance, can firms successfully compete and grow in the 21st century? Schumpeter himself thought that the desire to capture monopoly rents (by being the first in the market) and competitive pressures

Sources of product differentiation in a competitive marketplace range from trademarks, copyrights, and patents to new features enhancing the functionality and consumer appeal. Innovation has become associated with product differentiation. (Photos.com)

(the threat of entry from rival innovators) were the key drivers of competition and innovation. Since the 1940s—when Schumpeter produced most of his seminal writing on capitalism, competition, and entrepreneurship—the world has changed dramatically, with huge advances not only in technological and scientific knowledge but also in the very nature of competition and collaboration between firms and, perhaps more important, ecosystems of firms driven by common platforms and standard interfaces (like Apple). Competition has indeed evolved from competing within the market, through competing for the market, to competing to establish advantageous positions within value-creation ecosystems based on constant innovation and product differentiation.

One way to reappraise these issues is to see competition as static or dynamic in terms of technological innovation, according to L. G. Thomas (1996). On one hand, static competition takes technology as given, thus forcing firms to compete on price and costs. Greater competition lowers prices and/or raises costs, thus reducing profits. However,

competition solely based on prices and costs is only a small part of the equation for modern competition. On the other hand, dynamic (or Schumpeterian) competition takes technological change as endogenous, challenging firms to compete in completely new ways. As firms in an industry transform their technologies and products, they create new markets and also new streams of revenue. Thomas's study concludes that the overall nature of competition (in the U.S. economy) dramatically changed from the 1950s to the 1990s. In the early decades, static competition dominated. In later decades, dynamic competition clearly dominates.

In terms of firms' strategic approach, the 1980s had a focus toward competitive positioning of the firm through analysis of industry structure and competition. Michael Porter of Harvard Business School pioneered the application of industrial organization economics for analyzing the determinants of firm profitability. However, according to Paul McNulty (1968), the failure to distinguish between the idea of competition and the idea of market structure is at the root of much of the ambiguity concerning the meaning of competition.

The 1990s shifted toward the creation and development of internal firm resources and capabilities, and their unique leveraging as a primary source of profitability. In the mid- to late 1990s, the dimension of dynamic capabilities was added to the resource-based view, because of high-velocity industry and market changes. According to Davenport et al. (2006), the planning, balancing, positioning, and resource-based approaches can also be termed "predictive" approaches, as they all attempt to predict a particular competitive environment and probable position or fit of a company. In contrast, the learning approach, drawing from the work of Peter Senge, changes the character of strategic management to one of managing adaptation; the key proposition is that the only sustainable competitive advantage for an organization is the ability to learn faster than its competition.

Davenport et al. note that, as a new era of the knowledge-networked innovation economy is now being experienced, a shift toward competition based on new value innovation is becoming evident. Companies today must develop distinctive organizational capabilities, not just business strategies; they must focus on platforms and services, not just products; they must pull information from the market, responding to real-time changes in demand and competitive conditions, and not just push products out; they must achieve economies of scope, not just scale, by creating efficiencies across all of a firm's activities; and they must acquire flexibility, in addition to efficiency, to adapt quickly to volatile marketplaces.

A unique feature of this approach to competition is that the company providing the core technology in the platform relies heavily, and sometimes exclusively, on other companies—which can be called "ecosystem partners"—to make actual products or offer specific services that provide value to the end user. Some platform companies make their own products or products complementary to the platform; Microsoft, for example, makes both the Windows operating system and the Office application suite. Other platform companies primarily license their technology and allow other companies to make physical or software products. For example, Qualcom does this with its patent portfolio for data transmission, and Google does this with its Android operating system software. Successful platforms need to provide relatively easy access to their interfaces and be relatively modular in design to facilitate other companies adopting the technology, building around or on top of it, or adding to it.

Successful platforms should also exhibit what are called "network effects"—positive feedback that leads to more adoption. The more users and "complementary" products and services (such as Windows, Android, and iPhone applications) that outside companies create, the more valuable the platform becomes to users as well as to the platform owner. The more complementary applications there are and the more usage of the platform technology there is, the more other users or complementors appear to adopt the platform. In "multisided" platform markets, this momentum around platform adoption can also indirectly attract other players in the market, such as when advertisers become drawn to advertise on Google search pages or on Facebook as these platforms attract more users.

Angel J. Salazar
Manchester Metropolitan University

See also Advertising; Business Failure; Business-to-Business Marketing; Competitive Intelligence; Customer Orientation; Entrepreneurial Marketing; Focus Groups; International Markets; Market Evaluation; Market Orientation; Positioning a New Product or Service; Retailing; Target Markets; Test Markets; Wholesale Markets

Further Readings

Baumol, William J. *The Free-Market Innovation Machine: Analyzing the Growth Miracle of Capitalism.* Princeton, NJ: Princeton University Press, 2002.
Cusumano, Michael. *Staying Power.* New York: Oxford University Press, 2010.
Davenport, T., M. Leibold, and S. Voelpel. "Strategic Management in the Innovation Economy." In *Strategy Approaches and Tools for Dynamic Innovation Capabilities.* New York: Wiley, 2006.
Gawer, A. and M. Cusumano. *Platform Leadership: How Intel, Microsoft, and Cisco Drive Industry Innovation.* Cambridge, MA: Harvard Business School Press, 2002.
Mathews, John. *Strategizing, Disequilibrium and Profit.* Stanford, CA: Stanford Business Press, 2006.
McNulty, Paul. "Economic Theory and the Meaning of Competition." *Quarterly Journal of Economics*, v.82/4 (1968).
Thomas, L. G. "The Two Faces of Competition: Dynamic Resourcefulness and the Hypercompetitive Shift." *Organization Science*, v.7/3, 1996.
Vives, Xavier. "Innovation and Competitive Pressure." *Journal of Industrial Economics*, v.56/3 (2008).

COMPETITIVE INTELLIGENCE

Competitive intelligence is the ability to predict competitors' next moves. In the context of new ventures, the ability to anticipate incumbents' actions provides a preview of the future. Competitive intelligence is much more an art than an exact science, implying that predictions are inherently imprecise. However, approaching competitive intelligence both methodically and creatively increases the likelihood of spotting competitors' upcoming market-changing actions. The means of prediction include analyses of major changes in cash flow, product and service improvements in commodity markets, and scenario planning. Each of these provides anticipatory techniques for spotting competitors' impending actions.

First, predicting a major offensive based on a competitor's cash flow is typically the easiest method but yields the least specific predictions. Among the three major categories of cash flow—cash flow from operations, investing, and financing—cash flow from investing and financing are typically the most useful in competitive intelligence. Cash flow analysis, despite its simplicity, assists potential new ventures in spotting upcoming competitive actions. Sizable and sudden cash flow changes can point a firm in the right direction for further investigation.

A brief example may help clarify the point. Suppose that in the wake of a natural disaster, such as a massive earthquake, a company such as Caterpillar (an earth-moving equipment manufacturer) has a large outflow of cash flow from investing. Large, sudden cash outflows from investing indicate that a firm has made a present investment for future returns in property, plant, or equipment. In isolation, such movements of cash are not revealing; in the context of the external shock of the natural disaster, Caterpillar may have invested cash to ramp up production capacity. Simply put, the firm has traded one form of equity, cash, for another form of equity, production capacity. The strategic rationale is that Caterpillar may be anticipating an increase of new orders for earth-moving equipment in response to the natural disaster. This increase in inventory would heighten entry barriers for potential new ventures in targeting the same market space. Clearly, this example would simply provide a modest start for more investigatory work to confirm or reject the initial hunch.

Second, product and service improvements in markets characterized by commoditization may also be useful for potential new ventures. Spotting a commoditized market is readily accomplished by noting that the major differentiating attribute is price. Competitive intelligence predictions, if correct, may provide new venture opportunities even in the presence of established incumbents. In fact, established incumbents combined with market saturation can work to a potential new venture's advantage. The key is to recognize a pattern of product or service enhancement in conjunction with stable or decreasing pricing. In essence, this implies that product or service enhancement is not rewarded by increases in price. Rather, a firm is simply maintaining price as costs increase. The result is profit margins squeezed to a maintenance level; the typical case is flat margins between cost and price, despite product or service enhancements.

From the perspective of product or service features, incumbent firms paradoxically move in the wrong direction. The starting point for such patterns tends to be historically rooted in markets that have progressed insidiously toward more demanding rather than less demanding customers. This dilemma pits incumbents tightly against one another in a race toward elusive profit margins that evaporate at an increasing pace as firms chase the most lucrative but demanding buyers.

Competitive intelligence thus begins by recognizing industries composed of products or services that were historically novel and unique; these products and services have gotten better as their associated profit margins have gotten worse. This leaves open an unattended market of less demanding customers. Firms can tap into this profit pool of customers who are satisfied with "good enough" products or services. Finding these open competitive spaces enhances competitive intelligence through deliberate consideration of market opportunities that competing firms may utilize. Firms capitalizing on such competitive intelligence gain a broader view of market opportunities by considering the entire spectrum of product and service offerings from the lower end to the higher end of the spectrum. This inherently points toward the possibility of competitors' forthcoming actions as they attempt to maneuver away from commoditization of existing products and services.

Third, as noted previously, competitive intelligence can be addressed using techniques from the simplest, such as cash flow analysis, to the increasingly difficult but more insightful market opportunities based on industry commoditization. Both of these approaches provide potentially valuable competitive intelligence. However, they are limited in scope. A more flexible and comprehensive approach is scenario analysis. Scenario analysis gives a more holistic view by expanding the range of potential competitor moves. In the context of competitive intelligence, scenario analysis creates "stories" about possible competitor actions. In the strict sense, scenario analysis is not intended to predict competitors' next moves but rather to imagine the range of possibilities competitors may take. These imagined states then provide a range of options. This range of options may then be used to preemptively counteract potentially damaging competitor actions. However, scenario analysis is not solely a defensive practice; imagining the range of competitor actions provides the context for offensive moves as well.

Each of these methods of attaining competitive intelligence—analyzing major changes in cash flow, observing product and service improvements in commodity markets, and scenario analysis—helps firms focus present resource commitments that prepare for future situations. Competitive intelligence thus provides a preview not only of potential competitor actions but also of the shape of the industry as a whole. For new ventures, peering into the future supports more informed choices in the present. Competitive intelligence provides the basis for these choices.

Scott Droege
Western Kentucky University

See also Agility and Rapid Response; Championing New Ventures; Cognition; Commitment and Persistence; Competition; Knowledge; Negotiating Strategies; Obstacle Identification; Passion

Further Readings

Christensen, Clayton M. *The Innovator's Dilemma: When New Technologies Cause Great Firms to Fall.* Boston: Harvard Business Press, 1997.

Christensen, Clayton M., Scott D. Anthony, and Erik A. Roth. *Seeing What's Next: Using the Theories of Innovation to Predict Industry Change.* Boston: Harvard Business School Press, 2004.

D'Aveni, Richard A. *Beating the Commodity Trap: How to Maximize Your Competitive Position and Increase Your Pricing Power.* Boston: Harvard Business School Press, 2010.

Gadiesh, Orit and James L. Gilbert. "How to Map Your Industry's Profit Pool." *Harvard Business Review*, v.76/3 (1998).

Johnson, Mark W. *Seizing the White Space: Business Model Innovation for Growth and Renewal.* Boston: Harvard Business School Press, 2010.

Marcus, Alfred. *Strategic Foresight: A New Look at Scenarios.* New York: Palgrave Macmillan, 2009.

CONTEXTUAL MARKETING

This article proposes a conceptualization of the components of contextual marketing (CM) in light of the outcome of the Charleston Summit. While there is widespread acknowledgment of the importance of small firms and the individual actors within them to economic well-being, there remains a knowledge gap about many of the management actions that small firms take. This view is born out of debate and discussions that have been taking place within the sister domains of marketing and entrepreneurship and the ongoing challenge for researchers within those related fields to develop a research model to guide scholars at the "interface."

Background

The CM concept posits that independent theories of the marketing function exist alongside those that are already known—indeed, the history of marketing theory would appear, with exploration, to be predicated upon a limited number of hard-held constructs that have changed little over time and are perhaps best described as administrative marketing (AM) approaches. However, the CM independent, parallel, and emergent paradigm has yet to be fully understood and indeed appears within marketing texts used within both the academic and small business development fields. Furthermore, it is clear that aspects of CM stand outside the "accepted" or "normative" view of marketing. These especially (but not exclusively) include the use of language, the genderized process, communities of practice and shared interest (tribes), authenticity and heritage, and the application of effectual logic constructs.

Indeed, many attempts to define marketing within the small firm context run afoul of the inadequacies of lexicography and conceptualization. Therefore, CM questions the worth of the historical reductionist paradigm when used in the complex, irrational, emotional, egotistical, creative, and conversational world that comprises the small firm environment—where owners, managers, and entrepreneurs work at the edge of time and chaos, making sense of the world around them through relationships with others' independent cultural perspectives and metanarratives.

Debate within academic symposia as to the nature of marketing within the small firm and marketing's relationship with entrepreneurship appears to be increasing. Perhaps the answers scholars seek lie not so much with the words we use to describe the theory, application, or practice of marketing as in the meanings we (and the small firm) associate with these words and social actions, and how such meanings are vocalized (or physically expressed) in context. CM acknowledges that our "marketing" sense has been impaired through the aging process, but what we are yet to acknowledge is how much of the ongoing conversation we are missing.

The small-firm sector in particular is highly heterogeneous, complicated by social contexts and a high degree of individualism. The rationale of the owner is often the rationale of the firm. In such circumstances, the success of a standardized approach to marketing practice will be limited. The key actors within small firms, it would appear, like to be treated as individuals and communicated with in their own language. A review of the extant literature and current research activities within the field would suggest that there remains a lack of specific knowledge about the contextual nature of the meaning and operation of marketing within the small firm. Small firms base their market development activities—arguably all their business decisions—on knowledge that is derived at a socially constructed level. The socialized nature of this approach and the lack of formality in nearly all areas of business management lead to the acknowledgment that many, if not all, of these actions are at variance with "textbook" or "accepted" marketing management practices. CM has arisen as a result.

Marketing in Context

The central feature of much of CM is the concept of a situation-specific approach and application of marketing, which is contextualized to the individual focal firm and therefore has both a uniqueness and inherent complexity. While this activity is complex, essential key factors can be identified that offer insight into how marketing is performed within each context. However, these factors are interdependent, interrelated, and synergistically influential in that, for a successful interface to take place between the firm and the market, firms simply have to perform these activities; they cannot be overlooked if firms are to do business.

Marketing in context, therefore, is a process of building a marketing approach to accommodate the specific situation. As a starting point (note, not a foundation), the concept takes the parameters of marketing concepts, theories, and techniques at a general level—in essence, the textbook approach to marketing management—and renders them in the context of the aforementioned fundamental prerequisites of the small firm.

The next stage of the process is to consider the inherent characteristics of the small firm. These characteristics range from the explicit, such as the individual personality of the owner/entrepreneur and the influence of that person's traits on the marketing decision-making process of the enterprise, to the implicit, such as the limited resources that are available.

The result is a stratification of influence upon how a small firm does marketing within the unique context of its situation. A pivotal issue is that this uniqueness is not the uniqueness of a "generic" small firm but rather the uniqueness of the "individual" small firm—hence the importance of acknowledging the social constructive state.

Conclusion

This discussion has set out to explore the contemporary research issues posed by the debate and discussions culminating in the outcome report of the Charleston Summit, as reported in D. Hansen and F. Eggers (2010). As part of the debate, four perspectives of the interface were derived as seen in the table accompanying this article.

What this essay concentrates on is a development of perspective 4. This perspective has been described by Hansen and Eggers as follows:

> The fourth perspective could be considered the opposite to the first. Rather than commonalities among marketing and entrepreneurship, this perspective represents that which is unique to the interface—thus: the combination of marketing and entrepreneurship creates something distinctive, like an offspring.

Therefore, this article suggests that perspective 4 is "contextual marketing" and that, as such, CM is made up of or contains a number of components—one of which is the meaning and operation of a language for marketing in context. The importance of a "language" for marketing within the small firm is referred to both implicitly and explicitly throughout the entrepreneurship, marketing, and small and medium enterprise (SME) literature. However, the literature stops short of further and more detailed investigation—which is perhaps understandable, as the study of sociolinguistics has a body of literature of its own. The development of a contextual lexis for the meaning and operation of marketing may be dependent upon a number of conditions, which can be observed to exist within the dimensions of the individual owner/entrepreneur, the prevailing industry norms, and the strength of formality or

Four Marketing/Entrepreneurship Interface Research Perspectives

Perspective	Explanation
1. Marketing and entrepreneurship	Commonalities between both disciplines—the normative and historical perspective—where the interface appears at the intersection of the two domains
2. Entrepreneurship in marketing	Entrepreneurship issues framed in the field of marketing or viewed through a marketing theoretical lens—in essence, "entrepreneurship" as viewed by researchers in the marketing field
3. Marketing in entrepreneurship	Marketing issues framed in the field of entrepreneurship or viewed through an entrepreneurship theoretical lens—in essence, "marketing" as viewed by researchers in the entrepreneurship field
4. Unique interface concepts	Concepts that are distinct and unique to the interface and evolve out of the combination of marketing and entrepreneurship

Source: D. Hansen and F. Eggers, "The Marketing/Entrepreneurship Interface: A Report on the Charleston Summit." *Journal of Research in Marketing and Entrepreneurship*, v.12/1 (2010).

informality present in the use of language for marketing within the focal firm.

The field of sociolinguistics and the importance of vocal communication may hold the key to unlocking a paradigmatic foundation, which has hitherto been overlooked. Any academic myopia may be due in part to the reluctance of researchers to engage in this complex field and in part to the reluctance to fully accept an emergent and alternative paradigm (as seen in perspective 4).

This article sits at the interface between the concepts of marketing and entrepreneurship and language, socially constructed and in context—an acknowledgment of the "sound" of marketing within the small firm. It is considered, however, one of a number of components of CM that can be found within perspective 4. Furthermore, it is proposed that this perspective has, as antecedents, the foundational philosophical constructs of psychology, sociology, and anthropology.

Jonathan H. Deacon
University of Wales, Newport

See also Advertising; Business-to-Business Marketing; Competition; Customer Orientation; E-Commerce; Entrepreneurial Marketing; Focus Groups; International Markets; Market Evaluation; Positioning a New Product or Service; Retailing; Social Networks; Target Markets; Test Markets; Wholesale Markets

Further Readings

Bjerke, B. and C. Hultman. *Entrepreneurial Marketing: The Growth of Small Firms in the New Economic Era.* Cheltenham, UK: Edward Elgar, 2002.

Carson, D. et al. "Contextual Marketing." Seventh Annual Research Symposium on the Marketing-Entrepreneurship Interface, Oxford Brookes University, Oxford, 2002.

Carson, D. et al. "Contextual Marketing: The Language/ Vocabulary of Marketing in SMEs." Eighth Annual Research Symposium on the Marketing-Entrepreneurship Interface, University of Gloucestershire Business School, University of Gloucestershire, Cheltenham, 2003.

Carson, D. and A. Gilmore. "Characteristics of SME Marketing and a Conceptual Framework." In *Proceedings of the 1999 Academy of Marketing Conference.* Stirling, UK: University of Stirling, 2000.

Hansen, D. and F. Eggers. "The Marketing/ Entrepreneurship Interface: A Report on the Charleston Summit." *Journal of Research in Marketing and Entrepreneurship*, v.12/1 (2010).

Mead, G. *Mind, Self and Society.* Chicago: University of Chicago Press, 1934.

Morrish, S. C., J. H. Deacon, and M. Miles. "Entrepreneurial Marketing: Acknowledging the Entrepreneur and Customer-Centric Interrelationship." *Journal of Strategic Marketing*, v.18/4 (2010).

Sarasvathy, S. "Causation and Effectuation: Toward a Theoretical Shift From Economic Inevitability to Entrepreneurial Contingency." *Academy of Management Review*, v.26/2 (2001).

CONTRACTS AND TRUST

For new ventures, formal contacts are used as a means to impose control on an environment characterized by unpredictable actors and risky interdependence. From the employment relationships of key team members to questions of how control is shared between founders and investors, contracts are used to formalize parties' expectations and undergird those expectations with the force of legal sanctions. Contracts can clarify and codify agreements, but they also provide actors with the means to enforce those agreements and punish actors' failures to live up to their agreements.

Some dimensions of new venture management will always involve contracting: Venture capital placements in a portfolio firm inevitably include some degree of formal contracting, for example. However, it is costly, slow, and complicated to encode every last expectation or relationship into a formal contract, and it is nearly impossible to rely on legal enforcement to ensure that actors will live by their words. In fast-moving start-ups, enforcement is a nuclear option: the expense and time consumed by enforcement can cripple or kill the firm.

In practice, some key dependencies and relationships are maintained without explicit contracting. Others will be covered by boilerplate contracts chosen out of convenience, based on familiarity, or to adhere to industry norms. Even when entrepreneurs do pay careful attention to contracting, their contracts cannot cover every possible contingency. These contracts are said to be "incomplete" by transaction-cost economists. In the absence of contracting, or in the gaps left by incomplete contracts, the leaders of new ventures must rely on trust.

Trust refers to one party's willingness to make itself vulnerable to another party based on positive, confident expectations about how that other party will behave. This trust can help to limit the need for costly contracting. The degree to which an entrepreneurial venture can rely on trust rather than contracting can be a considerable source of advantage: Absent the costs and effort associated with contracting and monitoring, ventures can speed their decision making and respond more nimbly to their market environment: They can attract and deploy investment funding faster, particularly during the bootstrapping phase before formal investments are made into the firm. They can grow more quickly, adding staff and forging new partnerships with greater speed and ease.

Trust can be forged between key actors in the founding of a new venture in a number of ways. Strong reputational systems can build calculative trust. In hubs of new venture creation, such as the Bay Area or Boston, information about entrepreneurs' and investors' reputations spread easily through dense social networks. Insight into actors' previous behavior helps to create the basis for trust—as does the knowledge that word of any subsequent opportunism will spread through those same networks. The availability of this type of recourse is a noncontractual way of deterring opportunism.

However, trust can flourish for noncalculative reasons. In founding teams, for instance, vulnerability and interdependence are not simply a matter of reputation systems and mechanisms for deterrence. They are products of affective ties between the founding members and of identification with the firm as a social unit. Friendships, open communication, and shared commitment to the start-up serve to communicate that each team member is interested in mutual gain and team outcomes, rather than narrow self-interest. Through the mechanism of social

The concept of business being conducted on a handshake may be outdated, but new venture founders must balance their skills as contractors with an ability to create a sense of trust when making agreements. (Photos.com)

exchange, members of the entrepreneurial team initiate and escalate trusting and trustworthy behaviors. Minor acts of precipitous trust, absent the protections of formal contracting, are reciprocated, deepening over time the norms that guide the team and creating an increasing disincentive to engage in opportunistic behavior.

Research conducted by Sophie Manigart and her colleagues suggests that many investors want iron-clad contracting, even in the presence of high trust. However, the stakeholders involved in new venture management must be aware of the risks associated with formal contracting in trusting relationships. First, contracted parties may attribute their successes to the contract rather than the trustworthiness of their counterparts. The natural escalation and deepening of trust over time may be stunted as contracts crowd out trust. Second, contracts may signal distrust or make the risk of defection more salient. Complete contracts in particular require the parties to imagine the full range of ways in which defection and opportunism could occur, which can also deteriorate trust. Trust and contracts may ultimately give way to contracts alone.

Formal contracting is a useful tool. In situations of overt distrust, it can allow for cooperation that might otherwise prove impossible. The process of negotiating contract terms can be useful in revealing parties' assumptions and interests. In situations where there is a strong norm toward contracting, it can also confer legitimacy. For the small enterprise that wishes to grow via franchising or the start-up in search of venture capital investment, the presence and form of contracting may be a signal of competence. However, the management of new ventures should use formal contracts with caution. Used without discretion, contracting consumes resources, slows the pace of a new venture's operations, and may crowd out existing trust among the venture's key stakeholders. Although the image of business conducted on a word and a handshake may seem outmoded, new venture founders must balance their skill as contractors with their savvy as initiators and managers of trust.

Lukas Neville
Queen's University

See also Agency Theory; Psychological Views; Risk Management

Further Readings

Azoulay, Pierre and Scott Shane. "Entrepreneurs, Contracts, and the Failure of Young Firms." *Management Science*, v.47/3 (2001).

Barney, Jay and Mark Hansen. "Trustworthiness as a Source of Competitive Advantage." *Strategic Management Journal*, v.15/1 (1994).

Gompers, Paul and Josh Lerner. "The Use of Covenants: An Empirical Analysis of Venture Partnership Agreements." *Journal of Law and Economics*, v.39/2 (1996).

Manigart, Sophie et al. "The Impact of Trust on Private Equity Contracts." *Vlerick Leuven Gent Management School Working Paper Series*, v.1 (2002).

Shepherd, Dean and Andrew Zacharakis. "The Venture Capitalist-Entrepreneur Relationship: Control, Trust, and Confidence in Co-Operative Behavior." *Venture Capital*, v.3/2 (2001).

CORPORATE ENTREPRENEURSHIP AND INNOVATION

In the 1970s, early research in corporate entrepreneurship focused on understanding how new ventures may be formed within an existing organization. Since that time both the research focus and the definition of corporate entrepreneurship have evolved and changed. One currently accepted description of corporate entrepreneurship is the investment or funding of a new venture that is typically different from the organization's core business domain; however, the entity typically remains a part of the existing organization. It is important to point out that many researchers recognize that corporate entrepreneurship activities can be either internally or externally focused. Some researchers define external venturing as creating or investing in a semiautonomous or autonomous entity that resides outside the existing organizational domain, whereas internal venturing is the creating or investing in an entity within the existing organization.

Some researchers have considered corporate entrepreneurship to be an important growth strategy and a pathway to improving corporate performance. Other researchers suggest that it is important for organizations of all sizes and industries to adopt an entrepreneurial attitude and behavior in order to succeed and thrive in today's competitive environment.

Some suggest that organizations engage in corporate entrepreneurship to complement their innovation activities and strategies. Increasingly, creativity and innovation are becoming synonymous with organizational growth and sustainability. Thus, it is important to understand just how corporate entrepreneurship can impact or influence innovation activities (such as research and development, training, and education programs) within the organization. One concept that is gaining significant research momentum is the notion of open innovation, which owes its beginning to the success of the open-source software model.

The open-source software model has created a new paradigm in how to think about corporate innovation. Open-source software exploits the distributed intelligence of development teams all across the globe. Some suggest that open-source software can be described as a user-centric innovation. It is widely known that the open-source model uses the vast knowledge economy to deliver some very exciting software innovations, introducing products and systems that are interwoven into our daily lives. Researchers have noted that industrial research and development (R&D) is undergoing a paradigm shift from a closed to an open innovation model. In this new paradigm, an organization's business model must consider both external and internal ideas to create value—with one important caveat, however: The organization must define some internal mechanism to claim a portion of the newly created value. In considering the importance of innovation to organization survivability, what role should corporate entrepreneurship play? The strategic posture that an organization adopts regarding innovation activities has a significant impact; if the organization invests too early or blindly in new innovation activities, it may waste money, whereas if the investment is made to late, the organization may be unable to compete effectively.

Researchers have suggested that organizations can take a number of different strategic positions in terms of corporate entrepreneurship and investing in innovation activities. R. G. McGrath and I. C. MacMillan (2000) suggest four less costly corporate entrepreneurial options: (1) spin-offs, (2) joint ventures with competitors, (3) licensing, and (4) tight-focus strategies. They suggest that a spin-off can allow the parent or existing organization to benefit from innovation without having to fund the new entity independently.

The benefit of the joint venture with a competitor is to protect the valuable resources of the industry as well as protect the industry from outside attackers. Licensing a technology can provide new revenue as well as lock competitors into the technology, at least for a period of time. Using a tight-focus strategy, the organization utilizes its resources to capture the most profitable portion of a market and leave the other niches for competitors. W. Vanhaverbeke et al. point to another possible strategy: that of real options. The real-options strategy provides an opportunity to wait and see. During this wait-and-see period, the organization may gain additional information in order to reduce uncertainty prior to making an investment in any corporate entrepreneurship activities.

Along with the many other concepts and the ideas briefly discussed above, it is important not to forget the most important factor influencing corporate entrepreneurship and innovation: the customer. Eric von Hipple (2005), the thought leader in user-centric innovation, theorizes that innovation is becoming democratized. Users are developing and customizing products and services and freely sharing with others. These users can be both individuals and organizations. Additionally, many users are engage in "modding." Modding is the act of adapting a product or services to fit specific needs. Keith Sawyer (2007) suggests that approximately 10 to 40 percent of consumers engage in some form of modding. The plentitude of affordable and powerful information technology products as well as the free sharing of information around the world has now put know-how in the hands of the masses. Information that was once privy to a select few is now available to many. Some large organizations, including Procter & Gamble and Toyota, have tapped into the power of user-centric innovation and anticipate reaping the benefits.

What might corporate entrepreneurship and innovation look like moving forward? Key technologies of the early and mid-20th century were developed internally within large, diversified organizations, primarily in the United States and in Europe. They were able to capture a competitive advantage via economies of scale and scope. In the 21st-century information and knowledge era, innovation can originate anywhere. Therefore, for organizations to achieve a competitive advantage, it is becoming important that they adopt strategies allowing them flexibility to extract value from these burgeoning resources, although such ventures may require nontraditional business models.

Joe Anthony Bradley Sr.
Applied Research Associates, Inc.

See also Championing Corporate Ventures; Corporate Venturing; Innovation Management; Innovation Management: Corporate; Innovation Processes; Product Innovation; Radical and Incremental Innovation; Service Innovation

Further Readings

Barringer, B. R. and A. C. Bluedorn. "The Relationship Between Corporate Entrepreneurship and Strategic Management." *Strategic Management Journal*, v.20 (1999).

Chandler, A. *Scale and Scope: The Dynamics of Industrial Capitalism.* Cambridge, MA: Belknap Press, 1990.

Chesbrough, H. *Open Innovation.* Boston: Harvard Business School Press, 2003.

Chesbrough, H. and C. Tucci. "Corporate Venture Capital in the Context of Corporate Innovation." Working Paper, Hass School of Business, University of California, Berkeley, 2004.

Dess, G., G. Lumpkin, and J. McKee. "Linking Corporate Entrepreneurship to Strategy, Structure, and Process: Suggested Research Directions." *Entrepreneurship Theory and Practice*, v.23 (1999).

Hill, R. M. and J. D. Hlavacek. "The Venture Team: A New Concept in Marketing Organizations." *Journal of Marketing*, v.36 (1972).

Kogut, B. and A. Metiu. "Open-Source Software Development and Distributed Innovation." *Oxford Review of Economic Policy*, v.17/2 (2001).

Kuratko, D. F. *Corporate Entrepreneurship.* Hanover, MA: Now, 2007.

Kuratko, D. F. "Intrapreneurship: Developing Innovation in the Corporation—Advances in Global High Technology Management." *High Technology Venturing*, v.3 (1993).

McGrath, R. G. and I. C. MacMillan. *The Entrepreneurial Mindset: Strategies for Continuously Creating Opportunity in an Age of Uncertainty.* Boston: Harvard Business School Press, 2000.

Miles, M. and J. Covin. "Exploring the Practice of Corporate Venturing: Some Common Forms and Their Organizational Implications." *Entrepreneurship Theory and Practice*, v.26/3 (2002).

Morris, M. H., D. Kuratko, and J. G. Covin. *Corporate Entrepreneurship and Innovation.* Mason, OH: Thomson/South-Western, 2008.

Peterson, R. and D. Berger. "Entrepreneurship in Organizations." *Administrative Science Quarterly*, v.16/1 (1971).

Pinchott, G. *Intrapreneurship.* New York: Harper and Row, 1985.

Sawyer, K. *Group Genius: The Creative Power of Collaboration.* Cambridge, MA: Perseus, 2007.

Sharma, P. and J. Chrisman. "Toward a Reconciliation of the Definition Issues in the Field of Corporate Entrepreneurship." *Entrepreneurship Theory and Practice*, v.23/3 (1999).

Vanhaverbeke, W. and N. Peeters. "Embracing Innovation as Strategy: Corporate Venturing, Competence Building and Corporate Strategy Making." *Creativity and Innovation Management*, v.14/3 (2005).

Vanhaverbeke, W., V. Van De Vrande, and H. Chesbrough. "Understanding the Advantages of Open Innovation Practices in Corporate Venturing in Terms of Real Options." *Creativity and Innovation Management*, v.17/4 (2008).

Von Hippel, E. *Democratizing Innovation.* Cambridge, MA: MIT Press, 2005.

CORPORATE VENTURING

Creating new businesses within an existing corporation and integrating them into that company's current operations constitute one aspect of corporate venturing, the other being engaging in corporate renewal activities that allow the company to meet emerging business challenges. Corporate venturing as a topic of serious academic interest assumed prominence after publication of Gifford Pinchot's book *Intrapreneurship* in 1985.

Because of their very nature, established companies tend not to be as entrepreneurial as their smaller counterparts. Their large size, expanded structures, multidivisional operations, and widespread employee base make it challenging for them constantly to innovate and come up with new products and services. Some authors, such as N. Thornberry, note that the term *corporate venturing* is even taken to be an oxymoron. Managers in large firms are rewarded for minimizing risks rather than taking up additional risks, for conforming to rules and procedures rather than breaking them, and for achieving efficiencies in current operations rather than moving into uncharted business arenas when current activities are profitable and do not show any cause for immediate concern. In effect, large firms operate on the logic of utilizing existing capabilities rather than building new ones.

Literature on corporate venturing suggests that two groups of variables affect entrepreneurial activities within established firms: environmental factors and organizational factors. Among the former are factors such as extent of environmental dynamism or the pace of change in the external environment, growth rate of the industry, emerging technological opportunities, and demand for new products and services. Thus, companies tend to engage more in new business creation and innovation when the external environment is dynamic, highly competitive, and open to opportunities for growth. In contrast, entrepreneurial efforts take a backseat when the external environment is static, competition is low, and industry growth opportunities are limited. As a result in established and successful firms, the norm is to do more of current activities rather than engage in new tasks.

With regard to organizational factors affecting corporate venturing, previous research has identified several. Among these are included the firm's capacity to absorb knowledge, the role of board members as conduits of knowledge, the organization's ambidexterity or ability to engage simultaneously in knowledge exploration and exploitation activities, the company's strategic alliances with like-minded partners with complementary capabilities, the top management's vision and leadership, and organizational and management support for taking risks and engaging in innovation. S. A. Zahra, I. Filatotchev, and M. Wright find that boards and absorptive capacity complement each other in enhancing corporate entrepreneurship activities. When the firm's absorptive capacity is rather low (which means that it has difficulties in absorbing and utilizing external knowledge), boards can mitigate this to some extent.

Because corporate venturing requires a different mind-set, reward structure, and ways of working compared to mainstream organizational activities, creating a structural differentiation mechanism by keeping the unit in charge of new venture activities distinct from the rest of the organization also helps. At the same time, a supportive organizational culture incorporating a shared vision, participatory decision making, work discretion, and work in cross-functional teams has also been found beneficial in supporting new venture activities. Thus, it appears that as far as adopting a structural arrangement for the purpose of facilitating new venture activities is concerned, the firm has two possibilities open before it: either create an autonomous, distinct unit dedicated to the pursuit of new venture activities or instead embrace a culture of experimentation, risk taking, and engaging in new activities throughout the organization and especially based on cross-functional teams. Which of these two mechanisms is more effective in a specific context will depend on a range of other organizational factors, such as strategy, time orientation, and expectations of top management. Some researchers have found that corporate context perpetuates the role schemas that managers come to expect as guiding their day-to-day actions in large firms. Therefore, it is vital that the firm's senior leaders understand whether these applicable role schemas are facilitating or hindering new venture activities and take action as appropriate.

Although corporate venturing activities are of paramount importance to the company remaining competitive, the firm's current setup does not easily allow for engaging in these activities, especially if the firm has been successful in its current operations. Therefore, it requires foresight and sagacity on the part of the firm's senior leadership to create parallel structures and processes that allow employees to take risks, innovate, and consider creating new products, even as they maintain the continuity of current operations. In that sense, launching new ventures within established firms is both a top-down and a bottom-up process, relying on creation of an overall entrepreneurial climate as well as employee engagement in specific innovation and entrepreneurship projects.

Devkamal Dutta
University of New Hampshire

See also Championing Corporate Ventures; Corporate Entrepreneurship and Innovation; Culture and Entrepreneurship; Innovation Management: Corporate; New Product Development

Further Readings

Ginsberg, A. and M. Hay. "Confronting the Challenges of Corporate Entrepreneurship: Guidelines for Venture Managers." *European Management Journal*, v.12/4 (1994).

Jennings, D. F. and J. R. Lumpkin. "Functioning Modeling Corporate Entrepreneurship: An Empirical Integrative Analysis." *Journal of Management*, v.15/3 (1989).

Phan, P. H., M. Wright, D. Ucbasaran, and W. Tan. "Corporate Entrepreneurship: Current Research and Future Directions." *Journal of Business Venturing*, v.24 (2009).

Pinchot, G. *Intrapreneuring*. New York: Harper and Row, 1985.

Thornberry, N. "Corporate Entrepreneurship: Antidote or Oxymoron?" *European Management Journal*, v.19/5 (2001).

Zahra, S. A., I. Filatotchev, and M. Wright. "How Do Threshold Firms Sustain Corporate Entrepreneurship? The Role of Boards and Absorptive Capacity." *Journal of Business Venturing*, v.24 (2009).

CREATIVITY

Creativity is a welcome asset in almost any enterprise. For entrepreneurs or for the founding of a new venture, creativity can, however, be crucial. The very foundation of entrepreneurial activity is the production of new business ideas that originate from the entrepreneur's creative potential. Moreover, entrepreneurs use their creative potential for employing their often sparse financial resources in a new, innovative, and economic way. A number of empirical studies have found entrepreneurs to be generally more creative than the average population. They tend to be more capable of recognizing new business opportunities, of developing radically new business ideas, and of improving already existing concepts (so-called me-too enterprises). Research has found opportunity recognition to be a creative process and link creativity significantly to the radicalness of innovations, making creativity one of the most important success factors for entrepreneurs.

Definition and Early Research

Generally, the term *creativity* refers to the ability to come up with new, unconventional ideas or create novel realities. Whereas novelty is considered a sufficient condition in the field of arts, in business creative ideas also need to be perceived as useful, whether internally or by potential customers. In an organizational context, creativity refers to the generation of novel ideas, while the process of applying the original ideas in order to create novel and useful products is reserved to the term *innovation*. Hence, creativity can be seen as a source for innovation, rendering it a necessary but not sufficient condition for innovation.

Until the 20th century, when scientific interest in creativity emerged, the concept of creativity was confined to the world of the arts. Although some

Creativity is an intellectual process that results in generating new ideas, merging known concepts into something new, or solving problems in an innovative way. Entrepreneurial activity is based on producing new business ideas that originate from the entrepreneur's creative potential. (Photos.com)

attempts at characterizing and measuring creativity had already been undertaken by 1950, scientific research into creativity, its antecedents and correlates, became popular after Joy Paul Guilford's address to the American Psychological Association in that year. Since then, research on various aspects of creativity has been conducted in various disciplines.

Even though efforts have been put into the conceptualization and proper measurement of creativity, a universal taxonomy of creativity or widely recognized diagnostic methods do not yet exist. This is true for all fields of research that have studied the phenomenon of creativity, such as different areas of psychology, cognitive science, philosophy, history, economics, business, and management.

Creative Outcome and Creative Process

A number of creativity measures exist that are being widely used in research and practice. Harrison Gough added a scale on creativity to the Adjective Check List, a common inventory assessing personality traits with a list of descriptive adjectives. Guilford constructed several creativity tests in the 1960s, upon which Ellis Paul Torrance based his Torrance Test of Creative Thinking, one of the most often used creativity tests to date. The test measures creative outcome by scoring solutions to divergent thinking problems.

A number of theories exist about the process by which creative outcome is achieved. From a cognitive perspective, creativity is an intellectual process that can include the generating of inherently new ideas, the associative merging of several known concepts into something new, and the solving of problems in a novel way. A creative person is prone to finding more unusual and unexpected associations between given concepts. A recent empirical study has shown that radicalness of innovations rises in accord with an entrepreneur's creativity.

Mihály Csíkszentmihályi has divided the creative process into five basic elements (similar models of the creative process had previously been proposed by Graham Wallas and Mel Rhodes):

1. *Preparation*: knowledge/experience, interest, and curiosity that initiate the creative process

2. *Incubation*: intuitive and unstructured thinking on the idea/problem

3. *Insight*: the "Eureka!" experience, when the new idea is consciously recognized

4. *Evaluation*: checking the viability of the idea

5. *Elaboration*: refining and possibly implementing the new idea

Opportunity recognition, a crucial aspect of creating a new venture, has been described as the creative stage in the process of forming a new venture and is sometimes seen as a creative process itself. The five stages of the creative process as described by Csíkszentmihályi can be incorporated into a model of opportunity recognition where preparation, incubation, and insight reflect the first phase of opportunity recognition (discovery), while evaluation and elaboration constitute the second phase (formation).

Preparation as a facilitator for opportunity recognition encompasses previous work experience, market/domain knowledge, and social networks. Networks also play an important role during the insight stage, when opportunities may become clear during peer discussions, and the evaluation stage, when peer discourse backs up the viability analysis.

Factors Influencing Creativity

A number of personal characteristics as well as factors pertaining to the work environment have been found conducive to creativity. Whereas some researchers consider creativity to be a personality trait, others see it as a skill that can be acquired and learned. Most practitioners are convinced that creativity can at least be fostered—for example, by means of creativity techniques. The question of whether creativity and intelligence are linked or are even different aspects of the same concept has been widely discussed among some of the most influential researchers in the field of creativity, such as Teresa Amabile, Gregory J. Feist, Guilford, and Torrance. Correlations found between creativity and intelligence are consistently low, leading researchers to assert that creativity is distinct from intelligence, but overall, results remain inconclusive.

At the beginning of the 20th century, Sigmund Freud proposed that creativity emerges as a sublimation of unfulfilled desires and can be linked to neurosis. Whereas this proposition still lacks empirical evidence, the link between affect and creativity has been substantiated. Some researchers suggest that positive affect increases creativity by broadening the cognitive search process and defocusing attention, thereby expanding the number of elements viewed as essential for solving the problem at hand. This effect is especially pronounced when positive affect joins high levels of activation as well as a focus on achievement. Both of these are generally found in entrepreneurs, who are enthusiastic and exceedingly interested in reaching their entrepreneurial goals. It becomes apparent that positive affect is most likely to increase creativity in entrepreneurs. Interestingly, negative affect may also have a positive impact on creativity. In fact, a higher prevalence of affective disorders was found in highly creative individuals and their blood relatives when compared to the rest of the population.

Personality traits that also characterize most entrepreneurs—such as risk taking, being open to new experiences, and extroversion—have been linked to creativity. In addition, research in the fields of psychology and business (for example, by Amabile), as well as neurobiology, found a high level of specialized knowledge or expertise to be a necessary condition for creative innovation. Another crucial condition for creativity is motivation, especially intrinsic motivation originating from an individual's satisfaction with the task at hand rather than extrinsic rewards.

A study involving highly successful entrepreneurs revealed that creativity is strongly linked with opportunity recognition as well as with a number of factors that render a person enterprising (such as self-confidence, enthusiasm, and independence). Moreover, successful entrepreneurs generally view themselves as very creative. Consequently, it makes sense for entrepreneurs to create, for themselves as well as their employees, an environment conducive to creativity. Conditions of the work environment that foster creativity are a feeling of safety that entails a sense of self-worth, a nonjudgmental climate that allows one to make mistakes and suggest unconventional ideas, a certain amount of perceived freedom, and open communication.

Creativity Techniques

In addition to the right work environment, conditions that foster creativity may include techniques designed to boost a new venture's creative potential. Three popular techniques for fostering creativity are TIPS, brainstorming, and lateral or divergent thinking. These methods, introduced and promoted in the 20th century, have gained much attention among practitioners around the globe.

TIPS (also known as TRIZ) is a method originally introduced into the field of engineering in 1946 by Genrich Saulowitsch Altschuller, Rafael Borissowitsch Shapiro, and Dimitri Kabanov. The technique has since been expanded by various contributors. The acronym translates as "theory of inventive problem solving." TIPS provides a defined set of tools and problem-solving strategies to help formalize the innovative process. The essential problem-solving principles of the innovative process in TIPS are solving technical contradictions; focusing on the desired ideal result rather than the current situation; focusing on functionality (such as communication) rather than solutions (such as the telephone); and maximizing the use of every element in the product. TIPS has long since transgressed the border of engineering and is commonly introduced into all kinds of different organizations and industries.

Brainstorming was developed by Alex Faickney Osborn and became popular in 1953. It is a creativity technique most often used in groups for producing a large number of ideas in order to solve a specific problem. The basic rules of brainstorming are to produce a large amount of unconventional ideas while withholding judgment and to combine and improve ideas before evaluating their appropriateness for the problem at hand. Since the critical evaluation of ideas generated by other group members is put on hold, each participant is encouraged to voice even the most unconventional thoughts. The evaluation of the ideas is delayed to a later stage in the process. The combination and improvement of ideas are seen to result in better solutions as well as additional ideas by promoting associative processes. Research results suggest, however, that individuals working independently produce at least the same amount and quality of ideas as do brainstorming groups. These results may be due to various inhibitory group effects, such as social loafing.

Lateral or divergent thinking, introduced by Edward de Bono in 1967, disbands traditional ways of approaching a problem and promotes a process of creative problem solving. An essential technique applied in lateral thinking is the questioning of conventional solutions by purposefully searching for the most unlikely solution. Mental leaps and associations are valuable steps on the way to an ultimately appropriate solution, while not every intermediate step needs to follow a logical sequence. Basic premises and contexts are not taken for granted and are repeatedly questioned.

Economic Implications of Creativity

The professional creative workforce (the so-called "creative class") is becoming an increasingly important aspect of today's economy. About 10 million workers in the United States are estimated to work as creative professionals. Creative careers can be found not only in the "classical" creative professions (such as writing, theater, and fine arts or design) but also in marketing, research and development, scientific research, architecture, engineering, and even accounting and finance. Economists such as Richard Florida promote creativity as a crucial factor for inventing new technologies, products, and services that, in turn, will foster economic growth. In his 2002 book *The Rise of the Creative Class*, Florida proposed that a higher density of creative professionals is associated with a higher level of economic development in countries with the three T's of economic development: technology, talent, and tolerance.

Since creativity is also a prerequisite for finding flexible solutions to emerging problems, it is an essential element not only in launching new ventures but also in establishing and retaining an effective position in the rapidly changing economic world.

Sonja A. Sackmann
Nicola B. Klaus
University BW Munich

See also Innovation Management; Innovation Processes; New Product Development; Opportunity Recognition; Research and Development

Further Readings

Amabile, Teresa. "How to Kill Creativity." *Harvard Business Review*, v.76/5 (1998).

Baron, R. A., and J. Tang. "The Role of Entrepreneurs in Firm-Level Innovation: Joint Effects of Positive Affect, Creativity, and Environmental Dynamism." *Journal of Business Venturing*, v.26/1 (2011).

Csíkszentmihályi, Mihály. *Creativity: Flow and the Psychology of Discovery and Invention*. New York: HarperCollins, 1996.

De Bono, Edward. *The Use of Lateral Thinking*. London: Cape, 1967.

Florida, Richard. *The Rise of the Creative Class: And How It's Transforming Work, Leisure, Community and Everyday Life*. New York: Perseus Book Group, 2002.

Guilford, Joy Paul. "Creativity." *American Psychologist*, v.5/9 (1950).

Lumpkin, G. Thomas et al. "Opportunity Recognition." In *Entrepreneurship: The Way Ahead*, H. P. Welsch, ed. New York: Routledge, 2004.

Sternberg, Robert, ed. *Handbook of Creativity*. Cambridge, UK: Cambridge University Press, 1999.

CREATIVITY AND OPPORTUNITIES

While there is disagreement as to whether opportunities are something that exist external to an entrepreneur or are constructed or developed by an entrepreneur, there is little debate that opportunities are important to entrepreneurship. Definitions of entrepreneurship often involve the recognition or creation, evaluation, and pursuit of opportunities. Also, regardless of the view (recognition or creation) taken, most scholars acknowledge that recognizing, creating, or developing opportunities requires creativity. In fact, creativity is often described as a defining characteristic of entrepreneurs. Many

scholars suggest that the recognition or creation of opportunities either requires creativity to be successful or actually is a creative process itself. In the psychology domain, where creativity has traditionally found its home, scholars have also seen a connection between creativity and entrepreneurship in general and more specifically with opportunities, and many have also considered the process to be a specific case of creativity. The creativity literature is said to approach researching and understanding creativity from four perspectives, known as the four P's (not to be confused with the four P's of marketing): person, process, product, and press (the latter being environmental and external pressures). These four P's provide a useful framework for reviewing the relationship between creativity and opportunities.

Person

Person refers to the characteristics and motivation of the creative individual. Teresa Amabile, a well-known professor of creativity, innovation, and management at Harvard, believes that three aspects of a person influence creativity: creative thinking skills, expertise, and motivation. The typical entrepreneur, who is pursuing his or her passion, will have high levels of intrinsic motivation and thus likely have more creative ideas for pursuing the passion. Moreover, since the area of pursuit is something about which the individual is passionate, they likely have a high level of expertise. Thus, the one area in which an entrepreneur may need help is creative thinking skills. These can be enhanced with any number of creativity books, brainteaser puzzles, and creativity games. Also (as is discussed below in the section on press), creativity can be enhanced (or harmed) by the people with whom one interacts.

Studies show that a person who is intrinsically motivated will come up with a larger number of creative ideas. This motivation to pursue entrepreneurial opportunities comes from disequilibrium between the level of aspiration of an individual and that individual's perceived valuation in the market. Higher levels of potential financial reward are also associated with a larger number of opportunities identified and more innovative opportunities. However, results for this are mixed, as some studies show that financial reward actually reduces creativity. The less knowledgeable an entrepreneur is about customer problems, the more motivated by potential financial reward that person will be; however, if one does not solve a customer problem, one is not likely to be successful as an entrepreneur. Once again, it is important for an entrepreneur to pursue his or her passion.

Certain qualities may help an individual to be more creative. These include broad interests, high energy, attraction to complexity, intuition, self-confidence, flexibility, and a sense of self as "creative." These are also characteristics that help an individual successfully recognize and pursue an entrepreneurial opportunity. In addition to the ability to produce many ideas and evaluate to find the good ones, entrepreneurs should have a strong conviction of the worth of their ideas and persuasive capabilities to convince others of this worth. They need to invest in ideas that are currently unknown to the public, might be unpopular, or might otherwise be considered low in value and to develop and sell those ideas to others at a higher value.

Creativity is also considered by some to be one of two personality traits that are related to successful opportunity recognition. Studies have found a significant positive relationship between an individual's creativity level and the number of new business ideas, opportunities identified, opportunities pursued, and successes. It has also been proposed that high levels of creativity are related to high levels of entrepreneurial alertness and optimism or self-efficacy.

Process

One of the clearest connections between opportunities and creativity can be found in a well-established model of creativity that consists of five iterative stages: preparation, incubation, insight, evaluation, and elaboration. Preparation refers to the skills and knowledge one acquires or accesses to bring to the creative *process*. As will be described below in the discussion of product, to create truly novel ideas one should have diverse skills and knowledge. To acquire such diverse knowledge, one should try many different things, visit different places, and talk to different people. One good example is the combined knowledge of coffee being sold in Seattle and coffeehouses in Italy. These led Howard Schulz to what we know today as Starbucks. Incubation is the time away from the process, especially when one hits

a "roadblock," where the mind continues to explore options for solving the problem or generating ideas subconsciously. Incubation is often considered necessary for breakthrough ideas. The notion that ideas come while taking a shower is an example of incubation. An idea breaks through to the conscious mind during the insight stage. This is typically repeated many times—one rarely has just one idea. If an idea passes a "gut check" or is intuitively felt to be an idea with potential, it moves to more formal evaluation. Thus, this stage involves a range from informally talking to people about an idea to more formal evaluation methods such as what would be found in a feasibility analysis. Finally, it is generally accepted that ideas are not fully formed upon conception and thus need elaboration. This involves extensive effort to add details to the idea, such as the target market and competitive positioning.

Other process models link creativity and opportunities. Thomas Ward has suggested that using models of creativity that involve generative and explorative processes would be a useful way to examine entrepreneurial processes. Scholars have been examining opportunity development, which is said to be creative or at least require creativity. Several other models of opportunity have included creativity. Overall, there is a strong connection between processes of creativity and processes related to entrepreneurial opportunity.

Product

A creative *product* is defined in terms of two dimensions: novelty and usefulness. Novelty is also referred to as originality, newness, or innovativeness; usefulness, as value or appropriateness. Entrepreneurs aspire to seek opportunities that are both novel and useful. It is not difficult to see how to create usefulness in ideas. Usefulness can be based on filling a customer need or a market gap. Novelty, however, is more elusive. To understand novelty it is important to understand where an idea comes from. The easiest way to think about an idea is to think of it as a combination of bits of knowledge, which combine in one's brain to create ideas, similar to the way hydrogen and oxygen combine to create water. (As an aside, analogies such as this are often used in creativity and opportunity recognition, both for generating ideas and for communicating them.)

What makes one idea more novel than another is that the pieces of knowledge that are combined are very different from one another. Think, for example, of combining knowledge of waterskiing and snow skiing to come up with a new business idea. These ideas likely will not be very novel, since both are forms of skiing and have many similarities. However, if one were to combine knowledge of snow skiing and marine biology, the ideas would be much more novel. For example, perhaps an entrepreneur knows that scales of a particular fish enhance the fish's ability to swim fast. Replicating the design of that scale on a snow ski could allow skiers to ski faster. (The concept of biomimicry applies knowledge of nature to such innovations.)

One of the benefits of using a creativity perspective in examining opportunities is the relevance of creative products. Most conceptions of opportunity-related processes include some kind of outcome, such as business concepts, business models, and business plans or even the opportunities themselves. These are all forms of creative products. Ideas can also be measured as products of the creative process. Although not directly linked to creativity, several recent studies of opportunity have used measures similar to those used in creativity research. In such studies, subjects are usually given the task of listing as many ideas as they can, given some technology or situation. In the creativity literature this would be part of an "alternative uses task" where the subject lists as many uses as possible for an everyday object (such as a brick). Other measures used include ideas subjects have had in the recent past or asking respondents, for example, "How many opportunities for creating or purchasing a business have you identified within the last five years?" Some studies have also considered novelty by looking at the innovativeness of opportunities.

The number of and innovativeness of opportunities are two measures that have been used by scholars, and they represent two dimensions of divergent thinking: fluency (number of ideas) and originality (novelty or innovativeness of the ideas). However, according to the creativity literature, there are two other dimensions of divergent thinking: flexibility (diversity of opportunities, which concerns whether the ideas are all variations of one kind of business or vary greatly) and elaboration (the detail of the opportunities, that is, whether they are presented in only a few words or are fully described in several paragraphs). Creativity tests adapted for entrepreneurial opportunity research, such as the alternative uses task, permit both process and product to be measured from a creativity perspective.

Press

Press includes all of the environmental pressures that either nurture or impair creative activities. Entrepreneurs face many external pressures as they are developing opportunities. Most of the pressures serve to reduce the creative potential of the opportunities. For example, sharing initial ideas with friends and family may result in suggestions to change or even abandon ideas, especially if they are very novel and thus difficult to understand (thus the value of analogy mentioned above). However, entrepreneurs can put themselves in environments that enhance creativity. One example is networking. Weak ties, people with whom one infrequently associates, are found to be a good source of unique information, which can lead to more creative ideas. What makes an idea novel is combining diverse knowledge. Interacting with weak ties gives an entrepreneur access to different knowledge, creating a better environment for novel ideas to emerge. Likewise, teams comprising individuals with diverse backgrounds are more likely to be creative.

Press also includes goals, incentives, freedom from time pressure, and good role models. It also encompasses the social interactions that influence the conception and development of opportunities. Some models propose that factors in the work environment, such as supervisory support and group interactions, are important for enabling creativity. These environments promote the communication of ideas and the flow of information, which enhance creativity.

Social sources of information have been found to have direct positive effects on opportunity recognition. Studies have looked at how social capital influences creativity and have found that weak ties are preferable to strong ones when it comes to stimulating creativity but that the number of weak ties should be kept at an intermediate level, rather than at a lower or higher level, lest it becomes a constraint. In addition to the number of weak ties, the position of an individual in the network is important. Whereas being in a near-central location is beneficial to creativity, locating oneself on the fringe is also relevant, as it encourages boundary spanning.

David J. Hansen
College of Charleston
Javier Monllor
DePaul University

See also Creativity; Network Ties; New Product Development; Opportunity Development; Opportunity Identification and Structural Alignment; Opportunity Recognition; Opportunity Sources

Further Readings

Amabile, Teresa. "Entrepreneurial Creativity Through Motivational Synergy." *Journal of Creative Behavior*, v.31/1 (1997).

Amabile, Teresa. "How to Kill Creativity." *Harvard Business Review* (September 1, 1998).

Csíkszentmihályi, Mihály. *Creativity: Flow and the Psychology of Discovery and Invention*. New York: HarperCollins, 1996.

Dimov, Dimo. "Beyond the Single-Insight, Single-Person, Attribution in Understanding Entrepreneurial Opportunities." *Entrepreneurship Theory and Practice*, v.31/5 (2007).

Hansen, David J. et al. "A Multidimensional Examination of a Creativity-Based Model of Opportunity Recognition." *International Journal of Entrepreneurial Behaviour and Research*, v.12/5 (2011).

Lumpkin, G. Thomas et al. "Opportunity Recognition." In *Entrepreneurship: The Way Ahead*, H. P. Welsch, ed. New York: Routledge, 2004.

Ward, Thomas. "Cognition, Creativity and Entrepreneurship." *Journal of Business Venturing*, v.19/2 (2004).

CREDENTIALS

A credential is defined as a report, diploma, or status that evidences some level of competence. Credentials can take many forms, including academic degrees, certifications, years of experience, credit histories, or licenses. The credentials required to begin a new venture can vary (by industry, lender, location, or municipality) and often are undefined or difficult to identify. They can affect both whether or not an individual can begin a new venture and how that venture operates.

Credentials can affect one's ability to start a new venture in several ways. First, local, state, and federal governments have laws, statutes, and ordinances that may require individuals or ventures to possess certain credentials in order to operate. One good example of government credentialing comes from the local level. Many municipalities require occupational licenses, a type of credential that legitimizes the business within a specific area. Typically, these licenses are readily available and are merely a form of tracking businesses and generating tax revenue. However, not all local licenses are easily obtained. For example, individuals who wish to open a restaurant or bar that serves alcohol are usually required to purchase or possess a liquor license (a credential that allows the sale of alcohol). Often, the number of available licenses is limited and lack of possession of this credential could immediately prohibit one from beginning the new venture.

Second, each year both bankers and venture capitalists screen hundreds of potential new investment opportunities, often evaluating them at least in part on the credentials of the individual submitting the proposal. The credentials bankers look for are not always the same as those venture capitalists look for. When approving and underwriting a traditional small business loan, bankers typically want individuals to possess credentials in the form of a degree, several years of related experience, and licenses or certifications necessary for the venture to operate. Venture capitalists operate differently. Whereas bankers approach lending from a more scientific or calculated approach (experience + 20 percent capital + collateral + respectable credit history = minimal repayment risk, for example), venture capitalists view investing as more of an art form. Thus, venture capitalists may place more emphasis on the individual or the idea and less on any mathematical formula (at least when it comes to assessing credentials). Venture capitalists are highly skilled investors and typically know how to build resources around an idea they wish to fund. Whereas a banker may look at the total package and determine that one of the credentials of interest is not sufficient to warrant a loan (say, years of relevant experience in the industry of interest), a venture capitalist may see this as an irrelevant credential, given that they themselves have the experience necessary or know how to find individuals with the necessary credentials and make them part of the team.

When a new restaurant or bar opens and wishes to serve alcohol, the organization is required to either purchase or possess a liquor license—a credential that allows the sale of alcohol. Restaurateurs and bar owners face a number of hurdles in receiving this credential, including a limit on available liquor licenses. (Photos.com)

Credentials can also affect how a new venture operates in several ways. First, say one wished to open a restaurant. This type of venture typically requires that an individual have a food manager's certification, which sounds simple but may be complicated. In Florida, for example, the state requires that someone with this certification be present whenever food is prepared or served. In this case, it is not the entrepreneur or owner beginning the venture who must possess the credential; rather, it typically is the manager on duty and several of the staff who must possess the credential. Second, licenses may impose certain restrictions on a venture. Some credentials may prohibit business operations during certain hours of the day (as in the case of occupational or liquor licenses that mandate that the business must close by 2:00 A.M.); others may limit the type of work or business that can be done (many states limit the size of a truck a driver can operate or the type of drugs a pharmacy technician can dispense or handle based upon the individual's credentials). In this sense, some industries can be very "credentials intense" (trucking, medical professions, insurance, real estate), while others are not (retail, commercial, and residential cleaning and pet grooming, for example).

Eric W. Liguori
California State University, Fresno
Jeffrey Muldoon
Louisiana State University

See also Barriers to Entry; Business Angels; Credit; Licensing; Venture Capital

Further Readings

Bhide, A. "Bootstrap Finance: The Art of Start-Ups." *Harvard Business Review*, v.70/6 (1993).
Fleming, D. "Management Forecast Characteristics: Effects on Venture Capital Investment Screening Judgments." *Behavioral Research in Accounting*, v.21/2 (2009).
Fried, V. and R. Hisrich. "Toward a Model of Venture Capital Investment Decision Making." *Financial Management*, v.23/3 (1994).

CREDIT

Credit is one of the oldest systems of financial exchange known to humankind. It is the trust that one party extends to another party that allows the second party not to pay for (or reimburse) the first party immediately. Credit, in short, involves purchasing something with money that one does not have, whereupon the parties in question (buyer and seller) come to an agreement that the purchasing party will reimburse the party distributing the goods over a temporally structured duration, with each installment of payment possibly holding the weight of interest upon each subsequent reimbursement. Credit does not require money; as such, the concept of credit can be applied to barter economics when both parties agree to provide and exchange products, services, or other resources at an agreed-upon time.

The extension of credit is based on the reputation (or creditworthiness) of the buyer or entity. Creditworthiness is the creditor's judgment of an entity's current and future ability and proclivity to adhere to the agreed-upon debt obligation. Creditworthiness is determined by a combination of factors, including the buyer's history of borrowing and repaying debt obligations, a credit rating, and the entity's integrity.

A credit rating is a published ranking based on detailed financial analysis of the entity's (individual's, firm's, or debt security's) ability to repay a debt in a timely fashion. The credit rating includes the entity's financial history as it relates to fulfilling its debt obligations, the present financial position of the entity, and the potential future income of the entity. Firms such as Dun and Bradstreet gather, analyze, summarize, and provide this information for use in the decision for the extension of credit. The highest credit rating is usually AAA and the lowest rating is D; at the lowest rating, credit is sometimes not granted, because of the entity's financial instability or other difficulties.

Trade credit has multiple functions, one of which is the extension of credit to a firm by suppliers in commercial trade as an arrangement to buy materials, equipment, goods, or services without expending immediate cash payment. Within the extension of credit, the firm must consider both the positive and the negative costs of trade credit and the potential financial impact trade credit will have on the firm. Depending on the trade credit terms available from the supplier, the cost of trade credit can be detrimental to the firm; the interest rate or due date can be altered or have penalties imposed if payments are not received in accordance with the agreement. For example, a supplier might agree to extend trade credit to a firm with the terms of 1 percent 10 net 30. Under these terms, a 1 percent discount would be given if the total amount of the invoice were paid within 10 days, with the full amount of the invoice due within 30 days of the firm's receipt of said invoice. On an invoice of $1,000 and payment made within the 1 percent 10 terms of the trade credit, the firm would realize a discount of $10. Over a 12-month period, the firm would generate total discounts of $120, or 12 percent of one invoice. On the other hand, by surrendering the discount, the firm is able to use its money for 20 more days. This second option is actually costing the firm 18 percent on the items purchased from the supplier (360/20 days = 18 opportunities for discounted payment × 1 percent = 18 percent of missed discount). In addition to the cost of lost discounts, the firm must consider the cost of late payments and/or delinquency payments (upwards to 24 percent), applicable when the firm extends payment beyond the agreed-upon 30 days.

The use of trade credit requires intelligent planning to avoid unnecessary costs. When properly used, trade credit can provide a firm with an effective

Company credit ratings are published and include the entity's financial history as it relates to fulfilling its debt obligations, the present financial position of the entity, and the potential future income of the entity. This rating will affect the firm's ability to enter into credit agreements to buy equipment, goods, or services without immediate cash payment. (Photos.com)

tool in reducing its overall requirement for capital, a way to build a commercial credit history, and a means of establishing a record of financial stability. However, the lack of trade credit and the ineffective use of trade credit can lead to higher operating costs resulting from surrendered discounts, delinquency penalties, and damage to the firm's future trade credit rating.

Consumer credit is defined as short-term lending to individuals for the purchase of goods or services that are not intended for resale or for further use in the production of other products. Consumer credit is primarily used for personal, family, or household purposes. Common types of consumer credit include automobile financing, personal loans, retail loans, store credit cards, and bank credit cards. The costs to the borrower for consumer credit include interest fees, origination fees, and any other charges required by the lender as an integral part of the credit agreement and are additional to the amount borrowed for which the borrower must pay.

Individual creditworthiness is also considered when lenders extend credit to borrowers and is expressed in the form of the annual percentage rate (APR). The APR is the cost of funds for the entire year, including interest, fees, and applicable insurance (if required), and is expressed in a single percentage. The annual percentage rate is a number that consumers can use to compare the cost of funds for other loans or investments and allows a comparison to be made between competing products. The APR can be expressed in two ways: the effective rate (which includes compound interest and can be calculated in many different ways, depending upon how the various fees are factored) and the nominal rate (the nonadjusted simple interest rate).

Typically the APR does not account for compounding. For example, if the APR for a consumer credit card is 24 percent, the percentage rate is 2 percent per month, but the interest rate, or the cost of the loan for the entire year, may be greater than the 24 percent as a result of the compounding effect. Lenders must inform borrowers of the APR before any loan agreement is signed.

Credit is becoming increasingly important, given the increase in entrepreneurial activities globally. The shifting trend from classical foreign aid (whereby developed economies donate funds to developing countries) to social entrepreneurship has accelerated the pace of new ventures and the transition from the public to the private sector in terms of economic activity. The ability to secure credit is also sector dependent, based on prevailing "hot" sectors in the economy. For example, the technology sector, especially as it is involved in ventures related to social media, is better able to secure funding compared to other sectors. Thus, ventures not related to social media may face a higher cost of doing business given their required rate of return. This reality presents a catch-22, given that the increased cost of doing business translates to higher prices, which may ultimately undermine the long-term success of a new venture.

Alfred Lewis
Hamline University
Dan Kipley
Azusa Pacific University

See also Bankruptcy; Barriers to Entry; Barter; Capitalism; Cash Flow; Debt; Debt-Based Financing; Equity- and Debt-Based Financing; Microfinance

Further Readings

Cole, Robert Harzell and Lon Mishler. *Consumer and Business Credit Management*. Chicago: Irwin, 1995.
Connelly, Patrick O. *Trade Credit Risk Management*. BookSurge Publishing, 2007.
Elston, Julie and David Audretsch. "Financing the Entrepreneurial Decision: An Empirical Approach Using Experimental Data on Risk Attitudes." *Small Business Economics*, v.36/2 (February 2011).
Grath, Anders. *The Handbook of International Trade and Finance: The Complete Guide to Risk Management, International Payments and Currency Management, Bonds and Guarantees, Credit Insurance and Trade Finance*. Philadelphia: Kogan Page, 2008.
Reuvid, Jonathan. *The Business Guide to Credit Management: Advice and Solutions for Case-Flow Control, Financial Risk and Debt Management*. Philadelphia: Kogan Page, 2010.
Taub, Richard P. *Doing Development in Arkansas: Using Credit to Create Opportunity for Entrepreneurs Outside the Mainstream*. Fayetteville: University of Arkansas Press, 2004.
Weltman, Barbara. *The Rational Guide to Building Small Business Credit*. Rollinsford, NH: Rational Press, 2007.

Crisis Management: Corporate

Corporate crisis management is a process of programmed decision making, dynamic adjustment, staff training, and dealing with a major unpredictable event so as to remove or reduce the threat or losses incurred from the crisis. There are hundreds of potential threats existing for every organization; 30 years of hard work can be destroyed within 30 seconds. Corporate crises usually take the form of plant fires, product defects, workplace violence, sabotage, loss of competitive secrets, embezzlement and extortion, industrial accidents, or natural disasters. Any of these events can cause an immediate and prolonged financial loss to a company and requires an intensive communications effort directed to investors, employees, consumers, and other entities and may present a series of regulatory, community relations, and competitive challenges.

Corporate crises can be divided into several types. These include problems that can arise in the process of doing international business. When considering which country will be the next target, there will be a decision-making crisis if the nascent firm has made a decision that is not matched by the economic or political climate of the host country. If it concerns the legal system, such as tax laws, or abuse of power for personal gain, for instance, the top management team may face a crisis. An operation management crisis may arise because of inefficient management covering areas of quality control, environmental protection, and public relations. In order to expand market share, the business may face a financial crisis, especially if the company is in financial straits to begin with (as is common with new ventures) or if it is fluctuating in the stock market. It is very hard to borrow money from local banks abroad. When the new venture sets up a new branch, it needs to recruit new employees, and this may cause a human resources crisis, if the company is facing issues with recruiting, training, compensation, and benefits that are in line with the culture. Some employees may also accuse the company of wrongdoing, which can invite public attention, especially if the company has no suitable mechanism in place to communicate with the media; the ensuing public relations crisis can damage the reputation of the company and compromise its credibility, leading to loss of consumers' support and trust. This would be disastrous for a nascent firm hoping to root its business in the host country. Other crises can be the result of an unpredictable incident or "act of God," such as those resulting from natural disasters including earthquakes, volcanic eruptions, hurricanes, floods, landslides, and droughts.

A corporate crisis is often characterized by their abruptness (its unpredictable and sudden occurrence), destructiveness (the serious damage and loss it causes), uncertainty (the difficulty of determining its future effects), emergency (the need to make decisions quickly and react immediately), and attention (its attraction of negative media coverage and/or public scrutiny). Typically, a crisis has the capacity to visit negative financial, legal, political, or governmental repercussions on the company, especially if it is not dealt with in a prompt and effective manner.

Over past decades, high-profile disasters have thrown an intense spotlight on the issue of crisis management, as new ventures have witnessed the damage that poor crisis management can wreak on business fortunes. A growing percentage of start-ups have intensified their efforts to put effective crisis management strategies in place. In order to tackle a crisis effectively, experts have proposed a six-stage model that is commonly accepted by both the academic community and professionals.

The first stage in crisis management is to have in place strategies that will facilitate the avoidance of crisis insofar as that is possible. With some forethought based on the venture's particular enterprise, staff, plant, and other specifics, these measures can be simple and inexpensive.

The second stage is preparation—a plan to meet the emergency when a crisis occurs in the event that avoidance strategies do not work. Every entrepreneur should assume that crisis is inevitable; hence, procedures for meeting potential crises should be outlined in advance. For example, a business can establish a center that is designed to handle crises resulting from natural disasters, staffing it with personnel trained to test infrastructure and administer basic first aid and other medical procedures.

The third stage is to have in place methods of detecting potential crises; new ventures in particular can sometimes classify problems incorrectly and focus on technical issues rather than correctly identifying problems that can lead to crisis. In this endeavor, it is important to abide by the basic principle of putting the customer's interest first—a principle that is often forgotten during a crisis—in order to minimize losses in the long run. Keeping communications with customers open and accurately locating the source of a problem are essential and may involve outside investigators as well as insiders.

The fourth stage is crisis control, which involves the need to set priorities according to the specific crisis situation. The most urgent priority is to curtail losses, and that need entails making good decisions both rationally and promptly—which is particularly difficult given the pressures of the crisis and typically a lack of complete information. Chief executive officers (CEOs) should guard against conventional but potentially damaging wisdom, such as "tell them nothing" or (by contrast) "tell the truth slowly." In fact, it is important to communicate with media and the public in a timely fashion, honestly, and with discipline; otherwise, journalists may turn to those who are not well informed, and rumors and speculation may take on a life of their own. It is better to confront the public and honestly relate what is known—as well as what is unknown—than to avoid communication. It is also important for both employees and the public to see the CEO and senior managers at the location of the crisis, which makes it clear that the top managers care and are doing their best to resolve the problem and minimize damage. The aim of any company should be to take crisis seriously, handle it quickly and thoroughly, and solve it finally. Those who have a clear understanding of different areas of crisis management should be tasked to address the crisis; these specialists should focus on crisis management, allowing the rest of the staff to perform their standard tasks insofar as possible.

The fifth stage is to settle the crisis in a timely and effective manner. Those who stand motionless will be knocked down even if they are on the right track. It is crucial to solve the problem quickly. This stage, when properly addressed, will lead to the final stage: to benefit from the crisis, which means to learn something from it. This final stage can partially make up for losses by resulting in correction of the mistakes that led to the crisis in the first place. Of course, even when the six stages of crisis management are ideally executed, there is no assurance that crisis will not occur again; luck is a vital factor also.

This six-stage model of crisis management is often simplified as a five-stage model: signal detection, probe and prevention, damage control, business recovery, and learning. A four-stage model, based on a life-cycle approach, describes crisis using medical terms: prodromal, breakout or acute, chronic, and resolution (which correspond to identifying the source, evaluating the possibilities, dealing with the risk, and summarizing for future reference). Other experts divide crisis into three stages—including pre-crisis, crisis, and post-crisis—with each stage divided into substages.

Although entrepreneurs in both new ventures and established businesses can do much to prevent the crisis, it usually strikes at some point in the life of a company, and therefore it must be assumed that it will happen. When crisis occurs, it is important to accept it, handle it, and look ahead. For the long-term life of the firm, it is most important for crisis managers to tell the truth, and tell it to the media and public immediately. Nearly every crisis includes not only the root of failure but also the seeds of success. It is the essence of successful crisis management to find, cultivate, and harvest that potential for opportunity rather than misconstrue the situation and make things worse.

Finally, it is important to build goodwill and good relations on a daily basis before crisis occurs; that way, businesses are well positioned to be treated fairly by media and the public when crisis does occur. The way a venture weathers and emerges from crisis will in large part be based on its reputation. A reservoir of goodwill can do much to defend, preserve, and even enhance a reputation during crisis. When a

crisis does erupt, prompt and proactive communication should be a cornerstone of any business's crisis containment strategy.

Shuyi Zhang
Shanghai Finance University

See also Championing Corporate Ventures; Change Management: Corporate; Communication Styles; Risk Management

Further Readings

Augustine, Norman R. "Managing the Crisis You Tried to Prevent." In *Harvard Business Review on Crisis Management*. Boston: Harvard Business School Press, 1999.

Barton, Laurence. *Crisis in Organizations: Managing and Communicating in the Heat of Chaos*. Mason, OH: South-Western Publishing, 1993.

Gordon, Kim. "Under Fire: Will a Crisis Take Your Company Down? Here's How Deft Handling Can Turn Public Opinion Around." *Entrepreneur* (April 2001).

Keating, Lauren. "Proactive Approach Minimizes Damage to Image." *Atlanta Business Chronicle* (November 10, 2000).

CULTURE AND ENTREPRENEURSHIP

Most scholars and organizational leaders now recognize that an organization's culture has a powerful effect on many outcomes, including performance, job satisfaction, extrawork behaviors, and sustainability. E. H. Schein believed organizational culture is the most important facet in enhancing leadership and direction for the organization. Culture forms with or without coercion from leaders and must be managed to produce positive outcomes. Just as any ethnic group's culture contains many different and unique rituals, norms, values, and structures that guide behavior, an organization's culture contains the same principles. Therefore, an organizational culture is a set of rules, norms, values, structures, and principles that guide and constrain the behavior of its members and the processes and behavior of an organization.

In today's global business environment, business owners must coordinate business activities on a much larger scale. They must think not only about the internal systems of the business but also about how those systems fit into the market of the global environment. This global environment has expanded the market of every business, and business leaders must create a culture that facilitates growth in an external culture. As the market continues to change, leaders must adapt within the confines of cultural standards of community and national cultures.

Just as an organization's culture is based on a set of norms, values, and structures, entrepreneurs and other new business ventures must account for the cultural norms of the environment. These cultural attributes constitute one of the major determinants of a country's ability to develop and maintain high levels of entrepreneurial activity. Researchers have associated three main activities with entrepreneurial orientation: innovativeness, risk taking, and proactiveness. In addition to the cultural norms of the environment, research has indicated that other controls, such as the economic system, exchange rate, and governmental systems, can have an effect on entrepreneurial activities. A clear understanding of the definition of culture forms a stable foundation for all systems within an organization. Culture is to a group what personality is to an individual. Behaviors are easy to identify, but the underlying causes are difficult to distinguish. An entrepreneur who undertakes a new business venture must realize, anticipate, and adapt to the personality of the culture. Doing so strengthens the systems within the business.

Any group with a stable membership and a history of shared learning will develop some form of culture. Just as the culture of an organization forms when (1) founders or leaders of an organization make decisions and take action based on their personal views of the world, (2) the learning experiences of its members are implemented as the organization evolves, and (3) new beliefs, values, and assumptions are brought in by new members and leaders, the culture of a country or community is formed from these factors. Every culture experiences some common attributes, such as daily routines, activities, rules, language, and codes of social relations. How these attributes are formed and acted out differs from one culture to another. These unique attributes create a sense of community that causes the members to take on the culture's identity. The community of culture will exhibit commitment among its members. Entrepreneurs that create their business around these attributes create a system that results in members feeling that they have something in common. Employees are willing to commit themselves to a truly engaging purpose, which is larger than their personal self-interest. People are willing to give of themselves to help create the collective enterprise.

A culture can be viewed as a system through which execution of processes is determined and through which its members are identified. New business ventures that fail to account for the components of such a system set themselves up for failure. Entrepreneurs and business leaders must earn acceptance from the community. Aligning a business with the cultural values involves four elements: First, alignment with cultural values provides a business with structural stability. This helps define the organization, provides purpose, and acts as a foundation for the interrelated parts working toward one vision and goal. Second, the system receives depth, which is often the unconscious part of the system. This is less visible and is hard to identify because it is so deeply embedded. Third, congruency with the culture adds breadth to an organization. It covers all of the system's functioning and influences all aspects of how an organization deals with its primary task, its various environments, and its internal operations. Finally, integration allows all of the elements into a larger paradigm that ties them together. It implies that rituals, climate, values, and behaviors combine into a coherent whole.

An entrepreneur can be defined as anyone who organizes or assumes the risk of a business or enterprise. L. Y. Chen proposed that the process of organizational culture plays a much more important role in smaller entrepreneurial businesses than it does in larger organizations. Large organizations provide many levels where the aspects of culture can be shifted and changed to facilitate positive outcomes. In a smaller organization, however, there is little room for error. Any decision can have drastic effects on business outcomes. Therefore, the ability to adapt is crucial in an entrepreneurial setting. Creating and maintaining an accurate culture is a key element of the success of an organization. Therefore, a small business must be adaptable to outside environments and market trends while maintaining its core principles and the congruency between its mission and culture. It is imperative that the type of culture created be consistent with the business market that is being reached. For instance, an organization whose main function is the creation and design of printed material would not function well in a hierarchical culture where communication was primarily vertical instead of horizontal. This type of culture would diminish creativity and innovation, something that is crucial to the success of a graphic design organization. Therefore, it becomes the duty of the business owner and his or her executive staff to create, implement, and maintain a culture that fosters creativity and innovation. The behavior patterns of the leader permeate all levels of the organization to instill the norms, values, thinking patterns, and behavior of the members.

D. A. Shepherd, H. Patzelt, and J. M. Haynie described an entrepreneurial organization as one that continuously initiates and implements innovation through new ideas. Conversion of its human capital into new and fresh ideas, both outside and inside the organization, helps stabilize the organization, encouraging the organization to seize opportunities and engage in changing environments. This is crucial in hypercompetitive environments; market share is often achieved by organizations that implement new ideas and remain on the edge of innovation. Some suggest that this entrepreneurial approach requires a mind-set that must be developed first at the individual level and then at the organizational level. Regardless, it is the leader who must develop the guidelines of the culture that allow this type of thinking and behavior to occur.

The interaction of the entrepreneur, or leader, and culture is a reciprocal and complementary process. The psychological processes of the leader enhance the beliefs, norms, values, and behavior of the organization—its culture—which reciprocates to fulfill the needs of the entrepreneur. It is imperative that these internal processes be congruent with the external culture's constructs. Not only does the reciprocal behavior occur within the organization; the same precepts of reciprocation should occur between the organization and the culture in which it is located. Those who fail to adopt this reciprocative behavior conflict with the external culture. An adaptation must occur to minimize conflict and maximize integration of the business into the external culture.

It is imperative that organizations realize the spirit of entrepreneurship in their processes and external environments. Entrepreneurs in the 21st century will be required to foster an entrepreneurial culture that supports growth and initiative in order to adapt in a changing global environment.

Anthony D. Daniel
Ashford University

See also Communication Styles; Globalization; Leadership; Social Intelligence; Social Networks; Start-Up Teams

Further Readings

Cameron K. S. and R. E. Quinn. *Diagnosing and Changing Organizational Culture: Based on the Competing Values Framework.* San Francisco: Jossey-Bass, 2006.

Chen, L. Y. "Examining the Effect of Organization Culture and Leadership Behaviors on Organizational Commitment, Job Satisfaction, and Job Performance at Small and Middle-Sized Firms of Taiwan." *Journal of American Academy of Business,* v.5/1 (2004).

Daniels, J. D., L. H. Radebaugh, and D. P. Sullivan. *International Business: Environments and Operations,* 13th ed. New York: Prentice Hall, 2011.

George, Gerard and Shaker A. Zahra. "Culture and Its Consequences for Entrepreneurship." *Entrepreneurship Theory and Practice* (Summer 2002).

Hayton, James C., Gerard George, and Shaker A. Zahra. "National Culture and Entrepreneurship: A Review of Behavioral Research." *Entrepreneurship Theory and Practice,* v.26/4 (2002).

Kreiser, P. M., L. D. Marino, P. Dickson, and K. Weaver. "Cultural Influences on Entrepreneurial Orientation: The Impact of National Culture on Risk Taking and Proactiveness in SMEs." *Entrepreneurship Theory and Practice,* v.34/5 (2010).

Schein, E. H. *Organizational Culture and Leadership,* 3rd ed. San Francisco: Jossey-Bass, 2004.

Senge, P., A. Kleiner, C. Roberts, R. Ross, and J. U. Smith. *The Fifth Discipline Fieldbook.* New York: Doubleday, 1994.

Shepherd, D. A., H. Patzelt, and J. M. Haynie. "Entrepreneurial Spirals: Deviation Amplifying Loops of an Entrepreneurial Mindset and Organizational Culture." *Entrepreneurship Theory and Practice,* v.34/1 (2010).

CUSTOMER ORIENTATION

Customers are defined as end users who buy products and services. Since companies' highest priority is to make their customers satisfied, customers are considered to be the most important assets for all companies. In particular for new venture companies, it is necessary to rewrite the definition of "customer," because the concept of customer for new ventures is different from that of established companies. Generally, traditional large-scale and established companies have existing customers. New ventures, by contrast, have prospective customers or lead users who are expected to buy products or services after the new venture is created and the new product or service is launched. Therefore it is important for new venture managers to understand the positive role of prospective customers for the creation of the venture, and their impact on entrepreneurship should be emphasized.

Research on Customer Orientation

The literature on customers and entrepreneurship notes that new ventures' aim is to reach an emerging market that has yet to be exploited; new ventures are dedicated to identifying and adapting to unserved customer needs. In order to be successful in finding hidden customer needs, entrepreneurs must pay close attention to their ventures' customer orientation; new and small firms must learn from the experiences of the customers who are using current products or services. Basically, customer orientation focuses on meeting the needs of customers by learning end users' insights into product and services. This involves asking users—through face-to-face interviews, focus groups, surveys, or the Delphi method (which engages experts responding to questionnaires)—questions about a product's good and bad aspects, its side effects, and experiences the customer has had with the product or service.

Researchers have found that small or new organizations can have breakthroughs after learning from customers' complaints, problems, and insights. The success of new ventures is hidden inside the learning process from the customer. Scott Shane empirically tested the relationship between prior knowledge of customer problems and the creation of new ventures. He found that entrepreneurs' prior knowledge of customer problems influenced their decisions regarding which markets to enter and exploit. For example, an entrepreneur who was working on customer problems in clinical pharmacology was able to learn how a technology could be used to treat hypertension after his investigations of customers. A radical innovation can therefore be hidden inside users' experiences, although sometimes it may not be easy to gather this information from them. Matthew R. Marvel and G. T. Lumpkin researched 145 technology entrepreneurs for whom prior knowledge of technology was found to be positively associated with radical innovations developed in university-affiliated incubators.

Eric Von Hippel coined the term *lead user method* in 1986, noting that lead users are an excellent source of ideas for novel products. Lead users of products and services are customers who discover needs for products or services months or years in advance of most market participants. Von Hippel's lead user method starts with identification of needs and trends, identification of lead users and interviews, and finally concept design. The methodology is based on the idea that breakthrough products may be developed by identifying leading trends in the marketplace associated with the product to be developed. Once the trend or broader problem to be solved has been identified, the developers seek out "lead users," people or organizations that are attempting to solve a particularly extreme or demanding version of the stated problem. In contrast to traditional market research techniques, which focus on collecting information from the users at the center of the target market, the lead user method collects information about both needs and solutions from the leading edges of the target market and from analogue markets, that is, those markets facing similar problems in a more extreme form.

Because lead users are aware of problems related to products or services, they may help entrepreneurs identify and exploit opportunities before those opportunities are recognized by typical users and rival companies. Lead users may be customers of a competitor or totally outside the industry. For example, the computer industry identified the new technology of the touch screen by reference to lead users associated with telecommunications companies, who were interested in integrating touch screens into their phones; banks were also lead users, since automated teller machines (ATMs) use touch screens. These users' needs eventually led to technologies that created product categories such as smart phones and notepads.

Economist and professor of technological innovation at the MIT Sloan School of Management, Eric Von Hippel is best known for his concept of user innovation. Von Hippel coined the phrase *lead user method* to refer to customers who discover the need for a product or service long before the average user. (Wikimedia/Jean-Baptiste Labrune)

Learning From Customers

To learn and understand the likes and dislikes of the customer, entrepreneurs often consider the results of surveys and questionnaires or conduct face-to-face interviews and focus groups. As customers are experts in using the product, insights can be gained via the Delphi method as well. However, while it is important to gather and analyze facts and figures, for new ventures it is even more important to interact directly with customers. They provide "living data" that are up to date and that reflect changes in the marketplace and customers' evolving needs. New venture entrepreneurs can make use of these data to fully understand and respond rapidly to their customers' expectations. When firms analyze the ideas of their customers, they can learn their opinions, experiences, and insights into the firm's products and improve the products or services to match those customers' needs. They can even learn about their mistakes by analyzing customers' views and apply those lessons to make their products more profitable.

While doing customer orientation, the firm must analyze the needs and wants of the customers in depth and serve them with the objective of achieving the highest customer satisfaction possible. Each and every customer group should be treated differently, because customer problems are different in each market segment, whether shoes for teenagers, scissors designed for left-handed users, shampoo for those with curly hair, "lite" drinks for people who are watching their weight, books for university students, perfume for elderly men, handbags for young women, tennis rackets for professional tennis players, or hair dye for those with white hair.

In order to find suitable target markets, new ventures must devise an entrepreneurial marketing strategy, which includes developing an appropriate marketing mix involving product, price, distribution, and promotion. According to Neetu Andotra, there is a relationship between customer orientation and these four marketing elements. In terms of product, customers are most concerned with its attractiveness, image and identity, and packaging. In terms of price, reasonable and fixed prices and infrequent changes in price are found to be important. For distribution, timely information on new and improved products is important. Finally, for promotion, availability of products with wholesalers, efficient and adequate customer services, convenience in locating products, and cooperative and friendly dealers are found to be most important to customers.

After a new venture is established and new products are sold to customers, it is important to build strong customer relations. Philip Kotler defines this as customer relationship management (CRM), the overall process of building and maintaining profitable customer relationships by delivering superior customer value and satisfaction. In new ventures, CRM should be applied as a customer-focused strategy in which the firm's goal is to satisfy customers by requiring the proper products and providing high-quality customer services.

Small and new firms can face particular challenges in this regard. Rosalind C. Paige mentions in her study of craft micro-retailers that a large number of small businesses in the retail sector have failed within five years of start-up. Their small market size makes it necessary for such new ventures to develop unique customer orientations in order to outperform competitors in similar market conditions.

New ventures can be successful in the market only if they innovate and fill a gap or a niche in the market.

For new ventures, identifying and adapting to unmet and unserved customer needs are more important than ever. New venture managers must be driven by imagination, must be capable of negotiating occasional chaos, and must always be ready to adapt rapidly to changes. Above all, this involves remaining fully aware of customers' changing needs. Being adaptive to changes is very important in the eyes of the customers, as customers prefer innovative products and services. The strategies of small and new businesses must always be committed to creating higher value for the consumer and improving entrepreneurial performance. Entrepreneurs engaging in new ventures to solve customer problems should always be learning from their customers' experiences.

Asli Tuncay-Celikel
Isik University and University of Sussex

See also Change Management: Corporate; Focus Groups; Innovation Management: Corporate; Learning; Target Markets

Further Readings

Andotra, Neetu. "Optimising Customer-Orientation in Small Business Through Marketing-Mix Feedback Results." *Journal of Services Research*, v.6/2 (2006).

Gartner, William B. "A Conceptual Framework for Describing the Phenomenon of New Venture Creation." *Academy of Management Review*, v.10/4 (1985).

Kotler, Philip. *Marketing Management*. Upper Saddle River, NJ: Prentice Hall, 1997.

Kuratko, Donald and Jeffrey S. Hornsby. *New Venture Management: The Entrepreneur's Roadmap*. Upper Saddle River, NJ: Pearson Prentice Hall, 2009.

Marvel, Matthew R. and G. T. Lumpkin. "Technology Entrepreneurs' Human Capital and Its Effect on Innovation Radicalness." *Entrepreneurship Theory and Practice*, v.31/6 (2007).

Morrish, Sussie C., Morgan P. Miles, and Jonathan H. Deacon. "Entrepreneurial Marketing: Acknowledging the Entrepreneur and Customer-Centric Interrelationship." *Journal of Strategic Marketing*, v.18/4 (2010).

Paige, Rosalind C. "Profiles of Successful Craft Micro-Retailers." *Journal of Developmental Entrepreneurship*, v.14/4 (2009).

Shane, Scott. "Prior Knowledge and the Discovery of Entrepreneurial Opportunities." *Organization Science*, v.11/4 (2000).

Vesper, Karl H. "New Venture Strategies." University of Illinois at Urbana-Champaign's Academy for Entrepreneurial Leadership Historical Research Reference in Entrepreneurship, 1990. http://ssrn.com/abstract=1496217 (Accessed December 2010).

Von Hippel, Eric. "Lead Users: A Source of Novel Product Concepts." *Management Science*, v.32/7 (1986).

DEBT

The availability of financial resources is central to an entrepreneur's decision to start a business and for the venture's ongoing performance. Barriers to appropriate levels of financial resources can have a negative and enduring impact on entrepreneurs' decisions. The "bank-based view" argues that banks play a positive role in allocating capital effectively, improving corporate governance, and enhancing investment efficiency.

Despite the importance of financial resources, not all entrepreneurs have access to appropriate levels of finances. The problem is vital for entrepreneurs in developing countries. Given the poor financial infrastructure of most developing countries, entrepreneurs have limited access to the type of credit offered by formal institutions in developed countries. Traditional banks in developing countries are rarely willing to lend to entrepreneurs without collateral, given that "poor entrepreneurs" have limited access to tangible assets and personal wealth. This lack of collateral can make it difficult for entrepreneurs to obtain financing from formal institutions.

The location of entrepreneurs also influences the debt structure. Entrepreneurs in developed countries have options for financing their businesses that are different from and better than those of their counterparts in developing countries. Venture capitalists are an alternative source for entrepreneurs in developed countries. Also, contracts between the entrepreneur and a venture capitalist are enforceable through strong property rights laws in developed countries. In developing countries, the often poor enforcement of law makes this an unfeasible option for new entrepreneurs. The Grameen Bank, however, has been successful in serving the niche market of entrepreneurs with limited access to credit. In 2010, there were approximately 130–190 million borrowers worldwide, and the amount of loans from microfinance institutions (MFIs) totaled more than $43 billion.

Women in developing countries face additional barriers to financing over and above those of their male counterparts. Researchers have found that, in developed countries, women have less in personal savings than men since they work less than men. Women in developing countries are in a worse condition, however, when it comes to gaining access to credit. They have limited access to the workplace and lower wage rates. Additionally, they have less education, which limits their ability to attain well-paying jobs. Cultural norms can also limit their ability to accumulate tangible assets. This combination of limited assets and lack of personal savings eliminates access to credit from formal lending institutions.

The debt structure plays a different role for entrepreneurs at different stages of entrepreneurship. Established firms have different debt structures from those of newly established businesses. The majority of new entrepreneurs in developed as well as developing nations rely on the financial support from family members. In developed nations, however, entrepreneurs are able to gain access to credit from formal institutions as their new ventures become established. Given the importance of financial resources for new entrepreneurs, policy makers should adopt policies that allow entrepreneurs to have greater access to debt-related financing.

Farzana Chowdhury
Indiana University

See also Bankruptcy; Barriers to Entry; Barter; Capitalism; Cash Flow; Credit; Debt-Based Financing; Equity- and Debt-Based Financing; Microfinance

Further Readings

Allen, F. and D. Gale. *Comparing Financial Systems.* Cambridge, MA: MIT Press, 2000.

Allen, F. and D. Gale. "Diversity of Opinion and Financing of New Technologies." *Journal of Financial Intermediation,* v.8 (1999).

Armendariz, B. and J. Morduch. *The Economics of Microfinance.* Cambridge, MA: MIT Press, 2005.

Bencivenga, Valerie R. and Bruce Smith. "Financial Intermediation and Endogenous Growth." *Review of Economics Studies,* v.58 (1991).

Diamond, D. "Financial Intermediation and Delegated Monitoring." *Review of Economic Studies,* v.51 (1984).

Ramakrishnan, R. T. S. and A. V. Thakor. "Information Reliability and a Theory of Financial Intermediation." *Review of Financial Studies,* v.51 (1984).

DEBT-BASED FINANCING

After entrepreneurs have exhausted their own funds to start their venture, debt is the most widely used form of external financing by new firms. As such, debt is an important source of external financing for funding working capital and possibly growth in new firms. There are multiple theories on how firms will use debt to finance their operations, along with multiple sources available to new firms. Banks are the largest source of debt for new firms, with other debt sources also available. Creditors utilize various means to identify the creditworthiness of new firms, and new firms use various methods to try to signal to creditors that they are worthy. However, there is still a possibility that creditors ration credit to viable new ventures. As a result, viable new firms can face credit constraints that affect their survival and growth.

The two primary options for external financing are debt and equity, which compose a firm's capital structure. A debt claim gives a creditor the right to a set of cash flows, usually interest and principal payments. Debt claims differ from equity claims in that equity claims give an investor the right to residual cash flows that remain after the firm has met all other promised expenses.

There are multiple theories on how firms will craft their usage of debt and equity to finance their operations. One theory suggests that firms will try to balance their tax shields with the probability of bankruptcy and agency costs (static trade-off theory). Another theory says that firms have an order of preference in using internal equity, debt, and external equity (pecking order theory). A third theory suggests that a firm will go through a life cycle based on its growth, and its financing options change to support the stage of growth the firm is in (finance growth cycle theory). Finally, another theory suggests that entrepreneurs start their firms to be autonomous. Thus, entrepreneurs make financing decisions by balancing the survival and growth with their goal to be in control as they learn more about their entrepreneurial abilities (financial theory of entrepreneurial types). In all four of these theories, debt plays a prominent role.

Types of Debt

The most common forms of debt are term loans, lines of credit (sometimes called overdrafts), trade credit, and occasionally credit cards.

A term loan is a loan for a fixed amount and fixed duration with a regular payment schedule that is decided at the outset of the contract. The interest rate charge may be fixed or variable. If the rate is variable, it is usually based on the prevailing base or prime rate. Term loans are usually used to finance fixed and long-term assets as opposed to working capital or short-term assets.

A line of credit is a facility offered by banks that allow firms to borrow up to a maximum amount. Interest is calculated on a daily basis on the drawn-down amount with a minimum payment amount due on a regular basis (normally on a monthly basis). The bank can demand the outstanding balance be paid at any given time; however, it rarely can enforce this right except in special situations. Robert Cressy found that one third of new firms used lines of credit in 1988 with one half of them using lines of credit within three years of starting.

Trade credit is a means of borrowing from suppliers. New firms are able to purchase products and services from suppliers (who are usually not as credit constrained as new firms possibly are) and pay the suppliers at a later date, usually at a higher price for the product, or price plus interest. Allen Berger and Gregory Udell have found that trade credit constituted 16 percent of total debt in firms in 1992 and that the percentage did not change with firm age. Some studies have found trade credit to be used as a substitute for term loans and lines of credit, whereas other studies have shown a strong positive relationship between trade credit, term loans, and lines of credit.

Credit card usage has increased as a means to finance new ventures, because of the ease of obtaining credit cards. Credit card debt is unsecured debt but provides much lower amounts of debt and usually has higher interest rate costs than term loans. Some new ventures counter these negative traits of credit card debt by obtaining multiple credit cards and juggling the outstanding balances between the credit card accounts. It is unknown if credit card debt helps new ventures survive or grow.

Sources of Debt

Debt is provided by various sources, both formal and informal, which have different motivations. Banks, financial institutions (such as financing companies, thrift institutions, and insurance companies), credit card companies, governments, and other businesses (such as suppliers and strategic partners) are formal sources of debt. Family and friends are informal sources of debt (who can provide "love money"). Formal sources are more stringent with their terms, and their primary source of income tends to be the money they earn from the interest on the loan they provide borrowers. Informal sources of debt are usually trying to help entrepreneurs start their firms and might be more lenient with regard to terms and repayment schedules; their primary income comes from a source that does not depend on the interest they are possibly earning on the loan. Thus, they might let a payment or two lapse for a short period of time before asking for payment.

Banks are usually the first source that new firms approach, as entrepreneurs are familiar with banks from personal experience and banks have a large number of retail outlets that are easy to access physically. With the large number of retail outlets, there is a higher probability that the entrepreneur will know a banker at one of the retail branches who will be willing to sponsor that entrepreneur's bid for loan funds to start his or her venture; this is known as relationship-based lending. If the entrepreneur does not have a strong relationship with a bank or banker, the loan application approval is based strictly on transaction-based reasoning, which includes financial statement lending, credit scoring, and asset-based lending.

Governments are another source of debt, but usually not through direct loans. Rather, governments offer other support in the form of guarantees to banks that can provide term loans to new firms. In the United States, the guarantees that the Small Business Administration (SBA) provides banks allows banks to make the future cash flows of the new firm be a higher priority in determining which firms receive loans (as opposed to other factors, such as collateral from the entrepreneur). In addition, with the backing of the SBA, small business investment companies (SBICs) provide long-term loans as well as equity to firms, especially during the firms' growth stages.

It has been argued that new firms are credit constrained and are not able to borrow sufficiently in financial markets. This results in credit rationing, which occurs either when a firm with a net-positive present value receives a portion of what it needs (Type I credit rationing) or when that firm does not receive any of the funds required (Type II credit rationing, also called redlining). Credit rationing occurs as a result of information asymmetry between creditors and borrowers. Information asymmetry plays a greater role with new firms, because new firms lack a track record. Creditors are not able to raise interest rates to cover the increased risk because of adverse selection effects (good borrowers will drop out of the borrowing pool first) and competition from other creditors. The argument against the existence of credit rationing is that most firms do not wish to grow and thus are not asking for external financing.

There are various means to try to decrease the information asymmetry issue, including collateral, human capital, personal guarantees, and relationships. Collateral is used to reduce agency costs, debt expense, and the cost of debt. Collateral reduces agency cost by preventing the borrower from substituting the collateral that is pledged to invest in a riskier project. Collateral reduces debt expense by entitling the creditor to the collateralized asset in the event of default. Finally, collateral reduces the cost of debt by mitigating the dilution that occurs when additional debt is issued with higher priority. However, new firms do not have a large amount of collateral unless the entrepreneur is well endowed before starting the venture. In addition, any assets the new firm might have are mainly intangible. Human capital is an important determinant of whether a new firm will receive money from a bank and, if so, how much. Human capital can help ease the financial constraint felt by new firms, as entrepreneurs with higher education and more work experience encounter fewer barriers in obtaining debt. Personal guarantees tend to be used often with debt for new firms. The new firms do not have the assets on their balance sheets to provide collateral. Banks therefore require personal guarantees from the owners of the firm to mitigate their risk exposure. Relationships can also help new firms overcome information asymmetry issues. New firms do not have a track record and do not have long relationships with banks. However, the entrepreneur starting the firm may have relationships in the community. As a result, he or she may have a relationship with a bank through personal financing activities. Although collateral, human capital, personal guarantees, and relationships play a role in determining the willingness of a creditor to lend to a new firm, ultimately it is the firm's ability to generate the cash flow necessary to service the debt that is the creditor's primary criterion. However, many creditors do not have the ability to project the future cash flow of a new firm.

Because most entrepreneurs do not have the aspiration to grow their firms it is unlikely they will borrow from formal creditors except for the purpose of managing cash flow from daily operations (working capital). They use lines of credit for this purpose. Few new firms use term loans to finance the purchase of fixed assets (such as land, equipment, and machinery). Short-term debt is more important than long-term debt to new firms, and to small firms in general; by contrast, for large firms, long-term debt is more important and represents a constant percentage of their total debt.

New firms decrease their reliance on debt as they age, depending on their growth intentions.

New firms that stay small as they age will decrease their overall borrowing over time as they pay back loans from friends and family. Mitchell Petersen and Raghuram Rajan found that young firms use debt more than older firms. The amount borrowed from banks initially increases with age, supporting relationship banking, before decreasing and becoming less important. New firms that grow will increase their reliance on borrowing, suggesting that they use debt to finance their growth. However, growth firms also increase their reliance on external financing as a whole as they also increase their use of equity financing as they grow.

Some would argue that growth firms do not want to use debt because they do not want to increase regular interest costs associated with debt and they do not want to be bound by the legal downside imposed by debt claims, which could force them into bankruptcy involuntarily. Obtaining a bank loan too early in a firm's life could put a burden on the firm's cash flow. The counterargument is that entrepreneurs do not want to dilute ownership that is associated with equity financing and there is a fixed upside with debt—thus they do not have to share success with outside investors. This has been found to be especially the case with overly optimistic entrepreneurs. In addition, entrepreneurs do not want to share control of the firm, as many times they started the firm in order to be their own boss.

The role that debt plays in the survival of new firms is important, with capital structure being a factor that contributes significantly to whether firms survive within their first two or three years. Thereafter, capital structure, including debt, becomes less of a factor in survival of the firm.

John M. Mueller
University of Louisville

See also Bankruptcy; Business Angels; Credit; Debt; Equity- and Debt-Based Financing; Initial Public Offering; Venture Capital

Further Readings

Astebro, T. and I. Bernhardt. "Start-Up Financing, Owner Characteristics, and Survival." *Journal of Economics and Business*, v.55/4 (2003).

Berger, A. N. and G. F. Udell. "The Economics of Small Business Finance: The Roles of Private Equity and Debt Markets in the Financial Growth Cycle." *Journal of Banking and Finance*, v.22/6–8 (1998).

Berger, A. N. and G. F. Udell. "A More Complete Conceptual Framework for SME Finance." *Journal of Banking and Finance*, v.30/11 (2006).

Cassar, G. "The Financing of Business Start-Ups." *Journal of Business Venturing*, v.19/2 (2004).

Cressy, R. C. "Business Borrowing and Control: A Theory of Entrepreneurial Types." *Small Business Economics*, v.7/4 (1995).

Huyghebaert, N., L. Van De Gucht, and C. Van Hulle. "The Choice Between Bank Debt and Trade Credit in Business Start-Ups." *Small Business Economics*, v.29/4 (2007).

Parker, S. C. and C. M. Van Praag. "Schooling, Capital Constraints and Entrepreneurial Performance: The Endogenous Triangle." *Journal of Business and Economic Statistics*, v.24 (2006).

Petersen, M. A. and R. G. Rajan. "The Benefits of Lending Relationships: Evidence From Small Business Data." *Journal of Finance*, v.49/1 (1994).

Robb, A. M. et al. *An Overview of the Kauffman Firm Survey: Results From the 2004–2008 Data.* Kauffman Foundation, 2010. http://www.kauffman.org/uploadedFiles/kfs_2010_report.pdf (Accessed February 2011).

DISCOVERY AND EXPLOITATION

Entrepreneurship is concerned with the discovery and exploitation of opportunities for economic value creation. The opportunity can be in the form of new goods, services, raw materials, business models, or different organizing methods that can be exploited for profit. The term *discovery* implies the awareness or realization of potential opportunities and is based on two primary modes: search and recognition. *Exploitation* implies that the entrepreneur realizes a means-end relationship to utilize the discovered opportunity for profit. An embedded causal relationship exists between discovery and exploitation.

Entrepreneurial opportunities and their discovery are often distinguished from opportunities in general, since entrepreneurial opportunities are typically restricted to novel and/or new approaches to relationships and business models. Hence the refinement of existing models, improvements in processes to increase efficiency, and the like do not fall under the purview of entrepreneurial opportunities. An entrepreneurial opportunity, when discovered and exploited, typically results in a new means, ends, or means-end relationship.

Scott Shane and S. Venkataraman suggest that the discovery of entrepreneurial opportunities materializes as a result of (1) the existence of prior information regarding the opportunity or similar opportunities, and (2) individuals or teams that possess the necessary cognitive properties to evaluate the opportunity. Prior information, as referred to above, includes experience of the individual or the firm, the stock of knowledge acquired by the firm through market interactions, and research and developmental expenses incurred in the past. The discovery of an opportunity can also be due to a deliberate search for an opportunity. That opportunities exist and can be openly discovered implies that entrepreneurs know *ex ante* what they are seeking. The existing capabilities of a firm enable the discovery of new entrepreneurial opportunities and the exploitation of these discoveries in novel ways. In addition, the idiosyncratic information and experience allow certain individuals or firms to evaluate and exploit information more fully and better determine if and how to exploit the opportunity. Essentially, these opportunities enable the firm to create the means, ends, or both in the process of exploitation.

Adequate cognitive capabilities enable the entrepreneur or firm to assess the potential value to be created through an opportunity and/or the opportunity's (un)attractiveness. It is this combination of prior information and the cognitive capabilities of the entrepreneur that enables the evaluation and exploitation of these opportunities. This prior knowledge enables the entrepreneur to make sense of the patterns that emerge in the external environment and assimilate the new information. Jointly, the processes of discovery, evaluation, and exploitation allow the creation of new products and services.

Discovery is realized in multiple ways. The various types of discovery include the identification of valuable products and services, new markets (geographic or demographic), new ways of organizing and/or structures, new methods of production, and new raw materials. In addition, while theoretically achievable at the individual level, the process of opportunity discovery normally stems from the mutual contribution of various actors. Thus, the discovery process is a function of numerous resources (tangible and intangible) that are effectively identified and combined, resulting in the recognition of market opportunity.

Exploitation of these opportunities can take the form of creation of a new firm or the sale of the opportunity to existing firms. It should be noted that the term *exploitation* carries a different meaning within the search literature. Generally speaking, the search literature considers exploitation to be the refinement or enhancement of existing products or processes to increase efficiency or improve quality. As used here, however, exploitation implies the creation of new means-end relationships for profit. Exploitation involves new entries and is carried out through *de novo* ventures. Exploitation is achieved through a realized outcome of the process of discovery. Thus, exploitation, by definition, is action as a result of opportunity discovery.

The terms discovery and exploitation have also been used in the context of existing firms and their ongoing search for new and novel products and services. *Entrepreneurial orientation* refers to the processes carried out in a firm that lead to new entry. Discovery and exploitation both play a vital role in the ability of a firm to recognize and capture opportunity. Exploitation requires that the entrepreneur commit significant time and resources, collect information, perform market research, and deal with significant uncertainty, ambiguity, and market variability. Danny Miller initially viewed the processes leading to new entry or exploitation of these opportunities (entrepreneurial orientation) as a function of three main activities carried out within a firm: innovation, proactiveness, and risk taking. In his view, it is through the collective presence of all of these behaviors that a firm acts in an entrepreneurial fashion, resulting in market entry. The proactiveness element has direct ties to the discovery and exploitation of opportunity. By definition, proactiveness refers to the ability to identify opportunities in a market setting and then actively pursue these market opportunities. Thus, it is both a recognition process and an action. This, in essence, is the combination of discovery and the initial stage of exploitation and is essential to the pursuit of new market entry for existing firms. This proactive disposition is key in linking discovery to action (exploitation). In this way, exploitation is carried out through an entrepreneurial action or new market entry. The acceptance of risk allows the firm to act on identified opportunities. Thus, opportunity recognition without the willingness to accept risk will fail to result in exploitation (new entry).

Netflix and Amazon are excellent examples of entrepreneurial discovery and exploitation. Reed Hastings, the founder of Netflix, was unhappy with late fees being charged for video rentals; he believed this was a common feeling among consumers in this market and viewed this discontent of the customer as an opportunity to be exploited. Through this opportunity recognition process, the innovation of a new business model, and the willingness to accept the financial and market risks associated with entry into this already competitive market, Hastings was able to exploit a market deficiency. In addition, in this case the discovery process came as a result of market-specific knowledge that was accrued through past experience. Hastings exploited this discovered opportunity through his creation of a rental-by-mail business model that eliminated late fees for the consumer and provided structural flexibility for the firm itself. This venture has morphed into a very successful rental and streaming service.

Similarly, Amazon founder Jeff Bezos started an online book store during the mid-1990s when he saw the potential for the growth of the Internet. He recognized the futility of brick-and-mortar stores and foresaw a future where customers would be comfortable buying over the Internet. The Website also offered reviews from customers and allowed customers to research books before purchasing them. Amazon has since grown to be a portal for the sale of goods from multiple providers.

Dinesh N. Iyer
Justin L. Davis
Ohio University

See also Cognition in Experts and Novices; Creativity and Opportunities; Opportunity Development; Opportunity Identification and Structural Alignment; Opportunity Recognition; Search-Based Discovery

Further Readings

Companys, Yosem E. and Jeffery S. McMullen. "Strategic Entrepreneurs at Work: The Nature, Discovery, and Exploitation of Entrepreneurial Opportunities." *Small Business Economics*, v.28 (2007).

Miller, D. and J.-M. Toulouse. "Chief Executive Personality and Corporate Strategy and Structure in Small Firms." *Management Science*, 32/11 (1986).

Shane, Scott. "Prior Knowledge and the Discovery of Entrepreneurial Opportunities." *Organization Science*, v.11/4 (2000).

Shane, Scott and S. Venkataraman. "The Promise of Entrepreneurship as a Field of Research." *Academy of Management Review*, v.25/1 (2000).

DISTRIBUTION

The term *distribution* refers to the movement of products or services from the supplier of raw goods to the plant (producer or manufacturer) to end users (customers). Distribution exists in various forms: from supplier to factory, from producer to wholesaler, from wholesaler to retailer, from retailer to the end user, and (increasingly) directly from producer to the end user. The whole process of distribution, through all the actors involved, is called the distribution channel. In this respect, distribution can also be defined as the movement of products and services through the distribution channel to the final consumers from the original producer or supplier. The term *channel* refers to buying, selling, packaging, transporting, storing, and all other value-added activities.

Distribution in small and new ventures is similar to distribution in large and established companies, but there are some key differences due to the markets served and timing of delivery. In new ventures, products and services are served to niche markets, so the distribution channel will be simpler and leaner and will offer a higher speed of delivery than that offered by established organizations. However, establishment of the distribution channel as a process will be more difficult than it is for established companies, because new ventures have to build their own distribution actors and strategies (the whole channel).

At the beginning of the distribution channel is distribution from the supplier to the manufacturer. Basically, the supplier sells its materials or services to the producer. If the venture is producing a product, then in the plant of the manufacturer, the raw materials or the semifinished products coming from the supplier are manufactured or assembled as a finished product. If the venture is selling a service, other service suppliers may sell their services to the venture. For example, Turkish Airlines, one of the world's oldest and most popular airline companies (established in 1933), works with several suppliers of catering and cleaning. Catering firms supply food and beverages that are served during the flights, and cleaning firms are responsible for

Distribution takes place when products or services from a supplier of raw materials ships goods to a factory or producer, which continue down distribution channels to wholesalers, to retailers, and then to customers, or may move directly from a producer to an end user. (Photos.com)

cleaning and tidying the airplanes' cabins before each new flight.

An example of an airline with a relatively simple distribution channel is EasyJet, a venture airline company that aims to satisfy its customers with low-cost flights to the world's favorite destinations. In contrast to Turkish Airlines, all of EasyJet's services—including light snacks, beverages, speedy boarding, and luggage transport—cost the customer extra fees. If customers want these services, they pay for them. For example, EasyJet has a first-come, first-served seating policy, but customers can buy speedy boarding tickets to enable them to choose their seats ahead of other passengers. EasyJet was established to serve a niche market of travelers who want to explore different countries for a few days with minimal luggage or simply a backpack, and its planes typically depart from relatively small airports to decrease the time spent negotiating the systems of larger airports. In the EasyJet example, the distribution channel is leaner and simpler; there are no suppliers of huge loads of food, beverages, or luggage handlers, because passengers who use the service are interested in cost savings and therefore tend not to buy these services.

In the second phase of the distribution channel, the producer sells the finished goods or services to wholesalers. Wholesalers deliver to retailers, and retailers sell to end users (customers). Sometimes producers directly sell to end users without the intermediary agency of wholesalers and retailers. For example, airline companies can sell their services directly to end users via their offices or Website, or indirectly through other parties, such as travel agents, tour operators, and those parties' online Websites. Therefore, distribution may occur both indirectly and directly from the producer to the end user.

Most new venture companies look for channels of distribution that are both direct and indirect. Patricia Phillips McDougall and her colleagues tested a sample of 123 independent new ventures and found that successful new ventures in high-growth industries become developers of new channels of distribution behavior. For example, Apple uses both direct and indirect distribution strategies. Apple computers are sold by Apple itself via both brick-and-mortar and online Apple stores and via wholesalers and retailers. Wholesalers of Apple sell the computers to companies, whereas retailers sell them to individual customers in computer stores and online computer store Websites.

Michael Porter has indicated that distribution is one of the primary means whereby companies create value and competitive advantage. He developed the concept of the "value chain" or "value network," which works as a system of relationships to create value between suppliers and customers. In his value chain, suppliers ("inbound logistics"), production ("operations"), and collecting, storing, and distributing products and services ("outbound logistics") are three of firms' most important activities in value creation and competitive advantage. Michael Song and his colleagues conducted an empirical study that examined 11,259 new technology-based ventures in the United States over a period of five years and found that 36 percent survived after four years and 22 percent survived after five years. To explain the successes and failures of these ventures, the researchers reviewed 31 other key studies of technology ventures and found that value-chain management (defined as cooperation with suppliers, distribution, agents, and customers) was one of the most significant factors in the firms' success.

John Bessant and Joe Tidd have noted that small and newly established firms can be competent in extending or adapting existing products and services and applying existing products or services in newly created market segments or at different price points. In the new venture management literature, it is also emphasized that small firms have less bureaucracy and are able to serve smaller market niches with specialization, as opposed to large firms, which serve mass markets with high-volume global sales, high spending, and greater risks. Therefore, for small and new businesses, distribution will be made to niche market retailers or wholesalers as well as specialized suppliers.

In the 21st century, distribution can be customized to customers' needs in terms of the product's or service's packaging, its delivery schedule, and the delivery location, but the actual product/ service might be standard, without customization. For example, some new ventures have specialized in one-to-one distribution, which is a niche market. Using the online supplier, for instance, an Amazon customer can buy and send a book to a friend within a few minutes. The friend will receive an individually wrapped gift with a personalized message, and each step will be handled online. The product, a book, is not new, but the service, convenience combined with personalized and quick delivery, is. The establishment of the distribution channel is therefore one of the most important steps to success in new and small ventures.

Asli Tuncay-Celikel
Isik University and University of Sussex

See also Customer Orientation; Retailing; Selling Products and Services; Wholesale Markets

Further Readings

Bessant, John and Joe Tidd. *Innovation and Entrepreneurship*, 2nd ed. Hoboken, NJ: John Wiley and Sons, 2011.

McDougall, Patricia Phillips et al. "The Effects of Industry Growth and Strategic Breadth on New Venture Performance and Strategy Content." *Strategic Management Journal*, v.15/7 (1994).

Porter, Michael. *Competitive Advantage: Creating and Sustaining Superior Performance*. New York: Simon and Schuster, 2004.

Song, Michael et al. "Success Factors in New Ventures: A Meta Analysis." *Journal of Product Innovation Management*, v.25 (2008).

E-Commerce

E-commerce is the buying and selling of products through electronic services, especially over the Internet. Originally, "electronic commerce" was used to refer simply to the electronic facilitation of funds transfer, such as through an electronic funds transfer, which was introduced in the 1970s. Various methods and protocols at the time allowed businesses to send invoices, purchase orders, and similar documentation electronically. Dedicated electronic systems were soon introduced for airline and hotel reservations, car financing (systems used at dealerships), and business-to-business shopping and ordering.

The increased popularity of credit cards in the 1980s and the increased availability of the Internet in the 1990s—especially following the introduction of Web browsers—led to e-commerce as we know it today, which nearly always refers to shopping and purchasing conducted through the Internet. Pizza Hut offered online ordering of pizza through its Website as early as 1994, the same year Netscape released its first Web browser. That same year, SSL encryption was introduced to make transactions secure.

Secure transactions are key to e-commerce and continue to be of concern. Although most theft of credit card numbers still occurs in person, even in the 21st century—either through physical theft of the credit card or when the numbers are collected by an unscrupulous employee—there is genuine cause for concern over the transmission of credit card numbers, banking information, and other pertinent information over the Internet, particularly as wireless Internet usage in public places becomes more common and the average consumer may not know how to safeguard against information theft on his own initiative. The benefit of cash has always been that it is anonymous; no one can use cash to identify the payer and use that person's credit by assuming that person's identity. The opposite is true for those who pay using critical private information, which occurs when one writes a check, transfers funds electronically, or uses a credit card.

SSL encryption stands for secure sockets layer, and it and its successor, transport layer security (TLS), are used to encrypt information as it passes through the Internet—not only in Web browsing but also in e-mail, instant messaging, and voice-over intellectual property (IP). As in other cryptographic protocols, a handshake procedure between the client software and the server establishes the server's credentials through a digital certificate containing its name, the trusted certificate authority issuing the certificate, and the server's public encryption key; the credentials are validated with the certificate authority, and a random number is generated in order to produce session keys used for the encrypted session. This encryption helps protect against eavesdropping while ensuring that the encrypted information is going to the server it is actually supposed to go to. Users have proven to be remarkably lax in their personal online security—even those who are well informed about risks often make mistakes such as using the same password on all sites, using

E-commerce purchasers are surprisingly lax with their personal online security, even when they are informed of the risks of practices like using one password for multiple Websites, opening and forwarding e-mails from unknown addressees, and neglecting to install firewalls or securing their wireless connections. (Photos.com)

impractical passwords, maintaining public social networking profiles that reveal password hint answers, opening e-mail attachments from unknown senders, and failing to use firewalls and to secure their wireless routers. The burden of ensuring a minimum level of security has fallen to the software; without it, privacy breaches would be more common, and the public faith in e-commerce would diminish.

Amazon.com launched in 1995, as did eBay and a flurry of online stores. Many failed in the dot-com bust around 1999–2001, but Amazon and eBay have together transformed the world of commerce. By 1998, it was even possible to buy stamps online, which could be downloaded and printed out, and in 2010, online retail sales in the United States totaled about $173 billion.

Amazon

Amazon launched as an online bookstore, but today virtually anything can be purchased there, either through Amazon itself or through one of the Amazon Marketplace vendors, which range from full-fledged businesses (even vendors with their own online stores, such as igourmet.com, which maintains Amazon Marketplace accounts so that its offerings will turn up in Amazon searches). Amazon's own offerings include books, music, movies, software, video games and consoles, consumer electronics, kitchen and household appliances, toys, tools, gourmet food, jewelry and watches, health and personal care items, clothes, scientific supplies, and groceries. Still, the store has not abandoned its roots: Its Kindle, an electronic book reader, was the best-selling Christmas gift of 2010.

Selection has always been Amazon's strength. Amazon can offer many more books than a brick-and-mortar bookstore can, and finding a specific book does not require hunting through aisles or depend on the correct categorization and shelving of books. Whereas many companies died quickly when the dot-com bubble burst, Amazon's business plan did not anticipate turning a profit for its first four or five years (in fact, it took seven years from its incorporation and six years from the opening of its virtual doors to the public). Whereas shareholders complained about this slow growth after Amazon went public and initial profits were extremely modest, when they finally did appear, they proved substantial, and the company has lasted more than a decade longer than its dot-com littermates. It has also been persistent in acquiring other dot-com companies, including music retailer CD Now, the Internet Movie Database, the Mobipocket e-book software company, the print-on-demand BookSurge company, audiobook vendor Audible.com, AbeBooks, the online shoe store Zappos, and cult online vendor Woot.com.

Through its partnerships, Amazon operates the retail Websites for Target, Timex, Marks and Spencer, Lacoste, and Sears Canada, and the company has a growing number of enterprise clients for which it provides a multichannel platform. Profits have continued to grow, and Amazon's stock entered the S&P 100 index in 2008. In 2010, its market capitalization was higher than Barnes and Noble, Best Buy, Target, Costco, and Home Depot. It operates warehouses and fulfillment centers throughout the United States, as well as in Canada, the United Kingdom, France, Germany, China, and Japan.

One of Amazon's innovations has been Amazon Prime, an extension of the typical customer loyalty program. For an annual fee—$79 a year in

2011—customers get free two-day shipping for any eligible product (which includes nearly every product sold by Amazon itself, but not its partners or Amazon Marketplace) and overnight shipping for $3.99 per item. Although this program offers a significant savings in shipping, Amazon already offers free "super saver" shipping for orders over $25, so what Amazon Prime helps encourage is impulse shopping. Preordered items like books, DVDs, and CDs can be shipped before their street dates in order to arrive on the day of release. Customers can take advantage of sales to order cheap books, movies, and albums without searching for other items to bring their orders up to $25, and receive their items quickly—and will most likely order more items overall as a result of the added convenience they have paid for. A late 2010 *Wall Street Journal* article reported that Amazon had a plan to add free streaming movies to the Amazon Prime membership, putting it in competition with Netflix's streaming-only membership plan. Amazon's plans also included an expansion of its grocery section, originally limited to shelf-stable items (often by the case), to include grocery delivery of fresh, frozen, and perishable items within specific metropolitan areas.

One of the reasons for Amazon's popularity is the increasing perception by customers that anything available for purchase may be purchased there; it has long since graduated from its identity as a bookstore. In reality, it is much like a mall or enormous department store, allowing customers to buy from a vast array of different businesses with a single checkout transaction regardless of the number of businesses products are purchased from. It accomplishes this not only through its partnerships with specific vendors—including a large number of online stores—but also through Amazon Marketplace and third-party sellers. Amazon collects a fee but operates all of the e-commerce infrastructure and transactions. In addition, third-party sellers benefit from being listed in such a well-trod shopping space. Small businesses can easily jump onto the e-commerce bandwagon by creating a relationship with Amazon.

PayPal

The e-commerce site PayPal originated with the merger between Confinity, a Palm Pilot payment and cryptography company, and X.com, an Internet financial services company. PayPal enabled online payments through bank account transfers or credit card payments from registered users, which allowed anyone to pay anyone else on the Internet without needing to have a merchant account to process credit cards and without needing to worry about sending cash through the mail or having a check bounce. PayPal thus had a number of uses—musicians running their own Web pages could sell CDs and merchandise using it, personal debts could be repaid with it, start-up Internet businesses could use it, and so on—that enabled it to be much more successful than the eBay-only Billpoint, its most prominent competitor. In 2002, eBay acquired PayPal for $1.5 billion. Originally, eBay auctions could be paid for through a variety of means. Since its acquisition of PayPal, eBay has required that PayPal be offered as a payment option on all of its listings in the United States, and PayPal has become the standard method.

PayPal can be exceptionally useful for small ventures selling their products or services online, because customers need not give their financial information to the vendor, which may make them more confident in transacting business online. Merchant accounts, which are necessary if more than $500 is to be transferred out of the PayPal account in a given month (whether by check payment to the venture or by bank transfer), cost an additional fee but are generally cheaper than the cost of processing credit cards and reduce the business's risk exposure.

Woot

A specialized Internet retailer that is a perfect role model for a small e-commerce business, Dallas-based Woot opened in 2004 and has attracted a devoted cult following. Woot's model is simple: With special exceptions, every day from midnight until midnight the site sells one item. The item is offered at what is often a significant discount, and if it sells out, nothing else is sold until the following day. Often the items being sold are computer or electronics items, and the sales model means that defective items cannot be returned (a refund is given instead) and that customer service cannot be provided for any products. Shipping costs a flat $5.00.

The aforementioned special exception is a Woot-Off, in which every time a product sells out, it is replaced within minutes by a new product, which continues for one to four days. Woot-Offs are never announced ahead of time, and Woot never announces which product it will be selling in the future, so the community that follows Woot refreshes the site often (or uses software to monitor it), waiting for the next deal, often even purchasing the current deal simply to advance the Woot-Off to the next item. Most Woot-Offs at some point include among their items the "bag of crap" (BOC), an assortment of undisclosed items for a small flat fee. Often the BOC items are of little to no value and include novelty items and accessories such as key-chain fobs, but on rare occasions a BOC includes a disproportionately expensive item such as a laptop computer or a high-definition television. For this reason, when a bag of crap goes up for sale, it sells out so quickly that the site inevitably becomes overloaded—and for that reason, in turn, buying a bag of crap (even if it contains nothing worthwhile) has become a necessary rite for all true members of the Woot community.

Woot's niche is undoubtedly not yet fully filled; there is ample room for similar businesses, particularly catering to specific types of customers.

Retail Services

A number of retail services are offered through e-commerce companies. Pizza Hut enabled online ordering early on; many other restaurants now do the same, and in large cities an intermediary third party may offer a site that takes orders for food delivery and passes them on to the restaurant, which relieves restaurants from having to operate their own Websites. This allows for more participation by mom-and-pop restaurants that lack the infrastructure and labor resources to maintain an online presence.

In addition to food ordering—including grocery orders in large cities—there are many online flower delivery businesses, online travel agencies, online ticket vendors for sports and other events, and video rental outlets such as Blockbuster and Netflix. Netflix, an online DVD rental service, has been so successful that it has threatened the viability of brick-and-mortar DVD rental outlets.

Advantages

The advantages of e-commerce are, for some businesses, that the physical site is no longer important. Depending on the nature of the business, it may be operated in an office park, in a garage, or in the homes of a telecommuter while the inventory sits in a rented warehouse. For other businesses, e-commerce offers the chance to expand the business

(particularly if online ordering and shipping are available) far beyond the local customer base or better serve customers (as with online delivery of local goods).

Overhead costs can be significantly lowered when a physical storefront is not necessary, and fewer on-site employees are needed. Furthermore, e-commerce is ideal for niche businesses that cannot expect to drum up enough business locally or that are part-time endeavors for the owner.

Bill Kte'pi
Independent Scholar

See also Advertising; Agility and Rapid Response; Distribution; Entrepreneurs in Technology; Initial Public Offering

Further Readings

Childers, J., Jr. and E. Offstein. "Building Entrepreneurial E-Commerce Competitive Advantage: A Blending of Theory and Practice." *Advances in Competitiveness Research*, v.15/1–2 (2007).
Godin, Seth. *Tribes*. New York: Portfolio, 2008.
Gundry, L. K. and J. R. Kickul. "Leveraging the E in Entrepreneurship: Test of an Integrative Model of E-Commerce New Venture Growth." *International Journal of Technology Management*, v.33/4 (2006).
Hamilton, R. H. "E-Commerce New Venture Performance: How Funding Impacts Culture." *Internet Research*, v.11/4 (2001).
Longenecker, Justin G., J. William Petty, Leslie E. Palich, and Carlos W. Moore. *Small Business Management*. Stamford, CT: South-Western College, 2008.
Mueller, R. E. "E-Commerce and Agricultural Commodity Markets: E-Commerce and Entrepreneurship in Agricultural Markets." *American Journal of Agricultural Economics*, v.83/5 (2001).
Paper, D., E. Pedersen, and K. Mulbery. "An E-Commerce Process Model: Perspectives From E-Commerce Entrepreneurs." *Journal of Electronic Commerce in Organizations*, v.1/3 (2003).
Yrle, A. C. and S. J. Hartman. "E-Business: An Outsourcing Solution for Small Businesses." *International Journal of Management and Enterprise Development*, v.1/3 (2004).

EMOTIONS

One of the most salient characteristics of human life is emotion. Emotions color the way in which we make sense of ourselves and our surroundings. Affective processes are responsible for a plethora of behaviors, enacting and sustaining motivation. Research has identified important connections between affect and various dimensions of performance—such as task, organizational citizenship behavior, and counterproductive work behavior (CWB)—as well as turnover, creativity, and decision making, to name a few. Finally, the dynamic and contagious nature of emotion has propelled interest in its management. It has become increasingly important to look more closely at emotions in the workplace.

As a first step it is important to distinguish between affect, emotion, and mood. *Affect* can be considered an umbrella term under which affective constructs, such as moods and emotions, can be categorized. *Emotions* are brief, relatively intense physiological reactions to a stimulus elicited by a certain target. In contrast, *moods* are longer lasting, more diffuse, and not usually focused on a particular event. Both emotions and moods can be characterized by a positive or negative valence. Under this definition, affect is seen as a transient, short-term affective experience (or state).

A second way to approach affect is to view it as an individual's stable and enduring tendency to feel and act (that is, a trait). Although there is debate over the underlying dimensional structure of trait affect, the predominant approach in the organizational sciences has been to follow David Watson's formulation. Under this framework, affectivity is mapped on two orthogonal (distinct) dimensions: positive affect (PA) and negative affect (NA). Individuals high in PA experience a surge of positive feeling states, such as alertness and enthusiasm, whereas those low on PA experience feelings of lethargy and apathy. Scoring high on NA is associated with negative feeling states such as anxiety and fear; scoring low on NA is associated with feelings of serenity and tranquility. It is worth noting that personality has been consistently linked with workplace moods but not emotions.

Although the person is one factor affecting the experience of affect, he or she does not act in a vacuum. Therefore, it is important to consider the context in which the person is operating in order to understand what produces emotion. In general, research has found that work conditions, leaders, work group characteristics, physical setting, and organizational rewards and punishments influence an employee's emotional life. In turn, the emotion directly influences the employee's subsequent behavior (motivation and performance). Moreover, the nature of emotion is such that it does not stop at the individual but influences surrounding coworkers as well. For example, a humorous leader may put a follower in a good mood, who in turn decides to help (feels like helping) a troubled coworker with a task.

Three emerging streams of research have contributed to our understanding of emotions in the organizational behavior literature. These are the construct of emotional intelligence (EI), the process of emotional labor, and the mechanism of emotional contagion.

First, although there is a schism in the literature surrounding the conceptualization and operationalization of EI, John Mayer and his colleagues define EI as the "ability to monitor one's own and others' feelings and emotions, to discriminate among them, and to use this information to guide one's thinking and actions." Emotionally intelligent people can perceive emotional displays of others accurately, which grants them the ability to tailor their behavior to the needs of others. However, it must be noted that multiple models of EI exist, with some having questionable validities. This blurs the understanding of what EI exactly is and does. Hence, organizations should approach EI-related interventions with caution.

Emotional labor is a process of regulating one's own emotions in a manner that is in accord with organizational rules and policies. The construct was coined by sociologist Arlie Hochschild, who viewed it as managing emotions for pay. One can imagine the context as the stage and the employee as the actor delivering a congenial performance to an audience (customers). Like actors, the individual must suppress inappropriate feelings and change them into appropriate ones, a process called deep acting. An alternative method, called surface acting, is to fake the expressed emotion (for example, give a fake smile). The latter has been found to be detrimental to one's health, since being inauthentic causes discomfort and negative physiological reactions. Employees skilled in the art of emotional labor outperform their less skillful peers while benefiting the organization.

Finally, expressed affect carries the power to influence isomorphically surrounding others in a process called emotional contagion. The process starts with an individual exhibiting an emotional expression to a target. An ingrained physiological mechanism then mimics the individual's emotional expression, which in turn "contaminates" the target with the exhibited emotion. For example, upon hearing an unsuccessful joke, a person might nonetheless smile after the person who told the joke smiles. This process not only occurs at the dyadic level but also extends to the group level. Research has shown that emotional contagion contributes to effective leadership and desired positive subordinate and organizational outcomes, such as increased satisfaction, performance, cohesion, and productivity.

Emotions are an inherent part of human nature, and as such they are omnipresent. Moreover, ample evidence supports the existence and influence of affect on the self, others, and the organization.

Vias C. Nicolaides
George Mason University

See also Leadership; Passion; Psychological Views

Further Readings

Baron, Robert A. and Jintong Tang. "The Role of Entrepreneurs in Firm-level Innovation: Joint Effects of Positive Affect, Creativity, and Environmental Dynamism." *Journal of Business Venturing*, v.26/1 (January 2011).

Barsade, S. G. and D. E. Gibson. "Why Does Affect Matter in Organizations?" *The Academy of Management Perspectives*, v.21/1 (2007).

Brief, A. P. and H. M. Weiss. "Organizational Behavior: Affect in the Workplace." *Annual Review of Psychology*, v.53/1 (2002).

Cardon, Melissa S. et al. "A Tale of Passion: New Insights Into Entrepreneurship From a Parenthood Metaphor." *Journal of Business Venturing*, v.20/1 (January 2005).

Hayward, Mathew et al. "Beyond Hubris: How Highly Confident Entrepreneurs Rebound to Venture Again." *Journal of Business Venturing*, v.25/6 (November 2010).

Kaplan, S., J. C. Bradley, J. N. Luchman, and D. Haynes. "On the Role of Positive and Negative Affectivity in Job Performance: A Meta-Analytic Investigation." *Journal of Applied Psychology*, v.94/1 (2009).

Mayer, J. D., P. Salovey, and D. R. Caruso. "Emotional Intelligence: New Ability or Eclectic Traits?" *American Psychologist*, v.63/6 (2008).

Pugh, S. D. "Service With a Smile: Emotional Contagion in the Service Encounter." *Academy of Management Journal*, v.44/5 (2001).

Rhee, Kenneth S. and Rebecca J. White. "The Emotional Intelligence of Entrepreneurs." *Journal of Small Business and Entrepreneurship*, v.20/4 (2007).

Rubin, R. S., D. C. Munz, and W. H. Bommer. "Leading From Within: The Effects of Emotion Recognition and Personality on Transformational Leadership Behavior." *Academy of Management Journal*, v.48/5 (2005).

Shepherd, D. A. "Educating Entrepreneurship Students About Emotion and Learning From Failure." *Academy of Management Learning and Education*, v.3/3 (2004).

Watson, D. C. "Development and Validation of Brief Measures of Positive and Negative Affect: The PANAS Scales." *Journal of Personality and Social Psychology*, v.54 (1988).

ENTREPRENEURIAL MARKETING

Since the first research symposium devoted to it in the early 1980s, entrepreneurial marketing (EM) has developed rapidly. At the start, EM was regarded equal to marketing in small and medium enterprises (SMEs). Today, EM is regarded both as marketing conducted by entrepreneurs in new ventures and as a form of marketing with entrepreneurial characteristics—not related to firm size. With this latest view, EM is marketing to create change and destabilization and is especially suitable in highly dynamic markets. EM has obtained significant academic legitimacy in the past decades, partly because empirical research is beginning to document important differences between EM and traditional marketing practices.

In new and young ventures, marketing decisions are often made by the founding entrepreneurs. As some of these firms become large corporations, the influence from the individual entrepreneur, or from a small group of individuals, is still maintained. Well-known examples are entrepreneurs such as Richard Branson (Virgin) and Ingvar Kamprad (IKEA), both of whom have been able to create and expand firms to become large players in multinational markets and still maintain influence. In most business environments, it is possible to find both small and larger firms controlled by an entrepreneur or an entrepreneurial team, and we know that the firm's behavior is directly influenced from the personality and thinking of this individual or small team.

EM is about creating scholarly knowledge of successful entrepreneurs' behavior in the marketplace and its antecedents. Much of established theory in mainstream marketing, however, is based on empirical evidence from large and established firms. Such organizations generally have complex organizational structures with many layers of hierarchy and decision making, structures influenced by bureaucratic rules and information that has passed through these layers.

Industrialist Richard Branson at the *Time* 100 Gala in 2010. Branson appeared on the magazine's top-100 list of leaders, artists, entrepreneurs, and thinkers in 2008. (Wikimedia/David Shankbone)

Differences in behavior between entrepreneurs and managers are well discussed within the entrepreneurship literature. For example, Saras Sarasvathy has identified entrepreneurs' effectuation-related decision-making process. Guided by the entrepreneurial vision, entrepreneurs take action one step at a time within the limits of available resources. The vision and the marketing actions taken may be of a very strategic character but are taken as small, short-term business activities. Although the subject here is how entrepreneurs do marketing, it is also about the entrepreneur who takes actions devoted to developing a new or existing business. Hence, in principle EM is marketing actions taken by entrepreneurs. EM supplements existing marketing theory by adding the entrepreneurship dimension into the marketing discipline. EM also adds the marketing dimension into the discipline of entrepreneurship. It shares much with strategic entrepreneurship.

EM has gained more and more attention during the last 25 years in most parts of the world. Both education and international research are growing, manifested in many courses at both the undergraduate and the graduate levels and an increasing stream of articles, special issues of international journals, and international research symposia.

Although the EM is conceptually relatively clear, there is not a full consensus among researchers on how to define this new area. Many definitions of entrepreneurship relate successful entrepreneurs to those who are proactive, innovative, able to identify opportunities, and good at leveraging resources. Such behavior is generally regarded to characterize the activity of EM. Gerald Hills and Claes Hultman have proposed the following view: EM is a spirit, an orientation as well as a process of passionately pursuing opportunities and launching and growing ventures that create perceived customer value through relationships by employing innovativeness, creativity, selling, market immersion, networking, and flexibility. According to the same researchers, EM is characterized by the following:

- Marketing that permeates all functional areas
- Marketing decisions linked to personal goals
- Flexible, customized approaches to the market
- Speedy reaction to shifts in customer preferences
- Exploitation of smaller market niches
- Customer knowledge based on market immersion and interaction
- Marketing tactics that are often two-way with customers
- Planning that is done in short, incremental steps
- Vision and strategy driven by tactical successes
- Marketing decisions based on daily customer contacts and networks
- A focus on proactively creating and exploiting markets
- An inherent focus on recognition of opportunities
- Calculated risk taking
- Reliance on intuition and experience
- Product/venture development that is interactive, incremental, and informal, with little formal research/analysis
- Passion, zeal, and commitment
- Marketing that strives to lead customers (as opposed to following them)
- Value creation through relationships and alliances
- Marketing based on personal reputation, trust, and credibility
- Innovative behavior in creating products/services and devising business strategies

Origins of EM thinking can be traced back to Adam Smith, Joseph Schumpeter, Edith Penrose, Israel Kirzner, and Peter Drucker. More recently, a symposium jointly sponsored by the American Marketing Association and International Council for Small Business in 1982 can be seen as the start point for EM. In the years that followed, symposia have been held in all parts of the world on a more or less regular basis, especially since the beginning of the new millennium. As the EM research has evolved, new streams are supplementing the traditional approach. Like many other new research areas, the present research is scattered and heterogenic but at the same time studies in EM share many commonalities. In principle, three different views of EM can be identified.

First, some authors regard EM as a premature stage on the way to advanced marketing management. Philip Kotler has been an advocate of this view of EM in some of his books. With this perspective, marketing organizations as they grow should develop advanced marketing functions that analyze and plan marketing activities. In such early stages, EM is just rudimentary marketing compared to the well-developed marketing management procedures of large organizations. This, however, is not a well accepted view among EM researchers today.

The second view of EM represents an extensive stream of research, where EM is regarded as synonymous to small business marketing. We know from this research that such marketing is very informal, reflects the owner's personality and personal goals, is done with limited resources, often without formal planning and market analyses, and is also linked to the owner's personal network. David Carson and Audrey Gilmore state, for example, that the nature of SME marketing is that it is dominated by the inherent characteristics of the entrepreneur/owner/manager and the inherent limitations of the SME. It is often, but not always, innovative and opportunity driven. Today, this area is generally called SME marketing and shares much with EM but is not identical to EM. It is important to understand here that SME marketing is not regarded as rudimentary or undeveloped marketing; on the contrary, SME marketing can be very complex, often with fantastic achievements created with very limited resources, but without complex marketing-management procedures. Entrepreneurship researchers point out that there is a difference between ordinary small business owners and growth-oriented entrepreneurs. Based

on the same discussion, the difference between small business marketing and EM is obvious.

The potentially most promising type of research regards EM as marketing specially suited for the present business world. In this third category of research, EM is seen as a new school of marketing, though within the marketing discipline. As turbulence increases in many markets, the ability to deal with change becomes important indeed—not only for creation of growth but also for long-term survival. Entrepreneurial characteristics like innovativeness, proactivity, and ability to act on opportunities become vital, especially in dynamic markets. This stream of EM research deals with change, especially the ability to master change and turn it into a marketing advantage. Many organizations continuously behave in an entrepreneurial manner, deliberately searching for growth through change. EM brings the perspectives of the areas of marketing and entrepreneurship together; the resulting interface is the arena for research on deliberate change and disruptive marketing behavior.

This type of EM also covers a strategic orientation of firms, which—regardless of size—use entrepreneurship intentionally in order to sharpen and vitalize the organization's competitive advantage. On foundations laid by Edith Penrose, a focus on internal resources as the basis for gaining a competitive advantage has received strong acceptance. These resources must continuously be bundled, re-bundled, and refined into innovative and dynamic capabilities. In stable environments, which can be forecast, such processes can be manageable, performed by managers. In a turbulent and changing environment, this is an entrepreneurial process, with the ultimate purpose of continuously creating and improving the potential customer value. From Schumpeter and Kirzner a different view of how to gain competitive advantage can be derived. Schumpeter's view is that the entrepreneur creates imbalances in an economy by introducing innovations that destabilize the existing balance in the market. Kirzner had a somewhat opposite view, regarding the entrepreneur as someone with an ability to see opportunities other people do not see. By exploring unexplored opportunities or niches with a marketing vocabulary, the entrepreneur reduces existing imperfections in an economy.

EM, as seen by researchers within this category, is proactive and operates on, or causes, disequilibria conditions and thereby causes disequilibria in the market. Innovation is sometimes regarded as a key element in EM. Innovation is seen as the phenomenon or process that commercializes inventions. Marketing's role in innovation, then, is to provide the concepts, tools, and infrastructure to close the gap between innovation and market positioning to achieve sustainable competitive advantages. Innovations moreover enable an EM marketer to destabilize relations in a market.

Sussie Morrish, Morgan Miles, and Jonathan Deacon suggest that at the core of a firm that engages in EM are two equally important actors: (1) the customer and (2) the entrepreneur. The customer's needs are always fundamental to all marketers, but in EM, the needs, wants, resources, capabilities, experiences, and networks of the entrepreneur are of equal importance. What allows a firm that embraces EM to be innovative, risk accepting, and proactive is that the entrepreneur is passionate about creating value for him- or herself and others by creatively leveraging their capabilities.

EM involves intensity and motivation as compared to a dispassionate, analytical planning process. It typically encompasses flexibility and effectuation as a creative, incremental process. EM also focuses on opportunities. Opportunity recognition (OpR) today holds a prominent position in entrepreneurship theory and has become a central focus of entrepreneurship research. The importance of OpR is demonstrated by the fact that most basic definitions of entrepreneurship allude to opportunity recognition as central to the entrepreneurial phenomenon. Although OpR is an essential step in the early stages of formulating and launching a new venture, OpR may also occur to a greater or lesser degree throughout the life of the enterprise and the life of the entrepreneur. Whereas OpR has been prominent within theories of entrepreneurship, researchers have only recently begun to report the results of empirical studies on OpR. OpR research supports a number of different views of the opportunity recognition process, and a comprehensive model of OpR has not yet emerged. However, the marketing discipline has not yet embraced the recognition of opportunities, despite attention historically focusing on the evaluation of market opportunities. Further development of EM can be aided by integrating OpR knowledge.

Claes M. Hultman
Swedish Business School at Örebro University

See also Business-to-Business Marketing; Contextual Marketing; Entrepreneurial Orientation; Market Evaluation; Market Orientation; Target Markets; Test Markets; Wholesale Markets; Women's Entrepreneurship; Women's Entrepreneurship: Best Practices

Further Readings

Bjerke, Björn and Claes Hultman. *Entrepreneurial Marketing—the Growth of Small Firms in the New Economic Era*. Cheltenham, UK: Edward Elgar, 2002.

Carson, D., S. Cromie, P. McGowan, and J. Hill. *Marketing and Entrepreneurship in SMEs: An Innovative Approach*, London: Prentice Hall, 1995.

Carson, D. and Audrey Gilmore. "Marketing at the Interface: Not What but How." *Journal of Marketing Theory and Practice*, v.8/2 (2000).

Hills, Gerald, ed. *Marketing and Entrepreneurship: Research Ideas and Opportunities*. Westport, CT: Quorum Books, 1994.

Hills, Gerald and Claes Hultman. "Entrepreneurial Marketing." In *Marketing: Broadening the Horizons*, Stefan Lagrosen and Goran Svensson, eds. Lund, Sweden: Studentlitteratur, 2006.

Hills, Gerald, Claes Hultman, S. Kraus, and R. Schulte. "History, Theory and Evidence of Entrepreneurial Marketing: An Overview." *International Journal of Entrepreneurship and Innovation Management*, v.11/1 (2010).

Hills, Gerald, Claes Hultman, and Morgan Miles. "The Evolution Development of Entrepreneurial Marketing." *Journal of Small Business Management*, v.46 (2008).

Miles, Morgan and Jenny Darroch. "Large Firms, Entrepreneurial Marketing and the Cycle of Competitive Advantage." *European Journal of Marketing*, v.40/5-6 (2008).

Morris, Michael, Minet Schindehutte, and Raymond W. La Forge. "Entrepreneurial Marketing: A Construct for Integrating Emerging Entrepreneurship and Marketing Perspectives." *Journal of Marketing Theory and Practice*, v.10/4 (2002).

Morrish, Sussie, Morgan Miles, and Jonathan Deacon. "Entrepreneurial Marketing in SMEs: An Exploratory Case Study." *Journal of Strategic Marketing*, v.18/4 (2010).

Sarasvathy, S. D. *Effectuation: Elements of Entrepreneurial Expertise*. Northampton, MA: Edward Elgar, 2008.

Schindehutte, Minet, Michael Morris, and Leyland Pitt. *Rethinking Marketing: The Entrepreneurial Imperative*. Upper Saddle River, NJ: Prentice Hall, 2009.

ENTREPRENEURIAL ORIENTATION

The term *entrepreneurial orientation* (EO)—also referred to as firm-level entrepreneurship, entrepreneurial posture, strategic posture, strategic orientation, or corporate entrepreneurship—refers to firm-level practices or processes leading to an act of entrepreneurship (new entry). Entrepreneurial orientation is a multidimensional construct comprising various processes, including innovativeness, proactiveness, risk taking, competitive aggressiveness, and autonomy. The works of D. Miller and P. Friesen (1983), Miller (1983), and J. G. Covin and D. P. Slevin (1988, 1989) provided the foundational structure of the EO construct.

Early entrepreneurship research identified various characteristics of entrepreneurial firms. However, it was Miller (1983) who initially proposed a combination of factors that he found to be representative of the entrepreneurial nature, or strategic posture, of an organization. He defined an entrepreneurial organization as "one that engages in product market innovation, undertakes somewhat risky ventures, and is first to come up with 'proactive' innovations, beating competitors to the punch." Thus, the foundation of the entrepreneurial orientation construct was introduced, with the key elements being innovativeness, risk taking, and proactiveness. Miller's theory and research instruments have become widely used in the scholarly community when examining relationships among entrepreneurial, environmental, strategic, and organizational variables.

Entrepreneurial orientation has received an increasing amount of attention in entrepreneurship literature since the early 1990s, coinciding with the growth and legitimization of entrepreneurship as a field of study. Several empirical approaches have been used to measure the EO construct. However, the vast majority of research on EO has used the survey instrument initially developed by Miller (1983) and later modified by Covin and Slevin (1989). To develop their scale, Covin and Slevin created a survey that examined the innovativeness, proactiveness, and

risk-taking propensity of organizational leaders. Two additional dimensions of EO were later suggested by G. T. Lumpkin and G. G. Dess (1996): competitive aggressiveness and autonomy. Each of these five variables contributing to EO provides a unique contribution to the entrepreneurial behavior of an organization.

Innovativeness (new development of products and processes) was one of the first variables to be considered essential to successful entrepreneurship. It refers to an organization's proclivity to engage in the development or pursuit of new ideas, products, or processes. In Joseph Schumpeter's (1934) view, societal, technological, and market imperfections could be advanced through increased competition as a result of innovation. A considerable amount of research has linked innovation to organizational growth, suggesting that innovativeness is a key component of entrepreneurship. Innovation has been viewed in several ways by researchers in the field of entrepreneurship. Early researchers sought to dichotomize innovation as either product-market or technological (process) innovation. Innovation practices focusing on marketing or advertising functions, product design, and/or market research would be typical of product-market innovation. Technological innovation is characterized by innovative practices focused on product/market development, with primary emphasis on industry and technological expertise.

Proactiveness refers to a firm's intensity in identifying and capitalizing on available market asymmetries. Proactive firms place emphasis on capturing opportunity and the response speed needed once these opportunities are recognized in a market. Past research has noted the importance of introducing new products and technologies ahead of competitors rather than following other firms or simply responding to competitive threats in the environment. In this respect, proactive organizations seek to seize opportunities ahead of their competitors.

The propensity to accept risk is the third component of the entrepreneurial orientation construct. Entrepreneurs have been labeled as moderate risk takers compared to the general public and have even been found, compared with nonentrepreneurs, to categorize various organizational situations as having less risk. This highlights both the practical and the perceptual implications of risk for entrepreneurial behavior. Risk is viewed in this setting, according to Lumpkin and Dess, as a willingness to make large investments in resources or activities that have a reasonable chance of failure.

The two components of EO that are less commonly seen in research are competitive aggressiveness and autonomy. Competitive aggressiveness refers to the way firms react to trends and changing demand that exist in their market. More specifically, competitive aggressiveness is the degree to which a firm challenges new market entry by firms and outperforms rival firms in their particular market segment.

Autonomy refers to the independent action of individuals or a team in developing an idea or a vision and supporting its development from idea to completion. Two types of autonomy have been identified in the literature, labeled autocratic mode and generative mode. Autocratic mode is the autonomous action of individuals within the firm. Thus, this type of autonomy is high when the leader is entrepreneurial individually and leads the firm accordingly. In contrast, the generative mode refers to entrepreneurial action by members within the firm as ideas are generated and passed up to management. In this type of firm, the organizational culture of the firm is characterized by entrepreneurial action, and this culture is embedded throughout the organization. Many researchers have failed to distinguish between the entrepreneurial actions of the organization and the entrepreneurial actions of individuals within the organization. Many organizations have been labeled "entrepreneurial" or "not entrepreneurial" as a result of the actions of a single individual, rather than the actual actions of the firm as a whole. This oversight emphasizes the need for the use of the autonomy construct when examining the EO of an organization. In addition, failure to specify this variable has also led to the use of the EO construct at an individual level, as opposed to its intended use as a firm-level construct.

While literature in the EO stream has been able to circumvent any major theoretical or methodological controversies, a debate on the dimensional nature of the EO construct has continued since the mid-1990s. Beginning with the contribution of Miller (1983), the latent variables of innovativeness, proactiveness, and risk-taking were considered to be unique contributors of an overall measure. Following this view, EO has been treated as a unidimensional construct, comprising these three variables. Covin and Slevin (1988) developed what is the most widely accepted

measure of EO and argued for the aggregation of the dimensions of EO. In essence, both Miller and Covin and Slevin proposed models that required the mutual presence of all three variables for a firm to be considered entrepreneurial. Lumpkin and Dess (1996) then questioned this unidimensionality and suggested that the three variables should be considered unique contributors to the entrepreneurial nature of a firm. Thus, they posited the EO construct to be multidimensional in nature, with each variable having a unique relationship with proposed dependent variables.

In a more recent addition to this existing debate, Covin et al. (2006) reemphasize both the theoretical and the definitional grounding of EO as a unidimensional construct. Citing Miller's work, Covin et al. point out the interdependent nature of innovativeness, proactiveness, and risk taking for a firm to be considered entrepreneurial. The absence of any of these characteristics, even with the strong presence of the other two, would theoretically suggest the firm is not entrepreneurial. Whereas EO research has largely moved beyond this debate, it does still exist in that there has been no true resolution.

Justin L. Davis
Andrew Fodor
Ohio University

See also Cognition; Commitment and Persistence; Competitive Intelligence; Creativity; Credentials; Knowledge; Learning; Networks; Obstacle Identification; Passion; Risk Management; Time Management

Further Readings

Covin, J. G., K. M. Green, and D. P. Slevin. "Strategic Process Effects on the Entrepreneurial Orientation-Sales Growth Rate Relationships." *Entrepreneurship Theory and Practice*, v.30/1 (2006).

Covin, J. G. and D. P. Slevin. "The Influence of Organization Structure on the Utility of an Entrepreneurial Top Management Style." *Journal of Management Studies*, v.25/3 (1988).

Covin, J. G. and D. P. Slevin. "Strategic Management of Small Firms in Hostile and Benign Environments." *Strategic Management Journal*, v.10 (1989).

Lumpkin, G. T. and G. G. Dess. "Clarifying the Entrepreneurial Orientation Construct and Linking It to Performance." *Academy of Management Review*, v.21/1 (1996).

Miller, D. "The Correlates of Entrepreneurship in Three Types of Firms." *Management Science*, v.29 (1983).

Miller, D. and P. Friesen. "Strategy-Making and Environment: The Third Link." *Strategic Management Journal*, v.4 (1983).

Schumpeter, J. A. *The Theory of Economic Development.* Cambridge, MA: Harvard University Press, 1934.

ENTREPRENEURIAL SUPPORT SYSTEMS

Most economists agree that entrepreneurial activity is the lifeblood of a vibrant economy and is central to long-term, sustainable economic growth and development in different regional and national economies. In this context, an entrepreneur (whether social, rural, technological, academic, female, youth, immigrant, or corporative) could be an important agent who contributes to economic development. William Gartner argues that the business creation process is integrated by the individuals starting a new venture, the actions taken to create a new venture, and the environment in which the new venture is developed. Therefore, one of the most important elements in a new venture environment is an entrepreneurial support system. This system comprises interdependent components formed into an integrated whole with the purpose of guiding the development of a new venture. The main members of an entrepreneurial support system are economic and social agents such as the government, industry, academic institutions, and other public or private organizations. Examples include the Kauffman Foundation, the W. K. Kellogg Foundation, Doing Business (a World Bank group), and Global Entrepreneurship Monitor. These organizations provide a powerful network among individuals, entrepreneurial ventures, and communities that contributes to economic development and growth.

Devi Gnyawali and Daniel Fogel (1994) suggest that an entrepreneurial support system is required to develop several initiatives or programs targeted to the needs of entrepreneurs and small-business owners, such as (1) capital access and financial assistance, (2) technical assistance and support infrastructure, (3) entrepreneurial education programs to improve business skills, (4) access to mentorship networks to encourage peer learning, (5) a regulatory environment to facilitate business start-up and growth, and (6) an entrepreneurial culture that recognizes, embraces, and celebrates entrepreneurs, creating an environment in which entrepreneurs choose to live, work, and play.

The role of government in an entrepreneurial support system is extremely important, because it "sets the rules of the game," creating an effective regulatory environment for new and established enterprises (intellectual protection, business creation policies, committees of small business, collaboration networks, and so on). Most governments provide resources to serve the educational, technical, workforce development, and capital needs of entrepreneurs. However, some governments are building a more extensive support infrastructure through both public and private investment, which includes entrepreneurial education for business owners and youth, access to a wide variety of financing instruments ranging from micro loans to working capital loans to angel and venture capital investments, networking opportunities for business owners, tax-based incentives, protection of proprietary ideas and innovation, rewards for entrepreneurship, minimization of entry barriers, and other policies and programs.

Often these governmental programs are cosponsored by universities or other academic institutions, which view themselves within the entrepreneurial support system as crucial partners in economic growth. According to Maribel Guerrero and David Urbano (2010), this new type of university—known as an entrepreneurial university—is a natural incubator that promotes new business creation through its support mechanisms (business incubators, technology transfer offices, business creation offices, entrepreneurial education programs, rewards systems, alliances or investor networks, strong intellectual property and contract law systems, university technology commercialization programs, and education and mentorship for entrepreneurs) oriented to potential entrepreneurs inside the university community (students, faculty, and researchers). An entrepreneurial university is viewed as a relevant tool for facilitating the development of the contemporary knowledge-based economy through the generation and exploitation of knowledge, which is transformed into social and local development. Also, an entrepreneurial university can be viewed as a bundle of idiosyncratic and heterogeneous resources (financial, human, technological, and physical) that leverage intellectual, social, relationship capabilities to generate a sustained competitive advantage.

Another interesting member of the entrepreneurial support system is the industry, because it generates new technologies and new ideas that promote the development of new enterprises. For example, small and medium-sized enterprises often have interesting and innovative ideas but do not have the resources to implement them. For this reason, it is necessary to create alliances with government, academic institutions, and key industry players in order to develop collaborative agreements that help entrepreneurs generate innovations in their products, processes, and business models and stay focused on being more competitive and sustainable.

An entrepreneurial support system links all relevant service providers, operates according to common procedures, and offers a customized and comprehensive set of public and private services for entrepreneurs. Several characteristics are essential: common intake procedures, clear referral systems, straightforward guidelines, and regular collaboration. An entrepreneurial support system collectively contributes to the creation of more entrepreneurs and small-business owners who are better skilled and, in turn, create and grow stronger, more productive, and more competitive businesses. In this way, the support system contributes to economic development by creating jobs and generating wealth. David Audretsch (2007) identifies an entrepreneurial society as a place where knowledge-based entrepreneurship has emerged as a driving force for economic growth, employment creation, and competitiveness in global markets.

However, David Ray (2008) notes considerable differences in the type and number of support measures when comparing developed versus developing countries. The latter often lack institutions that comprise the entrepreneurial support system. A possible explanation would be the portion of gross domestic product (GDP) that is invested in research and development. In this respect, in developed countries, Babson College's Business Innovation Factory suggests that academic programs and policies are more focused on technology transfer and licensing opportunities, while in developing countries, the support systems are focused on creating an environment for students and faculty to pursue entrepreneurial activities. Some successful examples of entrepreneurial support systems are the Center for Rural Entrepreneurship in North Carolina, the Michigan Opportunities and Resources for Entrepreneurs Program, the Babson College Business Innovation Factory, Silicon Valley, and the Enterprise Support System.

Maribel Guerrero
Basque Institute of Competitiveness,
Deusto Business School
David Urbano
Autonomous University of Barcelona

See also Entrepreneurial Training; Entrepreneurship Education: Graduate Programs; Entrepreneurship Education: High School; Entrepreneurship Education: Undergraduate Programs; Infrastructure

Further Readings

Audretsch, David. *The Entrepreneurial Society*. Oxford, UK: Oxford University Press, 2007.

Clark, Burton. *Creating Entrepreneurial Universities*. Oxford, UK: Pergamon, 1998.

Cooke, Philip. "Regional Innovation Systems, Clusters, and the Knowledge Economy." *Industrial and Corporate Change*, v.10/4 (2001).

Economic Development America. *Creating Systems for Entrepreneurship Support*. Washington, DC: Economic Development Administration, 2005.

Fogel, Georgine. "An Analysis of Entrepreneurial Environment and Enterprise Development in Hungary." *Journal of Small Business Management*, v39/1 (January 2001).

Gnyawali, Devi R. and Daniel S. Fogel. "Environments for Entrepreneurship Development: Key Dimensions and Research Implications." *Entrepreneurship Theory and Practice*, v.18 (1994).

Guerrero, Maribel and David Urbano. "The Development of an Entrepreneurial University." *Journal of Technology Transfer*. DOI 10.1007/s10961-010-9171-x, 2010.

Inzelt, A. "The Evolution of University-Industry-Government Relationships During Transition." *Research Policy*, v.33/7 (2004).

Kirby, David, Maribel Guerrero, and David Urbano. "The Theoretical and Empirical Side of Entrepreneurial Universities: An Institutional Approach." *Canadian Journal of Administrative Sciences*, v.26 (in press).

Lalkaka, Rustam and Pier Abetti. "Business Incubation and Enterprise Support Systems in Restructuring Countries." *Creativity and Innovation Management*, v.8/3 (2001).

Mian, Sarfraz. "Assessing and Managing the University Technology Business Incubator: An Integrative Framework." *Journal of Business Venturing*, v.12/4 (1997).

Neck, Heidi M. "An Entrepreneurial System View of New Venture Creation." *Journal of Small Business Management*, v.42/2 (2004).

Ray, D. and I. Ray. *Entrepreneurship Support Systems: Preliminary Entry 100. Toward a Global Strategy of Applied Economic Theory*. New York: Springer, 2008.

Spilling, Olav R. "The Entrepreneurial System: On Entrepreneurship in the Context of a Mega-Event." *Journal of Business Research*, v.36/1 (1996).

ENTREPRENEURIAL TRAINING

New venture management is largely an entrepreneurial activity. Its creation and sustenance greatly depend on entrepreneurial training, which is the act of exposing individuals to a learning experience that promotes knowledge and skills for enhancing entrepreneurial capabilities. The training serves as a catalyst that drives entrepreneurship. A well-trained entrepreneur is able to thrive when there are obstacles in new venture development. Effective entrepreneurial training prepares people for a lifetime career in entrepreneurship. In both formal educational institutions and informal training centers, the emphasis on entrepreneurial training is gaining increased attention as a result of emerging global challenges that have shrunk employment and limited economic opportunities. The desire to minimize the social consequences, which has assumed a global dimension, explains the emphasis placed on entrepreneurial training by individuals, institutions, governments, and nongovernmental organizations. As a result, entrepreneurship has received much attention as a primary goal in most educational curricula in the developing, emerging, and developed economies of Africa, Asia, and the West.

Entrepreneurial training comes in different forms. Apart from the well-known and popular institutional methods of training in entrepreneurial centers of colleges and allied organizations, there is the mentoring approach that is common in sub-Saharan Africa, especially Nigeria. This apprenticeship type of entrepreneurial training occurs in the informal sector, where an entrepreneur recruits younger individuals to learn the art of entrepreneurship over a period of time, usually between two and five years. After the training, the apprentice sets up a new venture in the same line as the mentor's. This practice has survived and thrived over time across Africa, where most entrepreneurs in artisanship and commerce (buying and selling of goods and commodities, including jewelry, building materials, motor vehicle parts, educational materials, and oil and gas products) have gone through the apprenticeship entrepreneurial training program. Irrespective of the form of entrepreneurial training, there are many skill and knowledge areas that are usually covered. Some of the major ones are psychological and technical skills.

As a planned behavior, entrepreneurship involves psychological processes of innovation, creativity, and risk taking. Whereas innovation concerns the identification and adoption of new venture ideas, creativity occurs when there is a decision to pursue an idea in order to achieve the best possible outcome. Risk taking then follows when the individual embarks on the actual behavior of translating the idea into entrepreneurial activity. All of these are enabled by self-motivation and resilience—the inner drive to sustain effort and continue despite barriers. Therefore, training in the psychological skills of entrepreneurship is aimed at behavioral and attitudinal development to shape intentions and personality factors that enhance individuals' involvement in the risks and successes of entrepreneurship. When the human skills element has been adequately addressed through entrepreneurial training, it is possible to succeed in starting and managing new ventures.

Another area that is covered in entrepreneurial training concerns technical skills. These refer to the capacity to plan and deploy human, material, and financial resources for optimal utilization and productive outcomes. Apart from teaching budding entrepreneurs to recognize opportunities for cultivation, a well-tailored entrepreneurial training program enables potential entrepreneurs to deploy critical resources for maximum output. The ability to match input with maximum output may not be possible without technical skills. Potential entrepreneurs must therefore learn to develop adequate technical skills to place employees and prioritize the allocation of materials and financial resources. Thus, entrepreneurial training programs must develop both psychological and technical skills in sufficient degrees to allow new entrepreneurs and their new ventures to succeed.

Myles Mace first delivered an entrepreneurship lecture at Harvard University in 1947, according to Jerome Katz. Ever since, there has been increased attention by educational and allied institutions to prepare students and interested participants for careers in entrepreneurship as a model of economic empowerment and development. Educational curricula in the liberal arts, sciences, and technology have incorporated an orientation toward new venture creation, from setting up not-for-profit organizations to establishing small-, medium-, and large-scale enterprises. From the highly rated Harvard University to less celebrated African universities and training centers, the current global trend in promoting and developing new ventures through entrepreneurial training has reached a level of emphasis never previously witnessed.

Entrepreneurial training is important for anyone who is considering self-employment, either part-time or full-time, as well as others who are already in new venture management. This training makes it possible to handle challenges and optimize the resulting benefits. Although people have been known to engage in new venture creation without prior entrepreneurial training, such training offers the strategic and tactical platform for the effective application of innovation and creativity. As an economic exercise, creating and managing new ventures require that entrepreneurs are well equipped with sufficient knowledge and skills to effectively manage the associated challenges. For instance, the socioeconomic and political dynamics that continually shape opportunities and resource distribution have made it important to engage individuals with entrepreneurial training. Hence, this training is designed for people of all classes and strata, including men and women of all racial, religious, and other socially defined backgrounds.

In many African countries, entrepreneurial training has become a major component of preretirement planning programs. It provides an avenue to prepare participants to shift careers or to transition into retirement as one career phase ends and a new venture begins. The purpose is to empower people to maintain their economic relevance after paid employment and also help them to overcome the boredom and feelings of inadequacy that may accompany retirement, especially for those who enjoy good health in retirement. Many beneficiaries can combine the experience from this training with those experiences already acquired in previous careers (such as a certain level of risk taking, working with others, decision making, and financial management) to engage in successful new venture management.

In a bid to manage new ventures effectively, several issues are involved in the cost-benefit analysis. These are also the focus of entrepreneurial training. Programs are designed to cover wide areas that are considered appropriate and suitable for specific lines of business activity. They are undertaken to strengthen entrepreneurial capacity and make up for the possible shortfall in traits that bring about success in new venture management. There are no specific single training programs that serve as a cure-all for all the barriers and bottlenecks that may accompany entrepreneurship. For instance, Douglas Gray in 1995 reported that all the characteristics required to create and sustain new ventures are rarely found in a single entrepreneur. In many training curricula, however, participants are presented with a variety of topics that are carefully designed to address different aspects of new venture management. Through training, participants are encouraged to consider the array of benefits as opposed to the challenges of creating new ventures. Additionally, entrepreneurial training can provide the drive and incentive, in the form of empowerment, to overcome the fear of failure, fear of criticism, and fear of success usually experienced by aspiring creators of new ventures.

Entrepreneurial training addresses both situational and dispositional issues, which play key roles in new venture management. Situational issues are mainly determined by socioeconomic and political factors in the community and environment. Dispositional issues are personal to the individual aspiring entrepreneur. Through training, potential entrepreneurs are able to appreciate the impact of both issues on entrepreneurship and new venture outcomes. For instance, the availability of start-up capital is rarely sufficient to drive and sustain entrepreneurial intentions and behaviors. Experience from disbursement of microcredit financing shows that some beneficiaries have a tendency to divert such funds to more compelling and predictable economic activities rather than invest them in new ventures, whose survival and development are uncertain. This is one reason that personality and attitudes toward new venture management are deserving of attention: Although such personal issues seldom enjoy coverage in popular training programs and centers, entrepreneurial training needs to address them in order to prepare individuals for new venture management.

Never in history has entrepreneurial training been more popular among individuals, communities, and nations. The training available in educational institutions and vocational centers employs diverse criteria for evaluating program effectiveness. Successful venturing depends, in large part, on the quality of training available to the entrepreneur. As a continuous learning process, entrepreneurial training serves as a tool for dealing with the many challenges new ventures face, including survival and sustainability. Many ventures fail before they are established, casualties of the many challenges that can overwhelm the entrepreneur. The global economy is expected to witness phenomenal growth in new venture creation, and approaches to teaching entrepreneurship will likewise continue to grow in both diversity and popularity.

John Oselenbalu Ekore
University of Ibadan

See also Entrepreneurial Support Systems; Entrepreneurship Education: Graduate Programs; Entrepreneurship Education: High School; Entrepreneurship Education: Undergraduate Programs; Entrepreneurship Pedagogy; Leadership; Leadership: Training and Development; Leadership: Transformational; Learning; Learning Theory; Master of Business Administration; Networks; Social Networks

Further Readings

Gray, Douglas. *The Entrepreneur's Complete Self-Assessment Guide.* London: International Self-Counsel Press, 1987.

Katz, Jerome. "The Chronology and Intellectual Trajectory of American Entrepreneurship Education." *Journal of Business Venturing*, v.18 (2003).

Katz, Jerome and R. Green. *Entrepreneurial Small Business.* Burr Ridge, IL: McGraw-Hill, 2007.

ENTREPRENEURS IN CONSUMER PRODUCTS

The consumer products entrepreneur speculates about consumer demand for a particular good in the future. A consumer product can be any tangible good for sale, available for private use. Once the product is identified, methods to produce the product are set into motion. Utilizing packaging, marketing, and consumer expectations, the entrepreneur steers the growth, stability, and profitability of the product.

If necessary, the entrepreneur may identify a capital investor who is willing to provide funds used in exchange for some of the profits after product launch. Banking on consumer demands and ensuing success, such capital investors expect to be repaid. If anticipated demand and revenue are not met, however, both the entrepreneur and capital investors suffer a loss, and the entrepreneur experiences product failure.

From laptops to iPads, digital cameras to smart phones, wedding gowns to wrap dresses, the entrepreneur thrives in the world of consumer products. The entrepreneur in consumer products looks back to a legacy of success stories of profitable products born from both necessity and pure genius. For example, a homogenous product such as milk, under the entrepreneur's management, can be turned into a "hot" new consumer product with the addition of value that allows the product to be labeled "vitamin-enriched," "flavored milk," or "milk drink." An upgrade to product packaging, such as the juice box, can render the product a competitor of similar products in bulkier or less convenient containers; launched in 1986, this particular innovation—a portable, convenient, and aseptic box—created consumer demand that compelled 20 percent of the U.S. juice market.

Diverse cultural markets require breakthrough ideas and innovation. The entrepreneur in consumer products understands that his or her product must meet the specific needs of a diverse consumer population without ignoring a broad-spectrum customer. A small idea of providing consumable foods to the rich Spanish culture of Lower Manhattan stands as an example of entrepreneurial success in consumer goods. Starting in 1936 as the owner of a small store distributing Spanish foods, Don Prudencio Unanue, founder of Goya Foods, launched what would grow into a worldwide distribution of Hispanic food products.

As Goya's commercial presence reached a national audience, demand for its products grew, and supermarket shelves from Manhattan to Honolulu began stocking Goya products for retail sale. In 2010, Goya Foods was distributing

The 1980 introduction of an entrepreneur's packaging invention—selling juice in a portable, convenient, and sterile box—gave an existing product category new life. (Photos.com)

an extensive, diverse line that offered more than 1600 Hispanic food products; the firm had become the largest Hispanic-owned food company in the United States, ranked by Forbes at number 355 in 2010, with revenues of $1.10 billion.

In addition to considering diverse and rapidly changing cultures, entrepreneurs of consumer products must offer speed and convenience. Fast-moving consumer goods (FMCGs), also known as consumer packaged goods, are products manufactured and packaged to sell quickly. Examples include instant noodle soups, individual portions of ice cream, disposable razors, and toothpaste. FMCGs can be divided into three tiers: packaged foods, cosmetics and toiletries, and household care products.

One example of such a consumer product is the college food staple instant noodles. This FMCG—such as Ramen Instant Noodle, created by the late Taiwanese-born entrepreneur Momofuku Ando (1910–2007)—was inspired when he was in the streets of Osaka and drew lines of customers to wait in the cold for a cooked bowl of noodles. Ando experimented with making a dry, water-soluble noodle that could be cooked instantly by the addition of boiling water. He then added flavor, insisting on chicken, to make the noodles appealing and profitable to a world market, because no religion forbids the consumption of chicken. Ando launched Chicken Ramen in 1958. Japanese markets considered it a "luxury product" and continued to cook, steam, and retail noodles on site. Ramen noodles flew aboard the space shuttle *Discovery* and were advertised via a 60-foot steaming "cup of noodles" atop the famous Times Square Building, featured prominently during the U.S. New Year's Eve "ball drop" from 1996 to 2006. Instant noodles are now a staple in the FMCG market, and entrepreneur Ando's company Nissin produced revenues of US$3.2 billion in 2009 and operated plants in 11 countries.

A "fad" or "craze" niche product can be highly profitable for the consumer products entrepreneur, although often sustaining only a short market life. For example, Gary Dahl, the creator of the Pet Rock (literally a polished rock with an attached short leash), saw instant success for this fad product in 1975. Costing only $1.00 to produce and generating a profit of $5 million in 2009 dollars, the Pet Rock flew off retail shelves during the 1975 fourth-quarter holiday shopping season. Like any fad or craze, the Pet Rock's popularity diminished quickly and significantly; by Valentine's Day, 1976, the Pet Rock had disappeared. During its short market existence, however, Dahl's rock-with-a-leash concept amassed a small fortune.

The Silly Bandz craze hit U.S. stores in 2010. Rubber-band manufacturer Robert Croak developed a fast-selling consumer product, Silly Bandz, which consisted of silicone bracelets made in animal shapes (such as dogs, cats, and lizards) and marketed to children. Aimed at the young consumer market, Silly Bandz targeted the disposable incomes of adults, either through the child's allowance or through adult purchases of the product as a gift. Originally overlooked, the "tradability" aspect of Silly Bandz became a profitable marketing device. School-aged children began trading Silly Bandz with their friends and classmates. At the peak of its performance, Silly Bandz shipped 1,500 boxes per week at $5 per pack, translating into millions of dollars in revenues.

A different type of consumer product is the multi-type product, typified by the iPod, invented by Tony Fadell of Apple Inc. and launched in 2001. Defined as a personal digital device, the iPod is marketed to those seeking portability and access to large volumes of music. Additionally, it is considered a durable good, since the iPod is made for a long consumption life. However, it can also be recognized as an FMCG, since it is marketed for quick and easy use, ease of transport, and playback of large repositories of music. Apple then introduced new iPod models, dubbing them "generations" and adding more memory to allow picture storage, video viewing, and games, which were highlighted as new features. As new models debuted, early iPod generations were retired and no longer produced. Consumers owning older iPod models were not, however, tethered to purchasing a newer-generation model; the older models continued to function and with proper usage would work for a long time. However, consumers of early iPods often wished to purchase newer models, and even if they did not, the original models could still tie into a different market: the purchase of songs online, also through Apple. Thus, the iPod is a good example of a product that is attractive at several marketing levels: as a durable good, as an FMCG, and as a generator of revenue for Apple's music business. In 2010, first-quarter reports stated that 21 million iPods had been sold during the 2009 third (holiday) quarter.

The next great product may set the consumer world on "fire," but it would be best that it not burn down the house. Consumer product entrepreneurship is subject to federal scrutiny under the various consumer regulations that serve to protect the general public from undue harm caused through product use or consumption. The U.S. Consumer Product Safety Commission (CPSC) works to protect the consumer from unreasonable risk and serious injury. The Food and Drug Administration (FDA), operating as an agency within the U.S. Department of Health, works to protect the consumer's safety with regard to medical, biological, and metabolic products, including food, drugs and medications, cosmetics, and tobacco products. The Consumer Product Safety Improvement Act of 2008 created new rules for product testing and documentation, increasing fines and specifying imprisonment for certain safety violations. The legislation allowed for the creation of a publicly accessible database where consumers could learn about products considered harmful.

Product failures, or "failures to properly launch," result in what is termed a "crash and burn." A consumer product can be withdrawn from the open market as the result of a number of factors, including inability to achieve projected demand, an unsustainable product life cycle, or lack of profit. Automotive entrepreneurs have suffered from several failed product launches including those of the Ford Edsel, the Gremlin, and most famously the car made famous by the *Back to the Future* movie series, the DeLorean. The Internet, however, created a new life for these entrepreneurial product "failures" through fan sites, blogs, and parts sites.

The reward for a successful consumer product goes beyond revenues and sustained market life. For those who dare, Ernst and Young, a global leader in tax and advisory services, annually awards the prestigious Ernst and Young Entrepreneur of the Year award in the retail and consumer products category. The award recognizes the entrepreneurial spirit among those elite new venture entrepreneurs who have demonstrated vision, leadership, and the ability to grow a successful business. Past recipients include the Culver Franchising System restaurant chain (2005), Anvil Knitwear's chief executive officer Anthony Corsano (2008), Steven Nichols of K-Swiss (1994), and Bill Hay and Denise DuBarry of Thane International (1998).

With the advent of social media, entrepreneurs now have a global retail and marketing venue that is particularly suited to the start-up level. Facebook offers marketing tools that can take entrepreneurs and their products global via the World Wide Web. Social consumerism, a growing niche for entrepreneurs, is driven by the ability to purchase a product representational of social strata, such as products geared to upper-class or affluent individuals (or those who desire to improve their social status). In this market, whether it is a luxury car or a hot children's toy, sales are often compelled by the desire to appear affluent, an intrinsic value that can often outweigh the product price, or value.

Another market affected by social media is the rural market. It is predicted that the rural consumer market will constitute $1.3 trillion in purchasing power by 2020, thus representing one of the fastest-growing consumer niches. Instant access to product reviews and mobile price shopping can equalize the buyer's market for both wealthy affluent and rural poor consumers. Each group, through Internet and mobile technology, has access to products at prices tailored to their wallets. The future of consumer products therefore lies in the hands of purchasers, driven by the innovations of shrewd consumer products entrepreneurs.

Diane A. Carlin
Business Librarian and Development
Research Consultant

See also Advertising; Branding; Entrepreneurs in Entertainment; Entrepreneurs in Food; Entrepreneurs in Franchising; Entrepreneurs in Media; Entrepreneurs in Technology; Product Innovation; Selling Products and Services

Further Readings

Beyers, Tim. "Trend-Spotter: The Man Behind Silly Bandz." *Business and Small Business* (December 8, 2010). http://www.entrepreneur.com/article/217709 (Accessed December 2010).

Entrepreneur.com. "Fast Moving Consumer Goods." *Business and Small Business* (January 1, 2007). http://www.entrepreneur.com/tradejournals/article/158111743.html (Accessed December 2010).

Ernst and Young—Hall of Fame. http://eoyhof.ey.com (Accessed December 2010).

Goya Foods. "About Goya Foods." http://www.goya.com/english/about.html (Accessed December 2010).

Hevesi, Dennis. "Momofuku Ando, 96, Dies; Invented Instant Ramen." *The New York Times* (January 9, 2007). http://www.nytimes.com/2007/01/09/business/worldbusiness/09ando.html (Accessed December 2010).

Johnson, Robert. "Openers: Refresh Button; a Fad's Father Seeks a Sequel—New York Times." *The New York Times—Breaking News, World News and Multimedia* (May 30, 2004). http://www.nytimes.com/2004/05/30/business/openers-Refresh-button-a-fad-s-father-seeks-a-sequel.html (Accessed December 2010).

Starett, Charles. "Apple Q1 2010: 21 Million IPods, 8.7 Million IPhones Sold." *ILounge News* (January 25, 2010) http://www.ilounge.com/index.php/news/comments/apple-Q1–2010–21–million-Ipods–8.7–million-Iphones-Sold (Accessed December 2010).

TheMiddleClass.org. "Consumer Product Safety Improvement Act of 2008." http://www.themiddleclass.Org/bill/consumer-Product-Safety-Improvement-Act–2008 (Accessed December 2010).

U.S. Consumer Product Safety Commission. http://www.cpsc.gov/about/about.html (Accessed December 2010).

U.S. Food and Drug Administration. "Centers and Offices." http://www.fda.gov/AboutFDA/CentersOffices/default.htm (Accessed December 2010).

ENTREPRENEURS IN ENERGY

Renewable energy can be the new venture entrepreneur's oyster. From fuel cells to electric-battery cars, flexifuel, ecotourism, ecofriendly food packaging, green floors, energy-saving gas boilers, and energy-efficient cooking pots, the opportunities and ideas for entrepreneurship in renewable energy are limitless. The desire of energy entrepreneurs to place renewable energy in the hands of consumers outweighs the risks, with little to no worldwide policy structure.

Renewable energy or alternative energy (AE) is broken into four categories:

- *Biomass energy:* energy garnered from biological materials as wood, waste, hydrogen gas, and alcohol fuels
- *Hydroelectric power:* electrical energy generated by water such as rivers via dams, kinetic energy generators, tides, and waves
- *Wind power:* energy produced from giant windmills or wind turbines, often operating in groups called wind farms across large swaths of land, as well as off in oceans off the U.S. and now European coasts
- *Solar energy:* photovoltaic (PV) power utilizing light-sensitive panels to convert sunlight into electricity, as well as newer solar thermal technologies that capture the power of sunlight to heat water or air, which powers generators

Banks are reluctant to lend to such high-risk enterprises. Hence, venture capitalists serve as the main source of funding for energy entrepreneurs. However, they too desire a high and fast return on investment, which has motivated energy entrepreneurs to take their ventures and production outside the United States. For example, Chuck Provini of Natcore Technology developed a new solar panel production device. Unable to secure funding in the United States, Provini sought investors in China. Through this process, Provini discovered that the Chinese were willing to invest small amounts of money at start-up, with the knowledge that the technologies would take on life and provide return on investment (ROI). China's National Energy Commission (NEC) declared plans to invest

$738 billion in wind, solar, biodiesel fuel, and nuclear energy between 2011 and 2020.

Sometimes the most unlikely sources, such as nonprofit investment groups, stand out as entrepreneurial funding resources. As a finalist in the 2011 Zayed Future Energy Prize, which honors individuals, organizations, and companies focused on energy issues, E+Co Energy Capital Investors, a nonprofit organization headquartered in the United States, provides capital investment, business development funds, and carbon financing in the form of loans and equity investments to entrepreneurs around the world. In 2009, E+Co reported an average investment (in U.S. dollars) of $147,749 with a total portfolio of $39,596,588.

The National Renewable Energy Laboratory (NREL), under the auspices of the U.S. Department of Energy, is the country's foremost recognized research and development laboratory in renewable energy. NREL analyzes current energy policies, market trends, developing technologies, and the potentially positive or negative environmental impacts of infrastructure plans. Offering technology systems analysis, market analysis, policy analysis, and sustainability analysis, NREL works to increase public awareness of available renewable energy technologies and of market futures. Establishing partnerships with universities and other research and development institutions, NREL is able to work with a wide scope of resources.

New energy research and development are often undertaken or sponsored by U.S. institutions of higher education. For example, the Massachusetts Institute of Technology (MIT) sponsors the Clean Energy Prize, an award of $200,000 for new ventures in the area of clean energy. The prize was created to spur the best and brightest minds in clean energy, in the hope of creating new energy entrepreneurs. The 2010 prizewinner, C3Nano, focuses on the solar cell industry; it created a new transparent electrode for what is believed will make photovoltaic solar panels cheaper to produce and more energy efficient.

Playing an important role, social media serve to communicate new products, ideas, and advocacy in the renewable energy market. The U.S. Department of Energy's Office of Energy Efficiency and Renewable Energy (EERE) is available through several social media sources, including Facebook, blogs, Twitter, Widgets, and YouTube. For example, the Department of Energy uses Facebook to promote the Annual Solar Decathlon, a collegiate event that challenges teams to design and build functional and affordable solar-powered houses.

It is predicted that U.S. electricity demand will increase as much as 26 percent by 2030. Many believe that the United States needs to decrease its dependence on foreign oil. President Barack Obama's $787 billion renewable power initiative stimulus package was expected to increase state and regional growth in this area. The European Union (EU) predicts that by 2020, renewable energy should account for 20 percent of total EU energy consumption. As reported in the Enerdata yearbook, in 2010 Africa led the world with 46 percent renewable energy as the primary source of energy consumption. The U.S. Energy Information Administration's *Independent Statistics and Analysis* (ISA) reported in 2008 a total U.S. renewable energy consumption of 7.367 quadrillion British thermal units.

A small sample of current energy innovations that are capturing attention includes the following:

- The green energy machine, a modern-day trash compactor with a price tag of $850,000, made by the IST Energy Company; it compacts three tons of trash, turning it into pellets that are then converted into gas electricity.
- A kinetic energy adaptor created by Energy Solutions International and Green Revolution; when attached to gym equipment, this device converts the resistance into electricity used to power the gym.
- Biodiesel fuel made from the camelina plant, launched by the company Great Plains; this plant, which is not used for food consumption, requires little water, fertilizer, or pesticides, and Great Plains expects to plant a million acres of camelina, which would yield 100 million gallons of biodiesel fuel.
- A device to recycle household energy made by Little Foot Energy; the technology redistributes energy, such as the hot water used during a shower, converting it for energy to power the air conditioner.
- Energy systems consultants, such as Borrego Solar Systems, which works with clients to utilize traditional business solutions (such as feasibility analyses, marketing, and technology evaluations) to create a best-energy fit for their customers' energy needs, including cost-effective solutions for transitioning to renewable energy.

Diane A. Carlin
Business Librarian and Development
Research Consultant

See also Discovery and Exploitation; Entrepreneurs in Transportation; Geography of Innovation; Infrastructure; Patent Protection; Political Economy and Entrepreneurship; Research and Development; Risk Management; Sustainable Development; Venture Capital

Further Readings

Ashby, Michele. *The Modern Energy Matchmaker: Connecting Investors with Entrepreneurs.* Omaha, NE: Addicus Books, 2010.

Bluestein, Adam and Amy Barrett. "Revitalizing the American Dream: An Energy Policy for Entrepreneurs." *Small Business and Small Business Information for the Entrepreneur.* July 1, 2010. http://www.inc.com/magazine/20100701/an-Energy-Policy-For-Entrepreneurs.html (Accessed December 2010).

Enerdata. *Global Energy Statistical Yearbook 2011.* http://yearbook.enerdata.net (Accessed December 2010).

Heard, Earl B. and Brady Porche. *Energy Entrepreneurs: Insights and Inspiration From Self-Starters in Business and Industry.* Baton Rouge, LA: BIC Publishing, 2007.

MacBride, Peter. *Live Ethically.* Blacklick, OH: McGraw-Hill, 2008.

Mucha, Thomas. "The Energy Entrepreneurs: Green Power Meets the Bottom Line." July 14, 2010. http://www.globalpost.com/dispatch/africa/100705/green-Energy-Entrepreneurs-Renewable-Energy-News-Entrepreneurship (Accessed December 2010).

Spears, Larry. "Why Investors Will Start to Profit From Alternative Energy in 2011." *Stock Market News and Financial Analysis—Seeking Alpha.* http://seekingalpha.com/article/242781–why-Investors-Will-Start-To-Profit-From-Alternative-Energy-In-2011 (Accessed December 2010).

U.S. Energy Information Administration. "Renewable and Alternative Fuel Data, Reports, Analysis, Surveys." http://www.eia.doe.gov/fuelrenewable.html (Accessed December 2010).

ENTREPRENEURS IN ENTERTAINMENT

According to entrepreneurship scholars S. Venkataraman and Scott Shane, the study of entrepreneurship examines how individuals discover, evaluate, and exploit opportunities to create future goods and services. Joseph Schumpeter stressed that entrepreneurship occurs when an innovator implements change within markets through novel combinations. Essential entrepreneurial behaviors are described by Robert Baron as the generation of ideas for new products or services, the recognition of business opportunities, and the acquisition of necessary resources for new venture development. Entrepreneurs can be found in all types of industries, including the entertainment industry.

The entertainment industry at the wholesale level generates annual revenues exceeding $300 billion, according to industry expert Harold Vogel. Recorded music sales alone reached annual sales of $40 billion in the mid-1990s, and although sales have declined, annual sales of recorded music were close to $30 billion in 2010. Much of this decline has been attributed to the advent of illegal file sharing and digital downloads made possible by the Internet. Many entertainment industry professionals have directly blamed file sharing for their declining market share, but industry experts David Kusek and Gerd Leonhard suggest that the challenges faced by certain sectors of the entertainment industry are a result of these sectors' failure to adapt to the ways in which technology is altering the market. This supports Schumpeter's description of creative destruction—the process by which entrepreneurs disrupt the economic status quo through innovation, creating new market opportunities while destroying the old economic structure, and in which entrepreneurs use innovations that appeal to customers and take market share from oligopolists, thus creating new competition. Technological changes often bring upheaval to an industry and instigate the creative destruction process, and this is especially true for digitally related sectors such as the entertainment industry.

Throughout different periods in history, the entertainment industry faced a number of interrelated technological, market, and organizational changes that contributed to a more turbulent environment for the entertainment industry, and researchers Richard Peterson and David Berger found that these periods of environmental turbulence led to the emergence of entrepreneurship within the entertainment industry. They describe the entertainment industry as having a market environment of extreme turbulence, in part because of its dependence on the rapidly changing style preferences of its consumers. Market turbulence in the entertainment industry is also a result of the advent of new technologies. Therefore, technology plays a central role in entrepreneurial activities within the entertainment industry. Technologies continue to change at an ever-increasing speed. As technology continues to shift and new technologies are developed, entrepreneurs in entertainment will have increased opportunities.

The recording industry provides a prime example of how a turbulent market and technological change can lead to entrepreneurship within the entertainment industry. For decades, the recording industry has been dominated by a few major record labels that set and control the pricing and distribution of recorded music and earn the majority of their profits from selling a large number of recordings by a fairly small number of artists. Record labels have traditionally been a recording artist's only means for production and distribution of his or her recorded music, as well as the primary resource for marketing and connecting with customers. As new technologies have become available, however, recording artists have gained access to new resources with which to create and distribute their products, advertise, and connect with their customers.

As a result, many artists also become entrepreneurs themselves by taking on the responsibilities of production, marketing, and distribution of their

With new technologies emerging and the popularity of social networking, recording artists are no longer dependent on the record label as their only outlet for producing and selling music and can use entrepreneurial activities to distribute their music or to market to and connect with their customers. (Photos.com)

product. They often engage in "bootstrapping" activities, such as using their personal networks and fan bases to obtain low- to no-cost assistance to promote their products and events; to sell products at events; to fill positions such as sound, lighting, recording, and production technicians; and to secure assistance with other tasks. Other examples of these artists' entrepreneurial activities include offering a share or percentage of product or ticket sales, offering free products, and offering other low-cost incentives as a means of obtaining labor and other resources at little to no cost. Entertainers can use online social networking sites such as Facebook, YouTube, and Myspace to build their fan bases, promote events, and advertise products. Other tools, such as Websites, blogs, and Twitter accounts, are also used to build fan bases and market products. Technology also provides opportunities for entertainers to distribute their products directly to their customers. By taking advantage of technology, many entertainers are able to eliminate the "middle man" and reach their customer base directly, retaining creative control over their ventures. Artistic freedom and innovative products are often linked to independent producers and entertainers as opposed to larger bureaucratic firms, as illustrated by researchers John and Stephen Mezias.

At the consumer end, online tools such as Websites, YouTube, iTunes, Facebook, and Myspace provide opportunities for immediate distribution of product and for inexpensive promotion that has potential access to a worldwide audience. Tools such as Pandora and Rdio provide fans with the opportunity to discover new recording artists in genres they like—artists of whom they were previously unaware—without having to rely on the decisions of program directors at radio stations filtering the music before the audience has access to it. In addition to facilitating distribution and providing direct access to customers, technology has dramatically reduced the cost of music, film, and other products of the entertainment industry.

As these examples from the music industry demonstrate, entrepreneurs in the entertainment industry can leverage new technologies to take advantage of available resources and to facilitate creative control of their product. As a result, entrepreneurial entertainers are more innovative, making them more competitive, which allows them to gain a portion of market share from larger bureaucratic and less innovative entertainment firms.

Rebecca J. Franklin
Oklahoma State University

See also Entrepreneurs in Media; Entrepreneurs in Technology

Further Readings

Baron, Robert A. "Behavioral and Cognitive Factors in Entrepreneurship: Entrepreneurs as the Active Element in New Venture Creation." *Strategic Entrepreneurship Journal*, v.1 (2007).

Kusek, David and Gerd Leonhard. *The Future of Music: Manifesto for the Digital Music Revolution*. Boston: Berklee Press, 2005.

Mezias, John M. and Stephen J. Mezias. "Resource Partitioning, the Founding of Specialist Firms, and Innovation: The American Feature Film Industry, 1912–1929." *Organization Science*, v.11/3 (2000).

Peterson, Richard A. and David G. Berger. "Entrepreneurship in Organizations: Evidence From the Popular Music Industry." *Administrative Science Quarterly*, v.16/1 (1971).

Schumpeter, Joseph A. *The Theory of Economic Development*. Cambridge, MA: Harvard University Press, 1934.

Shane, Scott and S. Venkataraman. "The Promise of Entrepreneurship as a Field of Research." *The Academy of Management Review*, v.25/1 (2000).

Vogel, Harold L. *Entertainment Industry Economics: A Guide for Financial Analysis*. New York: Cambridge University Press, 2011.

Wacholtz, Larry, Mark Volman, Serita Stewart, and Cindy Heath. "Entertainment Entrepreneurial Opportunities Caused by the Creative Destruction of the Traditional Business Models Due to the Consumers Use of Digital Technology." USASBE Conference Proceedings, 2011.

ENTREPRENEURS IN FINANCE AND BANKING

The finance sector has always attracted entrepreneurs, and made many of their fortunes—though it is an industry that has also been prone to volatility and has by its nature tended to require larger amounts of starting capital than many other sectors might. However, it has been a consistent source of opportunities and can be expected to remain so.

Historical Entrepreneurs

Vermonter Henry Wells and New Yorkers William Fargo and John Butterfield were rivals in the highly competitive express industry—responsible for rapid delivery across a quickly expanding country—in the 1840s, and they dealt with their rivalry by joining forces and increasing their market share rather than risk destroying each other and letting some other competitor prosper in their stead. In 1850 they formed the American Express Company.

American Express was a joint stock corporation that merged Wells and Company, Livingston, Fargo, and Company, and Butterfield, Wasson, and Company. It established its headquarters in what is now the TriBeCa neighborhood of Manhattan and had an almost complete monopoly on express service throughout New York State. Its addition of financial services began in 1882, when it launched its money-order business. Soon after, Fargo's younger brother and successor, J. C. Fargo, instituted the American Express Travelers Cheque, after a trip to Europe during which he found it difficult to obtain cash despite his letters of credit. Eventually, financial services would become American Express's focus.

In the meantime, Wells and Fargo were anxious to capitalize on the California gold rush, but Butterfield and the other American Express executives had no interest in expanding west. Wells and Fargo remained on the board of American Express but formed Wells, Fargo, and Company in 1852 as an additional endeavor to provide express and financial services in California. Services offered included the buying and selling of gold dust, bullion, and specie; freight service between California and New York; express and banking offices in communities around the gold fields; and a freight and messenger route throughout California. When the California banking system collapsed in 1855 because of rampant uninformed speculation, Wells Fargo was forced to close its doors temporarily but reopened within days; although it had lost two thirds of its net worth, it was one of the only survivors of the bank panic and now found itself with virtually no competitors.

It rapidly became the preeminent banking, communications, and transportation business in the West, developed its own stagecoach business, and by 1866 it was able to consolidate the entire overland mail route from the Missouri River to the Pacific Ocean.

Junius Spencer Morgan (1813–1890) was born to a Welsh family in Massachusetts. He began his working life in the importing and retail business and was a partner in the J. M. Beebe and Co. dry goods importing company from 1836 to 1853. In his 40s, he met London banker George Peabody and was enticed to join Peabody's firm (with offices in London and New York City) as a partner. Ten years later, in 1864, he succeeded Peabody as head of the firm, which he renamed J. S. Morgan and Co. During the Civil War, the bank was designated the financial representative of England to the United States, and Junius brought in his son, John Pierpont Morgan (1837–1913), to head the New York office.

John had worked in the London branch of the Peabody firm briefly as a 20-year-old before relocating to New York City to work for Duncan, Sherman, and Company, Peabody's American representatives. Whereas running the New York offices of J. S. Morgan, John avoided military service in the Union army by paying a substitute $1000 to serve on his behalf (a not uncommon practice during the Civil War) while he helped to finance the war effort. In particular, he financed the purchase and repair of old carbine rifles to deal with the army's rifle shortage. In 1871, he partnered with the Drexel family in Philadelphia, with Anthony J. Drexel acting as his mentor in the banking business at Junius's request, to form the New York firm of Drexel, Morgan, and Company.

When Drexel died in 1893, the company was renamed J. P. Morgan and Company, retaining strong business relationships with J. S. Morgan and Company and Drexel and Company in Philadelphia. J. P. Morgan became one of the most important bankers in the world at the tail end of the Industrial Revolution, financing the formation of the U.S. Steel Corporation in 1901 as a merger between Andrew Carnegie's Carnegie Steel, the Federal Steel Company, and the National Steel Company. Prior to that, Morgan had formed General Electric through the merger of Edison General Electric and the Thomson-Houston Electric Company, in 1892, and had battled with Jay Gould and Jim Fisk for control of the railroads in the 1870s and 1880s.

The battle among the railroad tycoons was the main catalyst for Congress's passage of the Interstate Commerce Act in 1887, and similarly the formation of the enormous and enormously wealthy U.S. Steel prompted unsuccessful attempts at breaking it up via antitrust laws. At its founding, U.S. Steel controlled two thirds of the American steel production, but it expanded slowly rather than risk being broken up, and by 1911 its share had slipped to 50 percent as its much smaller competitors grew more quickly.

Morgan presided over businesses at a time when the Industrial Revolution had shed a light on the need to modernize management practices, and his own reorganizing of the businesses that he bought out was called "Morganization" by both his allies and enemies. Like Warren Buffet today, he took businesses that had potential and restructured them in order to see that potential realized—and bought successful companies with the aim of making them even better. By the 1890s he was wealthy and sufficiently well connected that when the latest bank panic depleted the Federal Treasury's supply of gold, Morgan formed a private syndicate to buy up $65 million worth of gold, much of it from Europe, in order to restore the Treasury in exchange for bonds.

Not all of Morgan's efforts were successful. He was the financier behind Nikola Tesla's Wardenclyffe Tower project, which not only was not successful but would not necessarily have benefited Morgan greatly even if it were: The project was an attempt to broadcast power wirelessly, and Tesla envisioned a transmission system that would make limitless electricity available for free to anyone in range of it, exactly the way radio broadcasts work.

Modern Opportunities

Changing times mean new opportunities. Even, if not especially, during a depression, there are banking opportunities in offering unconventional loans, such as the microloans many organizations have instituted or encouraged in the developing world. The line between offering loans to those who cannot obtain them from other sources and outright predatory lending can be thin, and in the United States, nontraditional institutions such as check-cashing outlets, payday loan lenders, and title loan lenders often make their profit by charging the maximum interest allowed by local law and sometimes effectively exceeding it by tacking on various fees and penalties. However, there are less opportunistic potential ventures as well.

For instance, a banking venture specializing in small businesses and sole proprietorships can charge higher banking fees than usual in order to offset a specialized personal service, part banking service and part consultancy, with business conducted electronically or through house calls. Such businesses have little overhead compared to a traditional bank, as they can be run out of the entrepreneur's home or a small amount of rented office space.

There is even room for traditional banks, in neighborhoods in need of them. Elwood Hopkins and Daniel Tellalian started Emerging Markets Inc. in 2000 as a sort of go-between between Los Angeles neighborhoods and banks. Emerging Markets constructs profiles of low-income neighborhoods, mapping out social dynamics and community politics to present a depth of information to which banks usually do not have access, and demonstrate to banks the missed opportunities in order to encourage one of them to open a branch in the neighborhood. Once that is accomplished, local community leaders are enlisted to educate their neighbors on good banking policies in an effort to free poor neighborhoods of their reliance on predatory lending palaces. In exchange, Emerging Markets is paid an annual retainer by each of the banks in its clientele.

Growing dissatisfaction with the traditional banking system has created opportunities for and interest in other forms of banking. For instance, although the first "virtual," or Internet-only, bank, a bank without a supporting branch network, began operations in 1995, the 21st century has seen a real surge in interest in such virtual banks. So far, most virtual banking ventures have been initiated by existing banks that possess the necessary capital. One of the best known, ING Direct, is operated by the ING Group financial services institution and conducts business in Australia, Austria, Canada, France, Germany, Italy, Spain, the United Kingdom, and the United States. Its focus is on high-interest savings accounts, which have become rare in traditional bank networks. Transactions may be conducted online, by phone, by mail, and sometimes by automated teller machine (ATM), but the focus is on long-term savings, complementing the account holder's other bank accounts rather than supplanting them. A potential venture opportunity might be

to create an alternative bank that would answer all the everyday banking needs of the average customer.

Digital currency, which is used for online transactions, may present future opportunities for the finance and banking entrepreneur. The legal status of digital currency is not yet clear in most jurisdictions, which should make entrepreneurs cautious, but the opportunity for new ventures is certainly there.

Bill Kte'pi
Independent Scholar

See also Business Angels; Entrepreneurs in Franchising; Entrepreneurs in History; Microfinance; Venture Capital; Venture Management Firms

Further Readings

Cruikshank, Jeffrey L. *Shaping the Waves*. Cambridge, MA: Harvard Business School Press, 2005.

Feldman, Gerald D. and Peter Hertner. *Finance and Modernization: A Transnational and Transcontinental Perspective for the Nineteenth and Twentieth Centuries*. Aldershot, UK: Ashgate, 2008.

Grossman, Richard S. *Unsettled Account: The Evolution of Banking in the Industrialized World Since 1800*. Princeton, NJ: Princeton University Press, 2010.

Gunderson, Gerald. *An Entrepreneurial History of the United States*. Washington, DC: Beard Books, 2005.

ENTREPRENEURS IN FOOD

Entrepreneurship in the food sector is about adding value to edible agricultural produce. This can involve growing, harvesting, processing, packaging, marketing, distributing, wholesaling, retailing, or serving of some kind of foodstuff. Opportunities for new enterprises have grown across this range of activities as a consequence of technological progress and changes in demand patterns. On the technological side, computerized production and logistics have facilitated the development of more flexible production and supply systems. On the demand side, consumers increasingly favor variety, healthy options, and convenience in the foods they buy.

The concentration of distribution among a small number of national and increasingly international supermarket chains has had a less clear impact on new enterprises. The buying power of national chain stores is a source of opportunity for new food entrepreneurs able to gain access to their huge customer bases, but meeting their requirements can be onerous for small suppliers. Alternative distribution channels that have opened either to address market gaps left by the big supermarket chains or in reaction against their market dominance may offer more promising prospects for new ventures. With increasing consideration of the environmental impacts of food production and consumption, books such as D. Suzuki and H. Dressel's *Good News for a Change: Hope for a Troubled Planet* have claimed that a counterrevolution in food production and consumption is under way; more food will be produced, distributed, and consumed within close proximity.

While health and environmental concerns are providing opportunities for new enterprises, the food industry has always attracted entrepreneurs. Food manufacturing and distribution are dominated by a small number of corporations, including Kellogg's, Kraft, Nestlé, Tesco, Unilever, and Walmart, but much of the innovation in food products and distribution starts with independent entrepreneurs. Ben & Jerry's ice cream is a well-known example.

Ben Cohen and Jerry Greenfield were childhood friends who reunited after college and decided to go into the food business together. They decided on ice cream because it required less equipment than other options and because they could market it in a college town that lacked an ice cream parlor. The first Ben & Jerry's opened in Burlington, Vermont, in 1978. The original shop succeeded with creative ice cream flavors and the owners' efforts to connect with the community. Distribution through local grocery stores started two years after the first store opened, and in 1983 the stage was set for further expansion after Cohen and Greenfield signed a deal with a Boston distribution company. In 1988, President Ronald Reagan named Cohen and Greenfield the U.S. Small Business Persons of the Year, and by year's end the company was operating shops in 18 states. Having helped expand the market for premium ice cream, in 2000 Cohen and Greenfield sold their brand to the international food giant Unilever for $326 million.

Cohen and Greenfield's experience illustrates why the food sector is attractive to people starting a new business. It can be easy to identify a market opening for fresh food products by observing the range of food outlets existing in any particular locality. Production can start with comparatively

After helping to revolutionize the premium ice cream market with their Ben & Jerry's brand, Ben Cohen and Jerry Greenfield sold their once fledgling, Vermont college-town brand to the Unilever Corporation for $326 million in 2000. (Wikimedia)

little investment based on distribution from the premises where a product is made. However, in addition to the comparative ease of entry, there are challenges particular to the food sector that need to be considered as well. To be successful, products must maintain consistent quality and taste, and often ingredients are natural products that can vary in their properties. Hygiene and public health standards must be adhered to, as well as labeling requirements when food is packaged for sale. Care is needed to warn consumers of potential food allergy issues arising from the ingredients used. Fresh food products have a limited shelf life and require careful planning of stock levels.

In addition to these business management issues, relations between food producers and retailers are frequently troublesome. The food industry as a whole is characterized by a fundamental imbalance between a distribution sector of large and powerful groups and a supply sector divided between a few major corporations and many small producers. Because fresh and chilled foods are perishable, suppliers can be vulnerable to buyers' insistence on price reductions or other changes of terms.

Food entrepreneurs also need to be aware that food and eating carry a large number of meanings that influence consumer behavior. Customers' country of origin can, for example, have an important influence on purchasing decisions. Origin effects are both cognitive and normative. Cognitive aspects relate to the feelings and emotions people associate with particular places. Normative aspects relate to personal and social judgments regarding the purchase and use of products of a particular origin.

Cognitively people may infer a certain level of product quality based on either the actual experience of tasting food of a particular origin or an inference derived from some known attributes of a locality. For example, knowing that California is a sunny state and believing that fruit tastes best when "sun ripened" may lead people to infer that fruit from California is of high quality. To make this kind of judgment, consumers must have confidence that they can make a reliable evaluation of the fruits' place of origin. Labeling that both states and guarantees the place of origin can increase consumer confidence. Feelings that consumers associate with particular places may be positive, negative, or both. This applies to all types of products, but food can have symbolic and cultural significance that heightens sensitivity to its geographic origin. Notions of authenticity, tradition, and status (for example, that the product is exotic or special) are frequently attached to particular food products produced in particular places. Scotch whiskey, Japanese sushi, French wine, and Spanish olives are examples of products whose association with geographic locale is particularly significant.

The normative meanings attached to the origin of food arise where consumers are influenced by moral judgments. At the extreme, consumers may boycott food from certain regions for political, economic, or ethnic reasons. It is claimed, for example, that French wine sales in the United States declined as a consequence of France's opposition to the military operation in Iraq that was led by the United States in 2003. Strong normative feelings can also exist about the health effects of food that become the focus of consumer campaigns. Urban school boards in some parts of the United States have, for example, banned the sale of soft drinks and other sugary beverages in schools.

Consumers may occasionally be positively disposed toward buying the products of a particular place as a reward or out of sympathy, perhaps following a natural disaster in that region. Moral considerations are not unique to food purchasing, but food is particularly susceptible, given the comparative ease of product substitution, frequency of purchasing, low price penalty, and emotions associated with eating. This can also explain why "buy local" campaigns can be especially effective for food producers.

The combination of the comparative ease of starting up, the need to adhere to food safety and sanitation controls, consumer sensitivities, and particular business management challenges are reflected in specialized sources of guidance. In the United States, for example, the Northeast Center for Food Entrepreneurship offers assistance to new and established food entrepreneurs, drawing on long-established centers attached to Cornell University and the University of Vermont.

The generic competitive strategies proposed by Michael Porter offer food-sector entrepreneurs a choice of either a cost or differentiation strategy. Cost-based approaches might target national supply contracts for basic or semiprocessed products where the competition is likely to be larger, established enterprises. This strategy is unlikely to be attractive to new enterprises, as they must match the cost advantages that incumbents derive from economies of scale in both production and logistics. A more feasible cost leadership strategy is to target a local or regional market, where a new enterprise can offset small-scale production with savings in distribution costs. Both cost strategies fail to respond to the potential for niche market strategies created by the increasing diversity in the demand for food products.

Two niche or differentiation strategies exist: market and product specialization. Market specialization targets a particular market segment, such as ethnic, organic, or health foods, and may develop a range of products to fit the chosen segment. Product specialization targets a specific product, such as a type of drink or fruit conserve (jam), that can be distributed nationally or at least across regions. Success in either of these differentiation strategies relies on the enterprise's having a new product or service that can compete with those of existing suppliers. As seen in the case of Ben & Jerry's, exploiting local market gaps can be a viable starting point, regardless of the long-term strategy. With the food industry dominated by national and multinational brands, making and distributing in localized markets can be a sufficient point of differentiation in itself, as there is much discussion of an increasing trend for consumers to favor locally produced food. This can apply whatever the stage in the value chain.

There has been much speculation about the trend favoring the local production of food for local consumption. Some see it as a reaction to concerns about the rise of capitalist agriculture, the ethics associated with globalized food production, and the loss of local distinctiveness. Associated with the reaction to globalization are suggestions that there is an increased desire to eat "real" rather than synthetic foods and to reject the products of industrialized agriculture. This is also discussed in terms of conscious consumption displacing conspicuous consumption and "slow food" displacing "fast food." The slow food movement started in Italy and is based on an agenda that blends politics, social consciousness, taste, and sensuality. It favors the promotion of regional foods and small producers and seeks to celebrate taste and cultural traditions. The movement now has adherents in many countries, including the United States, although some suggest that American culture is not as conducive to the pleasures of eating and drinking as are European cultures.

Beyond the slow food movement, affluent consumers are paying less attention to cheapness and quantity and more to quality, rarity, and esteem for artisan production methods. Concern over "food miles" is another expression of the trend favoring local food, as questions are asked about the long distances some food products travel to market, particularly when local alternatives can be substituted. In the United States, for example, it is estimated that the average distance traveled by a pound of fresh produce is 1,500 miles. This kind of statistic has the potential to gain consumer attention, although it is far from clear that local purchasing is better for the environment than purchasing food that has been distributed over long distances (at least not if the issue is reduced simply to that of food miles). The environmental impacts of transporting food products capture only part of the food production life cycle. The impact of long-distance freight can be offset by comparatively low environmental impacts during the production and harvesting phases. Nonetheless, alternative food agendas supporting local branding, farmers' markets, and buy-local campaigns have become a part of the food industry landscape.

In addition to the association of food with local commodities that are fresh, healthy, and nutritious, food has been linked to the demand for more civic engagement. Supermarkets are efficient environments for purchasing a diverse range of consumer items quickly and in large volume. They are less effective in providing environments that encourage social interaction, allow friends or neighbors to meet, or offer personalized service. Added to this

demand for environments that facilitate informal interaction, the relocation of retailing to shopping malls and retail parks has left behind a surplus of property in inner-city areas and small rural towns. These places, which once were thriving areas of commerce, can be well suited for new enterprises, offering property and potentially the ability to take advantage of historic areas of interest to tourists as well as local consumers.

Advocates of localized food enterprises claim several economic advantages over enterprises supplying conventional food markets. Growers do not have to sell as much produce to make the same income, as they can capture more of the final price received compared with what they can capture when using market intermediaries. A fourfold increase in the profit margin on each unit of sales is considered reasonable and only part of the gain for locally owned enterprise, since local producers utilize local resources. Overall, research based on studying the impacts of farmers' markets suggests that every $10 spent on local produce can return on the order of $24 to the local area, whereas the same expenditure at a supermarket would generate $14. Such economic advantages lie behind a new wave of food sector entrepreneurship.

A report, *Community Food Enterprise: Local Success in a Global Marketplace*, funded partly by the Bill and Melinda Gates Foundation, describes cases from the United States and internationally of new types of food enterprise. These include Lorentz Meats, based in Cannon Falls, Minnesota, which operates a meat-processing plant capable of handling species as varied as bison, pigs, and elk, as well as cattle. Lorentz's particular innovation is a business model providing a sufficient scale of processing capacity to offer small-scale ranchers access to processing costs that make it feasible to sell their meat commercially. Direct marketing has been an important part of this model, as it allows Lorentz and its suppliers to share income otherwise lost to retailers and distributors. This direct marketing includes a range of joint-venture-branded products to which suppliers can direct their meat and have it distributed to end buyers regionally and nationally.

The Californian-based Swanton Berry Farm, also featured in *Community Food Enterprise*, has demonstrated how to grow organic strawberries, manufacture value-added jams and pies, and sell them directly to the public. Swanton's business model rests on supplying three markets. The first and easiest to reach are quality-conscious, price-insensitive consumers in the top 20 percent of income earners. The distribution channel for this market segment comprises farmers' markets in affluent localities and grocery stores located in wealthy neighborhoods.

The second market is made up of people who favor Swanton's products because of a general preference for organic or locally produced food or both. These consumers are distinguished by their normative values rather than their incomes. As committed food people, these customers are addressed by selling through farmers' markets and other local networks.

The third market is made up of impulse buyers who individually purchase when it is convenient to do so and as long as they perceive value in their products. Swanton serves this large group of potential buyers through a variety of avenues to their products—from roadside farm stalls and pick-your-own locations to farmers' markets—and by incorporating their berries into a variety of value-added and packaged products, such as jams and shortcake. Swanton also makes use of secondary crops, which works as long as such products are genuinely superior to alternatives available in supermarkets.

Swanton Berry Farm shows that local producers of quality food products are not restricted to wealthy, elite customers. Evidence that a larger market exists for local and fresh foods as alternatives to the products of major food corporations can also be claimed from the experience of New York's Greenmarket program. This initiative is run by the Council on the Environment, a privately funded citizens' organization with a presence in the New York City mayor's office. The program promotes regional agriculture and ensures a continuing supply of fresh local produce through a network of local food markets, many operating year-round and located in low-income neighborhoods. The first of the markets was opened in 1976 by a civic entrepreneur who linked food assistance to the urban poor to improved market access for the state's farmers. Coupons distributed through the Supplemental Nutritional Assistance Program (formerly the Food Stamp program) are redeemable at the markets and account for a large share of the expenditures at the markets.

Social policy concerns have the potential to increase opportunities for food entrepreneurs targeting alternative, healthier food options. The present dominance of processed food in many people's diets is increasingly being associated with diet-related health problems such as obesity, diabetes, and heart disease. However, it is not necessarily the case that food entrepreneurs need to rely on alternative distribution systems. Supermarkets are increasingly looking for food products with qualities that can be labeled "traditional," "fresh," "local," and "organic." Indeed, supermarket chains have frequently acted quickly to source and promote local produce in their stores as part of their marketing strategy.

Martin Perry
Massey University

See also Advertising; Branding; Risk Management

Further Readings

Donald, B. and A. Blay-Palmer. "The Urban Creative-Food Economy: Producing Food for the Urban Elite or Social Inclusion Opportunity?" *Environment and Planning A*, v.38 (2006).

Luomala, H. "Exploring the Role of Food Origin as a Source of Meanings for Consumers and as a Determinant of Consumers' Actual Food Choices." *Journal of Business Research*, v.60 (2007).

Northeast Center for Food Entrepreneurship. *Small Scale Food Entrepreneurship: A Technical Guide for Food Ventures. Building Venture Capital Industries: Understanding the U.S. and Israeli Experiences.* Geneva, NY: New York State Agricultural Experiment Station, [n.d.].

Porter, Michael. *Competitive Advantage: Creating and Sustaining Superior Performance.* New York: Simon and Schuster, 2004.

Suzuki, D. and H. Dressel. *Good News for a Change: Hope for a Troubled Planet.* Sydney, Australia: Allen and Unwin, 2002.

Wallace Center at Winrock International and the Business Alliance for Local Living Economies. *Community Food Enterprise: Local Success in a Global Marketplace.* Arlington, VA: Author, 2009.

Entrepreneurs in Franchising

While not all businesses are equally well suited to franchising, franchising can be an effective way either to expand a business or to become a small business owner. Entrepreneurs and small business owners often find franchising an attractive option for expanding a business venture versus opening additional locations using their own capital. In fact, several companies that are now global icons can trace their origins to a single ambitious entrepreneur who chose to expand his business by selling franchises; Ray Kroc's McDonald's is perhaps the example immediately familiar to most people, though numerous other businesses in industries as diverse as restaurants, cleaning services, fitness centers, dry cleaners, moving companies, and muffler shops have followed similar trajectories from single-location to regionally or globally recognized brands. Likewise, those with entrepreneurial personalities may find becoming a franchisee an attractive opportunity to own their own business. Franchising, like any other contractual business arrangement, has several important advantages as well as some potential disadvantages, and therefore deciding whether franchising is suitable for a particular person and his or her business merits careful consideration. The International Franchise Association (IFA), a membership organization whose mission is to promote franchising, has estimated that franchised businesses account for at least $1 trillion of sales per year—about 40 percent of all retail sales. Clearly, the phenomenon of franchising is relevant to anyone interested in new venture management or expansion.

Entrepreneurs as Franchisors

A successful small business owner who determines that it is time to expand the business often faces a choice between opening and operating additional locations himself versus offering franchise opportunities—in other words, selling the right to offer products or services using the existing business name in exchange for an up-front fee and, usually, continuing royalty payments—to others. If he chooses to open and operate additional locations himself, he must have sufficient financial resources to do so. In addition to financial constraints, another significant constraint to expansion is personnel resources. The business owner must decide whether he will personally be able to successfully manage multiple locations or must hire a manager. The delegation of day-to-day operations to a hired manager always involves trust issues, but one must also consider that the manager may tend to be less motivated, diligent, or dedicated than a person with an

ownership stake will probably be. Any investment made in training a manager may also be lost if that person decides to leave and pursue other employment. Because a franchise arrangement passes these financial and labor issues on to the franchisee, many entrepreneurs find franchising an appealing option for expansion.

Certain kinds of businesses are better suited to franchising than others, and an entrepreneur who wants to expand in this way must determine whether it is truly appropriate. As with all other business expansions, there must be adequate consumer demand to sustain growth and the business sector itself should be healthy. Any business that might be considered merely a fad is not likely to be a good candidate for franchising, and it is no coincidence that a very high proportion of successful franchises belong to well-established market sectors, such as the food service and retail industries. In general, simple businesses are more easily duplicated successfully as franchises. A business with a complex operational model will render it inherently more difficult to recruit and train others to operate as franchisees and may require significantly more ongoing franchisor support to sustain their efforts. Simplicity and standardization will reduce the time required to educate a new franchisee and to start up each new location. Finally, if business success is largely dependent on an individual entrepreneur's charisma and personal connections, it may be difficult to find franchisees who share the characteristics necessary for success.

Assuming that the business model is sufficiently simple to reproduce in franchise form, franchising is often an affordable mechanism for facilitating expansion from the perspective of the entrepreneur who wants to grow their business, since each franchise location is opened using capital supplied by the franchisee. This arrangement enables the franchise network to grow rapidly, since the usual constraints of raising or borrowing capital to fund business development are not a burden on the franchisor. Additionally, since a franchisee assumes responsibility for the day-to-day management and operations of the franchise location, limited personnel resources do not constitute an obstacle to expansion, as they might if an entrepreneur contemplated opening and running additional locations. The franchise system also distributes the financial risk of expansion to multiple parties, which can make it easier to secure financing from banks or other lenders. Depending on the nature of the business and the size of the franchise network, expanding a business through franchising may provide additional advantages based on scale—for example, purchasing equipment or supplies in large quantities for the entire network may result in volume discounts not available to any single location owner.

Potential drawbacks must also be carefully considered in determining whether franchising is appropriate for any particular entrepreneurial business. By definition, an entrepreneur relinquishes some control over the business by becoming a franchisor and involving outsiders as franchisees. The franchisor has an incentive and a responsibility to protect the trademark or brand name, but will not necessarily have total authority over the operations of all franchises, and must therefore trust that each franchisee will be dedicated to protecting the brand's reputation rather than cutting corners which may have negative impacts across the entire franchise network. Whereas many people who choose to become franchisees possess an entrepreneurial spirit and are highly motivated to work hard, inconsistencies in personal priorities and management styles can have very tangible consequences for the entire network far beyond any single franchise location. In fact, research has shown that restaurant chains with large numbers of franchisees tend to have lower overall quality ratings than chains with locations owned by a smaller number of franchisees.

Conflict between franchisees and franchisors is not uncommon, and the relationship must be carefully maintained so that both parties are satisfied and the best interests of the entire network are protected, despite any potential disagreements about priorities or the level of support the franchisor provides to franchisees. Screening suitable franchisees before entering into a franchise agreement is therefore important.

Finally, although the potential for collecting royalty income from the franchise network is an attractive advantage, any entrepreneur who considers franchising a business for the first time should expect that it will take time for the franchise network to be built up before it is a significant source of additional revenue for the franchisor. Especially during the early phases, the franchisor must be prepared to provide some degree of training and support to franchisees, which requires a commitment of time and energy, as well as some additional expenses, if the franchisor visits franchises spread over a large geographic area.

Entrepreneurs as Franchisees

From the perspective of an aspiring entrepreneur, joining an established franchise network as a franchisee can be an attractive opportunity. Although there are several variations to franchise agreements, by purchasing a franchise one is at minimum gaining an association with an established trademark and is poised to benefit from its name recognition among customers. In many popular franchised businesses, the franchisee acquires a complete business model. Since the success of the business model has already been proven, the franchisee benefits from knowing what works and theoretically confronts less risk of failure than might an entrepreneur who attempts to launch an entirely new venture without any affiliation with an existing business or established customer base. For this reason, franchises have a much higher success rate than independent new business ventures. However, as a franchise owner, one still has the opportunity to employ one's entrepreneurial and leadership skills, and many franchisees relish the idea of being their own boss and having flexibility in their work schedule.

Becoming a franchisee can be a way of surmounting obstacles such as a relative lack of financial capital and business experience for competent and capable small investors, particularly women and minorities, who might otherwise be excluded from or underrepresented in business ownership. The IFA describes franchising as "being in business for yourself, but not by yourself." This motto highlights the fact that franchisors provide several valuable services to franchisees, such as proven operational procedures, managerial training, and ongoing assistance of many kinds, including the development of marketing plans and other strategies for reaching customers, depending on the nature of the business. In some cases, a franchisor may also help to select the business location and arrange for property leases and construction, assist franchisees in obtaining financing to start the venture, and even provide equipment financing.

Because franchising can take place in a wide variety of industries, an entrepreneur interested in becoming a franchisee must think not only about profit potential but also about what kind of franchise business might best suit his or her skills and preferences. People with certain personality traits may be more successful as franchisees, and it is therefore wise for anyone considering a franchise opportunity honestly to assess his or her own interests and capacities, as well as the information available about the franchise, its market, and its earning potential. A successful franchisee must be willing and able to sacrifice some independence in exchange for the security, training, and marketing power of the franchise trademark.

A person who tends to be a loner, is resentful toward authority figures, or prefers to make all decisions and to chart the course of the business single-handedly may not make an ideal franchisee, because that person could have difficulty complying with the various controls and procedures established by the franchisor. In recent years, some franchise companies, including Dunkin' Donuts and Sport Clips Haircuts, have provided incentive programs to assist U.S. military veterans in becoming franchisees. Veterans often make excellent franchisees, because their military training has usually endowed them with a respect for leadership and for following procedures; they also have access to pensions and preferential lending programs that may put the capital requirements of purchasing a franchise within reach.

While acquiring a franchise may be an opportunity to own a business with less risk than starting from scratch, this most emphatically does not imply that there is no risk involved. Even a proven business model can never be guaranteed to be successful in a new location. To ensure that potential franchisees fully understand the risks and obligations of a franchise agreement, the Federal Trade Commission requires franchisors to supply a franchise disclosure document (FDD) before any franchise agreement is signed. The purpose of the FDD is to make the potential franchisee aware of important information, including background on the franchisor, the costs of entering into the business, the legal obligations of both parties, statistics on existing franchised and company-owned outlets in the franchise network, and audited financial information. Also, if franchisors choose to make any financial performance representations such as projected revenues, the FDD must include additional disclosures and substantiation for those representations.

In the wake of the recession of 2008 and ensuing years, potential franchisees in many lines of business have found that standards are stiffer than they had been in more robust economies. In order to secure financing to purchase a franchise, entrepreneurs must have a significant down payment, often up to 30 percent, a healthy personal net worth, good credit, and, increasingly, relevant managerial or industry experience. These heightened standards, while often prudent, form a barrier to entry for some aspiring entrepreneurs.

Conclusion

Franchising is a business concept that provides many potential advantages for entrepreneurs, whether they are seeking to launch a new business venture or to expand an existing one. Because franchising arrangements can be flexible and versatile, they can be suitable for a variety of businesses and industries, and in fact, franchised businesses are a crucial component of the economy. However, franchising is not universally suitable for all business ventures, and therefore entrepreneurs must critically consider whether forming or joining a franchise network is likely to meet their specific needs and goals.

Sarah E. Fancher
Saint Louis University

See also Franchisee and Franchisor; Franchises: Legal Aspects; Franchises: Starting

Further Readings

Birkeland, Peter M. *Franchising Dreams: The Lure of Entrepreneurship in America*. Chicago: University of Chicago Press, 2002.

Entrepreneur. "2010 Franchise 500." http://www.entrepreneur .com/franchise500/index.html (Accessed December 2010).

Gillis, William E. and James G. Combs. "Franchisor Strategy and Firm Performance: Making the Most of Strategic Resource Investments." *Business Horizons*, v.52/6 (2009).

Holmberg, Stevan R. and Kathryn Boe Morgan. "Franchise Turnover and Failure: New Research and Perspectives." *Journal of Business Venturing*, v.18/3 (2003).

ENTREPRENEURS IN HISTORY

Much of modern history has been influenced by entrepreneurs, who have capitalized on the opportunities created by the free-market system, democracy, the expanding and diversified population of the United States, and the acceleration of technological innovation that began with the Industrial Revolution. In particular, the 19th century—which also saw the rise of the industrial tycoons and the cattle barons, groups that intersect with but are not coequal with the entrepreneurs—saw a flourishing of business success stories unlike what had been seen in previous years. Technology plays a role here: New industries and new markets opened by the railroads created new opportunities. Additionally, over the course of the 19th century it became more possible and more common for businesses to operate at the national level: Newspaper chains made the news business national, and railroads and canning and refrigeration helped encourage nationwide food brands.

P. T. Barnum and Entertainment

Phineas Taylor Barnum is sometimes called the first show business millionaire, having made his fortune in entertainment in the mid-19th century, long before the mass media that made so many fortunes in the 20th century. Born in 1810, Barnum started as a small business owner and newspaper publisher, before moving to New York City from Connecticut in 1834. His entertainment career began with Barnum's Grand Scientific and Musical Theater, a variety troupe, which he augmented by purchasing Scudder's American Museum and renaming it Barnum's American Museum. The museum appealed to families but was a perfect example of the charm of Barnum's work—which catered to the lowest common denominator but did so with more style and panache than his competitors. The museum not only included a wax museum and the usual displays of dioramas and scientific instruments; it was also filled with hoaxes, gimmicks, and sideshow attractions, including the trunk of a tree under which Jesus had allegedly sat, a weaving loom operated by a dog, a flea circus, a mummified monkey that a taxidermist had connected to a fish tail and billed as a mermaid, an aquarium that included beluga whales, a zoo that included bears trained by Grizzly Adams, and a variety of performers, some of whom also worked for his troupe. The performers included the famous conjoined ("Siamese") twins Chang and Eng, magicians, William Henry Johnson (the freak show performer better known as "Zip the Pinhead, the What-Is-It?"), ventriloquists, actors who performed

biblical tales and *Uncle Tom's Cabin*, and minstrels in blackface. The aquarium was the first in the United States. The museum had a capacity of 15,000 and operated for 15 hours a day, serving more than 30 million customers (about the population of the country at that time) in its first 20 years, each of them paying 25 cents for admission.

Barnum even took his show to Europe, bringing the dwarf known as General Tom Thumb with him to a meeting with Queen Victoria, which not only brought publicity to the Barnum enterprise but also resulted in invitations to the other royal courts of Europe. The tour through Europe considerably added to Barnum's collection of attractions, including a number of automatons once built to impress royalty and nobility. His return to the United States saw him on a spending spree, enhancing his New

"The Greatest Show on Earth," the Barnum and Bailey's Circus, was created by entrepreneur Phineas Taylor Barnum, sometimes referred to as the first show business millionaire. Barnum had an edge on competing circuses—he purchased a train at a time when paved highways barely existed and used it to transport his acts. (Public Domain via Wikimedia)

York museum and buying several others. The theater was widely seen as a low-class place of ill repute in America in the 1840s, which Barnum treated as a challenge to improve the theater's reputation and thus improve its profit potential. He built the largest theater in New York and called it the Moral Lecture Room, opening with a temperance-themed show called *The Drunkard*. Shakespearean plays were abridged in order to appeal to families, and these classics joined melodramas, farces, dog shows, beauty contests, and baby contests on his stages.

Barnum is best known today for his circus, but he did not enter the circus business until he was 61, long after he first came to fame and fortune and at a time when most would have considered winding down their careers. The museum, which had profited considerably during the Civil War because of the need for escapist entertainment, had burned down in the summer of 1865, and when he built a new one elsewhere in the city, it too burned down in 1868. He moved from the museum business to the circus business three years later, premiering P. T. Barnum's Grand Traveling Museum, Menagerie, Caravan, and Hippodrome, which went through a number of name changes, including the phrase that would become most associated with it: "The Greatest Show on Earth." After an 1881 merger, the circus became not P. T. Barnum's but Barnum and Bailey's, and for much of its history it was known simply as Barnum and Bailey's Circus.

The circus was the first to be transported by train, and Barnum purchased his own train for the purpose. In an America that lacked extensive paved highways, this gave him much greater geographic access than his competitors and, even without his gift for the dramatic and the entertaining, would have been sufficient to make him dominant in the industry.

Despite having exhibited so many hoaxes in his shows, Barnum wrote several books that not only promoted the Barnum brand but also debunked many of the popular hoaxes of the day, including spiritualist mediums and spirit photography. Although he was a promoter of blackface entertainment, his minstrel shows mocked racist institutions and white attitudes about blacks.

Louisa Knapp and Publishing

Louisa Knapp Curtis was the wife of Cyrus Curtis, the publisher of Boston's magazine *The People's Lodge*, and when a fire destroyed that business in the first year of their marriage in 1876, they moved to Philadelphia, where Cyrus founded *The Tribune and Farmer* and the Curtis Publishing Company, a magazine publisher. For a time he also published three nationwide newspapers.

But it was Louisa who left a lasting mark. Given a single column, "Women at Home," to write in *The Tribune and Farmer*, she turned that column into a one-page supplement, which soon became so popular that it was spun off into its own magazine, of which she was the first editor: *Ladies' Home Journal*. This magazine launched in 1883 and became one of the most popular magazines in the United States, with a circulation of one million by the 1890s (when the population of the country was about 65 million). At the beginning of the 20th century, the magazine began publishing the work of social reformers and muckrakers, expanding its scope well beyond its original focus on practical housekeeping. It was also the first magazine to reject advertisements for patent medicines, on the grounds that they were dangerous and at best ineffectual. It became known as one of the "Seven Sisters," the major magazines aimed at American women: *Ladies' Home Journal*, *Better Homes and Gardens*, *Family Circle*, *Good Housekeeping*, *McCall's*, *Redbook*, and *Woman's Day*. Until the 1960s, *Ladies' Home Journal* was the most successful of these.

Asa Candler and Soft Drinks

Coca-Cola, now one of the world's most recognized brands, was first developed by Georgia pharmacist John Pemberton as a nonalcoholic alternative to his popular French Wine Coca, a sweetened spiced wine. Atlanta and Fulton County passed prohibition legislation in 1886, and Pemberton developed Coca-Cola, a concentrated syrup to be diluted with carbonated water at soda fountains, in order to have a product to sell in those markets. He made the usual health claims about his sweet drink—that it cured headaches, impotence, and dyspepsia—and advertised in the local paper. The drink sold well enough to attract investors, and eventually businessman Asa Griggs Candler founded The Coca-Cola Company to sell Pemberton's creation. Candler was responsible for what is believed to be the first coupon, a ticket good for a free glass of Coca-Cola at any soda fountain, distributed in 1888. The coupons were designed by Frank Mason Robinson, who had been Pemberton's bookkeeper. Robinson also designed the Coca-Cola logo, using the Spencerian script standard in formal handwriting when Robinson was growing up and advertising signs that were put up on Atlanta streetcars. Early Coca-Cola advertising revolved around its refreshing taste and pictures of stylishly, often very formally, dressed young women, including well-known actresses.

Coca-Cola was one of many popular soft drinks in the 19th century, and many other brands remain around today—Pepsi, Dr. Pepper, Moxie, and Hires Root Beer (which also began as a temperance drink). However, Coca-Cola was successful on a scale rarely seen in any product category. For one thing, it almost singlehandedly created a flavor. Although "cola" is such a staple soft drink flavor that it will be found in virtually any soda company's product line, and among the offerings of any generic or store brand, it has little to do with the kola nut from which it takes its name. Since the end of the 19th century, cola has really meant "tasting like Coca-Cola and Pepsi," and both of those sodas derive their characteristic flavor from a blend of ingredients that includes multiple citrus oils, vanilla, cinnamon and other spices, lavender, and citric or phosphoric acid. It is from the complex combination of these flavors that the distinctive cola taste, both spicy and acidly sharp, emerges. In fact, while urban legends have always centered on the "coca" in Coca-Cola's name (a de-cocainized coca leaf extract is used to provide flavor), Coca-Cola itself no longer uses kola nut extract—there simply are not enough kola nut growers in the world to supply the vast company.

Before Coca-Cola, soft drinks had primarily been regional or local brands. Under Candler, Coca-Cola was quickly distributed much more widely. Ironically, while bottling was key to Coca-Cola's success—it easily survived the disappearance of soda fountains that reduced Moxie's popularity, and the hobble-skirt bottle design has become an important part of the brand's iconography—Candler was skeptical of the idea at first. He was used to dealing with soda fountains and did so proactively, using them to help protect the brand identity by threatening to cut them off if they served anything but Coca-Cola when customers asked for "a coke." Coca-Cola was fighting off dozens of imitators under Candler's watch, many of which Candler sued for trademark infringement because of their overly similar names,

like Koke. It was a fight not only against imitators but also against the trend of *coke* and *cola* becoming generic terms, which could not legally be protected. Candler failed with *cola*; Pepsi-Cola, most notably, and the scores of modern cola brands, are able to use that word without restriction. Legally, he won on *coke*, despite being opposed to that shortening of the brand—he far preferred to use the full name and insisted that employees and soda jerks do so. The name Coke never appeared on any Coca-Cola advertising until long after Candler's time. (Even then, its first usage was the "Coke Means Coca-Cola" slogan in 1941, not exactly a hearty embrace of the word.) Furthermore, in Atlanta and other parts of the South, lowercase coke did become a generic term for soft drink. However, it never spread to great degree beyond the South, and The Coca-Cola Company won sufficient trademark infringement cases to protect its exclusive right to use the word commercially.

Furthermore, Coca-Cola's identity was strongly associated with the soda fountain. Although they were not supposed to do so, soda jerks made many modifications at customers' requests. Long before the new limited-edition flavors of Coke introduced in the 21st century, customers were ordering cherry Cokes, lemon Cokes, vanilla Cokes, and coffee Cokes, among others, made by blending different syrup concentrates at the fountain. A "strong Coke" was made with an extra addition of syrup, typically a double dose, especially in sweet-toothed places like Atlanta and Texas. Some customers even ordered ammonia Cokes—Cokes adulterated with a small amount of aromatic spirits of ammonia, also known as "smelling salts." The ammonia Coke was a common remedy for hangovers, migraines, and persistent headaches, though caffeine was most likely the remedial ingredient in such cases.

Perhaps it is because of Candler's misgivings that The Coca-Cola Company itself did not begin bottling Coca-Cola. Instead, he granted the rights to bottle the soda to entrepreneurs Benjamin Thomas and Joseph Whitehead of Chattanooga, Tennessee, who formed the Coca-Cola Bottling Company. Relationships between the two companies became complicated over the years, especially once the Coca-Cola Bottling Company began to act as a parent bottler, subcontracting the bottling to regional companies. The hobble-skirt bottle design was introduced in 1915 after The Coca-Cola Company sponsored a competition among suppliers to create a new bottle that would be practical for distribution but distinctive enough in design that it could be recognized in the dark.

Candler stepped down from management of The Coca-Cola Company in 1916, when he was elected mayor of Atlanta, but the company continued to follow the innovative precedent he had set. In 1928, it became the first commercial sponsor of the Olympics, and it has remained a sponsor ever since.

Charlie Chaplin and Filmmaking

The actor Charlie Chaplin moved to the United States from England in 1910, and soon became one of the most famous actors in Hollywood and the world. The height of his career was during the silent era, when his unparalleled talent for mime, slapstick, and visual comedy and his skills as a director were well served by the short length of films of the era. Contrary to urban legend, the talkies did not end his career, but as production paradigms changed, he made fewer films in part because everyone was making fewer films once they became longer and the production more involved. Sound added little value to his movies, though, and it's true that the classics of his filmography are predominantly silent.

Chaplin's skills were not confined to the screen. Having begun on the British stage as a child performer, he had a mind for show business and recognized the value of creative control. With Mary Pickford, Douglas Fairbanks, and D. W. Griffith—one of the world's most beloved actresses, its star action hero, and one of its most esteemed directors—Chaplin cofounded United Artists in 1919, a film studio controlled by the creative talent. Each held a 20 percent stake in the company, with the remaining 20 percent held by their lawyer, William Gibbs McAdoo. The inspiration for the studio's creation was the evolving culture in Hollywood, where as studios accrued power they took greater control over the creative process and shared smaller portions of the profits with creative personnel. Originally, each partner was going to produce five films per year, but feature films were becoming more expensive as the technology evolved, and no one stuck to that plan. The sound era hurt Pickford's and Fairbanks's careers, but Chaplin's had made him rich enough that between his money and his studio, he was free to make whatever movies he wanted—the sort of opportunity that would not be afforded anyone else until the New Hollywood era decades later.

Berry Gordy and Popular Music

Born in 1929 in Detroit, Berry Gordy Jr. was the seventh of eight children in a middle-class family, and while his siblings had all taken jobs typical of the middle class, Berry dropped out of high school with a get-rich-quick scheme to become a professional boxer. He boxed for several years before being drafted for the Korean War and upon his return, in 1953, opened a record store. Although the store was not successful, Gordy continued to be interested in working in the music business in some form, and while he worked at the Lincoln-Mercury automotive plant, he got in touch with the owner of a local talent club, eventually meeting popular singer Jackie Wilson.

Meeting Wilson led to Wilson recording "Reet Petite," a song co-written with Gordy, his sister Gwen, and producer Billy Davis. It became a Top 10 hit in the United States. Gordy cowrote a number of other songs for Wilson in the next few years, as well as a song for Etta James. As he got to know the music industry, Gordy looked for opportunities in producing, and in 1957 he discovered the Matadors, a band that would soon be renamed The Miracles, led by Smokey Robinson. More discoveries followed, and with an $800 loan from his family, 30-year-old Berry Gordy started Tamla Records, a rhythm-and-blues label, in 1959. Later in the year, Gordy bought the building that would become known as the Hitsville USA studio, converting the photography studio in the back of the house into a recording studio.

Motown Records was Gordy's second label, founded immediately after Tamla and incorporated in 1960, merging with Tamla. It took its name from a nickname for Detroit, a portmanteau for Motor Town. The label soon had its first hit with the Marvelettes' "Please Mr. Postman," and in the next 10 years Motown Records—operating as several labels and imprints, and often producing music that was later picked up for distribution by larger companies such as Chess and United Artists—added Stevie Wonder, the Supremes, the Jackson 5, the Four Tops, and Marvin Gaye to its stable of artists. In that same period it had more than 100 top 10 hits.

Gordy diversified his company's genres, with Workshop Jazz releasing jazz records, Rare Earth producing rock, and Mel-o-dy focusing on country. At a time when some venues were still reluctant to book black artists, Gordy was methodical about maintaining his acts' public image in order to appeal to as wide an audience as possible.

In 1972, Gordy relocated to Los Angeles and began to produce movies, beginning with the Billie Holiday biopic *Lady Sings the Blues*, starring Diana Ross in a role for which she was nominated for an Oscar. One of his best-known films was the cult kung fu sensation *The Last Dragon*, co-starring Prince's protégé Vanity.

Bill Gates and Computers

The computer industry and subsequently the Internet have provided opportunities for a number of entrepreneurs, but perhaps the most significant is Bill Gates, who founded Microsoft with Paul Allen in 1975 and continued to serve as its chairman until 2008, overseeing an age in which desktop computers went from impractical rarities to ubiquitous necessities.

Like most pioneers in the early computer industry, Gates began as a hobbyist, teaching himself the BASIC programming language during his math classes and exploiting operating system bugs in DEC PDP microcomputers to give himself free computer time during which to test programs. When he, along with three other students, was banned from the computer for exploiting those bugs, they offered to troubleshoot software in exchange for free computer time. A similar arrangement was made with Information Sciences Inc., which hired the four students to write a payroll program in return for free computer time and royalties.

With a near-perfect score on the Scholastic Aptitude Test (SAT), Gates left Seattle for Harvard but took a leave of absence midway through his bachelor's degree to found Microsoft. He had stayed in touch with Paul Allen, one of the four high school students, and the two had developed a BASIC interpreter for the Altair 8800 computer built by Micro Instrumentation and Telemetry Systems (MITS). "Micro-Soft" was originally the name for the partnership between Gates and Allen, headquartered in Albuquerque because that was where MITS was located. In 1976, the hyphen was dropped, the name Microsoft was registered with the state of New Mexico, and Gates never returned to college. He took an early stand against the prevailing pro-piracy attitude in the hobbyist community when Microsoft's BASIC interpreter was leaked before completion, publishing an open letter to computer hobbyists declaring that they should not expect high-quality software without payment.

Microsoft continued to develop software for various companies, and although Gates was in charge of the business end of the venture, he continued to review and often rewrite every line of code the company produced in its first five years, in addition to writing his own. In 1980, shortly after the company's relocation to Washington State, IBM contacted Microsoft about developing the BASIC interpreter for its highly anticipated IBM PC, which would go on to become one of the first widely available personal computers. When IBM's discussions with other companies to develop an operating system for the PC ended fruitlessly, the company came back to Microsoft. In response, Gates made the shrewd decision to purchase the 86–DOS operating system outright, repackage it as MS-DOS, and deliver it—without a transfer of copyright—to IBM (as PC-DOS). IBM paid only a onetime fee, but because Microsoft retained the copyright, it sold MS-DOS again and again to the many hardware vendors who produced personal computers that were clones of IBM's hardware and thus needed a similar if not identical operating system—a class of personal computer which soon became known as "PC compatibles" and in time would outsell actual IBM PCs. In a way, this helped both Microsoft and IBM and laid the groundwork for the "I'm a Mac/ I'm a PC" dichotomy of computer culture between Apples and PCs.

Microsoft's in-house-developed operating system, Microsoft Windows, was launched in 1985. Only two years later, Gates became the world's youngest self-made billionaire. Just as MS-DOS had simply taken an operating system that Gates knew worked well and applied it to the circumstance where it was most needed and useful, Windows took the concept of the Macintosh operating system that were the most markedly different from MS-DOS—the graphical user interface—and created a PC version of it. It was Windows that made Microsoft's name and changed the computer industry, to the point that both consumers and industry people began referring to "Windows machines" rather than "PC compatibles," even though Microsoft continued to have nothing to do with the hardware. At the same time, Gates recognized the power that software's importance gave the company, and the development of Windows has shaped the development of hardware, as it is in every hardware vendor's interest to make sure that its hardware is compatible with current and forthcoming Windows releases.

Despite his reputation for an argumentative and often superior managerial style, Gates weathered antitrust litigation that could have ruined the company and has devoted himself to philanthropy, operating the Bill and Melinda Gates Foundation since 2000. From 1993 to 2007, he was number one on the Forbes 400 list, and from 1995 to 2007 he was number one on its list of the world's richest people (which excludes royalty and heads of state).

Bill Kte'pi
Independent Scholar

See also Entrepreneurs in Energy; Entrepreneurs in Finance and Banking; Entrepreneurs in Food; Entrepreneurs in Franchising; Entrepreneurs in Media; Entrepreneurs in Real Estate; Entrepreneurs in Technology; Entrepreneurs in Transportation

Further Readings

Cruikshank, Jeffrey L. *Shaping the Waves*. Cambridge, MA: Harvard Business School Press, 2005.
Gunderson, Gerald. *An Entrepreneurial History of the United States*. Washington, DC: Beard Books, 2005.
Walker, Juliet E. K. *History of Black Business in America*. New York: Twayne, 1998.

ENTREPRENEURS IN MEDIA

Currently, many people consider media to be the most entrepreneurial industry of all. Digitization had radically altered the way media content is produced, distributed, and consumed, leading to the emergence of many business opportunities. Much of the innovation in the industry is driven by media entrepreneurs. However, the level of innovation and rate of entrepreneurship vary widely among different media sectors. In Europe, more than one third of media companies are young firms, and the media sectors with most young firms are miscellaneous publishing activities (such as magazines) as well as motion picture production companies and allied services. In the United States, nearly all media sectors have been found to be more entrepreneurial than any other U.S. manufacturing or service industry. Many new media start-ups are built around user-generated content and open distribution platforms, which challenge traditional business models built around content produced by professionals and distributed through proprietary platforms. With the growth of the Internet, media consumption behavior has changed and interactivity has become important. Other media start-ups take advantage of digital technologies to disaggregate traditional business value chains, such as e-publishing in books or digital music downloads. Media ventures, for example, providing services such as aggregating content from other sources, are attracting significant audiences, and are often founded with the ambition to be sold to incumbent firms struggling to defend their market shares.

To provide an overview of the phenomenon of entrepreneurs in media, this entry will first line out the distinctive features of the media industries and how entrepreneurship in them differs from other industries, before moving on to present different typical types of entrepreneurs in media as well as examples of these types.

Characteristics of Media Industries and Companies

One distinctive feature of media companies is that they are often not entirely commercially oriented. Rather, many must or want to act in the public interest. For example, news media companies typically not only aim to provide accurate information and news but also critically monitor politics, the economy, and society at large. Also, many media companies have artistic and creative imperatives—for example, in music and film production. Thus, from their inception many media start-ups need to balance different, sometimes conflicting, interests and demands. A newspaper publisher, for example, must balance the demand of running cost-efficient operations and matching advertisers' interests while maintaining journalistic quality to sustain readership. The challenge for media entrepreneurs lies in developing a business model that balances such possibly conflicting demands with the generation of sufficient revenues.

Although many industries are currently facing technological changes, the scope and velocity of the changes in media industries make outcomes nonlinear and unpredictable for both established media companies and start-ups. For example, many traditional newspaper companies are struggling to compete with free (online) news offerings, which change consumers' reading patterns and lead not only to fewer print copies sold but also to reduced advertising revenues, both from classifieds (which are typically placed by individuals) and from advertisements placed by other businesses. For media start-ups, it is very difficult to predict whether consumers' attention might switch from one medium to another or whether a new media offering might be used in addition to existing media.

Many media companies depend on the creative content they develop and bring to the market. How the market will react to that content is difficult to predict, which makes, for example, the attempt of movie producers to create a blockbuster movie (which could be leveraged into cross-media sales as well as licensed products featuring the main movie characters) a very uncertain endeavor. Similarly, it is difficult to predict which songs will become hits in the music charts or which books will be best sellers.

Finally, demand for media products is influenced by the dual-product nature of commercial media. Revenue for media products carrying advertising is determined not only by the time and attention given by the product's audience but also by advertising. Thus, survival of media products—and ultimately media companies—often requires that they appeal to both audiences and advertisers. These different factors pose distinct challenges to media entrepreneurs, as advertisers might make conditional requests regarding design and content of the media product.

In the entrepreneurship field, much attention has been given to the importance of recognizing profitable business opportunities and exploiting them. However, as the outline of distinctive features of the media industries presented above has shown, media entrepreneurs might need to incorporate other important aspects into their media products, such as more missionary attempts to "change the world into a better place" and literary or artistic endeavors. Thus, for media entrepreneurs the rationales for starting an entrepreneurial venture might differ from those for "typical" ventures in other industries. Generally, the entrepreneurship literature associates motives for becoming entrepreneurially active with a relatively high need for achievement, an internal locus of control (the belief that one's personal actions directly influence the outcome of an event), self-efficacy (task-specific self-confidence), the setting of performance and growth goals, the desire for independence, drive (to realize one's idea), and egoistic passion for work. Whereas these motives can explain why purely commercial media ventures are founded, they do not fully explain the noncommercial characteristics of many media start-ups. For example, some media ventures are torn between aiming to make a profit and making the world a better place in which to live—by addressing and aiming to reduce a social problem or by providing artistic and cultural value, entertainment, or intellectual stimulation. This double ambition of founding a commercially feasible venture and pursuing some additional, noncommercial goal characterizes much media entrepreneurship, especially in the traditional media sectors of print, radio, and television.

This dual mission somewhat resembles the phenomenon of social entrepreneurship, which integrates economic and social value creation by pursuing opportunities to catalyze social change or address social needs. For many media entrepreneurs, just as for social entrepreneurs, the societal mission is explicit and central in founding and running a venture. This mission affects how media entrepreneurs perceive and assess opportunities. Mission-related, not wealth creation, impact often becomes the central criterion of success. Wealth may therefore be seen as a means to an end for media entrepreneurs. Another characteristic that some media entrepreneurs share with social entrepreneurs is that the value created can be difficult to capture—namely, a media start-up that has achieved an impact on society might not be able to capture much economic value from this impact.

More scholarly investigation of media entrepreneurship is needed, because drastic changes are occurring in media industries. Established companies are challenged not only by the new technologies that are changing their business logic but also by fundamentally different ways of bringing business concepts to market. For traditional print-media companies, it has even been suggested that their products (such as printed newspapers) will become extinct in the foreseeable future.

Start-up companies are taking advantage of the increased demand for media niche products. Technological advances have reduced barriers to entry in content creation, made professional-level production more widely available, and created new distribution and promotion channels—making it easy to match specialized content with niche audiences. The logic of such start-up companies deserves closer attention to understand more fully how media industries are evolving.

Types of Media Entrepreneurs

When asked to name famous entrepreneurs in media, many people think of Walt Disney, Rupert Murdoch, or Hugh Hefner. Indeed, these entrepreneurs have altered their media sectors through innovative products and services. More recently, different types of entrepreneurs have affected media industries.

Some media entrepreneurs have the main goal of adding a critical or creative voice and often run their start-ups as not-for-profit ventures. This neither means that the media product is necessarily free nor that the venture cannot make a profit, but rather that profits are reinvested into further developing media activities. A well-known "missionary" entrepreneurial media venture is the online site for investigative journalism ProPublica, http://www.propublica.org. Established and run by the former managing editor of the *Wall Street Journal,* Paul Steiger, this venture is financed by wealthy individuals who fear the impact on democracy and government accountability if printed newspapers were to go out of business as a result of decreased audiences and advertising revenues. Investigative journalism is resource- and time-intensive, differing significantly from content produced "for free" and distributed in blogs, Wikipedia, and similar outlets. A range of other not-for-profit media ventures have appeared over the past years and are similarly financed by donations or foundations.

Another type of media venture, typically aiming to improve the lives of people—whether they are found in ethnic niche markets or global audiences—has emerged in different countries, such as the United States and the Republic of South Africa: ethnic minority entrepreneurs, including the so-called "black media" ventures. One example is *InSpire* magazine, http://www.inspiremag.org, which is intended to "produce a highly interactive and quality publication that will provide its readers with constant positive and inspirational stories that will uplift the human spirit." Founded by professor and television talk show host Lee Jones, the magazine claims to reach an audience of 150,000 people. The most well-known example of a black media entrepreneur is Oprah Winfrey and her media house (http:// www.oprah.com), which has the mission to help the global audience "live your best life," is diversified into different media platforms (magazine, book club, radio, television, and online store), and also runs philanthropic projects such as one that assists economically disadvantaged girls in the Republic of South Africa to receive an education.

In recent years, social media have dramatically altered the way people use media and communicate. Tools such as YouTube, Facebook, Twitter, blogs, and Flickr provide users the opportunities to create a dynamic Internet presence that can be instantly updated. Social media invite media content coproduction by audiences, and the instant feedback the customer interaction provides is increasingly used for marketing purposes by companies from different industries and other types of organizations. Many entrepreneurs have founded social media-based ventures, and, beyond attracting a sufficient customer base, a major challenge lies in designing a sustainable revenue model. The issue is clearly illustrated by the 2010 feature film *The Social Network,* depicting Mark Zuckerberg, the founder of Facebook (http://www.facebook.com), who was believed to be worth an astonishing $6.9 billion in 2010. In 2008, Facebook surpassed its former main competitor, Myspace (http://www.myspace.com), which has since struggled with decreasing advertising revenues and has redirected its attention from social networking to music, videos, and games. Other examples of entrepreneurial social media ventures are Groupon (http://www.groupon.com), which provides discounted deals for different activities in a large number of different cities; LinkedIn (http://www.linkedin.com), a professional networking site aiming at facilitating deal-making and career advancement; and the gaming site Zynga (http://www.zynga.com), which raises money for social projects through online gaming. How sustainable these ventures are going to be is uncertain and will evolve over time in response to consumer demand and new media ventures.

Many entrepreneurial media ventures transfer established forms of media content to a new environment; that is, they mainly change the form of distribution. An example occurred as encyclopedias migrated from mainly printed volumes to CDs and DVDs to online content. The Swedish online trading site blocket (http://www.blocket.se) is a successful media start-up that has been acquired by Scandinavian media house Schibsted in an attempt to move classifieds online. Similarly, in the magazine sector, entrepreneurs often create new titles online only. Special-interest online magazines manage to attract a well-defined interest group, which provides a chance to attract revenues from advertising aimed at this specific customer segment. The Austria-based magazine 55+ (http://www.55plus-magazin.net) targets the still relatively neglected segment of people in their 50s and 60s, who often have high spending power and an interest in travel, health and wellness, and eating and drinking well. The magazine provides original content about these topics, attracting advertisers who target the group. The German venture Hitflip (http://www.hitflip.de) has become Europe's largest online consumer-to-consumer swapping platform for media products (DVDs, games, CDs, books, audio-books), using a sophisticated technological solution that allows for scalability of the business and securely manages the complex matching processes between customers' demands and supplies.

While the types of media entrepreneurs discussed above have dealt with entrepreneurs acting on opportunities, some entrepreneurs in media industries have been pushed into self-employment. For example, with newspaper and book publishing companies facing financial crises and cutting back on staff, many start-ups appear because unemployed journalists, editors, and graphic designers are now self-employed, sometimes developing innovative or successful venture ideas, for example, in investigative journalism and photojournalism. Similar processes can be noted in film-production companies, which have moved from companies integrated across the entire movie value chain toward specialized companies within disintegrated value chains. In the coming years, one can expect that many new entrepreneurial media ventures will be founded, altering our way of consuming media content.

Leona Achtenhagen
Jönköping International Business School

See also Entrepreneurs in Entertainment; Entrepreneurs in Technology

Further Readings

Achtenhagen, Leona. "Understanding Entrepreneurship in Traditional Media." *Journal of Media Business Studies*, v.5/1 (2008).

Aris, Annet and Jacques Bughin. *Managing Media Companies: Harnessing Creative Value*, 2nd ed. New York: John Wiley and Sons, 2009.

Hoag, Anne. "Measuring Media Entrepreneurship." *International Journal of Media Management*, v.10/2 (2008).

Knight Centre for Digital Media Entrepreneurship. http://www.startupmedia.org (Accessed February 2011).

McKelvie, Alexander and Robert Picard. "Growth and Development of New and Young Media Firms." *Journal of Media Business Studies*, v.5/1 (2008).

Saila.com. http://saila.com (Accessed February 2011).

ENTREPRENEURS IN REAL ESTATE

Real estate has always been a fertile area for entrepreneurship. Whereas the bursting of the 2000s housing bubble has slowed new construction and the house "flipping" that had become so popular by 2004–05, commercial development remains a vital sector and in the past has been the source of many fortunes.

Donald Trump

The grandson of Austrian immigrants and a native of New York, Donald Trump claims in his autobiography to have considered film school before turning to the real estate business, working for his father, real estate developer Fred Christ Trump, after college. Donald's first projects were in his father's specialty, middle-class rental housing in Staten Island, Brooklyn, and Queens. When he moved to Manhattan in 1971, three years after joining the company, he became interested in large Manhattan building projects and saw in them the potential for greater profits and public recognition.

Trump soon won the rights to develop the Penn Central yards and followed that project by taking advantage of the city government's need for investment in the midst of the city's 1970s economic crisis, getting a significant tax concession in his transformation of the old, bankrupt Commodore Hotel into a new Grand Hyatt. Trump's dissatisfaction with what he saw as government overspending and inefficient spending was made known early on, when a New York City government project that he had estimated should have cost $110 million ran up nearly $1 billion in costs for the city. His offer to take over the project and complete it at cost was rejected. Later in his career, he similarly offered to build a ballroom for the Obama administration at cost and complained that his offer did not even yield a response.

The Trump Organization—the elder Trump's development company, which Donald eventually took over—relocated to Trump Tower, a mixed-use tower Donald had built over a four-year period, finally completed at the end of 1983. Built next to Tiffany's flagship store—and using its air rights, as well as the designation of the tower's atrium as a "public space," in order to build a tower taller than zoning laws would otherwise permit—the tower boasted an interior heavily decorated with pink marble, mirrors, and brass, while the atrium featured a waterfall as well as shops and cafés. Trump Tower is now home to the television studio where the NBC show *The Apprentice* (starring Trump) is filmed and is the official residence of the Miss Universe, Miss USA, and Miss Teen USA pageants operated by Trump in conjunction with NBC. Trump's projects continued to expand, including Atlantic City casinos and other commercial developments. The recession of the late 1980s led him to business bankruptcy in 1991, in part because of the just-built $1 billion Trump Taj Mahal Casino, which had been financed with high-interest junk bonds. In order to avoid both personal bankruptcy (his personal debt was $900 million) and further losses to the Trump Organization as creditors sought relief in bankruptcy court, Trump restructured his business debts; among other measures, he ceded 50 percent ownership of the Taj Mahal to the bondholders in exchange for lower interest rates on the debt. He also gave up a 49 percent stake in the Trump Plaza Hotel to some of his lenders in exchange for better rates on the half billion dollars in debts the Trump Organization owed them.

Trump's recovery is one of the great business success stories. By 1994 he had eliminated much of his $3.5 billion in business debt and $900 million in personal debt, continually sacrificing assets or shares of assets in exchange for better loan terms and gambling on his ability to generate the income he would need to meet those terms. Further, he was able to retain Trump Tower and his three casinos—the projects

Donald Trump has become an iconic figure in real estate entrepreneurialism. He has built and developed a string of massive projects like the Trump Tower in New York and hotels and casinos across the United States. (Wikimedia/ David Shankbone)

most associated with the Trump who had emerged from his father's shadow while putting the family name on virtually everything he touched. Meanwhile, he had become a major celebrity, with frequent television appearances even before he starred in multiple seasons of *The Apprentice*. His casino holdings were combined in 1995 into the publicly held Trump Hotels and Casino Resorts (now Trump Entertainment Resorts Holdings), though the company struggled to stay afloat, restructuring its debt in 2004 and seeking voluntary bankruptcy protection.

Interestingly, when Trump was unable to repay a $40 million loan to Deutsche Bank in the aftermath of the 2008 global financial crisis and that bank filed suit against him, he initiated a countersuit for tarnishing his image, arguing that the financial crisis was an act of God and the terms of the contract thus did not require him to pay.

Steve Wynn

Real estate developer Steve Wynn, born in Connecticut and raised in Utica, New York, was instrumental in the 1990s resurgence of the Las Vegas Strip.

Wynn's father, Michael, ran a number of bingo parlors, which Wynn took over upon his father's death in 1963, shortly before Wynn's graduation from the University of Pennsylvania. The bingo business did well enough that four years later, Wynn moved to Las Vegas, purchased a stake in the Frontier Hotel and Casino, and started a wine-importing company. This venture soon led to casino acquisitions, including a controlling interest in the Golden Nugget Las Vegas, which he renovated and expanded from a simple gambling hall to a resort hotel casino. The Golden Nugget helped to attract high-rolling clientele to the downtown area. When Atlantic City legalized gambling in 1976, Wynn looked to expand there and purchased the Strand Motel in order to tear it down and replace it with the Golden Nugget Atlantic City, completed in 1980. After his renovation of the Golden Nugget in Las Vegas, the Atlantic City Golden Nugget was his first casino project started from scratch, and it became the city's top-earning casino by 1983, with Frank Sinatra included among its cadre of regular entertainers. Like Trump, Wynn enjoyed the spotlight and included his public image as part of his brand: Advertisements for the Golden Nugget, for example, featured Wynn delivering fresh towels to Sinatra in his room. However, his well-publicized problems with the city's officials led him to swear off further development in Atlantic City.

Wynn returned to Las Vegas to build the Mirage, which opened in 1989 and is one of the most significant casinos in the rejuvenation of the Las Vegas Strip. Financed with junk bonds from junk bond king Michael Milken, the Mirage was the most opulent casino in Las Vegas, with an indoor forest and an artificial volcano. Four years later, Wynn opened the Treasure Island Hotel and Casino next door to the Mirage, with Vegas's first permanent Cirque du Soleil show and a large artificial lake adjacent to the Strip. This project was followed by the Bellagio, the epitome of Wynn's luxury casinos. The $1.6 billion project included an indoor conservatory, an artificial lake, an art museum, boutique shopping, and branches of fine-dining restaurants from Paris, San Francisco, and New York. The high table limits at the Bellagio poker room have made it the center of professional poker culture in Las Vegas, and the venue has hosted several World Poker Tour tournaments.

These three casinos played a major role in creating new interest in Las Vegas and making it a major vacation and convention destination. Wynn consolidated his interests into Wynn Resorts Limited and took that concern public in 2002; in the next two years, his net worth doubled to $1.3 billion. When three gaming concessions opened in Macau, a region of China that in the 21st century became the largest gaming market in the world, Wynn was able to mount a successful bid for one of them and began developing the Wynn Macau casino. It opened in 2006, the first Las Vegas–style resort casino in Asia, with 600 rooms and suites, 212 table games, designer shops, a spa, and 22,000 square feet of multipurpose convention space. The Wynn Macau expanded in 2010 to add the Encore, an all-suite hotel integrated into the existing casino, with another 414 suites.

Mary Foote Henderson

One of the first women in real estate development was Mary Foote Henderson (1846–1931), the daughter of Judge Elisha Foote of Seneca Falls, New York. At 22 she married Senator John Henderson from Missouri, the senator who had introduced the constitutional amendment abolishing slavery. Shortly before the wedding, Henderson was one of the few Republican senators to vote against impeaching President Andrew Johnson, a vote that ended his political career. However, the couple soon found themselves very wealthy as the result of Henderson's purchase of Missouri county bonds issued after the Civil War and believed worthless. He purchased them at 10 cents on the dollar, but when the courts enforced the honoring of the bonds, he was paid the full face value.

Mary became interested in the Meridian Hill neighborhood surrounding the Washington, D.C., home, which led to her buying blocks of real estate that she developed by building elaborate, distinctive homes, which she then sold as embassies and diplomatic residences. She funded and was involved in many plans for beautifying and developing the D.C. area, and she supported a 1900 plan to replace the White House with a more impressive modern mansion on Meridian Hill. Although that project was unsuccessful, the District of Columbia did respond to another of her crusades: to change the name of 16th Avenue to the Avenue of the Presidents.

Current Opportunities for Real Estate Entrepreneurs

Realtors are generally slow to adopt new technologies and adapt to changing conditions. The industry still promulgates the myth that buying a house is a sound investment—the foundational myth of the modern real estate industry born in the 1960s. On the contrary, economists have made it clear that, for most homebuyers, the appreciation of their home's value over time will just about keep up with inflation, allowing them to break even on the sale. Even in the face of the housing collapse that began in 2008, the old myth is still part of the standard home purchase pitch and the industry has been slow to promote alternative justifications for purchasing a home. However, wherever there is an industry that is change-resistant, there is opportunity for innovation.

Alternative business models may be attractive for real estate entrepreneurs. One model charges lower commissions but offers fewer services. For instance, the realtor may do nothing more than list the property on the Multiple Listing Service for the seller, letting the seller handle contract negotiations with the buyer, arrange home showings, and perform other tasks. For the small commission or flat fee the realtor charges, the seller benefits from MLS exposure. The legality of such a stripped-down service may be questionable in some states; state legislation sometimes mandates certain minimum services be provided by a realtor. The listing-only service can be augmented with à la carte services, paid for individually rather than built into the price or commission, as in traditional realtor service.

Another area for new ventures is real-estate consulting, in which the realtor's revenue is generated not from a sales commission but from an hourly rate. Consultants are assured that their time is compensated, and customers are assured that they are paying only for time the consulting realtor actually spends helping them. This potentially protects both parties, as consultants do not need to worry about unpaid time spent driving potential buyers around looking at properties or about the seriousness of a potential buyer. Consultants can also work with investors who are interested in commercial properties or other real estate investments.

Bill Kte'pi
Independent Scholar

See also Entrepreneurs in History; Franchisee and Franchisor; Franchises: Starting; Insurance; Master of Business Administration; Sales; Venture Valuation

Further Readings

Gunderson, Gerald. *An Entrepreneurial History of the United States.* Washington, DC: Beard Books, 2005.
Kazmierski, Michael. *The Paths and Characteristics of Real Estate Entrepreneurs.* Cambridge, MA: MIT, 2008.
Randel, James A. *Confessions of a Real-Estate Entrepreneur.* New York: McGraw-Hill, 2006.
Rider, Stuart Leland. *Great Big Book on Real Estate Investing: Everything You Need to Know to Create Wealth in Real Estate.* Irvine, CA: Entrepreneur Press, 2005.

ENTREPRENEURS IN TECHNOLOGY

Entrepreneurs in technology are defined as individuals developing new ventures in a technology-intensive environment. Other terms for this type of entrepreneur are *technoentrepreneur* and *technopreneur*. The specific skills of these entrepreneurs are derived from their operations and experience in environments where technologies are key assets. It is important to note that today most entrepreneurs deal with technology at some level, even if they are florists or coffee-shop owners. The difference between these entrepreneurs and technoentrepreneurs, however, is the magnitude of importance of technologies in their value chain and the degree to which their ventures are considered "high-tech" or dependent on technology. As a consequence, technoentrepreneurs tend to be different and behave differently from entrepreneurs operating in more mature or less technology-intensive environments.

First, operating in technology-intensive environments means that entrepreneurs will be confronted on a regular basis with breakthroughs in their industries. As the founder of a new venture, the technoentrepreneur may even expect to be at the start of this breakthrough. New technology ventures are almost always created based on a technology (product or process technology) the founders expect will offer better performance than existing ones.

Technologies go through life cycles, known as technology life cycles, where an existing technology evolves in terms of performance (through incremental innovation) up to a plateau. It is then replaced by a newer technology offering better performance. For a new technology venture, this means that it can expect to need the capacity and resources to adapt to or ideally remain ahead of frequent changes in technology, whether these be the technologies that operate the venture or technologies that form part of the venture's products or services.

Characteristics of Technoentrepreneurs

The differences in behavioral characteristics between technoentrepreneurs and "regular" entrepreneurs are not obvious. However, it can be said that the characteristics that contribute to the success of all entrepreneurs—their thirst for freedom, aversion to authority, and risk-taking behavior—must be present in extra measure in technoentrepreneurs. The ability to undertake risk is particularly easy to understand. Starting a venture with an unproven technology requires a higher level of risk acceptance than opening a hair salon, a restaurant, or a car dealership.

The most common characteristic of technoentrepreneurs is that they are either themselves highly skilled in one scientific or technical domain or are part of a team with at least one highly skilled individual. For technoentrepreneurs with a scientific or technical background, two types of entrepreneurs will be found: those starting a business during or right after graduating (the founders of Google, for example) and those starting a business after extensive experience as a researcher. The latter type typifies ventures that are spin-offs from public research labs in Europe and the United States or even spin-offs from large companies. The researcher brings to the new venture a higher level of scientific knowledge.

On one hand, young graduates starting a high-tech business are mostly found in the information technology (IT) industry, where the accumulation of knowledge is less crucial than "getting the right idea." On the other hand, older technoentrepreneurs coming from a research background will tend to develop more sophisticated products in more technology-intensive industries (microelectronics, biotechnologies, and nanotechnologies, for example). In a study in Catalonia, C. Serarols and D. Urbano (2008) found that dot-com entrepreneurs tend to be younger than traditional entrepreneurs.

It can be noted that these characteristics have a direct influence on the development of start-ups in different regions. Venture capitalists from the United States tend to be fine with the financing of start-ups created by young and inexperienced technoentrepreneurs in new and unproven markets (Facebook being the latest important example). On the contrary, venture capitalists from Europe are generally wary of these profiles and prefer to invest in ventures created by older and more experienced people with strong scientific and technical backgrounds. As a consequence (even if it is not the only reason), start-ups in the Internet world are coming more from the United States than from Europe, and the few European success stories (Meetic, for example) have been backed mainly by non-European venture capitalists.

It is incorrect to assert that all technoentrepreneurs have a Ph.D. in a scientific field or have an extensive research background. Although that may be true for many technoentrepreneurs, there are also many examples of successful technoentrepreneurs without any scientific degree. Bill Gates is one; more recently, among the three founders of Twitter, only one has an engineering background, the other two are college dropouts (and serial entrepreneurs). Nevertheless, as Serarols and Urbano have found, the level of education is generally found to be related to the success of a start-up.

If they do not have deep scientific or technical skills, technoentrepreneurs have the skills to evaluate the potential of new high-tech ventures and to create adequate management teams. Most of the time through the use of their network, they will be able to transform a technology-based idea into a business model with the potential to generate revenues.

The most detailed study so far on the characteristics that have influenced the success or failure of technoentrepreneurs was done in 2009 for the Kauffman Foundation by V. Wadhwa et al. As it concerns only high-tech entrepreneurs based in the United States, the results cannot be extrapolated for application to other regions of the world. According to this study, their profiles are as follows:

- The vast majority have a middle-class or upper-class family background.
- 95 percent of them have at least a bachelor's degree, and the majority were in the top 30 percent of their classes.
- They are, on average, 40 years old, mostly married, with children.

Concerning their explanations for success, the main points highlighted by high-tech entrepreneurs are

- prior work experience,
- learning from previous successes and failures,

- the management team,
- professional and personal networks,
- a university education but not an alumni network, and
- availability of financing, although external sources of financing did not really influence the start-up.

For the entrepreneurs creating their venture for the first time, the report shows that 10 percent received money only from venture capital or from private investment (angels). We can note also that the support from regional or local public institutions is ranked as not important. This could be one of the differences between the United States and other countries, such as Finland, Singapore, or Malaysia, where governments are more involved in the development of technoentrepreneurial ventures.

When asked what may inhibit the creation of new ventures by others, the personal characteristics cited are the following:

- A willingness or ability to take risks
- Lots of time and effort required
- Business management skills
- Entrepreneurial knowledge (understanding how to start a business)
- Industry and markets knowledge
- Family and financial pressures

Finally, it is important to note that a large percentage of the technoentrepreneurs surveyed mention "good fortune" as an important factor in their success.

High-tech entrepreneurs often start with a strong motivation and an idea in which they really believe. For Michael Dell, that idea took the form of a PC business did not need intermediaries to sell them—in other words, computers that could be sold directly and could, moreover, be made to order at a cost cheaper than that of the competition. After the ideas come the technologies to support the ideas. In the case of Dell, a very powerful logistical system was rallied to source components, assemble the machines, and deliver them efficiently and effectively to end users. The motto "A good idea with the supporting technologies" could be applied also to the story of Apple, Google, and eBay.

Technoentrepreneurs and the Growth of the Venture

The growth of a technology-based venture can take many different turns. Obviously, growth will depend on the general success of the firm: whether it is able to recruit an adequate top management team, secure recurrent sales, grow sales, expand its market scope, cope with competition, and renew its technology portfolio. Numerous internal and external factors determine this success. However, the characteristics of the entrepreneur will also play a key role. Concerning the "intrinsic" characteristics of the technoentrepreneur, only scarce evidence is available in the literature. It was found by R. H. Trivedi and colleagues (2009) that entrepreneurial competencies and level of education are positively related to the growth of the start-up. However, the willingness of the entrepreneur to grow the business is one of the most important factors; growth is inherently related to the fit with the aspirations of the entrepreneur. In a situation where the founder is not comfortable with handling the growth of the company, two situations may evolve: First, and this is the most common case, the company will not grow but remain at a size that is satisfactory for the shareholders and the stakeholders. It is important to note that the vast majority of the businesses in most countries in the world are small or very small businesses. The second possibility is that the founder will give often give the executive responsibilities to a "professional" manager, usually a chief executive officer (CEO), who may have a successful background in a large company. By using this second strategy, the entrepreneur may keep the potential for growth of the venture open while staying in his or her comfort zone.

Stepping Down and Letting the Company Grow

Overall, the more a venture grows, the more the top management team will originate from large and established companies. It is obviously the duty of the founder who wants to grow the venture to hire and motivate the right people at the right time, choosing those whose abilities exceed and/or complement the entrepreneur's own characteristics.

An example includes Bill Gates transmitting the management of Microsoft to Steve Ballmer; similar developments have occurred at eBay with Pierre Omidyar and Meg Whitman or Google with Eric Schmidt, and there are numerous other examples where a technoentrepreneur has transferred the management role to somebody else while retaining another role in the company such as chairman of the Board or head of research and development. This is often how companies grow into global concerns.

On the contrary, there are many examples of companies with very promising technologies that never "took off," mostly because the founder remained the main manager. Bringing in a "nonfounder" as the CEO allowed these companies to benefit from more mainstream managerial competencies and from the experience gathered by these CEOs elsewhere. In the case of Microsoft, Steve Ballmer was one of the first employees of Microsoft, but he had sales and marketing competencies that were very well complementing Bill Gates's technological ones. For eBay or Google, the founders had no or few managerial skills and often no interest in growing the firm, preferring to remain on the technology or development side of the business.

François Therin
University College of Media Arts and Sciences

See also Entrepreneurs in Consumer Products; Entrepreneurs in Entertainment; Entrepreneurs in Franchising; Entrepreneurs in History; Entrepreneurs in Media

Further Readings

Serarols, C. and D. Urbano. "Do Dot.com and Traditional Entrepreneurs Succeed in the Same Way? A Multiple Case in Catalonia." *International Journal of Technoentrepreneurship*, v.1/4 (2008).

Trivedi, R. H., J. R. Savalia, and J. D. Patel. "Linking Technopreneurial Competence and Education to Business Growth." *International Journal of Technoentrepreneurship*, v.2/2 (2009).

Wadhwa, V., R. Aggarwal, K. Holly, and A. Salkever. *The Anatomy of an Entrepreneur: Making of a Successful Entrepreneur.* Kansas City, MO: Kauffman Foundation, 2009.

ENTREPRENEURS IN TRANSPORTATION

The convenience and affordability of transport services have changed radically over the last 50 years. Increased carrying capacity—through the development of wide-bodied jets and very large cargo carriers, for example—has extended distances and routes while reducing unit costs per mile traveled. Such innovations have facilitated the globalization of economic activity and the expansion of leisure travel. The continued search for convenient access, affordable travel, and reliable shipment of goods has provided and continues to offer opportunities for new ventures and new models for the conduct of business operations, although entrepreneurialism is more evident in some parts of the transport sector than in others.

Rail and sea freight remain big-business activities as a consequence of their high capital requirements, their use of dedicated infrastructure, and their large economies of scale. In some countries, the provision of rail services remains a state monopoly, whereas in others privatization has given an opening for new providers but typically in the context of regulation that continues to control market entry. Partly for reasons of ensuring safety and curbing the ability of monopoly providers to act against consumer interests as well as on the possibly more spurious grounds of controlling national interest, the transport sector as a whole continues to be highly regulated by governments and their agencies. The routes that individual operators can service and driver standards are frequently the subject of regulation. In addition, the public sector in many countries is often responsible for funding, building, and maintaining large parts of the transport system infrastructure, from expressways and other roads to airports and ferry ports, although various forms of public-private partnership may be employed to deliver these services.

Developments in technology and changes in public attitudes tend to create ongoing friction between the scope of government regulation and demands for open markets. Impatient entrepreneurs have frequently been at the forefront of efforts to expose unnecessary regulation and open markets to competition. This has been particularly the case for the air transport industry, where regulation was slow to respond to changing market realities and the glamour of air travel helps draw ambitious entrepreneurs to the sector.

Such an entrepreneur was Freddie Laker, who foresaw the likely direction of air industry deregulation in the United States in the 1970s and attempted to build a new type of airline. At a time when regulators were concerned to protect the position of established national airlines, Laker developed the concept for a new type of airline he dubbed the Skytrain. The Skytrain predates and in some respects aimed to go further than modern budget airlines in changing the affordability of air travel. Tickets for the London–New York Skytrain service were sold as walk-on fares available on the day of travel only, greatly reducing the cost by saving on the need for reservation systems and commission payments to ticket agents. Regulatory approval for the service was gained as Laker argued his service would create new demand rather than cannibalize the markets of the established carriers. The Skytrain concept was popular with the public, with people prepared to stand in line for up to five days to get on a flight. Expansion into other transatlantic routes and the introduction of advance booking contributed to the airline's collapse in 1982 through a combination of overborrowing, high interest rates, and the competitive retaliation. Laker airlines did not survive, but it

Innovations like the development of large cargo carriers in the 1910s and wide-bodied jets in 1970 have increased carrying capacity, extended possible distances and route options, and reduced the unit costs of goods per mile transported. (Photos.com)

can be credited with encouraging the introduction of more diversified pricing structures, including standby and advance purchase fares.

In the United States, another pioneering airline has had an even more enduring impact in providing a model that other low-cost airlines have followed as deregulation has opened space for new entrants. Southwest Airlines was established in 1971 with three aircraft to serve three cities in Texas: Dallas, Houston, and San Antonio. Operating within the state of Texas only, the airline was exempt from the controls enforced by the Civil Aeronautics Board, which regulated fares and service levels. With this freedom, it developed a winning, low-cost, friendly staff and "fun" formula. Academics who study service quality present it as a model for how a relaxed working environment, enjoyed by employees, can enable an organization to rely on staff commitment rather than having to employ scripts and other mechanistic devices to ensure customers remain satisfied with the level of service. With this advantage, the airline was well positioned to take advantage of the changes brought by the 1978 Airline Deregulation Act.

The 1978 act addressed the regulatory restrictions then affecting the growth of air travel, especially the effective control of fares by existing scheduled carriers and the prevention of new entrants into the domestic market from flying beyond individual state boundaries. This coincided with the second oil crisis, involving Organization of Petroleum Exporting Countries (OPEC), which caused a collapse in demand for air travel. That made the act particularly decisive in enabling new entrants such as Southwest Airlines to dislodge industry incumbents, including such long-established airlines as Pan Am and TWA. In 1990, Southwest passed the billion-dollar revenue turnover level and had a string of awards for its customer service. Indeed, such has been the impact of the airline that a "Southwest effect" has been identified whereby wherever the airline introduces service, across-the-board reductions in fares are made for all airlines providing service to and from the same and neighboring locations with consequent increases in passenger numbers. Reflecting this at one stage, it was reported that at any one time more than 50 communities were trying to persuade Southwest Airlines to introduce service to their localities.

Subsequent to the success of Southwest Airlines, imitators have found additional ways of lowering costs. An article in the *Journal of Transport*

Geography draws on several sources to distill the components that differentiate low cost from traditional airline companies. The core techniques are Internet booking, minimum cabin crews, lower wage scales, flexible working terms and conditions for employees relative to full-cost airlines, one class of seating to allow more seats per aircraft, short turnaround times at airports, no cargo carried (avoiding potential sources of delay as cargo is loaded and offloaded), a simple fare structure and pricing strategy, e-ticketing, no seat allocation, inflight sale of food and drink (rather than complimentary offerings), point-to-point services (rather than services connected through hub airports), a single type of aircraft, and the use of secondary airports that have capacity to ensure the swift turnaround of aircraft as a further contributor to maximizing aircraft utilization. Nonetheless, replicating some of these features alone is not sufficient to guarantee survival, with many of the start-up airlines following in the wake of Southwest Airlines having not survived. These include People Express in the United States and Debonair in Europe. The propensity for established carriers is to set up their own low-cost services, either by establishing low-cost subsidiaries or by adapting their core business model. A further reason is that the entrepreneurial flair and resources of the founder or founders are critical success factors for start-up airlines.

Charismatic leaders capable of inspiring staff loyalty and attracting customer support are a feature of the low-cost airlines that have succeeded. Such leaders include, in the United States, Herb Kelleher and Rollin King (Southwest); in Europe, Tony Ryan (Ryanair) and Stelios Haji-Ioannou (EasyJet); in Australia, Richard Branson (who has played an important role through Virgin Blue airlines); and in Asia, Tony Fernandes (who has built AirAsia into an airline that is claimed to have the lowest costs per passenger kilometer of the main budget airlines). Vision and commitment of individual entrepreneurs are important, but it is also significant that their start-up ventures have had capacity to expand rapidly. Attaining a critical mass is important for success in an industry where there are economies of scale and the need to secure a degree of market penetration. Entrepreneurs also need to be able to draw on financial backing to deter aggressive price and capacity behavior by established airlines. This is reflected in the way that many of the start-ups that

survive either developed from existing airlines (as in the case of Southwest, Ryanair, and Virgin Blue) or were led by entrepreneurs who had significant financial resources from prior business ventures.

Courier services are another area of transportation where entrepreneurialism has developed on the margins of regulated activity. The geographers Michael Taylor and Alan Hallsworth identify United Parcel Services (UPS) as the longest-established courier business among present-day participants. It was founded in 1907 in Seattle as a bicycle-based courier service mainly to deliver parcels above the weight limit that was reserved for the U.S. Postal Service. Over time it strengthened its position as a "shadow" post office by setting up collection points across the United States. It developed an attachment to efficient systems-driven operations that included requirements for UPS drivers of its brown and gold delivery trucks always to carry their cash in the same hand, to step down from the company's vehicles right foot first, and to adhere to other presentation requirements that included a ban on beards. The formalized and rigid work organization, combined with employee ownership and unionization, helped UPS expand across its home country but became harder to sustain when it expanded overseas.

UPS remained a purely ground-based delivery service up to 1982, when it also began to use air shipment. The possibility of using air transport to provide fast, overnight delivery services had first been identified by Federal Express (now FDX). Frederick W. Smith established Federal Express in 1973 in Memphis, Tennessee, as a service offering a guaranteed 24-hour pickup-to-delivery time for envelopes and light documents. As well as overnight air transport, Federal Express introduced a hub-spoke distribution service in which selected locations were used for assembling and distributing documents and computerized monitoring of items in delivery. It was initially restricted to the use of aircraft with a cargo capacity of up to 6,200 pounds. Above this limit, the Civil Aeronautics Board controlled the ability to offer air freight services. The same airline deregulation that opened the national market to Southwest Airlines enabled Federal Express to increase the size of its carriers, shifting it from being a specialized (and generally loss-making) niche operator in the courier industry into a leading player. In 1987 it gained regulatory approval for a U.S.-to-Japan express delivery service that had been permitted by an agreement between the respective governments and that initially allowed only one operator from each country to supply the service.

DHL, founded in 1969, is the third major player in the courier business. Its origins are closely tied to the accelerating internationalization of business and trade. The founders of DHL (Adrian Dalsay, Larry Hillblom, and Robert Lynn) set up a business to deliver documents relating to freight being shipped by sea ahead of the ship's docking. Using airmail delivery, DHL offered shipping companies a potential saving of two or three days in the time spent in port by enabling them to commence customs and other formalities in advance of a ship's arrival. From this base, Dalsay, Hillblom, and Lynn built a company specializing in the delivery of documents that were time-sensitive, low-weight, and high-value because of the transactions to which they related.

Internationalization of the operations of these companies, which commenced with separate business models, encouraged growing convergence among the leading courier firms by the end of the 20th century. Maintaining the relevance of their services has depended on the rapid adoption of new technology. Certainty of delivery has become as important as the speed of delivery, and this is reflected in the development of tracking technologies that enable courier companies to know where any item is between pickup and delivery. The development of e-commerce has brought two main responses: alliances with software companies to offer e-commerce services, and alignment with major e-commerce enterprises to offer complete logistical solutions that can take care of all delivery and warehousing needs. A further strategy has been to compete more directly with state-owned postal services, a move partly encouraged by the postal companies, which themselves have seen integration with international courier firms as a way of maintaining their own viability in the wake of the decline in traditional mail services.

Increasing concern with the environmental impacts of transport is affecting all modes of transport. This is a combined outcome of the growth in transport activity, the transport sector's reliance on petroleum, and the growing awareness of environmental issues arising from transport emissions, the loss of land for transport infrastructure, and the possibility of global environmental change. Whereas these concerns have yet to see a decline in the demand for air travel, in Europe, in Japan, and to a lesser extent in the United States it is reckoned that younger people are giving less priority to car ownership than the existing generation of car owners. This is not explained by environmental concerns alone; it is also the case that physical mobility, at least as it affects local travel, is not the same priority it was in the past. Market research indicates that increasingly the one technology young people say they cannot do without is a mobile phone, not a car.

Car clubs are one of the new forms of enterprise that are responding to changing markets for transport services. Zipcar is one of the best known, and it has expanded from its original base in Boston, Massachusetts, across big cities in the United States and then into Europe. Zipcar developed from a meeting in 1999 when Antje Danielson (an environmental science scholar at Harvard University) introduced Robin Chase (a graduate of the Massachusetts Institute of Technology Business School) to the concept of car sharing. Car-sharing schemes had been developing in certain European cities, where the basic model used information technology to increase the flexibility of car rental in ways that make it an option more feasible than car ownership for urban residents.

Car clubs work by locating a fleet of cars across a particular neighborhood and putting them in dedicated spaces on the streets or in car parks. People who join the club are issued smart cards and pin codes that, respectively, open the car door and allow them to start the engine. To book a car—whether for 30 minutes, several hours, or longer—members go online or telephone, locate the nearest available vehicle, and book it. All journeys are charged in a single, monthly bill. This makes car renting almost as convenient as owning a vehicle, but without the costs and management troubles (depreciation, the annual service, parking costs, and so on) that go with it. For people in big cities who do not have a daily need for a car, there can be significant financial savings in replacing car ownership with car club membership. With the focus on short-distance hires, it is possible that members get to use the same vehicle week after week—an advantage for the car club over traditional vehicle rental companies, where users have no sense of association with the vehicles that they use.

In developing this concept in the United States, Zipcar has been identified as a challenger brand, using the concept developed by Adam Morgan in his book *Eating the Big Fish*. Challenger brands have four attributes: deciding what they stand for and sticking to it; crafting a compelling story; building a "lighthouse identity" (whereby the consumer follows the venture's lead rather than the firm being led by existing consumer preferences); and being brave enough to challenge that part of the market the venture is seeking to reconfigure. This depiction of Zipcar is justified by its success in extending participation away from the early adopters to "average" consumers. It is less typical in that mainstream car manufacturers, including Daimler and PSA Peugeot Citroën, are competitors.

Martin Perry
Massey University

See also Entrepreneurs in Energy; Entrepreneurs in History; Geographic Location; Geography of Innovation; Infrastructure; Location Strategy; Service Innovation; Territorial Strategy and Regions

Further Readings

Bunz, U. and J. Maes. "Learning Excellence: Southwest Airlines' Approach." *Managing Service Quality*, v.3 (1998).

Francis, G., I. Humphreys, S. Ison, and M. Aickon. "Where Next for Low Cost Airlines? A Spatial and Temporal Comparative Study." *Journal of Transport Geography*, v.14 (2006).

Morgan, A. *Eating the Big Fish: How Challenger Brands Can Compete Against Brand Leaders*, 2nd ed. Hoboken, NJ: Wiley, 2009.

Taylor, M. and A. Hallsworth. "Power Relations and Market Transformation in the Transport Sector: The Example of the Courier Services Industry." *Journal of Transport Geography*, v.8 (2000).

Tomkins, R. "You Take the Hire Road." *Financial Times* (October 12, 2007).

Tyrrell, P. "The Value of Being an Underdog." *Financial Times* (November 22, 2010).

ENTREPRENEURSHIP EDUCATION: GRADUATE PROGRAMS

Entrepreneurship education has been part of the postsecondary curriculum since at least the 1970s. However, with the increasing number of entrepreneurship programs in universities and colleges and technical institutes, more importance has been placed on entrepreneurship education pedagogy and the appropriateness and effectiveness of entrepreneurship education at the postsecondary level. Surveys and analyses of different pedagogical methods in this area started in the mid-1980s, as the first master's of business administration (MBA) program in entrepreneurship was offered in 1971 at the University of South California; the field then started to pick up steam.

In providing an overview of entrepreneurship education in postsecondary institutions there are two major challenges. It is important to note that as recently as 1991 the literature acknowledged that entrepreneurship education may be challenged by the lack of a solid theoretical basis. Although significant strides have been made in developing a theoretical foundation for entrepreneurship education, the absence of an agreed-upon definition of entrepreneurship has limited its progress. This lack of a common definition of entrepreneurship has been cited by researchers as recently as 2009, although despite this limitation interest in entrepreneurship education and business schools has heightened. Also, the definition of entrepreneurship has been the subject of wide debate in academic literature. Discussions have ranged from how entrepreneurship differs from new venture creation and business start-up to whether entrepreneurship is defined by individual activity or through descriptors of individuals. In regard to the theoretical grounding, there generally have been three approaches to examining entrepreneurship: the psychological or trait approach, the behavioral approach, and the opportunity identification approach.

Early research on personality and trait determinants of entrepreneurship identified three psychological constructs—achievement motivation, locus of control, and high risk-taking propensity as necessary individual traits or characteristics for successful entrepreneurship activity. This approach has evolved into an approach characterized by traits and characteristics of entrepreneurs. The question being addressed is why some individuals become entrepreneurs to start new ventures while other individuals, under the same circumstances, choose not to start new ventures or fail in the attempt. There are obvious implications for postsecondary entrepreneurship education. If entrepreneurs are successful because of traits and characteristics, it begs the question of whether entrepreneurship can be taught at the postsecondary level or whether postsecondary entrepreneurship education programs should have personality or trait screening as part of their admission criteria.

The behavioral approach emerged out of criticism of the trait approach and held that researchers should focus on what the entrepreneur does and not who the entrepreneur is. This approach to the study of entrepreneurship focuses on the organization as the primary level of analysis and focuses on the individual to the extent that the individual's actions enable or cause the organization to come into existence. This approach leads to entrepreneurial education focusing on the organizational conditions and influences relative to new venture creation or entrepreneurial activity. Organizational analysis, motivational theory, and organizational design and structures are what the behavioral approach contends should be the focus for entrepreneurial education in postsecondary education.

The opportunity identification approach to entrepreneurship focuses on how opportunities that bring in future goods and services are discovered, created, and exploited. This resource-based approach to defining entrepreneurial activity sees such activity occurring when an individual is able to combine resources that he or she believes will yield a profit. In this sense, entrepreneurship is a nexus or crossroads of enterprising individuals acting in a way that allows them to take advantage of entrepreneurial opportunities. This approach finds a parallel in economic theory and focuses on the individual's ability to identify opportunities for entrepreneurial activity rather than on the characteristics of the individual or the individual's behavior.

It is important to note that many entrepreneurship education programs take a varied or combined approach to the pedagogy of entrepreneurship education. That is to say, some programs may acknowledge traits or characteristics as a piece of the entrepreneurial puzzle but provide education to build on those traits or characteristics (in order to develop the skills necessary to identifying possible opportunities) or education to build organizational structures and components to ensure successful new venture creation.

More recently, there has been some research linking emotional intelligence to successful entrepreneurial activity. The research model of Leonidas Zampetakis et al. (2009) provides supporting evidence that "students are more likely to formulate

the intentions of starting their own business when they are high in trait emotional self-efficacy—the belief that they can successfully feel, recognize, regulate, control, and evaluate their own and others' emotions."

Contemporary entrepreneurship education continues to wrestle with the issue of what constitutes entrepreneurial activity. L. Pittaway and J. Cope (2007) highlight a lack of consensus on what entrepreneurship actually "is" when implemented in practice. They go on to argue that it is unclear whether entrepreneurship education enables graduates to become more effective entrepreneurs. They report that research on graduate outcomes has typically sought to identify mechanisms that can help graduate entrepreneurship occur, what variables influence success, and whether graduate-led enterprises are more successful than nongraduate ventures. They conclude that "certain factors like access to early stage finance, mentoring, and business support have some impact on chances of successful venture creation but it is difficult to conclude to what degree these influence the process and whether or not other factors (e.g., proactive behavior) actually sit behind the variables so far investigated." The implication that successful entrepreneurship is some combination of internal and external factors suggests that while entrepreneurship education may develop some entrepreneurial and new venture creation knowledge and skills, an individual's predisposition toward certain behaviors (such as the ability to be proactive) may be influenced by personal traits or characteristics.

M. Binks, K. Starky, and C. Mahon (2006) take a different perspective on entrepreneurship education and appropriate pedagogy. They contend that it is important to avoid definitional debates surrounding "entrepreneurship" and necessary to consider the entrepreneurial process holistically alongside the breadth of applications to which it is relevant. They focus on "improvement and change through realized creativity" rather than just new business formation and suggest a multidisciplinary approach to achieve this.

D. Kuratko (2005) notes a similar legitimacy but lack of maturity in entrepreneurship education. "The trend in most universities," Kuratko remarks, "is to develop or expand entrepreneurship programs and design unique and challenging curricula specifically designed for entrepreneurship students"; he further notes that "recognition is now being given to entrepreneurial schools." However, this growing infrastructure still lacks full departments dedicated to entrepreneurship or faculty granted tenure purely on the basis of their research and teaching in entrepreneurship. In addition, pure entrepreneurial journals are rarely considered "A" journals.

C. P. Zeithaml and G. H. Rice (1987) highlighted the increasing fragmentation of business education into specializations, contending that education in entrepreneurship covered the entire scope of business administration. They believed the field had the opportunity to take a broad, integrative, pragmatic, and rational approach to business.

In contrast, G. T. Solomon, S. Duffy, and A. Tarabashy (2002) believe that entrepreneurial education is unique and different from business management education. In their review of entrepreneurial pedagogy, they argue that entrepreneurial education must address the nature of business entry and therefore must include the development of a particular skill set that includes negotiation, leadership, product development, creative thinking, sourcing capital, idea protection, and other characteristics that define the entrepreneurial personality.

Research increasingly uses case-study and longitudinal methodologies exploring the performance of graduate enterprises over time. The anecdotal nature of these studies, however, yields mixed results. W. E. McMullan and L. M. Gillin's research (1998) tracked the outcomes of entrepreneurship graduates of Swinburne University of Technology in Melbourne, Australia. The results showed that 87 percent started ventures, either independently or under the auspices of a corporation. From this McMullan and Gillin deduced that the program showed signs "not only of helping people begin meaningful entrepreneurial careers, but also of providing governments with an effective microeconomic response for job creation." P. Rosa (2003), on the other hand, finds that British and Scottish graduates of entrepreneurship programs "tend to develop small and unimaginative businesses."

A point on which the literature—including Pittaway and Cope (2007), C. L. Shook, R. L. Priem, and J. E. McGee (2003), and B. W. Clark, C. H. Davies, and V. C. Harnish (1984)—does seem to agree is that entrepreneurship education might have an effect on entrepreneurship intentions. However, the effect of entrepreneurship education on venture creation outcomes, such as whether courses in entrepreneurship have more or less impact on venture creation than more traditional business courses, begs further research.

Indeed, while the literature affirms a profound adoption of entrepreneurship programs, particularly in the United States and the United Kingdom, evidence in the literature on what works and why is fragmented. What confounds the issues of pedagogy in postsecondary entrepreneurial education even more is that despite successes in teaching methodologies, the policy climate outside the academic environment as a determinant for entrepreneurial success adds yet another layer of complexity to attributing causality to pedagogical components. Nevertheless, the growing literature on entrepreneurial education at the postsecondary level provides a suite of approaches and models that vary in structure. Thematic convergences in the literature can help guide institutions to confirm strengths and weaknesses in their own approaches.

Mike Henry
Grant MacEwan University

See also Entrepreneurial Support Systems; Entrepreneurial Training; Entrepreneurship Education: High School; Entrepreneurship Education: Undergraduate Programs; Entrepreneurship Pedagogy; Leadership; Leadership: Training and Development; Leadership: Transformational; Learning; Learning Theory; Master of Business Administration; Networks; Social Networks

Further Readings

Binks, M., K. Starkey, and C. Mahon. "Entrepreneurship Education and the Business School." *Technology Analysis and Strategic Management*, v.18/1 (2006).

Clark, B. W., C. H. Davis, and V. C. Harnish. "Do Courses in Entrepreneurship Aid in New Venture Creation?" *Journal of Small Business Management*, v.22/2 (1984).

Finkle, T. "Entrepreneurship Education Trends." *Research in Business and Economics Journal*. http://www.aabri.com/manuscripts/08034.pdf (Accessed December 2010).

Gartner, William B. "'Who Is an Entrepreneur?' Is the Wrong Question." *Entrepreneurship Theory and Practice* (Summer 1989).

Kuratko, D. "The Emergence of Entrepreneurship Education: Development, Trends, and Challenges." *Entrepreneurship Theory and Practice*, v.29/5 (2005).

McMullan, W. E. and L. M. Gillin. "Industrial Viewpoint: Entrepreneurship Education: Developing Technological Start-Up Entrepreneurs, a Case Study of a Graduate

Entrepreneurship Programme at Swinburne University." *Technovation*, v.18/4 (1998).

Pittaway, L. and J. Cope. "Entrepreneurship Education: A Systematic Review of the Evidence." *International Small Business Journal*, v.25/5 (2007).

Robinson, P. and M. Hayes. "Entrepreneurship Education in America's Major Universities." *Entrepreneurship Theory and Practice*, v.15/3 (1991).

Rosa, P. "Hardly Likely to Make the Japanese Tremble: The Businesses of Recently Graduated University and College Entrepreneurs." *International Small Business Journal*, v.21/4 (2003).

Shook, C. L., R. L. Priem, and J. E. McGee. "Venture Creation and the Enterprising Individual: A Review and Synthesis." *Journal of Management*, v.29 (2003).

Solomon, G. T., S. Duffy, and A. Tarabashy. "The State of Entrepreneurship Education in the United States: A Nation-Wide Survey and Analysis." *International Journal of Entrepreneurship Education*, v.1/1 (2002).

Zampetakis, Leonidas A. et al. "On the Relationship Between Emotional Intelligence and Entrepreneurial Attitudes and Intentions." *International Journal of Entrepreneurial Behaviour & Research*, v.15/6 (2009).

Zeithaml, C. P. and G. H. Rice. "Entrepreneurship/Small Business Education in American Universities." *Journal of Small Business Management*, v.25/1 (1987).

ENTREPRENEURSHIP EDUCATION: HIGH SCHOOL

Seven out of 10 high school youths want to start businesses rather than take jobs. The questions of whether entrepreneurship can be taught or entrepreneurship training is needed are obsolete. More appropriate questions should concern what should be taught and how it should be taught. Many of today's high schools do not address entrepreneurship education at all. Those that do include entrepreneurship among their courses offer few curricular options.

With the current shortage of entrepreneurs and the constant need to boost the country's economy, it is essential that high school students are able to compete in local, regional, and global marketplaces. There is a need to determine if the entrepreneurial curriculum used in typical American high school districts (that is, where it exists at all) will help prepare students to be entrepreneurs. The literature suggests that there is a critical need for entrepreneurship

education in all stages and levels of the educational realm, especially at the high school level.

It is a sign of progress that the National Foundation of Teaching Entrepreneurship (NFTE) curriculum is now part of the Los Angeles Unified School District (LAUSD), among other equally valuable districts, elective classes. Not all schools offer this curriculum. Nonetheless, the NFTE curriculum can easily be put into effect if and where teachers and administrators are interested, and as resources are allocated for the curriculum to be taught.

The need for clarity about entrepreneurship is growing, as evidenced by the high interest in entrepreneurship by academic journals, professional associations, conferences, and academic appointments. The students most in need of the NFTE high school courses fall into three main groups: ethnic/racial minority students, inner-city students, and rural students. Current research shows that jobs are scarce in the inner cities and unemployment is high. The economic and social decline of American central cities is well documented, and the flight of industrial jobs from inner cities to suburban areas has resulted in rising poverty and unemployment for inner-city residents. The state of American inner cities needs to be assessed, and other opportunities, such as entrepreneurship education, need to be addressed.

While widely accepted definitions of *entrepreneur* and *entrepreneurship* are readily available, there appears to be no consensus on a focused definition of entrepreneurial education among most business scholars. According to the Consortium for Entrepreneurship Education (CEE), entrepreneurship education seeks to prepare people, especially young people, to be responsible, enterprising individuals who can become entrepreneurs or entrepreneurial thinkers and thereby contribute to economic development and sustainable communities. The present state of research, though meager, shows that entrepreneurship programs provide a mixture of opportunities for youth. Most entrepreneurship education programs focus on best practices and incorporate interactive learning, experience-based learning, role models, and community and business connections.

In general, entrepreneurship curriculum for the K–12 classroom focuses on entrepreneurship and teaches the students general behaviors and life skills, besides skills in starting a business. This curriculum usually focuses on three different groups of skills: (1) opportunity recognition, (2) the collection and commitment of resources, and (3) the creation of an operating business organization. Opportunity recognition involves the identification of needs in the marketplace and the creation of ideas for products or services that meet them. Collecting resources involves the willingness to take risks as well as skills in securing outside investors. The creation of an operating business organization requires the capability to deliver the service or product and includes the knowledge of financing/accounting, marketing, and management/leadership skills.

Three NFTE-sponsored studies on entrepreneurship education and curriculum have been conducted at three distinct school districts. These studies examined entrepreneurship education and curriculum on the secondary level. The first was a qualitative study on an entrepreneurial education program called Entre Prep. It was conducted at a high school in Los Angeles, California, in 2001. A group of high school seniors who participated in the program were surveyed to see what entrepreneurial-related themes emerged during the internship. The results showed that males' views on entrepreneurship education were much different from those of the females. The males were more concerned with the business knowledge gained and individual business accomplishments. The females were more interested in meaningful relationships they developed with their mentors and others in the work setting. The study suggested the importance of understanding gender differences in supplying entrepreneurship education.

A second study included classroom observations and focus groups with NFTE alumni, as well as pre- and post-test analysis of almost 1,000 youths who participated in the entrepreneurship education programs during 1995–96 among individual northern California and Washington, D.C., school districts. The results of the study indicated that 62 percent of the NFTE students improved in their entrepreneurship knowledge, in contrast to only 3 percent of the control group. These NFTE students' belief in their ability to start a profitable small business increased 20 percent after participating in the program; among the NFTE alumni students, 95 percent were very satisfied or satisfied with the NFTE program and would strongly recommend it to others.

The third study was conducted in two Boston public high schools (East Boston High and Brighton High) as a two-phase, multiyear study. The first phase of this study was designed to address the role of NFTE in supporting and enhancing entrepreneurship, including entrepreneurial thinking and behavior. Results indicated that the NFTE student group's aspirations to become entrepreneurs were 44 percent greater, whereas the comparison group's aspirations to become entrepreneurs were only 10 percent greater. In the follow-up, phase two, researchers increased the number of schools (from two to six) and the number of students. Results indicated that the NFTE students' overall Entrepreneurial Behavior score increased significantly from pre- to post-test, and the Locus of Control dimension of the NFTE students increased 3 percent. This indicated that in both phases of the study the NFTE students were more likely than the comparison-group students to engage in a range of entrepreneurial behaviors, such as taking initiative and taking on leadership roles, in many different aspects of their personal and professional lives.

In summary, those students participating in high school entrepreneurship programs benefit from the programs even if they do not decide to become entrepreneurs. Empirical studies support the notion that the transformational experience resulting from entrepreneurship education can be profound, including increased self-confidence, skilled public speaking, hands-on business skills, decreased vulnerability to negative peer pressure, a sense of purpose, the motivation to complete high school and go onto college, and increased self-responsibility.

Henrique Barreto
Kaplan University

See also Entrepreneurial Support Systems; Entrepreneurial Training; Entrepreneurship Education: Graduate Programs; Entrepreneurship Education: Undergraduate Programs; Entrepreneurship Pedagogy; Leadership; Leadership: Training and Development; Leadership: Transformational; Learning; Learning Theory; Master of Business Administration; Networks; Social Networks

Further Readings

Doucet, L. *Post-Evaluation of an Entrepreneurship Program for Inner-City Youth*. Malibu, CA: Pepperdine University, 2010.

Fitzgerald, J. "Promoting Entrepreneurship Among Inner-City High School Students: Does It Improve Student Outcomes?" *Urban Education*, v.34/2 (1999).

James, Karen B. *Participation in a National Foundation for Teaching Entrepreneurship Program: The Impact on High School Students' Knowledge of Entrepreneurship and Evaluation of the Learning Experience*. New Castle, DE: Wilmington University, 2008.

Mariotti, S. "About/Mission and History of NFTE." http://www.nfte.com/what/mission (Accessed January 2011).

National Clearinghouse on Families and Youth. "Learning by Doing: Investing in Youth Entrepreneurship." http://www2.ncfy.com/publications/lbd/ent.htm (Accessed January 2011).

ENTREPRENEURSHIP EDUCATION: UNDERGRADUATE PROGRAMS

Entrepreneurship is one of the top-growing subjects at four- and two-year colleges. The 1990s and 2000s have observed a worldwide surge in interest and involvement in entrepreneurial education. A study published in 2006 showed that 1,600 U.S. universities and colleges offered over 2,200 entrepreneurial-related courses. The dynamics of the economy and political changes have also drawn attention to nontraditional forms of entrepreneurship training and education. Many educators, researchers, and policy makers now believe that entrepreneurship education should play a major role in the curricula of many universities and colleges—they see entrepreneurship as a relevant economic policy directly tied to globalization, involving entrepreneurial skills to meet worldwide marketplace requirements.

In 2005, the state of entrepreneurship education programs in the United States did parade more than 2,200 courses at more than 1,600 schools. Of these numbers, there were 277 endowed positions, 44 refereed academic journals and other entrepreneurship-related journals, and over more than 100 established and funded centers. It was estimated that entrepreneurship, as an academic discipline, was worth about $450 million. Main courses included marketing and negotiation, leadership, accounting and finances, business ethics and law, new product development, creative thinking, and technological innovation. Minor, yet crucial, courses included business plans, computer entrepreneurial simulations, behavioral and situational computer simulations, and group activities dealing with situations to find novel solutions under conditions of stress, ambiguity, and risk.

Although there is a lack of agreement regarding educational approaches to entrepreneurship education, it is often structured in practical and economic terms. Many business schools, for example, use entrepreneurship education to spearhead local economic growth, advance regional development, and create jobs. One of the main frameworks of entrepreneurship education is the action-oriented approach. The action-oriented approach is best characterized by educators giving practical tools and encouraging their students to take on a "get out and do it now" attitude. Nevertheless, some argue that these entrepreneurship programs have not done a good job of teaching creativity, instead focusing on the regimentation of prescribed analytical problem-solving techniques focused mainly on the administration and bureaucracy of new enterprises.

The main challenge of entrepreneurship education revolves around the question, "Can entrepreneurship be effectively taught?" Fortunately, there is support in the literature that it can, by using myriad teaching approaches and by replacing the "Can" in the previous question with "What" and "How." For example, (1) passive lecture approaches should be replaced by team teaching, (2) business-only instructors and professors should be replaced by instructors and professors from other disciplines, and (3) pedagogy should move away from focused experts and toward didactic expertise and learning-by-doing entrepreneurial knowledge.

Grouped by rising order of complexity, the most popular teaching approaches are the following:

- *Managing enterprises:* This approach represents most undergraduate entrepreneurship education programs. It requires technical business skills (in accounting, finance, operations, and so forth) with leadership and strategic abilities. Instruction is usually offered as a combination of lectures/discussions, team projects, presentations, and case studies.
- *Starting new enterprises:* Here the focus is on the skills and tasks needed to form new businesses: business plans, securing venture capital, marketing, and so on. Skills are taught by using case studies, classroom and computer simulations, and real-world projects.
- *Identifying existing (and creating new) opportunities:* Here the focus is on identifying new opportunities and creating value. Skills

developed range from financial analysis, market research, and team building to strategic leadership. These skills are usually taught using innovative problem-solving techniques, such as creative-thinking exercises.

- *Creating comfort with uncertainty, employing self-alertness, fostering technological and organizational innovation, and adjusting to change*: These skills are taught through activities involving economic functions, economic theories, and discovery. The focus is on the awareness of economic models and trends.

Growth of entrepreneurship education in undergraduate programs is measured chiefly in two related ways: by the number of schools offering courses in small business or entrepreneurship, and by the number of classes in small business or entrepreneurship, both within traditional business schools. The number of schools offering courses in small business or entrepreneurship increased significantly between 1977 and 2001: from 93 to 1,200. If the number of courses offered outside traditional business schools is included, the increase was from 1,200 to 1,600. Most of these courses outside traditional business schools are offered in engineering schools, medical schools, schools of allied health, and veterinarian schools. The growth is also marked in both endowed positions, from less than 10 to more than 200 during the same time period.

In summary, the chief purpose of entrepreneurship education does not have to be the creation of entrepreneurs and the creation of new businesses. However, its main focus and the need for entrepreneurial education are evident; research indicates that less than 30 percent of entrepreneurs with no entrepreneurial education are expected to remain self-employed over the next five years. Of those with entrepreneurial training, 35 percent are expected to employ 20 or more workers over the next five years. In addition, many students are launching business enterprises during college and following graduation. Influencing this trend are corporate and government downsizing and a dreary national economic outlook. As self-employment becomes an option for students in all academic disciplines, student interest will drive a demand for entrepreneurship education at universities and colleges.

Henrique Barreto
Kaplan University

See also Entrepreneurial Support Systems; Entrepreneurial Training; Entrepreneurship Education: Graduate Programs; Entrepreneurship Education: High School; Entrepreneurship Pedagogy; Leadership; Leadership: Training and Development; Leadership: Transformational; Learning; Learning Theory; Master of Business Administration; Networks; Social Networks

Further Readings

Béchard, Jean-Pierre and Denis Grégoire. "Entrepreneurship Education Research Revisited: The Case of Higher Education." *Academy of Management Learning and Education*, v.4/1 (March 2005).

Katz, Jerome A. *A Brief History of Tertiary Entrepreneurship Education in the United States*. Brussels, Belgium: Organisation for Economic Co-operation and Development, 1998.

Katz, Jerome A. "The Chronology and Intellectual Trajectory of American Entrepreneurship Education, 1876–1999." *Journal of Business Venturing*, v.18/2 (March 2003).

Katz, Jerome A. "Fully Mature but Not Fully Legitimate: A Different Perspective on the State of Entrepreneurship Education." *Journal of Small Business Management*, v.46/4 (October 2008).

Klein, Peter G. and J. Bruce Bullock. "Can Entrepreneurship Be Taught?" *Journal of Agricultural and Applied Economics*, v.38/2 (August 2006).

Kuratko, D. F. "The Emergence of Entrepreneurship Education: Development, Trends, and Challenges." *Entrepreneurship Theory and Practice*, v.29/5 (September 2005).

Kuratko, D. F. "Entrepreneurship Education: Emerging Trends and Challenges for the 21st Century." White Paper, U.S. Association of Small Business Education, 2003.

Mars, Mathew M. *The Emerging Domains of Entrepreneurship Education: Students, Faculty, and the Capitalist Academy*. Tucson: University of Arizona, 2006.

Myrah, Kyleen. *A Study of Public Post-Secondary Entrepreneurship in British Columbia: The Possibilities and Challenges of an Integrated Approach*. Vancouver, BC: University of British Columbia, 2003.

Neck, Heidi M. and Patricia G. Greene. "Entrepreneurship Education: Known Worlds and New Frontiers." *Journal of Small Business Management*, v.49/1 (January 2011).

ENTREPRENEURSHIP PEDAGOGY

Entrepreneurship pedagogy refers to the educational strategies deployed to teach and assess entrepreneurship. The focus is less on curriculum design than on the underpinning educational philosophies, irrespective of the learners' educational level (primary or secondary school, college or university programs, adult education or professional courses) and the intended learning outcomes (such as developing learners' entrepreneurial skills, creating empathy with the entrepreneurial life/world, or starting a new venture for real). Entrepreneurship pedagogy examines the most appropriate learning strategies, including experiential learning, constructivist learning, and inquiry-based learning, as well as related topics, such as the changing role of the entrepreneurship teacher (from academic tutor to business adviser), the complex issue of entrepreneurship evaluation (what should be assessed, how, when, and by whom), and the need to develop a research agenda (to help entrepreneurship educators, at both theoretical and practical levels).

Experiential learning is a pedagogy that values learning from direct experience, learning by doing, and learning by reflection on doing, as opposed to didactic learning, in which the teacher transmits knowledge to the learners. In natural sciences, experiential learning is well illustrated by lab work, experiments, and observation. In the context of entrepreneurship education, experiential learning means that learners do not simply propose business ideas and write business plans but ideally also establish and run business ventures, even on a small scale. The underpinning pedagogical principle is that learners should later be able to repeat that entrepreneurial experience successfully, having done it first in a supportive educational environment, with minimal financial risks yet with the opportunity to reflect and learn from mistakes and guidance received from both teachers and peers. A pedagogical limitation is the fact that some context-specific knowledge may not be transferable and replicable in other situations. For example, a group of youngsters who successfully run a school-based, not-for-profit social enterprise may not be optimally equipped to set up and manage a commercial venture.

Constructivist learning is a pedagogy based on the view that people understand only what they have constructed themselves. Learning is seen as the result of individuals' mental construction, learners matching new information against existing information, thereby establishing meaningful connections and internalizing their new knowledge and understanding. The emphasis is on the learners working together and learning from one another. The teacher's responsibility is to frame and facilitate the learning experience. Online courses that use collaborative tools such as discussion forums and wikis are a good illustration of constructivist learning. In the context of entrepreneurship education, constructivist learning will favor group projects, typically with teams of students working together to design and research a new venture. The underpinning pedagogical principle is that learners will contribute to the collective construction of knowledge, combining their strengths and areas of expertise; for example, learners who are good at marketing will help the others learn about it. Discussions about product development, sources of funding, or organizational structures will lead the whole group to learn about those topics. A pedagogical limitation is the fact that some members may dominate the group, while others may be less involved and therefore learn less.

Inquiry-based learning (also called open learning and problem-based learning) is a pedagogical approach that focuses on the process of learning as opposed to the end product. There is no prescribed target or result that learners have to achieve; learners are given a question, and they must conduct research to come up with a solution. Inquiry-based learning is common in medical education and nursing programs. Questions may be open-ended, without a single correct answer, in which case different groups of learners will come up with alternatives that may then be compared and contrasted. Rather than leading or imparting knowledge, the teacher initiates the scenario and monitors progress. In the context of entrepreneurship education, inquiry-based learning means that the teacher presents learners with an entrepreneurial problem. Demand exists, but not supply, or it is the other way around: Supply exists, but not demand. The underpinning pedagogical principle is that learners will benefit from having to solve a genuine entrepreneurial issue, actively carrying out research by themselves, as opposed to working at a purely speculative level or being taught facts in a passive way. A pedagogical limitation is the fact that some aspects of new venture management, such as taxation and legal frameworks, may need to be taught in a traditional manner, as opposed to relying on learners to come up with creative answers.

Experiential learning, constructivist learning, and inquiry-based learning are all learner-centered approaches that build upon the same pedagogical tradition, especially the works of John Dewey and Jean Piaget, now applied to entrepreneurship pedagogy. They are not mutually exclusive but rather complement one another and may be combined, for example, with groups of students commissioned by a local business to suggest and evaluate franchising opportunities or tasked by a community group to formulate a response to a local problem with a limited budget. The learning focus may vary, but the skill set remains the same: critical thinking, ability to work in teams, creative thinking, and problem solving—key educational and entrepreneurial values. Matching these skills and values with the overall program helps ensure a solid educational foundation. All participants should be made to understand the pedagogy of the program—not only the instructors, guest speakers, and support staff but also the students. This transparency helps set and clarify everyone's expectations. If learners understand why they are expected to carry out certain tasks (such as market research, feasibility studies, cash flow forecasts, prototype designs, scenario planning, or environmental audits), they are more likely to engage with them, realizing that these tasks are not ends in themselves but rather means to develop their entrepreneurial learning.

Entrepreneurship pedagogy has an impact not on learners but also on the teacher, whose role changes, with a marked shift from being an academic tutor to becoming a business adviser. Teachers who were trained according to a more didactic paradigm may require a new set of professional competencies, not just about subject knowledge (for example, as policy frameworks and legislation keep evolving) but also about managing interactions with the learners in a different way. As their business adviser, the teacher works alongside the learners, following a horizontal model in contrast to the vertical model of more traditional pedagogies, with the knowledgeable expert on top and the cohort of learners underneath. This reconfiguration reflects the power dynamics of would-be entrepreneurs supported by an adviser; it also shows how entrepreneurship learning is a tool of empowerment at odds with traditional educational

settings—hence the possible need for readjustment for educators new to entrepreneurship pedagogy.

Complementing the learning and teaching strategy of any course of education is its evaluation strategy. As entrepreneurship education is usually outcome-based, it is sometimes easy to ensure an instructional alignment of the intended learning outcomes, the teaching techniques, and the evaluation. In the case of a course designed to teach learners how to prepare, structure, and write up a business plan, the final assessment will logically be the business plan itself. However, intended outcomes—for example, motivating learners toward a career in entrepreneurship or inculcating key entrepreneurial values, such as a sense of independence and distrust of bureaucracy—are sometimes broader and harder to assess in an academic way. How can entrepreneurial motivation or an entrepreneurial mind-set be assessed? Other aspects also require close consideration, such as the selection of the most appropriate format and method of evaluation (elevator pitch, longer oral presentation, interview, written test, take-away exam, questionnaire, report, essay, reflective diary, portfolio of evidence, vita, performance, role-play, film, and so on) as well as the timing and goal: Is it formative or summative? How important is the feedback provided? Who should assess the would-be entrepreneurs and give them feedback: their teachers, their peers, successful entrepreneurs, possible investors, all of them sitting together in a panel? While criterion-referencing is increasingly the norm (with learners having to demonstrate certain levels of achievement against preset standards and benchmarks), there is also an argument to maintain norm-referencing, especially to identify the highest achievers: as entrepreneurship, ultimately, leads to the success of some to the detriment of others, elements of competitiveness may be legitimate and intrinsically coherent with the spirit of the subject. Educators and program designers should remain aware of the diversity of potential assessment practices in entrepreneurship, although institutional traditions and accreditation systems may provide some constraints.

As a field of study in its own right, entrepreneurship required time to differentiate itself from the subject of business management as taught in most business schools, with its corporate model of functions mirroring the departments of large organizations (marketing, finance, human resources, and so forth). Entrepreneurship pedagogy is currently going through a process to gain legitimacy and recognition. Journals about enterprise and new business ventures have started including articles about pedagogy, such as those by Luke Pittaway and Jason Cope (2007) and Norris F. Krueger (2007). Collected editions are also being published on the topic, including Alain Fayolle's *Handbooks of Research on Entrepreneurship Education*. Some scholars are becoming famous in the world of entrepreneurship pedagogy, such as Krueger in the United States, Allan Gibb in the United Kingdom, and Fayolle in France. As a new area of scholarship, entrepreneurship pedagogy does not have a set canon yet. Its agenda reflects the challenges faced by educators, both in theory and in practice: for example, the need to be flexible (to accommodate not only a diversity of learning styles but also a diversity of learners, most of whom do not come from a business management background), to maintain credibility (through the application of rigorous methodologies and conceptual frameworks, which is difficult in the absence of any firm consensus on what constitutes entrepreneurship), and to reflect entrepreneurial values (such as risk taking, which does not always fit well within educational contexts, where teachers are not supposed to take risks with their learners). Entrepreneurship pedagogy is still a niche subject in its infancy, but the next decade will see it grow and develop.

Loykie L. Lominé
University of Winchester

See also Entrepreneurial Support Systems; Entrepreneurial Training; Entrepreneurship Education: Graduate Programs; Entrepreneurship Education: High School; Entrepreneurship Education: Undergraduate Programs; Leadership; Leadership: Training and Development; Leadership: Transformational; Learning; Learning Theory; Master of Business Administration; Networks; Social Networks

Further Readings

Fayolle, Alain, ed. *Handbooks of Research in Entrepreneurship Education*. Vol. 1, *General Perspectives;* Vol. 2, *Contextual Perspectives;* Vol. 3, *International Perspectives*. Northampton, MA: Edward Elgar, 2007–10.

Jones, Brian and Norma Iredale. "Enterprise Education as Pedagogy." *Education + Training*, v.52/1 (2010).

Krueger, Norris F. "The Microfoundations of Entrepreneurial Learning and Education: The Experiential Essence of Entrepreneurial Cognition." In *Handbook of University-Wide Entrepreneurship Education*, G. Page West III et al., eds. Northampton, MA: Edward Elgar, 2009.

Krueger, Norris F. "What Lies Beneath? The Experiential Essence of Entrepreneurial Thinking." *Entrepreneurship Theory and Practice*, v.31/1 (2007).

Pittaway, Luke and Jason Cope. "Entrepreneurship Education: A Systematic Review of the Evidence." *International Small Business Journal*, v.25/5 (2007).

EQUITY- AND DEBT-BASED FINANCING

The importance of entrepreneurial activity to local and national economies has been established. In order for entrepreneurs to utilize their talents and flourish, they need access to appropriate levels of financial capital. New ventures need significant amounts of capital to purchase necessary equipment and supplies. However, entrepreneurs in developing countries have limited access to these precious resources.

The modes of financing have significant implications for entrepreneurs. The availability of financing for new ventures varies across countries. Underdeveloped capital markets pose significant challenges to new ventures in developing countries. Financial intermediaries play more prominent roles for new ventures in the developed countries than in developing countries. Generally, debt financing is not an option for people who live in rural areas and whose livelihoods depend on agricultural output and yield low household incomes. The majority of established financial intermediaries in developing countries require tangible assets, such as land, as collateral prior to qualifying borrowers for loans. This requirement puts female entrepreneurs at a particular disadvantage, because they receive limited amounts of land compared with their male counterparts.

Even entrepreneurs residing in countries with well-established credit markets can face hardship in obtaining appropriate levels of credit, as the result of the high costs associated with obtaining loans from the formal financial intermediaries. Small businesses are highly risky, so financial intermediaries balance that risk-taking behavior by increasing the cost of funds.

Microfinance institutions (MFIs) have been a great source of financing for the entrepreneurs in developing countries. Muhammad Yunus, for example, established Grameen Bank, the first MFI, in Bangladesh in 1976. MFIs usually lend to a group of members. The entire group as a whole is responsible for returning the borrowed funds. In the case of failure, borrowers lose the privilege of access to the loans in the future. Using the group-lending scheme, MFIs tend to overcome the default problem. Another tool used by MFIs to increase repayment rates is increasing the loan amount after clients repay the original loan.

Entrepreneurs in developed countries have access to venture financing. Venture financing allows entrepreneurs to generate necessary and crucial financial capital from outside sources in return for equity in the venture firm. Venture capitalists (VCs) are able to help entrepreneurs with managerial support. VCs help with screening, contracting, and advising, as well as networking opportunities. Entrepreneurs in developing countries generally do not have access to either venture financing or what are termed business angels. The reason has been suggested to be developing nations' poor legal structure and poor stockholders' rights.

Presumably, financial institutions in Islamic countries should adhere to the sharia, a set of Islamic principles based on the teachings of Quran (the Muslim holy book) and sunna (directions given by Prophet Muhammad). However, the practice of these principles varies across Islamic countries. According to Islamic principles, any form of exploitive transaction is related to *riba* (the Arabic word for usury, or interest). *Riba* literally means an excess or addition. There are verses in the Quran clearly stating the prohibition: "Trade is like usury, but God hath permitted trade and forbidden usury." Along with interest items, whose legitimacy is in question, other financing instruments, such as insurance, options, and futures, are forbidden under Islamic law. Muslim investors therefore cannot participate in these types of transactions.

Islamic financial institutions use mark-ups and profit-loss sharing as financing instruments. *Murabaha*, or cost-plus sales, and *ijara*, or leasing, are two forms of financing that fall under the mark-up principle. In *murabaha*, the bank or creditor purchases an asset on behalf of the entrepreneur and resells the asset to the debtor at a price that includes the original cost of the asset and a premium. The premium is negotiable between the two parties. However, if the debtor defaults, the seller/creditor cannot increase the price. The other form of financing, *ijara*, occurs when bank or financier purchases the asset and allows the entrepreneur to use it for a fixed charge.

Two other principles of Islamic financing, *musharaka* and *mudaraba*, fall under the category of equity investments. In Arabic, *musharaka* means sharing. In this form of financing, investor and entrepreneur jointly supply the funds. By doing so, they share the same risk, and the return is based on the ratio of each investor's investment. Another form of joint venture or partnership, *mudaraba*, involves the investor providing all the capital and the entrepreneur being responsible for management. Profit from the venture is negotiated between the two parties.

Farzana Chowdhury
Indiana University

See also Bankruptcy; Barriers to Entry; Barter; Business Models; Capitalism; Cash Flow; Credit; Debt; Debt-Based Financing; Entrepreneurs in Finance and Banking; Microfinance; Revenue: Current Versus Deferred

Further Readings

Chiang, Wei-Chih, Hui Di, and Steven A. Hanke. "Debt or Equity Financing? Analyzing Relevant Factors." *The Tax Adviser*, v.41/6 (June 2010).

Muhammad Yunus, Nobel Peace Prize winner, addresses an audience at the Houston World Affair's Council in 2008. Yunus is the founder and managing director of Grameen Bank, a pioneer of microcredit and an economic movement that has helped lift millions of families out of poverty worldwide. (Wikimedia/Ed Schipul)

"Equity vs. Debt: Financing Your Business When the Banks Still Won't Play Ball." *Businessweek* (December 2009/ January 2010).

Garai, Gabor. *How to Finance a Business: An Introduction to Equity and Debt Financing*. Boston: Massachusetts Continuing Legal Education, 1995.

Grau, L. and D. Koletic. "Debt and Equity Financing." *Urban Land*, v.62/10 (2003).

Hillstrom, Laurie. "Debt vs. Equity Financing." *Encyclopedia of Management*. Detroit, MI: Thomson Gale, 2000.

King, Ann C., T. Malcolm Sandilands, and John L. Whitlock. *How to Conduct a Corporate Closing: Corporate Transactions and Debt and Equity Financing*. Boston: MCLE, 1998.

Kuo, Horng-Ching. *Corporate Financing: Debt Financing and Equity Financing*. Hull, UK: Barmarick Publications, 1989.

Neumann, Rebecca M. "International Capital Flows Under Asymmetric Information and Costly Monitoring: Implications of Debt and Equity Financing." *Canadian Journal of Economics*, v.36/5 (August 2003).

Ryan, Graeme and Con O'Brien. *Sources of Finance: The Guide to Debt and Equity Financing in Australia*. Melbourne, Australia: Business Library, 1990.

Yunus, M. *Banker to the Poor: The Autobiography of Muhammad Yunus, Founder of Grameen Bank*. Oxford, UK: Oxford University Press, 2001.

ETHICS

New ventures present exciting opportunities because they are prospects for creating new products and services—even new markets. Such ventures are launched in turbulent environments with success marked by rapid growth, technological change, and unpredictable circumstances. Challenging issues emerge daily that call for swift yet ethically sound decisions. Because these operations are often marked by high risk, the need for quick action, and ongoing innovation, a focused effort to establish their ethical foundation may be overlooked. Much of the research on entrepreneurial behavior still focuses largely on corporate social responsibility (CSR) and small business in general, rather than the challenges posed to new venture ethics per se.

Leaders' attention to the ethical foundations of the organization—from its inception—is essential. Management must be explicit about the importance of workplace ethics, expressed through clear and compelling mandates. Such directives must be complemented with leaders' affirming and demonstrating the commitment to such beliefs in their own actions, represented in both word and deed. Like the broader category of business ethics, new venture ethics is based on leaders who enact a system of moral principles for their operations. In the case of start-ups, the values are foundational pillars of the firm, guidelines that serve as drivers for members' behavior in day-to-day operations. Creating this doctrine is especially important when the organization is new, as it will shape employee practices and help people conduct their tasks in ways that are consistent with the firm's principles, appropriate, just, and ethical. Such practices provide the means for determining right from wrong in achieving business goals. Like managers in all types of firms, those making ethical judgments need to be concerned with the rightness or wrongness of their decisions and affiliated actions, while also attending to the rules, regulations, and compliance requirements for their industry.

The ethical climate of entrepreneurial firms has been described through its formal and informal ethical structures, reflecting that those who create and develop firms pursue diverse approaches to the question of ethics. Formal codes typically emphasize compliance, while informal mechanisms are based on relationship-building efforts in support of ethical decision making, the latter contributing to a culture of ethical strength. A business risk shared among all firms includes a tendency to remain mute when faced with issues that violate personal or corporate values. Unlike established organizations, new ventures have a unique opportunity to establish their climate and shape their culture. For example, we know that fostering conversation and reflection about ethical issues as a way of doing business, helps promote moral awareness in ongoing decision-making efforts. Incorporating this practice into the fabric of the organization can help establish active use of the firm's stated ethical values. Engaging in such practices can also cultivate trust among members and the firm's stakeholders. Trust is an important aspect of working together to attend to compliance activities, while also encouraging creative ethical innovation in everyday business transactions.

Individual entrepreneurial values are typically represented by integrity, honesty, and a strong work ethic. In the United States, entrepreneurs also believe that good faith and sincerity in dealing with stakeholders are important along with the ability to make decisions. When comparing entrepreneurs with other managers, entrepreneurs demonstrate stronger ethical perceptions about the relationship they have with their business. They are often driven by duty and a responsibility to society, with a need to consider how their actions should be consistent. In the past, entrepreneurship has often been viewed as the pursuit of commercial objectives, distinct from, and perhaps even in conflict with, ethical behavior. Researchers distilled traits that distinguish entrepreneurs from others, showing that they have a marked ability to create personal wealth through opportunity identification. As described by Dinah Payne and Brenda E. Joyner, this led to an image of the entrepreneur as a solitary heroic type—a captain of industry—a person whose productive activity is governed largely by profit seeking and motives to achieve goals based on personal gain. Such a view became problematic, not only because of the lack of contextualized insight but also because the underlying idea of entrepreneurship as an individualized activity is simply not accurate. Far from being isolated private creations, new ventures largely emerge from collective endeavors. The lack of a proven track record, asset value, and immediate profitability finds entrepreneurs reliant on working relationships and network ties, their means to access resources to create and sustain their venture.

Ethical conditions in new ventures are known to influence the capacity for self-regulation using reflective judgment in creating value. Research has explained how entrepreneurs' strength in reflective judgment can foster nurturing environments for employees and infuse a concern for customer satisfaction and a dedication to the quality of the product or service the firm offers. The underlying values of entrepreneurs not only translate into actions for their customers but also have led to success, in the sense of their commitment to the value of giving back to their communities. In so doing, leaders of new ventures can create strong bonds that bolster their reputations as corporate citizens and worthwhile organizations. As a result, they may be more likely to have a stronger workforce applicant pool and, therefore, to build more durable organizations.

The challenges faced in the early phases of the operation must be managed ethically, as this sets the tone for future business operations. For example, is exaggeration used in presenting initial ideas to investors? Is stock ownership divided fairly? Are standards for product reliability appropriate and consistent? Is communication with the board open and honest, including announcements of disappointing news that might threaten plans and expectations? To develop ethical strength over time, ethics must become the central, core value of the nascent enterprise. This means that ethics must be addressed in the business plan, mission statement, and performance criteria. A commitment to ethics is made explicit by leaders being forthright with financial data and attending to accounting and compliance practices with ethical rigor. Leader-managers of new ventures need to prepare for and deal with the anticipated tensions present in their everyday decisions, understanding the difference between truth and optimism in reporting and daily communication. Staying open to questions and having the willingness to discuss and resolve tough dilemmas with transparency signal that ethics are critical in achieving success. Given that new ventures involve partnerships, strategic alliances, social networks, and other virtual relationships, there is great potential for conflicts of interest. An explicit and consistent stand against questionable behavior is essential. This means leaders must make a point to articulate their commitment to ethics continuously. Those employees who are unable to embrace these standards, despite their expertise, need to find employment elsewhere. To integrate ethics as a part of the firm's identity, founders should find ways to engage in community service and establish an active role in social responsibility. Instilling an ethics audit is an ongoing process; as the operation grows, new challenges and risks emerge. The operation's commitment to ethics must be recast and reviewed periodically, preparing members to look for and deal with new and emergent issues.

Leaders of new organizations are keenly aware that they need to address shareholder expectations in the context of addressing stakeholder concerns. The idea that profit and social responsibility are mutually exclusive values is a fallacy; both are expected in today's global marketplace. Clearly, entrepreneurs have a critical role to play in establishing their organization's identity, which can create value in terms of financial gain and in having a favorable impact on society. Those who embrace CSR as a part of their new identity are likely to be guided by well-articulated values and have strong ethical cultures that have been established from the very start of the venture's life. These firms tend to go beyond the legal requirements in how they view business ethics, making an explicit effort to interact with stakeholders and work to give back to the communities they inhabit. Critical resources for the emerging firm stem from the bonds it forms with its stakeholders. These bonds comprise the feelings, beliefs, and commitments that constitute the venture's belief system. Through the development of relationships, firms gain access to and make effective use of the resources necessary for launching and sustaining their operation. This underscores the essential nature of ethics in new ventures, with the moral component of capitalism deliberately embraced to ensure the firm's viability, health, and long-term prosperity.

Leslie E. Sekerka
Menlo College

See also Agency Theory; Barter; Entrepreneurs in Food; Exit Strategies; Family Business; Family Business: Research; Intentions; Leadership: Transformational; Stakeholders; Sustainable Development

Further Readings

Bucar, B. and R. D. Hisrich. "Ethics of Business Managers Vs. Entrepreneurs." *Journal of Developmental Entrepreneurship*, v.6/1 (2001).

Clarke, Jean and Robin Holt. "Reflective Judgment: Understanding Entrepreneurship as Ethical Practice." *Journal of Business Ethics*, v.94 (2010).

Hanson, Kirk O. "A Good Start: New Ventures Can Make Ethics Part of Their Business Plan." *Issues in Ethics: Markkula Center for Applied Ethics*, v.12/1 (2001).

Payne, Dinah and Brenda E. Joyner. "Successful U.S. Entrepreneurs: Identifying Ethical Decision-Making and Social Responsibility Behaviors." *Journal of Business Ethics*, v.65 (2006).

EXIT STRATEGIES

Exit strategies deal with how new venture management restructures business assets for enhanced value through divestitures. Economic and political factors influence the reasons for exit. The following economic and political factors determine both companies' decisions to exit and the types of exit that managers choose.

Underperformance at the company or the business level contributes to economic reasons for exit. A venture's poor performance may come from a failed diversification strategy. Exit from the poorly performing business then consolidates operations and reduces costs. Financially distressed companies are more likely to sell off a failing business to external buyers than spin it off to current stockholders, thereby generating liquidity and meeting short-term financial obligations.

Companies may also exit countries or businesses for political reasons, such as protests from stakeholders. Usha Haley identified how U.S. companies exited from South Africa in response to sanctions and boycotts from stockholders, consumers, and governments. Multinational companies in South Africa that engaged in symbolic actions for U.S. stakeholders, such as the signing of the Sullivan Principles, were more likely to sell their subsidiaries to managers and to form leaving facades than to liquidate their assets.

Barriers to Exit

Despite reasons for exit, ventures may have difficulties undertaking exit strategies. Industrial organization economists such as Joe Bain and Michael Porter initially identified and extrapolated on the barriers that companies face when undertaking divestment of their assets. These include structural exit barriers, strategy exit barriers, and managerial exit barriers.

Structural exit barriers, or characteristics of the businesses' technology, fixed capital, and working capital, may impede exit. The more durable the assets and the more specific the assets are to the particular industry, the particular venture, or the particular location, the less likely that the venture will benefit economically from selling off or shutting down an unprofitable business, and the larger will be the immediate loss the venture will face if it does exit the business. Asset specificity hinders the redeployment of assets and hence their value to other companies.

Strategy exit barriers, or relationships between a venture's businesses, can deter exit. The more complementary or linked the specific venture is to other businesses, the less likely it is that the venture can economically justify selling or shutting down an unprofitable business, and the larger the immediate losses the venture will face if it does so.

Interrelationships and synergies hinder efficient and profitable divestment.

Finally, managerial exit barriers, or aspects of a venture's decision-making process, can inhibit exit from unprofitable businesses. Usha Haley and Stephen Stumpf identified several cognitive biases that might impact ill-structured decisions on exit, including illusion of control, escalating commitment to a losing course of action, and reasoning by analogy. These can encourage managers to throw good money after bad. Irene Duhaime and Charles Schwenk argued that once managers decide on divestment, it may quickly become the single outcome considered, as managers vigorously defend this alternative over all others.

Modes of Exit

Exit from a venture can occur in different modes. Several researchers have distinguished between different degrees of sell-offs and dissolutions. Others have identified how companies maintain control over assets such as intellectual property through their modes of exit.

In a sell-off, a company sells a business as an individual operating unit to another owner. Sell-offs include spin-offs, buyouts, carve-outs, and asset sales. Spin-offs involve the sale of equity shares of a business to the parent company's current stockholders. Management buy-outs involve selling a business to its former managers, who become the new owners. In leveraged buy-outs, a company sells its business to an investor group, which typically includes the sold unit's former managers. A carve-out comprises sale of a business unit to new shareholders or another company. In an asset sale, a company agrees to sell all or certain assets and liabilities, not the entire company, to a buying company. Managers engage in asset sales when they need to raise funds but find alternative sources of financing too expensive. Dissolution involves the shut-down of entire businesses. Kathryn Harrigan noted that managers attempt to avoid dissolution, as they have to satisfy labor unions' contracts in dismissal, to persuade customers to substitute other products, and to explain why the company cannot cover particular customers' needs or recover the value of the millions of dollars the managers invested in competitive positioning. Dissolution can also occur through formal bankruptcy or through delisting from a stock exchange.

Usha Haley found that U.S. companies that left South Africa in response to stakeholders' boycotts and sanctions attempted to maintain economic ties with the operations they divested as part of an exit strategy. The exits formed a roughly ordinal scale of residual control by the company ranging from dissolution of assets to sale to a South African or European company, sale to another U.S. company, sale to local management, and the formation of a trust. At one end of the scale, some companies engaged in dissolution or total liquidation and piecemeal sale of assets where the company no longer existed as an entity. When a U.S. company sold operations to a South African or European company, it could not secure ongoing equity agreements or protect its technology, but it did receive a higher price for assets than through subsequent modes. In a sale to another U.S. company, cultural factors kept many business operations in place, but the sale price was lower. In a sale to local management, the purchase price was financed through managerial assets, commercial bank loans backed by the subsidiaries' assets, unsecured loans from investment banks, and financing arrangements with the parent company that also exercised formal and informal controls over technology and personnel practices. Finally, the formation of a trust comprised a leaving facade where an offshore or onshore trust, wholly owned by the company, bought the South African operation and maintained substantial control over future operations and personnel.

Determinants of Exit Strategies

Several factors influence companies' exit strategies, including managerial decisions on modes of exit. These include age of the venture, size, managers and owners, and sanctions and symbolic actions.

Some studies confirm that the older a business is, the less likely it is to exit. With new ventures in particular, studies have found that the dissolution rate tends to decline with greater business age. Researchers have often attributed this finding to older firms' having to overcome what Arthur Stinchcombe called the "liability of newness" by creating effective routines and thereby overcoming technical and market-related start-up problems. Although inertia-induced problems may appear as businesses age, empirical evidence suggests that younger organizations have much higher dissolution rates than older organizations. Will Mitchell found that dissolution rates declined with greater sales and age for start-up firms. However, diversifying entrants' dissolution rates also declined with greater sales. When researchers controlled for age, sales, and other businesses and corporate characteristics, little difference existed in the business-dissolution rates of start-up firms and diversifying entrants.

Business-unit size, in conjunction with poor performance, has a strong impact on exit decisions and choices of exit modes. The larger the business unit, the higher the likelihood of a spin-off rather than a sell-off because the likelihood of its failure as a stand-alone operation is lower. Researchers have attributed the relationship between greater size and lower dissolution rates to commercial success. Researchers have assumed that larger businesses have greater impact on their communities than do smaller businesses, and their better future prospects deter managerial decisions to shut them down. Because of their commercial success, larger businesses also tend to have larger pools of financial and managerial resources that help them overcome problems that threaten their survival. When managers do make decisions to shut down larger businesses' unprofitable assets, they tend to concentrate on unrelated, prior acquisitions.

Managers may resist business exit because they link it with failure and because external stakeholders may view exit as stemming from poor management. Managers often incur personal losses such as declines in pay and prestige when companies lose size through divestitures. Consequently, exit often correlates with turnovers in top management teams. In particular, the arrival of new chief executive officers (CEOs) increases the likelihood of divestiture of poorly performing businesses, especially when the CEOs' cognitive biases and heuristics favor exit. Similarly, CEOs recruited from the outside, or with tenure of less than 10 years, are more likely to make decisive decisions on exit strategies than are those with longer tenures, because they can resist inertial forces. The owners' retirement, especially in small and family-owned companies, also provides a reason for exit: In many cases, successors cannot be found.

Finally, stakeholders' sanctions and boycotts appear to have no effect on exit strategies. Rather, profits and the bottom line may comprise the strongest influencer of exit decision. Symbolic reassurances by companies may deflect the need to exit. Indeed, in South Africa during apartheid, the companies that stayed in the face of U.S. stakeholders' protests also engaged in regular and focused symbolic actions to reassure the stakeholders that foreign operations synchronized with U.S. stakeholders' values and ethics. Companies that stayed in South Africa engaged in significantly more symbolic actions, captured by adherence to the Sullivan Principles, than those that exited. These symbolic actions dealing with resolutions and pronouncements, rather than actual actions to integrate workforces, enabled the companies to continue to operate in South Africa during the time of apartheid, despite stakeholders' boycotts, resolutions, and divestitures. The symbolic actions provided goodwill and legitimacy at home, thereby affecting mode of exit. For example, multinationals with the greatest symbolic actions also maintained the greatest control over their companies by exiting through trusts and selling their subsidiaries to local managers. Those with the least symbolic actions engaged in dissolution and piecemeal sale of assets.

Usha C. V. Haley
Massey University

See also Bankruptcy; Barriers to Entry; Strategy

Further Readings

Bain, J. S. *Barriers to New Competition.* Cambridge, MA: Harvard University Press, 1956.

Bergh, D. D. "Predicting Divestiture of Unrelated Acquisitions: An Integrative Model of Ex Ante Conditions." *Strategic Management Journal,* v.9 (1997).

Bigley, G. A. and M. F. Wiersema. "New CEOs and Corporate Strategic Refocusing: How Experience as Heir Apparent Influences the Use of Power." *Administrative Science Quarterly,* v.47 (2002).

Carroll, G. and A. Swaminathan. "The Organizational Ecology of Strategic Groups in the American Brewing Industries From 1975 to 1990." *Industrial and Corporate Change,* v.1 (1992).

Decker, C. and T. Mellewigt. "Thirty Years After Michael E. Porter: What Do We Know About Business Exit?" *Academy of Management Perspectives* (May 2007).

Duhaime, I. M. and C. R. Schwenk. "Conjectures on Cognitive Simplification in Acquisition and Divestment Decision Making." *Academy of Management Review,* v.10/2 (1985).

Haley, U. C. V. *Multinational Corporations in Political Environments: Ethics, Values and Strategies.* River Edge, NJ: World Scientific Press, 2001.

Haley, U. C. V. and S. A. Stumpf. "Cognitive Trails in Strategic Decision-Making: Linking Theories of Personalities and Cognitions." *Journal of Management Studies*, v.26/5 (1989).

Harrigan, K. R. "Exit Decisions in Mature Industries." *Academy of Management Journal*, v.25 (1982).

Huyghebaert, N. and L. Van De Gucht. "Incumbent Strategic Behavior in Financial Markets and the Exit of Entrepreneurial Start-Ups." *Strategic Management Journal*, v.25 (2004).

Karakaya, F. "Market Exit and Barriers to Exit: Theory and Practice." *Psychology and Marketing*, v.17 (2000).

Lang, L., A. Poulsen, and R. Stulz. "Asset Sales, Firm Performance, and the Agency Costs of Managerial Discretion." *Journal of Financial Economics*, v.37 (1995).

Mitchell, W. "The Dynamics of Evolving Markets: The Effects of Business Sales and Age on Dissolutions and Divestitures." *Administrative Science Quarterly*, v.39 (1994).

Montgomery, C. A. and A. R. Thomas. "Divestment: Motives and Gains." *Strategic Management Journal*, v.9 (1988).

Nixon, T. D., R. L. Roenfeldt, and N. W. Sicherman. "The Choice Between Spin-Offs and Sell-Offs." *Review of Quantitative Finance and Accounting*, v.14 (2000).

Porter, M. E. "Please Note Location of Nearest Exit: Exit Barriers and Planning." *California Management Review*, v.19 (1976).

Stinchcombe, A. L. "Social Structure and Organizations." In *Handbook of Organizations*, J. G. March, ed. Chicago: Rand-McNally, 1965.

F

FAMILY BUSINESS

Although there are many different definitions of a family business, most researchers agree that a definition must include a combination of equity ownership and control. Thus, a family business is defined as a business in which the founding family owns more than 50 percent of equity and family members—those who are related to the founding family through blood, adoption, or marriage—sit on the board of directors or hold management positions in the company. If certain conditions exist, family businesses have the potential to yield superior strategic advantages over nonfamily firms. These advantages stem from their unique characteristics, or their "familiness."

Family businesses represent a large portion of the U.S. economy. They generate about 50 percent of gross domestic product (GDP), 60 percent of total employment, and 78 percent of all new job creation. Almost 35 percent of family-owned businesses are large companies, such as Ford, IKEA, Lowe's, and Walmart. Long-lasting companies such as Marriott International Inc., Heineken, Enterprise Rent-a-Car, Nordstrom's, BMW, and the *Washington Post* Company are only a few examples of successful family-run companies. Globally, too, family-run businesses represent the engine of the economy. In Canada, family-controlled businesses produce 45 percent of GDP, create approximately 70 percent of new jobs, and employ half of the workforce. In Australia, approximately 80 percent of all businesses are family-run. In the European Union,

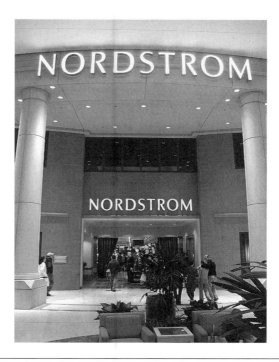

Family-owned businesses represent 35 percent of large companies and a large portion of the U.S. economy. Successful long-lasting, family-run operations include Ford, IKEA, Walmart, Marriott International, Nordstrom, Heineken, and BMW. (Wikimedia)

almost 700,000 businesses are established by first-generation entrepreneurs, who intend to transfer the business to their children.

Family businesses possess unique characteristics that distinguish them from nonfamily corporations. Often, family businesses are started by entrepreneurs with competitive, type-A personalities. Typically, these entrepreneurs are hardworking individuals, driven by a strong achievement need. They handle a variety of tasks and make decisions that cut across many functions, such as accounting, finance, manufacturing, and sales. Decision making is informal and ad hoc. In the first stage of a family business existence, there is a strong congruence between the values, goals, and principles of the family and those of the business. Thus, corporate governance issues that characterize public corporations do not exist or are very weak.

As the owner retires and the business is passed down to the second generation, it is run by a sibling partnership. The siblings may not agree on a common strategy of managing the business, and conflict may occur. In fact, survival to the next generation is often challenging. Seven of 10 family-owned businesses do not survive beyond the first generation. In this stage, the deciding factors in the survival of the business are the amount of trust, information sharing, and open communication among siblings. In contrast to formal oversight mechanisms that characterize public corporations, oversight mechanisms are still informal, based on trust and relationships.

In the third stage, the business is transferred to a set of cousins, grandchildren of the original owners, and family members related to them through blood, adoption, or marriage. Some family members play an active role, holding equity stakes and/or management positions in the company, while others have a passive role, limited to owning shares. In this and later stages, governance and decision making become more complex and formalized than in the first two stages.

Perhaps to enhance their prospects of survival, family businesses rely on relationships with other organizations to a larger extent than do public corporations. Family businesses form close ties with other family businesses, credit unions, homeowners' associations, banks, churches, local schools, nonprofit organizations, and local governments. The "social capital" that emerges from these ties allows them access to information, financial, and human resources and helps them hedge against risks in the economic environment.

Human resources functions, such as hiring, promotion, and performance evaluation, are often executed in an informal fashion in family businesses. It is very common to find that hiring is based on family ties or personal recommendations and acquaintances of owners or their relatives. According to a survey, about two thirds of family businesses do not require special qualifications of family members to enter the business. The work relationships in family-owned businesses are based on mutual trust and loyalty to a larger extent than one would find in a nonfamily corporation. However, this informality may lead to animosities between family and nonfamily members, as the latter may feel unfairly treated. Encouraging family members to get the necessary degrees and skills is important in order to reduce potential conflict and dissatisfaction. Clear communication of standards used for hiring, promotion, and performance evaluation is crucial to establish a performance-based human resources system.

Interestingly, family businesses engage in social responsibility to a higher extent than it is commonly believed. There are three main reasons for this occurrence. First, their organizational culture reflects the personal values and moral principles of the founder, which translates into a greater sense of awareness of their mission and vision. They are less likely to have a written code of ethics but more likely to lead by example to create an organization of integrity. Second, private, family-owned businesses are not pressured by shareholders to deliver short-term profits. Therefore, they have the freedom to engage in a variety of initiatives, ranging from downtown revitalization projects to funding local youth organizations. Their social responsibility strategy is often driven by personal reasons. For example, if a family member is affected by Alzheimer's disease, they might well fund charities that fight this disease. Third, the reputation of the business "spills over" into the reputation of the family, as the two are inextricably linked. Thus, family businesses have a strong incentive to avoid socially irresponsible behavior, since such behavior would permanently tarnish the reputation of the family.

The unique features described above yield family businesses superior competitive advantages over nonfamily businesses. These advantages are embedded in their *familiness*, which was defined by Timothy G. Habbershon and Mary L. Williams as "the unique bundle of resources a particular firm has because of the systems interaction between the family, its individual members, and the business."

Indeed, performance comparison studies found, for example, that family businesses have a long-term investment orientation, which makes them less vulnerable to market downturns and more alert to changes in the environment. They outperform the S&P 500 companies on indicators such as profit margins, debt-to-equity levels, and returns on investment. They are more creative and more focused on research and development activities. The practices of private family businesses are harder to copy because it is harder for competitors to gain access to information. They have an organizational culture that stimulates loyalty and commitment among employees. They energize their employees better through more flexible working practices, higher pay, and a more positive reputation. At the same time, they have lower recruitment costs and lower transaction costs overall, compared to nonfamily corporations.

However, one should not conclude that family businesses *always* outperform nonfamily corporations, all things being equal. Contingency factors, such as open communication and trust among family members, as well as between family and nonfamily members, the ability to establish a performance-based system in hiring, promotion, and succession; planning strategically for the future; and the ability to separate family issues from business issues, when necessary, are critical issues that determine whether a family business will be successful or not.

Looking into the future, an important challenge facing family businesses in the United States and abroad is of a demographic nature. As baby boomers approach and enter retirement age, approximately half of all U.S. and three fourths of Canadian first-generation entrepreneurs will retire by the early 2020s. In financial terms, approximately $1.2 trillion of assets in Canada and $4.3 trillion in the United States will be passed from the first to the second generation. This wealth transfer, the largest in North American history, will pose tremendous management and succession challenges for family businesses.

Cristina E. Ciocirlan
Elizabethtown College

See also Agency Theory; Family Business: Defining; Family Business: Research; Family Business: Stewardship; Family Business: Theory; Home-Based Businesses; Stakeholders; Succession Planning

Further Readings

Habbershon, Timothy G. and Mary L. Williams. "A Resource-Based Framework for Assessing the Strategic Advantages of Family Firms." *Family Business Review*, v.22/1 (1999).

MassMutual Financial Group, Cox Family Enterprise Center and the Family Firm. *American Family Business Survey*. Springfield, MA: Author, 2007.

Poutzioris, Panikkos, Kosmas Smyrnios, and Sabine Klein. *Handbook of Research on Family Business*. Northampton, MA: Edward Elgar, 2006.

Ward, John L. "How Governing Family Business Is Different." In *Mastering Global Corporate Governance*, U. Steger, ed. New York: John Wiley and Sons, 2004.

Ward, John L. *Perpetuating the Family Business: 50 Lessons Learned From Long-Lasting, Successful Families in Business*. New York: Palgrave Macmillan, 2004.

FAMILY BUSINESS: DEFINING

The term *family business* refers to a subset of business organizations within the economic landscape. Whereas many new ventures could be family businesses, firms are generally classified as family businesses by criteria or combinations of criteria, including family ownership, management by a family member, operational involvement of family members, and family member involvement across generations. This involvement presents opportunities to exercise influence over the business, its operation, and its culture. There is widespread consensus among scholars that the degrees of involvement and influence almost certainly ebb and flow along a continuum as a new venture develops, grows, and matures.

A new venture that is privately held, for example, would likely be influenced considerably by the family if it were controlled by one individual who participated proactively in daily operations and employed only immediate family members. As the firm matured, it might be influenced to a significantly lesser extent if the control and management were passed on to a collection of relatives (siblings, cousins, nephews, or nieces), all representing multiple generations of the same family who were absent from the management of daily operations while employing a substantially higher percentage of nonfamily employees. Still, as the firm matures further, it might become publicly traded, having yet a different level of family influence based on the formal governance structure. Therefore, the definition of "family" business can vary with regard to the involvement of family members.

It may seem surprising, but the meaning of the term *family business* has evolved and is still subject to some scholarly debate. Accordingly, various scholars have reviewed existing definitions, made attempts to consolidate thoughts, and offered some conceptualization of the definition of family businesses. In the current milieu, the debate has centered on whether the term *family business* should be reserved for those ventures where family involvement creates unique attributes or should encompass all ventures where family members are involved, regardless of whether this involvement leads to unique attributes. Most basically, a firm cannot be classed as a family business if the family is not involved. As noted, this involvement can be manifested in many different ways and can include ownership, governance, and/or management.

Still, several have suggested that that family involvement is a necessary but insufficient condition for a firm to be termed a family business. Beyond the precondition associated with involvement, the family must actively transform this involvement into distinctive attributes, behaviors, or cultures. Consistent with this idea, concepts like succession planning have been used to differentiate family and nonfamily firms, as succession planning demonstrates an intention of the family members to preserve the firm as a distinct entity. Others have incorporated both of these streams of thought where family firms have been differentiated from others by looking at the founding family's intentions to preserve family control through succession while simultaneously examining the family commitment, which reflects the extent to which the family takes an interest in firm activities and the family's goals are aligned with those of the firm.

Despite some theoretical debates, there is a consensus among scholars and practitioners on the importance of family business for economic development. Family firms account for the vast majority of businesses worldwide. Ramona Heck and her colleagues have demonstrated the prevalence of family businesses and have been especially influential in demonstrating how family businesses have positively influenced the U.S. economy. They have found that

family businesses are not evenly distributed across industries and regions, suggesting that family businesses dominate the agricultural, retail, wholesale, and distribution sectors of the economy and are most influential in the economies of the Midwest and rural areas. This empirical work, which demonstrates that family businesses are neither trivial nor random, has influenced the attitudes of public policy makers, who are in a position to positively, or negatively, alter the environment for family businesses.

Consistent with this, scholarly interests in family business have surged, as evidenced by the rapid growth in research devoted to the subject with special issues appearing in leading academic journals. Much of this scholarship has focused on distinguishing family businesses from nonfamily businesses and determining how their financial performance differs. Understanding the performance differences is essential to the study of family businesses. Family businesses are important not simply because of their large numbers but also because they represent a distinct subset of firms that may have, by virtue of their intangible resources, unique attributes that create competitive advantages. Accumulating the findings quantitatively across 78 articles with 95 samples and a total sample size of 80,421, Matthew Rutherford and Ernest O'Boyle found that family involvement did not significantly impact firms' financial performance but argued that some other moderators influence the relationship between family involvement and firm performance. That is, while the overall relationship may be insignificant across family firms, family firms are likely to vary dramatically, and there may be conditions under which family involvement and firm performance are significantly related.

Consequently, many have posited that the strategic decision making of family businesses is likely different from the strategic decisions made, actions taken, and goals pursued by nonfamily firms. Michael Carney, for instance, argued that family firms are distinct from nonfamily firms in that they are characterized by prudence with regard to the investment of family resources; greater liberty to act, because of unified ownership and control; and the tendency for idiosyncratic decision making. These characteristics are demonstrated as the controlling family exercises authority such that they pursue noneconomic goals, such as the perpetuation of family values through the business, preservation of the family's control of the firm, and fulfillment of family obligations. Whereas the pursuit of noneconomic goals has received support, the pursuit of noneconomic goals by family firms does not necessarily come at the expense of economic goals. Thomas Zellweger and Robert Nason argue that the balance between noneconomic and economic outcomes is reached as the demands of various stakeholders are examined, offering a theoretical model in which noneconomic performance outcomes have various relationships with financial outcomes. In essence, stakeholders (to include the controlling family, which is instrumental) are likely to influence a firm's goals, which, in turn, influence performance. These differing goals may be synergistic, where one performance outcome can enhance the other; substitutional, with one coming at the expense of the other; causal, where one performance outcome causes another; and overlapping, where performance outcomes can satisfy multiple stakeholders. This decision making and the pursuit of noneconomic goals have been found to have led to positive outcomes, behaviors, and practices (such as long-term orientation toward sustainability or prudent risk taking), as well as those that are negative outcomes (such as nepotism).

As researchers and practitioners move forward to further understand family businesses, they may profit from identifying and testing other characteristics that make family businesses distinct from nonfamily businesses. These may include succession patterns, types of ownership, and leadership styles. As researchers define such characteristics, the essence of the family business can be refined further. To date, two basic philosophies have emerged in differentiating family businesses from others. The first, which is termed the "components of involvement," assumes that family involvement is all that is necessary to make a firm a family business. The second, termed "essence," assumes that involvement is a necessary but insufficient condition for a firm to be a family business. Essence, instead, requires a deeper form of family involvement reflected in the culture of the firm and its value congruence with the family; this essence may lead to competitive advantage. As this exploration continues, researchers must address measurement issues, exploring the psychometric properties of family business measures such that findings are not an artifact based on measurement errors.

Daniel T. Holt
Mississippi State University
Matthew W. Rutherford
Virginia Commonwealth University

See also Agency Theory; Family Business; Family Business: Research; Family Business: Stewardship; Family Business: Theory; Home-Based Businesses; Stakeholders; Succession Planning

Further Readings

Carney, Michael. "Corporate Governance and Competitive Advantage in Family-Controlled Firms." *Entrepreneurship Theory and Practice*, v.29/3 (2005).

Chrisman, James J., Jess H. Chua, and Pramodita Sharma. "Trends and Directions in the Development of a Strategic Management Theory of the Family Firm." *Entrepreneurship Theory and Practice*, v.29/5 (2005).

Eddleston, Kimberly A., James J. Chrisman, Lloyd P. Steier, and Jess H. Chua. "Governance and Trust in Family Firms: An Introduction." *Entrepreneurship Theory and Practice*, v.34/6 (2010).

Heck, Ramona K. Z., Edward G. Rogoff, Myong-Soo Lee, and Kathryn Stafford. "The Economic Contributions of Family Business." Annual Conference of the United States Association of Small Business and Entrepreneurship, 2002.

Heck, Ramona K. Z. and Kathryn Stafford. "The Vital Institution of Family Business: Economic Benefits Hidden in Plain Sight." In *Family Business Gathering 2001*, Greg McCann and Nancy B. Upton, eds. DeLand, FL: Stetson University, Family Business Center, 2001.

Heck, Ramona K. Z. and Elizabeth S. Trent. "The Prevalence of Family Business From a Household Sample." *Family Business Review*, v.12 (1999).

Rutherford, Matthew W. and Ernest O'Boyle. "Exploring the Relation Between Family Involvement and Firms' Financial Performance: A Meta-Analysis of Main and Moderator Effects" (unpublished manuscript).

Shanker, Melissa C. and Joseph H. Astrachan. "Myths and Realities: Family Businesses' Contributions to the U.S. Economy." *Family Business Review*, v.9/2 (1996).

Zellweger, Thomas M. and Robert S. Nason. "A Stakeholder Perspective on Family Firm Performance." *Family Business Review*, v.21/3 (2008).

FAMILY BUSINESS: RESEARCH

In its 30-year history, family business research has made significant advancements. As researchers continue to explore the many facets of family businesses, there are several aspects that are worth considering and exploring in greater depth.

Academic research on family business started in earnest in the 1980s, when psychologists such as

Richard Beckhard, Elaine Kepner, E. J. Miller and A. K. Rice, Ivan Lansberg, and Manfred Kets de Vries consistently noticed important differences in families who worked together in business. Hence, from its inception, family business was strongly influenced by fields such as family therapy and clinical psychology. As researchers started to understand the relevance of family businesses and their contributions to economic and social welfare, more researchers from other fields, such as management and organizational behavior, gradually entered the field, which led to the first special issue on family business published in *Organizational Dynamics* in 1983. The interest culminated in the launch of a professional association in 1985, the Family Firm Institute, and in 1988 a journal exclusively dedicated to the study of family business was launched: *Family Business Review*. B. Bird, H. Welsch, J. H. Astrachan, and D. Pistrui (2002) and P. Sharma, F. Hoy, J. H. Astrachan, and M. Koiranen (2007) provide detailed overviews of the development of the field.

Since that time, family business has come a long way. The field currently hosts three print journals dedicated exclusively to research on family businesses: *Family Business Review* (Sage), *Journal of Family Business Strategy* (Elsevier), and *Journal of Family Business Management* (Emerald). The topic also sparks continuous interest in other specialized journals as well as mainstream publications. Likewise, there is a proliferation of dedicated family business chairs at universities and a variety of international academic conferences around the topic.

The growth prospects for the family business field are unprecedented. A recent review of manuscripts published on family business ProQuest's scholarly "business" journals section between 1985 and 2009 shows an annual growth rate of 12.4 percent, which is higher than the rate of growth in publications overall, according to A. Stewart and A. S. Miner (2011). These statistics concur with bibliometric research carried out by Elsevier indicating a 17 percent annual growth rate over the last 12 years in the number of authors writing on and papers concerning family business, according to J. H. Astrachan and T. M. Pieper (2010). This compares with typical 2 to 3 percent growth rates in most other fields. The field is growing and has produced several accomplishments.

Early writings on family business were limited to anecdotal accounts that largely demonized family companies as nonprofessional, conflict-ridden, and nepotistic entities. The successes of family business were all but ignored. This has changed over time. For one, researchers started to realize the positive effects of family involvement in business in terms of higher levels of commitment, continuity, and care for employees and communities at large. Furthermore, a series of large-scale surveys assessing the relevance of family businesses has changed the general position toward a more balanced attitude. Empirical research consistently shows that family businesses are major contributors to global economic production and employment, totaling 65 to 80 percent of all businesses worldwide. In the United States, family businesses generate approximately 60 percent of the country's employment, account for 50 percent of the gross domestic product, and account for 78 percent of new job creation.

With regard to new venture creation in particular, research at the United Nations level shows that families are the most important providers of start-up capital and financial resources to new and existing firms. The work indicates that 85 percent of all new ventures are started with family money, and future research will likely show that nearly every new venture requires family emotional and intellectual support to succeed. This role is particularly important in times of credit tightening and economic hardship as currently experienced at a global level.

Another important area of study that has sparked anew the interest of researchers is on the financial performance of publicly listed family businesses. Empirical research of the Fortune 500 companies by R. C. Anderson and D. M. Reeb (2003) showed that founding and influential families own stakes in about one third of Fortune 500 firms and account for more than 18 percent of the outstanding equity. Furthermore, and to the surprise of the researchers, Fortune 500 family firms outperform their nonfamily counterparts, demonstrating that family influence is an effective form of control, providing incentive structures that result in fewer agency conflicts and lead to greater financial and firm value performance. These findings triggered a host of follow-up investigations among large, publicly listed firms in the United States and other countries in the world, which consistently support the overperformance of family businesses. Obviously, the results need to be compared with respect to the underlying definition of family business used and distinctions made, whether the firm is run by the first or a subsequent generation. However, the positive correlation between family involvement and higher firm performance is generally supported.

The performance research also highlighted the existence of curvilinear relationships as another noteworthy characteristic of family businesses. In the case of Fortune 500 firms, according to Anderson and Reeb (2003), the relation between family ownership and firm performance was found to be nonlinear (inverted-U-shaped), such that firm performance first increases but then decreases as family ownership continues to increase. Empirical studies confirmed the nonlinear relationship between family ownership and firm performance for publicly listed family firms in Taiwan and Poland. Subsequent research has identified a host of nonlinear relationships in family business. Examples include nonlinear relationships between family ownership and the level of international entrepreneurship, dispersion of ownership among directors and use of debt, and the cultural dimension of individualism and entrepreneurship in family business.

Another stream of empirical research points to the superior social performance of family businesses. For instance, studies show that family businesses are more socially responsible, lay off fewer employees, and pollute the environment less than their nonfamily counterparts. These selected findings highlight some of the important differences of family businesses that warrant future investigation and analysis.

Extant performance research typically relies on financial measures of firm performance. However, unlike anonymously owned corporations, family businesses may set their own, possibly idiosyncratic performance metrics and goals. Families often value activities and products quite highly and may deemphasize financial performance, such as firm value, profits, equity, or asset returns. Family business goals and thus performance can be considered along multiple dimensions: financial firm performance, firm survival, family financial benefit, family nonfinancial benefit (such as emotional well-being), and societal benefit. Performance research in family business may be more complex than single-metric performance. Therefore, future studies of performance are well advised to measure accomplishments against the goals of the owning families.

Since most researchers in family business have a business or economic background, the focus of investigation typically revolves around the business and not so much the family. However, one can argue from a strategic point of view that businesses are mere vehicles that help owning families achieve their goals. For instance, prior research on multigenerational family businesses shows that large, extended business-owning families use their businesses as means to build family cohesion, a key driver of survival in the long run. Hence, a stronger research focus should be placed on the families that own businesses and what, beyond the business and financial resources, allows the families to be long-lived and prosperous, as well as the strategies conducive to these goals.

Another aspect worth further consideration is causality in how family affects business and business affects family. Drawing on the research previously presented, the common rationale is that family influence leads to higher firm performance. However, one can also argue that firm performance affects owning families such that better-performing businesses provide owning families with materialistic returns (such as money) as well as emotional returns (such as pride and identification) that contribute to family welfare and stability. As long as the business can provide such positive returns, the family probably maintains ownership in the business. Conversely, if the business can no longer provide such returns in a sufficient manner, the owning family may be more likely to divest from such underperforming organizations. In other words, it is not necessarily the family that causes better firm performance. It is equally plausible that firm performance may result in higher family ownership. Therefore, future studies are well advised to elaborate more profoundly on the causality between family influence and business outcomes.

Related to the previous point is the fact that family business scholars typically borrow established constructs from other disciplines and apply them to family business. Whereas this approach has contributed to a better understanding of family business, it uses family business as a mere context of research—not the content of scientific inquiry. Given their unique nature emerging from the marriage of family and business systems, family businesses have the potential to contribute new theoretical knowledge and conceptual insights and thereby inform other domains.

The development of specific family business constructs goes hand in hand with the application of research methodologies allowing for such discoveries to be made. Qualitative approaches that allow theory building from rich data obtained from a limited number of cases are well suited to develop content-based theories of family business. Mixed-methods approaches that combine qualitative and quantitative methods are desirable for this purpose as well. Quantitative approaches that show great promise are covariance-based and, in particular, variance-based structural equations modeling offering advanced scale development capabilities. Furthermore, experimental methods are well suited to test for causality, an area requiring more careful exploration as mentioned earlier. In summary, there are many approaches available to family business researchers, and choosing the adequate approach is contingent upon the type of research question and research setting faced.

Empirical evidence shows that 85 percent of all companies around the world are family businesses. Researchers need to recognize the significance of families as major owners of existing companies and sponsors of new ventures worldwide. Including family as a variable in research routinely would lead to further developments and advancements in current knowledge. Even greater progress would be made if family business systematically became the content of research and educational programs, as it would advance theory building and business practice in the long run.

Torsten M. Pieper
Joseph H. Astrachan
Kennesaw State University

See also Agency Theory; Family Business; Family Business: Defining; Family Business: Stewardship; Family Business: Theory; Home-Based Businesses; Stakeholders; Succession Planning

Further Readings

Anderson, R. C. and D. M. Reeb. "Founding-Family Ownership and Firm Performance: Evidence From the S&P 500." *Journal of Finance*, v.58/3 (2003).

Astrachan, J. H. "Family Firm and Community Culture." *Family Business Review*, v.1/2 (1988).

Astrachan, J. H. and M. C. Shanker. "Family Businesses' Contribution to the U.S. Economy: A Closer Look." *Family Business Review*, v.16/3 (2003).

Astrachan, J. H., S. A. Zahra, and P. Sharma. *Family Sponsored Ventures: The Entrepreneurial Advantage of Nations*. First Annual Global Entrepreneurship Symposium, Business Council for the United Nations, New York, 2003.

Beckhard, R. and W. G. Dyer Jr. "Managing Continuity in the Family-Owned Business." *Organizational Dynamics*, v.12/1 (1983).

Bird, B., H. Welsch, J. H. Astrachan, and D. Pistrui. "Family Business Research: The Evolution of an Academic Field." *Family Business Review*, v.15 (2002).

Burkart, M., F. Panunzi, and A. Shleifer. "Family Firms." *Journal of Finance*, v.58/5 (2003).

Chrisman, J. J. et al. "Management Journals as Venues for Publication of Family Business Research." *Entrepreneurship Theory and Practice*, v.32 (2008).

Chrisman, J. J., J. H. Chua, and L. P. Steier. "An Introduction to Theories of Family Business." *Journal of Business Venturing*, v.18 (2003).

Debicki, B. J., C. F. Matherne III, F. W. Kellermanns, and J. J. Chrisman. "Family Business Research in the New Millennium: An Overview of the Who, the Where, the What, and the Why." *Family Business Review*, v.22 (2009).

Dyer, W. G., Jr. and D. A. Whetten. "Family Firms and Social Responsibility: Preliminary Evidence From the S&P 500." *Entrepreneurship Theory and Practice*, v.30/6 (2006).

Heck, R. K. Z. and C. S. Mishra. "Family Entrepreneurship." *Journal of Small Business Management*, v.46 (2008).

International Family Enterprise Research Academy. "Family Businesses Dominate." *Family Business Review*, v.16/4 (2003).

Kaplan, T. E., G. George, and G. W. Rimler. "University-Sponsored Family Business Programs: Program Characteristics, Perceived Quality and Member Satisfaction." *Entrepreneurship Theory and Practice*, v.24 (2000).

Mandl, I. *Overview of Family Business Relevant Issues*. Study by the European Commission, 2008. http://ec.europa.eu/enterprise/policies/sme/documents/family-Business/index_en.htm (Accessed February 2011).

Rogoff, E. G. and R. K. Z. Heck. "Evolving Research in Entrepreneurship and Family Business: Recognizing Family as the Oxygen That Feeds the Fire of Entrepreneurship." *Journal of Business Venturing*, v.18 (2003).

Stavrou, E., G. Kassinis, and A. Filotheou. "Downsizing and Stakeholder Orientation Among the Fortune 500: Does Family Ownership Matter?" *Journal of Business Ethics*, v.72/2 (2007).

Stewart, A. and A. S. Miner. "The Prospects for Family Business in Research Universities." *Journal of Family Business Strategy*, v.2/1 (2011).

FAMILY BUSINESS: STEWARDSHIP

In the family business literature, stewardship theory is a central framework that is drawn upon to explain how a family can act as a resource to their family business. With its roots in sociology and psychology, stewardship theory views organizational members as collectivists, collaborative and trustworthy. Stewardship theory draws from the tenets of Douglas McGregor's classic Theory Y, which views organizational members as intrinsically motivated, pro-organizational, cooperative, and responsible. Regarding family businesses in particular, stewardship theory focuses on how the family contributes to family business performance, highlighting the psychological ownership and shared sense of responsibility the family feels for the business. Positive family relationships are seen as a unique resource to family firms, because they engender loyalty, shared identity, and a commitment to the success of the business.

Stewardship theory is often contrasted with agency theory in the family business literature. Researchers tend to view the behaviors of family employees on a continuum from opportunism to stewardship. Research acknowledges that family members can be motivated by self-interest and opportunism, as dictated by agency theory, or by organizational commitment and reciprocal altruism, as prescribed by stewardship theory. Those who prescribe to the logic of agency theory focus on the unique agency costs that arise from family involvement, such as nepotism, adverse selection, and entrenchment of ineffective family managers. The behavioral model of agency theory proposes that family managers are motivated by wealth preservation and the maintenance of ownership control and that they therefore exhibit risk-averse preferences that can result in stagnation, underinvestment in renewal, and poor business performance. Whereas agency costs have been shown to exist in some family businesses, thereby supporting agency theory, the tenets of agency theory do not explain when a family is a resource for a family business, contributing to the business's growth and survival. Stewardship theory fills this gap.

Stewardship theory portrays organizational members as trustworthy loyal stewards of the firm who contribute to the firm's goals through reciprocal altruistic behaviors. It views the family as a loyal collective that seeks to build enduring relationships with stakeholders and to sustain the firm for future generations. Stewardship behaviors can make family businesses especially successful, leading them to outperform and "outsurvive" their nonfamily business counterparts. By involving family members in the business, family owners create an intensely dedicated and loyal workforce who believe they have a common responsibility to see the business prosper. Their shared family identity motivates them to pursue business goals and to protect the reputation of the family business. As a result, the family commits to the long-term success of the business, seeking stable growth and prosperity.

Highlighting the shared sense of responsibility the family feels toward the business, stewardship theory research focuses on how the family contributes to family business performance. When family members display kinship obligation toward their business, feelings of personal and social fulfillment arise that cause them to guard the well-being of the business. Stewardship theory views positive family relationships as a unique resource to family firms, since these relationships engender loyalty and commitment toward the success of the business. Arguments in line with the stewardship perspective propose that involving family members in firm management allows family members to gain a better understanding of where the organization is headed, appreciate the challenges facing the firm, and make decisions that they believe will maximize firm performance. Family leaders behave as stewards when they protect the family's assets and attempt to create a healthier business for future generations. Stewards maximize their own utility by acting in the best interest of the family business to attain its goals, such as growth and profitability. Stewardship theory proposes that family members who behave as stewards are willing to put aside personal interests for the sake of the firm and to protect the business for the next generation.

There are numerous ways that stewardship may materialize in family businesses. J. H. Davis, F. D. Schoorman, and L. Donaldson's seminal work depicted stewardship theory as emphasizing strong identification and commitment to the organization, employee motivation based on self-actualization and intrinsic needs, involvement-oriented and collaborative decision making, long-term orientation, and the quality training of employees. Research on family businesses has characterized a stewardship philosophy as stressing longevity and long-term orientation, the nurturing of a talented workforce, aligned values between the family and business, family identification with the business, reciprocal altruism, strong and enduring relationships with external stakeholders, and participative decision making. Therefore, research rooted in stewardship theory has attempted to demonstrate how the family can be a resource to the family business.

Indeed, a stewardship philosophy has been shown to be common among successful family businesses. Stewardship theory proposes that because stewards believe their interests are aligned with those of the firm, they will work toward the pursuit of organizational goals. Kinship, a shared family name, common history, and familiarity can promote a strong shared identity in family firms, encouraging family members to uphold organizational values and pursue organizational goals. In turn, these firms can rely on mutual trust, intrafamilial concern, devotion to the family business, and clan-based collegiality. When family members assist other members, share responsibilities, and help each other accomplish organizational tasks, they can be seen as stewards of the firm. In particular, reciprocal altruism reinforces family members' interdependence, thereby encouraging them to place the business's objectives ahead of their own and to display citizenship behaviors. In line with stewardship theory, altruistic families possess collectivistic orientations that encourage family members to exercise self-restraint and to consider the effect of their actions on the firm. Further, family businesses that support a stewardship philosophy are believed to benefit from more proactive behaviors, entrepreneurship, and improved performance. Therefore, when trying to explain the unique benefits a family can bestow on a family business, researchers often employ stewardship theory.

Kimberly Eddleston
Northeastern University

See also Agency Theory; Family Business; Family Business: Defining; Family Business: Research; Family Business: Theory; Home-Based Businesses; Stakeholders; Succession Planning

Further Readings

Block, P. *Stewardship: Choosing Service Over Self-Interest.* San Francisco: Berrett-Koehler, 1996.
Chrisman, J. J., J. H. Chua, E. P. Chang, and F. W. Kellermanns. "Are Family Managers Agents or Stewards? An Exploratory Study in Privately-Held Family Firms." *Journal of Business Research,* v.60 (2007).
Davis, J. H., M. R. Allen, and H. D. Hayes. "Is Blood Thicker Than Water? A Study of Stewardship Perceptions in Family Business." *Entrepreneurship Theory and Practice,* v.34/6 (2010).
Davis, J. H., F. D. Schoorman, and L. Donaldson. "Toward a Stewardship Theory of Management." *Academy of Management Review,* v.22/1 (1997).
Eddleston, K. and F. W. Kellermanns. "Destructive and Productive Family Relationships: A Stewardship Theory Perspective." *Journal of Business Venturing,* v.22 (2007).
Le Breton-Miller, I. and D. Miller. "Agency vs. Stewardship in Public Family Firms: A Social Embeddedness Perspective." *Entrepreneurship Theory and Practice,* v.33 (2009).
Miller, D., I. Le Breton-Miller, and B. Scholnick. "Stewardship vs. Stagnation: An Empirical Comparison of Small Family and Non-Family Businesses." *Journal of Management Studies,* v.45/1 (2008).

FAMILY BUSINESS: THEORY

Researchers in family business believe that the family's influence in a family business makes these firms distinct from other business organizations, leading to intangible resources and unique attributes that create competitive advantages. To ferret out the extent to which this is so, researchers have often classified a firm as a family firm by criteria or combinations of criteria including family ownership, management by a family member, operational involvement of family members, and family member involvement across generations. Subsequently, researchers have applied mainstream management theories to explain how those firms classified as family firms may differ from nonfamily firms on several performance dimensions. Whereas several theories have been applied, most examinations have their roots in strategic management, and the theories used to examine family firms have converged around agency theory, the resource-based view of the firm, and stakeholder theory.

Agency Theory

Agency theory is concerned with the degree to which an agent will act in a principal's best interest. Within organizations like family businesses and new ventures, the theory is usually discussed as the relationship between a manager and how that manager represents an owner. However, agency theory has also been used to characterize the relationship between other dyads, such as manager–employee, owner–employee, owner–owner, investor–owner. Among these dyads, problems can appear in the forms of adverse selection and moral hazard. Adverse selection arises when a principal mistakenly enters into a contract with an incompetent or unsuitable agent who might be less committed, industrious, or ethical than the principal. Moral hazard occurs when an agent engages in activities that work in the favor of that agent but work against the principal. These problems exist because of asymmetric information—the agent generally possesses a greater understanding of the available information than the principal. Within the firm, these problems can be mitigated via incentives and monitoring.

Michael Jensen and William Meckling assert that the problems of adverse selection and moral hazard exist only when the interests of the principal and the agent diverge. Thus, problems, especially those arising from moral hazards, should be considerably reduced when the interests across a dyad overlap substantially—for example, when a manager and an owner share the same perspective and goals—thereby lowering the firm's overall cost structure, because the principal no longer must engage in substantial contracting and monitoring or risk the agent's behaving in ways that threaten the principal's interests (through shirking, free-riding, fraud, and so forth). In family firms, there is often significant percentage of family in any dyad (that is, there is high family involvement), which means these dyads should operate more efficiently. In other words, agency costs are mitigated because family businesses are characterized by unified ownership and management, alignment of interests, monitoring advantages, and shared concern for preserving the firm's wealth. Consistent with this, early studies proposed that family firms would have few or no agency problems, as the agent and principal are often the same entity. Increased family involvement, therefore, should lead to increased firm performance, all other things being equal, because individuals in the dyad care for each other and are more likely to act in the best interest of the family firm.

The dominant stance that has emerged within the literature, however, holds that family firms do indeed suffer agency-type problems, even if significant overlap exists between ownership and management subsystems. Agency costs are incurred because

Family members working together in businesses have a vested interest in ensuring the firm's future success. The dynamics of a family business can be examined by using agency theory, which is concerned with the degree to which an agent will act in the company's best interest. (Photos.com)

the owner/manager makes decisions that are inefficient or ineffective, failing to maximize shareholder return. Interestingly, these costs are not those that are traditionally described as agency costs, but, like traditional agency costs, they can be mitigated by using formal control mechanisms.

Resource-Based View of the Firm

Jay Barney introduced the resource-based view (RBV) of the firm, which posits that competitive advantages arise from valuable, rare, difficult-to-imitate, and nonsubstitutable resources within any firm. In some circumstances, family involvement in the firm may result in competitive advantage. Such competitive advantages have been described, broadly, as familiness. Familiness describes resources (tangible and intangible) that result from the interaction of family, ownership, and management in family firms. These three subsystems, and their interactions, are unique to family businesses. Although the techniques of measurement for the specific construct of familiness are still developing, manifestations of familiness have been identified. Family influence, for instance, offers the intangible resources related to reciprocal altruism to build a culture of stewardship where organizational members develop a responsibility to each other (and the firm) to see the business succeed. Another, more tangible, form of familiness is patient capital. Patient capital refers to the relatively long time horizon that family investors have regarding returns on investments. A final example of familiness is that of heightened brand equity, as family members desire to protect the family name and products/services associated with it.

David Sirmon and Michael Hitt provide a comprehensive framework to look at family businesses through an RBV lens. In this synthesis, they suggest that family firms evaluate, acquire, shed, and bundle their resources in unique ways such that family firms can effectively attain five unique sources of capital: human capital, social capital, survivability capital, patient financial capital, and governance structures.

Stakeholder Theory

According to R. Edward Freeman's explanation of stakeholder theory, various individuals and groups, termed stakeholders, influence firm decisions and, consequently, firm performance. Stakeholders represent any group or individual who can affect or can be affected by the fulfillment of the organization's goals. Whereas individual stakeholders or groups of stakeholders may all have a vested interest in the goal set of a specific firm, their specific demands may be in conflict with one another. Thus, conflicts arise as organizations with finite resources must make allocation decisions that limit their capability to satisfy all of the demands that are potentially conflicting. Accordingly, the power and legitimacy of the stakeholder group must be considered as their influence on goal performance is assessed. Powerful stakeholder groups known as dominant coalitions, for instance, would have more input into goal formation and the dedication of resources toward their pursuit than would less powerful groups.

When compared to nonfamily firms, family firms by definition have an additional stakeholder group to consider: the family. Perhaps most important, the family is likely a powerful stakeholder group, playing an instrumental role in the strategic direction of the firm as they have significant liberty to act, especially in cases when ownership and control are unified. Because of this, powerful family stakeholder groups often exercise authority such that the firm pursues noneconomic goals to include the perpetuation of family values through the business, the preservation of the family's control of the firm, and the fulfillment of family obligations. Clearly, this influence may have negative consequences for nonfamily stakeholders when a goal to maintain harmony and cohesion in the family leads to career opportunities for ill-prepared, incompetent, or poorly motivated family members. In contrast, nonfamily stakeholders may benefit from the relatively long time horizon that family investors have regarding returns on investments and the family's hesitation to pursue wildly risky and uncertain investments.

Daniel T. Holt
Mississippi State University
Matthew W. Rutherford
Virginia Commonwealth University

See also Agency Theory; Family Business; Family Business: Defining; Family Business: Research; Family Business: Theory; Home-Based Businesses; Stakeholders; Succession Planning

Further Readings

Barney, Jay. "Firm Resources and Sustained Competitive Advantage." *Journal of Management*, v.17/1 (1991).

Freeman, R. Edward. *Strategic Management: A Stakeholder Approach*. Boston: Pitman, 1951.

Habbershon, Timothy G. and Mary L. Williams. "A Resource-Based Framework for Assessing the Strategic Advantages of Family Firms." *Family Business Review*, v.12/1 (1999).

Jensen, Michael C. and William H. Meckling. "Theory of the Firm: Managerial Behavior, Agency Costs and Ownership Structure." *Journal of Financial Economics*, v.3/4 (1976).

Sirmon, David G. and Michael A. Hitt. "Managing Resources: Linking Unique Resources, Management and Wealth Creation in Family Firms." *Entrepreneurship Theory and Practice*, v.27/4 (2003).

FEASIBILITY STUDIES

In the new venture management literature, feasibility is an important concept identified in several phases of new venture creation: the individual behaviors or intentions necessary to be an entrepreneur; the arguments supporting the viability of the business idea prior to its development; and the entrepreneurship observed within organizations. In the following text, the concept of feasibility is analyzed within these three phases.

Studies about the individual's feasibility focus on the explanation and prediction of the entrepreneurial intentions of entrepreneurs, who create organizations to pursue opportunities, and potential entrepreneurs, who perceive one or several opportunities but have not initiated the process of creating an organization. Supported by the physiological and sociological literature, feasibility encompasses a strong element of control on behalf of the individual entrepreneur, meaning one has the talent, skills, and resources necessary to bring the activity to fruition. Since the 1980s, several entrepreneurial intention models have observed the thinking process of potential entrepreneurs to examine how individuals make decisions based on Albert Shapero's model, which integrates three elements: the personal attractiveness of starting a business, which includes both intrapersonal and extrapersonal impacts (desirability); the degree to which one is personally capable of starting a business (feasibility); and the individual's propensity to act. Albert Bandura suggests that the individual's feasibility for a particular course of action can best be understood through illuminating personal self-efficacy. Self-efficacy involves initiating and persisting at behavior under uncertainty, setting higher goals, and reducing threat-rigidity and learned helplessness. It is the individual's perception of his or her abilities and capabilities to execute some target behavior or perform a particular job.

This explains why, several years ago, governments, educational institutions, and private companies became involved in teaching and fostering entrepreneurship. Evidence suggests that these entrepreneurial education programs, which concentrate primarily on technical skills, have a positive influence on aspiring entrepreneurs. However, they often fail to address innovation, risk taking, and the philosophy and belief systems of the entrepreneur. When designing entrepreneurship courses and programs, educators might be advised to prepare students in cognitive entrepreneurial skills and belief systems to strengthen self-efficacy. Rather than focusing only on teaching competencies, these programs should also create opportunities for students to internalize these competencies through an ongoing exchange of experiences with mentors and role models. For instance, role models affect entrepreneurial intentions only if they affect self-efficacy.

Studies about the feasibility of a business idea look at the decision-making process behind the creation of a new venture, the creation of a new enterprise from an existing business, or the expansion of an existing business. These feasibility studies are based on the viability of the new business idea in the market. In this phase, the feasibility study helps to obtain data that allow entrepreneurs to determine whether the new business idea could succeed in the market. The entrepreneur is able to identify strengths, weaknesses, opportunities, and alternatives during this deliberation phase of the business development cycle, prior to formalizing the enterprise. The entrepreneur invests both time and money to generate an in-depth understanding of several dimensions: identifying opportunities, competitors, and commitments from customers in the market or market segment; determining the technical issues or regulations required to provide the service or manufacture the product; discovering the best form of efficient and consistent management; ascertaining the overall economic impact of the project; determining the reliability of the financial projections and the ability of the business to achieve the projected income, cash flow, risks, returns, and capital required; and establishing the different alternatives for an exit strategy.

In comparison with a business plan, the feasibility study provides an investigative function that outlines and analyzes several alternatives or methods to achieve business success, whereas the business plan provides a planning function to outline the actions needed to take the proposal from "idea" to "reality" with only one alternative or scenario. Therefore, with the feasibility study, the entrepreneur should be able to identify the true viability of the business idea based on its ability to generate cash flow and profits, withstand the risks it will encounter, remain viable in the long term, and meet the goals of the founders. In other words, the feasibility study reveals where and how the business will operate in different scenarios (conservative, optimistic, or pessimistic) and the implications, strengths, and weaknesses of each. Later, the feasibility study will be assessed by potential investors and stakeholders to analyze the potential entrepreneur's credibility and depth of argumentation.

Studies about feasibility within an organization concentrate on the entrepreneurial phenomena in a new or established enterprise. Deborah Brazeal explains that although the literature has unraveled the "black box," or mind-set, of the potential entrepreneur in the context of new enterprises, no effort has been made to detail the decision-making process within corporate entrepreneurship. Within this phase, however, the concept of self-efficacy again allows us to gain insight and estimate the capabilities of entrepreneurs to self-motivate, garner resources, and exercise autonomy over desire outcomes, particularly in a context in which employees believe they have, in their control, blueprints for innovative pursuits sanctioned by immediate supervision and congruent with organizational strategy.

Therefore, individuals with high self-efficacy exhibit a strong belief in their capabilities, choose challenging goals, invest significant time in carefully selected activities, and, most important, persevere in the face of insurmountable obstacles. In corporate entrepreneurship, a potential intrapreneur is inclined to engage in entrepreneurial behaviors when creative activities are jointly feasible (management allows time, resources, and support) and desirable (compensation is congruent with its expectative). Then, within organizations, the diversity of perspectives in a team helps to diffuse potential negative perception and raise feasibility, therefore playing a powerful role in managerial and employee behavior that leads to increased initiatives, persistence, and performance. Also, while intentions certainly seem to play an important role, it is clear that many highly motivated individuals are involved in favorable entrepreneurial environments. In this sense, gender and ethnic differences seem to be fully mediated by differences in self-efficacy.

Finally, to encourage economic development in the form of new enterprises, governments must first increase perceptions of feasibility and desirability. Policy initiatives will increase business formation. The growing trends of downsizing and outsourcing make this more than a sterile academic exercise. Even if we successfully increase the quantity and quality of potential entrepreneurs, we must also promote such perceptions among critical stakeholders, including suppliers, neighbors, government officials, and the larger community. Promoting entrepreneurial intentions by promoting public perceptions of feasibility is required.

Maribel Guerrero
Basque Institute of Competitiveness,
Deusto Business School

See also Business Models; Business Plans; Entrepreneurial Training; Entrepreneurship Education: Graduate Programs; Entrepreneurship Education: High School; Entrepreneurship Education: Undergraduate Programs; Entrepreneurship Pedagogy; Intentions

Further Readings

Ajzen, Icek. "Theory of Planned Behavior: Some Unresolved Issues." *Organizational Behavior and Human Decision Processes*, v.50/2 (1991).

Bandura, Albert. *Self-Efficacy: The Exercise of Control.* New York: Freeman, 1997.

Delmar, Frederic and Shane Scott. "Does Business Planning Facilitate the Development of New Ventures?" *Strategic Management Journal*, v.24 (2003).

Katz, Jerry and Richard Green. *Entrepreneurial Small Business.* New York: McGraw-Hill, 2009.

Krueger, Norris and Deborah Brazeal. "Entrepreneurial Potential and Potential Entrepreneurs." *Entrepreneurship Theory and Practice*, v.18/1 (1994).

Krueger, Norris, Michael Reilly, and Alan Carsrud. "Competing Models of Entrepreneurial Intentions." *Journal of Business Venturing*, v.15/6 (2000).

Shapero, Albert. "Social Dimensions of Entrepreneurship." In *Encyclopedia of Entrepreneurship.* Englewood Cliffs, NJ: Prentice Hall, 1982.

Stevens, Robert and Philip Sherwood. *How to Prepare a Feasibility Study: A Step-by-Step Guide Including Three Model Studies.* Englewood Cliffs, NJ: Prentice Hall, 1982.

Focus Groups

Focus groups are an efficient way of gathering insight into likely consumer reactions to a new business idea. They are a particularly useful tool for new ventures, allowing them to identify emerging needs in the marketplace that the established organization may miss and helping them to arrive at new solutions to an age-old problem. Focus groups have been used in market research since the 1920s, so there is a good understanding of the way to conduct focus groups for reliable results. Practical advice on the planning and recruiting of focus groups is summarized in many business research methods books. In addition to offering speed and comparative ease in conducting group interviews to collect information about new venture propositions, focus groups are useful because many consumer decisions are made in a social, group context.

In his book explaining real-world research methods, Colin Robson defines a focus group as a group of individuals who are interviewed on a specific topic—hence the label "focus" group. They are sometimes presented as a particular type of research interview—a focus group interview—to distinguish this approach to gathering business intelligence from other forms of interviewing. Whereas other forms of interviewing may be highly structured, offering respondents limited ways of responding to predetermined questions, focus groups can be open-ended, with discussions guided by the entrepreneur or a researcher and usually are expected to take at least one hour.

The sociologist Janet Ruane sees the give and take of focus group dialogue as an opportunity to learn more about *what* people think of the topic at hand as well as to learn more about *why* they think as they do. Advocates of the approach claim that when applied in ways that encourage interaction among participants, the group interview produces more insight into the issue of interest than is possible through multiple one-on-one interviews. Group dynamics can help in focusing on the most important topics, allowing the interviewer to assess the extent to which there is a consistent and shared view. Participants may include people who are reluctant to be interviewed alone, feel they have no insights to share, or generally do not respond to market research surveys. A particular advantage may exist when discussion touches on taboo subjects or issues liable to attract a strong social desirability bias (people professing support for something because of its perceived status but not actually reflecting this in their real decisions), provided that the group includes less inhibited members.

On the downside, the number of major questions that can be asked of a focus group is typically fewer than 10 per hour. There is a need for the interview

to avoid becoming dominated by more vocal participants, which runs the risk of emphasizing unrepresentative views. A danger of power struggles emerging between or among group participants as different perspectives emerge requires that the interviewer be sufficiently skilled to ensure that discussion covers the area of interest. Based on experience in the health sector, a researcher has noted a danger that the live and immediate nature of the interaction can lead focus group organizers to have greater faith in the findings than is warranted. Apple founder Steve Jobs, for example, is one entrepreneur who is quoted as discouraging reliance on focus group findings, believing that it is the entrepreneur's role to identify new product ideas.

Groups consisting of eight to 12 participants are generally thought to elicit a sufficient diversity of views. The decision about group size involves a trade-off between ensuring that there will be time for each participant to contribute and capturing a spectrum of experiences. Whatever the size and no matter how carefully participants are recruited, small groups will rarely constitute a representative sample. Entrepreneurs are well advised to use the focus group to help design a business concept but then use other forms of market research to gauge the strength of consumer interest.

The traditional use of focus groups has involved bringing together groups of strangers on the assumption that their unfamiliarity with one another leads to focus on the designated topic. Where participants are known to each other, the direction of dialogue may prove unsatisfactory. When group participants have different backgrounds, positions, and experiences, the discussion is stimulated and enriched, assisting group members to consider the focal topic from different perspectives and reducing the chances of "groupthink" (too little questioning of views and positions similar to one's own). These advantages may in practice need to be balanced against the difficulties of recruiting persons with diverse experience to discuss specific topics. Also, heterogeneous groups are generally considered more challenging to run than homogenous groups because of the risk that opinions expressed by some members will not be respected by others and because some members may show deference to apparently more knowledgeable persons in the group.

The focus group interviewer must combine two roles: moderator of group discussion, in the sense of keeping it within the bounds of what is of interest, and facilitator, in the sense of helping the group to run effectively while covering all the major questions. Hence the interviewer may be referred to as the group moderator or facilitator but in practice should expect to move between these roles as the interview progresses. Delegation to an expert interviewer is recommended, but entrepreneurs may observe proceedings at first hand or hidden from the participants.

Entrepreneurship research mainly uses focus groups for exploratory studies of issues that have not previously been studied. An example is a study that was designed to discover what management practices growth-orientated entrepreneurs adopt to sustain the growth of their enterprises. Owner-managers of enterprises that had grown consistently over the previous five years were recruited for the group interviews, each of which comprised nine entrepreneurs. In addition to such exploratory research, entrepreneurship studies use focus groups to make sense of findings from surveys. Surveys collecting quantitative data can explain what people's views are, whereas a focus group study can reveal why those views exist. The main risk to consider is that without a sensitive and effective moderator, a single dominant participant can shape the responses of other participants.

Martin Perry
Massey University

See also Advertising; Competition; Contextual Marketing; Customer Orientation; Market Evaluation; New Product Development; Sales; Test Markets

Further Readings

MacDougall, C. and E. Fudge. "Planning and Recruiting the Sample for Focus Groups and In-Depth Interviews." *Qualitative Health Research*, v.11 (2001).

Packham, G., D. Brooksbank, C. Miller, and B. Thomas. "Climbing the Mountain: Management Practices Adoption in Growth Orientated Firms in Wales." *Journal of Small Business and Enterprise Development*, v.12/4 (2005).

Robson, C. *Real World Research*. Oxford, UK: Blackwell, 2002.

Ruane, J. *Essentials of Research Methods: A Guide to Social Science Research*. Malden, MA: Blackwell, 2005.

FRANCHISEE AND FRANCHISOR

Franchising is a popular way of expanding a business, and the model has a very long history of success. Because franchise arrangements are so flexible, they can be implemented in a variety of industries. The professional relationship between the franchisor and his or her franchisees is unique, and the nature of the relationship can be a significant factor in a franchise venture's success or failure, as well as a factor in the overall satisfaction or frustration experienced by the individual parties. Unlike many other kinds of business relationships, the relationship between franchisee and franchisor is also particularly likely to change over time as the franchise matures and the franchisee becomes more confident in the operation of the business. Both parties have rights and obligations under the franchise arrangement, and the best results occur when the goals of both parties are honored as key objectives. Simply put, franchises would not exist without both parties, so those franchise systems that view the relationship as strategic and interdependent often fare best.

Role of the Franchisor

The majority of franchised businesses fit one of two models. The first model is that of chain-style business operations providing a standardized product or service; franchised restaurants, auto service businesses, and retail outlets fit this model. Distributorships are an alternative model, in which the franchisor authorizes the franchisee to sell its products to the public, as in car dealerships. The professional relationship between the parties may be different, depending on which franchising model the business venture fits; generally speaking, a franchisee in a chain-style operation will expect closer ties and more ongoing support from the franchisor than might a distributorship franchisee.

From the franchisor's perspective, advantages of a franchise arrangement include the opportunity to expand the business and therefore one's revenues relatively quickly and without assuming much additional financial risk. The franchisor's role is essentially to provide the trademark, business model, and in many cases training and support to the franchisee as the franchise venture prepares to open, as well as on a continuing basis after it is launched. Depending on the business, the franchisor may set recommended prices and provide inventory, often securing favorable pricing if supply or merchandise ordering is done in bulk for the entire franchise network. The franchisor may also be likely to spend time continuing to recruit new franchisees and expand the network.

Another important responsibility of the franchisor is to protect the trademark and the interests of the franchise system as a whole from infringement or from reputational damage. It is therefore essential that franchisors have authority and some control over franchisees. After all, a rogue franchisee who operates outside the guidelines does not really represent only himself. A customer will view the entire franchise network as one organization, and an unpleasant experience at a single franchise location will color that customer's opinion of the entire franchise network, which may have a negative impact on the business of many franchisees and ultimately the franchisor. Franchisors may need to audit or inspect franchisee-operated locations periodically to ensure that overall standards are being met.

Role of the Franchisee

The franchisee usually purchases the right to use an existing business concept, including its name and trademark or logo. The specific terms of franchising contracts can vary, but typically the franchisee obtains the right to operate the business franchise in a particular site or territory. In exchange, the franchisee usually pays some up-front amount as well as ongoing royalties to the franchisor, often based on a percentage of revenue.

From the franchisee's perspective, a major advantage is adopting a business model that has already been tested and proven to some extent to be successful, and acquiring the name recognition and goodwill associated with an established brand. Although no business venture can ever be guaranteed success, franchises are more likely to thrive than are other new ventures. Furthermore, many franchisees are drawn by the idea of being self-employed, but they may be lacking an entrepreneurial idea of their own.

Because of their financial ownership, a franchisee is quite different from a manager who is employed to handle day-to-day operations but does not usually have a personal financial stake in the business. Franchisees are usually quite motivated to work hard but may be reluctant to submit entirely to the franchisor's authority. Hired managers are perhaps more likely to accept higher levels of authority than are franchisees, who view themselves as their own boss, so a franchisor may be faced with the delicate task of persuading a franchisee to accept advice rather than expecting the franchisee simply to do as told. Of course, the franchise agreement is intended to ensure compliance, but litigation to enforce the contract is likely to be a last resort and one that all parties would prefer to avoid. Most would say that by the time the contract is invoked, the relationship between the franchisee and franchisor has already failed. Diplomatic handling of the relationship and an appeal to the franchisee's reasonableness in explaining any requests or policies that seem to inspire resistance or resentfulness are keys to success.

Potential Conflicts and Success Factors

For the franchise relationship to endure, both the franchisee and the franchisor must perceive that it is mutually beneficial and generally positive. Whereas a successful franchisee-franchisor relationship does benefit both parties, it is important to note that it is not legally a fiduciary relationship. This means that the parties do not necessarily have a legal obligation to protect each other's best interests and their compliance must be more intrinsically motivated. Since a typical franchise agreement is lengthy—often 20 years or more—it is vital that the relationship between franchisee and franchisor be managed with care to ensure positive interactions over the course of the business relationship.

There are several key areas in which conflict may be likely to arise. First, if a franchisor seeks to expand the franchise network and thereby his own revenues by selling additional franchises, he must be careful that these will not cannibalize sales from existing locations. The franchisor earns maximum income just by increasing sales volume throughout the franchise network, while any individual franchisee will be concerned with the profit at his own location and will be sensitive to any perceived encroachment on his territory being permitted.

Franchisees are also likely to become dissatisfied if they perceive that the franchisor provides inadequate training and managerial assistance. Since ongoing support from the franchisor is often touted as a key advantage to participation in a franchise arrangement, franchisees often have high expectations in this area. Depending on the nature of the business and the size of the franchise network, franchisors might be expected to provide centralized purchasing or marketing, legal or sales support, technical support, human resources management support, consultation on real estate purchase or leases, continued training and personnel development, and more. Unfortunately, franchisees may lack objectivity in evaluating the quality of the assistance they receive.

Some frustrations may arise when the franchisee views himself as an entrepreneur and chafes against the controls put in place by the franchisor. Franchisees are often likely to be highly motivated to work hard, but not necessarily for the benefit of the franchisor. For example, if the franchisee adds what she considers an innovative product or service not included in the original franchise concept, she may be reluctant to pay royalties on revenue derived from that source. As the franchise matures, such franchisees may be inclined to forget how much value the franchisor provided during the start-up phase and may become resentful about continuing royalties, viewing themselves as primarily or solely responsible for the success of the business. Franchise relationships have been compared to parent-child relationships in that in the beginning, franchisees are eager to learn and gladly accept the franchisor's wisdom and authority. Later, as the franchisee becomes more experienced, he may feel more confident and comfortable operating the business independently. As a result, he may become increasingly critical of the franchisor and resentful of or resistant to the franchisor's authority.

While franchisees do share an incentive to maintain and promote the brand's image and customer goodwill, franchisees are not always as strongly motivated to safeguard the brand if their own short-term profitability is not compromised. For example, a franchisee whose business does not rely strongly on repeat customers may be tempted to cut corners or otherwise undermine the brand if there is a potential for short-term gain. Franchisors will want to discourage this sort of free-riding and may need to find a way to supervise franchisees in order to prevent such behavior. Although such a situation can lead to conflict with the noncomplying franchisee, enforcing policies is usually viewed favorably by other franchisees in the network, because they realize that their reputation with customers can be negatively affected by the noncompliance of any franchisee. Fair, consistent enforcement of standards will build trust and

be a boon to relationships with all franchisees. Of course, any appearance of favoritism or unfair treatment of an individual franchisee by the franchisor will have a severely detrimental effect.

Likewise, a franchisor must not be perceived as draconian or overly aggressive in exerting control over franchisees. Whereas it is important to uphold policies, there should also be a respect for each franchisee's unique skills, expertise, and knowledge of the local market and a balance of control in the relationship. It may be appropriate for there to be flexibility in many procedures, leaving details of day-to-day operations to the individual franchise operator. For example, while recommended pricing and marketing campaigns might be designed with the entire franchise network in mind, it may be beneficial to permit franchisees to make final decisions about prices or promotions based on their local customers' needs and preferences.

As with most other kinds of relationships, trust and communication are crucially important to success. Trust will be established over time as both parties act in a way that reflects their commitment to the success of the franchise network overall. Clear, honest communication must be facilitated. Depending on the particular business, mechanisms to promote communication might include regional or national meetings and workshops, franchisee associations, field-based support teams, and intranet-based resources and documentation. All information must be delivered to franchisees in a way that is credible and genuine. It may be helpful to explicitly stress the essential interdependence of the relationship—for example, by using team-building language and pronouns like *we* and *us* rather than divisive terms like *you* or *them*.

Training is also important. If a franchisee is well trained in the preferred procedures and understands the rationale behind them, he is likely to abide by them without resentment or temptation to circumvent the policies. However, a truly positive franchise relationship will include some mechanism for feedback and flexibility. A franchisee might have excellent ideas for improving how business is done, and she must feel that her input will be valued and honestly considered by the franchisor.

Although conflict cannot always be avoided entirely, it is useful to screen potential new franchisees carefully to ensure that they not only meet financial requirements to invest in a franchise but also share priorities, values about which goals and policies are important, and commitment to protecting the best interests of the entire franchise network. Taking the time to evaluate and screen candidates can be an effective way of preventing conflict in the relationship further down the road. Potential franchisees are also well advised to consider not just the terms of the franchise offering, spelled out in the franchise disclosure document, but also their subjective impressions of the franchisor in evaluating what a long-term business relationship might be like. They are also wise to take advantage of any opportunity to meet with existing franchisees to get a sense of the tone of interactions and general level of satisfaction throughout the franchise network. Very large franchise networks may even have franchisee organizations, which will be a venue for sharing information and leveraging franchisee interests in interactions with the franchisor.

By its very nature, franchising involves a unique relationship between the franchisee and franchisor. Both parties enter into the relationship with a belief that their goals are complementary, but the relationship is complex and fraught with the potential for various conflicts. Managing the relationship skillfully and successfully is a challenge of paramount importance for franchisors.

Sarah E. Fancher
Saint Louis University

See also Entrepreneurs in Franchising; Franchises: Legal Aspects; Franchises: Starting

Further Readings

Luangsuvimol, Theeranuch and Brian H. Kleiner. "Effective Franchise Management." *Management Research News*, v.27/4–5 (2004).

Modell, Charles S. "Trust: Key to Successful Franchise Relationships." *Franchising World*, v.42/9 (2010).

Monson, Catherine. "Establishing and Maintaining an Effective Franchise Relationship." *Franchising World*, v.40/6 (2008).

Trivedi, Rajiv K. "Creating Winning Dynamics: Franchisees, Franchisors and Compliance." *Franchising World*, v.41/9 (2009).

Watson, Anna and Richard Johnson. "Managing the Franchisor-Franchisee Relationship: A Relationship Marketing Perspective." *Journal of Marketing Channels*, v.17/1 (2010).

Franchises: Legal Aspects

Establishing a business, especially when related to a franchise, is a project of great importance that involves numerous legal aspects. Franchising is a collaboration between entities joined by a contract. Franchising involves a balanced and fair written agreement that regulates the relationship between franchisor and franchisee. Different regulations may exist, depending on the country where a venture is started, and the contract is a fundamental pillar of the franchise relationship, the document in which the obligations and rights of each party are specified.

Attempts to regulate franchise systems in the United States emerged in the 1960s. The lack of laws governing franchise relationships led the Federal Trade Commission (FTC) in 1979 to implement some basic regulations to control such arrangements. The FTC requires franchisors to present a "franchise disclosure agreement" at least 10 days before the transfer between both parties. Franchisors must comply with norms indicated by the Uniform Franchise Offering Circular (UFOC), which gives basic information about the individual franchise system to potential franchisees. The FTC requires the creation of a UFOC for all franchises, and the North American Securities Administrators Association (NASAA) has created some guides showing what type of information any UFOC should contain, including those about the franchisor and the franchise system and the relationship expected by franchisees with regard to franchisors. The FTC concluded that the NASAA guides were sufficient, and most franchisors use the NASAA format when creating a document. In 2007, the FTC adopted a new set of rules for franchises known as the Amended FTC Franchise Rule. Beginning in 2008, all franchisors were required to prepare and distribute documentation that follows the Amended FTC Franchise Rule format for the development of the "franchise disclosure document" (FDD).

By law, a franchisor must provide the franchisee with a UFOC/FDD before a contract can be signed or any payment is made. The FDD is quite long (it can be up to 700 pages long). Information contained in the 23 sections of the FDD is related to management history and experience, contact and background information for key staff, financial history, legal history, and fee schedules pertaining to opening, running, and closing the franchise. The FDD must also offer some information about how many franchises have been opened, closed, or transferred. Moreover, it must include information about investment in capital, required purchases, and applicable territorial rights. Additionally, requirements of the relationship between franchisor and franchisee, as well as mutual prospects, must be established. Each state can require that the FDD include some specific information, but these requirements must be according to federal law managing federal regulation policy. Under the FTC rule, there is no private right of action against franchisor violation of the rule, but at least 15 states have passed statutes that provide this right of action to franchisees when fraud can be proven under these special statutes.

The following are the 23 points to be covered in the franchise disclosure document:

1. The franchisor and any parents, predecessors, and affiliates
2. Business experience
3. Litigation
4. Bankruptcy
5. Initial fees
6. Other fees
7. Estimated initial investment
8. Restrictions on sources of products and services
9. Franchisee's obligations
10. Financing
11. Franchisor's assistance, advertising, computer systems, and training
12. Territory
13. Trademarks
14. Patents, copyrights, and proprietary information
15. Obligation to participate in the actual operation of the franchise business
16. Restrictions on what the franchisee may sell
17. Renewal, termination, transfer, and dispute resolution
18. Public figures
19. Financial performance representations
20. Outlets and franchisee information
21. Financial statements
22. Contracts
23. Receipts

Finally, it is necessary to describe the franchise agreement. This document is the binding contract that rules the relationship, and it is different from the FDD. The franchise system uniformity creates an effective structure, but it may be a source of conflict between franchisor and franchisee. The franchise agreement defines specific requirements and conditions expected from the business management. This uniformity is beneficial for the franchisee, since it provides him or her with an established successful framework as shown in the market. In the United States, there is no general register of franchises, but each state gathers data about franchises and oversees compliance with rules and laws related to such activities in its jurisdiction.

Regulation about franchises in the European Union (EU) is more complex, mainly because the franchise is affected by laws both at the national level and at the EU level, in addition to a code of ethics known as the European Code of Ethics for Franchising. Although lots of norms are applicable in this issue, it is basically governed by European rules.

Franchise contracts must comply with rules related to activity, franchisee protection, and defense of the competence, at both the European and national levels. Although each member state of the European Union has specific norms with regard to franchises, European Union law presents enough regulation about the matter to be applied on the whole by the member states.

Currently, EU Commission Regulation 330/2010 establishes guidelines to define the framework in which franchise agreements can be developed. The contract itself represents the principal link between franchisor and franchisee. Reasons for and causes of firm commitment for business cooperation will be gathered in such contracts. It is not possible to indicate a general or unique type of franchise contract; however, it will always have to comply with national and European law, independently of its form or content.

Another case is China, which has the largest number of franchises in the world, although its volume of transactions is still low. In 2005, a new law about franchises appeared, called Measures for the Administration of Commercial Franchise. This law has 42 articles and eight chapters that refer to different obligations between franchisor and franchisee.

Although each country can establish its own regulations, a general structure must be taken into account when typing a franchise contract, which addresses (1) an explicit recognition of the franchisor's patent rights (logos, marks, symbols, and any other distinctive features of the business); (2) a statement of the registration process for the area where the chain plans to expand; (3) the cession of use (or even cession of transfer) of these patent rights in the preestablished geographic and temporal conditions; and (4) the financial conditions for the franchisee (right of entry and royalties).

The franchise contract must also describe the obligations for the franchisor, which generally include the following:

- Assistance before the opening of the business (search for premises and staff, market research, financing, and so on)
- Starting and continued training for the franchisee and its managers
- Delivery of franchise manuals
- Responsibility for supply
- Technical and commercial assistance for the franchisee while the contract is valid
- Commitment for a competitive price set offered to franchisee
- Permanent update and adaptation of expertise in market requirements and tendencies

Obligations for the franchisee should also be addressed, including the following:

- Payments to the franchisor for granting and provisions
- Exclusive purchases from the franchisor, purchase center, or providers, which are recommended
- Willingness to apply and respect both management methods and establishment norms and facilities proposed by franchisor
- Periodic information to the franchisor about management and sale course
- Willingness to allow the franchisor to control and supervise the accounts and facilitate inventory checks

- Maintenance of fair competition while the contract is valid, temporary, and after the contract has been canceled
- Assignment of a zone of territorial exclusivity for the exploitation of the franchise (if necessary, it will include a graphic description of the zone in contract enclosures)
- The contract validity period and renewal conditions; the duration must be long enough that the franchisee can recover the investment
- Causes for contract cancellation and provision of recovering the material or nonmaterial elements by the franchisor
- Stipulation for the resolution of disagreements between both parties and competent jurisdiction

Samuel Gómez-Haro
University of Granada

See also Entrepreneurs in Franchising; Franchisee and Franchisor; Franchises: Starting

Further Readings

European Franchise Federation. "Regulation." http://www .eff-Franchise.com/spip.php?rubrique7 (Accessed December 2010).
Keup, E. J. *Franchise Bible: How to Buy a Franchise or Franchise Your Own Business.* Irvine, CA: Entrepreneur Press, 2007.
Murphy, K. B. *The Franchise Handbook: A Complete Guide to All Aspects of Buying, Selling, or Investing in a Franchise.* Ocala, FL: Atlantic Publishing Group, 2006.
North American Securities Administration Association, "Franchise Registration and Disclosure Guidelines." http://www.nasaa.org/industry___regulatory_resources/ uniform_forms/3697.cfm (Accessed December 2010).
Uniform Franchise Offering Circular (UFOCs.com). "What Is a UFOC?" http://www.ufocs.com/articles/what_is_ ufoc.php (Accessed December 2010).
Wageman, R. "China's New Franchise Rules." *Franchise Update Magazine*, v.2 (2007).

FRANCHISES: STARTING

A franchise is a business opportunity whereby a company, the franchisor, grants exclusive rights to an individual, the franchisee, to market its products or services in a given territory or at a given location.

Essentially, it is a prepackaged, turnkey business that one can buy, lease, or sell. In return for this right, the franchisee typically pays royalties to the franchisor and agrees to follow certain quality standards. In the United States, franchising is a very common and well-regarded model for going into business, with more than 900,000 franchised retail outlets operating in 2009. The economics of franchising in the United States are large, with franchising accounting for 4 percent ($880 billion annually) of the U.S. private-sector economy and 8 percent (11 million) of all private-sector jobs.

Most franchising activity follows one of two models: product distribution franchising or business format franchising. In product distribution franchising, products are commonly made by the franchisor and sold by the franchisee. Examples of product distribution franchising are abundant, including car dealerships (such as Ford, Chrysler, and Chevrolet), beverage distributorships (Coca-Cola, Anheuser-Busch), and gas stations (ExxonMobil, British Petroleum). Under this relationship, the franchisee benefits from the existing infrastructure and brand identification, and the franchisor benefits from additional distribution and expansion. In business format franchising, the process or delivery system is

the key component, and the franchisor typically goes to a great deal of formal effort to train the franchisee in the business's established marketing, sales, inventory, and production systems. Examples of business format franchising include restaurants (such as McDonald's, Subway, and Taco Bell), tax preparation and financial services (H&R Block, Liberty Tax Service, Jackson Hewitt Tax Service), and cleaning services (ChemDry, Jani-King, MaidPro).

There are two ways an individual can get into franchising. Individuals with an existing business can become franchisors, packaging and selling (or licensing) their business as a turnkey operation to others. Individuals may also become franchisees, purchasing or leasing the rights to an existing business. Regardless of the route one chooses to take, much work and financial capital are often required, and neither arrangement should be entered without careful consideration of the pros and cons of franchising.

Starting New

From the perspective of a business owner or franchisor, franchising is simply a means of expansion and distribution. The franchisor benefits from increased expansion, brand recognition, larger purchasing power, higher front-line motivation (a franchisee with an ownership position in the business will be more motivated than an employee), and reduced risk resulting from individual unit failure. Additionally, franchisors customarily receive a franchise fee (typically a onetime fee paid by the franchisee at the onset of the relationship) and a portion of the sales from each franchise. For the existing business owner, franchising as a means of expansion can be very appealing, and many have made millions by franchising their small businesses. Subway founder Fred DeLuca is a textbook example. DeLuca began Subway in 1965 in Bridgeport, Connecticut, at the age of 17 using $1,000 he had borrowed from family and friends. Forty years later, Subway was one of the fastest-growing franchises in history, with more than 32,000 franchised locations spanning 91 countries, and DeLuca's estimated net worth was $1.5 billion.

Despite DeLuca's success, preparing to franchise a business to others often requires much more work and capital than one might think. Legal, administrative, systemic, and psychological factors all must be addressed. A standard disclosure document,

Most franchising operations follow either a product distribution franchising model or a business format franchising model. Opening a McDonald's restaurant, a business format franchising unit, requires a minimum initial investment of $300,000 of nonborrowed personal resources, such as cash, securities, or business or real estate equity. (Wikimedia/Stu Pendousmat)

the Uniform Franchise Offering Circular (UFOC), is required by the Federal Trade Commission for franchising in the United States; other nations have similar requirements. Additionally, many states have their own franchise disclosure and registration requirements. Preparation of the UFOC essentially requires the use of an attorney experienced with franchising, given this is a multifaceted legal document. Audited financial statements and other administrative filings are also required to begin the franchising process.

Systems are at the core of any successful franchise, and the systems necessary to start and effectively operate a franchise unit need to be fully developed, vetted, and well documented. Systems include not just standard operating procedures but also detailed training programs for owners, managers, and employees; marketing and sales plans (complete with supporting materials); and even plans for how to market and sell the franchise itself. Finally, but equally important, the potential franchisor must be psychologically prepared to begin the franchising process. New franchisors need to have realistic expectations of the financial future (most new franchisors do not realize a profit in the first three years); they must understand what it is like to work with franchisees (they behave very differently from employees and more like customers); and they must be prepared to work long hours and persevere through obstacle after obstacle.

In deciding whether or not to franchise a business, it is important to answer the following questions: Do I have the entrepreneurial spirit necessary to become a franchisor? Can I teach my system for operating the business to others? Is my system valuable enough that it can be sold? Are there enough potential customers to support multiple franchises? Do I have the estimated $500,000 necessary to complete the franchise development process?

Buying an Existing Franchise

Purchasing an existing franchise offers a great variety of opportunities for those looking to enter into business for themselves. An estimated 1,500 different franchise opportunities are available in the United States, spanning more than 100 different industries. Many programs exist to help individuals purchase franchising. The U.S. Small Business Administration has a list of preapproved franchises. Individuals

seeking to buy into one of these franchises benefit from expedited SBA loan processing and financial assistance (typically in the form of SBA-guaranteed loans). Likewise, VetFran (the Veterans Transition Franchise Initiative) is a national program supported by more than 1,300 franchisors and is committed to providing special incentives, discounts, and preferred financing to veterans of the U.S. armed services. In VetFran's nearly 50-year history, it has aided in the establishment of more than 10,000 franchise locations globally.

When purchasing a franchise, franchisees benefit in many ways. First, they immediately have a product or service that has a track record of success; for example, in real estate, Century 21 is a well-known franchise throughout the United States. Second, the franchisee is often provided with both technical and managerial assistance, such as training in how to recruit qualified tax preparation staff or advice on what balance of insurance and bonding is optimal. Third, established processes and quality-control metrics provided by the franchisor aid in ensuring that production waste is minimized; McDonald's, for example, has a predetermined routine for slicing tomatoes and assembling salads. Fourth, franchise units often require less financial capital to start than do similar nonfranchised units; the franchisor is able to provide architectural sketches and floor plans that would otherwise have to be purchased, franchisors often have bulk means of distributing necessary operating supplies at wholesale costs, and market saturation and research reports may already be completed. Finally, many franchisors offer defined territories in which the franchisee has exclusive rights to grow and expand the business, thus minimizing the competition that may arise in a defined geographic area.

Just as franchisors must be psychologically ready to undertake this type of venture and must possess realistic expectations, so must franchisees. Franchisees must come to accept that while they will "own" the business on paper, by entering into a franchise relationship they voluntarily are agreeing to follow a predetermined system, and most franchisors contractually require franchisees to adhere to specific quality, production, and distribution standards. Additionally, many franchisees grow increasingly unhappy with the continued remittance of franchise fees to the franchisor (often based on a percentage of sales), despite knowing at the beginning of the relationship that this was inevitable.

Franchisors typically control the branding standards, marketing, products, and services of the franchisees. To some entrepreneurs, the contractual standards required by franchisors are deal breakers. These individuals are unwilling to accept that, even as the owner, there are some things they cannot change. In most franchised restaurants, the menus are set and have little variation (a McDonald's hamburger franchise bought in Houston, Texas, should be the same as one bought in Tampa, Florida, for example). The franchisee typically cannot decide to order a different brand of ketchup packet or even one-ply as opposed to two-ply toilet paper. This level of standardization has its pros and cons. On one hand, by requiring a specific brand of window cleaner, the franchisor is able to provide the materials required to be on hand by the Occupational Safety and Health Administration. On the other, the franchisee loses the autonomy to choose the lemon-scented version over the traditional scent or to purchase a different brand at a liquidation sale to save some money.

In sum, franchising remains a common model of new venture formation both within and outside the United States. Pros and cons exist for both the franchisor and the franchisee, and having realistic expectations goes a long way toward franchisor and franchisee satisfaction. Whereas every business can be franchised, not every business should be franchised.

Eric W. Liguori
California State University, Fresno

See also Entrepreneurs in Franchising; Franchisee and Franchisor; Franchises: Legal Aspects

Further Readings

Dugan, Ann. *Franchising 101: The Complete Guide to Evaluating, Buying, and Growing Your Franchised Business*. Chicago: Dearborn Financial, 1998.

Elgin, Jeff. "How Do I Start a Franchise?" Entrepreneur.com. http://www.entrepreneur.com/article/66178 (Accessed December 2003).

International Franchise Association. *About Franchising: Help With Buying a Franchise*. http://www.franchise.org/aboutfranchising (Accessed November 2010).

Judd, Richard and Robert Justis. *Franchising: An Entrepreneur's Guide*. Mason, OH: Thompson, 2008.

Speinelli, Steve. "Franchising." In *The Portable MBA in Entrepreneurship*, W. Bygrave and A. Zacharakis, eds. Hoboken, NJ: John Wiley and Sons, 2010.

Uniform Franchise Offering Circular (UFOCs.com). "What Is a UFOC?" http://www.ufocs.com/articles/what_is_ufoc.php (Accessed December 2010).

G

GENDER AND ACQUIRING RESOURCES

During the past few decades, the impact of gender on starting a venture as well as on subsequent venture performance has attracted increasing levels of scholarly attention. Gender is a social construction of sex that ascribes characteristics to men and women. It is typically articulated through a binary division into different stereotypical behaviors associated with the masculine and the feminine, where the former is privileged over the latter and thereby supports a hierarchical valuation of traits and characteristics. Disentangling the influence of gender on different aspects of new venture management is highly challenging, as masculine and feminine behaviors are social constructs that can be adopted by any individual regardless of biological sex. Putting it simply, not all female entrepreneurs behave in stereotypically feminine ways, and not all male entrepreneurs behave in stereotypically masculine ways. This challenge naturally influences a discussion of the impact of gender on acquiring resources, which needs to be kept in mind when evaluating research findings on this gender and resource acquisition.

Acquiring resources is a crucial entrepreneurial activity. During the start-up process, it results in a certain initial resource endowment of social, human, and financial capital, which facilitates the access to further resources required for developing the venture and for pursuing subsequent growth. The resource types typically distinguished are financial resources, physical resources (such as machines and other technologies), and organizational resources (including human and social capital). During new venture development, the process of acquiring resources requires finding investors, employees, business associates, and customers. The acquiring of resources depends on how supportive the social system is of entrepreneurial activities, on the industry structure, but also on the entrepreneur's vision and strategy for the venture.

In terms of human capital, male and female entrepreneurs differ with respect to experience and education. Whereas the level of education is rather similar across the sexes, the type of education differs. Male entrepreneurs are more likely to have completed education of a technical nature, whereas female entrepreneurs are more likely to have an education of an administrative, economic/commercial, or personal-service nature. As a result, gender differences exist with regard to which the sectors in which entrepreneurs are active. Women entrepreneurs are overrepresented in the retail and service sectors, particularly personal services. Male entrepreneurs are overrepresented in manufacturing, wholesale trade, and financial services. Ventures of women entrepreneurs are often in supporting services within these sectors. Service sector firms are often cheaper to establish, facilitating the entry of female entrepreneurs into this sector, given their restricted access to funding.

Starting a new venture entails costs for entrepreneurs—for example, for registering the company and developing the product or service offered—and thus financial capital is needed. Two areas of gender preference have been found for those entering self-employment: personal savings (including contributions from family and friends) and bank lending. Women often have greater limitations in their access to personal savings than do men, which has been attributed to their higher likelihood of having worked part time or in jobs remunerated at a lower rate, and their previous careers are more likely to have been characterized by breaks for childbirth and care, interrupting their career progression. This constrains women's opportunities to develop adequate reserves of financial, personal, and business resources to invest into their start-ups. In consequence, female entrepreneurs use substantially less capital at start-up than do their male counterparts, and such undercapitalization can seriously impede the development of the venture. Bank financing is the most common source of external financing for new ventures. Gaining access to bank lending has been reported as problematic for both sexes in terms of access and costs, but women entrepreneurs might have to overcome greater hurdles than men. This might help to explain why female and male entrepreneurs differ in the ways they finance their businesses (even though research on the determinants and the direction of these differences delivers inconclusive results).

Gender plays a role in the type of industry entrepreneurs become involved in. Females skew toward entering retail and service sectors because their past experience is more likely to be based in administrative, commercial, or personal-service areas. Male entrepreneurs tend to have completed a technical-based education and are overrepresented in manufacturing, wholesale trade, and financial services. (Photos.com)

Gender discrimination might not fully explain why female entrepreneurs tend to allocate smaller amounts of start-up capital to their businesses than do male entrepreneurs. Not all women are restricted from high levels of capitalization. The tendency of women not to start businesses with large amounts of financial capital might also be attributed to a possible lack of confidence among women regarding their entrepreneurial abilities. This tendency might be, at least partly, a result of choice. For example, female entrepreneurs might have different ambitions and objectives for their ventures. However, gender does not appear to play a significant role on the composition of financial capital (meaning that the proportion of, for example, equity and bank loans has been reported to be roughly similar).

Social capital, understood as contacts (potentially) leading to successful outcomes, has also been claimed to play a major role in acquiring resources for the new venture. Entrepreneurs frequently access their network contacts when recruiting information, capital, skills, and labor to start and develop their business activities. No gender differences have been found for the size of social networks or for maintaining and developing networks. The social structure, however, has an impact on resource acquisition, as female entrepreneurs more often carry out other activities besides running their own ventures, such as full- or part-time employment and taking care of their families and households. Such multiple assignments may limit the time female entrepreneurs spend on their ventures and thereby also restrict their resource acquisition process.

Leona Achtenhagen
Jönköping International Business School

See also Gender and Industry Preferences; Gender and Performance; Home-Based Businesses; Human Capital Theory; Microfinance; Minorities in New Business Ventures; Motivation and Gender; Social Networks; Women's Entrepreneurship; Women's Entrepreneurship: Best Practices; Work-Life Balance

Further Readings

Bem, Sandra L. *The Lenses of Gender*. New Haven, CT: Yale University Press, 1994.

Brush, Candida et al. *The Diana Project—Women Business Owners and Equity Capital: The Myths Dispelled.* Kansas City, MO: Kauffman Center for Entrepreneurial Leadership, 2001.

Brush, Candida et al. "A Gender-Aware Framework for Women's Entrepreneurship." *International Journal of Gender and Entrepreneurship*, v.1/1 (2009).

Greve, Arent and Janet W. Salaff. "Social Networks and Entrepreneurship." *Entrepreneurship Theory and Practice* (Fall 2003).

Marlow, Susan and Dean Patton. "All Credit to Men? Entrepreneurship, Finance, and Gender." *Entrepreneurship Theory and Practice* (November 2005).

Verheul, Ingrid and Roy Thurik. "Start-Up Capital: 'Does Gender Matter?'" *Small Business Economics*, v.16 (2001).

GENDER AND INDUSTRY PREFERENCES

There has been a marked tendency for women to establish and own business ventures in a range of industries different from those of their male counterparts. Historically, majority-female-owned small enterprises have been more concentrated in the retail and service sectors than have male-owned enterprises of similar size. With increased participation of women in self-employment, gender differences have tended to decline. In the United States, for example, the increase in the number of women starting in business went from around 5 percent of American businesses to close to 40 percent between 1970 and 2000.

With such a massive expansion in female entrepreneurship, it is not surprising that women have broken into nontraditional sectors, such as construction, wholesaling, and transportation. A Canadian government investigation of women entrepreneurs found the traditional patterns remained strong only insofar as females were disproportionately represented in the ownership of tourist ventures. They remained concentrated in other retail and service activities but at a level no longer much greater than that of their male counterparts. Similarly, the Canadian evidence shows a small deficit only in the share of agriculture/primary, manufacturing, and knowledge-intensive industries among majority female-owned small and medium enterprises (SMEs), compared with majority-male-owned firms.

Aggregated statistics at the industry level do not tell the whole story, as gender differences may also be reflected in specialization within industries. There is widespread evidence that women, for example, establish firms with significantly less (typically only one third) of the financial capital invested by their

Despite a 10-fold difference in the number of men versus women working in construction (the Bureau of Labor Statistics estimated 8,270,000 men and 807,000 women employed in the industry as of 2010), the overall number of self-employed women has increased, resulting in more females entering nontraditional sectors such as construction, wholesaling, and transportation. (Photos.com)

male counterparts at start-up. They are also less likely than men to have previous work experience relevant to the enterprise that they start. Lack of prior work experience supporting entry into self-employment has been identified as a constraining force on the diversification of female enterprises. Without their own work experience naturally leading into self-employment, reliance on existing female entrepreneurial role models can result, and those role models are most likely to be found in traditionally female sectors.

Given that female enterprise ownership is less diverse than is male ownership, most research interest has been in explaining constraints on female entrepreneurship. Explanations broadly fall into one of two theoretical perspectives: liberal feminist theory and social feminist theory.

Liberal feminist theory assumes that women and men ultimately will be equal if they are given identical opportunities. Disparities in entrepreneurial activity are thus attributed to differences in social opportunities open to men as opposed to women. This focuses attention on institutions and values that present particular barriers to women's participation in entrepreneurial ventures. Socialization encouraging female responsibility for child caring and household management, unequal access to learning opportunities, and consequent differences in the ability to acquire skills and experience are seen to explain gender differences in business choices. Female concentration in the service industry, for example, is explained in terms of the difficulty of gaining access to sufficient financial resources to start capital-intensive ventures.

Social feminist theory emphasizes how socialization processes work to condition women to have different expectations with respect to their participation in economic activity. Socialization commences early in life and is thought to leave females at a disadvantage to males when it comes to starting and running a business. Typical social feminist perspectives include how females develop psychological traits such as compassion and higher levels of communal qualities such as selflessness, a concern for others, and interpersonal sensitivity. Men, in contrast, are expected to exude self-assertion, self-expansion, and the urge to master. The outcome is that women are placed at a disadvantage to men when it comes to starting and running a business. Female affinity to service enterprises is thus interpreted as part of the socialization process that encourages women and men to believe that they are most suited to people-oriented ventures.

A general supposition has been that females do not have the same performance aspirations in business as males, partly because they have a high priority for maintaining a balance between work and family pursuits. In practice there is no overwhelming evidence to indicate that female-owner-managed SMEs differ from male-controlled enterprises with respect to their financial performance and business growth, when differences in the characteristics affecting business performance are controlled for. What do seem to matter are the growth intentions of entrepreneurs when businesses are started, rather than the gender of the owner-manager. Nonetheless, a different female experience is indicated by studies that show how females employ particular strategies to address gender-related challenges. Depending on the context, this can involve avoiding personal or phone contact, relying on e-mail contact and delegating negotiations to male managers. Similarly, there is research suggesting that women adopt different patterns of firm growth from those established by men.

In addition to the initial choice of enterprise activity, there is much evidence that various enterprise characteristics (including the size of business, age, time dedicated to the business, and legal organization) differ according to the gender of the owner-manager. There is much interest in the way that the financing process may be influencing this through women's disadvantage in the ability to raise start-up finances and obtain further external funding. Explanations include a comparative lack of personal assets and credit track record and stereotyping and discrimination by bankers. An international project, The Diana Project, was started in 1999 to raise awareness and expectations of female business owners regarding the growth of their businesses. The project continues to support and advance research designed to aid the growth and development of women-owned businesses.

Martin Perry
Massey University

See also Gender and Acquiring Resources; Gender and Performance; Home-Based Businesses; Microfinance; Minorities in New Business Ventures; Motivation and Gender; Women's Entrepreneurship; Women's Entrepreneurship: Best Practices; Work-Life Balance

Further Readings

Cheyne, J. and C. Harris. "Women and Self Employment." In *Entrepreneurship and Small Business Management in New Zealand*, C. Massey, ed. Auckland, New Zealand: Pearson/Prentice Hall, 2005.

Johnsen, G. and R. McMahon. "Owner-Manager Gender, Financial Performance and Business Growth Amongst SMEs From Australia's Business Longitudinal Survey." *International Small Business Journal*, v.23/2 (2005).

Jung, O. "Women Entrepreneurs (October 2010)." SME Financing Data Initiative. http://www.sme-fdi.gc.ca/eic/site/sme_fdi-prf_pme.nsf/eng/h_02215.html (Accessed February 2011).

Orser, B., M. Spence, A. Riding, and C. Carrington. "Gender and Export Propensity." *Entrepreneurship Theory and Practice*, v.20 (2010).

GENDER AND PERFORMANCE

Historically, new venture creation and management have been viewed with a masculine lens, emphasizing concepts such as profit maximization, efficiency, and linear development. Because women's participation in new venture creation has been disproportionally less than men's participation, the study of new venture performance has often been steered toward problems, approaches, and questions faced by men-owned ventures primarily. In 2010, women made up about 38 percent of business owners in the United States and 20 percent of business owners among countries associated with the Organisation for Economic Co-operation and Development (OECD), thus calling for more attention to the role that gender plays in the management of new ventures and their performance.

The importance of considering the role of gender in new venture performance does not solely stem from the perspective that entrepreneurship entails masculine and feminine management approaches. It is also motivated by the erratic nature of new venture performance and the unfolding research showing that the determinants of new venture performance change with time, size, and the industry of the firm. Thus, while good research exists taking into account how new ventures perform in comparison to established ventures and how women-owned firms fare in comparison to men-owned ventures, less attention has been focused on the intersection between these two streams of research.

Related attempts to understand how gender affects the performance of new ventures has looked into the entrepreneur's level of access to human capital and financial capital, along with growth aspirations. Much of this research has been motivated by the need to explain why women-owned businesses grow at a lower rate, employ fewer people, are less profitable, and fail more often than those owned by men.

One proposed explanation for the lack of women entrepreneurs, especially in technological and emerging high-growth industries, centers on the low levels of educated women pursuing careers as scientists. Career stereotyping and socialization of women during childhood is thought to result in women's lower interest in entering the sciences and a consequent lower level of training and preparation leading to careers as scientists. Furthermore, when women do become scientists and choose to pursue new venture creation, they often face more difficulty than men in leveraging the services of technology transfer specialists, because they often lack adequate networks in what are often male-dominated industries. Thus, at the societal level, the lack of encouragement and emphasis on motivating women to pursue traditionally male-dominated technical and

scientific careers leaves women ill equipped to pursue new venture creation in the most technologically advanced industries.

Others have suggested that the reasons women-owned firms underperform their men-owned counterparts relate to differences in human capital and financial capital. Measuring human capital in terms of levels of education, employment, and industry experience, one researcher found that women-owned ventures tended to generate higher profits when the entrepreneur had higher levels of human capital. In contrast, profitability among men-owned ventures was marginally positively affected by the entrepreneur's higher level of human capital.

When looking at the role played by financial capital, many have suggested that the reason women-owned businesses underperform in comparison to men-owned businesses is associated with the systemic barriers to financing faced by women. In fact, research does show that gender affects the amount of loans and equity capital raised by entrepreneurs for a new business and that these differences have an effect on the early growth trajectory of new ventures. When examining how levels of financial capital affected the growth of women- and men-owned firms, one researcher found that men-owned firms were more responsive to higher levels of financial capital, while women-owned firms were not responsive to levels of financial capital. Thus, it is important to note that determining whether men- and women-owned firms differ in their performance requires carefully accounting for not only the effect of different control variables but also the effect of different types of performance measurements.

An alternative explanation for why women- and men-owned ventures differ in their venture performance centers on their growth aspirations. Thus, determining whether women entrepreneurs differ in their growth aspirations from their male counterparts and how growth aspirations are tied to new venture performance has received increased attention. In a study of women-owned ventures, one group of researchers found that women entrepreneurs seek new venture growth when they aspire to create wealth, overcome a challenge, or create long-term financial security. In addition, the growth aspirations of women entrepreneurs were not associated with personal demographics or perceptions of gender-based societal obstacles. Furthermore, women-owned businesses that were women-centered, such as those targeting women customers, suppliers, and causes, were more growth oriented than women-owned businesses that did not orient themselves toward a female identity. Finally, it was also determined that women-owned businesses that sought the highest growth were those whose entrepreneurs branded themselves as the business, saw the businesses as an important investment, had a high level of confidence, and viewed the external environment as a source of opportunities and surmountable challenges.

In conclusion, although generally research has shown that women-owned ventures tend to underperform in comparison to men-owned ventures, scholars still do not have a strong understanding of what conditions explain this trend. Whether the reasons are sociological, strategic, or individual, as well as whether these reasons apply to all types of performance measurement, remains to be determined.

Alejandro Amezcua
Syracuse University

See also Gender and Acquiring Resources; Gender and Industry Preferences; Home-Based Businesses; Microfinance; Minorities in New Business Ventures; Motivation and Gender; Women's Entrepreneurship; Women's Entrepreneurship: Best Practices; Work-Life Balance

Further Readings

Bem, Sandra L. *The Lenses of Gender.* New Haven, CT: Yale University Press, 1994.

Bird, B. J. and C. G. Brush. "A Gendered Perspective on Organizational Creation." *Entrepreneurship Theory and Practice*, v.26/3 (2002).

Brush, Candida et al. *The Diana Project—Women Business Owners and Equity Capital: The Myths Dispelled.* Kansas City, MO: Kauffman Center for Entrepreneurial Leadership, 2001.

Freeman, S. and R. J. Varey. "The Effects of Entrepreneur Characteristics and Gender-Based Management and Communication Styles From an Internal Marketing Perspective Within Both a Small and Large Business Environment." *Marketing Education Review*, v.7/3 (1997).

Johnsen, G. and R. McMahon. "Owner-Manager Gender, Financial Performance and Business Growth Amongst SMEs From Australia's Business Longitudinal Survey." *International Small Business Journal*, v.23/2 (2005).

Short, J. C., A. McKelvie, D. J. Ketchen, and G. N. Chandler. "Firm and Industry Effects on Firm Performance: A Generalization and Extension for New Ventures." *Strategic Entrepreneurship Journal*, v.3/1 (2009).

GEOGRAPHIC LOCATION

Selecting the geographic location for a business venture is one of the most important decisions that an entrepreneur will make. Entrepreneurs who select the best locations will have a competitive advantage over competitors who do not select their locations wisely. The geographic location of a company will vary depending on the nature of their business. In the past, companies selected locations with access to railroads and raw material. However, today companies are more likely to select locations with airport accessibility, with Internet access, and near universities for high-skilled labor.

The process for selecting a location requires gathering information from a set of selection criteria and then moving that information toward a decision. The entrepreneur should narrow the choices down first by region, next by state, and finally by city. The ultimate location should match the market for the product or service of the business. The entrepreneur should first consider in which region of the country the business should be located. Regions are defined by one or more distinctive characteristics or features and include, for example, the Midwest and the Southwest. Selecting the best region will provide numerous benefits to a business and may provide an advantage over competitors that do not locate in specific regions. The entrepreneur must consider its customer and the region that has the best conditions for business success. Typical regional characteristics to consider include rising disposable incomes, growth in population in specific age groups, the cost of doing business, availability of suppliers, availability of skilled labor, presence of needed infrastructure, and proximity to markets. For example, a technical firm that is doing business in the United States and Canada may select the Pacific Northwest region, which includes Washington, Oregon, and British Columbia. Within this region, the entrepreneur may select the state of Washington and the city of Seattle, which is near clusters of technical firms, offers access to highly skilled labor, and is close to Canada.

When assessing locations, entrepreneurs should also consider the location's regulations and laws, taxes and incentives, and tax credits for locating a business in that jurisdiction. Incentives such as tax breaks may influence location decisions. Economic development departments within each state can offer good financial information. Often, local governments may reduce taxes that businesses pay on

A crucial component in planning a new business venture is selecting a physical location. St. Louis, Missouri, has become a popular choice for manufacturing distribution centers because it is centrally located in the United States and features easy access to most methods of transportation. (Wikimedia/U.S. Army Corps of Engineers)

property and income. For example, the county of Manatee in Florida offered a tax credit that resulted in several companies relocating to the county, and LegalZoom.com made a decision to move part of its operations from Los Angeles, California, to Austin, Texas, after a dispute over city taxes (the company was considering moving other parts of its operation to neighboring cities, such as Burbank and Glendale, where taxes were lower).

The key to selecting the best location depends heavily on the components that are most critical to the company's success. A firm's performance may be enhanced by locating it within a cluster of similar businesses. For example, many technical firms locate in clusters, such as those of Seattle and California's Silicon Valley. These clusters can provide upward mobility to a new firm as well as the environment needed to innovate and create new ventures. Additionally, high-tech firms require highly skilled labor and therefore must locate in an area where highly skilled labor can be accessed easily. Entrepreneurs should also consider business climate, proximity to markets, wage rates, Internet access, tax rates, and proximity of raw materials. Manufacturers benefit from locating near the markets that they serve, because transportation can be costly. For example, St. Louis, Missouri, has become the location for many companies' distribution centers because of its location in the middle of the country and its access to various means of transportation. Goods can be shipped from St. Louis to customers in any part of the country in a quick and efficient manner.

Being close to markets and near customers is critical to remain competitive. Many service-related industries and retailers find that being located near their clients is essential. Both the size of the trade area and population trends are also important to location decisions. However, a home-based location may be a good strategy for service businesses whose customers do not need to visit their place of business physically. There are several benefits to setting up a home-based business. For example, because the business area is set up in a section of the residence, the entrepreneur avoids the cost of rent. However, the entrepreneur will need to consider zoning laws that may affect its home-based business.

In the past, entrepreneurs in the United States initialized their start-ups without international business in mind. Today, entrepreneurs are planning from the start to penetrate both domestic and international markets. This development has also influenced entrepreneurs' decisions about geographic location. There are significant challenges to entrepreneurs going global, but many countries are making it attractive for businesses to locate to their countries. For example, the government of Dubai has worked to enforce copyright laws and provides generous tax breaks in an effort to attract high-tech companies. As a result, Dubai has attracted hundreds of companies from the United States and other nations around the world. Entrepreneurs may also consider the financial advantages of locating near international markets. For example, the cost of labor can be considerably lower in countries such as Mexico, China, Taiwan, and India. When European countries began forming the European Union, many businesses, in fear of being blocked out, considered locating in Europe to ensure access to future markets. Additionally, entrepreneurs may consider locating in another country to be near a major client. For example, as large corporations move locations to international markets their suppliers find it necessary to move with them to ensure continued business. Profiles of international cities can be obtained from *Euromonitor International* (http://www.euromonitor.com) and the Organisation for Economic Co-operation and Development (http://www.oecd.org).

Successful companies are known to track population growth. The more potential customers that a business has, the better will its chance of success be. Service and retail industries may find *Demographics USA* a valuable resource; it provides data on income levels, retail sales by type of merchandise, growth trends, and employment and payroll rates. Entrepreneurs can use *Demographic USA* to analyze considerations such as competition and buyers' purchasing power. By analyzing these data, an entrepreneur can make an informed decision about where to locate a new venture. Entrepreneurs also need to consider competition, local laws and regulations, transportation, utility costs, and quality of life; the latter has an impact on the ease with which employees can be recruited.

Several other data sources are useful in conducting a regional search for the ideal location. The U.S. Census Bureau's Website (http://www.census.gov) is a good place to start. Demographic and population data can be extracted from databases such as the County and City Data Book and the U.S. Statistical Abstract. The U.S. Statistical Abstract and County and City Handbook contain information on population demographics, and through the Census Bureau's Website, entrepreneurs can create customized reports on any of the nation's more than 3,100 counties and more than 12,000 cities with populations greater than 2,500. Demographic data on income levels, education, age, housing, and other population characteristics can also be extracted from the database. Additionally, the Census Bureau's American Fact Finder site (http://factfinder.census.gov) contains maps and fact sheets on almost every community in the United States.

Entrepreneurs also rely on geographic information systems (GIS) applications to select the best location for their businesses. These applications combine mapping with databases that contain economic, social, and demographic information to help entrepreneurs analyze business locations and their characteristics, such as markets and model spending patterns of a given geographic location. For example, one type of GIS software, ArcGIS, will analyze the best location for a new business combining demographics and population data. The selected characteristics can be displayed on a variety of color-coded maps that will also show nearby competitors.

Another useful source is the Population Reference Bureau (http://www.prb.org). This organization provides the most recent and important data collected from the U.S. Census Bureau. PRB also offers useful data such as the consumer price index data and research articles on the economic and demographic profiles for the U.S. population. In addition to economic and demographic information, the *Editor and Publisher Market Guide* provides information on transportation networks for more than 1,500 cities in the United States. Two additional sources on trends and patterns are *The American Marketplace: Demographics and Spending Patterns* and the *Commercial Atlas and Marketing Guide*. *The American Marketplace* contains information on patterns in categories such as race and ethnicity, health, spending and wealth, labor, education, income, and living arrangements. The *Commercial Atlas and Marketing Guide* provides information on more than 120,000 areas in the United States and includes information such as manufacturing activity, population trends, income, and trade. Location analysis is available through the Small Business Administration's small business development centers (SBDCs) (http://www.sba.gov/SBDC). SBDCs offer entrepreneurs training, research, counseling, and other services at no cost.

Tracy L. Green
University of California, Los Angeles

See also Home-Based Businesses; Import/Export Businesses; International Enterprise Planning; Location Strategy

Further Readings

Gitman, L. J. and C. McDaniel. *The Future of Business: The Essentials*. Mason, OH: South-Western/Cengage Learning, 2009.

Hill, Charles W. L. *International Business: Competing in the Global Marketplace*. New York: Irwin McGraw-Hill, 2009.

Indarti, N. "Business Location and Success: The Case of Internet Café Business in Indonesia." *Gadjah Mada International Journal of Business*, v.6/2 (2004).

U.S. Census Bureau. *The 2010 Statistical Abstract: Guide to Sources of Statistics*. http://www.census.gov/compendia/statab/guide_to_sources.html (Accessed February 2011).

Geography of Innovation

Geography of innovation is an expression used loosely within the contexts of innovation management and policy research, rather than an analytic concept with a consensual definition. The expression is, however, commonly used as suggested by

Apiwat Ratanawaraha and Karen P. Polenske in the sense of showing how innovation may be spatially distributed or concentrated.

The term can be related to both so-called high-tech ventures and low- and medium-tech industrial processes. There may be vastly different rationales and mechanisms at work behind the clustering or dispersal of industries pertaining to different business models and knowledge bases. The economic geographers Bjørn T. Asheim and Meric S. Gertler have noted that a persistent trend toward geographic proximity is at the center of today's globalization processes and that two paradoxical characteristics belong to this contemporary global economy. One is that innovative activity is unevenly distributed. Asheim and Gertler contend that the more knowledge-intensive the economic activity is, the more geographically clustered it is likely to be. Examples of this tendency can be found in clusters of knowledge-intensive industries such as biotechnology and financial services. Second, although intuitively one might expect a trend toward the weakening of geographic concentration in parallel with the advancement of the economy, the tendency seems, on the contrary, to move in the opposite direction, toward greater concentration. New means for the transfer of knowledge across borders, such as the increasing use of information and communication technologies including video conferencing and real-time webinars, were once believed to be laying the foundation for more dispersed patterns of innovative activity; however, such predictions have yet to be fulfilled.

One explanation for these counterintuitive developments—suggested by theorists such as Staffan Laestadius, Bjørn T. Asheim, Meric S. Gertler, and others—is that distinct geographic patterns develop according to the requirements and influences of distinct types of knowledge. These researchers have illuminated the basic distinction between codified or explicit knowledge, on one hand, and tacit forms of knowledge, on the other hand. The innovation process invariably relies on both types of knowledge. Since it is difficult, or as some would contend even impossible, to codify and make it easy to transfer tacit forms of knowledge, the role of geographic concentration is indispensable even in a knowledge society. According to Peter Maskell and Anders Malmberg, this trend has been reinforced by the increased access to explicit or codified knowledge, since the creation of unique capabilities and products depends on the production and use of tacit knowledge.

Tacit knowledge is a key determinant of the geographic patterns, since it defies easy articulation or codification and is hence difficult to exchange over long distances. The innovation process itself and, in particular, socially organized learning processes are changing. Innovation has come to be based increasingly on the interactions and knowledge flows between economic entities such as firms (customers, suppliers, and competitors), research organizations (universities and other public and private research institutions), and public agencies (technology transfer centers and development agencies). Moreover, as AnnaLee Saxenian has found, the interaction between individuals at the same physical location is key to the success of innovation, as in the case of Silicon Valley. Geographical proximity thus matters for two reasons: the crucial need to transfer "sticky" tacit knowledge and the growing importance of social interaction.

There are numerous examples of such geographic concentration for ventures in both "new to the world" innovations and traditional industries relying on incremental innovation. As examples of the former within the United States alone (besides the famous Silicon Valley area), Michael Porter has pointed to the Boston area for ventures in analytical instruments, communications equipment, and education and knowledge creation; the Atlanta area for companies in construction materials, transportation and logistics, and business services; and the Houston area for construction services, oil and gas companies, and aerospace and defense firms. In Europe, clusters in the United Kingdom in healthcare are perhaps those that have attracted the greatest attention, and more recently the emergence of clusters elsewhere, such as India for its information and communication technology firms, has attracted attention.

A different and somewhat broader approach to this research has been suggested by Richard Florida, who has considered a number of new characteristics for determining whether a geographic region has a high propensity for innovation or not. The approach draws attention to diversity as a prerequisite for creativity and ultimately innovation, with metropolitan regions identified as diverse in the sense of having high concentrations of, for example, technology workers, artists, musicians, homosexuals, and people whom Florida calls "high bohemians."

These locales are more likely to show a high level of economic development, because they are home to a "creative class," consisting of the groups mentioned above, who contribute to an open and urban environment, which in turn attracts more creative people.

Additional analyses have contributed to insights into the geography of innovation while expanding or reflecting on the notion of geography itself. To the extent that collaboration around knowledge creation is based on tacit or codified knowledge aimed at innovation, the geographic aspect is just one of many possible types of criteria. Alain Torre and André Rallet, along with Arnoud Lagendijk and Anne Lorentzen, ask this question with the point of departure being the concept of proximity; they wonder whether, in addition to geographic proximity, there may be other types of proximity. The notion of geographic proximity is obviously based on the notion of space and distance; other kinds of proximity, which these theorists refer to as "organizational proximity," may approximate a social or cultural affinity that makes it easier to communicate and interact. There may thus be cases in which both geographic and organizational proximity work together to create environments extremely conducive to collaboration and innovation. In some cases, ventures in close organizational proximity but not necessarily close in geographic proximity may thrive at the "periphery"; these suggest that the thesis of geographic concentration is not a deterministic one and that under certain circumstances it is possible to succeed outside regional concentrations or clusters.

Terje Grønning
University of Oslo

See also Globalization; Innovation Diffusion; Innovation Processes; Research and Development

Further Readings

Asheim, Bjørn Terje, and Meric S. Gertler. "The Geography of Innovation: Regional Innovation Systems." In *The Oxford Handbook of Innovation*, Jan Fagerberg, David Mowery, and Richard Nelson, eds. Oxford, UK: Oxford University Press, 2005.

Boutellier, Roman, Oliver Gassmann, and Maximilian von Zedtwitz. *Managing Global Innovation: Uncovering the Secrets of Future Competitiveness*, 3rd ed. Berlin: Springer, 2008.

Feldman, Maryann P. *The Geography of Innovation.* Berlin: Springer, 1994.

Florida, Richard. *Cities and the Creative Class.* London: Routledge, 2005.

Laestadius, Staffan. "Technology Level, Knowledge Formation and Industrial Competence in Paper Manufacturing." In *Microfoundations of Economic Growth: A Schumpeterian Perspective*, Gunnar Eliasson et al., eds. Ann Arbor: University of Michigan Press, 1998.

Lagendijk, Arnoud and Anne Lorentzen. "Proximity, Knowledge and Innovation in Peripheral Regions: On the Intersection Between Geographical and Organizational Proximity." *European Planning Studies*, v.15/4 (2007).

Maskell, P. and A. Malmberg. "Localised Learning and Industrial Competitiveness." *Cambridge Journal of Economics*, v.23 (1999).

Porter, Michael. "Clusters and the New Economics of Competition." *Harvard Business Review* (November/ December 1998).

Ratanawaraha, Apiwat and Karen P. Polenske. "Measuring the Geography of Innovation: A Literature Review." In *The Economic Geography of Innovation*, Karen R. Polenske, ed. Cambridge, UK: Cambridge University Press, 2007.

Saxenian, AnnaLee. *Regional Advantage: Culture and Competition in Silicon Valley and Route 128.* Cambridge, MA: Harvard University Press, 1994.

Torre, Alain and André Rallet. "Proximity and Localization." *Regional Studies*, v.39/1 (2005).

Zachary, G. Pascal. "When It Comes to Innovation, Geography Is Destiny." *New York Times* (February 11, 2007).

Globalization

Today's new ventures take place in a business environment defined by rapid change in the world's social, economic, and governmental behavior. Globalization can be defined as the process and results of these changes. The world is transforming from one in which business was created and conducted primarily within political and geographic borders to one in which distance serves as neither a significant obstacle nor a significant advantage. This transformation has major implications in the selection, planning, and execution of new ventures and in the planning and management of careers.

Definitions and Trends

Globalization results from, and continues to build, a worldwide consensus around shared values, in spite of loud protests to the contrary. Roland Robertson, in a 1992 article, explained that globalization "refers both to the compression of the world and the intensification of consciousness of the world as a whole." This worldwide awareness is especially important for new ventures, as markets, supplies, and customers need to be selected, developed, and managed in this larger, evolving context.

Multinational or transnational corporations are large organizations that are headquartered in one country and have locations in other "host" countries. These organizations were among the first to recognize and respond to the shrinking world and in many ways continue as the leaders in adapting to globalization. Many of the multinationals now make significant portions of their profits from markets outside their home countries and conduct the majority of their manufacturing outside their home countries as well. The iconic U.S. company Coca-Cola, headquartered in Atlanta, Georgia, is a good example. Not only does Coke do most of its manufacturing outside the United States; it also employs more of its 90,800 people outside the United States than within and makes the majority of its annual profits from non-U.S. sales. Coke now boasts more than 500 international brands and employs 25,000 vendors in Africa alone.

The multinationals are both creating and responding to globalization, as they employ, buy from, and sell to what Dominic Wilson and Raluca Dragusanu call the "exploding middle class." In a 2007 article, these two authors contrast the shrinking middle class in developed countries with the rapid growth of the middle class in developing countries. Developing countries include both the BRIC nations—Brazil, Russia, India, and China—and a longer list referred to as the N–11 (new eleven) countries—Bangladesh, Egypt, Indonesia, Iran, Mexico, Nigeria, Pakistan, the Philippines, South Korea, Turkey, and Vietnam—identified by Goldman Sachs as most likely to be among the world's largest economies in the near future.

International economic trends confirm dynamic advances in world markets as well as shifts in the relative value of products produced within individual countries. In 2010, the estimated world's gross domestic product (GDP), based on figures derived by the International Monetary Fund and adjusted by purchasing power parity (PPP), was approximately US$74 trillion. That number was expected to reach $99.336 trillion by 2015. The United States was expected to go from $14.658 trillion in 2010 to more than $18 trillion by 2015, while China, the world's fastest-growing major economy, was expected to increase its 2010 GDP of about $6 trillion to more than $10 trillion by 2015. Goldman Sachs predicted in 2007 that the size of China's GDP would exceed that of the United States by 2050.

The traditional developing countries of Brazil, Russia, India, and China, the so-called BRIC nations, are expected to continue their upward trajectory, although some doubts are being raised about Russia, based on that nation's perceived failure to build a single successful multinational company. India's GDP grew to $480 billion in 2010 and is expected to reach more than $2.5 trillion by 2015. Brazil's 2010 GDP was just over $642 billion in 2010 and was expected to add another trillion by 2015.

Whereas the financial data are impressive, the results of these changes are even more powerful. Globalization includes changes in almost all aspects of business. Supply chains now include a complex and diverse network of organizations that design, sell, distribute, transport, and store particular products. These supply chains typically involve a variety of companies and countries around the world. The developing countries with substantial participation in these supply chains are producing rapid, positive changes for their citizens.

New opportunities in developing countries are moving people into urban areas to take advantage of new employment opportunities, creating new business opportunities for others. As a result, worldwide poverty is decreasing and new business opportunities continue to emerge. The growing new middle class in developing countries is generating intense entrepreneurial activity as people create businesses large and small to meet the needs of their new neighbors.

Changes in Entrepreneurship

The goal of new ventures is to create and deliver services and products that are valued by others in the world. Value may be recognized by people in the new venture's local market more easily than in other countries, but the most exciting opportunities and impressive successes are often found in the developing countries.

The shrinking world seems to be generating a new type of entrepreneur, according to an article by Anne Habiby and Dierdre Coyle in the September 2010 issue of *Harvard Business Review*. According to these experts, this new set of entrepreneurs is emerging from what may be the "new frontier" of global development: Saudi Arabia, Jordan, Kenya, and other parts of Africa. These entrepreneurs are starting new businesses with much less capital than their predecessors and appear to be starting or supporting the start-ups of other new businesses with amazing speed and dexterity. Whereas these emerging companies are headed by people with the characteristics of typical entrepreneurs, they are developing their businesses in countries where the number of people with discretionary income is increasing dramatically and where multiple opportunities to address unmet needs for services and products exist. These new companies also appear to be hiring more people and producing more spin-off businesses than those of the traditional entrepreneurs.

A new category of entrepreneurship focuses on social needs. Social entrepreneurism creates organizations, tools, and aids for Third World countries and people in poverty to make their lives a little better and healthier. For example, one group developed a simple water filter for use in Africa, where clean water is rare and millions die from contaminated water every year. The device is not sold to make a profit but to save lives.

Intellectual Property

A growing but still weak worldwide consensus on the importance and manageability of intellectual property (IP) exists. Major differences remain in the law and its enforcement in the various countries in the world. As a result, legal advice from those with significant expertise in protecting IP is very important when doing business across cultures. For example, in the manufacture of semiconductors, more than 60 percent of companies report losses resulting from violations of IP rights, in a survey by SEMI, including patent infringement, theft of trade secrets, and counterfeiting of products. These violations of IP resulted in loss of sales and market share, a loss

of more than 2 percent of annual sales, which then leads to reduced selling prices and shareholder value. For the semiconductor industry, the loss amounts to several billion dollars per year. Other industries experience similar losses, with subsequent losses of jobs and tax income to operate public systems. Clear, written agreements around IP and confidentiality issues are highly recommended, but the selection of partners who are known to be trustworthy and who value a long-term relationship with those with whom they are partnering is the safest strategy. Enforcing a business contract is always difficult, especially in foreign markets with very different values regarding confidentiality, intellectual property rights, and contracts in general.

Managing Culture Differences

Culture can be defined as a group's collective wisdom about how to cope with the challenges of life. This wisdom is expressed through a powerful and often unconscious set of values and norms that are created through experience and passed down through generations. Understanding culture succeeds only when it is possible to identify the values underlying the various norms and practices that define that culture.

One example of the power of culture is found in the story of a U.S. team working to build an information technology (IT) system to serve the needs of the Indian, French, and U.S. divisions of the company. Every week there was a conference call with the three groups to discuss how to move forward and what the system would involve. Every week the Indians agreed with and seemed to support everything proposed by the U.S. group, whereas the French appeared to argue and disagree with everything proposed. The project never moved beyond the discussion phase.

The truth is that neither the French nor the Indians had much interest in changing their IT system. Because the Indian culture values maintaining harmony and communicating indirectly, their resistance looked like support to the U.S. team. The French, on the other hand, often make decisions through a vigorous debate of the issues, and so their arguing should not necessarily be seen as resistance.

The best way to succeed in cross-cultural work is to research the cultural characteristics of one's colleagues, both through reading and through talking with other members of their culture. Immigrants can be very helpful in explaining the differences in their home culture and the one in which they now live and work.

Leadership and Credibility

Leading and building credibility in international environments requires adapting to the expectations and norms of the various cultures involved. Differing cultures have different definitions of effective leadership and appropriate subordinate behavior. For instance, in authoritarian cultures, leaders are expected to maintain some distance from their subordinates and to accept full responsibility for the decisions they make and the instructions they give. In more egalitarian cultures, leaders are expected to be more collegial with their subordinates, acting as if their leadership role was only minimally different from the role of their subordinates. If the leader's behavior is significantly different from the behavior that is valued in the culture of the subordinate or superior, then that leader can be viewed as incompetent and not worthy of trust.

There is good news about leading across cultures, however. R. J. House and his colleagues found in their 1999 Global Leadership and Organizational Behavior Effectiveness Project (GLOBE) that vision, foresight, providing encouragement, trustworthiness, dynamism, and being positive and proactive are universally valued leadership characteristics. People around the world recognize and value those behaviors.

Authoritarian as opposed to egalitarian leadership is just one of many differences in the ways in which cultures differ in their definitions of effective leadership and in the ways they approach work. Understanding and adapting to these differences are critical to success in cross-cultural leadership. Recognizing and adapting to the culture with which one is working greatly increases the chances of building productive relationships.

Collaboration

Global relationships depend on a number of work processes, including coordination, communication, and collaboration. Trust and knowledge sharing are essential for collaboration. Some companies, such as Bose in Germany, are finding that collaborative approaches are enabling them to streamline their supply-chain processes, so manufacturing and distribution become faster, which in turn leads to a competitive advantage. Product development teams provide another example in which sharing of knowledge is essential to effective work. If members are located in distant places such as Dallas and Malaysia, creative work in developing a new product depends on the skilled use of electronic communications, and that depends on training in both technology and interpersonal skills, including cultural competency.

Collaboration across boundaries starts with an attitude about possibilities. As Russell Osguthorpe and R. S. Patterson point out, "Because each partner sees things differently, each imagines different solutions to the same problem. This is at once the opportunity and the risk associated with collaborative renewal." Diverse perspectives from different cultural backgrounds must be integrated to find ways of working together that will produce win-win outcomes. Respect for the others involved and their local values, styles, and insights can lead to integration of ideas and information resulting in innovation. The story is local; the principles are global. This means that individual experiences of partners or customers from different cultures are located in the local environment and can vary significantly, but that the business and leadership principles can be global and applied across the borders.

Conflict Management

Conflict is inevitable in business and is even more likely when business is conducted across borders. Separation by distance, language, and culture offer a multitude of opportunities to misinterpret, misunderstand, and disagree. In addition, the ways in which people from different cultures communicate and manage conflict are significantly, sometimes dangerously, different. Those who work across cultures are required to recognize and adapt to these differences.

The rate and pervasiveness of the changes that define and accompany globalization are both frightening and exciting. New opportunities emerge at a dizzying pace while traditional approaches are left by the wayside. In the context of change, entrepreneurs have an advantage compared to some well-established organizations that insist on traditional approaches. Overall, opportunities and rewards favor those entrepreneurs and organizations that embrace the realities of a shrinking planet and are willing and able to learn and exploit varying opportunities that accompany globalization.

Sue Freedman
University of Texas, Dallas
Michael M. Beyerlein
Purdue University

See also Culture and Entrepreneurship; Geographic Location; Geography of Innovation; Import/Export Businesses; International Enterprise Planning; International Markets; International New Ventures; Measures of Entrepreneurial Activity Across Countries; Microfinance; Patent Protection; Political Economy and Entrepreneurship; Social Entrepreneurship; Territorial Strategy and Regions

Further Readings

Al-Rodhan, Nayef R. F. and Gérard Stoudmann. *Definitions of Globalization: A Comprehensive Overview and a Proposed Definition.* Geneva: Geneva Center for Security Policy, 2006.

Goldman Sachs. "The Expanding Middle Class." Global Economics Paper 170. https://360.gs.com (Accessed December 2010).

Goldman Sachs. "Global Economic Outlook." http://www2.goldmansachs.com/ideas/global-economic-outlook/index.html (Accessed December 2010).

Goldman Sachs. "The N-11: More Than an Acronym." Global Economics Paper 153. https://360.gs.com (Accessed December 2010).

Habiby, A. S. and D. M. Coyle Jr. "The High-Intensity Entrepreneur." *Harvard Business Review*, v.88/9 (September 1, 2010).

House, R. J. et al. *Culture, Leadership, and Organizations.* Thousand Oaks, CA: Sage, 2004.

Osguthorpe, R. T. and R. S. Patterson. *Balancing the Tensions of Change: Eight Keys to Collaborative Educational Renewal.* Thousand Oaks, CA: Corwin Press, 1998.

Robertson, Roland. *Globalization: Social Theory and Global Culture.* London: Sage, 1992.

Wilson, Dominic and Raluca Dragusanu. "The Expanding Middle: The Exploding World Middle Class and Falling Global Inequality." Global Economics Paper 170. GS Global Economic Website. 2007. http://www.ryanallis.com/wp-content/uploads/2008/07/expandingmiddle.pdf (Accessed February 2011).

GOAL SETTING

A goal is something that one is trying to accomplish and can be used to improve performance. Goal-setting theory is considered to be one of the most practical theories of motivation in most organizations. Goal-setting theory was first developed by Edwin Locke and Gary Latham in the 1990s. These authors and numerous others since then have shown a relationship between the specificity and difficulty of a goal and self-efficacy (self-confidence) in performance. Goals are what define entrepreneurs and lead to their success. In order to lead to higher performance, goals should be specific, should present a challenge in terms of difficulty, and concomitantly should not be too easy to achieve. Having such goals is better than having no goal at all or having a vague "do your best" type of goal. Some entrepreneurs may be more willing than others to take the risks associated with difficult and challenging goals and are motivated to do well. Those willing to take risks will set difficult goals that stretch their abilities. Specific and challenging goals lead to motivation and performance.

Goals should be agreed upon between employees and supervisors in order for the employee to accept the goals. The employees must both value those goals and believe that he can achieve them. Goals should be SMART (specific, measurable, attainable, realistic/relevant, and time-based) in order to be effective. Individuals should have a variety of goals that are short-term (require less than two years to achieve), medium-term (require between two and five years to achieve), and long-term (require more than five years to achieve). Goals should be linked to feedback and rewards. Having an appropriate deadline is very important.

In setting goals, people may be motivated internally by pride or achievement, independence or autonomy. Individuals often do well with goals that they enjoy working toward, finding their progress both pleasant and energizing. People may also be motivated externally to set goals by rewards such as a bonus, recognition, or other benefits. It is important to determine what motivates a person to achieve a goal. Entrepreneurs, for example, often seek financial rewards, personal rewards, independence and autonomy, freedom, control, achievement, wealth,

Goal setting is often part of an employee performance appraisal system. Once clear goals are established, they should be agreed upon between the employee and supervisor to ensure that the employee values the goals and believes they are achievable. At that point, an action plan can be created and performance evaluated. (Photos.com)

opportunity, flexibility, or some combination of these rewards. Entrepreneurs are generally motivated by a desire to achieve and often are willing to take risks to realize the success of a new venture. High among their motivators, then, are financial performance, personal satisfaction, responsibility, and control.

Both the intensity of goals and commitment to goals have been studied. Entrepreneurs are focused on commitment, achievement, perseverance, and drive. Those people who focus intently on achieving goals and who are committed to goals are more likely to achieve those goals. Those who are highly motivated to achieve their goals will persist. The determination and drive to succeed are often the most important predictors of success. Entrepreneurs often intently pursue their goals, and with confidence.

People with high self-efficacy (confidence) feel that they have the necessary knowledge and skills to complete a goal, even when it is a difficult goal. They will commit, persevere, and reach their goals even in the face of adversity. Those entrepreneurs with high self-efficacy often identify opportunities that they turn to their advantage. Individuals who have high self-efficacy are more likely to set goals

for themselves. Also, those individuals who are perceived to have high self-efficacy continue to increase the level at which they set goals for themselves. There is often a strong relationship between self-efficacy and goal performance.

D. C. McClelland's need for achievement involves setting goals, taking risks, taking responsibility for actions, and desiring feedback. High-achieving individuals often try to take moderate amounts of risk when they believe they can influence the results of the situation. They are more concerned about their personal achievements than getting a reward and they desire feedback. Self-rewards also help people achieve the goals they have set for themselves. Entrepreneurs are motivated to perform and to sustain their entrepreneurial activities.

In many organizations, goal setting is often associated with the term *management by objectives* (MBO) and is part of the performance appraisal system. This process often consists of establishing clear goals or objectives, developing and implementing an action plan, evaluating performance, taking correct action if needed, and setting new goals. Feedback is needed so employees can understand their progress toward their goals. Organizations should seek to integrate their goals for employees' performance with the goals of individual employees. To improve performance, organizations need to cultivate loyalty and commitment from their employees, as well as share the overall vision and goals of the organization and where the employee fits in that vision. The firm's performance, as well as the employee's, is linked to goal setting.

Entrepreneurs tend to be successful at goal setting, which helps them work smarter instead of harder. Entrepreneurs are oriented toward the future and motivated to achieve their goals. They have a results orientation that helps them to manage risks. To motivate others, the entrepreneur must determine how he or she "feels" about the goals.

People often engage in setting and working toward goals if they feel that their effort will lead to performance and that performance will lead to a reward; this is known as expectancy theory. The reward must be something that the person setting the goal values. People will set goals if they believe that they can perform the task, that they have control over it, and that they will get a valued reward. Positive feedback will help people gain confidence in their ability to accomplish a goal. Goal setting is one way that people engage in self-leadership. In addition to motivation, self-efficacy, expectancy, and an internal locus of control, individuals need appropriate tools and training in order to reach goals. Some goals may be unreachable without such tools and training.

One downside to goal setting is that the drive to reach some goals, especially when they are beyond the skills of the employee, may have negative consequences, such as when people cut corners or act unethically in order to achieve a goal. In this case goals may be too hard to reach or there may be too much pressure to perform. Individuals, entrepreneurs, and managers should check to make sure that goals are not too difficult and work to prevent frustration that leads to unethical actions. Cautious people may be afraid of failure, which can cause them stress.

Entrepreneurs and new venture managers need to recognize that, in setting goals, employees will set priorities. Setting and reaching a goal requires commitment, but some individuals are compulsive in terms of achievement and may work toward a goal to the exclusion of other priorities, such as time for friends and family. Often entrepreneurs themselves display this behavior. Sometimes there may be events outside a person's control that can either support or damage the ability to attain the goals set. Failure can also be demotivating and frustrating for entrepreneurs. Initially people are often excited about goals and plans, but as time passes they may engage in post-planning syndrome, returning to old behaviors. This can result from a lack of priorities, a lack of long-term focus, or a change in the direction or goals of the venture.

Other obstacles to reaching goals include failing to anticipate obstacles, lack of commitment, failure to learn from experience, failing to set objectives and make progress toward goals, and failing to reevaluate or revise unrealistic goals. Realistic goals need to be set. Entrepreneurs should be committed and should track progress. The best insurance that goals can be met is the realistic setting and subsequent achievement of goals. When new ventures achieve the entrepreneur's goals—whether internal or external rewards such as recognition, challenge, accomplishment, growth, or economic rewards—entrepreneurs and their employees will be motivated to continue the entrepreneurial behaviors that created those rewards.

Katherine Hyatt
Reinhardt University

See also Commitment and Persistence; Gender and Performance; Intentions; Locus of Control; Measures of Performance; Motivation and Gender; Overconfidence; Planning Fallacy; Time Management

Further Readings

Brännback, Malin and Alan Carsrud. "Do They See What We See? A Critical Nordic Tale About Perceptions of Entrepreneurial Opportunities, Goals, and Growth." *Journal of Enterprising Culture*, v.16/1 (March 2008).

De Clercq, Dirk, Teresa V. Menzies, Monica Diochon, and Yvon Gasse. "Explaining Nascent Entrepreneurs' Goal Commitment: An Exploratory Study." *Journal of Small Business and Entrepreneurship*, v.22/2 (2009).

Kuratko, Donald F., Jeffrey S. Hornsby, and Douglas W. Naffziger. "An Examination of Owner's Goals in Sustaining Entrepreneurship." *Journal of Small Business Management*, v.35 (January 1997).

Locke, Edwin and Gary Lathan. "Goal Setting Theory." In *Motivation: Theory and Research*, Harold F. O'Neil and Michael Drillings, eds. Hillsdale, NJ: Lawrence Erlbaum Associates, 1994.

Locke, Edwin and Gary Lathan. *A Theory of Goal Setting and Task Performance*. Englewood Cliffs, NJ: Prentice Hall, 1990.

McClelland, D. C. *The Achieving Society*. Princeton, NJ: Van Nostrand, 1961.

Noel, Terry W. and Gary P. Latham. "The Importance of Learning Goals Versus Outcome Goals for Entrepreneurs." *International Journal of Entrepreneurship and Innovation*, v.7 (November 2006).

Stewart, Wayne H., Jr. et al. "Entrepreneurial Dispositions and Goal Orientations: A Comparative Exploration of United States and Russian Entrepreneurs." *Journal of Small Business Management*, v.4/1 (January 2003).

Timmons, Jeffrey A. "Goal-Setting and the Entrepreneur." *Journal of Small Business Management*, v.16 (April 1978).

GROWTH

The literature does not provide a uniform definition of *venture growth* or *enterprise growth*. Growth is seen mostly as a positive phenomenon within the meaning of a positive change in terms of size. It is generally differentiated into two forms, quantitative and qualitative growth. The former may entail growth in terms of turnovers, profit, or number of employees; the latter may be captured in terms of job satisfaction, product quality, or the achievement of objectives from the perspective of the founder. The condition for the realization of growth is that the young venture be a commercially feasible business model with a sufficiently large market potential at its disposal. According to the criterion of degree of cooperation, three basic forms of growth can be distinguished: internal, external, and cooperative growth.

Internal, or organic, growth refers to situations in which a young venture grows from its own strengths and therefore with its own resources. In this case, sufficient resources must be available for carrying out internal growth, from both the quantitative and qualitative points of view. If no or insufficient internal resources are available, the new venture can try to generate them by pursuing a cooperative growth strategy.

Internal growth strategies form the basis for entrepreneurial activities. Young ventures, in particular, often do not have a choice and must realize growth by focusing on their own strengths as well as their own resources. The generation of internal or organic growth depends, however, on a number of factors. These include, in the first place, the core competencies and resources of a young venture. With the uniqueness of the product or service offer, which competitors would find difficult to imitate, the realization of an internal growth strategy becomes possible. It is therefore important for a young venture to develop and nurture its own core competencies and to exploit them purposefully to achieve long-term success in the market. Furthermore, it is necessary that the young venture has a well-founded business plan at its disposal, as an unsystematic approach to the generation of internal growth without a clear direction can lead the young venture into chaos.

Organic growth is often a slow process that requires not only a clear focus on one's core competencies but also patience and persistence from the venture founders. The availability of liquidity is a fundamental condition for the permanence of a venture and, therefore, for the realization of venture strategies. To achieve internal growth, liquidity is necessary in many ways, from the development and diversification of a product to the opening-up or extension of markets, hiring of new staff, or the introduction of a computer-aided management information system.

If a market grows as a whole, a young venture may be able to participate in this growth with its specific product offer and thereby to increase its sales or generate new sales. The young venture can also grow through product innovation and so force market growth. However, the products not only must be developed with internal resources but also must be marketed in order to follow the pure form of an internal growth strategy. In practice, it often occurs that a young venture develops a unique product, but the marketing is taken over by a partner. This is mainly the case when a young venture has too few of its own resources at its disposal. Distribution partnering occurs in particular in industries where initial costs for product development are high and subsequent marketing and distribution are complex and costly; examples include biotechnology and pharmaceuticals ventures, such as when young biotech start-ups team with established pharmaceutical companies. In general, by building up and using a specific network, young ventures can obtain the required resources through individual cooperation with strategic partners.

External growth refers to growth outside the internal value-creation process of a venture. External growth strategies are usually pursued by established ventures and young ventures in their later growth phases. They manifest themselves in practice mainly in merger and acquisition strategies. Systematically, mergers and acquisitions are transactions in which ventures change their ownership structure (partly or completely). An acquisition is understood as the purchase of a legally independent venture by another venture. An acquisition must be distinguished from a merger; a merger involves the voluntary combination of two previously legally independent ventures. The boundary between acquisition and merger is nonetheless fluid.

Through an acquisition, the taken-over venture loses its legal independence. The motives of young ventures for acquisitions are multiple. Fundamentally strategic, financial, or personal motives usually play an important role. Individual motives, for instance, can involve turnover growth, access to new markets or technologies, utilization of synergy effects, or the extension of the product and service range. In many cases, the purchasing venture wants to acquire resources that form a meaningful complement to its own resources and are in harmony with the strategic orientation of the venture. These resources can be tangible or intangible. For young ventures, important factors in this context are the takeover of new business fields, the experiences and competencies of the management team, the addition of protected know-how (such as patents), but also the takeover of a nonprotected know-how (such as operating instructions or secret recipes for the manufacture of a special sauce for catering business).

Possible advantages of an acquisition or merger are often seen in a quick generation of fixed cost degression effects (economies of scale), as well as synergy effects (economies of scope) through a new combination of the formerly independent resources of the two ventures. However, potential disadvantages can also be listed, primarily the possible acquisition and reorganization costs when merging the operations of the two companies. The young venture is confronted with the question whether the purchase price corresponds in fact to the fair value of the venture that has been taken over. In practice, problems often arise concerning the compatibility of the individual venture-specific resources. For example, such problems can occur in the area of information and communication structures and systems or in the area of software solutions (different planning systems), if the two ventures used different methods. Areas particularly subject to such issues include planning of procurement, logistics, production, finance and accounting systems, controlling, and human resources management. It is also possible that the two businesses use incompatible software programs for operations such as research and development. Under these conditions, high integration and subsequent costs can accumulate for the young venture.

The joining of different venture cultures is linked to great challenges for the ventures involved in the acquisition process. Differences in the venture cultures manifest themselves mainly in different values, norms, and the formal and informal rules and regulations of each venture. In many cases, it must be assumed that the incompatibility of these cultures is an essential reason that the desired advantages (in particular envisioned synergy effects) are not always achieved. Venture cultures have normally grown over a certain period of time and developed their own individual manifestations. Therefore, different attitudes toward working methods and processes, but also diverging moral-ethical worldviews, may become evident. Especially in young ventures, the venture culture can be shaped to a large extent by the founders, who usually occupy a central position within the venture, and employees may strongly focus on them.

Cooperative growth is a strategy that is a hybrid of internal and external growth paths. Cooperative growth is achieved via the utilization of formal or informal network structures or individual relationships. The primary aim is the acquisition and employment of complementary resources. An important condition for the successful realization of cooperation is that each partner can achieve an advantage, creating a win-win situation, through synergies incurred during the exchange of know-how. Motives for cooperation can, for instance, be created through core competencies in basic technologies or key functions. Forms of cooperation include joint ventures and strategic alliances. Types of cooperation can be differentiated according to the size structures of the partners. From the perspective of a young start-up venture, cooperative projects may occur with small ventures (those of a similar size structure within the context of entrepreneurship) or with large ventures (those with dissimilar size structures).

Cooperation between ventures involves that at least two economically and legally independent ventures working together with the purpose of reaching a common goal, whether that be to increase market share, improve their competitive positions, or reduce risk. In contrast to "going it alone," the cooperating ventures strive to reach a higher level of success. However, cooperation requires the ventures to proceed on the basis of labor division and in accordance with contractual agreements.

The various forms of cooperation can be differentiated according to various criteria, such as the intensity of the cooperation (which can range from the exchange of information and experience to joint formation of a new business entity), value-chain-related criteria (whether horizontal, vertical, or lateral), function-related criteria (such as procurement, production, or distribution), criteria related to geographic reach (regional, national, or international), or criteria related to the duration of the cooperative venture (short-, medium-, or long-term). Moreover, different cooperative forms of growth of a venture can be visualized. These may be networks, strategic alliances, and joint ventures.

Like other growth strategies, cooperative growth is associated with specific advantages and disadvantages for young ventures. Cooperation can help young ventures improve access to markets and resources, reduce costs, use technologies effectively, gain access to capital, or gain advantages relative to time.

Cooperation can also, however, be disadvantageous—for example, if the absorption of know-how serves only one partner's purposes. Cooperation between young ventures and large, established ventures can lead to the young partner's dependency on the established partner. The absorption of know-how may include certain product and production technologies and standards as well as organizational structures and concepts in a young venture that have not been secured through industrial protection rights. Also in the area of industrial protection rights, dependencies can be generated because a young venture is not in a position to protect its innovations through, for example, patents or registered designs, lacking the necessary finances, time, or knowledge (or simply because such needs have been overlooked in the product development process). An established venture, with its resources and knowledge, could file an application for a patent or register a design without including the young venture. Dependencies and lawsuits can also occur in connection with the registration of brand names. To avoid lawsuits relating to protection rights, all relevant points should be regulated by contract, in advance of the cooperation.

Overall, when young ventures enter cooperative projects with large, established ventures, the potential benefits and risks of cooperation must be weighed against each other and monitored continuously.

Kim O. Tokarski
Bern University of Applied Sciences
Christine K. Volkmann
University of Wuppertal

See also Business Models; Entrepreneurs in Franchising; Licensing; Networks

Further Readings

Churchill, Neil C. and Virginia L. Lewis. "The Five Stages of Small Business Growth." *Harvard Business Review*, v.61/6 (1983).

Greiner, Larry E. "Evolution and Revolution as Organizations Grow." *Harvard Business Review*, v.50/4 (1972).

Penrose, Edith T. *The Theory of the Growth of the Firm*, 4th ed. Oxford, UK: Oxford University Press, 2009.

Volkmann, Christine K., Kim Oliver Tokarski, and Marc Gruenhagen. *Entrepreneurship in a European Perspective: Concepts for the Creation and Growth of New Ventures*. Wiesbaden, Germany: Gabler, 2010.

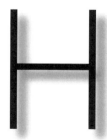

HISPANICS AND ENTREPRENEURSHIP

The tremendous growth of the U.S. Hispanic population is leading to fertile opportunities for existing businesses, as well as for Hispanic entrepreneurs. As entrepreneurs race to capture these opportunities, they should remain cognizant that while this market is similar in many ways to others, there are important differences. Hispanic entrepreneurship in the United States is vast, diverse, and vibrant, but concerns remain about factors that can inhibit its growth.

Hispanic entrepreneurs in the United States originate from more than 20 countries in North, Central, and South America, the Caribbean, and Europe. As a result, the culture, beliefs, opinions, and modes of doing business of Hispanic entrepreneurs are as varied as the countries and ancestry they represent.

According to the U.S. Census Bureau, the U.S. population is growing and becoming more diverse, with people of Hispanic origin leading this growth. With a projected population of nearly 48 million people, Hispanics remain the fastest-growing population group, increasing in size by 21 percent between 2000 and 2005. Caucasians, the slowest-growing population group, are not expected to contribute to growth after 2030 as the group will be declining in size. On the contrary, Hispanics will contribute an estimated 45 percent of the country's population growth from 2010 to 2030 and 60 percent from 2030 to 2050.

In 2006, the states with the largest number of Hispanics were California, with more than 13 million, and Texas, with nearly 8.4 million. The states with the next three largest Hispanic populations included Florida, New York, and Illinois, which, combined, accounted for an additional 8.5 million Hispanics. The challenges associated with an increasing population of immigrants also offer business opportunities for entrepreneurs.

Hispanics, like generations of immigrants before them, come to the United States seeking better lives and economic opportunities. Often, however, immigrants' only prospects lie in low-skill, low-paying jobs that lack opportunities for advancement. Immigrants sometimes do take these jobs, often finding this work to be more desirable than that in their native countries. However, Hispanic immigrants often develop an alternative to this less desirable job market through entrepreneurship.

Entrepreneurship offers a more attractive option for Hispanics because it promises higher earnings, enhanced professional standing, independence, and flexibility to accommodate family needs, as well as a means by which to create wealth to be transferred to the next generation. Indeed, family is central to the Hispanic culture. One study found that Hispanic business owners are more committed than other immigrant groups to keeping the business in the family. For Hispanics, entrepreneurship is a sensible path to pursue, as census data indicates that Hispanics who are self-employed have incomes that are 33 percent higher than those who earn wages.

Hispanics are attracted to entrepreneurship in part because equity created from the business can be transferred to family and the next generation. According to census data, owning a business contributes to a 33 percent higher income for Hispanic entrepreneurs than for Hispanics employed in traditional job settings. (Photos.com)

Many immigrants bring with them diverse cultures, which has proven to be an advantage for entrepreneurs. Hispanics are more likely to be self-employed and prosper by locating in populous Hispanic neighborhoods that retain a cultural distinction from their larger, surrounding areas. Hispanics are relationship-oriented, and entrepreneurs who locate in these neighborhoods maintain a deep commitment to their communities, with employees, suppliers, and customers drawn largely from within the community.

Entrepreneurs who locate their businesses in these neighborhoods also help to attract further Hispanic migration. By hiring Spanish-speaking employees with similar cultural experiences, targeting familiar products to consumers through Spanish-language advertising and bilingual store signage, businesses build rapport with new immigrants, helping to re-create their native culture in their adopted home. However, as many second-generation Hispanics do not learn to speak Spanish and assimilate into the larger American culture in greater numbers,

the viability of these Hispanic neighborhood businesses becomes threatened as the culture within the community changes.

Hispanic consumers are likely to be loyal buyers of brands that they recognize from their native country and typically spend more than non-Hispanics on many items. However, as many Hispanic customers live on a limited budget and send money to families in their native country, they are price-sensitive consumers who make running a profitable business challenging. In addition, a concentration of firms within a neighborhood, serving the same customers with products that are little differentiated from one another, creates fierce competition, driving down prices. Still, the greatest threat to the viability of these neighborhood businesses comes from mainstream businesses. National retailers are responding to the significant and growing Hispanic market by analyzing the cultural makeup of the communities they serve, tailoring their merchandise selection accordingly, and selling brands from their customers' native countries at a lower price.

In many of their native countries, Hispanic women have relatively few opportunities to launch a business and few role models with whom to interact. Thus, they may be more inclined to start a firm as new immigrants to the United States. In addition, American societal and gender roles may differ from those found in Hispanics' native countries. For example, in countries like Mexico, where gender roles are more traditionally defined, males dominate a significant portion of society culturally as well as professionally. Women have fewer options. Whereas they may have been raised to run a family, Hispanic women may choose entrepreneurship as an alternative to a traditional career. For these women, entrepreneurship allows them to contribute financially to the family, gives them a level of social equality, and provides them with the opportunity for better quality of life while balancing work and family. Even so, societal and gender roles persist, as is evidenced by the dramatic drop in start-up activity among Hispanic women in their mid-30s, as opposed to Caucasian and African American women in the same age category.

Although Hispanic entrepreneurship has increased, census data show that Hispanics are underrepresented among business owners in the United States. In 2007, Hispanics represented nearly

15 percent of the U.S. population and owned 2.3 million businesses, an increase of 43.7 percent since 2002. Of these, foreign-born Hispanics were more likely to start a firm than their native-born counterparts. Even so, with only 8.3 percent of all U.S. businesses, Hispanics have among the lowest self-employment rates of all minorities. Although the rate of Hispanic self-employment differs by country of origin, for some the picture is far worse. For example, the Mexican Hispanic self-employment rate is nearly half the rate of Caucasians.

Several problems contribute to the entrepreneurship gap and inhibit the growth of Hispanic businesses. A significant percentage of Hispanics are immigrants who have inadequate access to financial resources, low levels of formal education, and limited relevant business training. Low levels of educational attainment are particularly troublesome in that it may restrict access to more profitable industries.

Capital to launch or expand a business is difficult to obtain without collateral. As a result, Hispanic entrepreneurs typically limit the size of their businesses and target industries that are less capital intensive. Lack of capital may also mean that Hispanic entrepreneurs may not be able to focus exclusively on the business but rather continue to maintain outside employment to cover their families' financial needs. Thus, a lack of capital may help to explain why Hispanic-owned businesses are less likely to survive than those owned by Caucasians or Asians.

A lack of capital may also help explain why Hispanics may not be involved in different types of business at the expected rates. For instance, a franchise offers a ready-made business model but also requires a large amount of start-up capital and the payment of franchise fees. Different minority groups weigh these factors differently. For example, Asians, African Americans, and Native Americans are more likely to own franchises than are Hispanics.

In addition, research has shown that length of U.S. residency and English-language proficiency directly affect the likelihood of owning a business. Also, studies show that avoidance of uncertainty in Latin American countries, including Mexico, is significantly high, suggesting that those societies have very low acceptance of uncertainty and ambiguity, which may dampen entrepreneurial prospects.

Nonetheless, winds of change loom on the horizon. For Hispanics in particular, the level of educational attainment significantly predicts the rates at which they will become entrepreneurs. Approximately 20 percent of Hispanic men with some graduate education report efforts to launch a new business, compared with 10 percent of Caucasian men with the same education. In addition, the highest level of start-up activity was in the least urban areas, where levels of educational attainment are higher.

The desire to start a business is also reflected among young Hispanics. For example, Hispanic girls are more likely to be interested in entrepreneurship than are Caucasian girls, although their interest is more likely to be motivated by social and relational factors, whereas boys are more motivated by independence. Therefore, although issues that impede the development of Hispanic entrepreneurship remain, we continue to learn about Hispanic entrepreneurs and factors promoting positive new venture outcomes.

Enrique Nuñez
Ramapo College of New Jersey

See also African Americans and Entrepreneurship; Culture and Entrepreneurship; Family Business; Minorities in New Business Ventures

Further Readings

Bradley, D. B., III, and L. Stuckey. "Impact and Effect of Hispanic Growth on Small Business and Entrepreneurial Development." *International Journal of Entrepreneurship*, v.9 (2005).

Curci, R. and R. Mackoy. "Immigrant Business Enterprises: A Classification Framework Conceptualization and Test." *Thunderbird International Business Review*, v.52/2 (March/April 2010).

Robles, B. J. and H. Cordero-Guzmán. "Latino Self-Employment and Entrepreneurship in the United States: An Overview of the Literature and Data Sources." *Annals of the American Academy of Political and Social Science*, v.613/1 (September 2007).

Shinnar, R. S. et al. "Immigrant and U.S.-Born Mexican-Owned Businesses: Motivations and Management." *Journal of Developmental Entrepreneurship*, v.14/3 (September 2009).

Wilson, F., D. Marlino, and J. Kickul. "Our Entrepreneurial Future: Examining the Diverse Attitudes and Motivations of Teens Across Gender and Ethnic Identity." *Journal of Developmental Entrepreneurship*, v.9/3 (December 2004).

HOME-BASED BUSINESSES

Home-based businesses (HBBs) are generally understood to be ventures that operate at or from the owner's home residence. In a sense, all HBB activity is entrepreneurial, as HBB owners by definition have possession of a new venture based on an idea and have accountability for its inherent risks and outcomes. HBBs are very common entrepreneurial start-up businesses; many highly successful companies began in someone's kitchen, garage, or bedroom. HBBs can operate from rural or urban areas but most research about HBBs focuses on activity in cities and developed urban areas.

HBBs have been the focus of research in many countries around the globe since the late 1980s because of the rapid growth in their popularity as a business option. These countries have included Canada, the United States, Australia, New Zealand, and the United Kingdom, as well Ghana, Peru, Sri Lanka, and Zambia. Three reasons for the rapid growth in the number of HBBs are often given: the adoption of information and communication technologies (ICT), which has enabled more flexible modes of working; a "downshifting" movement, which has driven an increase in HBBs in response to companies' outsourcing and subcontracting of tasks formerly done by staff; and push factors such as government economic reforms (deregulation). Research on HBBs has examined it in relation to such themes as working at home, lifestyle and work-family issues, gender, the role of information technology, and the contribution of HBBs to economic development.

HBBs are based at or conducted from the home, so economic geography is an important foundation for understanding the HBB phenomenon. The modern workplace evolved because of the territorial separation between working and living, especially since the advent of the automobile, which created the suburbs and further separated the home and economic spheres of life. The newer technological innovation of the Internet is enabling economic geographic relationships to be reorganized yet again. Now institutions in cities are seen as part of a physical/digital network, providing telematic entry points into electronic space. As organizations become digital in nature, the conduct of entrepreneurial activity is also becoming more fluid as entrepreneurs become both place based and space based. Place is not less

important as people become more engaged with virtual spaces, but their routines of engagement with place and space are changing. Entrepreneurial activity now occurs in traditional workplaces; in third places such as cafés, restaurants, airports, and trains; and also in the home. Where work is being conducted has become more complex, and homes are now becoming more interconnected with traditional sites of work because of communications technology. Homes are now new "windows" into production and consumption opportunities, and home-based entrepreneurs have taken advantage of this opportunity. HBBs are now an increasingly accepted part of the economic landscape, although they still tend to be ignored in government economic policy and mainstream business research, despite the efforts of stakeholders to heighten their profile.

Consequently, HBBs are often misunderstood. They are assumed to be hobby or artisan types of businesses, operated on an ad hoc part-time basis, mainly by women and often away from metropolitan areas. Thus, they do not conform to ideas about what a business or entrepreneur is or should be. However, HBBs are legitimate businesses that generate real employment and make a significant economic and social contribution to their local communities, and HBB operators display entrepreneurial characteristics.

According to census data, the total number of people working from home increased from 3.47 million in 1999 to 4.34 million in 2005; the largest share (28 percent) of home-based businesses were in professional services like the legal, accounting, programming, and consulting fields. Home-based businesses often have strong family and ethical values, making them a valuable asset to a community. (Photos.com)

Most people operate from home simply because it is most convenient to do so. HBB operators do have some characteristics that can enable and/or constrain entrepreneurial opportunity, such as working part-time on the business while also engaging in traditional employment, having multiple income streams from more than one business, and having a high need for autonomy and control that sometimes limits the desire for expansion.

HBB operators' characteristics regarding the success or failure of ventures have been investigated in some depth. One major issue is how HBB owners define success, which highlights the importance they place on both financial and nonfinancial criteria such as personal satisfaction, achievement, pride in the job they do, and flexible lifestyle. Flexibility in lifestyle is often especially important to home-based entrepreneurs. Sometimes the two objectives of financial success and lifestyle come into conflict with each other, but many home-based entrepreneurs do not see the twin goals as being in conflict.

Other research has focused on the positive environmental, economic, and social benefits that HBBs can bring to communities since HBBs often have strong familial values and ethical components, tend to be environmentally sensitive, and add diversity to communities. These values can be reflected in product and service offerings as well as by the ways they operate. Craft-based ventures, for instance, often use the natural landscape for inspiration in the creation of products, and HBBs can be environmentally more sustainable as they provide necessary products and services close to people's residences, thus making travel less necessary.

Negative perceptions of HBBs are often grounded in erroneous historical assumptions associated with urban planning rules, which tend to see urban areas in unifunctional terms (such as commercial, industrial, and residential) and also because there tends to be a moralistic bias against private economic gain emanating from domestic homes. There is also some anxiety that homes may become the sweatshops of the future and provide only marginal economic opportunities.

However, despite their tiny size, research shows HBBs make a contribution to urban livelihoods and may well be essential to the well-being of regions' inhabitants and the development of the modern metropolis. There appears to be a relationship between wealth and the concentration of HBBs in particular regions, although this phenomenon is not well researched or understood. Current thinking suggests that HBBs should be supported and not hindered by urban planners, as these businesses are both resilient and able to adapt to changing circumstances, and therefore they may provide significant positive outcomes for local economic development initiatives.

HBBs appear to be viable business alternatives and are potentially economically and socially significant to the well-being of cities. Jane Jacobs advanced the idea that cities are the engines of economic development and cities are natural generators of diversity and prolific incubators of new ventures and ideas of many kinds. However, cities do not generate diversity automatically. Her prescription for diversity includes a high density of people; a mixture of work, leisure, and residence in the same area; a mixture of old and new buildings; and short street blocks. The combined effect of these conditions is to make it possible for people to interact and to communicate freely (thus creating "knowledge spillovers") and to try out new ideas. HBBs contribute to a city's diversity by enabling an environment needed for creative cities to flourish.

Another reason HBBs contribute to economic growth is that they provide a low-cost and easy entry option for entrepreneurs trying out new ideas. Although the mechanisms (and their respective importance) by which new and small businesses bring about economic growth are subject to considerable debate, it is clear that variety helps create economic growth. Evolutionary approaches to organizations and economies argue when there is more variety to select from, the eventual quality of what is retained is better. In addition, HBB owners have a high autonomy orientation, which is strongly associated with innovation and creativity more generally, and so it seems likely that HBBs are essential cogs in the innovative engine that powers modern cities, a notion now widely supported by urban planners and economists alike.

HBBs are a challenging model for entrepreneurs to use for a number of reasons. The major challenge for HBB owners is isolation. All business activity is fundamentally relational, as tasks take meaning from their position within an ensemble of activities that can be performed in series or parallel, usually by people working together. Technical tasks, including entrepreneurial actions, are embedded in currents of sociality, not individualism. Opportunity recognition and development are both complex and recursive and depend on social actors working together to find value in propositions. Proximity to others is therefore essential; multiple actors need to be together to create the "spark" of creativity that drives innovative action and to engage in other networking activities. Consequently, isolation is a challenge for HBB entrepreneurs because the modern home is physically and psychologically segregated from physical networks and therefore potential collaborators.

Effective HBB entrepreneurs overcome these challenges in a number of ways, including accessing the hybrid "third places" that are evolving to assist in the physical place-based communication necessary for the smooth running of economic activities, such as temporary meeting rooms and café precincts. Some HBB entrepreneurs develop innovative solutions to the problems of isolation by marketing linked products to a specific market under one brand. Online communities are also evolving in order to assist in overcoming poor networking opportunities and to help HBBs access resources catering to their needs.

The diversity of HBBs suggests that bundling them altogether in policy and research may be inappropriate. Instead, a "pathway" approach in policy would help differentiate certain types of HBBs from others so that the needs of regions, groups, and individuals can be catered to. For example, identifying ambitious HBBs with potential for expansion and supporting them may assist in regional economic development. HBBs are often used by enterprising new immigrants in their integration strategies. HBBs are often seen as an option for people about to retire as a way to move out of formal employment and into another income-generating activity. Targeting higher-potential HBBs with appropriate support is clearly one focus of economic and regional development policy, but this needs to occur alongside attitudinal shifts toward seeing HBBs more positively rather than ignoring them or actively discouraging them, as is often now the case.

Other issues for HBBs have to do with learning and management practice. The learning processes of HBB entrepreneurs and other micro- and small business operators tend to combine informally absorbed information, heuristics, and other shortcut methods in an approach that is more intuitively based than that of formal institutional processes of learning. In addition, home-based entrepreneurs tend to lack the knowledge and desire to apply best-practice systems used in larger organizations to achieve excellence, mainly because they are just not big enough to be systematized in the same ways. This suggests that learning and decision-making models, and even managerial paradigms designed for larger businesses, may not be directly applicable to HBBs. However, rapidly evolving standards around quality and excellence that are being adopted in larger institutions may make it more difficult for HBBs to qualify for service provision, making it difficult if not impossible for them to compete in many industries.

Despite these challenges, HBBs are here to stay, and understanding them is becoming more important. Increased adoption of communications technology makes economic activity more fluid, and the home is being reintegrated into economic flows of activity in many ways. HBB ventures are entrepreneurial, but they do not conform to stereotypes of the successful business. Further research into HBBs is necessary because not only do they challenge many stereotypes of the entrepreneur and of a successful business but they also bring into sharp focus the need to look at entrepreneurial activity as a contextual, place-based activity.

Janet Grace Sayers
Massey University

See also Family Business; Gender and Acquiring Resources; Gender and Industry Preferences; Gender and Performance; Microfinance; Minorities in New Business Ventures; Motivation and Gender; Women's Entrepreneurship; Women's Entrepreneurship: Best Practices; Work-Life Balance

Further Readings

Mason, Colin et al. *Invisible Businesses: The Characteristics of Home-Based Businesses in the United Kingdom.* Glasgow, UK: Hunter Centre for Entrepreneurship, University of Strathclyde, 2008.

Sayers, Janet and Nanette Monin, eds. *The Global Garage: Home-Based Business in New Zealand.* Melbourne, Australia: Dunmore Press, 2005.

Thompson, Piers et al. "Women and Home-Based Entrepreneurship." *International Small Business Journal*, v.27/2 (2009).

Van Gelderen, Marco et al. "Home-Based Internet Businesses as Drivers of Diversity." *Journal of Small Business and Enterprise Development*, v.15/1 (2008).

Walker, Elizabeth. "Home-Based Businesses: Setting Straight the Urban Myths." *Small Enterprise Research*, v.11/2 (2003).

HUMAN CAPITAL THEORY

Human capital theory posits that the costs associated with developing an individual's knowledge, skills, and abilities should be considered an investment because the outcome of these costs generates additional economic value. This theory has implications for both individual-level decisions and firm-level decisions. At the individual level, human capital theory posits that individuals may make investments in their own human capital in order to increase their earnings. At the firm level, the theory suggests that firms may make investments in developing the human capital of their workforces in order to increase firm performance. Because the abilities and talents of entrepreneurs, start-up teams, and early-stage workers are critical to the survival and success of nascent firms, human capital investments play an important role in the performance of new ventures.

Human capital theory was formalized in the mid-1960s by Gary Becker, who argued that investments in human capital directly affect an individual's productivity. For example, investing in education and experience may lead to an increase in individuals' productivity within an organization. Becker categorizes an investment in human capital that increases the productivity of an individual at multiple employers as an investment in general human capital. An example of investment in general human capital is investing in an employee with a master's degree in business administration. If the investment has value only to one employer, it is categorized as an investment in firm-specific human capital. An example of firm-specific human capital is investing in training employees how to use customized software that is used by only one firm. Human capital investments may also be specific to a task, a job, an occupation, or an industry.

Because investments in education and experience are costly, rational individuals weigh the returns associated with investing in these factors with the costs of making these investments and then make the optimal investment in acquiring human capital. For example, if individuals acquire firm-specific human capital, they do not increase their value to other

potential employers. As a result, these individuals cannot threaten to leave their current employers for a better external job and thus cannot appropriate any of the value of their firm-specific investments in human capital. Consequently, rational individuals should never bear the costs of investment in firm-specific human capital because they cannot reap the benefits. In this case, employers should bear the costs and reap the benefits of the investments.

However, for general human capital, individuals are able to reap the benefits of their investments. If individuals acquire general human capital, they increase their value to alternative employers and thus can use these multiple potential employers to bid up their wages and extract all of the value of their general investments. In this case, individuals should bear the costs and reap the benefits of the investments.

While one of the key implications of human capital theory is that employers pay for firm-specific human capital investments and individuals pay for general human capital investments, this core implication holds only in well-functioning labor markets. However, entrepreneurs are rare and new ventures often face uncertainty and limited information, so labor markets for new ventures may face significant frictions. As a result, human capital theory has different implications for new ventures from those it has for established ventures.

First, the human capital investments of individuals may increase their ability to be entrepreneurs. The traditional framework focuses on individuals as employees; however, the same investment decision also applies to entrepreneurship. Extending human capital theory to entrepreneurship suggests that potential entrepreneurs weigh the costs of investment in human capital with the returns associated with entrepreneurship and invest accordingly. Because entrepreneurs' educational background, general experience, industry experience, and prior new venture experience have all been shown to be positively related to the success of new ventures, there are positive returns for entrepreneurs' investments in human capital.

Also, working in an entrepreneurial context may facilitate the acquisition of additional human capital that would not have been gained from employment at an established firm. For example, experience in a new venture represents investments in understanding the challenges and opportunities specific to new ventures and leads to higher performance in subsequent entrepreneurial contexts; thus, the act of gaining experience in a new venture is an investment in entrepreneurial human capital. Similarly, if individuals at new ventures are more likely to perform tasks that span many functional areas than individuals at established firms, then experience at new ventures will generate broader human capital than experience at established firms that are large enough to implement job specialization.

Additionally, while all firms can adjust the human capital embedded in the firm through hiring new employees or by training existing employees, both of these options may be cost prohibitive for resource-constrained new ventures. As a result, new ventures may be more likely to engage in the bricolage of human capital, which entails reallocating, repurposing, and recombining existing human capital to respond to changing conditions.

In summary, human capital theory is an important tool in understanding the connection between individuals' knowledge, skills, and abilities and organizational performance. Because the human capital of entrepreneurs and employees at new ventures plays an important role in venture performance, this tool is particularly important in understanding the phenomenon of entrepreneurship and the management of new ventures.

Benjamin A. Campbell
The Ohio State University
Preeta M. Banerjee
Brandeis University

See also Human Resource Strategy; Human Resources; Knowledge; Knowledge-Based View; Labor Costs; Resource-Based View

Further Readings

Becker, Gary. *Human Capital: A Theoretical and Empirical Analysis, With Special Reference to Education.* Chicago: University of Chicago Press, 1964.

Dencker, John, Marc Gruber, and Sonali Shah. "Pre-Entry Knowledge, Learning, and the Survival of New Firms." *Organization Science*, v.20/3 (2009).

Lazear, Edward. "Balanced Skills and Entrepreneurship." *The American Economic Review*, v.94/2 (2004).

Robinson, Peter and Edwin Sexton. "The Effect of Education and Experience on Self-Employment Success." *Journal of Business Venturing*, v.9/2 (1994).

Shane, Scott and Rakesh Khurana. "Bringing Individuals Back In: The Effects of Career Experience on New Firm Founding." *Ind Corp Change*, v.12/3 (2003).

Human Resource Strategy

Strategy can be defined as the set of related decisions that an organization makes about how it will create value and thereby achieve competitive advantage. *Human resource strategy* represents the subset of decisions that an organization makes about how to use its personnel to create value. Human resource (HR) strategy is generally viewed as a supportive strategy to aid in accomplishing the corporate and business strategy of a firm. HR strategy determines the specific HR activities that an organization will use to influence the behavior of its employees and how it will develop their capabilities to accomplish its business strategy. New ventures are particularly well positioned to develop high-performance HR strategies to drive business results, since they are able to start with a blank slate, unfettered by legacy HR strategies that have accumulated from prior operations. New ventures have the flexibility to tailor their HR strategies to align closely with their business strategies.

HR strategy flows from the mission, vision, and values of the firm that shape its corporate and business strategies to achieve success. In the strategic management literature, corporate strategy is viewed as the fundamental decision about which industries, businesses, and markets a firm will compete with, given its mission and vision. Once this decision has been made, the firm's business strategy is developed for its competitive domain and in consideration of its organizational values. Business strategy is the set of decisions a firm makes about how it will create competitive advantage in the particular industry, business, and market it has selected.

Three generic business strategies have been identified and labeled as cost-leadership, differentiation, and focus. A cost-leadership strategy centers on delivering market-competitive products or services at low cost and thereby growing market share and profitability via high volume. A differentiation strategy aims at producing unique products or services for which customers are willing to pay a premium because of perceived added value. A firm with a focus strategy selects a subset of a larger industry, business, or market within which it chooses to compete. Within its chosen niche, the firm might use a cost-leader or differentiation strategy to achieve competitive advantage. A middle-of-the-road strategy describes firms that seek to simultaneously employ cost-leader and differentiation strategies. The particular business strategy pursued by a firm has profound implications for supportive strategies in each of its functional units (such as HR, marketing, production, management information systems, finance, and research and development).

These functional strategies are developed for each specialized area, such as HR, to support accomplishment of the firm's business strategy. Thus, HR strategy is the set of related decisions a firm makes about the HR activities in which it will engage to accomplish its business strategy to create value that leads to competitive advantage. For example, Walmart has been frequently cited as a firm with a cost-leader strategy, whereas Apple has been similarly cited as an example of a firm with a clear differentiation strategy. The HR strategy of these firms varies markedly. With a cost-leader strategy, Walmart focuses on limiting wage and benefit costs and operating with a relatively low-skilled workforce, thereby minimizing training costs and accepting higher turnover. However, Apple's HR strategy is much more focused on attracting and retaining skilled workers with higher pay and more extensive benefits and providing extensive training and development to these employees. Whereas these firms are in different industries, even firms within the same competitive space may have significantly different HR strategies. In a noted study, researchers documented significant differences between the HR strategies of Walmart and Costco, both of which compete in the mass retailing market space. It was found that, while Costco paid higher wages and provided significantly better benefits, it had lower average labor costs than Walmart as a result of its lower turnover and its more productive workforce. Similar differences in HR strategy can be seen in firms with focus and middle-of-the-road business strategies.

HR strategy requires translating a firm's business strategy into decisions about the specific HR activities the firm will use to shape employee competencies (what employees know how to do) and behaviors (what employees choose to do) to aid in achieving competitive advantage. A firm's set of HR activities is sometimes referred to as its HR architecture, or the specific set of HR programs, policies, and practices that it uses to influence its employees' competencies and behaviors. HR programs are ongoing structured initiatives intended to meet employee needs, develop employee abilities, and encourage employee behaviors important to the firm's performance. These programs assure uniformity in employee actions and provide predictability in the employment relationship. HR policies are pre-made decisions that provide guidelines for employee behaviors in order to assure consistency and equity in dealing with issues arising in the workplace; these policies are generally implemented to deal with recurring issues. HR practices are emergent decisions that are made on a day-to-day, as-needed basis to guide employment-related actions in situations that arise episodically. These practices provide precedents that can evolve into policies over time as the need for and benefits of ongoing standardization of employee behavior become apparent.

The goal of HR strategy is to implement a set of HR programs, policies, and practices that will shape employee competencies and behavior for enhanced employee performance that can be translated into enhanced firm performance. HR competencies encompass both compliance competencies, which are intended to assure reliable performance based on knowledge, skills, and abilities needed by employees to do their current jobs, and developmental competencies, which are focused on acquisition of new knowledge, skills, and abilities needed for future job performance. HR programs, policies, and practices are also intended to shape employee behaviors that can improve organizational performance. Six generic employee behaviors have been identified that organizations routinely promote through their HR strategies to increase efficiency and effectiveness. Generally, organizations develop strategies to increase the level of the following employee behaviors:

- *Attachment*, the willingness of employees to continue in an employment relationship with the firm (the opposite of employee turnover)
- *Attendance*, the employee's faithfulness in being available to accomplish work for the firm when scheduled or needed (the opposite of absenteeism)

- *Productivity*, the employee's degree of engagement and diligence in performing useful work activities that create value for the firm
- *Organizational citizenship behavior (OCB)*, the willingness of employees to engage in positive behaviors that go above and beyond minimum job requirements
- *Nondeviant behavior*, employee avoidance of dysfunctional behaviors such as theft, workplace violence, sabotage, malingering, and other negative behaviors that diminish workplace collaboration and performance
- *Satisfaction*, the degree to which employees have positive attitudes toward their job and the organization

Research indicates that firms with higher levels of these employee behaviors have higher levels of firm performance, because they are able to use these behaviors to achieve higher levels of efficiency and effectiveness in accomplishing organizational goals. Thus, in this context, HR strategy is the specific set of decisions that a firm makes about the HR architecture it will use to achieve higher levels of employee competencies and behaviors to achieve its business strategy.

HR strategy identifies the specific HR programs, policies, and practices needed in each of the major stages in the HR management process of acquisition, development, and engagement of a firm's personnel. HR acquisition primarily deals with strategies as to how organizations define and design needed jobs (job analysis and design); determine the number of workers needed at various points in time and develop supplies that will be available when needed (HR planning and scheduling); attract the best-qualified candidates to apply for available positions (recruitment); and determine the best-qualified applicants for hiring (selection and placement).

HR development typically involves strategies for introducing new employees to the job and to the organization (orientation); providing new employees with job and/or organization-specific knowledge and skills needed to do the job (training); enhancing the capabilities and competencies of employees for future positions and other contributions to the organization (employee development and career planning); and using performance appraisal results to improve current performance and future contributions (performance management).

HR engagement focuses on strategies related to economic and noneconomic rewards provided to workers to recognize current and motivate future contributions (fixed and variable compensation, recognition and promotion); provide economic and noneconomic rewards to retain employees via their safety and security needs (benefit plans, safety and health programs); implement mechanisms for ensuring fair and equitable treatment in the workplace and by the organization (grievance, justice, and dispute resolution).

Thus, a firm's HR strategy is ultimately the mix of specific programs, policies, and practices in each stage of the HR process designed to lead to a set of employee competencies and behaviors that will optimally contribute to achieving the venture's business strategy.

Tom J. Sanders
University of Montevallo

See also Human Capital Theory; Human Resources; Leadership; Resource-Based View

Further Readings

Anthony, William P., Michele K. Kacmar, and Pamela L. Perrewe. *Human Resource Management: A Strategic Approach*, 6th ed. Florence, KY: Cengage Custom Publishing, 2009.

Cascio, Wayne and John W. Boudreau. *Investing in People*, 2nd ed. New York: FT Press, 2010.

Huselid, Mark A., Brian E. Becker, and Richard W. Beatty. *The Workforce Scorecard: Managing Human Capital to Execute Strategy*. Boston: Harvard Business School Press, 2005.

Robbins, Stephen and Timothy Judge. *Organizational Behavior*, 14th ed. Upper Saddle River, NJ: Prentice Hall, 2010.

Ulrich, Dave and Wayne Brockbank. *The HR Value Proposition*. Boston: Harvard Business School Press, 2005.

Wright, Patrick M. *Human Resource Strategy*. Alexandria, VA: SHRM Foundation, 2008.

HUMAN RESOURCES

The term *human resources* (HR) generally refers to the administrative department in an organization that manages employee affairs. This group is often thought of as a maintenance cost: a necessary but expensive entity that spends money but does not bring in any of its own. Whereas it is certainly true that HR serves as the bureaucratic heart of most established organizations, the function and strategy of HR in new organizations is substantially different. In fact, the constraints of a strong bureaucracy in an established organization would likely prevent that organization from engaging in the flexible HR practices necessary to leverage employee skills and knowledge in the way required by the dynamic and uncertain environment of a new venture. Whereas employees are a source of competitive advantage in all companies, they are even more important in new organizations. Given the relatively small size of most start-ups, each employee has a much greater impact on the success or failure of the company compared to larger organizations, which have a much more substantial cushion in terms of manpower and funds. Thus, understanding and incorporating strong HR practices is particularly important for the survival of new organizations. In general, for new ventures HR is particularly important in addressing the following: formation of a new company, recruitment, selection, compensation, performance assessment, training and development, and employee rights.

In established companies, there is an employee life cycle, which refers to the path an employee takes through an organization, from his or her very first exposure to departure for another job. This life cycle begins the moment a potential employee is contacted by or shows interest in an organization as a potential employer. The earliest part of the life cycle is characterized by information gathering by both the potential employee and the organization. This includes the assessment of fit via selection procedures, the communication of important features of organizational culture through orientation activities, and the provision of mentoring and training.

While this life cycle is present in new ventures as well, the life cycle of the entrepreneur is different in that this process begins before the new venture even exists. There are three milestones for the creation of a new venture: (1) aspiring, which refers to the intent to begin or continue as an entrepreneur; (2) preparing, which represents an attempt to begin a new business; and (3) entering, which refers to the actual opening of a new business. Individuals who have current or previous experience as entrepreneurs (even if those experiences were negative), those who reside in areas with a great deal of unemployment, and those who reside in areas with many small businesses have a greater likelihood of reaching the aspiration milestone.

None of these milestones involves what is thought of as HR in established organizations. For new ventures, simply coming into existence represents its own unique form of HR. Of course, this uniqueness does not end at organizational conception. New ventures necessitate a number of specialized HR considerations, including specific recruiting and hiring strategies and individualized compensation. Additionally, before continuing, it is important to note that entrepreneurships are not always formed from scratch; many new organizations emerge as spin-offs of established ones, the result of an entrepreneurial spirit fostered within a parent company. Certain HR policies and organizational structures can foster an atmosphere of innovation and opportunity seeking, whether in a new organization or an established one.

An important part of creating such an intraorganizational entrepreneurial environment is to recruit talented individuals. Recruiting may be difficult for new ventures, because they lack the reputation and name recognition that established companies possess. For example, a major supermarket chain will have an easier time recruiting talented job applicants than will a local co-op. The purpose of recruiting is to increase the number of employees applying for a certain position, as well as to target specific types of desirable individuals. There are several strategies companies can adopt when recruiting, depending on the position the organization is trying to fill. These strategies can include targeting new high school or college graduates (if inexperienced, entry-level applicants are being sought) and targeting trade associations (if the position requires specific skills). Companies seeking to foster an entrepreneurial spirit are likely to focus on educated and technically skilled individuals. In this case, focus may be placed on establishing contacts with colleges, universities, and technical associations. Such targeting helps establish long-term relationships between the organization and desirable applicant pools, providing a steady stream of talent that is aware of and interested in the organization. For example, many large computer-oriented firms have long-standing relationships with prestigious computer science programs in order to hire their best graduates quickly.

Once potential employees have been recruited, there must be a system in place to select the best persons for the position. The purpose of selection is to determine which applicants have the most desirable characteristics that will enable them to perform a targeted job effectively. This includes both the hiring of new employees and the promotion of current employees. The first step in determining which characteristics are valuable for employees is a procedure called job analysis, which refers to the systematic collection of data on current successful employees so that their characteristics can be replicated in new hires. In a new venture, people are often hired for positions that do not yet exist. That is, the new hire will be the first to occupy the position and hold the job title, so additional information must be utilized. In these circumstances, historical data are often used. The best freely available source of such information is the Occupational Network Database (O*NET, available online at http://online.onetcenter.org).

Once the profile of a needed employee has been located in O*NET, various KSAOs (knowledge, skills, abilities, and other characteristics) necessary to succeed on the job can be identified as targets of the selection process. Perhaps as a consequence of this, job descriptions in entrepreneurial organizations are likely to be broader, less comprehensive, and based more on competencies than on more work-oriented constructs, as they would be for established positions.

For new organizations, several specific personality traits have been identified as key factors that can be used as criteria for selection of entrepreneurs, including need for achievement, need for autonomy, innovativeness, an internal locus of control, self-efficacy, and intrinsic motivation. Empirical research indicates that each of these personality traits has been linked to entrepreneurial success. Individuals high in need for achievement have a strong desire for skill mastery and accomplishment. Individuals who desire autonomy want to work independently and set their own goals. Innovative individuals challenge the status quo and seek new ways of doing things. Having an internal locus of control indicates that the individual believes he or she (as opposed to some outside force dictating success and failure) is in control of his or her own fate. Intrinsic motivation is motivation that is derived from enjoyment of a task itself as opposed to motivation that originates from

some external source (such as monetary compensation). Intrinsically motivated individuals are likely to persevere in spite of the difficult challenges that they will face in an innovative environment. This is not to say that intrinsically motivated individuals do not expect to be well compensated. Indeed, it appears that ample compensation is a minimum requirement for such entrepreneurial individuals to accept a job or to continue working in a job where innovation is expected. Rather, once proper compensation has been set, the main driving force for an intrinsically motivated individual is simply the enjoyment of the job. Determining pay for such individuals can be difficult and expensive.

One major consideration when placing someone in a position within a company is how much to pay that person. Several factors must be taken into consideration when determining an employee's compensation package, which includes both base pay and fringe benefits. Typically, employers refer to the average salary of other individuals employed in the position of interest (this information is available through the U.S. Bureau of Labor and O*NET), as well as the size of the available labor pool, the industry, the employee's years of experience, and other available data about similar positions. When hiring entrepreneurial individuals, it is likely that base-pay compensation will have to be above average to attract the most talented individuals in the field. Additionally, bonuses and recognition should be individually determined; these benefits must be perceived as the result of individual accomplishment rather than as part of a general, department-wide plan. Such wholesale rewards are actually likely to reduce motivation, as they may be perceived as mundane and thoughtless. Entrepreneurial individuals desire to succeed as individuals and to be rewarded as individuals.

Fringe benefits range from healthcare and retirement plans to prime parking spots and corner offices. For large companies, the cost of fringe benefits can be as expensive as base pay. For new or small companies, fringe benefits must typically be restricted to only the most important or cost-effective options. Healthcare is likely to be a particularly important benefit. Although it is expensive, it is critical for recruiting many employees and plays a crucial role in their decision to accept a job and continue with a company. Applicants who join an organization that does not provide healthcare may be less likely to remain over the long term.

An implicit consequence of any system requiring individualized rewards is that the role of managers and supervisors is vital. Supervising in such an environment requires a delicate balance of being available and facilitative without being intrusive. Supervisors should listen honestly to employees and consider their new ideas. As a result, employees feel heard but do not perceive their supervisors as meddlesome. It is also important for managers to provide time, resources, and a degree of freedom regarding which projects the employee works on and how that work gets done. Employees in entrepreneurial firms are more likely to be asked or to request to perform duties outside their job description. This extends to letting employees meet with customers or others outside the firm, which enables them to understand the marketplace and ultimately to be better employees or entrepreneurs. Furthermore, managers must provide challenging work and allow access to others with superior technical skills. Finally, the manager must be able to evaluate all of these activities properly if compensation and recognition are to be adequate yet not excessive.

Useful performance appraisal is a difficult task even in long-standing organizations, for several reasons. First, managers tend to give higher performance evaluation ratings when the ratings will be used for administrative decisions such as pay and promotion. Second, managers may find it tough to give negative feedback to employees for fear of damaging interpersonal relationships. Finally, given the nature of a manager's job, he or she may not have sufficient day-to-day contact with an employee on which to base a judgment. These issues may be even more salient in new organizations or organizations with an entrepreneurial strategy, given that entrepreneurial individuals as managers are more likely to be occupied with other critical responsibilities.

Performance can be measured in several ways. Objective measures include production and personnel data. Production data measure the quality or quantity of output, such as the amount and number of sales or units produced. Personnel data include information that has been collected during the day-to-day functioning of the organization, including absences, commendations, reprimands, and accidents. There are subjective measures as well, including supervisor,

peer, and subordinate evaluations. For these kinds of evaluations, an employee is rated across a variety of job activities. One potential problem for these kinds of evaluations is called the halo effect. These effects occur when one's overall judgment of an employee impacts that person's ratings of each individual facet of performance. For example, if a supervisor thinks very highly of an employee, these positive feelings are likely to influence the supervisor's ratings on all their individual tasks, even if the employee performs some of those tasks poorly. This leads to inaccurate performance ratings. For this reason, a key role of HR is to train supervisors to make them aware of halo effects and other psychological barriers to making accurate ratings, in order to reduce the impact of such effects. Accurate performance ratings are absolutely critical in an organization, as they ultimately serve as the basis for promotion and pay decisions.

It is particularly important that performance is adequately assessed in new ventures, because highly skilled and motivated employees are likely to leave an organization if they perceive that their performance is not being properly measured, appreciated, and compensated. For such organizations, it is especially important that there are objective, quantifiable performance measures and that assessments are results-oriented. These measures can include the completion of projects on time and under budget, the number of new patents acquired, or the degree of adoption and profit for new innovations. Regardless of the specifics of the assessment strategy, entrepreneurs expect to be accurately appraised and appropriately compensated.

Another HR function that plays an important role in a new business is training and development. Like selection, training should be based on a systematic investigation of what KSAOs are needed beyond those defined in the selection system. This process is called needs analysis. The first step in a needs analysis is to gain the support of key personnel in the organization so that everyone has the same expectations and goals for training. The second step, organizational analysis, considers the organizational goals, resources, transfer climate (the degree to which using the skills learned in training on the job is encouraged), and legal and external constraints to determine how these factors may impact the effectiveness of training. Finally, a requirements analysis is conducted to determine what materials will be needed for training, including the methods, participants, and facilities. After these analyses have been done, a task analysis can be done. Much like a job analysis, a task analysis is a process by which the most important KSAOs necessary to do a job are identified, and it is these skills that become the focus of training. There are some skills that may be important to make the focus of training in new organizations. If new ventures are small and employ relatively few individuals, the ability to work as a team may be crucial to organizational success. It is likely that work will require the input of several people, and if individuals have a hard time working together to complete an assignment, the quality of the work is likely to suffer. This skill is particularly important given the individualist nature of typical entrepreneurial employees.

Employers must always be aware of the legal context and the rights of their employees. In the United States, the Civil Rights Act of 1964 expressly prohibits discrimination on the basis of race, color, religion, sex, and national origin. These are collectively referred to as protected classes, and myriad other specific protections exist for various other groups. There are two major categories of discrimination: disparate treatment and disparate impact. Disparate treatment occurs when an employer or one of its agents engages in overtly discriminatory behavior toward an employee because of that person's status within a protected class. An example of this might be a supervisor making derogatory comments to an employee about the employee's race or ethnicity. Disparate treatment is always illegal in the United States. Disparate impact is more complex and is defined by situations in which, while there is no intentional discrimination, company policies adversely affect members of protected classes. This can occur when a company utilizes hiring practices that result in members of one class being disproportionally eliminated from the selection process. For example, fire stations often include weight-carry tests as part of their selection procedures. The purpose of this inclusion is appreciated; firefighters will need to carry people out of burning buildings and move heavy debris quickly and under intense pressure. However, on average, men have greater muscular strength than women. Thus, a greater proportion of men are hired from the applicant pool than are women. This is disparate impact and *may* be illegal.

By their nature, cases of disparate impact are class-action cases, because they involve members of an entire class of people being discriminated against, as opposed to cases of disparate treatment, which typically involve individuals. Employers can shield themselves somewhat from impact cases by ensuring that selection and other procedures that determine organizational outcomes have been carefully crafted and are based on business necessity. The "Uniform Guidelines on Employee Selection Procedures," issued by the Equal Employment Opportunity Commission, provide the legal guidelines regarding discrimination in the American workplace and should be consulted by any new business to avoid potentially adverse legal decisions.

The successful implementation of human resources for new ventures requires particular strategies and policies. First, it is important to recognize that the HR life cycle for new ventures begins before the organization even exists. Second, locating, hiring, and keeping entrepreneurs means developing specialized recruiting practices, individually rewarding good work, and properly assessing performance. Additionally, training must be provided to maximize the talent within the organization. Finally, all strategies and policies must adhere to legal guidelines in order to shield the organization from potentially disastrous litigation.

Craig M. Reddock
Old Dominion University

See also Human Resource Strategy; Labor Costs; Labor-Management Relations in Start-Ups; Leadership; Leadership: Training and Development; Learning Theory; Psychological Views; University Start-Ups

Further Readings

Gatewood, R. D., H. S. Feild, and M. Barrick. *Human Resource Selection*, 6th ed. Mason, OH: Thompson South-Western, 2008.

Goldstein, I. L. and J. K. Ford. *Training in Organizations*, 4th ed. Belmont, CA: Wadsworth, 2002.

Heneman, Robert L., Judith W. Tansky, and S. Michael Camp. "Human Resource Management Practices in Small and Medium-Sized Enterprises: Unanswered Questions and Future Research Perspectives." *Entrepreneurship Theory and Practice*, v.25/1 (Fall 2000).

Landy, F. J., ed. *Employment Discrimination Litigation*. San Francisco: Jossey-Bass, 2005.

Marvel, M. R., A. Griffin, J. Hebda, and B. Vojak. "Examining the Technical Corporate Entrepreneurs' Motivation: Voices From the Field." *Entrepreneurship Theory and Practice*, v.31/5 (2007).

Rotefoss, B. and L. Kolvereid. "Aspiring, Nascent and Fledgling Entrepreneurs: An Investigation of the Business Start-Up Process." *Entrepreneurship and Regional Development*, v.17/2 (2005).

Society for Industrial and Organizational Psychology. *Principles for the Validation and Use of Personnel Selection Procedures*, 4th ed. Bowling Green, OH: Author, 2003.

Import/Export Businesses

The import/export field has long been a fertile area for new venture creation. Even in the case of large economies such as the United States, international trade is vital to find markets for goods and services and to satisfy local demand. Whereas much international trade is carried out by large organizations, opportunities for niche traders abound. With modern communications decreasing the impediments to building and maintaining business relationships across international borders, along with improvements in international transport, entrepreneurial opportunities for import/export ventures are growing.

Opportunities for international trade exist for three main reasons: availability, status, and price. Some things cannot be grown or made in a country, or at least not using conventional methods. Even where they can, the country of origin may denote a particular status or quality that leads to a preference for importing over local production. In other cases, there can be a significant price difference in importing over local production, where one place has an abundance of resources needed to produce the item of interest.

The diffusion of technology around the world and the increasing diversity of consumption options are reducing some of the impetus for international trade. More than offsetting this, the rise of newly industrializing economies and growing affluence around the world are increasing opportunities for import/export businesses. These import/export businesses assume a variety of forms.

An export management company handles export operations for a domestic company that wants to sell its product overseas but that is either unable or unwilling to manage its own exporting. A management company contracted to undertake all the responsibilities would be involved in hiring dealers, distributors, and representatives; handling advertising, marketing, and promotions; overseeing marking and packaging; arranging shipping; and sometimes arranging financing. Management companies usually specialize by product, foreign market, or both and are paid by some mix of commission and base income. Where the company takes title to the goods, it effectively acts as a distributor in its own right.

An export trading company acts as the link between buyers overseas and local sources of supply. Its clients are companies in overseas markets that are looking to source raw materials, components, or services for whom the trading company locates and contracts suppliers to satisfy the client's need. The trader might take title to the goods or work on a commission basis.

An import/export merchant purchases goods in one market for distribution in another. The merchant purchases goods directly from a domestic or foreign manufacturer and then packs, ships, and resells the goods on their own account. This means that being a merchant is potentially riskier than being a management or trading company, but the potential rewards are correspondingly higher. Import/export merchants may operate without a specific client base for which the goods are imported or exported. Rather, they may have relationships with a large pool of potential buyers and seek to interest them in the individual goods they purchase.

For new import/export ventures, key decisions are to determine who the potential clients will be, which geographic areas will be drawn from or sold to, and what specific products or services will be handled. Potentially all products—from large, complex technological goods such as aircraft to components and consumer goods—are open to international trade. Typically, trading companies start through individuals who have knowledge and familiarity with a particular field of technology that leads them to identify trading opportunities. As a network of contacts and familiarity with industry jargon and procedures are required, this entrepreneur's prior industry experience gives the new trading venture a considerable advantage.

Whatever the starting point, identifying a specific niche is important too. As Kenneth Weiss says in his guide to building an import/export business, finding something new, different, and desirable to trade places the new venture entrepreneur at an advantage. If that is not feasible, it is still possible to succeed provided that the new venture performs better in purchasing and marketing, that is, more cheaply or more effectively than competitors. Finding a market niche helps achieve this. Such a niche might, again, be a specific type of product or service or might have to do with the end user targeted (whether that be the mass-market consumer, heavy industry, light industry, medical providers or hospitals, government, other businesses, or professionals). Niches can also concentrate on the locations dealt with and the trade channels utilized (by means of direct sales, representatives, or distributors).

Managing payment terms is a critical consideration for import/export businesses, because determining appropriate prices and setting payment terms is much more complicated when trading internationally than domestically. In international trade there are several means of payment, each of which has advantages and disadvantages. Open account is the most widely used method of payment in international trade, but it is also the riskiest for the independent trader. With an open account, goods are dispatched to the buyer and paid for subsequently in response to invoices requesting payment for specific batches of goods. As a small exporter setting out in business, this method may be the only one available. Conversely, a small importer is unlikely to be offered an open account.

Payment in advance is an arrangement whereby the entity acquiring the goods pays in advance of receiving them. It relieves the exporter of any uncertainty that payment will be received but exposes the importer to risk that the order will not be fulfilled, at least in the expected time or to the expected quality.

A letter of credit goes some way to allowing the trading parties to share the risks to which they are exposed. The letter of credit is basically a letter written by an importer's bank communicated to the exporter's bank indicating that, when certain specified documents are received (essentially documents confirming that the expected goods are in transit), payment for the shipment will be released. The risks of this method of payment involve mainly the uncertainty concerning the banks' credit standing and their trustworthiness in effecting the expected payment transfers.

The point at which goods change ownership, the allocation of responsibility for completing customs documentation, and the extent to which prices cover shipment costs are additional areas of negotiation. These terms may be settled individually, but most trade is conducted according to one of a choice of standard terms, the so-called International Commercial Terms (Incoterms). The most frequently utilized are free on board (FOB) and cost, insurance and freight (CIF). With FOB, the seller is responsible for all necessary documentation and costs in shipping the goods to an international carrier. CIF gives the exporter responsibility for all freight costs to the destination country and insurance costs to the point of arrival. There are 13 Incoterms and much subtlety in the operation of each, and import/export firms must be familiar with them all.

Many more enterprises are engaged in international trade than those operating as import/export businesses. With regard to this larger population of small enterprises, most research focuses on participation in exporting, as this is assumed to have more significance for business and economic growth than importing. Broadly, the factors encouraging participation in exporting can be classified as originating either internally or externally to the enterprise and according to whether a venture recognizes opportunities for exporting proactively or reacts to opportunities that are put in its way.

Internal and proactive stimuli involve the exploitation of economies of scale, growth and profit goals, possession of a unique product/technology, managerial aspirations, and marketing advantages. Internal and reactive stimuli are risk diversification, need for off-season sales, and the utilization of excess capacity.

External and proactive stimuli are the identification of overseas market opportunities and the influence of change agents in promoting export development (such as import/export agents, business development agencies, and business partners). External and reactive stimuli are receipt of unsolicited orders and problems in expanding sales in the domestic market.

The key decisions in developing an export venture involve market selection, export market entry strategies, product policy, pricing, financing, marketing, and distribution. Broad alternative strategies concern market concentration (focus on a small set of structurally similar countries) versus market spreading. Product policy involves decisions about new product development or redesign to fit demand overseas and then questions of whether to provide standardized offerings across markets or to customize them. Responses to these matters should be informed by the characteristics of the venture (such as the product type and production methods) and the characteristics of the market served (for example, some markets and some products may require adaptation to fit local tastes or regulatory standards). As scale economies and price-based competition are likely to be most important for standardized offerings, new ventures are expected to be associated with nonprice advantages, such as customer responsiveness and production methods, that are sufficiently flexible to adapt to local preferences.

Business strategy guru Michael Porter developed the idea that the level and nature of home-country demand are important influences on whether enterprises gain a competitive advantage to serve overseas markets. Supplying a sophisticated market at home requires firms to perform at a higher level than those supplying less well-developed markets. This idea has been challenged from the experience of small economies, where growth-minded entrepreneurs do not have the option of expanding their enterprises

Pricing and product availability, such as goods that cannot be grown or made in a country using conventional methods, create opportunities for international import and export trade. The U.S. Department of Commerce reports that American companies exported $509 billion in services in 2009. (Photos.com)

through domestic sales. Porter's idea is more geared to explaining which industries obtain a competitive advantage in overseas markets than to which enterprises do.

The study of enterprise participation in exporting has developed from simple resource-based perspectives to a more complex relational perspective and increasingly some form of contingency perspective. A resource-based interpretation explains participation in and success at exporting in terms of firm-specific capabilities and resources, such as the characteristics and experiences of enterprise managers. A relational perspective emphasizes how exporting depends on the development of a network of business relationships. This encourages a stages theory of small and medium enterprise (SME) internationalization in which there is an escalating commitment to serving overseas markets as firms accumulate experience and increase sales. Evidence that some new ventures— including so-called born-global enterprises— bypass a sequential process, internationalizing their operations from an early stage, challenges the relational perspective.

The contingency perspective on exporting has developed from the structure-conduct-performance framework for understanding business behavior. This framework makes two main assumptions: first, that the competitive intensity faced by an enterprise is a product of structural characteristics of the firm's market (such as the ability of rivals to replicate each other's actions), and second, that the firm's choice and execution of strategy can alleviate the competitive intensity by enabling the enterprise to build a position that rivals cannot match. Export ventures' competitive strategies are thus viewed as planned patterns of resource and capability deployments designed to address specific competitive contexts. The contingency perspective builds on this framework and examines exporting activity more broadly as a firm's strategic responses to the interplay of internal factors (such as managerial aspirations and capabilities) as well as external factors (such as market opportunity).

Martin Perry
Massey University

See also Culture and Entrepreneurship; Globalization; International Enterprise Planning; International Markets; International New Ventures; Measures of Entrepreneurial Activity Across Countries; Political Economy and Entrepreneurship

Further Readings

Bagchi-Sen, Sharmistha. "The Small and Medium Sized Exporters' Problems: An Empirical Analysis of Canadian Manufacturers." *Regional Studies*, v.33/3 (May 1999).

De Clercq, Dirk, Jolanda Hessels, and André Van Stel. "Knowledge Spillovers and New Ventures' Export Orientation." *Small Business Economics*, v.31/3 (October 2008).

Graham, John L. and Taylor W. Meloan. "Preparing the Exporting Entrepreneur." *Journal of Marketing Education*, v.8/1 (Spring 1986).

Light, Ivan, Min Zhou, and Rebecca Kim. "Transnationalism and American Exports in an English-Speaking World." *International Migration Review*, v.36/3 (Fall 2002).

Orser, Barbara, Martine Spence, Alan Riding, and Christine A. Carrington. "Gender and Export Propensity." *Entrepreneurship Theory and Practice*, v.34/5 (September 2010).

Sousa, C. and F. Bradley. "Antecedents of International Pricing Adaptation and Export Performance." *Journal of World Business*, v.43 (2007).

Sousa, C. and F. Bradley. "Effects of Export Assistance and Distributor Support on the Performance of SMEs: The Case of Portuguese Export Ventures." *International Small Business Journal*, v.27/6 (2009).

Weiss, K. *Building an Import/Export Business*, 4th ed. Hoboken, NJ: John Wiley & Sons, 2008.

INCORPORATION

In the United States, a corporation is formed, and therefore the life of the entity begins, with the filing and acknowledged receipt of a certificate of incorporation by the department of state of the state in which the entity is formed. In that home state, the corporation is referred to as a domestic corporation. The certificate of incorporation requires at a minimum the following information: the name of the corporation, the purpose for which the corporation is formed, the county within the state where the office of the corporation is to be located, the aggregate number of shares the corporation will have authority to issue, a designation of the appropriate state's secretary of state as the agent of the corporation upon whom process in any action or proceeding against it may be served, the post office address to which the secretary of state will mail a copy of any such process served, the duration of the corporation, and the signature of the incorporator.

Incorporation may be made by one or more natural persons age 18 or older. These persons are called incorporators. An incorporator may form a corporation whose shareholders, officers, and directors will be other persons. The incorporator is responsible for organizational procedures: filing the certificate of incorporation, electing original directors, and adopting the first bylaws.

A promoter is the person who typically comes up with the idea for the corporation and usually remains involved after the corporation is formed (as a director or shareholder). A promoter locates interested investors, finds needed personnel and property locations, and nurtures the idea or product that is the corporation's focus. The risk in being a promoter is incurring promoter's liability. When a corporate promoter enters into contracts on a corporation's behalf before the corporation comes into existence (before the certificate of incorporation is filed), the promoter can be liable when it is not clear to the other party to the contract that the promoter is acting on behalf of an entity. Promoters can also be personally liable when entering a contract for their own benefit or when entering a contract on the corporation's behalf and acknowledging to the other party that the corporation does not yet exist. The promoter can be liable under these scenarios especially if the contract requires performance prior to formation of the corporation. The promoter's only recourse is then to go back against the corporation and seek money to the extent that what he or she paid for actually benefited the corporation and not the promoter.

If the promoter is liable at some point in time, he or she remains liable on the contract even if the corporation takes on liability by adopting the contract liabilities at a board meeting or in the bylaws after the corporation is formed. At this point, the promoter can be released from liability only by the other party to the contract. A release of one party where another party (the corporation) steps in to pick up the liability (and this is all approved by the second party to the contract) is called novation.

A corporation is an artificial entity that is distinct from its owners (shareholders). Hence, the attractiveness of forming a corporation lies in the limited liability afforded the owners. A corporation can act only through its agents, directors, officers, or other corporate personnel. Thus, the only penal sanction against the corporation per se is to fine it, enjoin it from some illegal activity, or close it down (termed dissolution).

In addition to the required items, a certificate of incorporation may contain information regarding the internal affairs of the corporation or regarding the liability of directors. The name chosen for a new corporation cannot be confusingly similar to the name of any other corporation formed in the state, and the corporation's name must show that it is a corporation by using "Co.," "Inc.," or some similar designation as a part of the name.

Corporate bylaws are required by law. Bylaws may contain any provision relating to the business of the corporation, the conduct of its affairs, its rights or powers, or the rights or powers of its shareholders, directors, or officers. Bylaws relate to the internal workings of the corporation and are part of the corporation's records; they are not filed with the department of state.

Each state's statute addresses the responsibilities of the owners/directors of a corporation. Some responsibilities include maintaining the records of the corporation, including recording and retaining minutes of all meetings. The assets and liabilities of the corporation should be kept and maintained separately from those of the officers, directors, and shareholders of the corporation. The corporation must have a meeting of the shareholders annually for the election of directors and transacting other business. The corporation must also maintain records of these meetings in its corporate minutes. The corporation needs a checking account in its own name. Real estate taxes, franchise taxes, and other applicable taxes must be paid in a timely manner in order to maintain the corporation's good standing with the state in which it is formed. Under New York's state tax laws, for example, a corporation must file franchise tax reports and pay franchise tax annually even if the corporation does not conduct any business or loses money. Franchise tax obligations apply from the date the corporate existence begins, which is the date of filing by the department of state unless a later date is stated in the certificate of incorporation.

The certificate of incorporation may name the initial board of directors, but if it does not, the board of directors may be named at the corporation's "organizing meeting," which takes place after the certificate of incorporation has been filed. If the directors are named in the certificate of incorporation, the organization meeting is called the "organization meeting of directors"; if not, then the initial directors are appointed at the first meeting, which is called the "organization meeting of incorporators." Directors make initial decisions. These include accepting subscriptions to corporate stock, approving issuance of shares in return for consideration (usually money) exchanged for stock, designating corporate officers, and establishing their areas of authority. The bylaws are adopted, amended, or repealed by majority approval of either the board of directors or the shareholders entitled to vote. There are no technical requirements for bylaws, and no filing in a government office is required. Valid bylaws are binding on all shareholders, whether or not they expressly consent to them or even know what they state.

Corporate bylaws regulate the corporation's internal affairs. Generally, they deal with matters such as the date of annual shareholders' meetings, calling and conducting shareholders' and directors' meetings, titles and duties of officers, the number of directors, and any special quorum or voting requirements.

A fundamental difference in the formation of a partnership and a corporation concerns filing. Creating a corporation requires that a certificate of incorporation be filed with the secretary of state for the state in which the corporation is to be incorporated.

There are several types of incorporation available to an entrepreneur or new venture. The prevalent corporate structure is known as the C corporation, a general corporation that allows an unlimited number of shareholders. This is the form chosen by firms wishing to have more than 30 distinct shareholders or significant public stock offerings to raise funds. The advantage of the C corporation is limited liability for the shareholders whereby the maximum loss is the amount invested to purchase the shares. The shareholders' ability to influence the activities of the enterprise is dependent upon the percentage of ownership based on the amount of shares owned by an individual or block of shareholders.

A close corporation is more appropriate for an entrepreneur just starting out solo or with a limited number of associates. The major difference between a close corporation and a C corporation is that a close corporation is limited to 30 shareholders. Furthermore, several close corporation regulations stipulate that existing shareholders must first be offered potential new shares prior to offering shares to new shareholders. Another option for a new venture is to form a subchapter S corporation. The advantage of this form is that it allows entrepreneurs and small business owners to be taxed in a manner similar to that of a sole proprietorship or partnership. Specifically, the S corporation avoids the double taxation incidence, whereby the typical general C corporation pays taxes on profits and distributed dividends are also taxed as personal income. The S corporation provides the best context for new ventures and small business owners, given its single tax incidence, limited liability, and the legal status as an entity. Limitations include U.S. citizenship or permanent residency, a maximum of 75 shareholders, the fact that only one class of shares is allowed, and other legal limitations.

In practice, the most common form utilized by entrepreneurs and small business owners is the limited liability company (LLC) because of its combination of limited liability and taxation status of sole proprietor or partnership agreement.

Dominic DePersis
Broome Community College
Alfred Lewis
Hamline University

See also Branding; Business Models; Contracts and Trust; Partnerships; Patent Protection; Taxes; Trademarks

Further Readings

Diamond, Michael R. *How to Incorporate: A Handbook for Entrepreneurs and Professionals.* New York: Wiley, 2010.

Mancuso, Anthony. *The Corporate Records Handbook.* Berkeley, CA: Nolo Press, 2011.

Mancuso, Anthony. *Incorporate Your Business: A Legal Guide to Forming a Corporation in Your State.* Berkeley, CA: Nolo Press, 2011.

Petrova, M. with P. Arora. "Corporate Social Performance, Resource Dependence and Firm Performance." *Journal of Business Economics*, Special Issue, forthcoming.

INCUBATORS

The term *incubator* (or *business incubator*) is defined as a suite of resources that support and encourage the development of new businesses. Today, incubators have emerged as an economic development tool for nurturing new and small companies. Incubators can be seen as intermediate firms that perform a bridging function between promising start-ups and resources required in their developmental stages, while protecting them from potential failure. Incubators may also act as links between start-ups and other stakeholders that provide resources, such as governments, financial institutions, and business networks. In many ways, incubators function as mechanisms for technology transfer while encouraging the development of small businesses.

The term incubator is adopted from other fields, such as medicine and the health sciences, and relates to the notions of nurseries, starter units, and hatcheries. In hospitals, incubators are facilities where prematurely born infants are nurtured, receiving temporary care under controlled conditions to enable them to be viable and independent. Similarly, business incubators nurture young firms and help them survive during the early years of their establishment, when they are most vulnerable. The infrastructure of business incubators was first built in the United States. A real estate company in Batavia, New York, was recorded as the first business incubator when it bought a huge multistory building, divided it into small units, and leased those units to tenants.

Incubators also find their roots in universities aiming to give academic staff and students the opportunity to commercialize their research ideas. University-related incubators emerged as tools for fostering new-technology business ventures by merging the concepts of commercialization of university research and technology transfer. Later, this concept expanded and more actors were involved: from private business, business associations, governments, and financial institutions. Nowadays many more incubators have been established to meet regional economic objectives and facilitate business programs. Consequently, the primary objective of incubators has expanded to include not only commercialized research products from universities but also other privately and publicly driven initiatives to create new small firms.

With their expanding roles, incubators can differ by location (whether near a university, proximal to the inner city, or inside a science park), objective (whether oriented toward developing for-profit or nonprofit ventures, specific technologies, or new regional jobs), infrastructure (whether primarily physical, virtual, centralized, or distributed across different places), and actors involved (whether university, private, or government personnel).

The basic characteristics of incubators can be grouped into two dimensions, by objectives and by target areas. The first dimension, objectives, can be further divided into two extreme poles, profit-focused and nonprofit-focused. Profit-focused incubators are those whose objective is to see the new firm make a profit. Nonprofit-focused incubators, on the other hand, are those that focus on creating new firms with the goal of commercializing university technologies by developing them into products.

The objective of these nonprofit-focused incubators is to apply science to real products that can find a market.

The second dimension, target areas, can be broken down into incubators focused on local targets, regional targets, or industry-related targets. Incubators focused on local targets explore the potential of a local university or research center. Today, some big firms also have internal incubators to enable employees to start spin-offs as a part of their business strategy. Incubators with regional targets have a regional mission. Usually, government or business associations play a significant role in supporting this type of incubator. Finally, incubators can focus on industries, such as the electronics industry or the biotechnology industry, and are usually concerned with broad-reaching policies to increase the competitiveness of a nation.

Incubators have diverse characteristics, some of which are similar. In the first place, most incubators share the same objective: to support start-ups so they can survive and become independent. Next, most incubators function as policy instruments to transfer and commercialize technology, and thus most incubators have a link with universities or research centers as producers of knowledge, innovation, and new technologies that lead to new business ideas. In turn, universities and research centers have resources such as academics, libraries, and laboratories that can support product development once products are identified and spawn new-technology firms. Most incubators are flexible organizations, offering customized facilities and supporting services (although some of these facilities can be spread across different university buildings rather than reside in a central location).

During the incubation process, incubators offer several other types of support. These include shared business services (such as administrative support, accounting services, and security), shared equipment (such as phone systems, Internet connections, copier and fax machines), shared physical facilities (such as conference rooms and lunch rooms or cafeterias), and co-location in an incubator center (which provides the opportunity for networking with other entrepreneurs).

An important component of the incubation process is the procedure for selecting candidate "incubates." In this regard, two types of incubators have been identified: pure incubators and flagship models. Pure (also known as traditional) incubators are typically established by universities and seek to exploit university resources by producing firms that commercialize university research results. Flagship incubators, on the contrary, originate mainly from local (regional) governments or real estate developers and tend to be more profit-oriented. In the latter model, significant investment is required to initiate a project, and revenue streams are necessary to support operating costs. In pure or traditional incubators, founders of start-ups are often employed by or otherwise associated with universities, including research-focused scholars and faculty members (particularly scientists and engineers), most of whom lack entrepreneurial knowledge and skills. By contrast, the profit-oriented strategy urges incubators to attract as many new start-ups as possible and to open doors to potential entrepreneurs from outside universities.

During the incubation process, firms are located at incubators only on a temporary basis, typically three or four years, after which they are forced to leave the incubator, whose support will end. In practice, this time limit is often flexible. Overall, the incubation process can be seen as a function of several factors, external and internal. External factors include the involvement of stakeholders, regional economic conditions, and entrepreneurial culture. Internal factors are related to the various qualities of the incubator organizations themselves in managing resources to support start-ups, including procedures for selecting candidates, the mix of types of support provided, capability for monitoring and business coaching, and exit assessments. Studies of incubators have found that the roles of these external and internal factors relate positively to the survival of the new ventures they support.

Danny Soetanto
Lancaster University

See also Management Information Systems; Research and Development; Technology Transfer; University Start-Ups

Further Readings

Barrow, C. *Incubators: A Realist's Guide to the World's New Business Accelerators.* Chichester, UK: Wiley and Sons, 2001.

Bergek, A. and C. Norrman. "Incubator Best Practice: A Framework." *Technovation*, v.28/1–2 (2008).

Bollingtoft, A. and J. P. Ulhoi. "The Networked Business Incubator: Leveraging Entrepreneurial Agency?" *Journal of Business Venturing*, v.20/2 (2005).

Clarysse, B., M. Wright, A. Lockett, E. Van De Velde, and A. Vohora. "Spinning Out New Ventures: A Typology of Incubation Strategies From European Research Institutions." *Journal of Business Venturing*, v.20/2 (2005).

Grimaldi, R. and A. Grandi. "Business Incubators and New Venture Creation: An Assessment of Incubating Models." *Technovation*, v.25/2 (2005).

Hackett, S. M. and D. M. Dilts. "A Systematic Review of Business Incubation Research." *Journal of Technology Transfer*, v.29 (2004).

Hannon, P. D. and P. Chaplin. "Are Incubators Good for Business? Understanding Incubation Practice—the Challenges for Policy." *Environment and Planning C: Government and Policy*, v.21/6 (2003).

Knopp, L. 2006 *State of the Business Incubation Industry.* Athens, OH: National Business Incubation Association, 2007.

Phan, P. H., D. S. Siegel, and M. Wright. "Science Parks and Incubators: Observations, Synthesis and Future Research." *Journal of Business Venturing*, v.20/2 (2005).

Phillips, R. G. "Technology Business Incubators: How Effective as Technology Transfer Mechanisms?" *Technology in Society*, v.24/3 (2002).

Rice, M. P. "Co-Production of Business Assistance in Business Incubators: An Exploratory Study." *Journal of Business Venturing*, v.17/2 (2002).

Von Zedtwitz, M. "Classification and Management of Incubators: Aligning Strategic Objectives and Competitive Scope for New Business Facilitation." *International Journal of Entrepreneurship and Innovation Management*, v.3/1–2 (2003).

INFORMATION

Information is used throughout a new venture by all parties, including the entrepreneur, to initiate and develop the venture's foundation as well as to maintain and grow the business. It is the foundational building block for knowledge and is found in every facet of entrepreneurial and new ventures. Because "infoglut" can lead to an overload, there are tools to control the amount of information to which one is exposed; to discern the relevant aspects of information; to differentiate the forms of information; to assess integrity, veracity, and reliability; to enhance the security of data in areas such as privacy issues and confidentiality; and to educate entrepreneurs on numerous legal issues concerning ownership and duplication or use. Information is crucial to the entrepreneur, but the utility of the information must be weighed against the actual and perceived costs. These will vary and may become sunk costs, whether the entrepreneur is examining specific or general (publicly available) information. With various empirical studies linking new product success with the collection and utilization of information, the accessibility and utilization of information are very important to entrepreneurs.

In the new venture context, *information* is defined as meaningful, accurate, and timely data presented within a framework to enhance understanding and meaning. As such, it is a tool that can be used, transformed, molded, accepted, or ignored. Whereas information should be verifiable and reliable, some data given as information may be inherently false or may be proven false at a later time. Whereas information theory, introduced by Claude E. Shannon and Warren Weaver, looks to information as irrelevant when considering its transmission, the semiotics of words and situations deems all data to have meaning, regardless of its transmission. Information can be transferred to and by any one of all five senses.

Information is different and distinct from knowledge. Knowledge requires understanding, perception, or reasoning, whereas information simply requires an acknowledgment of fact or perceived fact. Knowledge combines information to create a more holistic picture or understanding than is possible when simply examining information. Whereas the possession of knowledge requires information, the passage or possession of information does not require knowing the information. Indeed, today, information can be transmitted without people actually possessing it, as occurs with the transmission of information via the Internet.

Information encompasses many aspects of the law. Not only is the law based on information; it also pertains to information usage, distribution, ownership, and creation. Whereas each nation has laws pertaining to information, nations are also governed in the international arena by treaties and agreements, such as the Buenos Aires Convention and the Berne Convention for the Protection of Literary and Artistic Works, both of which protect authors' ownership of their work for varying periods following the author's death. This protection recognizes the proprietary nature of information and is recognized nationally and internationally as copyright law, which is subject to nation-specific legislation that assigns ownership of the information and intellectual property.

Because new ventures are often founded on a unique advantage, the security of information is important. This involves numerous elements, such as integrity, privacy, and confidentiality. The exact use of information depends upon the type of information, authentication, and nonrepudiation to ensure security. Information security ensures the consistency of information and noninterference with that information. It further refers to the confidentiality, integrity, and availability (or CIA triad) of data or information. Although information can be utilized for numerous purposes, the actual data remain immutable. Different countries have different laws and different understandings of security of information such that in some countries the moral or intellectual rights of the creators are recognized. However, the application of this legislation varies extensively.

Some information accessed by entrepreneurs originates from perceptions and postulation that the information may or may not be verifiable. The veracity of the information is important when developing wealth-creating opportunities. This information may be discovered accidentally, through prior experience and knowledge, or by searching. The search may be facilitated by individuals and businesses with access to information channels. Some information is listed in databases or is published in written reports, requiring the entrepreneur to use data-mining tools, including algorithms, to find specific data or to explore multidimensional relationships to build new data or information. These databases may be computerized or facilitated through information and communication technologies (ICT), requiring both the tools to download the information and access to the databases, which may be proprietary. These channels offer information that must be scrutinized in light of the peculiarities of the new venture under consideration. When information that matches the needs is found, the information is incorporated into the knowledge base. Information ownership may exclude it from public dissemination or require those wanting access to the information to pay a fee that is structured by the owner. Once the information is collected or downloaded, it must be processed by the entrepreneur to supply additional information that can be analyzed to yield knowledge.

Accompanying the increasing access to information is the possibility of breaking down the silos into which information has been placed as the individual disciplines developed. This allows the entrepreneur easier access to information from the many disciplines—such as accounting, marketing, and management—necessary in new ventures. The growing use of ICT eases the passage of information and increases the firm's ability to interact with customers and the entrepreneurship's ability to collect and utilize information. The instantaneous passage of information exacerbates the difficulties of partial information and the tendencies for decisions to be made without complete information. Whereas information may have enhanced importance, it is only one facet of the knowledge necessary for new ventures.

Information is increasingly easy for entrepreneurs to access through Web 2.0 and the emergence of technologies such as cloud computing and 3-D communication accessible via mobile telephones and other handheld devices. Information stored in electronic networks or saved to desktops that are connected to the Internet is open to the risk of piracy, hacking, and other forms of information theft. Unfortunately, this has resulted in an increasing disregard of intellectual property and ownership. It also opens the entrepreneurship to examination by investors, venture capitalists, and angels. Thus, the security of information is of growing importance as the world increasingly connects through electronic and virtual networks. This is especially true given the potential for information to remain accessible long after the information is no longer valid, the individual owning or related to the information has died, or the circumstances creating the information no longer exist.

Within entrepreneurship, accurate and timely information is important in decision making and planning. The timeliness of information is a crucial element for entrepreneurs, given the utility of knowledge and the ease of exploitation of the preexisting information. The origins of the information may determine its value to the entrepreneur. For example, information obtained in the local marketplace may not be of significance to the entrepreneur who is looking to enter the national or global arena. The value of information is determined by its compliance with intended use. Similarly, information that is believed to be factual but is not, such as that obtained during a crisis, may be of mixed value in its application and may ultimately worsen the situation. Furthermore, information may be ignored, as when individuals acknowledge knowing about a breach of ethics, laws, or human rights, as in counterfeiting, all while unilaterally moving ahead despite the breach. Such cases may reflect the cultural dynamics of the region as well as the nonconformity of information and statistics provided by different countries. This delivery of information can take several forms, each with positive and negative perspectives. Thus, information for entrepreneurs choosing to enter the global arena necessitates additional work and verification.

Information searches may involve trusted information channels (such as friends and confidants), government offices, trade publications, trade shows, accountants, attorneys, and business associates. The context of information can take multiple forms, especially with the ease of accessibility afforded by the information age with the emergence of Web 3.0. Information can be developed and published by private individuals using online publishers and private Websites. This complicates the task of entrepreneurs. With the emergence of Web 3.0 and the ease of publication of video, documents, and pictures, the dissemination of information is easier. Few individuals are truly independent commentators or information providers and receivers, because each individual is subject to his or her own psychological and sociological history. Thus, although the responsibility for the use or knowledge created by (mis) information has now become an individual matter, the information and its veracity and reliability remain lodged firmly in the time frame and situation for the entrepreneur.

Information provided through theory and studies may change over the course of time as instrumentation is developed to enhance precision and disciplines continue to evolve. Theory is information that guides and facilitates the entrepreneurs' development of knowledge, but the knowledge that is cultivated may contribute to the evolution of new information. Thus, information that is accurate at one point in time may be incorrect at a later time or in a different situation, indicating that information is not necessarily a truth that will withstand time, environmental change, or examination using a different set of standards. That is, information may be peculiar to an individual or distinct group at a specific time in a specific environment. Information may not be universal or eternal, resulting in the need for entrepreneurs to continually monitor and explore the environment for updated and new information. One means of doing this is by monitoring RSS feeds, now offered through multiple electronic information channels.

The potential universal dispersal of information and the comprehension of the diversity of entrepreneurs raise the issue of information ethics. Whereas this field emerged in 1979 with work done by Barbara Kostrewski and Charles Oppenheim, it has evolved with time to include ICT, the media, libraries, and other sources of information. The field of information ethics looks to enhance the quantity, quality, and variety of information publicly available. These ethics have now become a topic of international and global organizations, such as the United Nations Educational, Scientific and Cultural Organization (UNESCO). With the globalization of information and information dispersal, the applicable ethics are hotly debated with regard to relativism and moral imperialism. Entrepreneurs also may be impacted by other codes of ethics, such as ethics for social entrepreneurs, or may develop their own codes of ethics specifically designed to apply to their industry or their new venture. These are based on the information and practices most pertinent to the entrepreneur.

The levels of risk concerning information are especially important for new ventures; risk affects entrepreneurs' ability to earn sufficient income to retain their assets in production of profit. Entrepreneurs' belief that they are able to manage information with privacy and limited distribution encourages them to enter markets. Their ability to read and interpret the information available through their private channels reduces their risk to an acceptable level by allowing them to select the most profitable environment with ready access to information channels and tolerable trade-offs between risk and cost. However, information that will reduce a risk can be proprietary and can be controlled by the entrepreneur to reduce others' chances of success in the same market.

The optimal reduction of risk for entrepreneurships occurs with innovation. Entrepreneurs innovate to create a sustainable, competitive, or unique advantage in the marketplace. Successful innovation

depends on information about the marketplace, competitors, and multiple environments, including political, social, economic, technological, and legal. Information forms the basis of knowledge. Entrepreneurs seek and find unseen opportunities within the environment in their quest to establish successful new ventures, and in order to do so they must incorporate information from many environments into their analyses. Thus, entrepreneurs are wholly dependent upon information, from the initial seed of an idea through the formation of a new venture to the successful implementation of strategies leading to expansion of the business.

Ina Freeman
Jones International University
Amir Hasnaoui
Groupe Sup de Co La Rochelle and Centre de Recherche Télécom École de Management

See also Communication Styles; E-Commerce; Globalization; Human Resource Strategy; Knowledge; Leadership; Learning; Management Information Systems

Further Readings

Fiet, James O. "The Informational Basis of Enterpreneurial Discovery." *Small Business Economics*, v.8/6 (1996).
Fiet, James O. "A Prescriptive Analysis of Search and Discovery." *Journal of Management Studies*, v.44/4 (2007).
Kirzner, I. *Discovery and the Capitalist Process*. Chicago: University of Chicago Press, 1985.
Kostrewski, Barbara and Charles Oppenheim. "Ethics in Information Science." *Journal of Information Science*, v.1/5 (1979).
Nelson, George W. "Information Needs of Female Entrepreneurs." *Journal of Small Business Management*, v.25/3 (July 1987).
Sanyal, Paroma, and Catherine L. Mann. "The Financial Structure of Startup Firms: The Role of Assets, Information, and Entrepreneur Characteristics." *Research Review*, v.14 (July–December 2010).
Shannon, Claude E. and Warren Weaver. *The Mathematical Theory of Communication*. Chicago: University of Illinois Press, 1949.
Subhash, K. B. "Venture Capital Financing and Corporate Governance: Role of Entrepreneurs in Minimizing Information/Incentive Asymmetry and Maximization of Wealth." *Journal of Wealth Management*, v.12/2 (Fall 2009).

INFRASTRUCTURE

Entrepreneurs contribute significantly to economic growth by innovating and creating jobs. An entrepreneur's personal characteristics can play an important role in this process, but without the availability of essential resources, including appropriate infrastructures, success can be limited. *Infrastructure* can be defined as both the physical and the social resources necessary to succeed in new ventures. Having access to appropriate infrastructures enhances the likelihood that entrepreneurs will exploit their personal characteristics, their ideas, and their potential. On the other hand, entrepreneurs in transitioning countries often face formal, informal, and environmental barriers that can block access to infrastructure and therefore inhibit their ventures' success.

Well-established infrastructures reduce transaction costs by reducing the effect of distance between regions and integrating markets, thereby reducing unnecessary burdens on entrepreneurs. A well-established transportation and communications infrastructure, for example, provides an opportunity for populations in the rural areas of less developed countries to get involved in new economic activity and access the information necessary for the new ventures. Effective and efficient modes of transportation require well-maintained roads and efficient and reliable air transportation; these are necessary not only to transport products and services but also to allow entrepreneurs to network with other entrepreneurs. A dependable communications infrastructure is important for the rapid flow of information as well as for the reduction of the "digital divide"; information allows entrepreneurs to communicate with decision makers and business communities and take all relevant considerations into account during the decision-making process.

For entrepreneurs, this adds an additional financial burden. Extensive and efficient physical infrastructures are important for creating and establishing new ventures as well as for the management of new ventures. These infrastructures are even more important for entrepreneurs in less developed countries, as these countries move from one stage of competitiveness to another. Michael Porter defined competitiveness based on the country's economic development. He identified three stages: the

After Kenya gained independence from the British in 1963, Nairobi, pictured above, became the capital of the new republic. The city grew rapidly, straining the existing infrastructure. In less developed countries, an efficient transportation and communications infrastructure provides the opportunity for economic activity and new business ventures. (Photos.com)

factor-driven stage, the efficiency-driven stage, and the innovation-driven stage. Countries positioned in the factor-driven stage have a competitive advantage in terms of supplying low-cost commodities; they have fewer value-added products and rely heavily on natural resources. Therefore, effective infrastructure is important to mobilize these resources. At the innovation-driven stage, consumers demand sophisticated products, which requires more innovative activity. At the innovation-driven stage, innovation, rather than primary or raw products, becomes the tool for attaining competitive advantage.

In many developing countries, government has monopoly power over the creation and management of infrastructures. There is little competition, which leads to inefficient infrastructure service to citizens. Users also have little say in demand, since cost does not truly reflect the demand. Therefore, adequate quantity and reliability of infrastructure are needed for entrepreneurs to transport their products and services or to participate in important events. Users and managers of these infrastructures lack adequate resources; roads might not always be accessible; telecommunications might not be always available. For instance, power is important to entrepreneurs in the manufacturing industry. Availability of power can improve workers' productivity by allowing them to use improved machinery. However, loss of power is common in many emerging countries. Therefore, the quantity of infrastructure as well as the quality of infrastructure is important for new ventures as a country moves through various stages of development.

Social infrastructures include education and healthcare. A population with a high level of human capital is important for moving through various stages of competitive advantage. Human capital also contributes to the entrepreneurial activity. Human capital can be acquired knowledge as well as the management of knowledge. For entrepreneurs and early ventures to thrive, they need access to significant amounts of human capital. However, both formal and informal rules that are influenced by culture influence the importance placed on attaining an education. In many developing countries, the social infrastructure dictates that earnings to support family are more important than attaining an education. Basic education increases the efficiency of individuals by enabling them to adapt to changing conditions better than those who have no education. Countries at the efficiency-driven stage can use populations with little education to attract low-innovation industries, since workers with little formal education can carry out simple manual work. However, as entrepreneurs create more technologically advanced products from simple production processes, having a workforce with higher education can be very valuable.

Another important factor is the poor distribution of healthcare resources in developing countries. Healthy entrepreneurs and healthy workers are vital for productivity, whereas unhealthy entrepreneurs and workers can contribute to the loss of productivity and a lower level of efficiency. The poor health of family members can also contribute to the loss of productivity by tying up workers' monetary resources as well as their time.

Culture influences the development of certain personality traits as well as various social norms. Formal and informal cultural rules can be maintained by a society even if these do not result in efficient and effective entrepreneurial strategies. Informal rules are harder to change than formal rules, since informal rules are habitual. Geert Hofstede's cultural components include four dimensions: power distance, uncertainty avoidance, individualism-collectivism,

and masculinity. Individualistic culture promotes risk taking, self-orientation, and the pursuit of individual goals, which in turn promotes the importance of education. As the pools of well-educated people in a population increase, entrepreneurs are better able to find workers who can adapt to the rapidly changing business environment.

On the other hand, collectivist culture promotes deference to collective goals at the expense of personal goals. In order for new ventures to succeed, it is imperative for society as a whole, including social infrastructures driving public policies, to support risk-taking behavior and the promotion of individual goals, since personal goals may not always align with collective goals. Individualistic societies are also more accepting of the failures of new ventures than are collectivist societies. Whereas an argument can be made in favor of the avoidance of failure, failure has positive effects; it gives entrepreneurs an opportunity to learn and improve their entrepreneurial competence rather than maintain the status quo. Job security is an important feature that attracts nonentrepreneurs to the status quo.

For developing countries, "job security" is more important for meeting the basic needs of families than is searching for or taking advantage of an opportunity. Given this social infrastructure, an entrepreneur in a developing nation is taking an enormous risk in starting a new venture. The organizational structure, institutional structure, and availability of resources may influence this decision. Moreover, for entrepreneurs in developing countries, poorly regulated institutional structures create an uncertain environment where the "rules of the game" are not known. For example, corruption is a social norm in many developing countries, where paying bribes to officials is often expected and serves as a deterrent to engaging in new ventures. Some have argued that corruption offers a means for underrepresented populations in the developing countries to pursue their entrepreneurial motivations. However, policies need to be set in place to encourage entrepreneurs to pursue their intentions and goals.

Starting a new venture and making it successful require a combination of various resources, not the least of which are physical and social infrastructures conducive to the success of new ventures. All entrepreneurs are faced by barriers, but governments, especially in developing nations, can make the task easier by creating and cultivating adequate infrastructures.

Farzana Chowdhury
Indiana University

See also Business Models; Distribution; E-Commerce; Entrepreneurial Marketing; Entrepreneurial Support Systems; Entrepreneurs in Energy; Entrepreneurs in Transportation; Family Business; Franchises: Starting; Geographic Location; Incubators; Insurance; International New Ventures; Location Strategy; Microfinance; Public Policy: Government Stimulation of Start-Ups; Technology Transfer

Further Readings

Hofstede, Geert. *Culture's Consequences: International Differences in Work-Related Values.* Beverly Hills, CA: Sage, 1980.

Hofstede, Geert et al. "Culture's Role in Entrepreneurship: Self-Employment Out of Dissatisfaction." In *Innovation, Entrepreneurship and Culture: The Interaction Between Technology, Progress and Economic Growth,* J. Ulijn and T. Brown, eds. Cheltenham, UK: Edward Elgar, 2004.

Inglehart, Ronald. *Culture Matters: How Values Shape Human Progress.* Lawrence Harrison and Samuel Huntington, eds. New York: Basic Books, 2000.

Porter, Michael. *The Competitive Advantage of Nations.* New York: Free Press, 1990.

INITIAL PUBLIC OFFERING

An initial public offer or offering (IPO) occurs when a company issues common stock to the general investing public for the first time. An IPO is a pivotal event, because it provides the first opportunity for a stock market to react to the publicly available information about a company's competitive strategies. Firms choose to raise capital in public equity markets for a number of reasons. The first, and most obvious, is to finance growth strategies. The IPO provides access to large amounts of equity capital and the ability to restructure the firm's balance sheet (for example, retire debt) and provide funding for new investment. An IPO also provides the firm's initial investors a mechanism for exiting or "harvesting" their investment. An IPO can help firms launch new products, enter new markets, attract employees, and potentially improve the firm's long-term survival.

Finally, an IPO increases a firm's legitimacy within the business community. The following review outlines the steps in the IPO process, identifies ways to measure and improve performance, and highlights the growth in IPOs around the world.

The first step in the IPO process is to secure an investment bank to serve as the lead underwriter. The company and the investment bank will meet to negotiate the amount of money the company wants to raise, the type of securities to issue, and the details in the underwriting agreement. In a "firm commitment" underwriting agreement, the underwriter guarantees that a certain amount will be raised. To accomplish this, the underwriter buys the entire issue from the corporation and then reoffers it to the public. In a "best effort" underwriting agreement, the underwriter does not guarantee the amount of capital raised by the issue. Underwriters often form syndicates with other banks in order to underwrite IPOs, share in the risk of underwriting the IPO, and aid in selling the new issue.

The next major step in the IPO process is for the underwriter and issuing firm to file a "registration statement" with the Securities and Exchange Commission (SEC) to comply with the Securities Act of 1933. The registration statement contains detailed financial statements, background information, and ownership levels of the issuing firm's officers and directors and discloses how the firm intends to use the IPO proceeds. After filing the registration statement, the SEC requires the firm to observe a "cooling off" period while the SEC reviews the registration statement. During the cooling off period, the underwriter will often issue a "preliminary prospectus" (also referred to as a "red herring"). The red herring contains much of the same information found in the registration statement. However, the final offer price and the issue date (effective date) of the new issue are not contained in the preliminary prospectus. The underwriter and issuing firm use the preliminary prospectus as a selling document when they go on a "road show" to create interest in the IPO among targeted investors. During the cooling off period, the underwriter can receive only "indications of interest" from those interested in the issue. Once the registration statement has cleared SEC approval, a final prospectus, which includes the final offer price and the underwriting spread, is made available.

Industry experts and academics use a handful of ways to gauge IPO performance. These measures include the total proceeds raised and the percentage premium investors pay for the firm's shares above their pre-IPO book value. However, the most widely used method is to assess the degree in which the IPO is "underpriced" by calculating the percentage difference between the initial price of the stock (offer price) and the price of the stock at the end of the first day of trading. An underpriced IPO represents "money left on the table" in that the issuing firm fails to fully capture the value investors place in a new issue. IPO underpricing is quite pervasive across capital markets, and in the United States it was 7.4 percent in the 1980s, 15 percent in the 1990s, and averaged 65 percent in 1999–2000. Some consider underpricing to be a mechanism underwriters use to ensure that they sell all of their available shares so they can retain their full selling commission. Others see underpricing as a means to generate interest in the IPO and boost the public profile of the firm. Academics often attribute informational asymmetries between issuers and investors as the underlying reason for poor IPO performance.

Strengthening the issuing firm's corporate governance is a primary mechanism firms can use to reduce informational asymmetries with potential investors and improve their IPOs' performance. Incentive alignment mechanisms with company insiders in the form of retained ownership, stock options, or similar mechanisms can help convey to potential investors that managerial interests are aligned with those of minority investors. Likewise, monitoring mechanisms, such as boards with a majority of independent directors (or similar mechanisms), convey to potential investors that company executives will be actively monitored. The certification or endorsement of influential third parties, such as highly reputable underwriters, venture capital, and audit firms, can also improve IPO performance. However, it is important to note that the governance and certification mechanisms that affect IPO performance on one stock exchange may not necessarily work the same way in other capital markets.

Today, increasing numbers of private firms from around the world are taking advantage of public equity markets to raise capital. Historically, firms were confined by legal reasons to offer their shares only on the exchanges of their countries of origin. However, decreased regulation along with increased competition for financing sources has prompted many nondomestic firms, especially those from emerging market countries, to bypass their local stock exchanges and issue IPOs on the New York, London, or Asian stock exchanges. Indeed, the accelerating pace of global capital market integration since the 1990s has greatly increased the opportunities available to firms around the world, from small entrepreneurial firms to former state-owned entities, to raise capital through an IPO.

R. Greg Bell
University of Dallas

See also Agency Theory; International Markets; Measures of Performance

Further Readings

Bell, R. Greg, Curt Moore, and Hussam Al-Shammari. "Country of Origin and Foreign IPO Legitimacy: Understanding the Role of Geographic Scope and Insider Ownership." *Entrepreneurship, Theory and Practice*, v.32 (2008).

Carter, Richard, Frederick Dark, and Ajai Singh. "Underwriter Reputation, Initial Returns and the Long-Run Performance of IPO Stocks." *Journal of Finance*, v.53 (1998).

Certo, S. Trevis, Tim Holcomb, and R. Michael Holmes Jr. "IPO Research in Management and Entrepreneurship: Moving the Agenda Forward." *Journal of Management*, v.35 (2009).

Loughran, Tim and Jay Ritter. "Initial Public Offerings: International Insights." *Pacific-Basin Finance Journal*, v.2 (1994).

Innovation Advantage

The topic of innovation garners a great deal of interest, but it is most salient to the new venture context. Zoltan Acs and David Audretsch compared data from numerous studies that assess innovation and found that small firms contribute about two and a half times more innovations per employee than large firms. Despite the large firms' reputation, resources, and expertise, it is in the new venture context that the majority of innovations in society are created. Whereas entrepreneurs are recognized as a leading source of innovation, they may also be unique in the nature of innovations they systematically introduce.

History shows that technology evolves through periods of incremental change that are then punctuated by breakthroughs that either enhance or destroy the competence of existing firms across multiple industries. Competence-enhancing innovations are those improvements that build on existing know-how within a particular product category. These competence-enhancing innovations can substitute for older technologies, although the knowledge and skills required to create them are similar to those used to produce the previous generation. On the other hand, competence-destroying innovations are fundamentally unique. They are typically brought about by new firms and can either create a new product class or substitute for an existing product—such as steam versus combustion engines. Competence-destroying innovations often lower barriers to entry, allowing new firms to enter previously impenetrable markets by exploiting the technology. These types of innovations favor new ventures at the expense of established firms because they take advantage of new and fundamentally different knowledge.

James Utterback first discussed how varying types of innovation and their rate over time changes as an industry matures. For example, early in the industry life cycle, the rate of product innovation is considerably greater than the rate of process innovations. He referred to this period as the fluid phase, during which a great deal of experimentation with product design and operations takes place among rivals. During the fluid phase, there is a high degree of product innovation and much less attention is given to the processes that develop the product. After the fluid phase is the transitional phase, during which the rate of product innovation begins to decrease while the rate of process innovation increases. At this point in time within an industry, the product variety begins to give way to standardized designs that have been accepted in the market. As the product becomes more standardized, the rate of innovation in the way it is developed increases. Some industries enter a final specific phase in which both product and process innovations are greatly reduced. Another well-known scholar, Clayton Christensen, has described innovation in terms of disruptive versus sustainable and has illustrated the effects using the disk drive industry. He describes a disruptive innovation as a new technology, product, or service that eventually overturns the existing dominant technology in the market despite the facts that the disruptive technology is both fundamentally different from the leading technology and may initially perform worse than the leading technology in

terms of existing performance measures. Disruptive technologies eventually dominate a market either by fulfilling a role that the older technology could not fill or by moving up market through performance improvements until finally displacing other incumbents. In contrast, a sustaining technology refers to the successive incremental improvements to performance that incumbents incorporate into their existing products.

Among the most common ways of framing innovation are incremental as opposed to radical. Radical innovations are revolutionary discontinuous changes; incremental innovations are conventional extensions of a line of historical improvements. Scholars have long distinguished among radical and incremental innovations, although not always using these words. For example, James March distinguished between exploitation of existing technology and exploration of new technology. Exploitation involves refining or expanding existing products or processes, whereas exploration requires something fundamentally new. Some innovations may be divided into two poles, radical breakthroughs and incremental improvements, although many new products fall into neither extreme category. As William Baumol explained, the electric light and the combustion engine must have surely been deemed radical, whereas successive models of dishwashers and refrigerators, with each model improving to some degree on the previous version, illustrate incremental innovation. When comparing inventions throughout history, it is clear that entrepreneurs create the vast majority of breakthroughs. For example, studies have examined innovation through patenting, and results show that a patent filed by a small firm is more likely than a patent filed by a large firm to be among the top one percent of most frequently cited patents. Most of the radical innovations of the past two centuries have been, and likely will continue to be, developed by new ventures.

Large established firms have historically not performed well in terms of creating breakthrough innovations. When a high degree of change is required, there are organizational challenges in large firms and resistance from groups with the required knowledge and expertise. Numerous explanations have emerged as to why new ventures tend to have an innovation advantage. The bureaucratic nature of large firms may not be conducive to the required risk taking. Breakthrough innovation, by its very nature, is

Entrepreneurs like Thomas Edison create the majority of breakthroughs and innovations in business. Edison's 1879–80 electric lamps were seen as radical at the time, whereas over the decades new models featuring new technology illustrate incremental innovation. (Wikimedia)

characterized by high degrees of uncertainty, which may be tolerated to a greater extent in new ventures. Given the profound impact of innovation on creating wealth and improving society, there is little doubt that interest in the topic will continue to surge. Innovation creation is a fundamental research issue in the field of entrepreneurship, and the topic is certain to receive increasing attention. Entrepreneurs remain the main catalyst for innovation, and evidence suggests there is much to learn from the new venture context.

Matthew R. Marvel
Western Kentucky University

See also Cognitive Schemas and Scripts; Corporate Entrepreneurship and Innovation; Feasibility Studies; Geography of Innovation; Incubators; Technology Transfer

Further Readings

Acs, Z. J. and D. B. Audretsch. "Innovation and Technological Change." In *Handbook of Entrepreneurship Research*, Z. J. Acs and D. B. Audretsch, eds. Boston: Kluwer Academic, 2003.

Baumol, W. J. *The Microtheory of Innovative Entrepreneurship*. Princeton, NJ: Princeton University Press, 2010.

Christensen, C. *The Innovator's Dilemma*. Cambridge, MA: Harvard Business School Press, 1997.

Leifer, R. et al. *Radical Innovation*. Boston: Harvard Business School Press, 2000.

Leonard-Barton, D. *Wellsprings of Knowledge*. Boston: Harvard Business School Press, 1995.

March, J. G. "Exploration and Exploitation in Organizational Learning." *Organization Science: A Journal of the Institute of Management Sciences*, v.2/1 (1991).

Marvel, M. R. "Knowledge Acquisition Asymmetries and Innovation Radicalness." *Journal of Small Business Management*, forthcoming.

Tushman, M. L. and P. Anderson. "Technological Discontinuities and Organizational Environments." *Administrative Sciences Quarterly*, v.31 (1986).

Utterback, J. M. *Mastering the Dynamics of Innovation*. Boston: Harvard Business School Press, 1994.

INNOVATION DIFFUSION

The diffusion of an innovation is the process by which an innovation is communicated to and adopted by potential users. Understanding why an innovation will be adopted or not, and at which pace, is obviously very important for new ventures. The understanding of the diffusion process goes hand in hand with the understanding of what is an innovation. An innovation is a product, a service, or an object that is perceived as new by potential adopters. Therefore, most new ventures will base their early development on an innovation (something perceived as new) and will aim at having this innovation adopted by (sold to) the highest number of potential clients.

Studies on the diffusion of innovation started in the 1960s, based on the seminal work conducted by the sociologist Everett M. Rogers. Although there have been many recent developments in and refinements of the diffusion processes, diffusions of innovation have always followed a basically similar process. Theoretically, the diffusion of an innovation follows a bell-shaped curve (or an S curve in cumulative percentage):

Adopters are categorized depending on how early or late they will adopt an innovation. The first

2.5 percent of adopters are named innovators; the next 13.5 percent are opinion leaders (or early adopters); and the next 34 percent are called the early majority. Together, these three groups form the first half of the total number of adopters. The next 34 percent are named late majority (late adopters), and the remaining 16 percent are termed laggards. This artificial categorization of adopters is used mostly to highlight the different behaviors of adopters and the consequences in terms of strategy and marketing. For example, the marketing mix for an early adopter (opinion leader) will not be the same as the marketing mix used for the late majority.

The most important point to understand before going more deeply into the details is that, for the developers of this theory, innovation is linked to perception. An invention is thus something new to *the* world, whereas an innovation is something perceived as new to *a* world of potential adopters. If there is no perception of newness and obviously if there is no knowledge about the new product or service, the model is not applicable. This implies that the first task of a company is to make sure that the innovation is known among the target population of potential adopters and that there is a clear perception of newness.

Once this is achieved, the main theoretical framework states that the rate of adoption of an innovation will be influenced by five perceived attributes: the relative advantage, the compatibility, the complexity, the trialability, and the observability.

The relative advantage is the most obvious attribute. It is defined as the degree to which an innovation is perceived as better than the available products or services. This can be measured in terms of quality, convenience, satisfaction, or price, but also as a social prestige factor.

The compatibility can be of two types. First, the compatibility in terms of technical features is obviously important: Is this application designed for the operating system of my computer or smartphone? Is this machine operating with the voltage used in my country? Is this television accepting full high-definition broadcasts? The second type of compatibility is at a higher level and has to do with the social norms in a group or a country. For example, eating snakes or insects is a common practice in some countries and would be seen as inappropriate

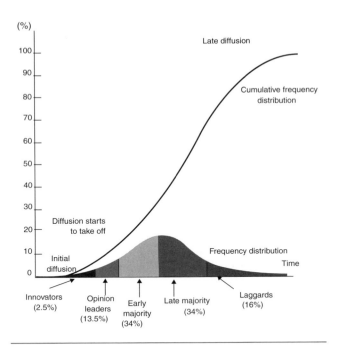

in others. Another example is the use of genetically modified organisms (GMOs) in agriculture, which is accepted in some regions of the world and forbidden in others. Social compatibility can also be connected to the religious beliefs or norms in certain countries, which would disapprove of or forbid certain practices, attitudes, or behaviors.

The complexity is also a rather obvious component in the decision to adopt an innovation. It concerns the perception of the difficulty of understanding, implementing, integrating, and using an innovation. If an innovation is easy to integrate (a new device as part of a home theater system or a new machine in a manufacturing plant) and to implement, potential adopters will have a positive attitude toward its adoption. Again, as we are dealing with perception, companies deal with the complexity factor through the design of the product or service and through the marketing strategy. For example, Apple has been doing this for decades when designing and presenting its products. From the iMac (with only two plugs) to the Apple television, this company has always favored a positioning of its products as less "complex" than the competition's.

Trialability refers to the possibility to experiment with an innovation before adopting it. The "try before you buy" is already widely used in many industries. From shoes to cars or even trial versions of software, there are many products or services that customers do not buy unless they have an opportunity to use and test them before making a purchase decision.

The last attribute, observability, is defined as the degree to which the results of the implementation of an innovation are visible. If a potential adopter can witness what happens after an innovation is implemented, he or she will be reassured on the other factors and also on the potential concerns in terms of health and safety. On the contrary, if the results are not visible, a precautionary principle may be the rule. The absence of observability is, for example, one issue that has deterred Europe from adoption of genetically modified crops. Because the general population, governments, and scientists do not have any information on the potential side effects of these crops, they have been forbidden in Europe and allowed only on a experimental basis under a very tight administrative control by governments.

Among the developments based on this theory, we can mention the technology acceptance model, developed by R. P. Bagozzi et al., and the concept of "crossing the chasm," by Geoffrey A. Moore. Moore defends the idea of a gap between the early adopters and the early majority. According to him, the needs and expectations of the different groups are different, and the real issue is to close this gap or cross the chasms. Several marketing techniques are suggested to overcome this issue, including creating enough buzz or momentum around the innovation to push the adoption beyond the chasm. It should be noted that chasms are found mostly for disruptive or radical innovations and are not systematic.

François Therin
University College of Media Arts and Sciences

See also Corporate Entrepreneurship and Innovation; Feasibility Studies; Geography of Innovation; Innovation Advantage; Innovation in Low-Tech Industries; Innovation Management; Innovation Management: Corporate; Innovation Measurement; Innovation Processes; Product Innovation; Radical and Incremental Innovation; Service Innovation

Further Readings

Bagozzi, R. P., F. D. Davis, and P. R. Warshaw. "Development and Test of a Theory of Technological Learning and Usage." *Human Relations*, v.45/7 (1992).

Moore, Geoffrey A. *Crossing the Chasm, Marketing and Selling High-Tech Products to Mainstream Customers*, Rev. ed. New York: HarperCollins, 1999.

Rogers, E. M. *Diffusion of Innovations*, 5th ed. New York: Free Press, 2003.

INNOVATION IN LOW-TECH INDUSTRIES

Innovation in low-tech industries is an expression that has not yet attained a universal definition. The term *innovation* is defined by the Organisation for Economic Co-operation and Development (OECD) as "the transformation of an idea into a new or improved product introduced on the market or a new or improved operational process used in industry and commerce" or "a new approach to a social service," whereas "low-tech" can be understood, by reference to the OECD's sectoral list, as those industries that have a low degree of research and development (R&D) intensity over longer periods of time. Examples of low-tech industries within this framework, as explained by Thomas Hatzichronoglou, include paper printing and the manufacture or processing of textiles, clothing, food, beverages, tobacco, wood, and furniture. In contrast, there is the medium-low-technology group of industries, including rubber and plastic products; the medium-high-technology group, including motor vehicles; and the high-technology group, including aerospace, computers, office machinery, pharmaceuticals, electronics, and communications. Hartmut Hirsch-Kreinsen and his colleagues estimate that between 3 and 10 percent of industries may be characterized as "high-tech" within modern economies today.

The OECD has pursued its policy development activities based on these definitions while at the same time acknowledging that weakness inherent in R&D intensity is a factor that determines the industry's technology status. This aspect has also been the focus of much scholarly research into the topic. Nick von Tunzelmann and Virginia Acha, for example, point to the contradiction between assuming, on one

Textile businesses are understood to be "low-tech" industries in that they generally have a low degree of research and development intensity over longer periods of time. Low-tech industries are rarely studied and reported on in the same way that innovative companies are. (Photos.com)

hand, that R&D is the main activity behind innovation and subsequently, on the other hand, operating with a term such as "low-tech innovation industries" when such industries are characterized as conducting no or little R&D. Thus, although being forced to refer to the OECD definition, business and social sciences studies are looking into possible determinants of innovation other than R&D.

Based on results from their extensive field studies, Hirsch-Kreinsen and colleagues divide the kind of knowledge advancement and potential innovation that may occur in even low-tech industries into three different levels. The first fosters the knowledge that may already be internally available within a company; this can take the form of principles, tricks, and knacks related to the processes that are in use and that may be improved further, usually in the form of process innovations but sometimes also in the form of product innovations. At a second level, the ability to recombine various types of knowledge and technologies that are already available may result in innovations. At a third level, one additional and important characteristic concerns the firm's relationship to its environment and questions the notion of low-tech firms and industries as such: A presumably low-tech industry is most often the customer of medium- or high-tech equipment or goods, and the low-tech industry will thus need to have capabilities in order to absorb these innovations originating

in other industries. Hirsch-Kreinsen and colleagues include examples, such as the experience of sales personnel in view of changing market conditions and absorption of scientific research results. Many companies are thus forced to integrate new knowledge into their own existing knowledge base in order to develop further.

Moreover, the actual implementation of new technology invariably necessitates adaptations in the form of process innovations, which in turn may be transferred elsewhere. The OECD's *Oslo Manual* highlights the absorption aspect when stressing that innovation in low- and medium-tech industries involves more complex processes than the simple adoption of new technologies. In many cases, it involves the incorporation of high-technology products and technologies, such as the use of information and communication technology in production processes and the use of biotechnology in, for example, food processing. Thus, high-tech innovations play a part in the development of new products and production processes. The use and application of high-tech advancements also place new demands on workers' skills and can influence organizational structure, interactions with other firms, and relationships with public and semipublic research institutions.

This relatively recent way of thinking about innovation in low-tech industries has several implications, perhaps first and foremost regarding the role of geographic proximity in connection with the third type or level of low-tech innovation. The low-tech industries may be high consumers of advanced machinery, and adapting and maintaining such equipment necessitate close collaboration with those who developed it in the first place.

Perhaps not surprisingly, the policies and research on low-tech industries are most prevalent in countries considered to have a high concentration of such industries. Canada, Australia, and Norway, for example, are different from many other Western countries in that they experience a high degree of industrial activity focused on the extraction of natural resources. Another case in question is Finland, which was for decades dominated by low-tech industries but in recent years has taken a swing toward high tech. International comparisons that make the high-tech/low-tech distinction are in a way biased toward the high-tech end of the continuum; however, countries with low-tech industries are interested in seeing how and even why these industries also contribute on a continuous basis to growth, welfare, and innovation, albeit perhaps according to some other mechanisms and indicators than those of high-tech industries.

Terje Grønning
University of Oslo

See also Geography of Innovation; Innovation Diffusion; Innovation Processes; Location Strategy; Radical and Incremental Innovation

Further Readings

Hatzichronoglou, T. *Revision of the High Technology Sector and Product Classification.* STI Working Papers 2. Paris: Organisation for Economic Co-operation and Development, 1997.

Hirsch-Kreinsen, Hartmut and David Jacobson, eds. *Innovation in Low-Tech Firms and Industries.* Cheltenham, UK: Edward Elgar, 2008.

Organisation for Economic Co-operation and Development and Eurostat. *Oslo Manual: Guidelines for Collecting and Interpreting Innovation Data,* 3rd ed. Paris: Author, 2005.

Von Tunzelmann, Nick and Virginia Acha. "Innovation in 'Low-Tech' Industries." In *The Oxford Handbook of Innovation,* Jan Fagerberg, David Mowery, and Richard Nelson, eds. Oxford, UK: Oxford University Press, 2005.

Innovation Management

Innovation is defined by the online *Business Dictionary* (www.businessdictionary.com) as the "process by which an idea or invention is translated into a good or service for which people will pay. To be called an innovation, an idea must be replicable at an economical cost and must satisfy a specific need. Innovation involves deliberate application of information, imagination, and initiative in deriving greater or different value from resources, and encompasses all processes by which new ideas are generated and converted into useful products." M. A. Maidique suggested that there are five stages in the innovation process: recognition, invention, development, implementation, and diffusion. Bruce D. Merrifield, former U.S. assistant secretary of commerce, in a speech given in 1986 on the forces of change affecting high-technology industries, defined the process of innovation as "invention, translation, and commercialization."

George Land and Beth Jarman concluded that "innovators can hold a situation in chaos for long periods of time without having to reach a resolution . . . will not give up, . . . have a long-term commitment to their dream, . . . [and] introduce a maximum of tension into the thinking process, unifying concepts that often appear to be opposed, solving problems which appear impossible."

The importance of innovation to economic development was recognized by J. Botkin et al.:

Innovation cuts across a broad range of activities, institutions and time spans. If any part of the pipeline is broken or constricted, the flow of benefits is slowed. This is felt ultimately in lower productivity and lowered standards of living. In this sense, the cost of capital is crucial not only at the early stages of research and product development but also at the later stages when high-technology products are installed in production processes, in both manufacturing and service industries, as new tools to improve worker effectiveness.

In general, the process of innovation is divided into two broad categories; evolutionary and revolutionary. Evolutionary innovation is further expanded into the categories of "continuous" and "dynamic continuous." In the continuous evolutionary process, a product is simply altered in terms of characteristics; it is not a new product. Dynamic evolutionary innovation requires additional effort by consumers to properly utilize the modified product. Revolutionary innovations often result in discontinuity; hence they are also called discontinuous innovations. Product offerings resulting from revolutionary innovation require consumers to adapt in order to take advantage of the new features of the new product. Management of innovation will vary based on whether the innovation involves an evolutionary or a revolutionary innovation process.

J. Heskett, in his article "What Is Management's Role in Innovation?" (2007), solicited responses from several scholars, and some of the responses were as follows: Umesh Gupta stated, "Innovation . . . is directly proportional to the attitude of senior management." Ginny Wiedower commented, "Without a corporate strategy to reach defined corporate goals, innovation will be misdirected and unguided." D. R. Elliott, however, pointed out that "innovations and inefficiencies are persistent anomalies in organizations." Actions of top managers, according to Marc Sniukas, should "set the context, guide the process, . . . clearly communicate reasons, . . . shield creative teams, . . . appreciate distinctiveness in people and their thinking, and welcome change." As Dan Hoch put it, "The real question revolves not around whether the managers have the courage, but does the CEO have the vision and fortitude to stand before the board and defend the opportunity to explore and fail?"

In 2007, the *Wall Street Journal* commented that managing innovation is one of the biggest challenges that companies face. They not only must come up with new ideas but also must foster a culture that encourages and rewards innovation. Otherwise, they risk being overtaken by their competitors.

Ultimately, innovation signals change, and organizations that are able to manage this process should achieve better performance than competitors. Evolutionary innovation can be best achieved through proper implementation management, whereas revolutionary innovation requires managers to create and nurture a culture of creativity that permeates the various functional areas of the organization.

Small businesses and new ventures are particularly well placed to cause disruptions in industry structures via convergence or radiation. The challenge to this pipeline of new ideas could be the ability to secure adequate funding to fully develop promising ideas or processes. Christensen found in his study of the disk drive industry that "despite the established firms' technological prowess in leading sustaining innovations, from the simplest to the most radical, the firms that led the industry in every instance of developing and adopting disruptive technologies were entrants to the industry, not its incumbent leaders."

Alfred Lewis
Hamline University
Dan Kipley
Azusa Pacific University

See also Corporate Entrepreneurship and Innovation; Feasibility Studies; Geography of Innovation; Innovation Advantage; Innovation Diffusion; Innovation in Low-Tech Industries; Innovation Management: Corporate; Innovation Measurement; Innovation Processes; Product Innovation; Radical and Incremental Innovation; Service Innovation

Further Readings

Botkin, J., D. Dimancescu, and R. Stata. *The Innovators: Rediscovering America's Creative Energy*. New York: Harper and Row, 1983.

Christensen, Clayton M. *The Innovator's Dilemma: When New Technologies Cause Great Firms to Fail*. Boston: Harvard Business School Press, 1997.

Heskett, J. "What Is Management's Role in Innovation?" *Harvard Business Review* (November 30, 2007). http://hbswk.hbs.edu/item/5821.html.

Land, G. and B. Jarman. *Breakpoint and Beyond: Mastering the Future Today*. New York: HarperCollins, 1992.

Maidique, M. A. "Entrepreneurs, Champions and Technological Innovation." *Sloan Management Review* (Winter 1980).

Wall Street Journal. "Managing Innovation." 2007. http://online.wsj.com/article/SB119023924039732943.html (Accessed February 2011).

Innovation Management: Corporate

Corporate innovation management involves corporations' processes for managing innovation, which includes organizational, technological, managerial, and strategic innovation. Innovation management focuses on allowing the company to respond to external or internal opportunities by using its creative efforts to introduce new ideas, processes, or products. Corporate innovation management involves employees at every level of the organization in contributing creatively to a company's research and development, manufacturing, and marketing. Corporate innovation management comprises a set of tools that allow the top management team, as well as lower-level managers and engineers, to cooperate with a common understanding of goals and processes. By utilizing appropriate innovation management tools, top management can trigger and deploy the creative juices of the whole workforce toward the continuous development of a company.

Corporate innovation can be categorized as either incremental or revolutionary. Incremental innovation applies to situations in which market needs and size are well understood and where technologies that can serve the market are perceived to be gradual improvements of existing technology platforms. The innovation in this category is typically evolutionary and involves product and process refinement. Revolutionary innovation, by contrast, may be underpinned by some understanding of market needs but is always accompanied by uncertainties about potential market size and product adoption rates, because the innovations typically bear little resemblance to existing technologies and may be poorly understood for considerable time. These innovations are found to be disruptive only after successful innovation and, frequently, only after some market adoption.

For corporate innovation managers, the most important type of innovation is technological innovation. Joseph Schumpeter defined it as the portfolio of productive factors never used before, including those used to introduce a product, technology, method, market, source of materials, or industrial organization. Several effective models of such innovation management have been invented; these include linear management, chain-linked management, new technology exploitation, and network innovation.

The linear process involves several stages in sequence, such as research, development, manufacturing, marketing, and ultimately customer relationship management. In each step, a group of employees takes the idea as it is passed to them from the previous stage, modifies it to accomplish a specific function, and passes it on to the next stage. The linear model, however, has proven to be somewhat impractical; it does not always play out in reality because it omits interactions between upstream and downstream processes.

An alternative method of innovation management is the expanded, chain-linked form. This strategy takes into account the interactions between the different stages of innovation in a more complete fashion, and it is ultimately more rewarding, as it tracks more closely to the way innovation actually progresses from idea to implementation, from the laboratory to the marketplace.

Another type of innovation management is new technology exploitation, defined as the testing of novel technical approaches specifically aimed at achieving a predetermined result. It is an iterative process, allowing for the more cyclical learning process of scientific discovery.

Network innovation refers to innovation that can be accomplished by team members located in different places around the world, who collaborate to work out the solution to a specific problem using virtual networks such as those built on the Internet. Instead of helping the company's products or services run faster in the distant future, networked teams and companies learn how to make themselves and their partners run faster today, adding value to already installed networks in addition to focusing on entirely new networks.

Regardless of the method used, it is essential for managers of corporate innovation to understand both the market and the technical issues. By creating multifunctional development teams, consisting of strategists, department and division heads, engineers, marketers, and even external investors and financial managers, managers of innovation can address both dimensions. The methods for organizing this set of people form the basis of the discipline of corporate innovation management. Usually, corporate innovation is demonstrated by product innovation and process innovation. Product innovation involves launching a new product as well as improving products on the basis of technology or managerial climate change. Such a product may be an entity, such as a machine, or a virtual service, such as the development of a financial portfolio. While process innovation is based on process change, it can either be pushed or pulled through development. Based on existing or newly invented technology or new regulations, a pushed process refers to what the organization has access to and tries to find profitable applications for such technologies or regulations, whereas a pulled process tries to find fields where the customer's needs have not been met and then focuses on developing solutions to those needs.

Innovation management uses a set of tools that allow innovators such as managers and engineers to cooperate with a common understanding of goals and processes. Common tools include brainstorming, virtual prototyping, product life-cycle management, idea management, TRIZ (or TIPS, the theory of inventive problem solving), stage-gate processes, project management, product line planning, and portfolio management. In product life-cycle management, for example, the life cycle of a new product is understood to be steadily shorter; increased competition forces companies to reduce the time it takes to get the product to market. Innovation managers must therefore decrease development time without sacrificing quality or the needs of the market.

In today's knowledge society, the continuous creation of knowledge is the only way for an organization to survive. In order to get more knowledge, the company must pay more attention to research and development, which can be used to develop both new products and organizational innovation. When this is done within the company itself, it is referred to as closed innovation: Within the walls of an individual company, the corporation seeks to discover new technology breakthroughs, initiate new organizational forms, and put new managerial models into practice. By contrast, open innovation usually combines creative technology, creates managerial systems, and uses external networks to generate innovation not only within the company but also across organizational boundaries, which ultimately yields a boost in value for the company.

Shuyi Zhang
Shanghai Finance University

See also Innovation Processes; Product Innovation; Radical and Incremental Innovation; Service Innovation; Technology Transfer

Further Readings

Clark, Charles H. *Idea Management: How to Motivate Creativity and Innovation.* New York: AMACOM, 1980.

Kelly, P. and M. Kranzburg. *Technological Innovation: A Critical Review of Current Knowledge.* San Francisco: San Francisco Press, 1978.

Trott, Paul. *Innovation Management and New Product Development.* Upper Saddle River, NJ: Prentice Hall, 2005.

INNOVATION MEASUREMENT

Innovation is of considerable importance to individuals, organizations, and nations as a source of business value generation that can be leveraged economically. Innovation has been central to economic indicators of growth and prosperity. Furthermore, innovation has grown in importance during recessionary periods as well. This is because economists and business analysts view innovation as the most sensible route to economic recovery and stability.

Innovation, like other critical business functions that involve an investment of resources, requires effective management. Companies with a well-managed innovation system are likely to derive maximum and sustained value from their innovations, while the brightest innovation can languish

without adequate resources or management attention and may fail to deliver its promised value to the company or shareholders.

As the adage goes, to manage anything, it must first be measured. Measurement of innovation therefore is necessary to deliver high business value and returns. Broadly speaking, innovation may be measured at two levels: the organizational level (relating to individuals, teams, and companies) and the national level (relating to country or regional competitive advantage from innovation).

The importance of measuring innovation has been recognized by many governments. In the United States, for example, various bodies, such as the U.S. Congress, Office of Science and Technology Policy, National Science Foundation, Bureau of Economic Analysis, and Department of Commerce, have been actively involved in innovation measurement initiatives. They have created task groups, workshops, presidential councils, committees, initiatives, and surveys that are intended to improve framework conditions for innovation and trigger economic growth.

Similarly, in the international arena, organizations such as the Organisation for Economic Co-operation and Development (OECD) have developed measures to compare innovation across nations and have ranked nations for innovation. OECD's approach to measuring innovation is broad-based and includes actors, processes, and framework conditions besides aggregate numbers or indices. Hence, OECD has attempted both to provide traditional positioning indicators of innovation and to go beyond the positioning indicators for a more nuanced interpretation of innovation.

The Global Innovation Index is another metric at the country level. Produced jointly by the Boston Consulting Group, the National Association of Manufacturers, and the Manufacturing Institute, it looks at business outcomes and governments' ability to support innovation by public policy. The Global Innovation Index measures innovation inputs (government and fiscal policy, education policy, and the innovation environment) and innovation outputs (patents, technology transfers, business performance on labor productivity, shareholder returns, impact on business migration, and economic growth).

At the organizational level, a survey of senior managers by the Boston Consulting Group suggested that companies believe that they are more effective at measuring innovation outputs (end results such as revenue and shareholder returns) than they are in tracking innovation inputs (such as people or funds invested) or innovation processes (which act to transform the inputs). Profitability, customer satisfaction, and incremental revenue from innovation appeared to be the most commonly used components of innovation metrics.

Generally, while organizations and nations are aware of the importance of measuring innovation, there is no agreement as to how, exactly, one should go about measuring it effectively. This stems in part from the nature of the innovation phenomenon itself. Innovation no doubt creates business value, but it is multifaceted and complex. Considering only the outcomes of innovation—by taking into account the number of patents granted, for example (a commonly used measure)—does not give a full understanding of the innovation process or the infrastructure required to enable its emergence. Also, the quantification of such measures does little to provide an appreciation of the value generated by the measure. For example, a company with six patents in a year that are largely incremental and did not result in a substantive increase in performance or revenues should not be equated with another company with six patents in a year that resulted in significant business value, revenue generation, and customer satisfaction. Hence, qualitative metrics measuring impact on brand, number of citations, and consumer satisfaction ratings, and the like need to be combined with statistical counts. The metrics should include both soft, or qualitative, data (that may encourage key people to think deeply for example) and hard, or quantitative, data (data subject to statistical analysis). Using only one type of data would not paint a full picture.

Another dilemma of measuring innovation is that, while inputs and outputs are relatively easy to track, this is not true of the processes involved. For example, inputs such as investment in research and development and outputs such as business revenue generated from new innovations are objective, quantitative data that may be easily gathered and interpreted. On the other hand, the innovation processes that transform the many inputs into valued outputs are much more intangible and harder to pinpoint or measure. Furthermore, innovation processes are context specific and may have differential impacts or weight for companies or industries. Consequently, measures of innovation generally capture only inputs or outcomes, while disregarding the processes.

Furthermore, innovation is too complex to be fully captured by a single summative measure. The measurement of any phenomenon tends to drive behavior and results, and innovation is no exception to this. Innovation can and should be measured and linked to incentives, both financial and nonfinancial. Without this linkage of innovation measurement to incentives, it is difficult to ensure behavioral change. The role of leadership in incentivizing and motivating innovation is instrumental in a firm's desire to innovate continuously and stay ahead of competition.

In summary, it is clear that innovation measurement is by no means robust or standardized anywhere in the world. The state of innovation metrics and measurement is still in its infancy. It is encouraging to note that much work is being done to create a valid and widely relevant framework for its measurement at organizational and national levels. Future research agendas on measuring innovation should consider both qualitative and quantitative metrics. Additionally, the measures should be linked to incentives so as to ensure behavioral and organizational outcomes. Finally, innovation measures should reflect inputs, processes, and outputs in an evaluative framework that considers relevant factors that impact various stages of innovation.

Manjula S. Salimath
University of North Texas

See also Change Management: Corporate; Innovation in Low-Tech Industries; Innovation Management; Innovation Processes; Product Innovation; Service Innovation

Further Readings

Andrew, James P. et al. *Measuring Innovation 2009: The Need for Action.* Boston: Boston Consulting Group, 2009.

Arundel, Anthony and Rick Garreifs. *Innovation Measurement and Policies.* European Commission, 1997.

Bloch, C. "Assessing Recent Developments in Innovation Measurement: The Third Edition of the *Oslo Manual.*" *Science and Public Policy*, v.34/1 (2007).

Organisation for Economic Co-operation and Development. *Measuring Innovation: A New Perspective.* Paris: Author, 2010.

Polenske, Karen R. *Economic Geography of Innovation.* New York: Cambridge University Press, 2007.

INNOVATION PROCESSES

Successful new businesses contribute to overall sustained economic development and growth. Also, a firm's capacity to innovate determines its capacity to compete. Successful firms venturing into new markets and technologies often devise novel ways to manage the processes that can help them continuously develop and refine new products and services, and also accelerate learning so that failing strategies can be quickly modified. Large companies can be particularly vulnerable to the type of creative destruction brought by the high levels of innovativeness by newcomers. Compared to established mature firms, new ventures' entrepreneurs have unique advantages (such as a fresh and up-to-date vision or freedom from organizational inertia) to identify commercial opportunities and combine intangible and tangible resources to exploit these opportunities in a novel and timely fashion. Likewise, although many entrepreneurial firms develop unique and attractive products, in the long run it is firms that repeatedly exceed customers' needs and that allocate their resources effectively that succeed.

Regardless of firm size and age, entrepreneurs and managers must continuously devise novel ways to adapt and nurture the processes that sustain the whole spectrum of their innovation activities. Whether internally developed or externally sourced, firms need to be able to orchestrate innovation processes and align them to the requirements of the competitive environment. Highly volatile and competitive external environments require more frequent radical innovations, for example. Most incremental innovations build on what has already been developed, requiring minor modifications to existing functions and organizational practices, but more radical innovations may require changing the entire organizational logic and order of things, making established practices obsolete. Sustaining innovation may require entrepreneurial firms to consider acquisitions, alliances, and the adoption of new management skills, and may also involve systematically learning from the mistakes and failures that are an unavoidable aspect of current uncertain and high-risk business environments.

Thus, what are the key innovation processes on which managers and entrepreneurs should focus their attention? What are the vital ingredients and enabling conditions that allow these processes to effectively promote innovation?

Traditionally, industrial-age firms have adopted linear "multistage" processes, whereby projects navigate through a structured sequence of steps from concept to development to production and commercialization; as each step is completed, the project is passed to the next step. Building from interactive theories of innovation, R. Rothwell (1994) emphasized the processes of adoption and interaction between units and teams within the firm; how the firm organizes itself and its interfaces with technology sources and potential customers becomes critical for its success. More refined models emphasize innovation as a parallel rather than sequential process; integrated research and development (R&D), production, and marketing teams are simultaneously engaged. More recent models account for networking processes, where customers and suppliers play an active role through diverse forms of informal and also formal collaboration, such as joint ventures and strategic alliances.

In today's highly competitive and volatile environments, however, the key features of effective innovation processes involve experimentation, improvisation, flexibility, and knowledge transfer, translation, and recombination. Firms that enable experimentation are able to recognize and pursue new opportunities earlier than their competitors. A business that promotes improvisation through flexible ways of working ensures creative and innovative behavior. Successful firms coordinate across functions and projects, enabling smooth knowledge transfer between and within projects, as well as setting routines for migrating from old practices and initiating new projects by recombining resources and capabilities. For instance, organizational practices such as cross-project and cross-divisional evaluation help link individuals from different functional units, thereby facilitating the exchange of ideas and the collaborative efforts of a variety of people concurrently working on different aspects of a project.

In the 21st century, learning and co-innovation have emerged as the most remarkable features of the innovation process. Despite the growing importance of learning and co-innovation, some managers still struggle to recognize technological and market opportunities. The existing literature tends to focus on technological know-how and prescriptive linear processes, while neglecting a more thorough description and explanation of the organizational dynamics;

why, when, and how organizational processes and routines emerge or are set in place by managers and innovators. A key challenge for effective learning and co-innovation is the increasing number of R&D collaborations across an increasingly large network of partners.

Learning and co-innovation are linked to the notion of "social embeddedness" and the role of cognitive, collective, and social structures. Nancy Napier and Mikael Nilsson (2008) present six principles and fresh examples that would help practitioners reflect on how to foster an innovative culture and enabling processes within and across organizations. The core element of their framework is establishing a "disciplined" process that would foster the mastery of "within discipline" and "out of discipline" thinking. Within this disciplined process, practices to help executives juggling between front-end and back-end foci (swinging between exploration and exploitation) and "surf" idea waves (whether big or incremental) are essential to foster creativity and innovation. This disciplined process is supported by additional factors that can enhance (or inhibit) creative and innovative processes. These include human resource policies, culture, and networking spaces. Adopting a similar lens, Peter Denning and Robert Dunham (2010) provide a unique set of thinking practices to boost the innovation process, namely sensing, envisioning, and embodying, among other strategies.

In the current knowledge-intensive age, acquiring a deep understanding and applied knowledge of these cognitive and relational skills is a major challenge for firms wanting to improve their innovation processes and aspiring to lead and stay in the lead.

Angel J. Salazar
Manchester Metropolitan University

See also Corporate Entrepreneurship and Innovation; Feasibility Studies; Geography of Innovation; Innovation Advantage; Innovation Diffusion; Innovation in Low-Tech Industries; Innovation Management; Innovation Management: Corporate; Innovation Measurement; Opportunity Recognition; Product Innovation; Radical and Incremental Innovation; Service Innovation

Further Readings

Brown, S. L. and K. M. Eisenhardt. *Competing on the Edge: Strategy as Structured Chaos.* Boston: Harvard Business School Press, 1998.

Denning, Peter J. and Robert Dunham. *The Innovator's Way: Essential Practices for Successful Innovation.* Cambridge, MA: MIT Press, 2010.

Napier, Nancy K. and Mikael Nilsson. *The Creative Discipline: Mastering the Art and Science of Innovation.* Westport, CT: Praeger, 2008.

Rothwell, R. "Towards the Fifth-Generation Innovation Process." *International Marketing Review,* v.1/11 (1994).

INSURANCE

Insurance for businesses operates on the same fundamental principles as insurance in general. The insurance business depends on risk management to identify the risks of the situations that will result in claims and to determine the premium and the limits to coverage accordingly. The basic principle of insurance is to pool money from the many insured customers in order to pay for the losses of the few. This requires a large number of similar customers, in order that resources can be pooled; furthermore, the losses that can be covered must be large, accidental, definite, and calculable. That is, the loss must be meaningful to the insured; its occurrence must be outside the control of the beneficiary; it must have taken place at a known time and place from a known cause; and it must be possible to establish the probability of the loss (in order to construct the terms of the insurance coverage) and its cost (in order to know what to pay out to the beneficiary). Furthermore, the risk of catastrophically large losses must be limited—and, more broadly, once the cost and probability of possible losses have been weighed against the pool of insured customers, the resulting premium must be affordable, or operating the insurance is untenable.

Insurance is one of the costs often overlooked in business planning, especially by small businesses whose owners do not have previous business owner experience. However, owners should not overcompensate for this lack of experience by buying the wrong insurance. Each organization should carefully consider which kinds of insurance are necessary and applicable to the kind of business it intends to conduct. There are a variety of types of insurance applicable to a business. Buildings and vehicles owned by the business should be insured, for instance, and will usually be included as part of a business owner's

Planning for the cost of insurance is often overlooked or underestimated when creating a business plan, especially for small businesses. Insurance coverage for business ventures needs to include coverage for property and assets and an appropriate amount of liability coverage. (Photos.com)

policy, which packages into one policy the various types of insurance coverage applicable to a business's needs.

There are also a variety of liability coverages applicable to businesses. As a broad category, liability insurance protects the insured against legal claims and is usually incorporated into things like property insurance (protecting against a lawsuit in the event of someone slipping and falling) and vehicle insurance (protecting against lawsuits after accidents). However, businesses are exposed to much more legal liability than this, and their insurance policies cover more varieties of liability. As a rule of thumb, liability coverage applies to negligence, not to willful acts.

The legal concept of liability is complicated, depending on a principle called the duty of care, as established by common law and reinforced by case law. A successful lawsuit demonstrates that the defendant—the business, its owner, or an individual—breached duty of care, resulting in an injury (including financial harms). Duty of care varies from state to state. The basic principle is that of a legal obligation requiring an individual to adhere to a standard of reasonable care when engaged in any activity that could foreseeably bring harm (again, physical or otherwise) to others. In Florida and Massachusetts, all that is necessary to establish a duty of care is foreseeability: If a business owner could have foreseen the harm, that person had a duty to take reasonable care to avoid it. California,

on the other hand, has criticized this as too simplistic, making foreseeability only one of many factors for courts to consider. The others are

- the degree of certainty that harm was suffered;
- the proximity of connection between the defendant's actions and the harm;
- the moral blame attached to the defendant's actions;
- the policy of preventing future harm;
- the extent of the burden to the defendant and the consequences to the community of imposing a duty of care in this circumstance;
- the availability, cost, and prevalence of insurance for the risk involved; and
- the social utility of the defendant's conduct from which the harm resulted.

Many states have followed in California's footsteps, sometimes with slight modifications (in particular, the social utility factor was added in 1997 in California and is not used by all states). The insurance and burden factors merit further discussion. The insurance factor is similar to foreseeability but more concrete: If it is possible to insure oneself against a certain risk, then it does make sense to consider oneself responsible for being aware of that risk and conducting oneself accordingly. This is a type of risk awareness that is easier to prove and more reasonable to assume than foreseeability. As for the burden, factors like this (coupled with moral blame) account for the difference between states in which a customer can successfully sue after burning themselves with hot coffee served at a normal steaming temperature and states in which it is far more difficult to do so—just to pick one example of a liability lawsuit. When foreseeability is the only factor needed to establish a duty of care, then serving hot coffee can indeed be construed as negligence, since it can result in harm. However, a reasonable examination taking into account other factors would find that there should be no breach of the duty of care in serving hot coffee at the temperature at which coffee is usually served, when hot coffee is ordered and when reasonable care is taken (that is, when it is not spilled or sloshed around). The practice of adding a warning, declaring that the contents are hot, to to-go cups of coffee (which, when lidded, may not visibly emit steam, as would a mug of coffee served inside a restaurant) is a protection against such liability suits; anyone who is burned by the coffee now has a more difficult time establishing negligence on the part of the establishment, as a warning of the risk that they assume by consuming or handling the coffee has been issued.

Once the extent of a duty of care is established, it must further be established that the defendant breached it, which is called the second element of negligence. The defendant's actions are compared against the standard of a "reasonable person," a legal fiction from the common-law tradition. Specifics of this reasonable person vary from case to case—most important, professionals are held to a higher standard in performing the tasks associated with their profession than are members of the general public. When a sick or injured person suffers further harm in the care of a member of the general public, the caregiver may be innocent of negligence even if the exact same actions would constitute malpractice if performed by a doctor, nurse, or emergency medical technician. Such liability suits are the stuff of late-night talk show jokes, but they present a real concern to business owners and are an everyday fact of life when working with the public. Differences in the measure of the duty of care from state to state can be an important factor in opening a business that caters to the public.

The closely related business judgment rule derives from case law and states that "directors of a corporation are clothed with the presumption, which the law accords to them, of being motivated in their conduct by a bona fide regard for the interests of the corporation." This establishes a duty of care on the part of the directors to the best interests of the business—but at the same time, it is assumed that the directors are acting in good faith unless it can be proven otherwise and that a lack of success on the part of the business cannot be assumed to be the result of negligence on the part of the directors. The business judgment rule makes it very difficult to appeal to the courts to interfere with the internal operations of a business unless fraud (or some other crime) or misappropriation of funds can be demonstrated.

Directors' and officers' liability protects a business entity from the lawsuits resulting from the actions of its directors and corporate officers. Typically both the directors and officers, and the corporation itself are protected. Directors and officers will often be named in suits made by regulators (who can bring criminal as well as civil actions), shareholders, customers, or competitors in the event of anticompetitive practices.

Professional liability insurance is a broad subcategory of liability insurance and includes all forms of malpractice insurance. The policy name will vary according to the profession but in essence insures a professional against negligence claims made by patients, clients, customers. Outside the medical and legal professions, this is generally synonymous with errors and omissions liability insurance, which covers the financial harms caused to others by errors or omissions in the course of the professional's operations. Virtually any business professional can benefit from errors and omissions liability coverage; a Web designer may be sued by a client for business lost because of a Website failure, a real estate broker may be sued over problems with the property he sold, appraisers may be sued for errors in their work, and so on.

There are also numerous nonliability options that can be packaged into business insurance, beyond insuring the physical assets, buildings, and vehicles owned by the business. Business interruption or business income insurance is additional disaster insurance which covers the loss of income experienced by a business while waiting for facilities to be rebuilt in the aftermath of a disaster. Without this, it can be difficult or impossible to retain employees while waiting to resume business, as they are forced to seek work elsewhere; furthermore, unless the business was especially healthy, the business itself may not be able to afford to continue operating, because of payments that need to be made on debts, revenue needed for upcoming projects, and other issues. Some policies will also cover the cost of operating from a temporary location, much like homeowner's insurance policies sometimes pay for hotel expenses while a homeowner is waiting for damage to be repaired. The insurance company determines, on a case-by-case basis, what constitutes the business interruption period; the covered period may end before the business is fully prepared to resume operations, as long as the damaged property has been repaired.

Business overhead expense disability insurance pays the policyholder's overhead expenses for a period of time if he or she becomes disabled; this form of insurance is intended to cover small businesses with a small number of employees. Expenses covered include rent, utilities, salaries, payroll taxes, office supplies, equipment maintenance and leasing, property taxes, accounting fees, and sometimes other expenses—but do not cover income taxes, inventory, or the salaries of new employees hired to do the disabled person's work. The benefit period is typically less than two years.

Some insurance companies also offer key person insurance, the specifics of which vary from policy to policy as the circumstance dictates. The underlying concept is that of an insurance policy on the life or health of an employee who is especially important to the company, so that in the event of that employee's death or incapacity (but not his or her quitting or being fired), the company is compensated for the loss of the employee's competence and contribution to the business. This key person can be a director, partner, or executive but can also be someone with special skills required to keep the business's operations flowing smoothly or an important project manager. One example, working both literally and figuratively, would be the drummer in a band. In the event of the drummer breaking his arm in a car accident, an upcoming tour or the recording of an album might have to be delayed. Depending on how the policy is structured, it can compensate for temporary personnel hired to replace the key person while the key person is recovering, for lost profits resulting from the delay or cancellation of projects the key person was involved with, and protect partnership interests by making funds available for existing partners to purchase the key person's partnership interests, as applicable.

For the self-employed, health insurance becomes a serious consideration. The health insurance industry has not traditionally kept the self-employed in mind. For a long time this has been remedied by guilds and unions for various kinds of contractors. For instance, the Writers Guild, representing screenwriters, allows qualifying writers to buy into the group's health coverage, although eligibility must be periodically renewed in order to retain insurance coverage. The Screen Actors' Guild (SAG) performs the same service for actors. Many other unions, trade associations, and professional associations for professions that typically attract contractors—carpenters and plumbers, for instance—offer similar options.

What many entrepreneurs do not realize is that if they previously had health insurance from an employer, they are probably entitled under federal law to continue that coverage for 18 months after their employment ends. They will have to pay their own premiums, with added fees, but this insurance—required under the Consolidated Omnibus Budget Reconciliation Act (COBRA)—is nearly always the least expensive option available to the self-employed, particularly if they are not yet eligible for insurance through a professional association. When that 18-month period ends, other arrangements will have to be made. Money can be saved on the open market by opting for a plan that has a high deductible or emphasizes emergency coverage over preventive care in exchange for low premiums. However, to really understand the cost of insurance, it is important to remember that the premium is often only half of the cost of insurance coverage, and excessively high copayments will not lead to savings.

Bill Kte'pi
Independent Scholar

See also Accounting; Business Failure; Cash Flow

Further Readings

Crain Communications. *Business Insurance: Broker Trends and Profiles*. Chicago: Author, 2010.

DeBaise, Colleen. *The Wall Street Journal Complete Small Business Guidebook*. New York: Three Rivers Press, 2009.

Jackson, Scott. "Mulling Over Massachusetts: Health Insurance Mandates and Entrepreneurs." *Entrepreneurship Theory and Practice*, v.34/5 (September 2010).

Pinson, Linda. *Keeping the Books*. New York: Kaplan Business, 2007.

Scroggin, John J. "Life Insurance and Business Succession." *Journal of Financial Service Professionals*, v.60/1 (January 2006).

Stevick, Glenn E., Jr. *Essentials of Business Insurance*. Bryn Mawr, PA: American College, 2006.

INTENTIONS

Intentions are an interesting and relevant topic for researchers from several areas of knowledge, such as psychology, sociology, and education. In the entrepreneurship field, intentions help to predict attitudes and to identify different pathways of behaviors of people in certain situations. In general terms, an intention is defined as the determination to act in a certain way in order to achieve a purpose or guide an action. Michael Morris and Foard Jones identify two seminal components in the study of intentions in any area: (1) an event that represents the implementation of an idea or achievement of an objective, and (2) an agent or individual who has carried out the event.

Norris Krueger explains that intentions are considered one of the main forces that make a new venture possible. Behind entrepreneurial actions are intentions, and behind intentions are attitudes such as desirability and feasibility. Perceived desirability is the degree to which people feel an attraction for a given behavior (to become an entrepreneur), and perceived feasibility is the degree to which people consider themselves personally able to carry out certain behavior. Several researchers have investigated entrepreneurial intentions models that try to explain and predict new venture creation, analyzing the personalities, social connections, labor experiences, and demographic characteristics (age, gender, ethnicity, and so on) of the agent or potential entrepreneur. Jerome Katz and William Gartner define entrepreneurial intention as the search for information that can be used to help fulfill the goal of venture creation.

The most representative intentions-based models have been Albert Shapero and Sokol's Entrepreneurial Event Model, Icek Ajzen's Planned Behavior Model, Norris Krueger and Alan Carsrud's Intentional Basic Model, and Norris Krueger and Deborah Brazeal's Entrepreneurial Potential Model. However, the predictive capacity of most of these models has been very limited, because they comprise static analysis, do not consider the influence of external environments, and are mostly tested on business students. Only two models have been more predictable of entrepreneurial intentions: (1) the Entrepreneurial Event Model, which identifies key social factors and the individual's perceptions that led to the act of starting a business, and (2) the Planned Behavior Model, which explains that the intentions are the result of attitudes formulated through life experiences, personal characteristics, and perceptions drawn from these prior experiences.

Entrepreneurship is a relevant instrument to promote economic growth and development in different regional and national economies, and the entrepreneur is a major contributor to economic development. It is important to identify the best mechanism to guide the development and enhancement of entrepreneurial intentions. Therefore, the study of entrepreneurial intentions should focus on the evolution of pedagogical approaches. In this respect, the Global Entrepreneurship Monitor found that training is more effective in contexts with favorable institutional environments, where the training-induced positive skills, perceptions, and intentions can be translated into action. For example, Jerome Katz, Nicole Peterman, Jessica Kennedy, and Kermit Kuehn provide a list of learning activities that could affect entrepreneurial intentions toward perceived desirability (exposure to successful experiences and ideas) and perceived feasibility (interactions with entrepreneurs, consulting and internships in entrepreneurial organizations, courses with essential knowledge and skills, and relevant networks). Further study should also investigate the factors that motivate individuals (employees) to start an entrepreneurial new venture within an existing business (termed intrapreneurship). This would allow for the establishment of the best strategies to provide the most beneficial conditions for potential entrepreneurs in all scenarios.

Although many studies focus on intentions, none analyzes the gaps among intentions, actions, and behaviors and whether such intentions really lead to start-ups. It is necessary to conduct longitudinal studies in order to bring insights about this relevant component in new venture management.

Maribel Guerrero
Basque Institute of Competitiveness,
Deusto Business School
David Urbano
Autonomous University of Barcelona

See also Cognition; Entrepreneurial Training; Entrepreneurship Education: Graduate Programs; Entrepreneurship Education: High School; Entrepreneurship Education: Undergraduate Programs; Entrepreneurship Pedagogy; Ethics; Strategy

Further Readings

Ajzen, Icek. "Theory of Planned Behavior: Some Unresolved Issues." *Organizational Behavior and Human Decision Processes*, v.50/2 (1991).
Bagozzi, Richard. "Self-Regulation of Attitudes, Intentions and Behavior." *Social Psychology Quarterly*, v.52/2 (1992).
Bagozzi, Richard and Youjae Yi. "The Degree of Intention Formation as a Moderator of the Attitude-Behavior

Relationship." *Social Psychology Quarterly*, v.52/4 (1989).

Coduras Alicia et al. *Global Entrepreneurship Monitor Special Report: A Global Perspective on Entrepreneurship Education and Training.* 2008. http://www3.babson.edu/ESHIP/research-publications/upload/GEM_Education_Training_Report.pdf (Accessed February 2011).

Gartner, William. "'Who Is an Entrepreneur?' Is the Wrong Question." *American Journal of Small Business*, v.12/1 (1988).

Guerrero, Maribel, Josep Rialp, and David Urbano. "The Impact of Desirability and Feasibility on Entrepreneurial Intentions." *International Entrepreneurship and Management Journal*, v.4/1 (2008).

Katz, Jerome. "The Chronology and Intellectual Trajectory of American Entrepreneurship Education: 1876–1999." *Journal of Business Venturing*, v.18/2 (2003).

Krueger, Norris. "What Lies Beneath? The Experiential Essence of Entrepreneurial Thinking." *Entrepreneurship Theory and Practice*, v.31/1 (2007).

Krueger, Norris and Deborah Brazeal. "Entrepreneurial Potential and Potential Entrepreneurs." *Entrepreneurship Theory and Practice*, v.18/1 (1994).

Krueger, Norris, Michael Reilly, and Alan Carsrud. "Competing Models of Entrepreneurial Intentions." *Journal of Business Venturing*, v.15/6 (2000).

Kuehn, Kermit W. "Entrepreneurial Intentions Research: Implications for Entrepreneurship Education." *Journal of Entrepreneurship Education* (2008).

Liñán, Francisco, David Urbano, and Maribel Guerrero. "Regional Variations in Entrepreneurial Cognitions: Start-Up Intentions of University Students in Spain." *Entrepreneurship and Regional Development*, v.23/3–4 (April 2011).

Peterman, Nicole and Jessica Kennedy. "Enterprise Education: Influencing Students' Perceptions of Entrepreneurship." *Entrepreneurship Theory and Practice*, v.28/2 (2003).

Shapero, Albert. "Social Dimensions of Entrepreneurship." In *The Encyclopedia of Entrepreneurship*. Englewood Cliffs, NJ: Prentice Hall, 1982.

INTERNATIONAL ENTERPRISE PLANNING

Because of the association between new venture performance and the internationalization of new ventures, many scholars, business experts, and government agencies advise all firms, including new and small ventures, to try internationalization. As a matter of fact, higher levels of internationalization—measured by foreign sales as a percentage of total venture sales—have been associated with higher relative market share a few years later and subsequently a good return on investment for U.S. firms.

According to research conducted at the University of Pennsylvania, it is quite possible that international operations might cost more than expected in the short run; however, corporate ventures' market share increases in the medium run. This might be interpreted as a higher return on investment as scale benefits translate into higher profitability. Obviously, a short-term period may simply not be long enough for investments in higher market shares to generate superior profits. Hence, a significant number of U.S. ventures—previously strictly domestic, with no international sales whatsoever—have expanded quickly into international markets over the short term and have successfully increased their percentage of international sales. Ventures that have enlarged international sales exhibit positive associations between the degree of strategic change and performance, as calculated in terms of both relative market share and return on investment. Therefore, increased international sales in technology-based new ventures seem to require simultaneous strategic changes in order to impact venture performance positively.

According to Patricia McDougall, technology-based new ventures that had sales in foreign markets had significant global strategies in comparison to similar ventures that sold their products only domestically. Seemingly, there are correlated changes in degree of internationalization, the adoption of a global strategy, and venture performance. Consequently, start-up entrepreneurs who intend to pursue internationalization should note that internationalization alone does not lead to increased profitability. Indeed, internationalization of sales does not appear to be an easy affair of applying conventional strategies and procedures initially developed for the domestic arena. In fact, successful internationalization appears to require changes in the venture's strategy as well. Consequently, three types of factors new entrepreneurs should consider before going international include, first, the characteristics of the lead entrepreneur; second, the start-up processes undertaken during the founding of the firm; and finally, the firm behaviors after start-up, including management practices and strategic behaviors, all strongly associated with new venture success and failure.

By and large, effective start-up or purchase requires broad planning efforts that consider all aspects of the industry and firm. In fact, successful firms spend more time planning than do unsuccessful firms. The advice and information provided by other industry participants, particularly customers and suppliers during start-up, are vital for success. Indeed, the lead entrepreneurs of successful firms are likely to spend more time communicating with partners, customers, suppliers, and employees than are the lead entrepreneurs of unsuccessful firms. Most successful firms want to become larger firms and embark upon sales to large sectors of the market. These thriving firms achieve high market shares, and with greater market share comes greater financial returns. Likewise, less successful firms are restricted to narrow market sectors consisting of fewer customers who are also more difficult to service. For a good reason, international entrepreneurship has been defined as the development of international new ventures or start-ups that, from their inauguration, engage in international business, thus viewing their operating domain as international from the initial stages of the firm's operation.

Moreover, the strategy and industry structure profiles of international new ventures are significantly different from those of domestic new ventures. Hence, the internationals pursue much broader market-based strategies, seeking a strategy of broad market coverage through developing and controlling numerous distribution channels, serving numerous customers in diverse market segments, and developing high market or product visibility. Furthermore, international ventures stress a more aggressive entry strategy, building on outside financial and production resources to penetrate numerous geographic markets on a large scale as well. Securing patent technology has also always been a significant constituent of their strategy. It is obvious that international ventures compete by entering the industry on a large scale, seeking to penetrate multiple markets and accepting the need for external resources to support such an entry. Whereas both the domestics and the internationals characterize domestic competition as relatively intense, the international new ventures compete in industries with higher levels of international competition. Hence, there are significant differences between new venture firms competing

domestically and new ventures choosing to enter international as well as domestic markets.

Djamel Eddine Laouisset
Alhosn University, Abu Dhabi

See also Entrepreneurial Marketing; Globalization; Import/Export Businesses; International Markets; Territorial Strategy and Regions

Further Readings

Alder, N. and Niron Hashai. "Knowledge Flows and the Modeling of Multinational Enterprise." *Journal of International Business Studies*, v.38/4 (2007).

Amin, Ash and Patrick Cohendet. "Organizational Learning and Governance Through Embedded Practice." *Journal of Management and Governance*, v.4/1–2 (2000).

Andersson, Ulf, Mats Forsgren, and Ulf Holm. "The Strategic Impact of External Networks: Subsidiary Performance and Competence Development in the Multinational Corporation." *Strategic Management Journal*, v.23 (2002).

Barney, Jay. "Firm Resource and Sustained Competitive Advantage." *Journal of Management*, v.17 (1991).

Bartlett, Christopher and Sumantra S. Ghoshal. "Cross-Border Management Motivations and Mentalities." *Text, Cases, and Readings in Cross-Border Management*. New York: McGraw-Hill, 2000.

Birkinshaw, Julian and Neil Hood. "Multinational Subsidiary Evolution: Capability and Charter Change in Foreign-Owned Subsidiary Companies." *Academy of Management Review*, v.23/4 (1998).

Bjorkman, Ingmar, Wilhelm Barner-Rasmussen, and Li Li. "Managing Knowledge Transfer in MNCs: The Impact of Headquarters Control Mechanisms." *Journal of International Business Studies*, v.35 (2004).

Fletcher, Denise. "International Entrepreneurship and the Small Business." *Entrepreneurship and Regional Development*, v.16 (2008).

Gamboa, Ernesto C. and Lance Eliot Brouthers. "How International Is Entrepreneurship?" *Entrepreneurship Theory and Practice*, v.32/3 (May 2008).

McDougall, Patricia and Benjamin M. Oviatt. "International Entrepreneurship: The Intersection of Two Research Paths." *Academy of Management Journal*, v.43/5 (October 2000).

O'Cass, Aron and Jay Weerawardena. "Examining the Role of International Entrepreneurship, Innovation and International Market Performance in SME Internationalization." *European Journal of Marketing*, v.43 (2009).

INTERNATIONAL MARKETS

Although many new ventures tend to operate locally or online, there is considerable potential in international markets. Often the potential to start a venture in a particular international market originates as a discovery during a systematic search, in which an entrepreneur examining all of the information available about a given area of business detects an idea for a venture that answers an existing need. Different markets have very different needs, and the existence of multinational corporations should not be taken as proof to the contrary: Toyota, for instance, develops different vehicles in each of its major markets. The Toyota 4Runner sells very well in the United States but not in Europe, where roads are narrower and the market puts a higher priority on fuel efficiency. Multinational corporations can afford to spend hundreds of millions, even billions, of dollars on market research, brand promotion, and product development, in order to address many markets' needs at once. Newer and smaller ventures need to approach their businesses differently.

It is important to establish the foreign market's potential, including the number of sales that would occur if there were no competition and every interested customer made a purchase. This is an obvious idealization, but the purpose is to identify the absolute maximum market potential, which in some cases may still be too low to be worthwhile. In order to assess countries relative to one another, it is important to use the same criteria and process for establishing the market potential of each country. It can also be wise to determine the market potential even of unavailable markets, as they can often be expected to become available eventually—as happened with many formerly communist countries after the dissolution of the Soviet Union in the early 1990s and as will one day likely happen with North Korea and Cuba.

Determining the market potential of a country usually requires data from the Commerce Department's International Trade Administration (ITA), which is tasked with assisting American companies in international trade and employs trade experts in 70 different countries. The ITA can supply product-specific market research reports, trade statistics, and up-to-date information on regulations,

product standards, tariffs, and customs requirements. Much of the information the ITA handles is unavailable from other sources. The related Office of Export Trading Company Affairs encourages American companies to export products and assists with the use of export trade intermediaries, long-term joint ventures, and the development of joint ventures between American competitors (which may benefit from working together in foreign markets). Trade associations and banks are secondary sources of information.

Market research is critical to entering a foreign market, and test-marketing a product by offering it in a limited area of the foreign country can be helpful when this is feasible and practical. Market research can help not only with determining the right market for the product (or the right products, from a company's product line, for a given market) but also with identifying the best advertising approach and the norms of what the market expects from similar products. Determining price is also key; few products can be sold for the same price worldwide, and costs may need to be reexamined if a given price is not tenable in a given market. Furthermore, information needs to be established about distribution, customer service, ongoing product support, and other matters.

Global positioning requires a familiarity with both local and global competitors; a new beer introduced to New York is going compete not only with Budweiser and other international brands but also with New York State and northeastern regional brands, as well as popular imports from Canada, Australia, Germany, and the Netherlands.

The regulatory environment varies wildly from country to country, both in industry-specific ways and in ways that are applicable to all businesses. Such issues as minimum wages, other labor laws, environmental laws, tax laws, definitions and extent of liability, and required permits, licenses, and other filings must be considered. The World Bank maintains an extensive business law library, accessible from its Website, that provides a valuable resource for exploring a foreign market venture. Cultural and societal norms—such as the typical (or legally guaranteed) amount of vacation time, the length of the workday and workweek, the scheduling of lunches and breaks, practices related to overtime and hazardous work, and maternity leave—also have an impact. Although many of these may not be relevant to a company that simply wants to export its products, they must be taken into account if a direct investment or the opening of a new business is being considered.

Entrepreneurs have been an important force in the increasingly global economy. Even new ventures that are not initially international in scope often internationalize in their first few years of operation. Obvious examples include recent Internet success stories such as Amazon and eBay, which began with a domestic focus and within a few years added services in many other countries. Other ventures are "born global," intended as international enterprises from the start. International entrepreneurship combines innovation and risk taking at an even larger scale than other entrepreneurship and may be able to capitalize on opportunities that would otherwise go unexploited. It is the most innovative ventures that are best able to leverage their competencies in order to succeed in international markets, and to maintain a competitive advantage.

Bill Kte'pi
Independent Scholar

See also Barriers to Entry; Globalization; International Enterprise Planning; Systematic Search

Further Readings

Gamboa, Ernesto C. and Lance Eliot Brouthers. "How International Is Entrepreneurship?" *Entrepreneurship Theory and Practice*, v.32/3 (May 2008).

Godin, Seth. *Purple Cow*. New York: Portfolio, 2009.

O'Cass, Aron and Jay Weerawardena. "Examining the Role of International Entrepreneurship, Innovation and International Market Performance in SME Internationalisation." *European Journal of Marketing*, v.43/11–12 (2009).

Stack, Jack. *The Great Game of Business*. New York: Doubleday, 1994.

Terjesen, Siri and Amanda Elam. "Transnational Entrepreneurs' Venture Internationalization Strategies: A Practice Theory Approach." *Entrepreneurship Theory and Practice*, v.33/5 (September 2009).

Zahra, Shaker A., Juha Santeri Korri, and JiFeng Yu. "Cognition and International Entrepreneurship: Implications for Research on International Opportunity Recognition and Exploitation." *International Business Review*, v.14/2 (April 2005).

INTERNATIONAL NEW VENTURES

Small and young ventures play a pivotal role in generating most new jobs and innovations, and as a result they are of premier interest in improving the economic wealth across countries. In today's increasingly competitive business environment, many new ventures pursue opportunities and use resources outside the home country of origin. Interest in international entrepreneurship (IE) has surged, and as a result academic study of IE has grown rapidly in the 21st century. According to Benjamin Oviatt and Patricia McDougall, international entrepreneurship involves the discovery, enactment, evaluation, and exploitation of opportunities across national borders to create future goods and services. Research on international entrepreneurship has focused on small and young (often referred to as "born global") ventures: business organizations that, from their inception, seek to derive significant competitive advantage from the use of resources and the sale of outputs in multiple countries.

Numerous studies in the international entrepreneurship literature have defined international new ventures (INVs) as those that gain a substantial degree of internationalization before they become six years old. However, this unique focus is counterintuitive and even surprising from the international business (IB) perspective. International business scholars have shown that the vast majority of companies, far from being "born global," enter new foreign markets in a slow, stepwise process in order to accumulate experience from unfamiliar foreign markets before committing resources to internationalization. These scholars have found that domestic firms decide to become multinational enterprises (MNEs) by expanding into foreign markets only after developing their home-country market successfully. When going abroad into foreign countries, multinational enterprises have tended to cultivate nearby countries first and then expand into more remote countries to reduce costs from operating their businesses under unfamiliar foreign environments.

After a firm decides to internationalize into foreign markets, the question becomes where to internationalize and ultimately what countries or regions will be most favorable for acquiring resources or generating customers from foreign operations.

Many studies draw on Alan Rugman's geographic conceptualization of a triad comprising the Asia Pacific region, the European Union, and North America. Overall, each of these regions shares commonalities, such as relatively low macroeconomic growth, similar technological infrastructures, the presence of capital, and knowledge-intensive firms across most industries. Most international new ventures do not appear to be truly born global, and even large firms, with vast resources, tend to favor regions for internationalization within their home region of the triad, as opposed to outside their home region. Despite popular belief, in the case of large multinational enterprises on the Fortune Global 500 list, most actually operate on a regional basis within their home region of the triad. Using a sample of 380 multinational enterprises with geographic sales segments, Rugman and Alain Verbeke found that 320 firms realized about 80 percent of total sales from their home regions of the triad. An explanation may be that established firms suffer from difficulties in replicating their firm-specific advantages (FSAs) in remote foreign countries and/or regions that are dissimilar to their own.

Unlike the largest Fortune Global 500 multinational enterprises, international new ventures are subject to the liabilities of smallness and newness, making internationalization even more challenging. Instead of the born global phenomenon argued by early international entrepreneurship scholars, successful international new ventures are expected to show a stronger home region orientation than large, well-established multinational enterprises; they tend to select nearby countries in their home region as their internationalization strategy. Consequently, a more appropriate term than "born global" for international new ventures may be "born regional."

A particularly relevant theory is that when new ventures internationalize, they are better able to realize firm-specific advantages in the home region of the triad, compared with other nonhome regions. Firm-specific advantages are unique resources and capabilities that may be based on marketing, distribution channels, and innovation systems, among other strategies. The advantages possessed by an internationalized firm are based ultimately on its internalization of an asset, such as production, marketing, or research and development (R&D) capabilities over which the firm has control. Essentially intraregional foreignness is preferable compared to interregional foreignness when considering internationalization. For example, firms are better able to reduce transaction costs by operating in markets similar to those of their home country. Another explanation is that by internationalizing within the home region of the triad, firms are better able to acquire information about local business practices as well as consumer tastes. Learning can take place more efficiently and effectively within the home region, because the countries in it are culturally related and in close geographic proximity. Evidence also suggests that firms are better able to deal with the institutional constraints of countries located within their intraregions than they are with the constraints of countries across interregions.

Despite a substantial increase in research on international new ventures over the past decade, most empirical studies are based on case studies or employ small samples of firms. Although there are examples of born-global firms in a number of case studies, these may be outliers from the standpoint of a large sample of firms. In a recent study utilizing a large, countrywide sample of 2236 Korean firms, In Hyeock Lee found evidence that 90 percent of all export sales for international Korean ventures came from the Asia Pacific region—their home region in the triad. Although additional research is needed, this notion challenges the dominant paradigm of international new ventures that are born global, suggesting instead that the regional relationship may be more dominant and the methods for most effectively internationalizing new ventures into foreign markets should be reassessed.

In Hyeock "Ian" Lee
Western Kentucky University

See also Geographic Location; Globalization; International Markets; Territorial Strategy and Regions

Further Readings

Delios, A. and P. W. Beamish. "Regional and Global Strategies of Japanese Firms." *Journal of International Business Studies*, v.45 (2005).

Ghemawat, P. "Semiglobalization and International Business Strategy." *Journal of International Business Studies*, v.34/2 (2003).

Johanson, J. and J.-E. Vahlne. "The Internationalization Process of the Firm: A Model of Knowledge Development and Increasing Foreign Market

Commitments." *Journal of International Business Studies*, v.8/1 (1977).

Johanson, J. and J.-E. Vahlne. "The Mechanism of Internationalization." *International Marketing Review*, v.7/4 (1990).

Lee, I. H. "The M Curve: The Performance of Born Regional Firms From Korea." *Multinational Business Review*, v.18/4 (2010).

Ohmae, K. *Triad Power: The Coming Shape of Global Competition.* New York: The Free Press, 1985.

Oviatt, B. M. and P. P. McDougall. "Defining International Entrepreneurship and Modeling the Speed of Internationalization." *Entrepreneurship Theory and Practice*, v.29 (2005).

Oviatt, B. M. and P. P. McDougall. "Toward a Theory of International New Ventures." *Journal of International Business Studies*, v.25/1 (1994).

Rugman, A. M. *The Regional Multinationals.* Cambridge, UK: Cambridge University Press, 2005.

Rugman, A. M. and A. Verbeke. "Liabilities of Regional Foreignness and the Use of Firm-Level Versus Country-Level Data: A Response to Dunning et al." *Journal of International Business Studies*, v.38/1 (2007).

Rugman, A. M. and A. Verbeke. "A Perspective on Regional and Global Strategies of Multinational Enterprises." *Journal of International Business Studies*, v.35/1 (2004).

JOB CREATION

In socioeconomic terms, any activity that provides opportunities for people to be engaged in income-generating occupations—either from new venture creation or from an already established business—is referred to as job creation. People seek paid employment to provide a living by allowing them to pay for their basic needs. Moreover, an inverse relationship exists between job creation and social problems. Hence, job creation remains a critical focus of governments in both developed and developing countries. New ventures, business expansions, and project development create new jobs. With labor statistics on job creation and high rates of unemployment telling the story of the state of the economy, it has become more important than ever for new ventures to thrive and thus enhance job creation.

Despite its well-established role in the history and theories of economics, job creation continues to generate concern in most parts of the world. It has acquired the status of a "best practice" by which to gauge the extent to which a government has performed successfully in terms of stimulating growth and development through policies that promote small-, medium-, and large-scale entrepreneurship. Microcredit and other financial services for businesses are examples of such programs. They are usually undertaken so that people are able to develop new businesses. When created, new ventures hire individuals to further the goals of the organization.

Job creation is associated with new ventures more than with existing businesses. When new ventures are created, people are hired to perform tasks that are required for the business or enterprise to survive and grow. No new venture is created without jobs being created. In contrast, existing large corporations sometimes ship jobs abroad to countries where labor is cheap. When businesses are established, they must hire employees; existing businesses, which already have a workforce, may freeze hiring over a long period of economic uncertainty to minimize costs. Downsizing or right-sizing as a cost-cutting strategy can occur only within existing firms, including big corporations, and not with new ventures. Cutting down on staff and freezing hiring remain popular with management as a best practice in restructuring. Hence, new venture creation deserves more attention as a job creation mechanism. Job creation expands when start-ups increase. This explains the principle behind microcredit financing as a global strategy for stimulating economic growth and development through small-scale entrepreneurship.

The global population is growing at a phenomenal rate. Expanding the rate of those who are accommodated by paid employment demands more job creation. When the population of a nation in the 18–60 age group grows astronomically, more people are available for work. Thus, planning new jobs through new ventures to accommodate the excess population so as to protect them from idleness, restlessness, poverty, despair, and crime becomes critical. Job creation requires governments to devise both

When a nation's economy is in a downturn, labor statistics studies generally report a decline in jobs created and high levels of unemployment. Job creation has become a critical focus of governments in both developed and developing countries in the early 21st century. (Photos.com)

micro- and macroeconomic policies to bring about an optimal engagement of the citizenry in the labor force. At times, job creation could involve the deliberate generation of new projects to employ large numbers of people.

Issues and Challenges

Creating new jobs is not easy anywhere. This problem results from the competitive demand for money across all sectors of the economy. Job creation programs are sometimes capital-intensive, requiring long-term investment. Moreover, the mobility of labor (both horizontal and vertical) within a country blurs the actual unemployment index, such that an accurate picture of the employment situation becomes difficult to ascertain; this, in turn, makes it difficult for policy makers to devise job creation strategies geared toward employment goals. Complicating this analytical difficulty is the fact that (according to statistics from the International Labour Office) support for new ventures and hence

job creation has declined among most central banks. Exacerbated by a world recession that began in 2008, this lack of support for new entrepreneurs has compounded global unemployment, underemployment, and poverty.

Another major problem bedeviling job creation, according to G. Epstein and E. Yeldan (2008), is financial globalization, which helps to redistribute limited jobs across countries, rather than accelerate capital accumulation and job creation across the globe. The authors view "global growth as highly uneven and geographically too concentrated to generate sufficient jobs worldwide with too little fixed capital formulation." Similarly, job creation by small and large firms has been comparatively examined, and these firms have been found to play different roles in the labor market. Whereas small and large firms provide roughly equivalent numbers of jobs, most job generation and destruction take place in small firms, which, according to Brian Headd (2010), generate the greater share of net new jobs. This is in line with David Birch's (1987) position on the role of small firms in creating opportunities for most people to work. Studies by researchers such as D. Johansson (2004) and others consistently support new businesses, especially small firms, as the critical source of new job creation and employment growth. It follows that job creation would be expanded through the effective creation of new small and medium-sized ventures, contrary to the stereotype that most small firms start small, stay small, and close just a few years after opening.

Benefits of Job Creation

The benefits derivable from job creation are numerous: At the individual level, jobs are needed to support people's material needs. Jobs also engage idle minds. Jobs improve people's quality of life and provide both psychological and obvious material benefits, which take the form of routine, structure, status, and avenues for social interaction. At the national and global levels, job creation provides security by lowering inactivity that can lead to crime. Jobs result in productivity, raising a country's gross national product (an index of the per capita income) through the doctrine of the "invisible hand." For a nation in transition, job creation increases the volume and quality of international trade through comparative advantage and discourages "brain drain" that arises from the mobility of labor. Job creation is a useful tool to stabilize developing economies with growing populations. When the working population is adequately engaged, there will be social and economic stability with fewer people available to engage in destructive conflict and agitation.

Finally, environmentally concerned advocates for green jobs hold the view that greener technology for power generation, transport, and food production will require more labor per unit of output than do nongreen or conventional methods, according to a study by R. H. G. Pollin, J. Heintz, and H. Scharber (2008). This type of new venture could check the problems of global warming and climate change while creating new jobs.

The challenges of shortage of capital, inflationary trends, downsizing, and the myriad other issues existing businesses face in surviving times of economic downturn require that more attention be directed at creating new ventures, which in turn will promote new job creation. During the 2008 global recession, existing businesses were either closing shop or downsizing. On the contrary, new businesses were hiring—once a business starts, it must hire. Expanding opportunities for job creation through new businesses consequently promotes talent identification, development, and the utilization of skilled individuals, which will in turn guide the 21st century in capacity building and development. Thus, a strong correlation exists between new venture creation and job creation.

John Oselenbalu Ekore
University of Ibadan

See also Community/Government Buy-Ins; Growth; Human Capital Theory; Human Resource Strategy; Human Resources; Managing Human and Social Capital; Public Policy: Government Stimulation of Start-Ups; Social Capital; Social Networks

Further Readings

Birch, D. *Job Creation in America: How Our Smallest Companies Put the Most People to Work.* New York: Free Press, 1987.

Epstein, G. and E. Yeldan. *Inflation Targeting, Employment Creation and Economic Development: Assess the Impacts and Policy Alternatives.* Abingdon: Routledge, 2008.

Headd, B. "An Analysis of Small Business and Jobs." SBA Office of Advocacy. http://www.sba.gov/advo (Accessed February 2011).

International Labour Office. *Global Employment Trends.* Geneva: Author, 2004.

Johansson, D. "Is Small Beautiful? The Case of the Swedish IT Industry." *Entrepreneurship and Regional Development*, v.16/4 (2004).

Pollin, R. H. G., J. Heintz, and H. Scharber. "Green Recovery: A Programme to Create Good Jobs and Start Building a Low Carbon Economy." 2008. http://www.americanprogress.org/issues/2008/09/pdf/green-Recovery.pdf (Accessed February 2011).

KNOWLEDGE

Knowledge is the representation of contextualized information in individual mental models exploited as both accessible facts and tacit skills or values of a fluid nature. In organizations, knowledge is a core resource, which is allocated by individual members and becomes a system's good when shared either within or between units. Knowledge transfer among units provides an opportunity for mutual learning, creation of new knowledge, and thus an organization's ability to innovate.

Modern perspectives on knowledge are based on far-reaching metaphysical discussions on what it means to know something. In antiquity, Plato and Aristotle promulgated theories on the origin of knowledge, claiming deductive thinking or pure sense experience as its source. In the early 1950s, the cognitive approach evolved, defining knowledge on a micro level as structured cognitive representation. According to this stream of research, the human being processes either direct or communicated information into cross-linked knowledge of the environment, subsequently saved as internal maps, according to American psychologist Edward C. Tolman. Data, mere discrete and objective facts, have to be interpreted by the user in order to be transformed into information. According to Ikujiro Nonaka, knowledge is derived from information by drawing comparisons and connections. In cognitive science, knowledge is described by distinguishing it in different types, according to John Robert Anderson: the representation of the facts about objects and phenomena (declarative knowledge) and the representation of skills and activities (procedural knowledge). Similarly, Michael Polanyi established the two dimensions of explicit and tacit knowledge. He described explicit knowledge as consciously accessible, because phenomena were perceived actively; in contrast, tacit knowledge is generated by performance but remains implicit and hardly expressible in propositional form. Both descriptions of knowledge are marked by the same idea: one type is an easily verbalized knowing-what, the other an experience-based knowing-how. Playing chess is a convenient example for illustrating the difference between knowing-what and knowing-how. Somebody who knows what chess is and even knows the rules does not necessarily know how to win. Particularly all implicit dimensions of knowledge become more and more important for interdisciplinary research.

From the macro perspective of organization theory, organizational knowledge is focused. The possessor of knowledge not only is delimited to actors but also can be located in the organization as a social system itself. The previously introduced concepts of "explicit" and "tacit" knowledge are applied analogically in the organizational context. Explicit knowledge is present in any organization, internally and externally. Inside an organization it is documented in files such databases, reports, the organization's intranet, or wikis, whereas external knowledge is available in any type of publication—in journals, in reports, or on the Internet. Tacit organizational knowledge is difficult—if not impossible—to articulate or codify, since it is growing in the collective (for example, as a component of organizational culture or daily routines). The knowledge of an organization is larger than the sum of the knowledge of its individuals, since it comprises interaction processes. In the past decades, the level of knowledge intensity in organizations has increased, heightening the importance of the management of those interactions. Thomas Davenport and Laurence Prusak, in their praxis-oriented book *Working Knowledge* (1998), understand knowledge as an interaction between actors that can strategically be changed with management processes. They describe those processes using the metaphor of brokers, buyers, and sellers dealing with good knowledge on open markets. All market actors negotiate about prices affected by supply and demand. Prices are established, influenced by factors such as reciprocity, reputation, trust, or altruism. Without a bilateral agreement on prices, the goods will not be exchanged; thus, the knowledge contents are not attaining further diffusion.

Davenport and Prusak's work strongly relates to the social network approach. Here the definition of knowledge is shifted completely toward a definition of shared knowledge, which is considered an interactive communication process between at least two actors. The approach is based on the importance of relationships among interacting units. Characteristics and explanations of shared knowledge are associated with various communication relations (or ties), such as the aforementioned factors, but also characteristics like frequency of knowledge exchange or multiplexity of knowledge contents. Mark Granovetter, who forwarded the term *ties*, in the 1970s exposed the vital importance of the quality of the relations for an operating communication by highlighting the role of trust. The network analysis enables the measurement of the knowledge flows in networks and illustrates the strength of ties, the cohesion between the actors, and the position of the actors in networks, to reveal possible patterns that facilitate the knowledge exchange. Knowledge sharing is also seen embedded in broader organizational networks, where ties among individuals assist the transfer and enhance receiving quality.

Knowledge is a significant resource for all ventures, providing sustainable advantage in a dynamic and competitive economy. In explaining the effects of knowledge in the context of entrepreneurship, both micro and macro approaches are used. From a micro perspective, innovative performance and other entrepreneurial outcomes are examined with a finer-grained approach to knowledge focusing on the individual. Understanding how the entrepreneur creates breakthrough innovations is here of vital importance. Many studies therefore investigate different types of knowledge. For example, Teresa Amabile posited that the combination of technological and market knowledge is beneficial for developing new ideas. Creativity is enhanced when the individual's cognitive representation facilitates the ability to link divergent knowledge types. However, before the creation of new ideas results in entrepreneurial exploitation, opportunities to apply them need to be discovered. The Austrian economists believe that the possession of certain knowledge contents allows people to see particular opportunities others cannot see. In line with that, Scott Shane (2000) demonstrated that prior knowledge combined with technology knowledge enhances entrepreneurs' ability to recognize opportunity and exploit new technologies. Therefore, three major dimensions of prior knowledge are important in the process of opportunity discovery: knowledge of markets, knowledge of ways to serve the market, and knowledge of customers' problems.

Matthew Marvel and G. T. Lumpkin (2007) integrated those three dimensions in their study on the influence of human capital on innovation radicalness and identified technology knowledge and knowledge of ways to serve the market as strong predictors of radical innovations. Counterintuitively, however, they found that knowing less about developing and packaging new products or services at an early point seems to be advantageous for radical innovations. The authors argued that a rather high level of knowledge about customers, markets, and development standards may inhibit the ability to detach from standards and norms and therefore may stifle creativity. However, next to the very specific types of knowledge, a rather broad understanding of the notion, referring to general work experiences or nonformal education such as training, is essential for entrepreneurs' innovativeness. The more diverse a person's work experience is, the greater will be his access to new information that provides answers to existing conjectures.

Furthermore, Diamanto Politis (2005) developed a conceptual framework focusing on entrepreneurial experience and entrepreneurial knowledge. In this model, entrepreneurial knowledge is regarded as "effectiveness in recognizing and acting on entrepreneurial opportunities and coping with the liabilities of newness." Corresponding to Shane (2000), this view posits that entrepreneurs learn via transforming prior, current, and shared experiences into new and useful knowledge, which supports the entrepreneurs' ability to discover, seize, and exploit entrepreneurial opportunities and helps them to cope with the barriers new ventures traditionally face.

In addition to the aforementioned micro approaches, there are macro approaches for examining various types of knowledge in the context of entrepreneurship. For example, Bjorn Asheim and Lars Coenen (2005) distinguish between two types of knowledge on which ventures can rely. They argue that firms' innovative performances are highly dependent on their specific knowledge bases, which include either analytical or synthetic contents. An analytical knowledge base is created independent of facts or experiences with a rather deductive reasoning. In contrast, the synthetic knowledge base refers to reasoning that establishes truth inductively, by observations or other proven facts. In their view, analytical knowledge bases exist in industrial settings, where scientific knowledge is highly important. In the innovation process, firms create their knowledge based on cognitive processes through their own research and development (R&D) departments or draw on external knowledge through results of studies from universities or other research institutions. They assert that analytical knowledge application results in new products and processes that constitute radical innovations, which frequently leads to the formation of new spin-off companies. Synthetic knowledge exists in industrial settings where innovation takes place primarily through the application of novel combinations of prevailing knowledge. Here, knowledge is created with inductive processes, such as those often found in applied research (which involves testing or experimenting through simulations and prototypes). The innovation process is regularly oriented toward novel efficient and practical solutions and leads to rather incremental innovations, which rarely results in founding new companies. Hence, new processes and products that constitute radical innovations are more likely to be born from analytic rather than synthetic knowledge.

From a macro perspective, knowledge about technology is important, but in addition market knowledge is essential for successful innovation processes. Here market knowledge refers to the firm's knowledge about its customers and competitors. Luigi Luca and Kwaku Atuahene-Gima (2007) examined various dimensions of market knowledge, such as breadth, depth, tacitness, and specificity. In their study they underlined the importance of a firm's broad understanding of diverse customers and competitors in product innovation. Furthermore, they investigated the role of the firm's knowledge integration mechanisms. They refer to formal structures and processes that ensure capturing, analyzing, interpreting, and combining knowledge within the firm via information-sharing meetings, analysis of failed and successful projects, or external consultancy. Those mechanisms enhance the effect of market knowledge depth and specificity on product innovation performance. Here the need for a more fine-grained notion of (market) knowledge is supported, as the effects of dimensions vary in strength and directness. Moreover, this contributes to the need to shed light on knowledge-sharing processes.

As posited in the social network approach, organizations must consider the process of knowledge sharing in the firm itself. A great amount of knowledge content abounds in organizations and the networks in which they are embedded. Existing cognitive resources within a unit remain unused if knowledge-sharing processes are not seen as critical to create new knowledge. A successful exchange of knowledge concurs with organizational theory on learning, as learning is seen as a process whereby individuals acquire and develop both explicit and tacit knowledge based on existing knowledge by exchanging and recombining it, according to W. Cohen and D. Levinthal (1990). Such intra- or interunit links enable ventures to gain competencies or capabilities and contribute to enhanced performance. Hence, partners in joint ventures who acquire and assimilate new external knowledge increase their performance; firms that learn about customers, suppliers, or competitors have better chances to adapt their products or services to emerging needs. Firms that seek to develop new applications benefit from those sharing processes by provoking innovative behavior. However, sharing diverse knowledge brings forth exploratory innovations, whereas the exchange of specific knowledge related to traditional topics of the firm tends to result in rather exploitative innovations.

Entrepreneurs who develop bonding networks from frequent interaction accrue a high level of knowledge exchange. Entrepreneurs who participate in incubator networks share common values for being linked and thus exchange experiences, overcoming the status of novice during business start-ups.

Maura Kessel
Jan Kratzer
Hans Georg Gemünden
Technical University of Berlin

See also Cognition; Information; Knowledge-Based View; Learning Theory; Social Networks

Further Readings

Amabile, Teresa. "How to Kill Creativity." *Harvard Business Review*, v.76/5 (1998).

Asheim, Bjorn and Lars Coenen. "Knowledge Bases and Regional Innovation Systems: Comparing Nordic Cluster." *Research Policy*, v.34 (2005).

Asheim, Bjorn, and M. S. Gertler. "Geography of Innovation." In *The Oxford Handbook of Innovation*, J. Fagerberg, D. C. Mowery, and R. R. Nelson, eds. New York: Oxford University Press, 2005.

Cohen, W. and D. Levinthal. "Absorptive Capacity: A New Perspective on Learning and Innovation." *Administrative Science Quarterly*, v.35 (1990).

Davenport, Thomas and Laurence Prusak. *Working Knowledge: How Organizations Manage What They Know*. Cambridge, MA: Harvard Business School Press, 1998.

De Luca, Luigi and Kwaku Atuahene-Gima. "Market Knowledge Dimensions and Cross-Functional Collaboration: Examining the Different Routes to Product Innovation Performance." *Journal of Marketing*, v.71 (2007).

Granovetter, M. "The Strength of Weak Ties." *American Journal of Sociology*, v.78/6 (1973).

Marvel, Matthew and G. T. Lumpkin. "Technology Entrepreneurs: Human Capital and Its Effects on Innovation Radicalness." *Entrepreneurship Theory and Practice*, v.31 (2007).

Politis, Diamanto. "The Process of Entrepreneurial Learning: A Conceptual Framework." *Entrepreneurship Theory and Practice*, v.29/4 (2005).

Shane, Scott. "Prior Knowledge and the Discovery of Entrepreneurial Opportunities." *Organization Science*, v.11/4 (2000).

Van Wijk, Raymond et al. "Inter- and Intra-Organizational Knowledge Transfer: A Meta-Analytic Review and Assessment of Its Antecedents and Consequences." *Journal of Management Studies*, v.45 (2008).

KNOWLEDGE-BASED VIEW

An emerging theory of the firm, the knowledge-based view (KBV) considers a firm's knowledge as the most strategically significant resource of a firm. Originating from the strategic management literature, this perspective builds upon and extends the resource-based view (RBV) of the firm initially promoted by Edith Penrose in her book, *The Theory of the Growth of the Firm* (1959) and later expanded by others. Although the RBV recognizes the important role of knowledge in firms that achieve a competitive advantage, the KBV argues that knowledge, unlike generic resources, has special characteristics. In fact, proponents of the KBV argue that firms exist because they better integrate and apply specialized knowledge than do markets and can better protect knowledge from expropriation and imitation than can markets. Thus, KBV suggests that knowledge generation, accumulation. and application may be the source of superior performance.

The study of KBV and how firms generate, leverage, transfer, integrate, and protect knowledge often overlaps with the study of knowledge management and knowledge (technology) transfer. Knowledge management requires that firms define knowledge, identify existing knowledge bases, and provide mechanisms to promote the creation, protection, and transfer of knowledge. Whereas information systems provide a technological repository of knowledge, increasingly firms recognize that the key to successful knowledge management requires attending to the social and cultural systems of the organization. The proponents of KBV argue that because knowledge-based resources are usually difficult to imitate and socially complex, heterogeneous knowledge bases and capabilities among firms are the major determinants of sustained competitive advantage and superior firm performance. This knowledge is embedded and carried through multiple entities, including organizational culture and identity, policies, routines, documents, systems, and employees. Firms are repositories of knowledge and competencies, and firms have superior capability in creating and transferring knowledge. Knowledge creation and innovation arise from new combinations of knowledge, where a firm can accumulate that knowledge and utilize that knowledge in new productive opportunities.

Regarding the study and management of new ventures, the notion that different knowledge is needed in the different phases of the new-venture life cycle is important for practitioners seeking growth, especially in knowledge-based industries. Both explicit (articulated, codified, and storable) and tacit (difficult-to-transfer) knowledge can be very important. It is generally argued, however, that tacit knowledge is more strategically important, as it is embedded in people and extremely difficult for competitors to replicate. In RBV terminology, it is inimitable. Additionally, when we look at the need for resources to change over time to maintain their market relevance, we require adaption and learning for this change to occur. This learning that facilitates the change relates to knowledge, one of the most flexible resources to which a firm has access. Firms and the people who compose them can change their knowledge over time. Ikujiro Nonaka and H. Takeuchi identified four knowledge-creation processes, including socialization, externalization, combination, and internalization. Socialization is a process that focuses on converting new tacit knowledge through shared tacit experiences. Firms gain new knowledge from outside organizational boundaries—for example, through interacting with customers, suppliers, and investors. Combination is a process whereby explicit knowledge transforms into new explicit knowledge. Examples include sorting, adding, categorizing, and other creative uses of databases. Externalization is a process focusing on tacit-to-explicit knowledge linking, that is, where knowledge is crystallized. In the internalization process, explicit knowledge is created by cataloging tacit knowledge and is shared across the organization, such as when codified tacit knowledge is read or practiced by individuals. These four processes have been found to mediate new venture strategy and firm performance across a variety of entrepreneurial firms.

Central to the understanding of the KBV is the definition of knowledge. Additionally, it is important to understand that while the KBV focuses on firm knowledge, individuals and their human capital contribute to the knowledge found at the firm level. Knowledge has long been a topic within the human capital and human resources management (HRM) literature. In fact, the major distinction between the KBV and HRM literatures with regard to knowledge has to do with the focus of the knowledge and its level. HRM literature focuses on testing applicants for job-related knowledge, training employees to build their job-related knowledge, developing participation and communication systems to transfer knowledge, or providing incentives for individuals to apply their knowledge. KBV focuses on knowledge as broadly accessible, organizationally shared, and transferable, that is, particularly market relevant, such as knowledge regarding customers, competitors, or knowledge relevant to the creation of new products. In KBV, knowledge can be viewed as something that characterizes individuals (human capital), but it can also be shared within groups or networks (social capital) or institutionalized within organizational processes and databases (organizational capital). The processes of creation, transfer, and exploitation of knowledge provide common ground across the two fields.

Preeta M. Banerjee
Brandeis University
Benjamin A. Campbell
The Ohio State University

See also Adaptation; Human Capital Theory; Human Resource Strategy; Human Resources; Knowledge; Resource-Based View

Further Readings

Conner, K. R. "A Historical Comparison of the Resource-Based Theory and Five Schools of Thought Within Industrial Organization Economics: Do We Have a New Theory of the Firm?" *Journal of Management*, v.17/1 (1991).

Grant, R. M. "Prospering in Dynamically-Competitive Environments: Organizational Capability as Knowledge Integration." *Organization Science*, v.7/4 (1996).

Grant, R. M. "Toward a Knowledge-Based Theory of the Firm." *Strategic Management Journal*, v.17 (Winter 1996).

Kogut, B. "The Network as Knowledge: Generative Rules and the Emergence of Structure." *Strategic Management Journal*, v.21 (2008).

Kogut, B. and U. Zander. "Knowledge of the Firm, Combinative Capabilities, and the Replication of Technology." *Organization Science*, v.3/3 (1992).

Liebeskind, J. P. "Knowledge, Strategy, and the Theory of the Firm." *Strategic Management Journal*, v.17 (Winter 1996).

Nonaka, I. and H. Takeuchi. *The Knowledge-Creating Company: How Japanese Companies Create the Dynamics of Innovation.* New York: Oxford University Press, 1995.

Penrose, E. *The Theory of the Growth of the Firm.* New York: John Wiley and Sons, 1959.

Saarenketo, S., K. Puumalainen, O. Kuivalainen, and K. Kyläheiko. "A Knowledge-Based View of Growth in New Ventures." *European Business Review*, v.21/6 (2009).

Spender, J. C. "Making Knowledge the Basis of a Dynamic Theory of the Firm." *Strategic Management Journal*, v.17 (Winter 1996).

Wright, P., B. Dunford, and S. Snell. "Human Resources and the Resource Based View of the Firm." *Journal of Management*, v.27 (2001).

LABOR COSTS

Labor costs are those expenses incurred by a new venture in the acquisition, development, engagement, and disengagement of the human capital necessary for its current and future operations. It is useful to think of labor costs as falling into three major categories— direct, indirect, and overhead. Direct labor costs usually refer to payroll-related expenses, such as direct wages and salaries, whether base pay or incentives; the employer's portions of payroll taxes and contributions required by national law, state law, and union agreements; and the costs of benefits paid directly to the employees or on their behalf during the period. Indirect labor costs are expenses that will be incurred in future periods to provide compensation or benefits, where the employee has a vested claim against the firm. Overhead labor costs are all of those indirect expenses involved in hiring, training, and maintaining the workforce. Managing these categories of labor costs needs to take place at the strategic, tactical, and operational levels in a new venture.

Strategic labor cost management involves making policy decisions about all aspects of the employment relationship that influence future labor costs. These decisions have the most impact on labor costs, as they determine the number of employees, the nature of the employment relationship, the type and level of compensation and benefits, and the overhead costs that will be incurred. Strategic labor cost management begins with job analysis and workforce planning to determine those jobs the firm requires and the number of employees needed in those jobs as the firm ramps up its volume of operations. Strategic decisions must be made on which jobs will be performed by firm employees and the mix of full-time or part-time workers; which jobs may be outsourced or offshored to other firms; and which jobs might be accomplished by nonemployee contingent labor such as consultants, independent contractors, and temporary staff. These decisions will influence the methods of recruitment, hiring, and training by the firm and consequent overhead costs. If a firm decides to employ most of its workforce directly, then this will usually require more overhead costs in its human resource (HR) function. Hiring employees requires policy decisions on pay and benefits and whether the firm will lead, match, or lag compensation in its labor market. Whether to use incentive compensation via bonuses paid in current periods and deferred compensation in cash or stock options is an important decision that influences future costs, as are decisions about the number and level of voluntary benefits that will be provided to employees. These decisions influence the amount of direct, indirect, and overhead labor costs the new firm will incur and how much flexibility it will have in varying these costs in the future.

Tactical labor cost management primarily focuses on how strategic decisions can most cost-effectively be implemented. These are most often "make versus buy" decisions; the new venture must determine whether or when it will establish a formal HR management function or contract for all or part of the services provided by this function. For example, outsourcing firms are available that provide all HR services and can provide economies of scale in payroll and benefit processing. However, as a new venture grows in employment, in range of 50 to 100 employees, it usually finds it more cost-effective to establish its own in-house HR function that either provides or oversees provision of employment-related services and functions as a central point to control labor costs. In this case, outsourcing of certain individual HR services may be cost-effective. As the venture grows, it will continue to face "make versus buy" decisions as to whether it is more cost-effective to bring a program in house or continue contracting.

Operational labor cost management focuses on the day-to-day control of direct labor expenses, since most indirect and overhead expenses are determined primarily at the strategic and tactical levels. Controlling hiring and scheduling are the most common methods of managing operational labor costs by matching workers to operational demands. To the degree that a firm uses contingent, nonemployee labor, it greatly increases its ability to ramp up or down labor costs based on volume fluctuations, while the use of part-time and overtime provide flexibility with its own employees. In terms of compensation, the more a firm is able to use variable and incentive compensation that is tied to performance, productivity, and volume, the more flexibility it retains. Benefit costs tend to be much more difficult to flex. Policy decisions that retain the firm's discretion in providing matching versus fixed retirement contributions and the employer's ability to vary contributions to other benefit plans can provide flexibility. Mandatory dispute resolution programs that require arbitration of employment disputes can reduce legal costs. Safety programs that prevent workplace injuries can significantly reduce workers' compensation costs, as can carefully managing employment levels to avoid costs of downsizing and resulting unemployment compensation and severance expense.

Tom J. Sanders
University of Montevallo

See also Human Capital Theory; Human Resource Strategy; Human Resources; Labor-Management Relations in Start-Ups

Further Readings

Corporate Executive Board. "Finding New Reductions in Labor Costs." *Bloomberg Businessweek* (April 30, 2010).

Dessler, Gary. *Human Resource Management*, 11th ed. Upper Saddle River, NJ: Pearson Prentice Hall, 2008.

Drager, Colette and Leah Davis. "Managing Labor Costs to Improve Your Bottom Line." http://www.mnpork.com/producers/documents/managing_costs_bottom_workforce.pdf (Accessed December 2010).

Milkovich, George T., Jerry M. Newman, and Barry Gerhart. *Compensation*, 10th ed. New York: McGraw-Hill Irwin, 2011.

Stevenson, Paul B. "Five Simple Tools for Managing Labor Costs." *Healthcare Financial Management* (January 2004).

LABOR-MANAGEMENT RELATIONS IN START-UPS

Labor-management relations in start-ups can be described from two perspectives: as part of a wider corporate strategy (for example, when new subsidiaries are established overseas) and in terms of start-ups from scratch, based on the initiative of an individual entrepreneur together with partners. The latter type of start-up is the focus here, particularly "high-tech" or knowledge-intensive start-ups, which have special needs.

Conceptualizing the birth, youth, and mature age of a firm as a life cycle, the start-up period coincides with the venture's birth as well as its childhood and even youth; there is no consensus regarding the precise time one reserves for the start-up period. However, according to the *Farlex Financial Dictionary* a start-up is defined as a company in its earliest stage of development, usually before its initial public offering (IPO). The start-up usually concentrates on product prototype development and the build-up of capitalization, and hence operates at least in the very beginning at a loss rather than gaining quick profits. The start-up is therefore dependent on venture capital or loans to continue operations during this phase. It could be noted that a business model alternative to the one described above is to aim for an "exit" different from an IPO—for example, by demonstrating convincingly the possession of a technology attractive enough for an acquisition by an incumbent firm.

There is no blueprint regarding the optimal way to staff or manage a start-up. Researchers have, however, described several types of start-ups and various challenges associated with these types. Expanding on a theme developed by Robert K. Kazanjian, Christine S. Koberg and her colleagues have illuminated how there tend to be contingencies among ownership structures and the organization of work determined according to the developmental stage of the high-tech company in question. Thus, where the start-up (and the preceding "embryonic") company is led by the owner-founder, or in some exceptional cases by a manager, the more mature firm is led by technical experts. Continuing with such start-up versus mature firm comparisons, the hierarchical complexity tends to be work groups versus functional specialization, incentives in the form of (anticipated) stocks versus salaries or bonuses, decisions that are decentralized versus centralized, and strategies that are focused versus differentiated. The ambitious start-up firm tends to be founded on an idea where both the product to be developed and the potential market are of an extremely insecure nature, and this insecurity in turn explains the need for an extra degree of flexibility when it comes to organizational forms, including labor-management relations.

Amar V. Bhidé has identified some useful distinctions in evaluating the possibilities and constraints surrounding the managerial challenges of start-ups: whether the start-up may be characterized as a "corporate initiative," "marginal start-up," "revolutionary venture," "promising start-up," or "venture capital-backed" start-up. Each of the types has its specific history and context, as well as appropriate managerial processes. Regarding the latter two types, the promising start-up is characterized by the founding entrepreneur's personal capacity to adapt and persuade resource providers, whereas the venture-capital-backed start-up also includes the potential for personal initiative but is, for better or worse, subject to monitoring.

One overriding concern is thus the challenge in connection with achieving a balance between a creative entrepreneurial spirit, on one hand, and a more systematic and professional structure, on the other hand. This challenge may be particularly evident in cases where the founder has a scientific background, as occurs with many university spin-offs, and where she or he thus might become overly concerned with scientific or technological visions at the expense of day-to-day management of the company. Gary P. Pisano has highlighted this dilemma for biotech firms by stressing that science

Scholars have found that the key to providing a team with leadership and motivation is to develop management systems that can sustain a balance between creative and structural types of workers. (Photos.com)

and business work in different ways, in the sense that they have different cultures, values, and norms. Within science, the methodology is held in the highest esteem, whereas in the business world, results are in the high seat. When these two worlds come together in biotech, the challenges that may stand in the way of success are considerable, at both the company and industry levels.

The creativity versus structure topic was elaborated on in a paper by Antonio Davila and his colleagues in which they pointed to (and, to a certain extent, countered) the widely held notion of structures being able to kill off innovative activity. In connection with the "entrepreneurial crisis" that many companies experience when they reach a certain size, generally between 50 and 100 employees, the management methods suddenly and invariably have to be transformed from a personal to a professionalized style. Davila and his colleagues argue that an earlier implementation of a professionalized style is better and that there is little risk in losing the entrepreneurial spirit if such systems are implemented earlier in a good way. Indeed, start-ups funded by venture capital may have some incentive toward or guidance related to the implementation of structured systems and may take advantage of this opportunity.

Apart from showing the need for balance between creativity and structure, one additional insight from research has been to point to the challenge of managing a heterogeneous workforce. In other words, the labor-management relations of a start-up will invariably be influenced by the fact that the workforce will be formed by people of rather different, albeit complementary, competencies. Labor-management relations must consequently be molded on a belief that although there should be structures and rules referring to collective values and common goals, the management of individual organization members must simultaneously take the differences in roles and competencies into consideration. Edward B. Roberts and Alan R. Fusfeld have provided an overview of competencies typically found in such organizations, ranging from the "technical innovator" (an expert in one or two fields who generates new ideas) to "project leader" (one who provides the team with leadership and motivation). The key, according to Roberts and Fusfeld, is then to accommodate both the creative and the structural (types) and develop management systems that can sustain a good balance between the two.

Following up on this theme, albeit while focusing on some characteristics that may also be common for mature companies with "knowledge workers," Sue Newell and her colleagues have emphasized the need to manage "skillfully"—in other words, acknowledge that this type of employee necessitates special measures. Considering the competitive situation for this kind of labor, there is a need for good employment terms and conditions. Furthermore, organization modes should be conducive to the type of creative work people are expected to do. One should therefore pay attention not only to structural aspects but also to the cultural conditions within the venture.

Terje Grønning
University of Oslo

See also Human Resource Strategy; Human Resources; Labor Costs

Further Readings

Bhidé, Amar V. *The Origin and Evolution of New Businesses*. Oxford, UK: Oxford University Press, 1999.

Davila, Antonio, George Foster, and Ning Jia. "Building Sustainable High-Growth Startup Companies: Management Systems as an Accelerator." *California Management Review*, v.52/3 (2010).

Kazanjian, Robert K. "Relation of Dominant Problems to Stages of Growth in Technology-Based New Ventures." *Academy of Management Journal* (June 1988).

Koberg, Christine S., Yolanda Sarason, and Joseph Rosse. "A Taxonomic Approach to Studying High-Technology Firms: Deciphering the Tower of Babel." *Journal of High Technology Management Research*, v.7/1 (1996).

Lester, Donald L., John A. Parnell, and Shawn Carraher. "Organizational Life Cycle: A Five-Stage Empirical Scale." *International Journal of Organizational Analysis*, v.11/4 (2003).

Nesheim, John L. *High Tech Start-Up: Creating Successful New High Tech Companies*. New York: Free Press, 2000.

Newell, Sue, Maxine Robertson, Harry Scarbrough, and Jacky Swan. *Managing Knowledge Work and Innovation*, 2nd ed. New York: Palgrave Macmillan, 2009.

Pisano, Gary P. *Science Business: The Promise, the Reality, and the Future of Biotech*. Cambridge, MA: Harvard Business School Press, 2006.

Roberts, Edward B. and Alan R. Fusfeld. "Staffing the Innovative Technology-Based Organization." *Sloan Management Review* (Spring 1981).

LEADERSHIP

Leadership is generally a process whereby a person influences others to accomplish a set of goals or objectives within an organization. Leadership and authority can be confused with each other. Authority describes the assigned power one person has over another; however, having authority does not make someone a leader—it makes him or her a boss. Effective leaders have the ability to cause followers to want to achieve desired outcomes, so the exercise of power becomes less important. Herein lies the art of leadership. Leadership in new or entrepreneurial ventures may be considered as a special case or subset of leadership in general.

The conditions affecting new ventures may be sufficiently different from those of established businesses to favor individuals with specific leadership traits or styles. A study done in South Africa identified a set of important entrepreneurial characteristics that are distinct from transformational leadership characteristics. The study found a medium degree of positive correlation between high scores on both sets of traits. Another study, of 112 start-up firms housed in business incubators in Taiwan, used the number of patents created as a measure of success. This study found no correlation with leadership style. Team members' assessments of leaders' traits of risk taking, innovativeness, and proactiveness correlated with assessments of creativity.

One can reasonably question whether entrepreneurial leadership is distinct or different from leadership in any firm. Warren Bennis has found that there are four traits common to all leaders, including management of attention, meaning, trust, and self-esteem. Bennis also noted that entrepreneurs are far likelier to have business-owning fathers or other relatives. However, Bennis also noted some distinct differences between start-up owners and seasoned managers, including a greater need for autonomy, more creative tendencies, and a higher calculated risk-taking orientation.

Although the differences between entrepreneurial leadership and leadership in general are subtle, both types benefit from the study of trait and process theories of leadership to help explain and identify successful leaders. Traits, which include the leader's knowledge, skill, physical appearance, and extroversion, for example, have a unilateral effect on followers because traits reside in the leader, and the follower simply reacts to them. Process leadership is generally defined by the relationship developed between the leader and his or her followers. Whereas

A company's human capital cannot be owned, but leaders often overlook the value of human assets, in part because they are not a balance sheet item. Herein lies the art of leadership. (Photos.com)

the processes can be influenced by the leader's traits, the primary focus is on what the leader does with his or her assets. What processes the leader chooses and how they are used is further influenced by philosophies of leadership, business, and by culture.

The "Be, Know, Do" model of leadership helps to describe why followers are willing to be guided by leaders. *Be* describes the character of the leader, *Know* describes his or her abilities, and *Do* describes the implementation of the leader's skills in ways that cause followers to be motivated and the goals and objectives of the organization to be met. Ultimately, leaders are most effective when they have earned the respect of their followers.

Studies have shown that social and emotional intelligence are the cornerstone traits of the best leaders. Perhaps the best way to understand what makes the most effective leaders is to deconstruct the leader's attributes.

Traits of Leaders

Part of the deconstruction of effective leaders relies on the concept of emotional intelligence. Emotional intelligence refers to the capacity to understand and explain emotions, on one hand, and of emotions to enhance thought, on the other. According to Daniel Goleman, the elements of social and emotional intelligence (EI) that are most closely correlated with a leader's effectiveness include self-awareness, self-regulation, motivation, empathy, and social skills. Self-awareness is a reflective action and describes one's understanding of how emotions affect actions and decision making. A critical piece of self-awareness includes an accurate self-assessment. Self-regulation refers to the ability to control one's actions in a positive and effective way; it also includes trustworthiness. Motivation causes one to embrace challenges and enjoy stimulation. Empathy allows one to understand things from other points of view. Finally, social skills enable better communication, listening, and negotiating.

There are four branches to emotional intelligence; perception, facilitation, understanding emotions, and emotional management. The perception and facilitation branches most closely relate to feelings, and the understanding and management branches relate to calculating and planning with information about emotions so that decisions can be made more effectively. As John Mayer and David Caruso pointed out, "findings suggest that people high in EI form strong relations with others and have reliable support networks. Other people come to help these individuals in times of need. By contrast, people low in EI are socially perplexed, and are relatively more prone to drug and alcohol use, and to using aggressive and violent behavior to solve problems." Furthermore, research is suggesting that leaders high in EI develop stronger teams, communicate better, and build a stronger social fabric. Those low in EI have more problems through their behavior in the workplace.

The leader's ability to use introspection when assessing decisions is an important application. Many studies support the notion that leaders who perform best on emotional intelligence tests are more effective overall and that the need for emotional intelligence becomes even more critical as the leader gains more seniority. In a study that tracked 80 scientists from Berkeley from 1950 to 1980, researchers discovered that those with high emotional intelligence were four times more likely to enjoy success and prestige than were those who had lower emotional intelligence scores and higher IQs.

Emotional intelligence requires a great deal of introspection, or the act of objectively assessing the impact one, as a leader, is having on organizational effectiveness. A person's emotional intelligence can be assessed through testing, and that might be beneficial. Emotional intelligence can also be learned to some degree. Generally, the older a person is, the more emotionally intelligent he or she has become. This finding suggests that emotional intelligence is learned through life experiences. Other findings indicate that courses on improving emotional intelligence can cause both short- and long-term gains.

In business, measuring a leader's emotional intelligence will provide little information regarding the leader's actual effectiveness in a particular organization. Measurements of profitability, customer and employee satisfaction, and public perception are the metrics most useful in that endeavor. However, unless the leader exercises emotional intelligence, the introspection necessary to react to these metrics will be mostly absent.

Leader Process Philosophy and Goals

Leaders do not exercise their traits in a vacuum. Leaders are influenced by philosophical choices in the subjects of leadership, business and economics, and culture. Often, an organization's success is measured by its ability to create value for its shareholders. For example, shareholder and stakeholder theories address what should be important for businesses. Shareholder theory espouses that a business's only responsibility is to its shareholders, and therefore increasing profitability is all that matters. In business schools and on Wall Street, the profitability metric has become the overriding standard. Stakeholder theory holds that businesses have a responsibility to all individuals and constituencies that have an interest in the business. These stakeholders will include employees, customers, communities, and governments.

When one subscribes to the stakeholder theory of corporations, one is acknowledging the importance of success metrics beyond profitability. It can also be argued that without good relations among employees, customers, communities, and governments, profitability is harder to attain. Assuming nonprofitability metrics are important, it follows that they must be measured. Within a business, it is easiest to measure employee and customer satisfaction.

Keeping employees satisfied helps organizations thrive. Nearly 70 percent of all operating costs are ultimately attributable to people. Human capital cannot be owned, and therefore it is critical to both lead and manage it wisely. However, considering the power paradox, it is unlikely that many leaders will value human assets, because they are not a balance sheet item, and as the leader advances, she or he tends to become oblivious to why others matter. The same holds true for customer satisfaction. If a leader fails to see things from another's point of view, he or she will lack the ability to understand and respond to customer complaints. These tendencies could be exaggerated in a leader who subscribes to the shareholder philosophy rather than to the stakeholder philosophy, because the application of shareholder theory tends to focus on short-term gain.

If one were to take the Machiavellian view, the best leaders are those who strive to be great and remarkable through the concealment of their intentions, the seeking of attention, being selectively honest, and ruling through fear. Eastern thought espouses the benefits of just the opposite: modesty and social intelligence.

Two fairly recently evolved theories of leadership have attempted to address focusing on others as the leader's primary concern. One of these theories is called transformational leadership, and the other is called servant leadership. The primary theorists behind transformational leadership are James Burns, Bruce Avolio, and Bernard Bass. Transformational leadership is defined as the ability to identify necessary changes, create the vision to drive the changes, inspire people to embrace the changes, and execute the changes. Transformational leadership manifests itself in four ways; individualized consideration, intellectual stimulation, inspirational motivation, and idealized influence. Jim Kouzes and Barry Posner elaborated on the transformational type of leadership in their writings on the "leadership challenge." Their five practices of exemplary leadership include modeling the way, inspiring a shared vision, challenging the process, enabling others to act, and encouraging the heart.

A 2010 study conducted by Daniel J. McCarthy and his colleagues, focusing on exemplary entrepreneurs in Russia over a period of four years, found that their leadership styles were similar to those found in U.S. entrepreneurs. The open transformational style was predominant in two thirds of the leaders studied, and a balanced style was found in another 25 percent. Furthermore, the percentage exhibiting the open style increased over the years 2003 to 2007. It seems that, despite a long history of authoritarian and autocratic leadership in Russia, successful entrepreneurial leaders seldom used that style.

Robert Greenleaf coined the term *servant leadership*. The primary focus of servant leadership is to serve colleagues, employees, customers, and other stakeholders. In this case, the leader is seen as a humble steward of all organizational resources. Servant leaders exemplify qualities such as empathy, the ability to listen, awareness, persuasion, conceptualization, foresight, stewardship, and community building. Servant leaders practice self-awareness, listening, changing the pyramid, developing colleagues, coaching and not controlling, unleashing the energy and intelligence of others, and foresight. Obvious similarities exist between the concepts of servant leadership and the elements of emotional intelligence, specifically self-awareness, empathy, and social skills.

Jim Collins, author of *Good to Great*, wrote about his research that identified "level 5 leadership." He stated that level 5 leaders build greatness through a "paradoxical combination of humility and professional will" and they are at once shy and fearless. The personal humility level 5 leaders exemplify includes modesty, the shunning of public attention, inspiring standards (not charisma) to motivate others, assuring ambitions are directed to the company and not him- or herself, taking personal responsibility for poor results (never blaming other factors), and having an unwavering resolve. Collins noted that often a significant life experience causes leaders to ascend to level 5 leadership. This significant event can be so compelling that the leaders learn that introspection is the key to their ability to withstand problems and overcome them. Level 5 leaders transformed their companies' performance to a degree not seen in companies run by level 4 leaders. Level 4 leaders tend to offer a compelling vision, and they have the ability to stimulate groups to a higher performance. These abilities correlate with a number of the transformational leadership characteristics. However, the introspective nature of servant leaders and highly emotionally intelligent leaders is missing. The significant differences in outcomes between level 5 and level 4 leaders is that the former are able to sustain great companies over long periods of time. Level 4 leaders engender success, but the success is far shorter lived and of a lower level.

The concepts of Burns, Bass, and Avolio's transformational leadership, Kouzes and Posner's leadership challenge, and Collin's level 5 leadership have many commonalities. The leaders are outwardly, rather than inwardly, focused as pertains to outcomes as a result of their efforts. This outward focus incorporates employees, the business itself, and colleagues and customers. Transformational leadership emphasizes the leader's role as the charismatic and visionary person at the helm. Collins challenges this concept, adding that the best leaders are humble and shun the spotlight. However, in all theories, the leaders are compelled to inspire, motivate, develop employees, and encourage greatness in others. Additionally, great leaders are introspective as it pertains to how they apply their skills. They continually reassess their motives and the effects they have on others.

Unfortunately, once leaders have earned respect and gained power, their effectiveness in leading often becomes compromised. Dacher Keltner, a professor at the University of California, Berkeley, has noted that "the skills most important to obtaining power and leading effectively are the very skills that deteriorate once we have power." This is referred to as the power paradox. Keltner points out that once leaders are in a position of power, they "tend to behave more selfishly, impulsively, and aggressively, and have a harder time seeing the world from other people's point of view." The power paradox explains that the very attainment of greater leadership and power tend to cause one's effectiveness to decline. The best way for a leader to prevent the power paradox from having this effect is to employ emotional and social intelligence.

The lesson for entrepreneurs is to be aware that for their businesses to grow and thrive, they cannot simply be the technicians (see Michael Gerber's *The E-Myth*) producing the good or service of the enterprise. As employees and customers are added, the complexity of the business intensifies. The entrepreneur needs to take on a professional manager's role or hire someone to fill that role. This professional manager will likely be at least one of the leaders in the organization, and the person chosen will have power. He or she will be chosen based on personal and professional attributes that make him or her ideal for the position, but once that person occupies the power position, the attributes will likely be diminished. Applying the concepts of emotional and social intelligence, servant leadership, transformational leadership, and level 5 leadership in the hiring of the manager/leader will help in the selection of the right person for the position. If the founder adopts the role, he or she will need to be aware of the social and emotional intelligence attributes necessary to be an effective leader, and practice applying them.

Carol Hancock
Kaplan University

See also Entrepreneurial Orientation; Entrepreneurship Education: Graduate Programs; Goal Setting; Leadership: Training and Development; Leadership: Transformational; Team Composition; Women's Entrepreneurship

Further Readings

Bennis, W. "Ten Traits of Dynamic Leaders." In *Managing People Is Like Herding Cats*. Provo, UT: Executive Excellence, 1997.

Chen, Ming-Huei et al. "Entrepreneurial Leadership and New Ventures: Creativity in Entrepreneurial Teams." *Creativity and Innovation Management*, v.16/3 (2007).

Collins, Jim. *Level 5 Leadership: The Triumph of Humility and Fierce Resolve*. Boston: Harvard Business Review, 2001.

Dencker, John C., Marc Gruber, and Sonali Shah. "Individual and Opportunity Factors Influencing Job Creation in New Firms." *Academy of Management Journal*, v.52/6 (December 2009).

Goleman, Daniel. *Emotional Intelligence: Why It Can Matter More Than IQ*. New York: Bantam, 1995.

Greenleaf, Robert K. *The Servant as Leader*. Indianapolis, IN: Robert K. Greenleaf Center, 1991.

Kouzes, James M. and Barry Z. Posner. *The Leadership Challenge*. San Francisco: Jossey-Bass, 2002.

Mayer, John D. and David Caruso. "The Effective Leader: Understanding and Applying Emotional Intelligence." *Ivey Business Journal* (November/December 2002).

McCarthy, Daniel J., Sheila M. Puffer, and Sergei Darda. "Convergence in Entrepreneurial Leadership Style: Evidence From Russia." *California Management Review*, v.52/4 (Summer 2010).

Smith, H. "The Shareholders vs. Stakeholders Debate." *MIT Sloan Management Review*, v.44/4 (2003).

Todorovic, Elimir William and Francine K. Schlosser. "An Entrepreneur and a Leader! A Framework Conceptualizing the Influence of Leadership Style on a Firm's Entrepreneurial Orientation—Performance Relationship." *Journal of Small Business & Entrepreneurship*, v.20/3 (2007).

Visser, D. J., T. J. De Coning, and E. v.d. M. Smit. "The Relationship Between the Characteristics of the Transformational Leader and the Entrepreneur in South African SMEs." *South African Journal of Business Management*, v.36/3 (2005).

Webb, K. "Why Emotional Intelligence Should Matter to Management: A Survey of the Literature." *SAM Advanced Management Journal*, v.74/2 (2009).

LEADERSHIP: TRAINING AND DEVELOPMENT

The concept of leadership training and development refers to the expansion of an individual's capacity to be effective in leadership roles and processes through informal and formal mechanisms. The development of leadership capabilities is essential for the growth and success of any new venture. However, leadership requirements for the entrepreneur are dependent on the stage of growth of the firm. At the early stages of a new venture, an entrepreneur must fulfill many functional roles, including finance, marketing, sales, and accounting, thus relying on more informal leadership practices. As the firm grows, these formal functional roles are delegated, and the entrepreneurial role evolves primarily to a leadership position with formal demands.

Conventionally, leadership training and development have been seen as an intrapersonal strategy; focus was on the leader's desired behaviors, attributes, and styles related to self-awareness (self-confidence, emotional awareness, accurate self-image), self-regulation (self-control, trustworthiness, personal responsibility, adaptability), and self-motivation (initiative, optimism, commitment). This traditional approach is referred to as *leader development*, in contrast to *leadership development*, which expands the intrapersonal model to emphasize the leadership process—specifically, the interaction of the individual with his or her social and organizational context. These interpersonal programs emphasize the relational aspects of leadership and focus on social awareness (including empathy, service orientation, and political awareness) and social skills (such as building bonds, team orientation, becoming a catalyst for change, and conflict management).

An effective leadership development strategy that drives change requires three distinct elements: (1) assessment, (2) challenge, and (3) support. Assessment provides information concerning one's current strengths, level of effectiveness, and areas in need of improvement. Assessment can be provided through informal means or formal assessment practices such as personality inventories, 360-degree feedback, and performance reviews. Challenge refers to elements of the situation that are difficult and pushes an individual to go beyond his or her comfort zone, thus providing the impetus for growth. These circumstances include new roles that require fresh skills or a novel situation that triggers one to question one's time-honored ways of thinking and behaving. Support affirms a participant's strengths, guides him or her to acquire new skills in order to meet challenges, and enhances self-confidence.

Specific developmental practices are ubiquitous, falling into three primary categories: (1) learning from work experience (such as job rotation or project management), (2) learning from others (such as mentors and coaches), and (3) course work (class-based training or ropes courses).

Developmental assignments expand leadership capacity through the roles, tasks, and responsibilities encountered in a job assignment. For a job assignment to be developmental requires intentionality; otherwise the focus most likely will be on the performance of the new task. Development assignments are particularly valuable in learning about team building, strategic thinking, and the development of influence skills.

Developmental course work has traditionally utilized classroom training as the primary formal developmental strategy. Today it is augmented and even replaced by nonconventional pedagogical practices, such as high ropes courses, action learning, and reflective journaling. The key elements of successful developmental course work are that it is connected to one's work and is part of an integrated group of interventions.

Developmental relationships are workplace associations that form a key component in the expansion of a person's capacity to be effective in leadership roles and processes. Formation and maintenance of these interactions are customarily spontaneous and the responsibility of the worker. Examples include, but are not limited to, mentoring, coaching, apprenticing, action learning, peer coaching, networks, team learning, and executive coaching. Both researchers and practitioners alike have acknowledged that they are one of the most useful, cost-effective, and enjoyable leadership development interventions.

Entrepreneurs cite the leadership competencies of people abilities (which include intrapersonal and interpersonal competencies) and strategic/analytical abilities as the two most important skills in performing their role. They develop these leadership competencies informally in their own social arena utilizing mentoring, observation, and contact with other managers and entrepreneurs, and on-the-job experience. Although their social relationships may be adequate in the early stages of their new venture, access to broader social, industry, and professional networks is essential to entrepreneurs' leadership development as their organizations grow.

Lisa Rosh
Yeshiva University

See also Entrepreneurial Training; Entrepreneurship Pedagogy; Leadership; Leadership: Transformational

Further Readings

Allen, Scott J. "Leadership Development: An Exploration of Sources of Learning." *Organizational Development Journal*, v.26/2 (2008).

Browning, Henry and Ellen Van Velsor. *Three Keys to Development: Using Assessment, Challenge, and Support to Drive Your Leadership.* Greensboro, NC: Center for Creative Leadership, 1999.

Day, David V. "Leadership Development: A Review in Context." *Leadership Quarterly*, v.11 (2000).

Hernez-Broome, Gina and Richard L. Hughes. "Leadership Development: Past, Present and Future." *Human Resource Planning*, v.27/1 (2004).

Kempster, Stephen and Jason Cope. "Learning to Lead in the Entrepreneurial Context." *International Journal of Entrepreneurial Behaviour and Research*, v.16/1 (2010).

Macpherson, Allan and Robin Holt. "Knowledge, Learning and Small Firm Growth: A Systematic Review of the Evidence." *Research Policy*, v.36 (2007).

McCall, Morgan W., Michael M. Lombardo, and Ann M. Morrison. *The Lessons of Experience: How Successful Executives Develop on the Job.* Lexington, MA: Lexington Books, 1988.

McCauley, Cynthia D. and Stéphane Brutus. *Management Development Through Job Experiences: An Annotated Bibliography.* Greensboro, NC: Center for Creative Leadership, 1998.

McCauley, Cynthia D. and Christina A. Douglas. "Developmental Relationships." In *The Center for Creative Leadership Handbook of Leadership Development*, 2nd ed., C. D. McCauley and E. Van Velsor, eds. San Francisco: Jossey-Bass, 2004.

Perren, Lew and Paul Grant. *Management and Leadership in UK SMEs: Witness Testimonies From the World of Entrepreneurs and SME Managers.* London: Council for Excellence in Management and Leadership, 2001.

Van Velsor, Ellen and Cynthia D. McCauley. "Our View of Leadership Development." In *The Center for Creative Leadership Handbook of Leadership Development*, 2nd ed., Cynthia D. McCauley and Ellen Van Velsor, eds. San Francisco: Jossey-Bass, 2004.

Van Velsor, Ellen, Cynthia D. McCauley, and Marian N. Ruderman, eds. *The Center for Creative Leadership Handbook of Leadership Development*, 3rd ed. San Francisco: Jossey-Bass, 2010.

LEADERSHIP: TRANSFORMATIONAL

Transformational leadership in entrepreneurial firms may be an important key to success. Important factors include the viewing of employees as important assets, the ability to inspire a shared vision with the firm's staff, and excellent communication skills. Entrepreneurial leaders engender creativity and provide an environment where employees feel encouraged and supported. Generally, a firm is created and sustained through a strong commitment to a vision regarding what the firm provides and the importance of those provisions to the market it serves. Visionary leaders are often considered charismatic: able to exude personal warmth and charm and show concern for employees outside work. Each of these traits is strongly associated with facets of transformational leadership, and so understanding its theoretical underpinnings is critical to an entrepreneurial firm's success.

Transformational leadership helps to motivate followers by emphasizing morals and ethics. Transformational leadership style inextricably links the leader and follower in a transforming process. This type of leadership is measured by the Multifactor Leadership Questionnaire (MLQ) developed by Bernard Bass and Bruce Avolio. The research from this construct shows that charismatic leadership is an important component of transformational leadership, as are individualized consideration, orientation to development of subordinates, intellectual stimulation, and inspirational leadership.

Charismatic leadership and idealized influence are often combined and characterize leaders who are role models, are trustworthy and respectable, and act ethically. Inspirational leaders are visionary and arouse a sense of team spirit in followers, causing them to feel excited and enthusiastic about their work. Eliciting creativity and innovation characterizes the leader who exemplifies intellectual stimulation. Leaders help subordinates develop themselves socially and emotionally through their individualized consideration traits. Bass argued that transformational leaders motivate followers by encouraging them to understand the value of ideal goals, by getting them to transcend their self-interests for the interests of the whole, and by self-actualizing.

Idealized Influence

The idealized influence factor of transformational leadership is based on Robert House's theory of charismatic leadership. Max Weber originally discussed charisma in management writings, positing that the trait gave leaders superhuman powers, perhaps of divine origin. House wrote that charismatic leaders display a strong sense of self, are highly moral, are dominant, and are influential.

Many theorists have described idealized influence. The idealized influence or charisma factor today defines leaders who are role models for their subordinates. Their followers want to emulate them because of their conduct and dependability. These leaders are highly respected and trusted and provide a vision for the future. Warren Bennis and Bert Nanus's work supported the successful effects of transformational type leaders who use vision, are social architects, create trust, emphasize their strengths, and minimize their weaknesses. Noel Tichy and Mary Ann Devanna found that transformational leaders recognize the need for change, create a vision, and then institutionalize change. They are able to do this through transformational processes that cause the people around them to see the vision and be inspired to follow it. Jim Kouzes and Barry Posner noted that exemplary leaders model the way and inspire a shared vision as defined in the transformational leadership model.

Inspirational Motivation

Leaders who use inspirational motivation encourage their followers by having high expectations of them and convincing them that the shared vision in the organization is worthwhile. They often do this through using symbols and other appeals that cause subordinates to believe that they will accomplish more through teamwork than they will through seeking their self-interests. Meaning and challenge are provided, partially through the use of team spirit and partly through inspiring enthusiasm and optimism. Jim Kouzes and Barry Posner felt that leaders inspire a shared vision by being forward looking and envisioning the future. They enlist the help of others through a shared sense of destiny. Inspired motivation helps free employees to contribute to the company without fear of criticism and with the assurance their ideas will be considered valid and useful. Glenn A. Valdiserri and John L. Wilson noted, "Encouragement from leaders gives employees inspiration to achieve personal satisfaction. Giving employees the authority to make decisions demonstrates flexibility in leadership [that is] viewed as an attribute of transformational leadership style and a critical factor for increasing profitability in the small business."

Intellectual Stimulation

Transformational leaders challenge followers to question their own beliefs and values as well as those of the leader and the organization. Problem solving is the hallmark of this approach, and followers are allowed the leeway to be creative in reframing problems without ridicule or criticism. Followers are included in decision making and problem solving. Transformational leaders will encourage subordinates to challenge the process, make the challenge meaningful, and take risks.

Individualized Consideration

This is the last factor in the transformational leadership construct. In line with Abraham Maslow's hierarchy of needs, the leader acts as a coach, mentor, or adviser in his or her attempt to allow the follower to self-actualize. Leaders will often create venues or opportunities that allow followers to exercise new skills. Enabling others to act through collaborating to improve performance, creating a climate of trust, supporting face-to-face interactions, and facilitating positive interdependence all help to ensure success. Kouzes and Posner pointed out that leaders can help to strengthen individuals through assuring that power is equally distributed, people can lead themselves, they are provided choices, they develop competence and confidence, and they recognize their interdependence through fostering accountability.

Even though the transformational leadership concept appears to be based on trait characteristics rather than behavioral ones, when leaders have made the effort and have received training regarding how to improve their transformational leadership abilities, they have experienced generally positive results. The specific training that precedes improvement includes education regarding leadership theory. Leaders in collectivist cultures tend to have an easier time adopting or learning transformational leadership concepts and behaviors. A collectivist culture is one in which people tend to view themselves as members of groups and usually consider the needs of the group to be more important than the needs of individuals. Many Asian cultures tend to be collectivist. Furthermore, women have shown more transformational leadership qualities than men, which have resulted in greater employee satisfaction and effectiveness of the organization. Whereas specific leadership traits have not been correlated to specific cultural traits, overall employees have viewed their organizational culture more positively when their supervisors were more transformational. A study done in small and medium-sized enterprises in South Africa evaluated a set of six important entrepreneurial characteristics, distinct from transformational leadership characteristics. The study found a medium degree of positive correlation between high scores on both sets of traits.

Consideration and initiating of structure are considered dichotomous factors of leadership. These two factors have been shown to lead to the highest levels of job satisfaction. The consideration factor correlates highly with employees' supervision, advancement, and total job satisfaction, and the initiating of structure correlates highly with employees' supervision, happiness with coworkers, working conditions, pay advancement, and total job satisfaction.

Leadership styles are strong predictors of organizational culture, and these styles can affect two types of culture that, in turn, affect productivity of organizations. The two types of culture that leadership styles can affect are innovative and competitive, which are externally oriented cultures, but style has little effect on bureaucratic and community cultures, which are internally oriented. The implication is that leadership style has an indirect effect on productivity through organizational culture. A possible solution to greater effect of transformational leadership on innovative and competitive cultures is provided in the "double-portfolio" design. In one portfolio are the four stages of product life cycle, named entrepreneurs, growth strategists, economists, and recyclists. The other portfolio is made up of the human resources. As G. David Hughes noted in 1990, "Instead of managing a portfolio of products, the executive engages in the continuous matching and rematching of a portfolio of strategists to a continuously changing portfolio of market opportunities."

There are significant questions regarding the four factors of transformational leadership that include idealized influence, inspirational motivation, intellectual stimulation, and idealized consideration. The constructs may not be clearly delimited, and they may be measuring the same concept. Some of the transformational leadership factors have been found to correlate highly with a laissez-faire type of leadership, which suggests that they may not be unique to transformational leadership. However, the concept of transformational versus transactional leadership is clear. Whereas both styles can help to increase employee satisfaction, most research indicates that transformational leadership styles are highly correlated with employees' satisfaction in their jobs.

Carol Hancock
Kaplan University

See also Goal Setting; Labor-Management Relations in Start-Ups; Leadership; Leadership: Training and Development; Team Composition; Women's Entrepreneurship

Further Readings

Ardichvili, Alexander, Richard N. Cardozo, and Alexander Gasparishvili. "Leadership Styles and Management Practices of Russian Entrepreneurs: Implications for Transferability of Western HRD Interventions." *Human Resource Development Quarterly*, v.9/2 (Summer 1998).

Bass, B. M. and B. J. Avolio. *MLQ Multifactor Leadership Questionnaire*. Redwood City, CA: Mind Garden, 1995.

Bass, B. M. and B. J. Avolio. "Transformational Leadership and Organizational Culture." *Public Administration Quarterly*, v.17/1 (1993).

Bennis, W. and B. Nanus. *Leaders: Strategies for Taking Charge*, 2nd ed. New York: HarperCollins, 2003.

DeCaro, Frank P., Nicole DeCaro, and Frances O. Bowen-Thompson. "An Examination of Leadership Styles of Minority Business Entrepreneurs: A Case Study of Public Contracts." *Journal of Business and Economic Studies*, v.16/2 (Fall 2010).

Ensley, Michael D., Craig L. Pearce, and Keith M. Hmieleski. "The Moderating Effect of Environmental Dynamism on the Relationship Between Entrepreneur Leadership Behavior and New Venture Performance." *Journal of Business Venturing*, v.21/2 (March 2006).

House, R. J. "A 1976 Theory of Charismatic Leadership." In *Leadership: The Cutting Edge*, J. G. Hunt and L. L. Larson, eds. Carbondale, IL: Southern Illinois University Press, 1976.

Hughes, G. David. "Managing High-Tech Product Cycles." *Executive*, v.4/2 (May 1990).

Kouzes, J. M. and B. Posner. *Leadership: The Challenge*, 3rd ed. San Francisco: Jossey-Bass, 2002.

Kouzes, J. M. and B. Posner. "A Prescription for Leading in Cynical Times." *Ivey Business Journal Online* (July/August 2004).

Maslow, A. H. *The Farther Reaches of Human Nature*. New York: Viking Press, 1971.

Maslow, A. H. "A Theory of Motivation." *Psychological Review*, v.50 (1943).

Roodt, J. "Self-Employment and the Required Skills." *Management Dynamics*, v.14/4 (2005).

Tichy, Noel and Mary Ann Devanna. *The Transformational Leader.* New York: John Wiley, 1986.

Valdiserri, G. A. and J. L. Wilson. "The Study of Leadership in Small Business Organizations: Impact on Profitability and Organizational Success." *The Entrepreneurial Executive*, v.15 (2010).

Weber, M. *The Theory of Social and Economic Organization.* New York: Free Press, 1947.

LEARNING

Learning refers to the intake of new information for the purposes of later recall and usage. Learning is integral to success, as new information is required in virtually all areas of new venture management. Those managing the new organization must learn new technologies, new procedures, new products, new employees' names, and so on. New employees must learn the structure of this new organization, their new job duties, the names of their new coworkers, the specifications of their new projects, and the like. To better understand how all of this can be accomplished most efficiently when managing a new venture, it is important to understand learning itself, so that one can get the most out of time spent attempting to learn, whoever might be doing the learning.

Learning can be thought of physiologically as changes in the chemical composition and structure of the brain. Such changes occur as memories are created. Learning is thus the process of encoding new information to be stored as memories. These memories are typically stored by association. People better remember information that is closely associated with information they already know. For example, it would be easier to remember information about five new vendors if one already knew their sales representatives. Because one has preexisting memories about the salesperson, it is easier to form related memories connected to those that one already has. This is because the brain builds memories by creating neural pathways, linking all pieces of new information to information that already exists there.

Information is typically stored in one of three ways: sensory memory, short-term memory, and long-term memory. Sensory memory is the quickest of these. Any time a person is exposed to information through the senses (as when seeing a picture, smelling a scent, or hearing a sound), it is temporarily stored in sensory memory but lost within a few seconds. If the person wishes to retain this information, it might be encoded to short-term memory, which is where information that needs to be actively processed is held. For example, in conversation with a client, a person might try to remember key facts about that client from that person's file to reference during that conversation. Two common beliefs about short-term memory are that people can hold approximately seven pieces of information in their minds at any given time and that information stored in short-term memory is typically available for immediate recall (sometimes more technically called retrieval) for less than 20 seconds. For example, a person might try to remember a phone number that someone has told to them long enough to write it down. This information is stored in short-term memory, and if it is not written down quickly enough, the information may be lost. The type of memory most relevant to learning for an organization is long-term memory, which is where people store information more permanently. Information stored in long-term memory can last anywhere from a few days to the remainder of a person's life. The goal of learning is to thus ensure the information desired is stored in long-term memory, where it can be recalled as needed later. Anyone who has forgotten the name of an acquaintance or where an important document was placed knows that encoding information in long-term memory is sometimes less than perfect, which can be extremely frustrating. Although researchers have learned much about what can increase or decrease the effectiveness of this process, there are many conflicting theories regarding how memories are actually created.

Research has found that one of the ways the time spent learning can be maximized, and therefore enhance later retrieval, is to enrich the learning experience itself. When a person is learning a new concept, his or her brain does not focus solely on that concept but rather takes in the information about the environment as well, which becomes integrated into the learning experience. For example, if a person attempts to learn something in a particular room, the view from the desk in the room, the music that was played at the time, and even the smell of the room may trigger memories the person created in that room long afterward. If a person's goal is to recall

Learning with others is beneficial as it gives the learner added perspective on the topic at hand. The type of memory most relevant to learning for an organization is long-term memory, which can remain in a person's memory bank anywhere from a few days to the rest of a person's life. (Photos.com)

information learned in the past, but in many different locations, it is thus advantageous to change locations while learning, creating many different environmental associations with the information, enriching the learning experience, and resulting in better retrieval of that information later. This can be as simple as attempting to learn in a different area of the office every day instead of sitting at the same desk.

A common belief about learning is that reading something again and again is enough to commit it to memory. Everyone has heard "practice makes perfect," and this is true to some extent. Repetition is a powerful tool when learning. If a person wants to learn a new list of clients' names and commit them to memory, practicing speaking the names aloud repeatedly can help. It is most effective, however, to spread the learning effort out over multiple periods of time, rather than in one long practice session. The brain requires rest in order to consolidate memories that it has gained. Just as a person should not exercise the body for six hours straight to improve physical health, a person should not stare at the same list of information for several hours trying to create new

memories. Instead, one should practice a little each day, or even during multiple sessions in one day, which gives the brain time to digest the information and solidify new neural pathways. Although cramming is a technique many college students rely upon, it is ineffective for long-term information storage.

This principle applies to new ventures well. According to the research literature, entrepreneurs do not learn how to manage a business effectively with a single pivotal learning experience. Instead, entrepreneurs learn constantly throughout their careers as their businesses change and grow. Some authors have suggested that the challenges new business owners face are the most valuable learning experiences of all. Furthermore, the experience of overcoming such obstacles and the lessons learned in the process build upon one another to create an invaluable body of knowledge based on experience. Challenges that force an entrepreneur to reexamine his or her point of view and change underlying assumptions and perspectives have been described by some researchers as "higher-order" learning. An important component of this kind of learning is the inherent self-reflection during which the learner must critique his or her own reasoning and assumptions in order to better him- or herself. For example, a saleswoman could face a difficult customer whom she would normally try to pass off to a coworker rather than handle the problem directly. In an effort to engage in higher-order learning, this saleswoman might decide to invest time understanding the customer and how to meet the customer's needs in a way that is mutually beneficial. In doing so, the saleswoman might discover that her perceptions about this customer were incorrect and that a change of perspective was all that was needed to meet the customer's needs. Although in this example the saleswoman had a positive experience that contributed to her learning, it is important to note that even situations that result in a failure are equally, if not more, important for learning. The experience of confronting problems and solving them successfully helps anyone improve their skills. As ideas are challenged, the successful entrepreneur will adapt and learn rather than maintain a routine that is no longer sufficient.

As a person learns about a topic, it is also highly effective to engage in metacognitive strategies—thinking about thinking. As a person learns, it is effective for that person to consider how much he or she has learned, what he or she still needs to learn, and what might be the best way to fill in knowledge gaps. This process, called monitoring, should take place during all learning efforts to maximize the effectiveness of those efforts. Monitoring one's own learning is a skill that can be taught, and it can be helpful to put some monitoring strategies to use when investigating a new topic. One popular strategy is asking oneself questions such as, "How does this fit into what I already know?" and "Do I fully understand this concept? What needs to be clarified?" However, this is not the only strategy that can be implemented, and the strategy selected will depend on what is being learned. Alternative strategies include making knowledge maps, writing about the knowledge as it is acquired, and simply thinking aloud during the learning process.

A person does not need to go through the learning process alone. Learning with others is typically beneficial, as it helps the learner monitor his or her own learning with added perspective. For example, explaining a new concept to another individual can allow the learner to reinforce the retrieval pathways and better understand the material themselves. The listener can ask questions and probe the learner, which enables the learner to engage in better metacognitive strategies. The listener also benefits by having the opportunity to ask questions and better understand the concepts themselves. This technique is more beneficial if the learners make an effort to pose thought-provoking questions to one another. Questions like "How do you know that?" and "Why does it work that way?" are examples of the kinds of questions that are most useful. For these reasons, learning with a partner or in small groups can be extremely helpful and enhance the learning experience for those involved.

Experience is an important aspect of entrepreneurial learning, perhaps even more important than in traditional education. In fact, research suggests that prior experience is an important predictor of both entrepreneurial performance and the success of the new venture itself. Experience affects learning by influencing how and what an individual learns such that those with little experience increase knowledge to a greater degree during a learning experience than do those with greater experience. However, those with experience in an area that requires specialized

or complex knowledge may experience learning more deeply by enhancing their specific knowledge. This kind of experience would not be possible for a newcomer, because a foundation of knowledge is required for this deeper level of learning to take place. For this reason, a novice entrepreneur will have altogether different learning experiences from those of an expert entrepreneur in objectively identical situations.

The learning process itself can also change over time as a person learns more about a particular subject. Novices tend to seek out large amounts of information and pay less attention to the quality of that information. Because the novice is new to the topic, there is some difficulty in knowing what is important to learn and what information is irrelevant. As a result, the newcomer's strategy tends to involve casting a wide net and gathering the information that is easiest to access. When experts need to learn something new related to their expertise, on the other hand, they gather less information, but the information collected is generally of a higher quality. This reinforces the need to monitor when learning about a new topic: By utilizing self-monitoring, the novice can gather information more like the expert, which streamlines the process.

Another difference between novices and experts is how the information is organized mentally. Experts more often employ a technique called chunking, in which groups of information are stored together, which speeds recall and guides future information seeking. For example, when considering additions to the product line, an expert on the current product line would be more likely to consider previous product categories and place the new items in those categories. A novice can employ this expert technique during the learning process to improve organization during memory storage and thereby aid later recall.

Learning and memory may at first glance seem like abstract concepts unrelated to new venture management, but they are actually critical to the everyday functioning of any organization. A new venture brings with it a new business model, clientele, skills, terminology, and much more. By putting into practice what scientists have discovered about learning, an entrepreneur can make the most of his or her time. Simple techniques such as monitoring the learning process and repetition can improve recall substantially. By using the best practices when learning and gathering new information, one can have a much more successful and effective experience, which can pay off in the long run.

Richard N. Landers
Rachel C. Callan
Old Dominion University

See also Cognition; Cognition in Experts and Novices; Cognition Theory; Entrepreneurial Training; Entrepreneurship Pedagogy; Knowledge; Learning Theory; Psychological Views

Further Readings

Cope, J. "Entrepreneurial Learning and Critical Reflection: Discontinuous Events as Triggers for 'Higher-Level' Learning." *Management Learning*, v.34 (2003).

Cope, J. "Toward a Dynamic Learning Perspective of Entrepreneurship." *Entrepreneurship Theory and Practice*, v.29 (2005).

Minniti, M. and W. Bygrave. "A Dynamic Model of Entrepreneurial Learning." *Entrepreneurship Theory and Practice*, v.25 (2001).

Sardana, D. and D. Scott-Kemmis. "Who Learns What? A Study Based on Entrepreneurs From Biotechnology New Ventures." *Journal of Small Business Management*, v.48 (2010).

Squire, L. R. and B. Knowlton. "The Structure and Organization of Memory." *Annual Review of Psychology*, v.44 (1993).

Wickelgren, W. A. "Human Learning and Memory." *Annual Review of Psychology*, v.32 (1981).

Zhao, Hao, Scott E. Seibert, and Gerald E. Hills. "The Mediating Role of Self-Efficacy in the Development of Entrepreneurial Intentions." *Journal of Applied Psychology*, v.90/6 (November 2005).

LEARNING THEORY

An understanding of learning theory and how it relates to entrepreneurs is invaluable for anyone pursuing new ventures. Knowing *how* learning occurs in the entrepreneurial context, one can better take advantage of learning opportunities as they arise. Many perspectives on learning theory have been explored in the research literature, but each perspective integrates two constructs embedded in entrepreneurial research: experience and innovation. Entrepreneurs gain valuable experience throughout their careers, which informs their business decisions and stimulates innovation.

Behavioral learning theory focuses on the precursors to and changes surrounding organizations, as well as how the organization reacts to these changes. Learning occurs whenever an organization is not meeting its customers' needs or is underperforming in some way and the organization is forced to adapt in order to remain competitive. Without this initial pressure, the organization will not learn or change, according to this theory. An example would be an Organization A that finds its sales dwindling after a competitor, Organization B, begins offering the convenience of online shopping to its customers. Organization A may react by also providing online shopping or by providing some extra service the competitor does not provide, such as superior customer service. In either case, the downturn in business causes the organization to change its approach to business. It is important to note that this process is ongoing; as the market changes, the organization reacts to these changes and learns which approaches are most effective.

Learning can also occur in the day-to-day routine of an organization and its members, which is the basis of action learning theory. According to this theory, the entrepreneur must attend to discrepancies between the organization's statements on how it should behave and its actual behavior. For example, if an organization's motto is "The customer is always right" and a survey of the customers shows that customer service is not being rated well, the organization will seek to make the behavior more consistent with the company's values. Like behavioral learning, action learning involves an ongoing process; the organization must be constantly watchful to make sure that its actions align with its espoused belief system. In doing so, the venture is more likely to be successful and meet consumer needs.

In contrast to these first two theories, which focus on behaviors, cognitive learning theory concentrates on how the act of acquiring knowledge leads to innovation. As an entrepreneur learns more about a new field or business area, he or she gains knowledge resources, which then influence future business decisions. For example, an entrepreneur may be familiar with one field while developing a new venture in another. Knowledge gained from one field can be applied to this new context, driving innovation in the new venture. By utilizing these cognitive resources, the entrepreneur may be able to conceptualize key areas of the new venture in ways his or her competitors cannot because they lack this knowledge advantage.

The constructivist approach to learning also frames learning in the context of knowledge acquisition. This theory recognizes that the learner brings with him or her a unique perspective that shapes how knowledge is acquired and utilized. Furthermore, rather than viewing knowledge as a static list of facts or theories waiting to be discovered by the learner, this theory regards knowledge as including the learner's thoughts, feelings, and interpretations of these data. Constructivists also view the purpose of learning as adaptive, centered on skill development that helps the learner cope with the outside world. Finally, the learner takes an active role in knowledge acquisition, creating new meaning in the process. This theory has been applied to entrepreneurs specifically because entrepreneurs learn how to be successful with new ventures by seeking out opportunities and learning from their experiences. Entrepreneurs need support from their teachers and mentors throughout this learning process. Traditional classroom instruction cannot provide all of the information needed, and thus advisers should encourage critical thinking and independent exploration. As with the other theories, because innovation is such an important aspect of developing new ventures, entrepreneurs must have the freedom to learn from experience to foster business growth.

D. A. Kolb (1984) developed experiential learning, which can be defined as the acquisition of knowledge through experience. This model of learning theory includes experience as well as reflection, thought, and experimentation. Learners acquire knowledge in a cyclical fashion, whereby concrete experience leads to reflective observation, abstract conceptualization, and active experimentation, ultimately returning to concrete experience. Each of these stages provides unique learning opportunities. Kolb stated that people acquire knowledge either through their own direct experiences (apprehension) or through conceptual interpretation and symbolic representation (comprehension), such as reading a book on a topic of interest. However, knowledge is also transformed, and this is done either by experimentation (extension) or by reflecting on experiences and ideas (intention). Researchers believe that individuals learn best when they cycle through all stages, experiencing each type

of acquisition and transformation, although there are individual preferences for one form of learning over another.

Some entrepreneurial researchers have noted that cognitive theory is part of experiential learning theory, while behavioral learning theory is not. Whereas cognitive learning theory focuses on transforming existing knowledge into new knowledge, behavioral learning theory emphasizes outcomes and routines. Researchers note that although behavioral learning may be crucial to maintaining an organization's current level of performance, new ventures require innovation and creativity rather than static but proven methods. Instead of refining existing procedures, entrepreneurs must seek out new opportunities and transform knowledge from previous experience into novel ideas. As a result, research investigating entrepreneurs has shifted away from theories focusing on behavior toward theories emphasizing experience. A relationship has been demonstrated between entrepreneurial success and experience—especially start-up experience. Those with more start-up experience are better able to capitalize on new venture opportunities when they arise and have increased performance in their firms, compared to entrepreneurs with less start-up experience. Researchers argue that the effects of this experience can be explained with Kolb's model; rather than simply acquiring knowledge from experience, entrepreneurs transform this knowledge, which allows them to apply it as novel opportunities and problems arise.

Although learning theory has been investigated for many years, the unique aspects of entrepreneurship, such as the role of experience and the importance of innovation, have led researchers to develop new theories with a focus on these characteristics. Rather than simply memorizing facts, entrepreneurs must take previous experiences and transform the knowledge gained to seize new opportunities effectively and solve problems quickly. In doing so, entrepreneurs can improve their chances of success by gaining new experience and reflecting upon it to prepare for what the future may hold.

Rachel C. Callan
Richard N. Landers
Old Dominion University

See also Cognition; Cognition Theory; Human Resource Strategy; Human Resources; Knowledge; Learning; Psychological Views

Further Readings

Kolb, D. A. *Experiential Learning: Experience as the Source of Learning and Development.* Englewood Cliffs, NJ: Prentice-Hall, 1984.

Löbler, H. "Learning Entrepreneurship From a Constructivist Perspective." *Technology Analysis and Strategic Management,* v.18 (2006).

Lumpkin, G. T. and B. B. Lichtenstein. "The Role of Organizational Learning in the Opportunity-Recognition Process." *Entrepreneurship Theory and Practice,* v.29 (2005).

Merriam, S. B. and R. S. Caffarella. *Learning in Adulthood: A Comprehensive Guide,* 2nd ed. San Francisco: Jossey-Bass, 1999.

Politis, D. "The Process of Entrepreneurial Learning: A Conceptual Framework." *Entrepreneurship Theory and Practice,* v.29 (2005).

Licensing

A license agreement consists of a licensor and a licensee. The licensor is the person who gives or grants a license. The licensee is the person who has the right or privilege and then the responsibility to use, carry on an operation, or act as representative under certain terms and conditions. A licensing agreement gives permission to do or carry on some trade or business that would otherwise be unlawful absent the agreement. The language of the agreement will grant the authority from an inventor, owner, or holder of a right to use the original works of the creator; in the case of a business operation, it will provide the licensee the right to represent the licensor. Licensing may pertain to technology or business matters. Governments may also provide licenses to companies to perform business operations. For example, a government may provide rights to serve the public to an energy company whose operations have a direct effect on the flow of water into an interstate river or a municipal entity established as a joint venture with encouragement of regulatory authorities in multiple states.

A standard type of licensing agreement used in business ventures will often allow one venture to represent another or resell the goods or services produced by the first. The agreement will often exist in business for the benefit of a business seeking to expand its reach to potential new customers. The license in certain instances will be in the form of a franchise. A franchise agreement will generally consist of permission by an originator or supplier of a product or service or an owner of a trademark or copyright and a reseller to do business under the first party's name. This arrangement is typically exercised under tight controls to ensure a standard quality, presentation, target market, and warranty. The reputation of the licensor is at stake in a license agreement. The license will come with requirements for training of those selling or explaining the good or service, retail space requirements or limitations, mandates for certain aesthetic presentation, and a defined territory for representation.

Other considerations include the mode of representation, whether virtual, by phone, or face to face. Printing of catalogs, languages in which materials are offered, and price points both high and low will be addressed in the license agreement. The amount of time allowed for orders to be filled will be addressed in the license agreement. Modifications allowed to be made to a product or service will be written into the license agreement. Policies regarding packaging, return of goods or rejection of services not performed as bargained, obligations to market the product or service on behalf of the licensor, maintaining a certain level of inventory so that the offering can be made readily available without delay—all such concerns will also be addressed.

The license agreement may not leave much room for negotiation between the licensor and the licensee and may consist of several mandates for the licensee. The reason for this boilerplating of the license is that the good or service being licensed must maintain a uniform representation of the owner to all consumers, no matter where they are located. This uniformity is more important in today's economy than ever before. Today, consumers are able to travel across the world relatively easily and inexpensively or see a virtual presentation of a good or service in different parts of the world in a matter of seconds via the Internet. If the presentation or pricing of the good or service varies widely from one place to another, the entire strategy or viability of the licensor could be undermined.

The use of a trademark or proprietary license during the term of a license agreement may include trademarks, trade names, logos, and designs. A reseller's advertising and promotion will likely need to be in accordance with current trademark usage policies or be preapproved by the licensor. Licensees will be prohibited from removing or destroying any copyright notices, trademarks, or other proprietary markings on the goods, software, documentation, or other materials related to the license. Upon termination of the agreement, any continuing representation by the licensee will be illegal. The license will have a stated term or length and will address specifics on how to end the relationship or terminate it for cause.

Other terms included address confidentiality. The parties will agree to maintain the confidentiality of information relating to products, sales data, and other business information shared by the parties and not generally known to the public. These include agreements for trade secrets, customer lists, and ingredients or component parts. Accounting and auditing procedures and processes will be clearly stated. Whether the license is assignable or not is a very important element of the agreement, key to maintaining control over who is involved. The choice of governing law is also extremely important; the agreement will very likely address the jurisdiction in which any disputes will be settled and the body of law that will be applied to any controversy, as well as whether the third party who decides the outcome of a controversy will be a court or an arbiter.

The license will further address modification to the agreement and waivers of any rights. Generally any such changes will be required to be in writing and signed by both licensor and licensee to be effective. The license agreement will also discuss severability. In any complex contract, there is a section that states that if, for any reason, any provision of the agreement shall be held to be invalid or unenforceable, the remaining provisions of the agreement shall remain in full force and effect.

There will also be a section that discusses the time during which one party may bring an action against the other to enforce any rights under the contract. For example, the agreement may state that any legal action arising out of the license shall be barred unless commenced within one year of the act or omission giving rise to the action.

There will likely also be provisions that attempt to plan for changes in technology during the license term. Additionally, minimum investments and market development funds will be required of the licensee or on a shared basis to ensure that the agreement has a good chance for success. Advertisements will be required to be approved by the licensor. Approved activities must be fully completed as promised and verified within the time limits agreed to in advance. The license arrangement should take into account local culture, economy, language, practices, laws, and regulations.

The agreement will speak to patent rights, sales, royalties, end users, and distribution and redistribution of materials. Licensing can go both ways in terms of new ventures or entrepreneurial undertakings. New ventures are sometimes started based on ideas generated by the research activities of university faculty and then licensed to start-ups to commercialize the idea. Likewise, entrepreneurs, if they lack funding or interest, can license their ideas to third parties and thus reap the benefit of the idea via royalties and other financial arrangements. The income generated by the licensing fees often acts as seed money for entrepreneurs to develop other ideas and also establish production facilities.

It is also customary for small enterprises to forge linkages with universities in order to ensure success and survival, especially in technology-intensive industries. Large enterprises are also increasingly making use of small firms to extend their research capabilities and capacities.

Dominic DePersis
Broome Community College
Alfred Lewis
Hamline University

See also Business-to-Business Marketing; Championing New Ventures; Community/Government Buy-Ins; Corporate Entrepreneurship and Innovation; Credentials; Entrepreneurial Support Systems; Franchises: Starting; Patent Protection; Technology Transfer; Territorial Strategy and Regions; Trademarks; University Start-Ups

Further Readings

Bagchi-Sen, Sharmistha. "Strategic Considerations for Innovation and Commercialization in the U.S. Biotechnology Sector." *European Planning Studies*, v.15/6 (July 2007).
Gans, Joshua S., David H. Hsu, and Scott Stern. "The Impact of Uncertain Intellectual Property Rights on the Market for Ideas: Evidence From Patent Grant Delays." *Management Science*, v.54/5 (May 2008).
Nguyen, Xuan-Thao N., Robert W. Gomulkiewicz, and Danielle Conway-Jones. *Intellectual Property, Software and Information Licensing: Law and Practice.* Washington, DC: Bureau of National Affairs, 2006.

Siegel, Donald S., David A. Waldman, Leanne E. Atwater, and Albert N. Link. "Commercial Knowledge Transfers From Universities to Firms: Improving the Effectiveness of University-Industry Collaboration." *Journal of High Technology Management Research*, v.14 (Spring 2003).

Weston, Glen E., Peter B. Maggs, and Roger E. Schechter. *Unfair Trade Practices and Consumer Protection*. St. Paul, MN: West Publishing, 1992.

LOCATION STRATEGY

A location strategy is, as defined by Marilyn M. Helms's *Encyclopedia of Management*, "a plan for obtaining the optimal location for a company by identifying company needs and objectives, and searching for locations with offerings that are compatible with these needs and objectives." A location strategy is based on formulating a number of factors deemed relevant to the business in question. A quantitative-qualitative technique may consist in applying weights to the overall evaluation—in other words, assessing what weight each of the factors should have when developing a list of relevant factors. The plan can then include the assignment of weight to each factor in order to reflect its relative importance in the company's overall objective. There should be a scale for each factor, and management, sometimes in conjunction with external consultants, must subsequently apply a score for the prospective location for each factor using the scale. After having multiplied the score according to the weights for each factor, the total score for the location appears. Finally, a recommendation is made based on the score.

The factors may range from the issue of overall feasibility to details of labor relations and the existence or absence of incentives. A feasibility analysis consists of assessing operating costs and other factors. One can try to calculate the long-term costs and revenues by first determining fixed and variable costs. To the extent possible, one should assess the costs of, for example, raw materials, taxes, wages, and energy. A feasibility study can thus constitute a starting point, where the location is portrayed as advantageous or disadvantageous according to a number of objective factors. Logistics evaluation is especially relevant to manufacturing operations and concerns the transportation options and costs for the prospective manufacturing and storage facilities. Facilities planning involves determining what kind of space a company will need, given its short-term and long-term goals.

Labor analysis should determine whether labor needs will be met in both a short-term and a long-term sense. Again, costs will be an important part of the assessment, ranging from information on labor productivity and wage rates to intangible aspects such as the quality of education and attitude of employees. Community and site evaluation concerns the relationship between the company and the prospective community, in other words, the question of whether the company's activities and the traits of the site will fit. This issue can, for example, be relevant in the case of particular forms of research and development, where a community may be found to be hostile toward the kinds of research and development the company intends to conduct.

Regulations and incentives in the form of trade zones or other types of regulation or deregulation may be relevant, since a company may be highly motivated toward or against localizing based on the existence of such incentives or constraints. In Europe, for example, there are to a certain extent different rules according to whether the country is a member of the European Community or not. In China, the United States, and several other countries, free-trade zones have been instituted in designated areas, facilitating the exchange of goods, services and labor into and out of the zones. There may, on the other hand, be barriers or restrictions that function as disincentives. Environmental regulation may also have an impact on the relationship between a company and the community around a prospective location. Incentive negotiation is a process by which a company and a location negotiate any benefits the company may receive, such as tax breaks. Finally, political risk may be a factor to be considered in a location strategy. If the political environment is deemed to be unstable, the company can risk discontinuation of its operation at some time in the future.

Based on an overall consideration of these or selected factors, a company can make a qualified decision on where to locate its operations. In the case of several competing prospective sites, a purely economic comparison of the location alternative can be made by selecting the location that has the lowest total cost for the expected activity volume. However,

Business locations with a possibility for the transfer of knowledge from nearby related companies or institutions are desirable. SRI International (founded as the Stanford Research Institute) based their main campus in Menlo Park, California, part of Silicon Valley, an area popular among research and technology firms. (NASA)

depending on the type of business, companies also may have to examine other aspects. The foregoing includes factors that are especially relevant to industrial factories, where one important objective is to minimize costs. Other operations may be service oriented and aimed at, for example, establishing a presence in a hitherto unexplored market. The relative importance of each factor varies even within the same company, as a result of the characteristics of the various activities of a firm.

In the case of knowledge-intensive operations, the location strategy may need to take a number of additional factors into consideration. Indeed, these "extended" factors are more random and context-specific when compared to the structured and cost-focused approach presented above, which is taken from more traditional management and business methodologies. Issues surrounding knowledge infrastructures and considerations related to innovation capacity may be decisive factors in connection with the location strategy of a knowledge-intensive venture. In 1967, Paul R. Lawrence and Jay M. Lorsch argued, for example, that manufacturing, the finance function, or research and development, within one and the same company, may face different types and levels of uncertainty vis-à-vis the organization's environment. They subsequently underlined the need for varying organizational structures at different times;

one could extend this logic to acknowledging that different parts or functions of an organization will be attracted to different locational attributes.

In descriptive as opposed to prescriptive research, there have been a number of examples of knowledge-related factors. Locations where there is a possibility for knowledge "spillovers" from other companies or institutions are particularly desirable, since such locations may support innovation activities. For example, according to Bjørn T. Asheim and Meric S. Gertler, in science-based and similar clusters spillovers may occur within the established local social networks of scientists well before these individuals have access to published results. Such spillover effects incentivize new ventures to locate near similar knowledge-based companies.

Terje Grønning
University of Oslo

See also Culture and Entrepreneurship; Geographic Location; Geography of Innovation; Globalization; International Enterprise Planning; International Markets; International New Ventures

Further Readings

Asheim, Bjørn Terje and Meric S. Gertler. "The Geography of Innovation: Regional Innovation Systems." In *The Oxford Handbook of Innovation*, Jan Fagerberg, David Mowery, and Richard Nelson eds. Oxford, UK: Oxford University Press, 2005.

Helms, Marilyn M. *Encyclopedia of Management*, 5th ed. Detroit, MI: Thompson Gale, 2006.

Lawrence, Paul R. and Jay M. Lorsch. "Differentiation and Integration in Complex Organizations." *Administrative Science Quarterly*, v.12/1 (1967).

LOCUS OF CONTROL

The construct known as locus of control (LOC) was introduced by J. B. Rotter in 1966 and refers to individuals' beliefs about the underlying main causes of events happening in their lives. Individuals with an internal LOC believe that the outcomes they experience are the result of their own actions. They are often described as believing themselves to be the masters of their own fate and to be in control of their own destinies. In contrast, individuals with an external LOC believe that external factors—such as fate, luck, God, or powerful others—determine the outcomes that they experience in their lives. They are often described as taking a passive approach toward their lives.

Having an internal or external LOC has motivational and behavioral consequences. Because of these consequences, LOC is argued to be a personal characteristic that influences entrepreneurial success. Entrepreneurship requires actions by individuals and involves shaping and changing the environment. People with an internal LOC, in contrast to people with an external LOC, should be more likely to take action, show higher levels of effort and persistence, and seek situations in which they can exert active control over their environment. They should thus be more likely to engage and succeed in the entrepreneurial process.

The tendency to have an internal or external LOC develops through mechanisms of social learning. If individuals are consistently rewarded for their efforts, they acquire an internal LOC because they see a causal relationship between their actions and rewards. If people do not succeed and are not rewarded, despite showing high levels of effort, they develop an external LOC.

LOC is argued to have motivational consequences similar to other individual beliefs and expectations, such as self-efficacy, optimism, and focus on opportunities. People with an internal LOC believe that there is a strong link between their actions and attainment of desired goals. This should lead to higher levels of effort and persistence, because they perceive a causal relationship between their levels of effort and persistence and the attainment of desired outcomes. LOC is also argued to have behavioral consequences. People with an internal LOC believe that they are able to exert an effect on outcomes, and they consider themselves to be choice-making agents. Therefore, they seek situations in which control is possible and avoid or leave situations in which they have only little control over their environment.

Because of the motivational and behavioral implications, LOC is argued to exert an influence on entrepreneurial success. In fact, meta-analytic research by A. Rauch and M. Frese revealed that an internal LOC is significantly related to start-up and performance of new ventures. Starting a

new business requires taking action and investing a considerable amount of effort and persistence. Furthermore, starting a new business implies that the entrepreneur shapes and changes the environment by recombining resources. Therefore, people who have an internal LOC should be more likely to engage in the start-up process because they seek situations in which they can exert control and change the environment. Once they have taken the initiative to start a new business, they are also more likely to succeed in the start-up process, because they show higher levels of effort and persistence. In contrast, people with an external LOC should be more passive and thus less likely to engage and succeed in the start-up process. They believe that outcomes are not contingent on their behavior and that external reasons determine success or failure. This should reduce the willingness to take the risks involved in entrepreneurship because of the high penalties in case of business failure.

Once the new business is running, people with an internal LOC should be more likely to achieve higher performance levels. Research has shown that entrepreneurs in their roles as business owners/ managers have a considerable effect on the firm's level of performance. Furthermore, if new businesses are to succeed, they must constantly exert an influence on their environments to gain larger market shares. Therefore, entrepreneurs of new businesses who show more effort and persistence and who are more inclined to change their environments should be more likely to lead their businesses to higher performance levels. Additional lines of reasoning on why LOC should be related to entrepreneurial success state that an internal LOC leads to setting more challenging goals and to developing more detailed action plans.

It is sometimes assumed that, as people age, they become less internal and more external, but data here have been ambiguous. It has been suggested that internality may increase up to middle age and thereafter decrease. Other research has suggested that LOC is two-dimensional and that changes in LOC in later life relate more visibly to increased externality rather than reduced internality. In terms of gender, there appear to be no general differences. Finally, there is some evidence that people from different cultures vary in LOC.

For example, Japanese people tend to have a more external LOC than people in the United States.

Hannes Zacher
The University of Queensland
Michael M. Gielnik
Leuphana University of Lüneburg

See also Agency Theory; Cognition; Overconfidence; Psychological Views

Further Readings

Ng, T. W. H., K. L. Sorensen, and L. T. Eby. "Locus of Control at Work: A Meta-Analysis." *Journal of Organizational Behavior*, v.27 (2006).

Rauch, A. and M. Frese. "Let's Put the Person Back Into Entrepreneurship Research: A Meta-Analysis on the Relationship Between Business Owners' Personality Traits, Business Creation, and Success." *European Journal of Work and Organizational Psychology*, v.16 (2007).

Rotter, J. B. "Generalized Expectancies of Internal Versus External Control of Reinforcement." *Psychological Monographs*, v.80 (1966).

M

MANAGEMENT INFORMATION SYSTEMS

Management information systems (MIS) existed in organizations well before computers and dematerialization of transactions. Management information systems and information systems should not be confused. A management information system is designed to facilitate decision making with the provision of information and reports on every aspect of the business. To do this, MIS often use information systems to collect, manipulate, store, and diffuse information in unabridged form, such as raw data, text, photographs, and sounds within organizations. This is completed using computerized resources such as hardware and software as well as the personnel involved to conduct specified operations with data deemed relevant to the organization.

MIS have numerous objectives, including those related to operations, technological issues, and transactions, each resulting in a unique definition but always including the integration of multiple areas of the firm through enterprise resource planning (ERP) for optimal usage of all resources. This centralizes information with management, giving MIS accountability to and including information that is relevant and pertinent to various stakeholders, including operations, finance, consumers, and others. Whereas the use of MIS is often low in new ventures and start-ups, these systems can assist in the management of business, giving the entrepreneur time to focus on other areas to help the business grow.

Definition of MIS

There are no universal definitions of MIS. However, most definitions agree that MIS are composed of manual or computer-based systems utilized to collect, store, and produce reliable information that responds to the needs of management in planning and achieving the strategic goals and objectives of the company. MIS perform three distinct but interrelated functions. First, MIS generate the reports prescribed by management to meet the corporate operational needs. Second, MIS develop reports and discloses data that allow management to simulate future scenarios from a number of alternatives.

Management information systems can be defined as manual or computer-based systems used to collect, store, and produce reliable information to enable a company's management team to plan and achieve the strategic goals and objectives of the company. (Photos.com)

Third, MIS supports decision making with the provision of timely, accurate, and reliable information that can be stylized specifically.

MIS are important within a firm because lodged within them is the information and planning for the future of the firm. For optimal effectiveness, MIS must be developed, maintained, and used with a consistent and unified purpose and goal. That is, MIS should have clearly defined guidelines, policies, standards, and procedures for operation and use. Through this consistency, the MIS can optimize synchronization of the firm's strategies, goals, and objectives across and among the multiple layers of the firm. Whereas not essential, MIS are often based on information and communication technologies (ICT). This guarantees the use of a larger volume of nonredundant data within a shorter time frame to optimize analysis and decision making.

Implementation of MIS

These systems are often implemented in medium-sized and larger organizations, but small and entrepreneurial organizations can benefit from them as well. Their implementation can be done in a number of ways: directly or in one massive change; in parallel with existing systems to ensure the new system captures and manipulates the data old system continues to capture and manipulate the data during the transition; piecemeal or by implementing different modules at different times to localize risks and facilitate training; or phased, which allows the implementation to segment the changes to one system at a time, again localizing the risk of failure and training opportunities.

Implementation of an MIS must be carefully planned and executed to include identification of all requisite and potential tasks to be undertaken during this step; diagrammed and networked to ensure activities disrupt or inconvenience the fewest people; and designed to include development of the procedure for monitoring the implementation and control of the implementation within either existing or new facilities that have been structured specifically for the system. Once the system has been physically located and established, master files and formats must be structured for storage, retrieval, and other activities. Once the files are structured, the system can be tested to determine its effectiveness and efficiency and to revise or rework those components that are not as effective and efficient as initially planned. This monitoring and evaluation constitute an ongoing process that must be completed on a regular basis.

The storage and ready access to information provided by MIS allow for the monitoring of information concerning activities, employees, customers, and all other records. The continual monitoring allows for the development of accurate and timely reports and presentations of information and its analysis, in the format developed by the users. That is, MIS can produce information in the format that best meets the needs of the users, both regularly and when needed.

Because of the importance of the reports and information originating with the MIS, the quality of the information inputted into the MIS must be ensured. As a prerequisite to guarantee this quality, security systems must be developed, structured, and implemented. This entails an identification of risks as well as the establishment of controls to alleviate the risks encountered.

MIS Risks

Like any other system, MIS have risks, including the distribution of sensitive information to the wrong individual, either purposely or accidentally; the input of wrong data, resulting in flawed decision making; and illegal hacking or destruction of data, rendering the system useless. The value of the MIS is in the timeliness, accuracy, consistency, relevance, and wholeness of the information. Any element that interferes with any one of these functions is a risk to the system. MIS are facing many challenges, including risks from humans (intentional and unintentional). However, because of the progress and advances of technology, technical failures are minimal.

MIS Value Creation

The first obstacle to the implementation of a MIS is the financial cost. Managers must overcome this constraint, because these systems contribute significantly to value creation within firms. MIS create value by highlighting the operations of the whole company such that all operations can be evaluated, increasing the transparency of the organization. This transparency assists in the identification of areas where costs are higher than expected so that the overruns can be addressed. MIS also allow management to see a clearer picture of the whole operation, enabling them to better understand possible innovations and improvements, as well as opportunities to reinvest or divest. With a whole picture, the divestiture of suboptimal or declining operations is facilitated, allowing management to increase efficiency in those locations that demonstrate the strongest profit potential. Furthermore, with the use of MIS, projects can be adequately evaluated to decrease the potential of taking unnecessary risks when chances of success are limited.

MIS Governance

MIS governance is similar to corporate governance, but its focus is on the planning, development, implementation, monitoring, evaluation, and growth of MIS. Sarbanes-Oxley and Basel II laws continue to demand higher accountability of those making decisions using these systems. However, as discussed, MIS not only require an understanding of their capacity within the firm but also require resources, which many smaller firms may not have. However, with the growing attention by key stakeholders to operations of companies, MIS governance now includes a growing number of stakeholders having access to information and systems.

Urbanization of MIS

The development and evolution of MIS within firms are partially dependent upon the evolution of technology but also dependent upon the willingness of a firm to adapt to existing systems, the comprehension of executives and users of what MIS are capable of doing, the development of the skills to redirect MIS, and the foresight to see what may be needed or be of benefit in the future. This requires firms to perform a cost-benefit analysis of the acquisition and implementation of new MIS, and one component of the cost-benefit must also examine the costs of not remaining current with technology. This must be oriented by the firm's information systems master plan. Thus, all business processes of the firm will be coherent with the global strategy.

Evaluation

MIS has three performance dimensions: technical, economic, and operational. To evaluate an MIS on these three criteria necessitates that those using the system understand the needs the system fulfills, the requirements of the system, and the system's capabilities. This information may not be in the hands of either the technicians or the management, but it should be at hand, meaning management and technicians must have open lines of communication. Management must be able to clearly and critically discuss the needs of the organization within the environment at the time of the evaluation. Those doing the evaluation must understand these needs, potentially anticipating future needs.

Today, information technology is pervasive in many places of business. Both the developed and the developing world are benefiting from the instantaneous communication and transfer of information. Management information systems allow businesses to use this plethora of information in a timely manner to optimize their operations and their profits. With many people having access to information technology, business is now mandated not only to stay current but also to be on the cutting edge.

Ina Freeman
Jones International University
Amir Hasnaoui
Groupe Sup de Co La Rochelle and Centre de Recherche Télécom École de Management

See also Entrepreneurial Support Systems; Entrepreneurs in Technology; Globalization; Information; Radical and Incremental Innovation; Technology Transfer

Further Readings

Govardus, Johannes and Maria van der Heijden. *Designing Management Information Systems*. New York: Oxford University Press, 2009.

O'Brien, James A., and George M. Marakas. *Management Information Systems*. Boston: McGraw-Hill, 2006.

Oz, Effy. *Management Information Systems*. Boston: Thomson Course Technology, 2006.

Schniederjans, Marc J., Ashlyn M. Schniederjans, and Dara G. Schniederjans. *Outsourcing Management Information Systems*. Hershey, PA: Idea Group, 2007.

Managing Human and Social Capital

The image of the inventive entrepreneur building a revolutionary product in his or her garage with nothing to guide the way but passion and persistence is a powerful mental picture in entrepreneurship.

In the life of every successful new venture, however, the time comes when one must make the leap from the garage to the office building. This leap requires assistance and ushers in a new set of challenges associated with selecting, building, and retaining valuable human and social capital to help the new venture reach its potential.

A firm's human capital results from the aggregate combination of knowledge, skills, and abilities embedded within a firm's human resources. This represents a particularly important resource in emerging new ventures, which are heavily reliant upon the efforts of individual employees. Compared to their more established counterparts, new firms are less able to hide poor performers and must rely heavily upon the knowledge, skill, and ability of each employee to meet strategic and operational objectives. This limited resource base places a premium on the human capital management practices that new ventures employ.

Successful new ventures work to enhance human capital by putting processes and structures in place that are geared toward attracting, selecting, and retaining valuable employees. In work on human resource management systems, Mark Huselid and a host of others have begun to establish the connection between several human resource (HR) practice dimensions and firm performance. Whereas the bulk of these connections have been assessed in larger firms, it stands to reason that new ventures may benefit from similar practices.

Specifically, new ventures that utilize structured approaches to recruitment and selection have greater levels of human capital, which ultimately enhances firm performance. New ventures that invest in recruitment strategies increase the pool of qualified applicants that are energized by the possibility of joining a start-up or an emerging organization. In addition, new ventures are well served by selecting individuals based upon their operational and technical proficiency, their ability to fit within the organization, and their willingness to be flexible with job responsibilities. New venture employees frequently have to "wear many hats," and a strong division of labor is often a misfit for the environment of fast-growing firms.

New ventures also increase their success rate in selecting employees by putting in place structured approaches to reviewing applications and conducting interviews. Utilizing structured selection

New firms can use tools like job fairs to recruit talent. A new venture relies upon the knowledge, skill, and ability of each employee to meet strategic and operational objectives and cannot afford to retain poor performers. (Wikimedia/Arvind Grover)

techniques that are derived from the demands of the position and the organization helps focus selection efforts on applicants' past behavior and actual capabilities and minimizes reliance on the perceptions or "gut feelings" of entrepreneurs and managers.

A rigorous and structured selection system is further supported by the use of firm- and industry-specific training. Whereas formal training activities may lie beyond the resource reach of new ventures, firms that take care to orient and socialize newcomers into the norms of the organization are often more successful. In addition, firms seeking to maximize their human capital implement proper knowledge transfer activities. Such practices help newly minted employees to understand the mission and goals of the organization and their specific operational and functional roles within that structure. Managing expectations early in the employment relationship helps new employees to reduce the ambiguity and anxiety associated with joining the venture.

Beyond selection and training, human capital is developed and motivated by firms that establish appropriate compensation systems. New ventures are generally not able to offer the same salary levels as larger counterparts; however, emerging organizations are able to promote the uniqueness of the opportunity, greater responsibility, faster promotions, and higher levels of autonomy. These nonfinancial benefits are attractive to some employees who are willing to trade lower initial salaries for greater responsibility and advancement opportunity. In addition, many new ventures are able to attract and retain valuable human capital by putting in place extensive profit- and ownership-based compensation practices. The Silicon Valley model of offering large ownership stakes to talented employees is a powerful motivator that helps a firm to maximize the return on its human capital investments.

In addition to benefiting from high-quality human capital, new ventures benefit from practices that help to enhance the level of social capital within the firm. Social capital refers to the strength of relationships both inside and outside the firm, which facilitate the sharing of vital information and knowledge. Social capital is enhanced by creating organizational structures and information-sharing practices that diffuse knowledge throughout the organization. Entrepreneurial leaders willing to provide employees with key information pertaining to the strategic, technical, financial, and operational aspects of the business are able to develop employees with a more comprehensive understanding of the business, who are able to make stronger contributions. Furthermore, new ventures that put processes in place to allow employees to provide feedback on the key issues affecting the business are often more successful than are their counterparts that fail to capture this knowledge.

Social capital is also enhanced through a firm's compensation system. By tying individual compensation to the performance of the firm, young ventures are likely to see improved performance. Incentivizing people to work together by establishing profit- and ownership-based compensation enhances communication and collaboration, which may ultimately lead to higher rates of growth and success. Finally, new ventures that actively build internal labor markets by promoting from within enhance the continuity of their teams and minimize dissonance with the original mission of the firm.

The research literature points to a strong connection between some of the specific practices discussed previously and the performance of new ventures.

For instance, in a study of firms that completed an initial public offering (IPO) Theresa Welbourne and Alice Andrews demonstrated that firms emphasizing organizationally based rewards and human capital in their initial filings had greater longevity than their counterparts. Similarly, Jake Messersmith and Jim Guthrie suggest a relationship between a system of such practices and firm sales growth.

In sum, new ventures that place an emphasis on building structure and processes that enhance the levels of human and social capital within the firm are likely to improve their performance relative to rivals. As Neil Tocher and Matthew Rutherford report, this is not an easy transition for many entrepreneurs to make; however, the growth of the firm depends, in part, on the ability of entrepreneurial leaders to build human and social capital in their organizations.

Jake Messersmith
University of Nebraska, Kearney

See also Human Capital Theory; Human Resources; Measures of Performance

Further Readings

Huselid, Mark A. "The Impact of Human Resource Management Practices on Turnover, Productivity, and Corporate Financial Performance." *Academy of Management Journal*, v.38 (1995).

Messersmith, Jake G. and James P. Guthrie. "High Performance Work Systems in Emergent Organizations: Implications for Firm Performance." *Human Resource Management*, v.49 (2010).

Tocher, Neil and Matthew W. Rutherford. "Perceived Acute Human Resource Management Problems in Small and Medium Firms: An Empirical Examination." *Entrepreneurship Theory and Practice*, v.33/2 (2009).

Welbourne, Theresa M. and Alice O. Andrews. "Predicting the Performance of Initial Public Offerings: Should Human Resource Management Be in the Equation?" *Academy of Management Journal*, v.39 (1996).

MARKET EVALUATION

Over the past 50 years, research has shown that most new innovations are unsuccessful. In fact, if success is defined as providing a reasonable return on initial investment, less than 1 in 100 projects achieve this milestone. Most business development efforts are seen to be unsuccessful; for example, G. Stevens and S. Burley found that of 3,000 unwritten raw ideas, only 1 resulted in commercial success. Whereas many factors can influence opportunity outcomes, one of the most common causes of failure is that the innovation does not meet the market need at a competitive price.

The introduction of a market evaluation and validation process into the commercialization path can reduce the likelihood of failure. By adopting a formal market evaluation process, which the innovator does not bias, the new venture can increase both the likelihood of success and return on investment. Research conducted by the Canadian Innovation Centre into the effectiveness of a formal market evaluation process provides evidence of the positive impact such processes can have on the likelihood of success. When entrepreneurs validated their market opportunities, 70 percent were successful within five years, whereas only 18 percent were successful if they did not conduct a validation study. Furthermore, a market evaluation study identifies fatal business flaws, thereby helping entrepreneurs identify what to fix, or even whether to proceed.

Market Evaluation Versus Market Research

Traditional market research is done by large companies to provide evidence for them to use internally to justify the market opportunity they wish to attack. Market research is often concerned with existing markets: determining the size of the market, trends in that market, and market segmentation. Furthermore, market research is often undertaken independent of the innovation being proposed; it can also be carried out retrospectively, to confirm the effectiveness of a launch strategy. However, this approach is not as useful to new ventures, which attack new markets or focus on small market segments.

Market evaluation, in contrast, takes a bottom-up approach to validate the presence of a new market and provide insight regarding the most appropriate way to exploit that opportunity. Market evaluation uses interviews with market stakeholders to answer specific market evaluation questions that help the innovator confirm the opportunity and approach first (and sometimes second or third) potential customers. Identifying, attracting, and obtaining these initial customers is critical to the long-term success of the business. Undertaking market evaluation is a formal process that involves disclosing specific (but sometimes limited) information about the innovation to validate market assumptions in the business plan and sometimes to make the necessary changes that might facilitate success. The following six fundamental questions are answered by market evaluation:

1. Do customers in the target market see value in the proposed innovation?

2. Do the pricing and proposed features and benefits meet customer expectations (and provide a significant benefit over competitor solutions)?

Links Between Market Evaluation and Successful Commercialization of an Idea

Market Evaluation Theme	Clients Who Successfully Commercialized (%)	Clients Who Struggle to Commercialize (%)	Clients Who Did Not Commercialize (%)
Validated the market	70	18	0
Aligned the innovation to the market	100	39	0
Pursued the customer's voice	60	14	0
Understood their competitive position	70	21	0
Formalized their marketing strategy	73	39	0

Source: Based on research conducted by the Canadian Innovation Centre.

3. What would be the first application of the product/service?

4. What is the purchasing process for acquiring this type of product or service?

5. Are there organizations that would be interested in promoting the product or service?

6. Are there adjacent markets that offer greater potential than the originally envisaged market?

The process of undertaking market validation provides detailed answers to innovation-specific questions and helps identify initial market segments, how purchase decisions are made, what distribution channels should be selected, how the product/service should be priced, and how features and benefits should be decided. Correctly interpreted, this feedback can provide guidance on market potential and evolution, and ultimately whether the innovation can form the basis of a new venture. Market validation therefore provides valuable insights that enhance the dialogue between entrepreneurs and funders, advisers, and researchers. The result is better-informed decisions.

Third-Party Market Evaluation

Market validation is most valuable if conducted by an independent third party, who can provide an impartial marketplace perspective on a given opportunity. There are two internal benefits to having an independent evaluation done. In the first case, the individual asking the questions will pose them in such a way as to gather maximum insights from interviews without the biases that might be introduced by the innovator. In the second case, market stakeholders are much more likely to share profound insights with an independent third party, whereas they might be reluctant to do so with the innovator. Even large organizations, such as IBM and Hewlett-Packard, use third-party organizations to validate their strategies and enhance the value proposition of a new product or service launch. Whereas market evaluation often requires cash expenditures, there are ways of undertaking this cost-effectively, perhaps by accessing support agencies or students.

There is also an external benefit of using third parties to perform market evaluation: It provides a validation of the business that can be shared with other individuals and businesses interested in partnering with the innovator. Clearly, self-collected data

are likely to be less useful in this regard. The value of market evaluation in assessing an innovation's market potential, as well as the impact of trends, competition, and the industry, cannot be overstated in moving a project forward. A good market evaluation process has the ability to provide a negative answer to discourage proceeding and to benchmark the likelihood of success against other studies. It can also be used as a diagnostic tool to help increase the likelihood of success.

Andrew Lewis Maxwell
Josie Graham
Canadian Innovation Centre

See also Advertising; Business Models; Business-to-Business Marketing; Competition; Contextual Marketing; Customer Orientation; E-Commerce; Entrepreneurial Marketing; Focus Groups; International Markets; Positioning a New Product or Service; Retailing; Target Markets; Test Markets; Wholesale Markets

Further Readings

Astebro, T. and D. J. Koehler. "Calibration Accuracy of a Judgmental Process That Predicts the Commercial Success of New Product Ideas." *Journal of Behavioral Decision Making*, v.20/4 (2007).

Canadian Innovation Centre. *Value of Market Validation for Early Stage Commercialization.* Waterloo, ON: Author, 2004.

Stevens, G. and J. Burley. "3000 Raw Ideas = 1 Commercial Success." *Research Technology Management*, v.40/3 (1997).

MARKET ORIENTATION

Market orientation was first defined within marketing literature in the early 1990s as an organization-level culture comprising values and beliefs about putting the customer first in business planning. Market orientation is rooted in the marketing concept, which was developed in the 1950s and 1960s by academics such as Peter Drucker and Theodore Levitt. Essentially, market orientation is a firm-level measurement of the behaviors and activities that reflect the marketing concept, and as such it is a cornerstone of the marketing management and marketing strategy paradigms.

The emergence of market orientation construct in the early 1990s was a part of a larger movement within the marketing discipline which, since the beginning of the 1980s, had experienced increasing interest in interactions between buyers and sellers and the relationships they build. In 1990, two influential articles on market orientation were published. In an article by John Narver and Stanley Slater, market orientation was profiled as a perspective based in organizational culture: "The organizational culture that most effectively and efficiently creates the necessary behaviors for the creation of superior value for buyers and, thus, continues superior performance for the business." In the same year, an article by Ajay Kohli and Bernard Jaworski defined market orientation in more behavioral terms as "the organization-wide generation of market intelligence pertaining to current and future customer needs, dissemination of the intelligence across departments, and organization-wide responsiveness to it."

Since these seminal research articles, market orientation has been studied both as (1) a cultural phenomenon and (2) a set of behaviors relating to (a) organization-wide market intelligence generation through decision support systems, marketing information systems, and marketing research efforts; (b) dissemination of the intelligence across functions in a firm; and (c) organization-wide responsiveness (actions) based on this intelligence. Market intelligence covers both customers and competitors. The two widely used measurement scales for market orientation, namely MARKOR (for the measurement of behavioral market orientation) and MKTOR (for the measurement of cultural market orientation), reflect the behavioral versus cultural division and are also rooted in the work of Narver and Slater (MKTOR) and Kohli and Jaworski (MARKOR). It should be noted that even though the cultural and behavioral aspects of market orientation are sometimes presented as competing views, they actually complement each other; a holistic market orientation consists of both behavior and cognition.

The importance of market orientation is based on the underlying assumption that profit maximization and long-term profitability are ultimate goals of firms. At the same time, however, these goals can be achieved only by understanding customers' needs and problems as well as competitors' strategies. The rationale behind the study of market orientation presupposes that analyzing a firm's competitive environment can generate exceptional advantages that lead to above-normal returns. This opposes the economics assumption that both the methodologies for collecting environmental information and the conceptual models for analyzing it are in the public domain, which would lead to firms reaching similar conclusions about the potential of strategies.

Indeed, the notion that market orientation has a positive impact on business performance is well documented in scholarly research. Comprehensive reviews of research that has empirically investigated the market orientation-performance relationship have been published in multiple meta-analyses on the topic. For example, in a 2004 study Cynthia Rodriguez Cano and colleagues found that the disattenuated weighted mean effect size (Pearson's correlation coefficient) of the relationship between market orientation and business performance is 0.35; the degree of market orientation of a firm explains about 12 percent of the variance in business performance. In another meta-analysis, from 2005, A. H. Kirca and colleagues found that the market orientation-performance relationship was significant, and stronger in samples of manufacturing firms, in low power-distance and uncertainty-avoidance cultures, and in studies that use subjective measures of performance. Furthermore, their analysis showed that market orientation affects performance through innovativeness, customer loyalty, and quality.

In addition to being a predictor of firm performance, market orientation may have a particularly important role in the recognition of opportunities to introduce new products or services to the markets, either through existing firm structures or through establishment of new organizations. For example, Scott Shane (2000) finds that three major dimensions of prior knowledge are important to the process of entrepreneurial discovery: prior knowledge of markets, prior knowledge of ways to serve markets, and prior knowledge of customer problems. Entrepreneurial new ventures emerge to fulfill unmet market needs, and they grow when they are able to serve these needs better than incumbents do. This suggests that staying customer- and market-oriented is an essential quality of entrepreneurial ventures in market economies. In new firms market intelligence generation is a less formal, more informally organized activity than market research conducted by incumbents. Yet entrepreneurs are known for being keen to listen to their customers and integrating customers' ideas into new products and services. Overall, new ventures tend to be less formalized and often also less centralized than established firms. These characteristics allow information on customer needs and competitor moves to be disseminated internally, even when formal dissemination channels are scarce.

Despite its overwhelmingly positive long-term effects on firm performance, market orientation may be hard to achieve in new, resource-poor ventures, particularly if these firms are focused on technology and science. Sometimes information on customer needs can be too costly or complex to access, especially for smaller technology ventures. In addition, especially in developing radically new products, conventional market research tools may be of limited utility; many firms do not incorporate users' or customers' opinions into their development processes because of the customers' limited domains of expertise, their inability to articulate their underlying needs, and the belief that user-developed concepts tend not to be innovative or creative.

Maija Renko
University of Illinois, Chicago

See also Contextual Marketing; Customer Orientation; Entrepreneurial Marketing; Entrepreneurial Orientation; Focus Groups; Market Evaluation; Opportunity Recognition; Target Markets; Test Markets

Further Readings

Drucker, P. F. *The Practice of Management*. Englewood Cliffs, NJ: Prentice-Hall, 1954.

Kirca, A. H., S. Jayachandran, and W. O. Bearden. "Market Orientation: A Meta-Analytic Review and Assessment of Its Antecedents and Impact on Performance." *Journal of Marketing*, v.69/2 (2005).

Kohli, Ajay and Bernard Jaworski. "Market Orientation: The Construct, Research Propositions, and Managerial Implications." *Journal of Marketing*, v.54/2 (1990).

Levitt, Theodore. *Marketing Myopia*. Boston: Harvard Business Press, 2008.

Narver, John C. and Stanley F. Slater. "The Effect of a Market Orientation on Business Profitability." *Journal of Marketing*, v.54 (October 1990).

Renko, M. *Market Orientation in Markets for Technology: Evidence From Biotechnology Ventures*. Turku, Finland: Turku School of Economics, 2006.

Rodriguez Cano, Cynthia, François A. Carrillat, and Fernando Jaramillo. "A Meta-Analysis of the Relationship Between Market Orientation and Business Performance: Evidence From Five Continents." *International Journal of Research in Marketing*, v.21 (2004).

Shane, Scott. "Prior Knowledge and the Discovery of Entrepreneurial Opportunities." *Organization Science*, v.11/4 (2000).

Master of Business Administration

The master's degree in business administration (MBA) is offered by universities with business or management schools that cater to students seeking to develop managerial skills in the multifaceted aspects of business and financial theory. The traditional structure of the MBA program, as initiated in the Gilded Age boom of the early 1900s, was that of a two-year program course to instill in the captains of industry the knowledge needed to guide their technical groundwork (typically in engineering) into a practical, human application.

The program originated when the Tuck School of Business, Dartmouth College, conferred an advanced degree in commercial science. In 1908, two early American schools of business, Wharton and the University of Chicago, offered two of the world's first MBA programs. As the popularity of these programs spread, however, the duration of the programs grew. Traditionally, MBA programs stem from universities in the United States but now are found throughout the world, a response to globalization and the laws of supply and demand in the job market as well as the demand for business students to remain competitive. In the United Kingdom, MBA programs were adapted to suit the needs of the domestic academic system; a one-year program is the norm for most candidates, with major programs developing in universities in such industrial centers as Manchester and London.

MBA programs are accredited by several academic institutions external to the business schools. These have been established over the years to maintain the integrity of the offerings of each school and thus ensure that the schools are teaching appropriately. In the United States, three major accrediting bodies are responsible for setting the parameters of what is acceptable to be taught in an MBA program: the Association to Advance Collegiate Schools of Business (AACSB), the Accreditation Council for Collegiate Business Schools and Programs (ACBSP),

The Wharton School of the University of Pennsylvania in Mack Plaza, pictured above, is the world's first collegiate business school and the first business school in the United States. Wharton, along with the University of Chicago, offered the first MBA programs in the world. (Wikimedia/Bruce Andersen)

and the International Assembly for Collegiate Business Education (IACBE), which accredits institutions outside the United States as well. Both the ACBSP and the IACBE are accredited by the Council for Higher Education Accreditation (CHEA). The Commission on Accreditation of Healthcare Management Education (CAHME) accredits MBA degrees that specialize in managerial positions in the healthcare field.

Not only must the MBA program be accredited; the university itself must be accredited prior to establishing an MBA program. These accreditations are both regional and national and are determined by the CHEA, based on the university's or college's geographic location. In the United States, location is determined by region: Western, Southern, North Central, New England, and Middle.

There are several basic types of MBA programs. The full-time or two-year program is conducted over the course of 18 months. The accelerated MBA program provides a variation of the two-year program and typically involves a higher course load as well as a more intense regimen of classes and test schedules; the accelerated program typically allows less vacation time between terms and is designed to get students in and out of the program as quickly as possible. The part-time MBA program is designed to work around the schedules of those already engaged in full-time careers; in this type of program, the student attends classes after normal working hours, on weekends or in the evenings and on holidays, when other schools or classes are not held. The executive MBA (EMBA) program was developed to meet the educational needs of executives and business managers. This type of MBA program allows students to participate in a business-oriented environment while working full time. Participants focus on their specializations, earning a degree based on the field or industry in which they are currently employed. The EMBA program often requires the student to have up to 10 years of experience working in his or her industry as a prerequisite to admission. The popularity of the executive MBA program is founded on the higher standards for applicants, the rigors of the course work, and the historically higher percentage of graduates who find employment upon completing the program.

MBA programs are also offered off campus. Distance-learning MBA programs have become increasingly popular, offering flexibility in both course structure and scheduling as well as allowing the student to engage in learning through several platforms, such as correspondence courses, video broadcast courses, and online courses.

Admission to graduate schools depends on a complex mix of several different factors. Schools review letters of recommendation, statements of purpose, grade point averages, and scores on either the Graduate Management Admission Test (GMAT) or the Graduate Record Examination (GRE). Acceptable scores on the GMAT typically range from 680 to 720. The GRE scores two areas, quantitative skills, or GRE-Q, and verbal skills, or GRE-V. The average GRE-Q score for MBA admission is 767, and the average GRE-V score is 679. Although there are more than 400 full-time MBA programs and half the top 30 programs accept the GRE, critics have argued that the examination's format is so rigid that it effectively tests only how well a student can conform to a standardized test-taking procedure. Decisions regarding admission to MBA programs also take into account the percentage of international students enrolled in a particular program, as well as the male-to-female ratio.

Students in MBA programs typically specialize in areas such as accounting, economics, entrepreneurship, finance, international business, marketing, operations management, organizational behavior, project management, real estate, or strategic management, among other areas. Many universities also have hybrid programs, such as the JD/MBA and the healthcare MBA.

The MBA can certainly enhance the knowledge base of entrepreneurs, including those involved in start-ups and new ventures. The degree allows them a better perspective from which to understand growth management and establish a network of similarly minded people, such as those from other industries, who can help the new venture as it moves forward.

Alfred Lewis
Hamline University
Dan Kipley
Azusa Pacific University

See also Entrepreneurial Training; Entrepreneurship Education: Graduate Programs; Entrepreneurship Education: High School; Entrepreneurship Education: Undergraduate Programs; Entrepreneurship Pedagogy

Further Readings

Baron, Robert A. "Effectual Versus Predictive Logics in Entrepreneurial Decision Making—Differences Between Experts and Novices: Does Experience in Starting New Ventures Change the Way Entrepreneurs Think? Perhaps, but for Now, 'Caution' Is Essential." *Journal of Business Venturing*, v.24/4 (July 2009).

Bouknight, Omari and Scott Shrum. *Your MBA Game Plan: Proven Strategies for Getting Into the Top Business Schools*. Franklin Lakes, NJ: Career Press, 2003.

DeMartino, Richard and Robert Barbato. "Differences Between Women and Men MBA Entrepreneurs: Exploring Family Flexibility and Wealth Creation as Career Motivators." *Journal of Business Venturing*, v.18/6 (November 2003).

Dew, Nicholas, Stuart Read, Saras D. Sarasvathy, and Robert Wiltbank. "Effectual Versus Predictive Logics in Entrepreneurial Decision-Making: Differences Between Experts and Novices." *Journal of Business Venturing*, v.24/4 (July 2009).

Heffler, Janet. *The EMBA Degree: An Examination of Career Issues*. Halifax, NS: Saint Mary's University, 2010.

Navarro, Peter. *What the Best MBAs Know: How to Apply the Greatest Ideas Taught in the Best Business Schools*. New York: McGraw-Hill, 2005.

Stralser, Steven. *MBA in a Day: What You Would Learn at Top-Tier Business Schools (If You Only Had the Time!)*. Hoboken, NJ: Wiley, 2004.

Wilson, Fiona et al. "An Analysis of the Role of Gender and Self-Efficacy in Developing Female Entrepreneurial Interest and Behavior." *Journal of Developmental Entrepreneurship*, v.14/2 (June 2009).

MEASURES OF ENTREPRENEURIAL ACTIVITY ACROSS COUNTRIES

The relationship between national culture and entrepreneurship has been explored from a variety of perspectives and using a variety of measurements for entrepreneurship. Much of the research on national culture has been based on Geert Hofstede's work, which examines the cultural dimensions of individualism-collectivism, power distance, uncertainty avoidance, and masculinity-femininity. Hofstede defined individualistic societies as "societies in which the ties between individuals are loose: everyone is expected to look after himself or herself and his or her immediate family"; defined collectivist societies, by contrast, are "societies in which people from birth onward are integrated into strong, cohesive in-groups, which throughout people's lifetime continue to protect them in exchange for unquestioning loyalty." Masculinity versus femininity refers to differences in emotional roles and values, with masculine values occupying a dimension of very assertive and competitive and feminine values more focused on modesty and caring. Power distance is the extent to which the less powerful members of organizations and institutions accept and expect that power is distributed unequally. A society's power distance level reflects the extent to which individuals are socialized toward obedience as opposed to initiative. Uncertainty avoidance reflects a society's tolerance for ambiguity and indicates "to what extent a culture programs its members to feel either uncomfortable or comfortable in unstructured situations. Unstructured situations are novel, unknown, surprising, and different than usual."

James Hayton and colleagues provided a review of behavioral research on national culture and entrepreneurship in which researchers predominantly used Hofstede's conceptualization of national culture and generally hypothesized that the cultural dimensions of high individualism, low uncertainty avoidance, high masculinity, and low power distance facilitate higher levels of entrepreneurship. Their review included empirical studies that examined the association between national cultural characteristics and aggregate measures of entrepreneurship, individual characteristics of entrepreneurs, and features of corporate entrepreneurship. The studies focused primarily on national differences among a diverse set of entrepreneurial motives, comparisons of values and beliefs, cognitions, and traits associated with entrepreneurship. In some studies entrepreneurship was measured based on entry mode into new markets, national rates of innovation, and rates of new-firm formation. Other entrepreneurial characteristics examined in the context of national culture include entrepreneurial traits such as innovativeness, locus of control, risk taking, and energy.

The Global Entrepreneurship Monitor

The Global Entrepreneurship Monitor (GEM) is an international research consortium that examines the relationship between entrepreneurship and economic development. GEM has been measuring and comparing entrepreneurial activity across countries since 1999. The best-known measure of entrepreneurship used by the GEM research consortium is the Total early-stage Entrepreneurial Activity (TEA), which measures the percentage of a nation's adult population who are nascent entrepreneurs and those who own and manage a business less than 3.5 years old. GEM reports have provided a source of comparable data across as many as 54 different countries on attitudes and aspirations toward entrepreneurship as well as start-up and established business activities. GEM's main objectives are to measure differences in the level of entrepreneurial activity among countries, identify factors determining national levels of entrepreneurial activity, and identify policies that may enhance the national level of entrepreneurial activity.

GEM data have been used in a variety of research studies. Comparisons of multiple countries have linked GEM data with other national-level data, including data from the Heritage Foundation/*Wall Street Journal* 2003 Index of Economic Freedom, the gross domestic product, the World Bank, Transparency International's corruption index, the World Economic Forum, the International Telecommunication Union, the KOF Swiss Economic Institute, the United Nations human development index, and the Coface country risk rating. Individual-level data from GEM have been

linked with national-level data on social capital from the World Values Survey (WVS), finding that high levels of generalized trust at the national level lead to an increased likelihood of opportunity perception and higher levels of weak-tie investment.

GEM data have been used to examine the development of entrepreneurship in a single country and in cross-country comparisons. GEM results have led to gender-based studies on topics such as perceived financial barriers for women, an examination of the differences in entrepreneurial activity between women in different ethnic groups, levels of entrepreneurial resources among women, comparisons between male and female entrepreneurs, and the relationship between norms supporting women's entrepreneurship and rates of female-to-male entrepreneurs. In addition to gender comparisons, GEM data have been used to compare minority and white entrepreneurs on demographic variables, socioeconomic variables, and perceptions related to entrepreneurship. Individual variables within GEM data that have been examined in comparison to other individual-level variables include entrepreneurial aspirations, entrepreneurial motivations, socioeconomic variables, innovativeness, educational attainment, unemployment, self-confidence, informal investment activity, fear of failure, and start-up skills. Studies based on GEM data are often used to develop recommendations for policy development.

GEM includes an Adult Population Survey and a National Expert Survey. The National Expert Survey examines entrepreneurial framework conditions that reflect aspects of the country's socioeconomic climate that influence entrepreneurship within the nation, adapted from the Global Competitiveness Report (GCR). GEM identifies framework conditions specific to entrepreneurship and innovation and includes nine entrepreneurial framework conditions (EFCs). The EFCs are financial support, government policies, government programs, education and training, research and development transfer, commercial and professional infrastructure, internal market openness, access to physical infrastructure, and cultural and social norms. For each of the EFCs, Likert scale items are completed by experts in each country.

The Adult Population Survey uses phone and face-to-face interviews to collect information on entrepreneurial attitudes and perceptions, entrepreneurial activity, and entrepreneurial aspirations.

Entrepreneurial attitudes and perceptions are attitudes toward entrepreneurship and include the extent to which individuals believe there are opportunities for business start-ups, the type of status they believe entrepreneurs hold, the level of risk they are willing to take, and perceptions of their own knowledge and skills related to business creation. Entrepreneurial attitudes and perceptions indicate whether entrepreneurship is a socially desirable activity within each nation's culture. Entrepreneurial activity examines the extent to which individuals within the population are engaged in new business activity. Entrepreneurial aspiration indicates the qualitative nature of entrepreneurial activity, reflecting differences such as how entrepreneurs differ in the aspirations toward innovation, introduction of new processes or products, engagement with foreign markets, and organizational growth. GEM also identifies individuals who have discontinued a business in the past 12 months, as they may reenter the entrepreneurial process. Variables measured by GEM are defined as follows:

- *Perceived capabilities*: The percentage of the adult population who believe they have the required skills and knowledge to start a business.
- *Perceived opportunities*: The percentage of the adult population who see good opportunities to start a firm in the area where they live.
- *Fear of failure rate*: The percentage of the adult population with positive perceived opportunities who indicate that fear of failure would prevent them from setting up a business.
- *Entrepreneurial intention*: The percentage of the adult population (individuals involved in any stage of entrepreneurial activity excluded) who intend to start a business within three years.
- *Know start-up entrepreneur rate*: The percentage of the adult population who personally know someone who started a business in the past two years.
- *Entrepreneurship as desirable career choice*: The percentage of the adult population who agree with the statement that in their country, most people consider starting a business as a desirable career choice.
- *High status successful entrepreneurship*: The percentage of the adult population who agree with the statement that in their country, successful entrepreneurs receive high status.

- *Media attention for entrepreneurship*: The percentage of the adult population who agree with the statement that in their country, one will often see stories in the public media about successful new businesses.
- *Nascent entrepreneurship rate*: The percentage of the adult population who are currently nascent entrepreneurs (that is, actively involved in setting up a business they will own or co-own); these businesses have not paid salaries, wages, or any other payments to the owners for more than three months.
- *New business ownership rate*: The percentage of the adult population who are currently an owner-manager of a new business, (that is, they own and manage a running business that has paid salaries, wages, or any other payments to the owners for more than three months but not more than 42 months).
- *Total early-stage entrepreneurial activity (TEA)*: The percentage of the adult population who are either nascent entrepreneurs or owner-managers of a new business (as defined above).
- *Established business ownership rate*: The percentage of the adult population who are currently owner-managers of established businesses (that is, they own and manage a running business that has paid salaries, wages, or any other payments to the owners for more than 42 months).
- *Business discontinuation rate*: The percentage of the adult population who have, in the past 12 months, discontinued a business, either by selling, shutting down, or otherwise discontinuing an owner/management relationship with the business (not a measure of business failure rates).
- *Necessity-driven entrepreneurial activity: relative prevalence*: The percentage of those involved in TEA who are involved in entrepreneurship because they had no other option for work.
- *Improvement-driven opportunity entrepreneurial activity: relative prevalence*: The percentage of the those involved in TEA who (1) claim to be driven by opportunity as opposed to finding no other option for work, and (2) indicate that the main driver for being involved in this opportunity is being independent or increasing their income, rather than just maintaining their income.

- *Total early-stage entrepreneurial activity for male working-age population*: The percentage of the male adult population who are either nascent entrepreneurs or owner-managers of new businesses (as defined above).
- *Total early-stage entrepreneurial activity for female working-age population*: The percentage of the female adult population who are either nascent entrepreneurs or owner-managers of new businesses (as defined above).
- *Informal investors rate*: The percentage of the adult population who have personally provided funds for a new business, started by someone else, in the past three years.
- *Growth expectation early-stage entrepreneurial activity: relative prevalence*: The percentage of the TEA who expect to employ at least five employees five years from now.
- *New product early-stage entrepreneurial activity*: The percentage of the TEA who indicate that their product or service is new to at least some customers.
- *International orientation early-stage entrepreneurial activity*: The percentage of the TEA who indicate that at least 25 percent of the customers come from other countries.

Entrepreneurial Orientation

Entrepreneurial orientation (EO) is a construct that describes the degree to which an organization can be characterized as entrepreneurial versus conservative. EO describes the entrepreneurial process and how entrepreneurship is undertaken. EO refers to the strategy-making processes upon which entrepreneurial decisions and actions are based. Pioneered by Danny Miller in the 1980s and refined by Jeffrey Covin and Dennis Slevin, EO has three primary dimensions: innovativeness, proactiveness, and risk taking. Innovativeness refers to the tendency toward new ideas, experimentation, and creative processes that may result in departure from established technologies or practices. Proactiveness reflects the tendency to anticipate and act on future needs or wants in the market, which sometimes results in first-mover advantage over competition. Risk taking refers to the willingness to commit resources when the outcomes are unknown or when the cost of failure may be high. Being entrepreneurial is contrasted with a conservative model. Miller and Peter Friesen explain that the entrepreneurial model "applies to firms that innovate boldly and regularly while taking considerable risks in their product-market strategies," and innovation is seen as "a vital and central part of strategy."

G. T. Lumpkin and Gregory Dess suggest that there are two additional dimensions that should be included as aspects of an entrepreneurial orientation. These dimensions are competitive aggressiveness and autonomy. Competitive aggressiveness is described as "the type of intensity and head-to-head posturing that new entrants often need to compete with existing rivals." Autonomy is the ability and desire to be self-directed when pursuing opportunities and is defined as "the independent action of an individual or a team in bringing forth an idea or a vision and carrying it through to completion."

EO is one of the most widely used constructs in entrepreneurship. A meta-analysis by Andreas Rauch and colleagues examined the relationship between EO and business performance. The examination of 53 samples from 51 studies with 14,259 organizations indicated a moderate to large relationship between EO and performance. A multicountry analysis of the psychometric properties of the EO scale found strong support for the cross-cultural validity of the scale. EO has been used in a large number of studies in both the international and multinational contexts. Dimensions of EO have been linked to Hofstede's cultural dimensions. Studies have found that uncertainty avoidance and power distance have a negative influence on risk taking and on proactiveness. International studies on EO have found differences between countries on all EO dimensions. EO is frequently linked to firm performance in international studies. Additional variables linked to EO across countries include networking, strategic alliances, market orientation, resource allocations, and dynamism.

Country Institutional Profiles

Lowell Busenitz, Carolina Gomez, and Jennifer Spencer developed and empirically validated a survey instrument that measures the country institutional profile for entrepreneurship. The measure consists of regulatory, cognitive, and normative dimensions. The regulatory dimension of the institutional profile includes regulations, laws, and government policies that are supportive of new business, reduce risks for entrepreneurs, and facilitate the acquisition of resources. The cognitive dimension includes the amount of knowledge and skills held by individuals in the country related to establishing and running a business. The normative dimension addresses values and attitudes of the country's residents toward entrepreneurial activities and toward innovative and creative thinking.

The measure was created to be specific to the domain of entrepreneurship and for exploring broad country differences. Busenitz and colleagues suggest that the country institutional profile measure provides a resource for examining specific country-level institutional differences related to different levels of entrepreneurship and for exploring why entrepreneurs in some countries have a competitive advantage over entrepreneurs in other countries.

Rebecca J. Franklin
Oklahoma State University

See also Culture and Entrepreneurship; Globalization; Import/Export Businesses; International Enterprise Planning; International Markets; International New Ventures; Political Economy and Entrepreneurship

Further Readings

Acs, Zoltán J. and László Szerb. *The Global Entrepreneurship Index (GEINDEX)*. Boston: Now Publishers, 2009.

Bosma, Niels and Jonathan Levie. *Global Entrepreneurship Monitor: 2009 Global Report*. London: Global Entrepreneurship Research Association, 2009.

Busenitz, Lowell W., Carolina Gomez, and Jennifer W. Spencer. "Country Institutional Profiles: Unlocking Entrepreneurial Phenomena." *Academy of Management Journal*, v.43/5 (2000).

Covin, Jeffrey G. and Dennis P. Slevin. "The Development and Testing of an Organizational-Level Entrepreneurship Scale." In *Frontiers of Entrepreneurship Research*, R. Ronstadt, J. A. Hornaday, R. Peterson, and K. H. Vesper, eds. Wellesley, MA: Babson College, 1986.

Hayton, James C., Gerard George, and Shaker A. Zahra. "National Culture and Entrepreneurship: A Review of Behavioral Research." *Entrepreneurship Theory and Practice*, v.26/4 (2002).

Hofstede, Geert. *Cultures and Organizations: Software of the Mind*. Berkshire, UK: McGraw-Hill, 1991.

Lumpkin, G. T. and Gregory G. Dess. "Clarifying the Entrepreneurial Orientation Construct and Linking It to Performance." *Academy of Management Review*, v.21/1 (1996).

Miller, Danny and Peter H. Friesen. "Innovation in Conservative and Entrepreneurial Firms: Two Models of Strategic Momentum." *Strategic Management Journal*, v.3 (1982).

Rauch, Andreas, Johan Wiklund, G. T. Lumpkin, and Michael Frese. "Entrepreneurial Orientation and Business Performance: An Assessment of Past Research and Suggestions for the Future." *Entrepreneurship Theory and Practice*, v.33/3 (2009).

MEASURES OF PERFORMANCE

The measurement of new ventures' performance is crucial, because these organizations are a major source of job creation and the improvement of their performance is vital to their sustained existence and growth. For the new venture owner or manager, this means that competitors of new ventures are often well-informed of the sales and profitability of new ventures.

A new venture is the end result of the process of creating and organizing a new business that develops, produces, and markets products or services needed to satisfy unmet market demand for the sole purposes of profit and growth. Entrepreneurship can be defined as the creators' new ventures. New ventures are sometimes founded by individuals and sometimes by teams of entrepreneurs; in the latter case, the comprehensiveness of the team has an affirmative impact on new venture performance.

A venture is considered new if it has not yet reached a phase in its development where it can be considered a mature business. The precise moment in time at which a new venture becomes a mature business has not yet been defined. However, the idea of business maturation could be equated with a firm that has fully completed its transition to a point of stability or, more generally, has overcome the "liability of newness" and can be reasonably evaluated. The time span taken by a new venture to mature will differ depending on its industry, resources, and strategy. It seems logical to suppose that the earliest this might occur would be three to five years after its formation and, more usually, not until the venture is eight to 12 years old.

New venture performance is influenced by both industry structure and venture strategy, as well as by the characteristics of the entrepreneur. Recent research has shown the dialectic effects of industry structure, strategy, and the entrepreneur have a far greater impact on new venture performance than of any of these variables in isolation, as suggested by Julia Kirby in her 2005 article "Toward a Theory of High Performance." The new venture game is an intricate one, which is one reason it is so risky. It also means that success can be enhanced by specialization in any one of the three basic variables (industry structure, strategy, or the entrepreneur), as this will both significantly diminish the complexities involved and allow the venture capitalist to develop greater expertise in managing them. Disregarding interactive effects, industry structure has a greater impact on new venture performance than either the strategy or the personality of the entrepreneur. This strongly supports the practice of many venture capitalists to specialize by industry. It also emphasizes, although indirectly, the remarkable importance of timing to new venture success.

Since industry structure has a major impact on new venture performance and since structure can change quickly in the early stages of market development, timing is particularly decisive in new venture success.

The conditional impact of strategy on new venture performance is far greater than its nonconditional impact. Differentiated strategies surpass focused strategies, as Harvard competitive strategist Michael Porter would say. This supports venture capitalists' belief that every successful new venture must have some type of unique selling proposition, other than price, that is not easily duplicated by competitors.

Beyond this, however, the key strategy message is that it all depends on circumstances. Also, strategy insights may be venture capitalists' key "value added" contribution—other than money—to a new venture. Entrepreneurs should select venture capitalists, much as venture capitalists select entrepreneurs, seeking those with the preeminent knowledge of their industry and the strategies suitable for it.

Sabine Sonnentag, author of *Psychological Management of Individual Performance*, emphasizes the fact that the personal characteristics of the entrepreneur have a slight impact on new venture performance. Entrepreneurs are not trivial to new venture success, but their individual profiles are not the key to such success, even if venture capitalists have a strong belief in the value of the entrepreneur and their past performance. The key characteristics of entrepreneurs that may affect new venture performance are their individual behavior patterns.

Venture capitalists in general have been right in disregarding traditional academic research in entrepreneurship. The wisdom of venture capitalists is that their practices disagree with the new venture performance model that has dominated academic research. Academics should move beyond studies of entrepreneurial personality and psychology by including in their research the behavioral distinctiveness sought by experienced venture capitalists.

The performance of a new venture is the corollary of a convergence of factors that include attributes of the entrepreneur, strategy, and industry structure. Industry structure and strategy, in isolation and in combination, influence new venture performance.

Other variables can shape the performance of a new venture that go beyond the skills and behaviors of its founders, the form of its strategies, and the structure of its industry. Some of these include the resources upon which a venture's strategy must be based and the organizational structure, processes, and systems by which the venture's strategy must be implemented, as Robert Kaplan notes in his 1996 article "Using the Balanced Scorecard as a Strategic Management System."

The determinants of new venture performance from the perspective of strategic management theory describe why the concepts of resources and organizational structure, processes, and systems are crucial elements of any fully specified model of new venture performance.

Djamel Eddine Laouisset
Alhosn University, Abu Dhabi

See also Innovation Measurement; Measures of Entrepreneurial Activity Across Countries

Further Readings

Cooper, Arnold C., F. Javier Gimeno-Gascon, and Carolyn Y. Woo. "Initial Human and Financial Capital as Predictors of New Venture Performance." *Journal of Business Venturing*, v.9 (1994).

Haber, Sigal and Arie Reichel. "Identifying Performance Measures of Small Ventures: The Case of the Tourism Industry." *Journal of Small Business Management*, v.43 (2005).

Kaplan, Robert and David P. Norton. "Using the Balanced Scorecard as a Strategic Management System." *Harvard Business Review* (January/February 1996).

Kirby, Julia. "Toward a Theory of High Performance." *Harvard Business Review* (July/August 2005).

Meyer, Christopher. "How the Right Measures Help Teams Excel." *Harvard Business Review* (May/June 1994).

Neely, Andy. *Business Performance Measurement.* Cambridge, UK: Cambridge University Press, 2002.

Niven, Paul. *Balanced Scorecard Step-by-Step for Government and Nonprofit Agencies.* New York: John Wiley and Sons, 2001.

Robinson, Kenneth C. and Patricia Philips McDougall. "Entry Barriers and New Venture Performance: A Comparison of Universal and Contingency Approaches." *Strategic Management Journal*, v.22 (2001).

Robinson, Kenneth C. and Patricia Philips McDougall. "The Impact of Alternative Operationalizations of Industry: Structural Elements on Measure." *Strategic Management Journal*, v.19 (1998).

Smith, Douglas. *Make Success Measurable.* New York: John Wiley and Sons, 1999.

Sonnentag, Sabine. *Psychological Management of Individual Performance.* New York: John Wiley and Sons, 2002.

MICROFINANCE

Microfinance is the collective term used to describe the process of providing funding to poor people who have no access to traditional finance institutions, such as credit unions and banks. Microfinance was championed by Muhammad Yunus with his revolutionary experiment in the early 1970s of providing finance to poor people, initially only women in Bangladesh. He later founded the Grameen Bank in 1983. Microfinance institutions (MFIs) can be characterized as banking or financial institutions for the poor, since they provide small loans and small savings programs. Numerous institutions have emerged dedicated to providing credit to poor entrepreneurs, especially in developing countries. According to a report by the World Bank, about 160 million people benefit from the services of microfinance providers.

In 2006, Brigit Helms categorized microfinance providers as follows:

- Informal financial service providers, such as moneylenders and savings collectors
- Member-owned organizations, such as self-help groups and credit unions
- Nongovernmental organizations (NGOs)

- Formal financial institutions, such as some commercial banks, state banks, agricultural development banks, savings banks, rural banks, and nonbank financial institutions

Since Helms identified these MFIs, technology has revolutionized their reach and scalability. Today, for example, ordinary mobile phones can be used to process transactions.

A study compiled by the Consultative Group to Assist the Poor (CGAP) suggested that MFIs have provided positive contributions to very poor households by allowing them to attend to basic needs. The increasing use of microfinancing also indicates an improving economic climate for this segment of the economic strata and in particular has been vital to improving the lives of women and bringing about gender equality. The CGAP study stated that

empirical evidence shows that, among the poor, those participating in microfinance programs who had access to financial services were able to improve their well-being—both at the individual and household level—much more than those who did not have access to financial services. In Bangladesh, Bangladesh Rural Advancement Committee (BRAC) clients increased household expenditures by 28 percent and assets by 112 percent. The incomes of Grameen members were 43 percent higher than incomes in nonprogram villages. In El Salvador, the weekly income of FINCA clients increased on average by 145 percent. In India, half of SHARE clients graduated out of poverty. In Ghana, 80 percent of clients of Freedom from Hunger had secondary income sources, compared to 50 percent for nonclients. In Lombok, Indonesia, the average income of Bank Rakyat Indonesia (BRI) borrowers increased by 112 percent, and 90 percent of households graduated out of poverty. In Vietnam, Save the Children clients reduced food deficits from three months to one month.

The World Health Organization studied the impact of microfinance institutions from a macro perspective and reported that

thousands of microfinance workers travel to poor communities to provide microfinance services, often to groups of women convening on a regular basis over months and years to repay loans and deposit savings. Many microfinance institutions in Africa, Asia, and Latin America already successfully offer services beyond microfinance, including training in business and financial management. An increasing number also offer health-related services, such as education, clinical care, health financing (loans, savings, and health insurance) and establishing linkages to public and private health providers to facilitate access to healthcare. This is a vast, private-sector infrastructure of service delivery that is mostly self-financed by interest on loans.

There have been several criticisms about the impact of MFIs. Some assert that MFIs and their success have helped absolve governments of their responsibility for developing adequate infrastructures in public health, social welfare, and education. As noted by Microfinanceinfo.com, some doubt that microfinance really has an impact on poverty. Others describe microcredit as a privatization of public safety-net programs. There are also concerns that some microfinance institutions have charged excessive interest rates. Some studies of microfinance programs have found that women are used as collection agents for their husbands and sons, such that the male relatives enjoy the proceeds while the women bear the credit risk. In some cases borrowers become dependent on micro loans rather than investments for regular living expenses.

A report by Microfinanceinfo.com surmised that the key debate about microfinance is whether

A financial transaction being conducted at a community-based savings bank in Cambodia. Microfinancing, an alternative to traditional financial institutions for people who have no access to credit unions or banks, has improved the lives and social status of women worldwide. (Wikimedia/Brett Matthews)

it should focus on improved welfare or financial sustainability. The two different approaches are usually named as "poverty lending" or "the welfarist approach" and "the institutionist approach" or "financial system approach." The welfarist approach might, for example, supply the customer with education and health, whereas the institutionists focus primarily on financial services, reasoning that only with a total focus on financial sustainability can the huge demand be met. MFIs that take the welfarist approach include the Grameen Bank and Women's World Banking. Examples of institutionists are ACCION International and BRI Unit Desa.

Alfred Lewis
Hamline University
Dan Kipley
Azusa Pacific University

See also Debt; Equity- and Debt-Based Financing; Gender and Acquiring Resources; Gender and Industry Preferences; Gender and Performance; Globalization; Home-Based Businesses; Motivation and Gender; Social Capital; Social Entrepreneurship; Social Intelligence; Social Networks; Sustainable Development; Women's Entrepreneurship; Women's Entrepreneurship: Best Practices

Further Readings

Armendariz, Beatriz, and Jonathan Morduch. *The Economics of Microfinance.* Cambridge, MA: MIT Press, 2005.

Consultative Group to Assist the Poor. http://cgap.org (Accessed February 2011).

Forbes.com. http://www.forbes.com (Accessed February 2011).

Helms, Brigit. *Access for All: Building Inclusive Financial Systems.* Washington, DC: World Bank, 2006.

La Torre, Mario, and Gianfranco A. Vento. *Microfinance.* New York: Palgrave, 2006.

Microfinanceinfo.com. http://www.microfinanceinfo.com (Accessed February 2011).

Sundaresan, Suresh. *Microfinance.* Northampton, MA: Edward Elgar, 2008.

World Health Organization. http://www.who.int/bulletin/volumes/88/6/09–071464/en/index.html (Accessed February 2011).

Yunus, M. *Building Social Business: The New Kind of Capitalism That Serves Humanity's Most Pressing Needs.* New York: Public Affairs, 2010.

MINORITIES IN NEW BUSINESS VENTURES

The issue of minority participation in new business ventures can be viewed from a variety of perspectives in an increasingly globalized economy. Historically, discussion and research surrounding minority participation in new venture creation centered on the North American experience of the immigrant in a growing nation and economy. Long before academic researchers in the field of business turned their attention to this emerging phenomenon, the social sciences addressed entrepreneurship in the context of the capitalist economy dominant in North America.

This discussion will begin with an overview of the history of the study of minorities in new business ventures, followed by a review of key terms used in the literature, and then will provide a brief discussion of the determinants/consequences model and economic and noneconomic benefits of minority participation in new ventures. The discussion will conclude with identification of new trends and potential future research directions.

There is some crossover in the use of the terms *ethnic entrepreneurship* and *minority participation in new venture creation*. While the terms have distinct meanings, this overview assumes that they are two dimensions of one domain: the participation of minority groups (established minority groups and recent immigrant groups) in the establishment of new ventures—that is, in entrepreneurial activity.

History of Research in Social Science: Sociology, Anthropology, Migration Theory

A body of literature has grown since the early 20th century around the economic behavior of ethnic groups, minorities, and immigrant communities. Most theories around the concept have taken root in the field of sociology, beginning with texts such as Max Weber's *The Protestant Ethic and the Spirit of Capitalism* (1906) and Werner Sombart's reply, *The Jews and Modern Capitalism* (1911). Models to study ethnic entrepreneurship have been adapted from other social sciences as well. For example, theories from anthropology and migration theory have been used to explain business behavior and venture creation based on ethnic categories, cultural histories, and migration experiences.

Economic theories of ethnic entrepreneurship also began to appear in the early 20th century, particularly in the United States, where the foreign-born have been overrepresented in small businesses since 1880. This literature notes that immigrants and ethnic minorities are more likely to start a new business when faced with limited opportunities in the host country. Where barriers exist to entrance in the more traditional labor force, venture creation and self-employment form a strategy for profit maximization and upward socioeconomic, often intergenerational, mobility. Nevertheless, a number of studies, theories, and critiques have been developed to explain not only differences in entrepreneurial tendencies among individuals of various ethnic groups, minorities, and immigrant communities but also disparities in the overall motivations for and performance of ethnic entrepreneurial firms.

Middleman Minorities, Enclave Economies, and Embeddedness

Within the ethnic entrepreneurship literature, key terms have emerged in the discussion on ethnic-minority involvement in new venture creation. E. Bonacich is recognized as coining the term *middleman minority*. Middleman minority entrepreneurs, sometimes described as sojourners, are recognized for their role in negotiating products between producers and consumers (such as owners and renters) and often negotiating between their ethnic community (or culture) and that of the host economy. Middleman minority entrepreneurs are thought to have few ties to the social structures of the host community and strong elements of solidarity among their coethnic members. Common examples of middleman minority entrepreneurs are Irish and Jewish immigrants who lived in New York in the 19th century. These entrepreneurs filled roles that brokered relationships, such as moneylending and trading, between their communities and the larger community.

The notion of the enclave economy is utilized to examine the development of ethnically or minority-owned enterprises within a bounded geography. Firms within this bounded geography are also unique in that their employment network is also coethnic, which can (but does not necessarily) include unpaid family labor. M. Zhou (2004), in his discussion of the ethnic entrepreneurship literature, further refined this concept of the enclave economy, attributing to it an increased level of institutional completeness. Community building and the creation of social capital are included as important characteristics. Therefore, in enclave economies, entrepreneurial activities move beyond those attributed to the middleman minority and are not just commercial. Rather, they are much more common to the variety known in the general economy, such as professional services and production. In his research, Zhou references Chinatown in New York City and Koreatown in Los Angeles as specific examples of these enclave economies; these communities certainly provide a network for commercial interaction, but they also serve to strengthen social cohesion in the communities. From outside the communities, it can often be difficult to distinguish between the social, community, and commercial dimensions of enclave economies.

Embeddedness is another important concept used widely in ethnic entrepreneurship literature. Embeddedness recognizes the institutional structures in which ethnic entrepreneurship arises. Embeddedness can refer to the structure of the host economy, including market conditions and the legal-political structures, as well as the structures of the ethnic or minority community, such as its specific location and ethnic networks. A. Martinelli (2004) goes as far as to suggest the concept of double-embeddedness to describe the context in which ethnic entrepreneurship arises. His central thesis is that there are two dimensions to the ethnic entrepreneurial context. Both the politico-institutional structure that shapes the market environment and the sociocultural background of the entrepreneur influence the entrepreneurial attitude, the resources mobilized, the opportunities and constraints for firm expansion, and other factors that can legitimize or hinder the entrepreneurial role. From this perspective, there are two drivers that influence the nature of entrepreneurial activity in minority groups. The external environment, made up of the institutions and politics that define the market, present or restrict successful entrepreneurial entrance into the market. The second driver emanates from the entrepreneur's sociocultural background, the degree to which entrepreneurial activity is embedded in the

sociocultural background. This may present itself as a predominance of entrepreneurial activity in the entrepreneur's cultural experience or as a predominance of the determinants of entrepreneurial activity (such as high risk tolerance).

Determinants/Consequences

The notion of determinants/consequences reflects a consistent tension within the literature between cultural and structural determinants of ethnic entrepreneurship. Cultural theory suggests that ethnic and immigrant groups are equipped with distinctive features such as dedication to hard work, acceptance of risk, skills attributed to human and cultural capital, a sense of community, and the strength of their national or cultural identity. An empirical study by L. Edelman and colleagues into the start-up and growth intentions of white and black entrepreneurs in America is an example of a culture-centric approach to theorization. Structural theory suggests that it is the institutional variables that allow opportunities for ethnic entrepreneurship to arise. Theories revolving around resource mobilization and management are structural in nature and remark on the availability of not only resources in the host economy—such as access to credit or legal instruments to protect and perpetuate a business—but also resources from the cultural or enclave networks of any individual. Moreover, push-pull factors of migrant entrepreneurs are structural in nature, as they remark on the conditions in the native environment that impel the decision to leave (push) and positive attributes perceived to exist in the new location (pull). Many models have been designed to conceptualize the cultural/structural dynamics that motivate or influence the ethnic entrepreneurship phenomenon, but it is very difficult for one theory or model to explain the phenomenon as a whole.

Also, tensions arise in discussions between economic and noneconomic motivations or outcomes of ethnic entrepreneurship. Whereas the literature generally recognizes that ethnic entrepreneurship is an effective option to circumvent labor market barriers in the host country and increase social and generational mobility, studies are increasingly recognizing benefits beyond economic and individual success. Alternative benefits include social status and recognition, role modeling, and a nurturing entrepreneurial spirit. An enclave economy provides a material base for the ethnic community to function effectively. One researcher who looked at Koreatown in Los Angeles used the example of ethnic Korean children and their knowledge of the networks available to reach higher academic goals, as compared to children of other ethnic or nonminority groups. This research notes that the critical institutional role an ethnic community has in the knowledge transfer process is not only firm-oriented but value-oriented as well.

Transnationalism: Networking and Resource Mobilization

Research during the 1990s and early millennium has provided insight into the effects of globalization on ethnic and minority entrepreneurship. In particular, interest in transnational networking trends has expanded from studies that previously focused on networking strategies within the enclave economy. This globalization of ethnic and minority entrepreneurship mirrors the globalization of capital and increased labor mobility. The interest in ethnic and minority entrepreneurship has moved from a focus on entrepreneurship that serves solely the local community or brokers between the local and broader communities to a focus on how immigrants use embedded social capital to create international trade activities between their home country or region of origin and their adopted country or region. Whereas historically the ethnic entrepreneur has been best positioned to broker between the local ethnic or minority community and the larger community, globalization has created the opportunity for these entrepreneurs to broker between the larger community, the local ethnic community, and the minority entrepreneur's country of origin.

D. Kariv et al. (2009) argue that one of the reasons business performance differs across ethnic entrepreneurial firms is that they engage in dissimilar types of transnational networking. M. Carney (2007) notes that ethnic entrepreneurial firms play a leading role in international trade because of their access to foreign capital and geographically dispersed networks. Zhou (2004) also observes the bicultural and often multinational ethnic networks of ethnic entrepreneurs, as well as new flows of capital and labor, and so anticipates new structures and forces emerging to determine ethnic entrepreneurship.

Research for the Future

Globalization and transnationalism have added yet another dynamic to the phenomenon of ethnic, minority, and immigrant entrepreneurship. Many consequences of ethnic entrepreneurship are noted in the literature but lack further investigation, particularly the noneconomic impact, such as the study of relationships and the development of social capital. Changes in entrepreneurial immigration patterns also provide avenues for more research. Contemporary immigration goes beyond largely conventional (at least North American) economic refugees with limited capital to a mix of immigration, including highly capitalized immigrants. The interaction of these ethnic community subsets in transnational entrepreneurial activity warrants further research.

Concepts are continually being refined and developed, and new innovative mechanisms to conceptualize ethnic entrepreneurship can be held to further scrutiny. In terms of scope, investigations into ethnic entrepreneurship continue to take place in industrialized countries, assuming only particular environments play the role of host economy. The economic behavior of minorities in emerging economies remains relatively unexplored. Ethnographic research and case studies have been for the most part the primary research methodologies utilized to investigate ethnic, minority, and immigrant entrepreneurship. However, the heterogeneity and complexity of entrepreneurial activities among these groups lead to mixed findings about outcomes. Therefore, any one investigation has limited analytical or deductive utility. Researchers have pointed out that too much attention to technical details may sometimes detract from the "big picture." Surveys have been widely used to get larger data sets. Puryear et al., for example, see ethnic entrepreneurship research as benefiting from studies that couple in-depth questions about business operations, family, and community contexts with a sample of adequate size and representativeness for rigorous and deep analysis of the minority entrepreneurial experience.

Mike Henry
Grant MacEwan University

See also African Americans and Entrepreneurship; Gender and Acquiring Resources; Gender and Industry Preferences; Gender and Performance; Hispanics and Entrepreneurship; Motivation and

Gender; Women's Entrepreneurship; Women's Entrepreneurship: Best Practices

Further Readings

Aldrich, H. and R. Waldinger. "Ethnicity and Entrepreneurship." *Annual Review of Sociology*, v.16/1 (1990).

Bonacich, E. "A Theory of Middleman Minorities." *American Sociological Review*, v.38/5 (1973).

Carney, M. "Minority Family Business in Emerging Economic Markets: Organization Forms and Competitive Advantage." *Family Business Review*, v.10/4 (2007).

Dana, L. P. "Toward a Synthesis: A Model of Immigrant and Ethnic Entrepreneurship." In *Handbook of Research on Ethnic Minority Entrepreneurship: A Co-Evolutionary View on Resource Management*, Dana Leo-Paul, ed. Cheltenham, UK: Edward Elgar Publishing, 2007.

Edelman, L., C. Brush, T. Manolova, and P. Greene. "Start-Up Motivations and Growth Intentions of Minority Nascent Entrepreneurs." *Journal of Small Business Management*, v.48/2 (2010).

Greene, P. and J. Butler. "The Minority Community as a Natural Business Incubator." *Journal of Business Research*, v.36/1 (1996).

Johnson, C. and V. Thomas. "Advancing Research on Minority Entrepreneurship." *Business Journal of Hispanic Research*, v.2/3 (2008).

Kariv, D., T. Menzies, G. Brenner, and L. Filion. "Transnational Networking and Business Performance: Ethnic Entrepreneurs in Canada." *Entrepreneurship and Regional Development*, v.21/3 (2009).

Light, I. *Ethnic Enterprise in America: Business and Welfare Among Chinese, Japanese, and Blacks.* Berkeley: University of California Press, 1972.

Light, I. and Bonacich, E. "Immigrant and Ethnic Entrepreneurs in North America." *Ethnic and Racial Studies*, v.7 (1984).

Martinelli, A. "The Context of Entrepreneurship: The Case of Ethnic Entrepreneurs." *Tocqueville Review*, v.25/2 (2004).

Mitchell, B. "Ethnic Entrepreneurship: Preliminary Findings From a South African Study." *Journal of Small Business and Entrepreneurship*, v.17/1 (2003).

Puryear, A. et al. "Sampling Minority Business Owners and Their Families: The Understudied Entrepreneurial Experience." *Journal of Small Business Management*, v.46/3 (2008).

Volery, T. "Ethnic Entrepreneurship: A Theoretical Framework." In *Handbook of Research on Ethnic Minority Entrepreneurship: A Co-Evolutionary View on Resource Management*, Dana Leo-Paul, ed. Cheltenham, UK: Edward Elgar, 2007.

Zhou, M. "Revisiting Ethnic Entrepreneurship: Convergencies, Controversies, and Conceptual Advancements." *International Migration Review*, v.38/3 (2004).

MOTIVATION AND GENDER

The word *motivation* comes from a Latin word *movere*, meaning to move. It is often associated with behaviors. Motivation involves expending effort toward a goal. Needs and other motives propel our behaviors to achieve those goals. Motives may be intrinsic (internal) or extrinsic (external). Individuals who are internally motivated are motivated by job satisfaction and pride in their work, among other factors. Those who are motivated externally are motivated by rewards such as pay, benefits, and status. Research on motivation began with needs theories. Frederick Herzberg suggests in his two-factor theory of motivation that some factors are motivators or satisfiers, and other factors are hygiene factors or dissatisfiers. Motivators include achievement, recognition, growth, responsibility, and the job itself. Hygiene factors are money, job security, policies, status, interpersonal relationships, and working conditions.

Women are often more satisfied with work, pay, and other factors than men. Women typically have lower incomes than men. Males focus more on having a career that affords them autonomy and creativity. Women may use autonomy as a way to be able to focus more on family-oriented pursuits. Women are concerned with growth, challenge, prestige, and flexibility to pursue personal goals. Women also tend to focus more on activities outside work, such as home and family, whereas men focus more outside the home. Women are concerned with social factors, self-expression, and good working conditions. Women tend to be more relationship oriented, which can motivate them to seek entrepreneurial activities. Men are more focused on starting a business to gain power or wealth. However, there is little or no difference between women and men in a variety of performance factors, such as sales and profits. Women work toward self-satisfaction and fulfillment as well. These preferences, whether shared or different, tend to motivate both men and women to become entrepreneurs.

There is some controversy over whether or not money is actually a motivator, but combined with another motivator it can increase motivation. Money seems to be attractive to people because it is a symbol of power, but it is most often considered motivating when the benefits of money outweigh other negative consequences. In order to motivate people through money to work harder, then, the entrepreneur should establish an incentive plan (something extrinsic) for employees to increase their earnings. Employees with an incentive plan have increased motivation and work toward that plan's goal. Job enrichment can also serve as an important motivator. Job enrichment involves adding responsibility, challenging tasks, autonomy, and decision-making authority, as well as a variety of different tasks.

Theorists have provided ideas on motivation and expectations in relation to new venture creation. Men tend to focus their businesses on wealth creation, whereas women seem to care less about making money when starting businesses; they are focused on achievement and fulfillment. Women also have a tendency to micromanage their new business ventures instead of delegating work.

Expectancy theory states that motivation equals expectancy times instrumentality times valence. Expectancy means that one expects one's effort to lead to performance. Instrumentality means that one expects performance to lead to a reward. Valence means the reward is something one will value. If one has high expectancies that one can accomplish a task, then one will have high self-efficacy (self-confidence) and will be more motivated. For example, people start businesses because they expect to achieve their goals. People who believe they have the necessary skills are motivated to be entrepreneurs. As a result of socialization, women often do not have the necessary skills or do not expect to be successful in new ventures, so they do not become entrepreneurs. They may have a lack of business background or education. Male entrepreneurs tend to have more confidence in their abilities because of their socialization to the business environment.

Abraham Maslow developed a hierarchy of needs that identified people's motivations; in hierarchical order, these are physiological, security, social, self-esteem, and self-actualization needs. People are motivated first by the need for food, clothing, or shelter (that is, their physiological needs must be met), then by the need for security, and so on. In general, based on Maslow's hierarchy, we can say that once their basic needs are met, people have three important needs: for security, social outlets, and personal growth.

Motivation is also discussed in terms of the push-pull theory. Things that "push" us to do something could be factors such as economic necessity, whereas "pull" factors include autonomy, achievement, and satisfaction. All these factors can motivate individuals to become entrepreneurs. Both men and women entrepreneurs tend to be pulled toward entrepreneurship through its promise of autonomy, achievement, and satisfaction or pushed toward entrepreneurship as a result of job loss or a need for alternative or additional employment and income.

D. C. McClelland suggested that people have three needs: achievement, power, and affiliation. The characteristics of male and female entrepreneurs are similar, and both men and women have similar risk-taking propensities, but women may tend to be more cautious in their entrepreneurial ventures. Female entrepreneurs often have the following characteristics: They are firstborns, are middle class, have a college education, have supportive spouses, have children, and have a business in a traditionally female-dominated industry.

Both men and women have a "need to achieve" (drive) and are motivated by job satisfaction, economic incentives (money), and independence. For example, money has been found to motivate both women and men to become entrepreneurs, especially where job loss or lack of jobs is concerned. For women, however, this motivator may result more from economic necessity than from a desire for wealth. Men, in contrast, are more likely to become entrepreneurs in order to be their own boss. Men are focused on wealth creation or advancement, whereas women are less motivated by these rewards. Many women become entrepreneurs in order to achieve a work-family balance, flexible schedules, personal challenge, job satisfaction, security, and also to circumvent careers in organizations where there is no possibility of breaking the "glass ceiling." They might start businesses as a way of transitioning to another career or to reenter the workforce after bearing or raising children.

The desire for independence can also motivate people to become entrepreneurs or to work at home, particularly if they can achieve the same or more pay. For women, this motivation is often tied, again, to work-family balance and the flexibility that affords them schedules that allow them to focus on many different personal as well as professional obligations and goals.

In reviewing the motivating factors and intentions of women, several other factors emerge from the literature that involve the venture's size and industry sectors, as well as women's goals, risks, and reasons for starting a business. Women tend to keep their businesses at a manageable size and typically are not focused on expansion or growth. They therefore tend to have smaller ventures. The size of their business is often related to their lifestyles and comfort levels. Family orientation may lead women to earn less in the businesses they start. Again, however, money is often not their primary motivator. They like the flexibility and freedom of entrepreneurship. Neither women nor men, it turns out, are concerned with employment growth.

While both women and men face similar barriers to venture start-ups, the differences between their entrepreneurship may also depend on the industrial sectors they choose to go into. Women are more driven toward service sectors, whereas men are more motivated toward manufacturing sectors. For women, personal goals are their dominant motivators instead of business goals. Women tend to be more cautious but crave the flexibility of owning their own business. Men have more confidence and are willing to take more risks. Several reasons women are motivated to start their own businesses are: necessity, opportunity, partnerships with others, interest, and passion. Women tend to start twice as many businesses as men. Often the tendency to start a business has to do with dissatisfaction with their current employers as well as the already mentioned motivation to attend to family needs.

Women tend to be more motivated by relationships and focus on relationship-promoting behaviors. These behaviors are desirable for all business owners. Many people are attracted to entrepreneurial ventures because of the personal gratification they may enjoy not only from profits but also from opportunities for challenge, advancement, and job satisfaction. With their orientation toward people and relationships, many women find that they can succeed and excel in the areas of entrepreneurship that concern leadership and management of people,

such as motivating employees to put effort into their jobs or successfully linking performance to pay.

Finally, both men and women may have a passion for entrepreneurship. Passion is often not discussed in the entrepreneurship literature as a motivating factor. The intentions of both men and women will guide goal setting, communication, and commitment. The factors can influence the decision to become an entrepreneur and to stick with this decision. Women who have a relatively high locus of control (LOC) are more likely to enjoin this passion and become entrepreneurs. People with high LOC are more likely than those with low LOC to believe that their skills and actions allow them to control or shape the events that happen in their lives. Hence, high-LOC women feel as though they will be able to manage whatever happens to them, so they are willing to take the risk of doing something new or using their skills in new ways, including starting a new venture. Such women are high in self-efficacy (self-confidence) and tend to take on risk and set goals that can lead to successful ventures.

Katherine Hyatt
Reinhardt University

See also Commitment and Persistence; Gender and Acquiring Resources; Gender and Industry Preferences; Gender and Performance; Goal Setting; Home-Based Businesses; Intentions; Locus of Control; Microfinance; Minorities in New Business Ventures; Women's Entrepreneurship; Women's Entrepreneurship: Best Practices; Work-Life Balance

Further Readings

DeMartino, Richard and Robert Barbato. "Differences Between Women and Men MBA Entrepreneurs: Exploring Family Flexibility and Wealth Creation as Career Motivators." *Journal of Business Venturing*, v.18 (2003).

Fischer, E. M., A. R. Reuber, and L. S. Dyke. "A Theoretical Overview and Extension of Research on Sex, Gender, and Entrepreneurship." *Journal of Business Venturing*, v.8/2 (1993).

Hisrich, R. D. and C. Brush. "The Woman Entrepreneur: Management Skills and Business Problems." *Journal of Small Business Management*, v.22/1 (1984).

Kirkwood, Jodyanne. *One Size Doesn't Fit All: Gender Differences in Motivations for Becoming an Entrepreneur*. Dunedin, New Zealand: University of Otago, 2004.

Ljunggren, E. and L. Kolvereid. "New Business Formation: Does Gender Make a Difference?" *Women in Management Review*, v.11/4 (1996).

McClelland, D. C. *The Achieving Society*. Princeton, NJ: Van Nostrand, 1961.

Shabbir, A. and S. di Gregorio. "An Examination of the Relationship Between Women's Personal Goals and Structural Factors Influencing Their Decisions to Start a Business: The Case in Pakistan." *Journal of Business Venturing*, v.11/6 (1996).

Still, Leonie V. and Wendy Timms. "Women's Business: The Flexible Alternative Workstyle for Women." *Women in Management Review*, v.15/5–6 (2000).

NEGOTIATING STRATEGIES

A critical precursor to new venture growth is the attainment of initial legitimacy, which is a social judgment of acceptance and appropriateness. Thus, before new ventures are able to gather the tangible resources necessary to survive and grow, such ventures must receive initial legitimacy from resource providers. However, a new venture cannot take legitimacy; rather, stakeholders must grant it to the venture. Hence, new ventures face a conundrum: The founder needs to persuade key stakeholders to grant the new venture legitimacy, yet the new venture does not possess many attributes of a legitimate firm. Entrepreneur negotiation strategy is a tool that will enhance new firms' chances to be granted legitimacy.

Negotiation and the Legitimacy Threshold

The pre-legitimacy juncture in a new venture's existence is possibly best captured by the idea of a legitimacy threshold. The notion of a legitimacy threshold holds that there exists a point in the early stage of most new ventures where the firm compiles some base level of legitimacy that enables it to survive and possibly grow. Thus, pre-legitimate ventures can be clearly contrasted with legitimate ventures, in that pre-legitimate firms are just getting off the ground, are financed entirely by seed money, have few substantial customers, and possess highly untenable resources. Alternatively, legitimate ventures have been granted at least a base level of legitimacy by key stakeholder groups such as customers or financiers. Such initial legitimacy will both signal to other stakeholders that the venture is legitimate and allow the firm to acquire the resources it needs to survive and grow.

Interestingly, the granting of legitimacy can be viewed as a function of the relative power of the two parties. Definitions abound, but power is often operationalized as an ability to get another individual to do what one wants him or her to do. In general, founders operating pre-legitimate firms are likely to have much less power than stakeholders. However, such founders can use proper negotiation strategies to leverage the power they do possess intelligently and thus increase their firms' chances of being granted legitimacy.

Power and Negotiation

The power-dependence model provides a solid framework by which to link power and negotiation strategy. The model theorizes that power in negotiations is a function of alternatives and commitment. As a result, the more alternatives that a negotiator has available, the more power she has. Commitment, on the other hand, is related to power in a different way. The greater is one negotiator's commitment to bargaining outcomes or issues, the more power the other party has. Therefore, an individual's power during negotiations is dependent on both the number of alternatives that the individual has and the degree of commitment that the individual is giving the negotiation. Thus, the founder can work to

A founder of a new venture needs to use negotiation strategy to convince stakeholders to grant the new venture legitimacy, yet the new venture does not possess many of the attributes defining a legitimate firm. (Photos.com)

(1) increase the number and/or quality of her own alternatives, (2) decrease the number and/or quality of the stakeholder's alternatives, (3) decrease her valuation of the stakeholder's commitment to bargaining outcomes, and (4) increase the stakeholder's valuation of the entrepreneur's commitment to bargaining outcomes.

Increasing the Number and/or Quality of the Entrepreneur's Alternatives. Negotiators will become more effective by increasing the number of alternatives available to the party that the negotiator is representing. The concept is straightforward: if the stakeholder is aware that the founder has other alternatives, legitimacy is more likely to be granted. To best leverage this strategy, founders should prepare extensively before negotiation sessions. Both the development of additional alternatives as well as researching the other party's alternatives will take extensive preparation. Founders also need to ensure that alternatives are valid and realistic options. Alternatives will generate power during negotiations only if they are indeed viable. Finally, since alternatives are not always

apparent to stakeholders, founders must signal to stakeholders the availability of such options.

Decreasing the Number and/or Quality of the Stakeholder's Alternatives. Once negotiations have begun, negotiators can consider attempting to influence the other party's perception of the viability and/or quality of the other party's alternatives. However, given the rather weak power of founders operating prelegitimate firms, this type of method is dangerous and is something that should probably not be tried.

Decreasing the Founder's Valuation of the Stakeholder's Commitment. A very effective way to decrease one's valuation of the stakeholder's commitment to bargaining outcomes is to develop other options. Thus, to decrease her commitment to the stakeholder's contribution, a founder should develop viable additional alternatives and signal those alternatives to potential stakeholders during negotiation.

Increasing the Stakeholder's Valuation of the Founder's Commitment. One way the founder can increase the stakeholder's valuation of the founder's commitment to bargaining outcomes is through demonstrating how the founder can create value for the stakeholder. The obvious way to create value for the stakeholder is for the founder to control a valuable outcome or resource that no one else controls. If a founder does indeed possess unique resources, the stakeholder will lack options, which should escalate the stakeholder's commitment to the bargaining process, increasing the chances that the stakeholder will grant legitimacy.

Summary and Critical Actions

In summary, during interactions with potential stakeholders, founders should attempt to increase the perceived value of their venture's offerings to stakeholders as well as continuously work to develop viable alternatives and signal such alternatives to stakeholders. To effectively leverage such strategies, founders will likely want to imitate certain aspects of legitimate firms as well as utilize interpersonal abilities and social networks. Given that firms perceived as legitimate tend to have more power in negotiations, founders operating pre-legitimate ventures will want to imitate certain attributes of legitimate firms by appearing professional, designing effective communication materials, and securing suitable office space. Additionally, socially proficient founders with many network contacts will have an easier time both developing and signaling their suitable alternatives to stakeholders, which will in turn enhance their firms' chances to be granted legitimacy.

Matthew W. Rutherford
Virginia Commonwealth University
Neil Tocher
Idaho State University
Kenneth Anderson
Gonzaga University
Paul Buller
Gonzaga University

See also Agility and Rapid Response; Barter; Championing New Ventures; Communication Styles; Competitive Intelligence; Contracts and Trust; Leadership; Licensing; Networks; Psychological Views; Risk Management; Sales; Selling Products and Services; Venture Valuation

Further Readings

Aldrich, H. E. and C. M. Fiol. "Fools Rush In? The Institutional Context of Industry Creation." *Academy of Management Review*, v.18/4 (1994).

Aldrich, H. E. and M. A. Martinez. "Many Are Called, but Few Are Chosen: An Evolutionary Perspective for the Study of Entrepreneurship." *Entrepreneurship Theory and Practice*, v.25/4 (2001).

Bacharach, S. and E. J. Lawler. "Power and Tactics in Bargaining." *Industrial and Labor Relations Review*, v.34/2 (1981).

Baron, R. A. and G. D. Markman. "Beyond Social Capital: The Role of Entrepreneur's Social Competence in Their Financial Success." *Journal of Business Venturing*, v.18/1 (2003).

Delmar, F. and S. Shane. "Legitimating First: Organizing Activities and the Survival of New Ventures." *Journal of Business Venturing*, v.19/3 (2004).

Kim, P. H. and A. R. Fragale. "Choosing the Path to Bargaining Power: An Empirical Comparison of BATNAS and Contributions in Negotiation." *Journal of Applied Psychology*, v.90/2 (2005).

Rutherford, M. W. and P. F. Buller. "Searching for the Legitimacy Threshold." *Journal of Management Inquiry*, v.16/1 (2007).

Tornikoski, E. T. and S. L. Newbert. "Exploring the Determinants of Organizational Emergence: A Legitimacy Perspective." *Journal of Business Venturing*, v.22/2 (2007).

Zimmerman, M. A. and G. J. Zeitz. "Beyond Survival: Achieving New Venture Growth by Building Legitimacy." *Academy of Management Review*, v.27/3 (2002).

NETWORK TIES

Entrepreneurs' network ties are thought to provide numerous benefits. The purpose of this contribution is to describe some of the main network-tie characteristics frequently examined within the entrepreneurship literature. To set the stage for a review of network-tie characteristics, a few definitions are needed. First, a network is defined as a set of actors (such as individuals) that are connected by a set of ties (relationships between the individuals). The actors within networks have been discussed at many levels of analysis, including individuals, teams, organizations, groups of organizations, and so forth. The term *network ties* is used to describe the connection, or relationship, between actors in a network. Characteristics of network ties have been characterized primarily through their relative structure, the nature of the connections, and the content ties provide.

The majority of studies examining network ties within the entrepreneurship literature have attempted to understand the structural nature and value of different network configurations relative to entrepreneurial outcomes. Specifically, structural characteristics of networks that have been extensively investigated include the size of the network and the strength of network ties. Overall findings suggest that the larger the size of the network, up to a point, the more information and positive benefits the entrepreneur will gain. In a study focused on identifying opportunities, Robert Singh and colleagues found a positive relationship between network size and the number of opportunities developed. Supporting this view, Sea Jin Chang found that the size of a start-up's network was positively related to the start-up's performance. In the context of this study, performance was measured as the venture's time to initial public offering (IPO). More recent work examining network size has sought to integrate other concepts related to size in the hope of providing finer-grained explanations for the influence of size on outcomes. Diane Sullivan and Matthew Marvel found that entrepreneurs who have a greater number of network ties are better positioned to create more jobs. Specifically, their research suggests that entrepreneurs who seek to grow their venture in the number of employees should increase their network ties, particularly in their early stages of venture development.

Beyond network size, entrepreneurship scholars have been very interested in studying the strength of network ties in terms of weak and strong ties. Weak tie relationships like work associates or acquaintances are characterized by infrequent interactions, a short duration of relationship, and a lack of socioemotional closeness. Weak ties are from diverse backgrounds and areas of expertise, and are those who possess different friends relative to the focal actor. On the other hand, people such as family members and friends are considered strong network-tie partners. Strong ties are characterized by frequent interactions, long duration of relationships, and close socioemotional bonds. Strong ties also possess trust and will share information in depth. Scholars have regularly investigated the relative impact of strong versus weak ties on the attainment of entrepreneurial outcomes. Weak ties have been associated with the frequency with which entrepreneurs develop opportunities. The reasoning behind this finding is consistent with Mark Granovetter's strength of weak ties argument, whereby weak ties are associated with the acquisition of novel information that can lead to the identification of opportunities. Scholars generally agree that both strong and weak ties are important, but for different purposes during venture development. For example, entrepreneurs may utilize strong ties to obtain crucial resources and weak ties for achieving legitimacy and discovering opportunities. Although the empirical findings on the strength of ties have been somewhat mixed, it is generally accepted that weak ties facilitate the attainment of informational resources and are helpful in highly dynamic industries and for identifying opportunities. Furthermore, strong ties are seen as useful in stable environments and when firms are concerned with exploitation activities and gaining access to certain, often more sensitive, resources.

Although a newer area of interest within the entrepreneurship literature, recent research has focused on the *content* flowing across network ties. Initially, researchers were interested in the idea

that important resources such as information, technologies, and emotional support are individually transferred across network partners. Several studies focused on identifying which types of content (information, technologies, and support) were the most advantageous and what structural properties of networks could help transfer these types of resources by individual network partners. More recent approaches to investigating content have looked at the overall composition of the resources present within the network, where resources can be tangible (such as financial capital) or intangible (such as information). The term *diversity* is often used to describe this property of networks. Others have used the term *compositional quality* to describe the extent to which network ties can provide the resources needed by the entrepreneur. Still others have used terms such as *relational mix* to describe the mix of resources available in networks. For example, Stephen Borgatti, Candace Jones, and Martin Everett developed the concept of compositional quality. They define the compositional quality of an entrepreneur's network in terms of the number of partners that have high amounts of the required characteristics, or resources (expertise, power, and so forth). That is, the more comprehensive the set of resources provided by a single or a limited number of resource providers, the higher the compositional quality of that network. They relate high levels of compositional quality to positive entrepreneurial outcomes such as an entrepreneur's social capital.

Researchers have increasingly examined entrepreneurship and network ties. The brief review above, while by no means comprehensive, highlights some of the main network-tie characteristics examined within the entrepreneurship literature. Given the inherent need for entrepreneurs to interact with others during new venture creation and development processes, it is of little doubt that this research area will remain an important research topic in the future.

Diane McMeekin Sullivan
University of Dayton

See also Managing Human and Social Capital; Networks

Further Readings

Borgatti, S. P., C. Jones, and M. C. Everett. "Network Measures of Social Capital." *Connections*, v.21 (1998).

Chang, S. J. "Venture Capital Financing, Strategic Alliances, and the Initial Public Offering of Internet Startups." *Journal of Business Venturing*, v.19/5 (2004).

Granovetter, M. "The Strength of Weak Ties." *American Journal of Sociology*, v.78/6 (1973).

Singh, R. P., G. E. Hills, R. C. Hybels, and G. T. Lumpkin. "Opportunity Recognition Through Social Networks of Entrepreneurs." *Frontiers of Entrepreneurship Research*. Wellesley, MA: Babson College, 1999.

Sullivan, D. M. and M. Marvel. "How Entrepreneurs' Knowledge and Network Ties Relate to the Number of Employees in New SMEs." *Journal of Small Business Management*, v.49/2 (2011).

NETWORKS

Entrepreneurs are intimately tied, through their social relationships, to a broader network of actors. Such actors include, among others, customers, suppliers, and competitors and often extend across industries and even cultural, political, and geographic boundaries. Entrepreneurial networks provide multiple benefits for the founding and growth of the new venture: They facilitate the search for opportunities, provide access to vital resources, and help gain credibility and legitimacy.

Research into entrepreneurial networks emerged in the mid-1980s within the field of entrepreneurship. Scholars began to recognize the embeddedness of the entrepreneurial process and that entrepreneurs are not isolated. Since then, entrepreneurial network research has looked at the impact of the network on the new venture performance and has examined which types of tie (connection) matter when. Other views on networks are found in social network research and the business network approach. Social network research investigates the impact of the network on the social group or organization, and the business network approach examines the interactions that create dyadic relationships (connections between two actors) within the broader network.

Networks comprise a set of actors (individuals or organizations) connected by a set of ties. Mark Granovetter defined the strength of ties as the intensity and diversity of relationships. Strong ties bind similar people in longer-term and intense relationships. Additionally, strong ties facilitate the transfer of fine-grained information and tacit knowledge, the development of trust, and joint problem solving.

Weak ties, in contrast, provide access to new business contacts and novel industry information through a diverse set of people with whom one has some business connection and infrequent or irregular contact. Brian Uzzi brought forward the idea that the ideal entrepreneurial network includes a particular mix of such strong and weak ties. Moreover, the entrepreneur aligns the mix of strong and weak ties to the changing needs of the venture over time.

Finding the right mix of weak and strong ties is very much at the heart of the debate about network benefits. Generally, weak ties support the search for new opportunities of the new venture, strong ties are useful for the acquisition of resources, and a mix of weak and strong ties promotes legitimacy for the new firm.

Especially for the analysis of the impact of entrepreneurial networks on new ventures, it is important to take into consideration the initial founding conditions of the firm. The initial founding conditions relate, on one hand, to whether the new venture holds the position of an insider or an outsider in its particular industry and, on the other hand, to whether the new venture pursues an incremental innovation (the exploitation of an existing product) or a radical innovation (the exploration of a new product idea). Research has found that insiders rely principally on their strong ties to gain access to new opportunities and resources and for legitimacy, whereas outsiders rely on their weak ties to search for information that provides them access to the inner circles of their particular industry. In regard to radical innovations, they often require new combinations of diverse knowledge. Weak ties, therefore, allow the entrepreneur to search for information among a diverse network of rather loose connections. Incremental innovations, however, are pursued using strong ties.

There is much debate in the literature about whether networks increase over time in density, complexity, and interdependency among actors or if networks shift from an initial cohesive network to one that is sparse or loosely integrated. In an effort to reconcile these conflicting findings, Tom Elfring and Willem Hulsink suggested three distinct patterns of network development of new ventures, taking into consideration their initial founding conditions and the three post-founding entrepreneurial processes (opportunity seeking, acquisition of resources, and legitimacy seeking). *Network evolution* is characterized by insiders pursuing incremental innovation. Their focus is on acquiring resources in the emergence phase and the search for new, additional opportunities during early growth. Hence, they initially rely on their strong ties and grow by adding weak ties. *Network renewal* describes insiders that pursue radical innovations. Those firms rely on both weak and strong ties. Weak ties are needed to search for new information regarding the development of their innovation. Strong ties, in contrast, provide the needed legitimacy that ventures pursuing radical innovations often lack. Strong relationships to well-known players in the particular industry are able to provide the needed credibility. Furthermore, strong ties are able to connect to additional weak ties for the search of new information. *Network revolution* is characterized by outsiders pursuing radical innovations. These ventures rely initially, during the emergence phase, on a large number of weak ties in their search for information on business opportunities and ties that lead them to the inner circle of their industry.

Networks may also have a negative effect on the new venture. A large number of weak ties, for instance, may cause a network overload. Strong ties, in contrast, may lead to overembeddedness within the network and contribute to the new venture becoming blind to new developments and exposed to the risk of being locked in with its close ties. In such cases, a dropping of ties or tie dissolution may provide a solution.

Sascha Fuerst
Universidad EAFIT

See also Partnerships; Social Networks

Further Readings

Clegg, Stewart, Karen Wang, and Mike Berrell. *Business Networks and Strategic Alliances in China.* Northampton, MA: Edward Elgar, 2007.

Elfring, Tom and Willem Hulsink. "Networks in Entrepreneurship." *ERIM Report Series Reference No. ERS-2001-28-STR* (May 2001).

Granovetter, M. "The Strength of Weak Ties." *American Journal of Sociology*, v.78/6 (1973).

Hoang, Ha and Bostjan Antoncic. "Network-Based Research in Entrepreneurship: A Critical Review." *Journal of Business Venturing*, v.18/2 (2003).

Slotte-Kock, Susanna and Nicole Coviello. "Entrepreneurship Research on Network Processes:

A Review and Ways Forward." *Entrepreneurship Theory and Practice*, v.34/1 (2010).

Todeva, Emanuela. *Business Networks.* Hoboken, NJ: Taylor & Francis, 2006.

Vervest, Peter, Diederik Fillem van Liere, and Li Zheng. *The Network Experience: New Value From Smart Business Networks.* Berlin: Springer, 2009.

NEW PRODUCT DEVELOPMENT

Improving and updating product lines is crucial for the success for any organization, and the failure of an organization to change could result in a decline in sales with competitors racing ahead. The process of new product development (NPD) therefore becomes crucial within an organization. Indeed, products go through the stages of a life cycle, which mean that eventually they will have to be replaced.

According to marketing guru Philip Kotler, there are eight stages of new product development: first, idea generation; second, idea screening; third, concept development and testing; fourth, marketing strategy and development; fifth, business analysis; sixth, product development; seventh, test-marketing; and finally, commercialization.

In the first stage, organizations obtain their ideas for new products from within the company: employees, competitors, customers, distributors, and suppliers. This first step of new product development requires gathering ideas to be evaluated as potential product options. For many companies, idea generation is an ongoing process with contributions from inside and outside the organization. Many market research techniques are used to encourage ideas, including running focus groups with consumers, channel members, and the company's sales force; encouraging customer comments and suggestions via toll-free telephone numbers and Website forms; and gaining insight into competitive product developments through secondary data sources.

The second stage involves selecting ideas that are feasible. In this step, the ideas generated are evaluated by company personnel to detach the most attractive options. Depending on the number of ideas, screening may be done in rounds, with the first round involving company executives judging the feasibility of ideas, while successive rounds may utilize more advanced research techniques.

In the third stage, the organization may find a feasible idea; however, the idea needs to be proposed to the target audience. In this step, and with a few ideas in hand, the marketer now attempts to obtain initial feedback from customers, distributors, and its own employees. Generally, during focus groups with customers the marketer seeks information that may address potential customers' like and dislike of the concept; level of interest in purchasing the product; frequency of purchase, used to help forecast demand; and price points, to determine how much customers are willing to spend to acquire the product.

In the fourth stage, a proposed marketing strategy will clarify the marketing mix for the product, including the segmentation, targeting and positioning strategy, and expected sales and profits. By this stage, the marketer has reduced a potentially large number of ideas down to one or two options. The key objective at this stage is to obtain useful forecasts of market size: overall demand, operational costs (production costs), and financial projections (sales and profits).

In the fifth stage, by which the company has a feasible idea and the marketing strategy also seems feasible, the long-run financial feasibility of the product is examined. This business analysis stage looks into the cash flow the product could generate, the product's cost, the market share the product may achieve, and the product's expected life. In this stage, ideas passing through business analysis are given serious consideration for development. Companies direct their research and development teams to construct an initial design or prototype of the idea. Marketers also begin to construct a marketing plan for the product. Once the prototype is ready, the marketer seeks customer input.

In the sixth stage, a prototype is finally produced. The prototype will run through all tests and be presented to the target audience for improvement. In this stage, products are ready to be tested as real products. In some cases, the marketer accepts what was learned from concept testing and skips over market testing to launch the idea as a fully marketed product.

The seventh stage is test-marketing, which means testing the product within a specific area. In this stage, if market testing displays promising results, the product is ready to be introduced to a wider market.

In the eighth stage, if the test-marketing has been successful, the product will be launched nationwide. However, there are certain factors that need to be taken into consideration before a product is launched nationally, such as timing, how the product will be launched, and where the product will be launched.

Marketing strategies developed for initial product introduction almost certainly need to be revised as the product settles into the market. Whereas commercialization may be the last step in the new product development process, it is just the beginning of managing the product. Adjusting the product's marketing strategy is required for many reasons, including changing customer tastes, domestic and foreign competitors, economic conditions, and technological advances.

Today's successful firms learn and relearn how to deal with the dynamics of consumers, competitors, and technologies, all of which require companies to review and reconstitute the products and services they offer to the market. This, in turn, requires the development of new products and services to replace current ones, a notion inherent in the discussion of Theodore Levitt's 2008 book titled *Marketing Myopia*.

Djamel Eddine Laouisset
Alhosn University, Abu Dhabi

See also Innovation Management; Innovation Management: Corporate; Patent Protection; Positioning a New Product or Service; Research and Development

Further Readings

Bernstein, Jerry and David Macias. *Engineering New Product Success: The New Product Pricing Process at Emerson Electric*. New York: Elsevier, 2001.
Gruenwald, George. *New Product Development: Responding to Market Demand*. Lincolnwood, IL: NTC Business Books, 1992.
Husig, S. and S. Kohn. "Factors Influencing the Front End of the Innovation Process: A Comprehensive Review of Selected Empirical NPD and Explorative FFE Studies." International Product Development Management Conference, Brussels, Belgium, June 2003.
Kim, J. and D. Wilemon. "Sources and Assessment of Complexity in NPD Projects." *R&D Management*, v.33/1 (2002).

Koen, F. et al. "Providing Clarity and a Common Language to the 'Fuzzy Front End.'" *Research Technology Management*, v.44/2 (2001).

Levitt, Theodore. *Marketing Myopia*. Boston: Harvard Business Press, 2008.

Smith, Preston G. and Donald G. Reinertsen. *Developing Products in Half the Time*. New York: John Wiley and Sons, 1998.

Ullman, David G. *The Mechanical Design Process*. New York: McGraw-Hill, 2009.

Ulrich, Karl T. and Steven Eppinger. *Product Design and Development*, 3rd ed. New York: McGraw-Hill, 2004.

OBSTACLE IDENTIFICATION

Anticipating obstacles in new venture management is the act of recognizing potential obstacles to the creation and growth of a new venture prior to the obstacles having a negative effect on the organization. Whereas anticipating obstacles requires an understanding of possible future events, it also makes possible preemptive decisions and actions that may mitigate the negative affect of obstacles. If anticipation is timely and the decisions made and the actions taken are sound, then the management of the new venture may be able to avoid or overcome the obstacles altogether. In contrast, identifying obstacles once they are encountered requires an accurate analysis of the current situation and calls for understanding the obstacles and responding to them quickly and effectively. The discussion that follows provides a framework for identifying which obstacles to be concerned with, and when, in terms of a new venture's life cycle, the entrepreneur or manager should anticipate that they will arise.

Although anticipation and avoidance (being proactive) are preferable to identification and reaction (being reactive), it is unlikely that all entrepreneurs and entrepreneurial teams will be able to anticipate every obstacle that confronts them, nor should they expect to. Nonetheless, it is important that they acknowledge and recognize the obstacles that they may encounter and be prepared to take the appropriate corrective action. It is interesting to note here that, although obstacles are generally considered to be negative things to be avoided, in part it is the existence of obstacles and the challenges they present that provide the opportunity for profitability to those new ventures that can avoid or overcome them more effectively than their competition.

To anticipate obstacles that the management teams of new ventures may encounter, it is important to understand the wide array of obstacles that exist. To do this, it is useful to view them in terms of the domains in which they exist and when, during the new venture's life cycle, they may arise. The table shows that obstacles can exist within four domains: within the individual entrepreneur, within the entrepreneurial team/organization, within the market (consisting of the interface between the product/service and the customer), and within the industry in which the new venture operates. Using this framework, we can differentiate among the different types of obstacles and better anticipate which ones the management team will encounter during the various stages of a new venture's life-cycle.

The following description of obstacles will start with the entrepreneur and progress through each of the domains of interest during the creation/start-up phase of the life cycle. This process will be repeated for each of the later stages of the life cycle. This approach is taken because successful new venture management requires the organization's leaders to look across and integrate their understanding of the various important domains at any one point in time.

Start-Up/Creation Phase

The first obstacle the entrepreneur faces is himself or herself in terms of limitations associated with

Obstacles to New Ventures by Domain and Life-Cycle Stage

Domain	Stage of the New Venture's Life Cycle			
	Start-Up (Creation)	Growth	Maturity	Decline
Industry	• Barriers to entry	• Barriers to entry • Mobility barriers	• Competitive positioning • Sustaining competitive advantage	• Declining industry attractiveness • Diversification issues
Market	• Meeting a need • Creating value	• Market share growth • Maintaining quality	• Continued innovation • Refining service	• Product, technology spin-offs
Entrepreneurial team/organization	• Recruitment/ selection • Value-chain connections	• Systems development • Profit and cash flow	• Alignment of individual and organizational goals	• Leadership succession
Individual owner or entrepreneur	• Knowledge, time, energy, finances	• Delegation • Sharing control	• Need strategic abilities • Loss of entrepreneurial spirit	• Exit strategy

knowledge, skills, abilities, and other characteristics (KSAOs), such as risk tolerance, available time, personal energy and motivation, self-efficacy, self-confidence, personal finances, and professional and social support networks. Performing a self-assessment that identifies strengths and weaknesses among these dimensions may help the entrepreneur to anticipate self-development needs as well as the scope of recruitment needs in building an effective entrepreneurial team.

Assuming that the entrepreneur has an objective of creating a new venture with growth potential, he or she will be faced with the challenge of recruiting and selecting an entrepreneurial team whose members possess complementary and perhaps compensatory KSAOs that help to create the foundation of resources and capabilities available to the organization. One critical aspect of these resources associated with the entrepreneurial team involves the collective profile of their value-chain connections. In other words, who does the leadership team know and how strong are their relationships with the external network of individuals that occupy important positions along the value chain? How many of these relationships are there, and what is the quality of the relationships between entrepreneurial team members and potential suppliers, buyers, and strategic alliance partners?

As the entrepreneur and his or her team look toward the market, the primary obstacle is to identify a need (some refer to this as identifying "the pain") that is unmet, a target market that is unserved or underserved, and to discover a way to meet the need (mitigate or cure the pain) by creating value for the target market. The process of opportunity recognition often involves creativity, yet if the insight generated by the creative process is not adequately anchored in the reality of the market, it will be difficult to create value. Obstacles to creating value may arise if the entrepreneurial team does not adequately understand the customer, does not comprehend the competition and its product and/or service offerings, or is unable to differentiate its product or service in the minds of the individuals comprising the target market.

Barriers to entry into the competitive space of an industry increase the cost of entering that industry. Specific obstacles here may include cost disadvantages because of a lack of economies of scale relative to the competition, a lack of economies associated with not having had the opportunity to benefit from learning-curve effects, or having to overcome the brand recognition that established competitors may possess, among many others.

Growth Phase

One obstacle or challenge that exists across all businesses during the growth phase is the challenge of determining the optimal growth rate. There is a well-established literature associated with the difficulties encountered when an organization grows too fast, at a rate that outpaces its financial or managerial resources. However, the objective of many entrepreneurs is to expand their operations at a rapid pace, particularly when the scalability, the potential market size, has been identified as expansive. With a large potential market identified, the notion that "we better get there before the competition does" can enter the new venture leadership team's decision-making processes.

As the new venture grows, it becomes physically and cognitively impossible for the individual owner or entrepreneur to make all the decisions and to be involved in all the processes of the now larger organization. Managerial hubris, the notion that the entrepreneur believes that he or she can make better decisions than everybody else in the organization (after all, he or she created the organization), is one contributor to the resistance to delegation and to sharing control. Taking a long time to delegate or share control can slow down the development of a larger and more capable management team as well as slow down the process of buy-in and commitment to the future of the organization.

A growing organization transitions from a sole proprietorship or partnership, in which coordination of organizational tasks is accomplished via direct supervision and face-to-face communication, to an organization requiring more complex coordinating mechanisms that often require the development of detailed organizational policies and procedures. Creating an effective and efficient bureaucracy with systems for communication, information management, customer relationship management, operations scheduling, value-chain integration, financial controls, and human resource and performance management can be an obstacle to entrepreneurs who like "the way we do things around here" and can require the allocation of additional resources that may be scarce during the growth phase, as investment in creating and meeting customer demand is frequently the primary focus.

Although there exists continuous pressure for profit and cash flow, between the two, cash flow is the primary concern in the growth phase. Inadequate cash flow is the ultimate obstacle not just to growth but to the organization's survival. It is useful to think of inadequate cash flow as a critical disease that requires immediate attention, whereas below-normal or lack of profit is more of a chronic disease that can be addressed or cured over time. Many firms fail in their early start-up and growth phases from lack of adequate cash flow. By anticipating that cash flow is the critical concern in the early stages, the entrepreneur and his or her team can manage the organization's growth so that its costs and expenses do not rapidly outpace the organization's ability to generate revenue and establish sufficient lines of credit.

Market share growth is a measure of how well the new venture is performing relative to its competition. Increased production or service provision is required to realize growth in market share attributable to the rising popularity of product or service offerings. Although leadership of the new venture should welcome market share growth, for it indicates that customers are perceiving the product or service as valuable, leadership must also be cognizant of the potential obstacles in meeting a rapidly growing demand. The capacity of the physical plant and limitations of the human, technological, or financial resources of the organization can serve as constraints to expansion. It is important to anticipate production and service provision levels by paying attention to sales trends. If the selling process specific to the new venture involves relationship building and an extended time line of activities (a pipeline), then the sales pipeline should be analyzed to allow for more accurate anticipation of when the sales will be made and at what volume level they are they likely to occur.

Rapid growth can introduce more variables or contributors to the value chain, and thus it is important to continually assess the quality of the new venture's processes, production, and service inputs. Adequate job analyses, process analyses, performance metrics, and evaluation systems need to be updated to reflect the changing scale and scope of a new venture's operations. On the face of it, one might expect that growth and quality create a natural tension, but it is useful to understand that quality throughout all of the processes will enhance the likelihood of market share growth.

Just as barriers to entry presented obstacles to the start-up, the growing venture will face these same barriers until, in a relative sense, the barriers (presented by the learning curve, for example) present the growing venture with the same level of challenge as that faced by incumbent competitors. Competitive positions in the industry may be preferred positions within the industry: preferred combinations of technologies, marketing processes, target markets, and product mixes, for example, that will provide one competitor with an advantage over the others. Moving from one technology to another or from one target market to another can require a reallocation or expenditure of resources that will range from inexpensive to very costly. The extent that moving from one competitive position in the industry to another is costly captures the notion of mobility barriers. A new venture may have been able to overcome the initial barriers to entry into the industry, but in order to realize the favored competitive positions in the industry, further process or product innovation may be required.

Maturity Phase

The obstacles faced in the maturity phase range from psychological through strategic. At the individual owner/entrepreneur level, he or she may experience a diminished entrepreneurial spirit and expression. A feeling that "I have accomplished what I set out to do, and now all that remains is to manage this organization" can be less rewarding to individuals who prefer to seek new challenges and build organizations, as oppose to managing them. In addition, depending on the scale and scope that the organization achieved, the initial founder of the organization may not be prepared to make and execute strategic plans that may call for a combination of business-level and corporate-level efforts such as cost leadership, differentiation, strategic alliances, diversification moves, merger and acquisition activities, or international strategies. In the event that the entrepreneur has limited interest or knowledge, skills, and abilities associated with the strategic management of the larger organization, he or she needs to identify a succession plan that includes recruiting, selecting, and placing a qualified management team.

As the leadership team sets goals for the mature organization, a primary challenge is to ensure that individual and group goals throughout the organization are aligned with the overarching goals of the organization itself. Implementation and evaluation should exist on short time cycles (daily, weekly, monthly) as opposed to relying on annual reviews. In addition, the feedback provided in the goal-setting and evaluation process should be utilized as a developmental tool as opposed to a punitive one.

Although mature, the venture should maintain a culture of continuous innovation with attention being paid to refining both product and service offerings. Work time, encouragement of leadership, and financial incentives should be included in designing an organizational culture that remains entrepreneurial. Lack of any of these three elements will serve as an obstacle to creating an optimally innovative workplace.

A mature industry is associated with slower growth, and thus the competitive rivalry can be higher as organizations attempt to capture the opportunities remaining. In this stage, the product and service offerings of the competition will be well known and the key to sustaining a competitive advantage will stem from the intangible, difficult-to-imitate processes and technologies that are embedded within each organization.

Decline Phase

Although one might not think about the decline phase when considering obstacles in new venture management, it is associated with tasks and obstacles that ought to be considered long before decline begins, with the first task being the entrepreneur's consideration of an exit strategy. Knowing the exit strategy before creating the new venture will facilitate decision making throughout the venture's life cycle. Building a strong team, creating a leadership and ownership succession plan, and considering the possibility of spinning off suitable products and technologies should be planned long before the organization enters the decline stage. A declining industry puts financial pressure on member firms but creates opportunities for diversification that need to be explored.

Anticipating and identifying obstacles is an ongoing process for entrepreneurs and their teams. As new ventures are created, launched, and grow the array of potential obstacles to be anticipated and identified will vary in content and in the severity of the challenges they present. Management of the new venture that effectively anticipates or identifies and effectively reacts to obstacles will enhance the likelihood of creating and sustaining a competitive advantage over time.

Dale B. Tuttle
University of Michigan, Flint

See also Barriers to Entry; Creativity; Emotions; Exit Strategies; Feasibility Studies; Goal Setting; Overconfidence; Passion; Resource-Based View; Tolerance for Failure; Work-Life Balance

Further Readings

Barringer, Bruce B. and R. Duane Ireland. *Entrepreneurship: Successfully Launching New Ventures*, 3rd ed. Upper Saddle River, NJ: Prentice Hall, 2010.

Entrepreneur's Toolkit: Tools and Techniques to Launch and Grow Your New Business. Boston: Harvard Business School Press, 2005.

Mullins, John. *The New Business Road Test: What Entrepreneurs and Executives Should Do Before Writing a Business Plan*, 3rd ed. Harlow, UK: Financial Times Prentice Hall, 2010.

Reuer, Jeffrey J., Africa Arino, and Paul M. Olk. *Entrepreneurial Alliances*. Upper Saddle River, NJ: Prentice Hall, 2011.

OPPORTUNITY DEVELOPMENT

Opportunity development is a process in which an initial rough idea for a new venture is continuously modified, refined, and developed into an opportunity. This view contrasts with many of the other opportunity-related processes (such as opportunity recognition, discovery, and identification), which come from the perspective that opportunities are objective—they exist in the world, separate from the entrepreneur. The objective view suggests that one need only recognize the existing opportunity and that knowledge is what enables one person to see an opportunity that is missed by another. However, there has been growing attention to the idea that opportunities are not separate from the entrepreneurs—that it is entrepreneurs who make opportunities. Furthermore, an opportunity does not emerge fully formed, as the objective perspective would suggest. Development is necessary because the ideas that lead to opportunities begin very fuzzy or with little detail and thus are highly uncertain. They must be fleshed out, shaped, and refined in order to reduce uncertainty and build confidence that one truly has an opportunity.

For example, one may see an opportunity to open an ecofriendly gym. However, before one can really say there is an opportunity, much more detail is needed. Who would use such a gym? What would make it ecofriendly? What is the ideal location? What kind of offerings should it have (equipment, classes, a pool, and so forth)? What would make it profitable? As these questions are answered, the opportunity becomes clearer and thus further developed. A recent summary of the opportunity literature suggests that opportunities begin with ideas or dreams, which become opportunities only once they have been evaluated and developed. Thus, we can say that opportunity development consists of at least three processes: a process for conceiving ideas, an evaluation process, and finally an elaboration process whereby the ideas are fleshed out.

There are several descriptions of opportunity development, but they have much in common. One set of scholars describe opportunity development as the process in which initial raw concepts are elaborated. Several other scholars offer similar descriptions, such as progressing, shaping, growing, or advancing an idea. Some scholars have described similar processes, involving elaborating and modifying ideas, but called the process something other than opportunity development. One thing that is clear from most descriptions is that opportunity development begins with some initial idea or concept that requires some form of elaboration to become an opportunity. It is also clear that this process takes time because it involves a lot of iteration.

Several studies have noted that entrepreneurs frequently have ideas that they do not pursue. That is, they come up with many ideas but pursue only one or a few of them. Some scholars have defined or measured opportunity development as adding new ideas or new elements to an initial idea. Several studies have used brainstorming exercises to measure opportunity. Dimo Dimov has written extensively about opportunity development and describes it as including a continuing stream of insights and ideas, rather than a single insight. The ideas and insights may emerge through experimentation. Thus, rather than considering the starting point of opportunity development as a single idea, it would be more accurate to think of opportunity development as including a process of conceiving many ideas. This ties in with the understanding that the process takes time and involves iteration.

Scholars also note that evaluation takes place throughout the opportunity development process. For example, the many ideas that entrepreneurs have that they choose not to pursue must be evaluated and determined not to represent viable opportunities. Evaluation is initially informal and becomes more formal as resources become committed to a concept. Thus, the initial evaluation may be a "gut check" or simply intuition. Some scholars suggest that ideas can follow a "stage-gate" procedure (a common practice in new product development) in which ideas are evaluated at various stages of development. Evaluation may result in abandoning, elaborating, or modifying concepts. According to Dimov, for ideas to be seen as opportunities, entrepreneurs must take action to acquire evidence that the idea is viable, has market potential, can offer the entrepreneur profit, and meet all other requirements for success. Other scholars, including Mahesh Bhave in a well-known study leading to a model of the entrepreneurship process, suggest that evaluation is required before elaborating and refining opportunities. Therefore, opportunity development includes not just the conception of ideas but also their evaluation.

Ideas, when initially conceived, are raw, rough, and rudimentary, and thus they require elaboration. In fact, the rougher the idea when first conceived, the more elaboration it needs. Ideas can be elaborated into many forms, including business concepts, business models, business plans, and ultimately new businesses. However, even these may not be fully elaborated and well articulated. There are many ways to elaborate ideas. One study examined both the degree and direction of change of ideas. In that study, ideas that changed either broadened or focused in scope. Another study measured elaboration as adding more detail to any of five elements of opportunity (offer, customer, value, revenue model, or technology). A study looking at social influences on opportunity development found two broad-level cognitive activities related to different social contexts in opportunity development. Information gathering included information scanning and information seeking, which were conducted with weak network ties (people with whom one has infrequent encounters). Concept creation involved interaction with strong network ties (people with whom one has frequent interactions,

such as family and good friends) to perform resource assessment and thinking-through-talking. In some studies, elaboration is found to happen after launch of a new business and involves providing greater detail and improvements to the value-creation capability of the business.

David J. Hansen
College of Charleston

See also Creativity; Creativity and Opportunities; Network Ties; New Product Development; Opportunity Identification and Structural Alignment; Opportunity Recognition; Opportunity Sources

Further Readings

Bhave, Mahesh. "A Process Model of Entrepreneurial Venture Creation." *Journal of Business Venturing*, v.9/3 (1994).
Corner, Patricia Doyle and Marcus Ho. "How Opportunities Develop in Social Entrepreneurship." *Entrepreneurship Theory and Practice*, v.34/4 (2010).
Dimov, Dimo. "Beyond the Single-Person, Single-Insight Attribution in Understanding Entrepreneurial Opportunities." *Entrepreneurship Theory and Practice*, v.31/5 (2007).
Sanz-Velasco, Stefan. "Opportunity Development as a Learning Process for Entrepreneurs." *International Journal of Entrepreneurial Behavior and Research*, v.12/5 (2006).

OPPORTUNITY IDENTIFICATION AND STRUCTURAL ALIGNMENT

The identification of promising opportunities is at the root of entrepreneurial pursuits. Stated broadly, opportunity identification involves entrepreneurs' efforts to find or imagine promising business ideas for their new ventures. The main difficulty of opportunity identification is that opportunity ideas are about the future; this implies that opportunity ideas are fundamentally uncertain. Even if an entrepreneur's idea is to copy a business that already exists and was successful in a different part of the country (or of the world), it is still not possible to know for sure what is really needed to make this business successful in one's own particular context, with the particular customers and competitors one is facing. Indeed, this problem becomes even more significant if the idea is about a completely new product, service, or business model.

In practice, this challenge of uncertainty not only affects entrepreneurs' efforts to exploit opportunities. It makes it particularly difficult to find, imagine, or identify new business ideas in the first place. To understand how entrepreneurs face this unique challenge of identifying promising business ideas, entrepreneurship scholars have studied the thinking processes that support opportunity identification. For instance, J. O. Fiet and his colleagues have conducted a series of studies on the merits of systematic search. Building on the notion that entrepreneurs identify opportunities through processes of pattern recognition, R. A. Baron and M. D. Ensley showed that the opportunity prototypes of expert entrepreneurs were more articulated and placed more emphasis on revenue considerations than the prototypes of novice entrepreneurs (who placed more emphasis on novelty and gut feelings). Denis Grégoire, P. S. Barr, and D. A. Shepherd showed that entrepreneurs used cognitive processes of structural alignment to identify meaningful connections between technologies and markets, and built on these connections to form beliefs about opportunity ideas for new products, new services, or new business models. The rest of this entry expands on this line of research and discusses the implications of structural alignment for relevant aspects of entrepreneurship.

Structural Alignment

Structural alignment is a cognitive process that underpins the perception and interpretation of similarity. When we encounter a new object, we ask ourselves whether anything in this new object resembles anything we have seen before. In other words, we use similarity to "make sense" of the world around us. Research has shown that structural alignment plays a role in a number of reasoning tasks and is particularly useful in tasks that demand creativity and "out-of-the-box" thinking. The particular relevance of structural alignment for opportunity identification rests on the notion that, from an economics standpoint, entrepreneurial opportunities are about creating new "matches" between products, services, or business models, on the one hand, and customers and markets, on the other. Accordingly, entrepreneurs can use processes of structural alignment to form beliefs about possible opportunity matches.

In this regard, an important insight from structural alignment research is that there are different kinds of similarities, and that the differences between them matter. At a basic level, our minds perceive and process superficial similarities. *Superficial similarities* consist of parallels between the basic elements of two objects or ideas: Do they have the same components, the same building blocks, the same parts? Do these elements have the same attributes or characteristics, such as their color, form, and composition? In addition, our minds also perceive and process structural similarities. *Structural similarities* consist of parallels between the "relationships" between the components of a first object or idea and the "relationships" between the components of a second object or idea. By "relationship," we mean the ways different components work together or act on each other. For more complex objects or ideas, relationships culminate in networks of higher-order "relationships between relationships." In practice, these higher-order structures of relationships serve to capture the overall functions of an object, or more complex ideas like cause-effect relationships or the goals or purposes of an object or an idea.

Interestingly, cognitive research shows that the human mind's "default mode of operation" is first to focus on superficial similarities. When an infant who has grown up with house pets first sees a wild squirrel or a fox, it intuitively assumes that the furry four-legged animal will behave the same way other house pets do. Inevitably, any attempts to call or approach the animal fail. Although the superficial features of wild animals look the same as those of domesticated pets, their underlying modes of functioning (structural relationships) are completely different. As we grow older, we learn to pay more attention to the structural similarities (and dissimilarities) of objects. For instance, we learn to look at the demeanor of animals (for example, how they walk, look, and relate to their environment) as cues to their level of domesticity. By the same fashion, we learn to apply solutions learned in one problem situation to other problem situations that share the same structural relationships. Better, we learn to make these knowledge transfers even if the superficial features of the original problem are different from those of the new problems—effectively making logical leaps across different domains. Observing that the burr seeds of burdock kept sticking to his clothes and his dog's fur on his way back from a hunting trip, Swiss engineer Georges de Mestral realized that the structural relationship "tiny hooks cause burrs to attach to clothes and dog's hair" could be transferred from the world of plants to a host of other domains that did not involve plants or seeds: he then spent the following year developing the large-scale manufacturing of Velcro.

Implications for Opportunity Identification

A first implication of structural alignment research for opportunity identification is to provide a cognitive explanation for where the inspiration for an opportunity may come from. In line with Baron's arguments about opportunity prototypes, structural alignment provides a framework for the analogies that entrepreneurs may make between their ideas and other businesses. When asked about his idea for a textbook rental Website, Chegg.com's chief executive officer Jim Safka simply retorted, "Well, it's a lot like Netflix, but for college textbooks." In the same vein, J. P. Cornelissen and J. S. Clarke suggested that by using metaphors and analogies between their new ideas and more familiar businesses, entrepreneurs could find it easier to explain their ideas and convince other people of the merits of these ideas.

A second implication of structural alignment research for opportunity identification is to draw attention to the specific mental connections that entrepreneurs make, not just between their ideas and other ideas but between the fundamental components of entrepreneurial opportunities. In this regard, Grégoire, Barr, and Shepherd showed that in their efforts to find opportunities for new technologies, entrepreneurs pay particular attention to the structural parallels between the capabilities of new technologies (what they can do well and why they can do it so well) and the underlying causes of latent demand in particular markets (why this is a particular problem or need). Conversely, their data suggest that entrepreneurs who focus too much on the superficial matches or mismatches between new technologies and markets may find it much more difficult to identify promising opportunities for these technologies.

Finally, a third and important implication of structural alignment for opportunity identification is to help explain why some opportunities are more difficult to identify than others—and what individuals and organizations can do to help meet this challenge. In this regard, Grégoire and Shepherd have found that even at very early stages, entrepreneurs are most positive about opportunity ideas where a new technology and a market for this new technology share high levels of both superficial and structural similarity. Conversely, entrepreneurs are most negative about opportunity ideas characterized with low levels of both types of similarity. One particularly interesting finding of their study is that, on average, entrepreneurs were highly uncertain about opportunity ideas where the technology shared low levels of superficial similarity but high levels of structural similarity with the market. This finding is interesting because, in their study, these were the "real-life" opportunities pursued with these technologies.

This research suggests that the similarity attributes characterizing opportunity ideas (the superficial and structural similarities between new products, services, and business models and the customers and markets to which they would be introduced) can pose significant challenges for individuals and organizations trying to identify promising entrepreneurial opportunities. Because our mind's "default mode of reasoning" centers on superficial similarity, we may dismiss opportunities because the superficial features of the new product or service idea simply do not match the superficial features of the targeted customers or markets. However, this may mask relevant structural parallels, such as when the structural capabilities of new products or services (what the new products or services can do and when they can do this) directly match the underlying causes of market needs and problems (the reasons customers in a market have the particular needs they have and why current products cannot meet these needs). In other words, the superficial dissimilarities between products/services and markets make some opportunities much less obvious than others.

The practical implication is to encourage more careful thinking about opportunity ideas, especially at the early stages of identification. In this regard, Grégoire and Shepherd have found evidence that those entrepreneurs with more defined intentions to start another new business in the near future tend to pay more attention to structural similarities than entrepreneurs who do not have such intentions. In other words, it appears that to the extent that they have more affirmed entrepreneurial intentions, some entrepreneurs may be more motivated to think a little more deeply about new technologies they encounter.

Implication for Decisions About International Entrepreneurship

Interestingly, entrepreneurship research on structural alignment is starting to have important implications beyond the identification of entrepreneurial ideas for new products, services, or business models. Building on the notion that new ventures' expansion to foreign markets also rests on an opportunity logic, David Williams examined the role of structural alignment in how entrepreneurs evaluate and exploit internationalization opportunities. He found that structural alignment underpins entrepreneurs' internationalization decisions such that entrepreneurs used different types of similarities and differences when deciding where to internationalize as opposed to when to internationalize their ventures. His results suggest that, in their evaluations of and decisions to exploit internationalization opportunities, entrepreneurs may focus heavily on similarities between the home market and the internationalization opportunities they are considering. At the same time, this focus on similarities may cause them to neglect important nonalignable differences, that is, features that exist in the home country but not in an internationalization opportunity (or vice versa). Take, for example, the case of a U.S.-based entrepreneur who has a solid network in her home country but has no network in the United Kingdom, where she is thinking about expanding her firm's sales. The lack of a network in the United Kingdom is a nonalignable difference between the United States and the United Kingdom. Because of the cognitive difficulties of identifying and processing nonalignable differences, however, this entrepreneur is unlikely to consider whether her lack of a network in the United Kingdom could place her at a disadvantage.

The practical implication, again, is to encourage entrepreneurs to think more broadly about internationalization opportunities and to devote particular attention not only to similarities but also to the alignable and nonalignable differences characterizing the set of possible internationalization opportunities they are considering. In this regard, knowledge provides one powerful means to improve entrepreneurs' considerations of more opportunity features and to better process nonalignable differences. Williams found that entrepreneurs with greater prior knowledge of an internationalization opportunity identified more similarities and more differences, including nonalignable differences in particular, between their home country and an internationalization opportunity.

Implications for New Venture Funding

As they do for entrepreneurs' efforts to identify and evaluate opportunities at home and abroad, structural alignment dynamics can influence investors' assessments of funding opportunities. To date, prior research on the decision models of angel investors and venture capitalists has focused mostly on investors' consideration of venture-specific information, such as the quality of the top management team, the intellectual protection of the venture's products or services, and the growth rate or rivalry of the industry. By contrast, fewer studies have considered the influence that investors' reference points can have in their funding decisions. In this regard, J. Gregan-Paxton and J. Cote showed that investors routinely draw from their knowledge of other businesses to evaluate new funding proposals. More important, they highlighted that such knowledge transfers rest on cognitive mechanisms of analogical reasoning and structural alignment. Focusing on the simple yet important structural notion that chances of success are higher for online businesses whose target market matches the demographics of people who regularly use the Internet, they observed that investors who have encountered a series of cases from which to abstract this structural rule are more likely to use it in their prediction of new venture success than investors who do not encounter such cases. In this latter case, investors are more likely to use superficial cues to guide their predictions of success, such as basing their prediction of success of an online pet food store not on the online business rule above but on what they know from other pet food businesses.

Concluding Remarks

Over and above the rich opportunities ahead for research on structural alignment in entrepreneurship, the key practical implication of this research is to draw attention to the simple yet powerful notion that not all similarities are equal. Although they may be easy to identify and process, superficial similarities may sometimes be misleading. Conversely, structural similarities demand more cognitive effort to identify and process, especially when they are not accompanied with superficial similarities. However, it is in these very cases that creative and "out-of-the-box" insights can be made.

Denis A. Grégoire
Syracuse University
David W. Williams
University of Tennessee

See also Creativity; Creativity and Opportunities; Discovery and Exploitation; Opportunity Recognition; Opportunity Sources; Passion; Systematic Search

Further Readings

Baron, R. A. "Opportunity Recognition as Pattern Recognition: How Entrepreneurs 'Connect the Dots' to Identify New Business Opportunities." *Academy of Management Perspectives*, v.20/1 (2006).

Baron, R. A. and M. D. Ensley. "Opportunity Recognition as the Detection of Meaningful Patterns: Evidence From Comparisons of Novice and Experienced Entrepreneurs." *Management Science*, v.52/9 (2006).

Blanchette, I. and K. Dunbar. "Analogy Use in Naturalistic Settings: The Influence of Audience, Emotion and Goals." *Memory and Cognition*, v.29 (2001).

Cornelissen, J. P. and J. S. Clarke. "Imaging and Rationalizing Opportunities: Inductive Reasoning and the Creation and Justification of New Ventures." *Academy of Management Review*, v.35/4 (2010).

Dahl, D. W. and C. P. Moreau. "The Influence and Value of Analogical Thinking During New Product Ideation." *Journal of Marketing Research*, v.34 (2002).

Davidsson, P. "The Domain of Entrepreneurship Research: Some Suggestions." In *Advances in Entrepreneurship, Firm Emergence and Growth*. Vol. 6, *Cognitive Approaches to Entrepreneurship Research*, J. A. Katz and D. A. Shepherd, eds. Oxford, UK: Elsevier/JAI Press, 2003.

Davidsson, P. *Researching Entrepreneurship*. New York: Springer, 2005.

Di Gregorio, D., M. Musteen, and D. E. Thomas. "International New Ventures: The Cross-Border Nexus of Individuals and Opportunities." *Journal of World Business*, v.43/2 (2008).

Díaz De Leó, E. and P. Guild. "Using Repertory Grid to Identify Intangibles in Business Plans." *Venture Capital*, v.5/2 (2003).

Dimov, D. "Grappling With the Unbearable Elusiveness of Entrepreneurial Opportunities." *Entrepreneurship Theory and Practice*, v.35 (2011).

Dunbar, K. "Concept Discovery in a Scientific Domain." *Cognitive Science*, v.17 (1993).

Fiet, J. O. "A Prescriptive Analysis of Search and Discovery." *Journal of Management Studies*, v.44/4 (2007).

Fiet, J. O. *The Systematic Search for Entrepreneurial Discoveries*. Westport, CT: Praeger, 2002.

Gentner, D. "The Mechanisms of Analogical Learning." In *Similarity and Analogical Reasoning*, S. Vosniadou and A. Ortony, eds. Cambridge, UK: Cambridge University Press, 1989.

Gentner, D. and J. Colhoun. "Analogical Processes in Human Thinking and Learning." In *Towards a Theory of Thinking*. Vol. 2, *Thinking*, B. Glatzeder, V. Goel, and A. von Müller, eds. Berlin: Springer, 2010.

Gregan-Paxton, J. and J. Cote. "How Do Investors Make Predictions? Insights From Analogical Reasoning Research." *Journal of Behavioral Decision Making*, v.13 (2000).

Grégoire, D. A., P. S. Barr, and D. A. Shepherd. "Cognitive Processes of Opportunity Recognition: The Role of Structural Alignment." *Organization Science*, v.21/2 (2010).

Grégoire, D. A., D. A. Shepherd, and L. S. Lambert. "Measuring Opportunity-Recognition Beliefs: Illustrating and Validating an Experimental Approach." *Organizational Research Methods*, v.13/1 (2010).

Markman, A. B. and D. Gentner. "Structural Alignment During Similarity Comparisons." *Cognitive Psychology*, v.25 (1993).

McMullen, J. S. and D. A. Shepherd. "Entrepreneurial Action and the Role of Uncertainty in the Theory of the Entrepreneur." *Academy of Management Review*, v.31/1 (2006).

Oviatt, B. M. and P. P. McDougall. "Defining International Entrepreneurship and Modeling the Speed of Internationalization." *Entrepreneurship Theory and Practice*, v.29/5 (2005).

Patel, P. C. and J. O. Fiet. "Systematic Search and Its Relationship to Firm Founding." *Entrepreneurship Theory and Practice*, v.33/2 (2009).

Sarasvathy, S. D. *Effectuation: Elements of Entrepreneurial Expertise*. Northampton, MA: Edward Elgar, 2008.

Shepherd, D. A. "Venture Capitalists' Assessment of New Venture Survival." *Management Science*, v.45/5 (1999).

Venkataraman, S. and S. D. Sarasvathy. "Strategy and Entrepreneurship: Outlines of an Untold Story." In *The Blackwell Handbook of Strategic Management*, M. A. Hitt, E. Freeman, and J. Harrison, eds. Oxford, UK: Blackwell, 2001.

Williams, David W. *Why Do Different New Ventures Internationalize Differently? A Cognitive Model of Entrepreneurs' Internationalization Decisions.* Atlanta: Georgia State University, 2010.

Zacharakis, A. and G. D. Meyer. "A Lack of Insight: Do Venture Capitalists Really Understand Their Own Decision Process?" *Journal of Business Venturing*, v.13/1 (1998).

OPPORTUNITY RECOGNITION

Opportunity recognition and pursuit of opportunities are critical for the economic development and activity of all nations. Without opportunities and entrepreneurs to recognize them, there is no entrepreneurship. The widely accepted definition of entrepreneurship by H. H. Stevenson and J. C. Jarillo focuses on pursuit of opportunities, emphasizing the role of opportunity in the context of entrepreneurship. Scott Shane and Sankaran Venkataraman suggest that opportunities involve identifying new combinations, new means, new ends, or new means-ends relationships that have the possibility of generating a profit for a new or existing business. These may include the introduction of new goods, services, raw materials, markets, ways of organizing, or various combinations thereof.

There are two competing theoretical perspectives concerning the origins of opportunities. Joseph Schumpeter argued that the entrepreneur creates disequilibrium in the economy by introducing innovation in several different ways. These include the introduction of new products or new means of production, the creation of a new market, the development of a new way to organize, or access to a new supply of resources. In contrast, Israel Kirzner suggested that opportunities are recognized by the entrepreneur as inefficiencies in the marketplace, and the exploitation of these opportunities facilitates the economy back to a state of equilibrium.

Regardless of the theoretical perspective, whether opportunities are recognized or created, there is general agreement on the role of individual human agency in the process. Even though opportunities are triggered by environmental changes, they are recognized by individuals. Shane and Jonathan Eckhardt call this intersection the "individual opportunity nexus." Individuals have access to varying amounts of different kinds of information and differ significantly in their values and beliefs about the changing nature of the world and their immediate environment. Factors such as education, prior knowledge, specific experiences, entrepreneurial self-efficacy, entrepreneurial alertness, pattern recognition, and an individual's social networks significantly influence one's perceptions, values, and general perspective on various changes in the immediate and extended environments. These unique and individualized experiences create what Robert Ronstadt calls the information corridors. These information corridors enable some people but not others to recognize and/or create new business opportunities.

Opportunity recognition has been described as an act, a process, and an ability. Peder Christensen and colleagues suggest that opportunity recognition involves the *act* of perceiving a possibility to create a new business or to significantly improve existing business to generate new profit potential. Opportunity recognition as an *ability* has been associated with the cognitive processes of perception, discovery, creation, pattern recognition, and their interaction with new, novel, or ill-defined problems or situations requiring creativity. Furthermore, Denis Grégoire, Pamela Barr, and Dean Shepherd suggest that opportunity recognition is a *process* of making sense of signals of change and forming beliefs regarding the profit potential of a course of action.

Jeffery McMullen and Dean Shepherd proposed opportunity recognition is a two-part process. Individuals may perceive opportunities as third-person opportunities, that is, opportunities that may be valuable for the economy that someone should pursue. From the identified third-person opportunities, first-person opportunities are those the individual perceives as appropriate to exploit himself or herself. Thus, opportunity recognition is a critical first step in the process sequence of entrepreneurship, which involves opportunity recognition, evaluation, and exploitation. The process of opportunity recognition, moreover, is recursive and may iterate through the components of recognition and evaluation as the opportunity is shaped.

Opportunity recognition is a complex phenomenon, involving the interactive and iterative output of individuals and environments. Past opportunity recognition research has faced several methodological challenges, as most of the research has focused on retrospective accounts. However, new methodological advances, including experimental, qualitative, and observational approaches, as well as methods from cognitive sciences and creativity literature, are improving our understanding of opportunity recognition.

The research on opportunity recognition is not limited to a focus on individuals or industries. Both opportunity recognition and the associated opportunity shaping are influenced by many social and contextual factors, which create room for multilevel constructs and research involving opportunity recognition. For example, corporate entrepreneurship literature has extended the construct to organizations and how they may recognize opportunities for strategic renewal. Overall, opportunity recognition is a key construct in entrepreneurship literature, spanning individual, firm, industry, and social contexts.

Shruti Sardeshmukh
University of South Australia
Ronda M. Smith-Nelson
University of Georgia

See also Creativity and Opportunities; Discovery and Exploitation; Opportunity Development; Opportunity Identification and Structural Alignment; Opportunity Sources

Further Readings

Baron, Robert A. "Opportunity Recognition as Pattern Recognition: How Entrepreneurs 'Connect the Dots' to Identify New Business Opportunities." *The Academy of Management Perspectives*, v.20/1 (2006).

Casson, Mark and Nigel Wadeson. "The Discovery of Opportunities: Extending the Economic Theory of the Entrepreneur." *Small Business Economics*, v.28/4 (2007).

Christensen, Peder, R. Peterson, and O. Madsen. *Opportunity Identification: The Contribution of Entrepreneurship to Strategic Management*. Aarhus, Denmark: Institute of Management, University of Aarhus, 1990.

Grégoire, D. A., P. S. Barr, and D. A. Shepherd. "Cognitive Processes of Opportunity Recognition: The Role of Structural Alignment." *Organization Science*, v.21/2 (2010).

Kirzner, Israel. *Competition and Entrepreneurship*. Chicago: University of Chicago Press, 1973.

Lumpkin, G. Tom and Benyamin Lichtenstein. "The Role of Organizational Learning in the Opportunity-Recognition Process." *Entrepreneurship Theory and Practice*, v.29/4 (2005).

McMullen, Jeffery and Dean Shepherd. "Entrepreneurial Action and the Role of Uncertainty in the Theory of the Entrepreneur." *The Academy of Management Review*, v.31/1 (2006).

Ronstadt, Robert. "The Corridor Principle." *Journal of Business Venturing*, v.3/1 (1988).

Sarasvathy, Saras, Nicholas Dew, Ramakrishna Velamuri, and Sankaran Venkataraman. "Three Views of Entrepreneurial Opportunity." In *Handbook of Entrepreneurship Research*. Dordrecht, Netherlands: Kluwer, 2003.

Schumpeter, Joseph. *The Theory of Economic Development*. Cambridge, MA: Harvard University Press, 1934.

Shane, Scott and Jonathan Eckhardt. "The Individual-Opportunity Nexus." *Handbook of Entrepreneurship Research*. Dordrecht, Netherlands: Kluwer, 2003.

Shane, S. and S. Venkataraman. "The Promise of Entrepreneurship as a Field of Research." *Academy of Management Review*, v.25/1 (2000).

Stevenson, H. H. and J. C. Jarillo. "A Paradigm of Entrepreneurship: Entrepreneurial Management." *Strategic Management Journal*, v.11 (1990).

Opportunity Sources

The identification and exploitation of opportunities are central to the process of starting a new venture. In an influential *Academy of Management Review* article, Scott Shane and S. Venkataraman argue that how opportunities to create future goods and services come to exist, through whom, and how they are exploited cover most of the questions that are asked by scholars of entrepreneurship.

Broadly defined, opportunities are circumstances that provide profit-earning possibilities. The most frequently exploited opportunities are based on improvements to existing business activities and involve efforts to optimize business models that are already known to work. As defined by Mark Casson, entrepreneurial opportunities form a subset of all opportunities involving the discovery of new goods, services, raw materials, and organizing methods that can be introduced and sold at more than their cost of production. Further developing this definition, Jonathan Eckhardt and Scott Shane add that entrepreneurial opportunities involve creativity in devising new means, ends, or means-ends relationships that have previously been undetected or underutilized by market participants.

Opportunities for new enterprise may come from a wide variety of openings. Peter Drucker described three categories of opportunity: (1) the creation of new information, as occurs with the invention of new technology; (2) the exploitation of market inefficiencies that result from information asymmetry, as occurs across time and geography; and (3) the reaction to shifts in the relative costs and benefits of alternative uses for resources, as occurs with political, regulatory, or demographic changes. Eckhardt and Shane offer another tripartite classification that distinguishes opportunities according to (1) the locus of the changes that generate the opportunity (whether it arises from a new product or service, new market area, raw material discovery, or new form of organization); (2) the source of opportunity (such as whether it arises from information asymmetry, arises from wholly new information, and affects supply or demand); and (3) the initiator of change (which might be a new or existing independent entrepreneur or other commercial or public-sector entity).

Whatever their origin, opportunities may exist without being identified. For example, the Internet has created new opportunities for communication that exist irrespective of whether they are recognized and acted upon. Opportunities arise from objective circumstances, but their identification is a subjective process.

The Internet has created new opportunities for communication that exist whether or not industries recognize and act upon them. When it is expected that an opportunity will be in high demand and will sustain high profit margins, it is considered more likely to be pursued than those with less favorable returns. (Photos.com)

The essence of entrepreneurial opportunities is that they are not obvious to everyone all of the time. The range of options and consequences of pursuing novel ideas is unknown and not simply resolved through the kinds of relatively mechanical calculations that can be used to optimize an existing process. Ultimately, opportunities exist because people differ in their assessments of the relative value of the resources that are to be drawn upon and created by a new venture. Without differences in the perceived value of resources, entrepreneurs may be challenged to obtain the necessary raw materials at a price that makes their venture viable. Similarly, if conjectures are shared among would-be entrepreneurs, competition may reduce the individual share of potential profit to a level below that needed to create a successful venture. Uncertainty plays a key role in sustaining differences in the evaluation of entrepreneurial opportunities, as people's response to uncertainty is conditioned by their individual life experiences, including formal education, and their capacity to visualize new means, ends, or means-end relationships.

Opportunities vary in their attractiveness to entrepreneurs and their likelihood of being exploited through a new venture. Opportunities with high expected value, for which there is anticipated to be high demand and based on activity that can sustain high profit margins, are considered more likely to be pursued than those with less favorable returns. Other characteristics suggested to favor exploitation are being at the early stages of a technology life cycle, facing some but not too many competitors, and having scope to learn from the experience of other entrants. Attributes that increase the probability of opportunity exploitation are not the same as those that increase the likelihood of success. The speed with which opportunities can be converted into commercial ventures is significant in determining whether incumbents are able to react to new ventures with the potential to disturb existing markets.

Explanations of opportunity identification and exploitation have focused on the acquisition and processing of information by the entrepreneur as well as the role of knowledge. This leads to expectations that the novice and experienced entrepreneur differ with respect to their access to and methods of appraising new venture opportunities.

Novice entrepreneurs may have fewer benchmarks than more experienced entrepreneurs for assessing whether the information they have collected is likely to be a fruitful source of new venture ideas. This limited insight into where a search effort might be most appropriately concentrated may lead the novice to rely on a broader range of information sources. The novice may also be more likely to rely on analytical or systematic information-processing styles than the experienced entrepreneur. The application of formal information-processing techniques can make opportunity identification a comparatively slow process, but it has the advantage of yielding more accurate results than where information is processed based on heuristics derived from personal experience.

Experienced entrepreneurs may engage in a focused search based on their established routines and information sources that have worked for them in the past. This may include the use of a network of contacts that maintain a good flow of information from sources of known reliability. A business track record may lead financiers, advisers, other entrepreneurs, and business contacts to proactively present business proposals to them. At the same time, experience may bring its own barriers to identifying and correctly assessing opportunities. Past experience may be of limited helpfulness in new and changing environments, especially where experience leads people to think that they know enough and infer too much from limited information sources. A tendency to want to confirm prior beliefs can constrain entrepreneurs to concentrate on what is familiar, limiting the ability to notice and react to information that does not conform to familiar patterns. Similarly, overconfidence may result in overly optimistic assessments of opportunities and to a focus on opportunities for implanting previously implemented models without recognizing that circumstances have changed. In this context, experience is ideally combined with the recognition of a need sometimes to revert to the use of systematic information-processing methods rather than relying on experience-based decision making alone.

The role of prior business ownership experience in shaping opportunity identification and exploitation is complicated by the diversity among established entrepreneurs. Paul Westhead and colleagues have, for example, found differences between serial and portfolio entrepreneurs in terms of the number of opportunities appraised, as well as differences between novice and experienced entrepreneurs as a whole.

Martin Perry
Massey University

See also Creativity and Opportunities; Discovery and Exploitation; Opportunity Development; Opportunity Identification and Structural Alignment; Opportunity Recognition

Further Readings

Casson, M. *The Entrepreneur*. Totowa, NJ: Barnes and Noble, 1982.

Eckhardt, J. and S. Shane. "Opportunities and Entrepreneurship." *Journal of Management*, v.29/3 (2003).

Shane, S. and S. Venkataraman. "The Promise of Entrepreneurship as a Field of Research." *Academy of Management Review*, v.25/1 (2000).

Westhead, P., D. Ucbasaran, and M. Wright. "Information Search and Opportunity Identification: The Importance of Prior Business Ownership Experience." *International Small Business Journal*, v.27 (2009).

OVERCONFIDENCE

New ventures are launched into difficult and dynamic environments, which can be quite risky; most new ventures fail. In the face of these odds, entrepreneurs must convince themselves and others that investing in their ventures is a good idea. Entrepreneurs should exude the confidence necessary to convince others to invest with them. They analyze the appropriate risks against potential returns before they begin the new venture. Risk and return are continually reviewed as the venture launches and begins to operate. Before launching a venture, entrepreneurs should discard ideas that do not meet appropriate risk-to-return criteria. During the operation of the new venture, they should exit when the risk-to-return criteria indicate that continuing operations will fail. However, entrepreneurs sometimes launch new ventures or continue to operate ventures against overwhelming negative odds. Individuals who ignore realistic risk assessments to launch or operate ventures are often displaying overconfidence.

Because most start-ups fail, it could be said that the failing entrepreneurs were overconfident. Whereas there is some truth in that statement, overconfidence is not merely a post facto label applied to an entrepreneurial failure. Because risk is associated with all new ventures, there will be normal failures based on unforeseen factors. Overconfident individuals are those who were more confident than was sensible. They ignored the reality of the situation.

Moreover, overconfidence is not a label applied because of a single error in judgment. Overconfidence is an attributional bias that leads an individual to expectations of success that are greater than the facts merit. Overconfidence, in other words, is not a single miscalculation but rather is a habitual bias toward miscalculating probabilities. This bias leads individuals to make routine judgments that exceed or are not in line with the realities or accuracy of a situation. Overconfidence is further viewed as the propensity to continually ignore objective feedback that counters initial subjective judgment. Entrepreneurs are more vulnerable to cognitive errors such as overconfidence. Therefore, overconfidence is a bias of interest to the social scientist looking to explain entrepreneurial behavior.

For example, entrepreneurs are generally considered more overconfident than business managers. At least two theories attempt to explain this phenomenon. First, new venture creation attracts a different kind of person. Perhaps people attracted to new ventures are less formal in their decision making; they may be rasher in their decision making, more spontaneous in their actions, and blinder to additional information. Second, the entrepreneurial environment is fraught with difficult conditions. The complicated nature of the environment creates information overload, high time pressure, and uncertainty. Bounded rationality suggests that all individuals have a limited ability to process information. Therefore, entrepreneurs especially rely on heuristics and other cognitive biases to make decisions in their noisy environments. Any resulting poor decisions might be attributable to overconfidence biases.

Given that overconfidence is a bias that affects those who start new ventures, entrepreneurs should be sensitive to this issue. Sensitivity is generated through awareness. Metaknowledge is awareness about the limits of our knowledge, and it includes the understanding of uncertainties associated with decisions. It can be said that metaknowledge is an appreciation of what we know and what we do not know.

Questionnaires designed to investigate metaknowledge include questions that can be verified but are not generally known. They force participants not only to answer questions but also to state their confidence ranges. Sample questionnaire items from a confidence quiz in Edward Russo and Paul Schoemaker's work include the following:

- How many patents did the U.S. Patent and Trademark Office issue in 1990? (*answer:* 96,727 patents)
- What is the shortest navigable distance (in statute miles) between New York City and Istanbul? (*answer:* 5757 miles)
- How many German automobiles were sold in Japan in 1989? (*answer:* 147,324 automobiles)

Participants are asked to answer with a low guess and a high guess such that they are 90 percent confident that the true answer would fall somewhere in that range. A majority of participants do far worse than they expect on this questionnaire.

Scholars have suggested a few ways to minimize the overconfidence bias. Since there is an overload of information in the entrepreneurial environment, entrepreneurs should actively seek out the critical information that may not be readily apparent. Looking for negative information, instead of merely focusing on the positive information, may minimize the overconfidence bias. Furthermore, prioritization could allow formerly unprocessed yet critical information to be utilized. Additionally, a phenomenon known as anchoring occurs when decisions are made without considering a range of confidence. When individuals are asked to create a range of confidence, their original answer anchors the range to a smaller spread than is warranted. Individuals who outline a probability range of confidence concurrently with the initial answer are more accurate in the assessments.

The overconfidence effect is not a new phenomenon. Confucius addressed overconfidence when he made the following widely attributed statement:

"To know that we know what we know and that we do not know what we do not know—that is true knowledge."

Wm. Camron Casper
Oklahoma State University

See also Business Failure; Cognition Theory; Commitment and Persistence; Locus of Control; Obstacle Identification; Opportunity Sources; Passion; Planning Fallacy; Risk Management; Tolerance for Failure

Further Readings

Baron, Robert A. "Counterfactual Thinking and Venture Formation: The Potential Effects of Thinking About 'What Might Have Been.'" *Journal of Business Venturing*, v.15/1 (2000).

Lichtenstein, Sarah and Baruch Fischhoff. "Do Those Who Know More Also Know More About How Much They Know?" *Organizational Behavior and Human Performance*, v.2/2 (1977).

Russo, J. Edward and Paul J. Schoemaker. "Managing Overconfidence." *Sloan Management Review*, v.33/2 (1992).

Partnerships

Developing a great idea into a new venture depends on establishing key relationships at different stages of business growth. Partnerships may be formal, with specific legal meanings, or informal, such as working with family or friends. Important partnerships involve investors, customers, developers, suppliers, marketers, sales people, and administrative and legal support. These partnerships bring unique skills or resources to the table.

No firm succeeds in isolation. Every successful venture is embedded in a value chain, a network of indirect relationships enabling products, information, ideas, and services to flow across the firm's boundaries. Ventures have direct relationships and partners at different stages of their evolution, including phases of initial, rapid, and continuous growth. Partnering across firm boundaries includes finding ways to enhance the relationships with all the people and organizations that impact performance. For example, large companies, such as Raytheon, offer development programs for small suppliers that enhance internal quality control. As the supplier's processes improve, so does the quality of the parts delivered to Raytheon.

Entrepreneurs and new venture managers must bring in the right partner at the right time. Partnerships will evolve and new partnerships will be needed throughout the product development life cycle. Managing these transitions is very challenging. Entrepreneurs need key partners sooner rather than later. Getting the right partners early on establishes the venture in many ways. For example, the right public relations firm and media exposure can position a company as experts in a field. Having one or two highly respected customers early in the firm's life cycle will validate the product or service and financial support. While it is important to seek out such early adopters, however, some early adopters may seek exclusivity if the product is unique and provides them with competitive advantage or differentiation.

Luck and timing are everything in new venture development. For example, one might readily find early funders, encounter unpredicted delays during development, or introduce a new product in the wrong economic conditions. However, developing smart and solid partnerships early can overcome hurdles and leverage opportunities. For example, one start-up computer service company in the direct marketing industry kept operating costs variable until growth made that operating model unsustainable. Its fixed cost model effectively reduced costs and improved service. However, this company failed to see a recession on the horizon, and both the company and its largest customers' businesses were adversely impacted by negative market conditions early in the cycle. As a result, the company went from being in the black to being in the red, even though decisions appeared prudent at the time.

Most good ideas that fail to become successful ventures lacked partners. Inability to develop the right partners can also hamper growth. It is crucial that at an early stage core team members know one another's strengths and weaknesses and communicate well and often. Partnerships, in other words, must be nurtured. Below, four types of partners are described that align with four stages of business development.

From Great Idea to Working Concept: Initial Funding

Stage 1 success depends on support from family and friends. If a venture is not well funded, there may be too much work for too little reward. This stage reflects sacrifice of time and energy far surpassing a normal job. Family can undermine the venture, unless the entrepreneur wins their support. For example, do family members pitch in to help do the work, tolerating crazy hours, or do they exert pressure to return to normal life?

Funding comes from three sources at three phases of stage 1. First, seed capital often comes from family or friends of family, so these relationships can become delicate. Credit card lines and home equity loans are common sources of funds. At this initial stage, development of proof of concept leads to creation of a prototype that builds the case for venture capital or winning over an initial group of customers.

Second, angel investors may be interested in developing the prototype. They are fairly sophisticated about business growth and may be persuaded to provide some money in advance of venture capital in response to a presentation, demonstration, or prototype. With a working proof of concept or prototype, the new firm can attempt to develop customer awareness, begin to deliver services or products, and experience initial income. However, ramping up to this stage probably takes an infusion of money. That usually means partnering with venture capitalists.

Third, venture capitalists are the most sophisticated early investors and typically provide the largest cash infusion. It takes a strong case to motivate their investment in an idea. It is important not to give away too much to family or angels during phases 1 or 2 of stage 1, as venture capitalists as a result may not see an adequate return on investment. Early investors need to cooperate and agree to dilution of ownership or early payout to get this third-round funding.

Stage 1 can take from six months to five years. Timing is different for each venture, depending upon capital intensity, time requirements, and the complexity of the necessary value chain.

Creating a Working Prototype: Partnering for Product Development and Building the Supply Chain

In stage 2, new venture success often depends on developing relationships with larger organizations. Getting attention from big companies can be challenging. Finding the receptive ones with little capital is difficult. Sporadic cash flow can also jeopardize supply of parts and sustained supplier relationships. Some new ventures seek to sell their products directly to larger companies. This is often the case for businesses in pharmaceuticals, medical devices, and high technology.

At this stage, as more people see the idea, intellectual property issues become salient. Filing for patents is expensive, must be done country-by-country, and may have a lengthy approval process. Intellectual property rights can be at risk, as many large organizations will not guarantee nonconfidentiality as they examine the product. However, entrepreneurs must always try to get a tight confidentiality agreement and at least file a provisional patent covering the most sensitive parts of the invention.

Getting the Idea to Market: Sales, Marketing, and Outsourced Manufacturing

In the third stage, distribution partners, such as those focused on logistics and sales, build customer awareness and product availability. As the firm gains market share, the owner-manager shifts attention from creativity to the bottom line and the challenge of building an organization. Developing trust outside the core team and delegating control to others are particularly difficult during this necessary transition.

At this point, improving profitability, reducing operating costs, and reducing waste become priorities. Organizations go through cycles of diversification and consolidation—creating varied products, processes, and parts and then integrating them for greater effectiveness and efficiency.

The company has grown too large for informal meetings among a small core team to provide smooth operations. Human resource development and working standards become essential in building effective relationships across the organization's levels and divisions. Everyone should have a voice, and the flow of communication should be optimized. Decision making should be pushed down to the level where the work is done. This avoids micromanagement. Building relationships of trust downward with managers and supervisors also frees up the executive team from operational concerns and prevents micromanagement.

Many problems can arise when transitioning and delegating power and control across organizational levels and stages of venture development, such as conflicting visions and egos, fighting for authority, lack of cohesiveness in the small group, erosion of trust, blurred spheres of authority, lack of a single voice inside or outside the organization, overlooked decisions and actions, divided employee loyalties, delayed decision making, and confused accountability.

In stage 3, the leadership team initially focuses on operational thinking, then on tactical operational thinking, and finally on thinking strategically to produce sustainability, process improvement, and long-term growth. Success at stage 3 generates resources for exploring new possibilities.

Keeping the Idea Relevant: The Customer

During the fourth stage, customers' feedback is analyzed and marketing becomes crucial. A new venture often fails because of an introspective focus on the technology and not on market needs or product usability.

Customers provide references, legitimacy, and market recognition. They help define the product and the brand. They also help fund development and growth. As Peter Drucker put it, "Because it is its purpose to create a customer, any business enterprise has two—and only these two—basic functions: marketing and innovation."

With an efficient organization in place and satisfied customers established, it is time to think about innovation. New ideas can come from anyone inside the organization. They can also come from customers. Partnering with customers means the changes in products and services will be market driven.

Conclusion

Partnering depends on building and sustaining good relationships that enable entrepreneurs to apply talent, energy, funds, and self-interests of others to the development of a new venture. Effective partnerships can determine the return on investment, the retention of great employees and valued customers, and the ultimate success of the venture.

Michael M. Beyerlein
Purdue University
Phyllis R. Kramer
New Venture Management
Jon Cordas
Purdue University

See also Communication Styles; Community/Government Buy-Ins; Customer Orientation; Human Capital Theory; Managing Human and Social Capital; Network Ties; Networks; Social Capital; Social Intelligence; Start-Up Teams; Team Composition

Further Readings

Doganova, L. "Entrepreneurship as a Process of Collective Exploration." 2009. http://www.csi.mines-Paristech.fr/Items/WorkingPapers/Download/DLWP.php?wp=WP_CSI_017.pdf (Accessed February 2011).

Drucker, P. F. *The Practice of Management*. New York: Harper and Row, 1954.

Ruef, M. "Entrepreneurial Groups." 2009. http://www.gsb.stanford.edu/FACSEMINARS/events/ob/documents/ob_02_09_ruef.pdf (Accessed February 2011).

Ruef, M. *The Entrepreneurial Group: Social Identities, Relations, and Collective Action*. Princeton, NJ: Princeton University Press, 2011.

Schutjens, V. and E. Stam. "The Evolution and Nature of Young Firm Networks: A Longitudinal Perspective." *Small Business Economics*, v.21/2 (2003).

PASSION

Passion is that elusive quality that hovers between enthusiasm and obsession, adds richness and excitement to a task, and provides the momentum to keep going even in the face of great obstacles. Whereas it fires enthusiasm and provides the energy to persevere in the face of weariness, passion alone is not sufficient to achieve success, and it can have a dark side.

We sense intuitively that passionate entrepreneurs do better than their less passionate counterparts. Apple's Steve Jobs, Virgin Atlantic's Richard Branson, and Ben & Jerry's Ben Cohen and Jerry Greenfield are modern role models of passionate entrepreneurs. Passion involves intense positive and palpable feelings associated with a venture or activity. Passionate entrepreneurs seem to have a real liking for what they do, which makes their significant investment of time and energy worthwhile. Passion seems to foster success by fueling the vision, self-identity, and self-efficacy necessary to achieve goals.

Whereas passion has been considered an innate characteristic or personality trait within entrepreneurs, some have suggested that it has more to do with the relationship between entrepreneur and venture—that is, that certain ventures somehow kindle strong emotions within the entrepreneur that other ventures do not. Passion involves powerful identification with a role that the entrepreneur values highly and finds meaningful. Passion is deeply rooted in the entrepreneur's sense of self and acts as a strong bond between the venture and the person.

Melissa Cardon and her research team have identified three prominent entrepreneurial roles: inventor, founder, and developer. The inventor is powerfully drawn to innovation, invention, and the creation of new venture opportunities. The founder, concerned mainly with the venture itself, is drawn to design and establishing the venture. The developer is attracted by the opportunity to market and grow the entity. Whereas a venture has the best chances for success when the entrepreneur can move fluidly among the roles, it is not uncommon for an entrepreneur to favor one role over others. Problems arise when an entrepreneur favors one role to the exclusion of the others.

The success of entrepreneurial teams is as dependent on passion as is the success of individual entrepreneurs. The degree of passion within the team is influenced by the personalities of the individuals as well as external variables not controlled by the team. Besides influencing the outcome of the team venture, passion affects how the team deals with conflict and other team dynamics. Teams are most successful when the members can correctly assess the levels and types of passion of the members.

While having strong positive feelings is necessary to venture success, it is not sufficient. According to George Odiorn, the key component of a successful venture is a good dose of competence and skill, which unlike passion, which can wax and wane, are steady and long lasting. Odiorn also suggests that while it is true that passion can be influential in setting and fulfilling goals, it is also true that having goals, especially "noble" goals, can kindle passion where there was none before. In cases where the goals are more

Entrepreneurs like the late Steve Jobs from Apple (photographed here at a press announcement for the MacBook Air), Virgin Atlantic's Richard Branson, and Ben & Jerry's Ben Cohen and Jerry Greenfield are modern role models of passionate innovators. (Wikimedia/Matthew Yohe)

mundane, competence and skill are required to carry the venture forward.

Some experts believe that competence and skill, or "cognitive preparedness," actually is a dimension of passion itself. Cognitive preparedness is the component of passion associated with the intellectual heavy lifting that is necessary in putting together a convincing and viable business strategy and in scanning the venture landscape for threats and opportunities. Venture capitalists cite cognitive preparedness as the most influential element in their choice to invest.

However, passion can have a dark side. Whereas positive feelings and identification with the entrepreneurial roles and activities can increase an entrepreneur's chances of success, excessive or obsessive passion can reduce them by fostering dysfunctional behavior. Obsessive entrepreneurs can become stubborn, unwilling or unable to seek out or accept disconfirming information, and dogged in their adherence to failing strategies, even in the face of powerful evidence. This severely impacts their decision-making and problem-solving abilities. Likewise, obsessive passion in teams can result in dysfunctional group behaviors, including group-think and group shift, conditions that cause team members to support group decisions they believe to be flawed. Passion is like the proverbial horse that, with its power and spirit, pulls the coach but, if left uncontrolled, can quickly destroy the coach and itself. Thus, the passionate feelings that drive the activity must be moderated by reason.

The role that passion plays in the success of an entrepreneurial venture is indisputable. Entrepreneurs' passion enables their creativity, diligence, resilience, and joy. Impassioned entrepreneurs define themselves in terms of their work or venture, and their excitement energizes others and propels their success. However, strong positive affect toward the venture is not sufficient to achieve success. Also needed are the cognitive skills and competencies that make the venture a reality by informing the strategy and moderating obsessive thinking.

Ariane David
California Lutheran University

See also Championing Corporate Ventures; Championing New Ventures; Commitment and Persistence; Competitive Intelligence; Creativity; Emotions; Entrepreneurial Orientation; Leadership; Leadership: Transformational; Negotiating Strategies; Overconfidence; Psychological Views; Social Intelligence

Further Readings

Baum, Robert J. and Edwin A. Locke. "The Relationship of Entrepreneurial Traits, Skill and Motivation to Subsequent Venture Growth." *Journal of Applied Psychology*, v.89/4 (2004).

Burke, Ronald J. and Lisa Fiksenbaum. "Work Motivations, Work Outcomes, and Health: Passion Versus Addiction." *Cross-Cultural Research*, v.43/4 (2009).

Cardone, Melissa S. et al. "The Nature and Experience of Entrepreneurial Passion." *Academy of Management Review*, v.34/3 (2009).

Chen, Xiao-Ping, Xin Yao, and Suresh Kotha. "Passion and Preparation in Entrepreneurs' Business Plan Presentations: A Persuasion Analysis of Venture Capitalists' Funding Decisions." *Academy of Management Journal*, v.52/1 (2009).

Mageau, Genevieve A. et al. "On the Development of Harmonious and Obsessive Passion: The Role of Autonomy Support, Activity Specialization, and Identification With the Activity." *Journal of Personality*, v.77/3 (2009).

Odiorn, George S. "Competence Versus Passion." *Training and Development*, v.45/5 (1991).

PATENT PROTECTION

With the World Trade Organization (WTO) Trade-Related Aspects of Intellectual Property Rights (TRIPS) agreement, most developed and developing nations have an established system for protecting intellectual property. Intellectual property, the product of a person's or company's originality and creativity, is usually protected in one of four forms: through copyrights, trademarks, protections of trade secrets, or patents. Of all of the forms, patents are the most complex and tightly regulated, although differences exist across national systems. Patents are defined by the U.S. Patent and Trademark Office (USPTO) as "any new and useful process, machine, manufacture, or composition of matter, or any new and useful improvement thereof." In general, patents protect the idea or design of an "invention" rather than the tangible form of the invention itself. The term *invention* is defined loosely so that it can encompass a wide variety of objects and processes, including computer programs, industrial processes, technological machines, and genetically engineered organisms.

To patent an invention, an inventor must meet a number of requirements. The invention must be sufficiently novel, nonobvious, and useful. To be considered novel, an invention must be substantially unlike anything that is already patented, has already been on the market, or has been written about in a publication. In fact, in the United States, an inventor cannot patent even his or her own invention if it has been on the market or discussed in publications for more than a year. Adaptations of earlier inventions can be patented as long as they are nonobvious, meaning that a person of standard skill in the area of study would not automatically come up with the same idea upon examining the existing invention. The last condition for patenting is that the invention is considered useful. This means that the invention serves some purpose and that it actually works. Unproven ideas generally fall into the realm of copyright law.

To get a patent, an inventor needs to complete an application, which requires extensive research and, in most cases, hiring a lawyer. Patent lawyers are attorneys with a science or technical degree who have met the patent office's certification qualifications. The application includes a list of any "prior art," earlier inventions that are relevant to the invention under consideration; a brief summary outlining the new invention; a detailed account and/or drawing of the "preferred embodiment" of the invention; a description of how the idea will actually be put into practice; and one or more "claims," actual legal descriptions of the scope of protection granted by the patent.

After its inventor submits an application to a patent examiner, the invention may be labeled "patent pending." When the examiner finally reviews the application, he or she may approve the application as it is submitted or reject the application. When an examiner is satisfied with an application, an inventor is issued a "notice of allowance." From that point throughout the life of the patent, an inventor is required to pay periodic maintenance fees to keep patent protection. The entire patenting process can take anywhere from a year to five years. In the United States, the life of the patent actually begins at the application date, not the approval date, so inventors do not wait for final patent approval to begin commercialization. An inventor's claim to an idea is also based on the invention date. Whoever completes an original invention first is granted the patent. In some cases, two or more inventors submit an application regarding the same invention around the same time. When this happens, the patent office must declare "interference," a trial that determines who was the first inventor. When something is invented as part of a person's work for a company, the company is typically given control over the invention and becomes the assignee, although the patent may officially go to the individual inventor or inventors. This arrangement varies depending on the country and the nature of the employee's contract.

There are two perspectives on the impact of patent protection. In obtaining a patent, an inventor acquires the right to exclude others from making, using, offering for sale, or selling the invention in the United States. For the life of the patent (20 years in the United States), patent holders retain the monopoly rights to profit from their inventions by going into business for themselves or licensing the use of their invention to other companies. On one hand, granting inventors the ownership of their original ideas and giving them temporary control over who can use those ideas are believed to encourage the advancement of science and technology. The process of inventing a new device or process is an extremely difficult one, and few people would go through it if there were no financial reward. Inventors are given an opportunity to profit from their creations. Patents also help disseminate technological information to other inventors, as application descriptions become part of the patent office's database, which is public record. Finally, once the patent has expired, the idea is more readily available than it would have been if it had never been patented. Thus, patents motivate individual inventors, as well as companies. They are particularly important to chemical, computer technology, and pharmaceutical firms. In these markets, success might be wholly dependent on having exclusive rights to innovative products, as product development can be long and costly.

On the other hand, the tragedy of the "anticommons," coined by Michael Heller, describes a coordination breakdown that arises from the existence of numerous rights holders frustrating the actual achievement of a socially desirable outcome. It is up to the patent holder to enforce the patent; the government does not go after patent infringers. If an invention is of worldwide interest, an inventor should consider applying for patents in other nations. Patenting in the United States offers protection only in the United States. To enlist the government's help in stopping infringement, the patent holder must take any infringers to court. Firms have been known to follow different patent strategies, including exclusivity (developing and maintaining a strong proprietary position), leveraging (use patent rights to obtain better terms in interfirm transactions), and defensive measures (prevent other patent owners from holding up business). For example, patent thickets (also known as patent floods or patent clusters) are used to defend against competitors designing around a single patent and become a dense web of overlapping intellectual property rights at which a company must hack away in order to commercialize a new technology.

While initial studies on patent protection found that patents were not the most important means to appropriate returns for innovation, scholars of new ventures utilize patent measures in accessing the economic and innovative success of the firm. The value of individual intellectual assets is rarely observable. Thus, to determine the value of an individual patent, inductive approaches must be chosen and a definition for the latent construct "patent value" is needed. Measures include backward citations (number of inventions listed as prior art), forward citations (number of future inventions that cite the invention as prior art), number of claims (scope of the patent), and technological area of impact (the patent classes to which the patent applies). The validity of patent data on studying new ventures depends on the appropriability regime, or those factors that influence a firm to appropriate return to innovation.

Preeta M. Banerjee
Brandeis University

See also Innovation Measurement; Licensing; Measures of Performance; Technology Transfer; Trademarks

Further Readings

Cohen, W. M., R. R. Nelson, and J. P. Walsh. *Protecting Their Intellectual Assets: Appropriability Conditions and Why U.S. Manufacturing Firms Patent (or Not)*. Cambridge, MA: National Bureau of Economic Research, 2000.

Hall, B., H. A. Jaffe, and M. Trajtenberg. *Market Value and Patent Citations: A First Look*. Cambridge, MA: National Bureau of Economic Research, 2000.

Heller, M. A. and R. Eisenberg. "Can Patents Deter Innovation? The Anticommons in Biomedical Research." *Science*, v.280/5364 (May 1998).

Lanjouw, J. O. and J. Lerner. *The Enforcement of Intellectual Property Rights*. Boston: NBER, 1997.

Levin, R. C., A. K. Klevorick, R. R. Nelson, and S. G. Winter. *Appropriating the Returns From Industrial R&D*. New Haven, CT: Cowles Foundation for Research in Economics, 1988.

Reitzig, M. "Improving Patent Valuations for Management Purposes: Validating New Indicators by Analyzing Application Rationales." *Research Policy*, v.33 (2004).

Somaya, D. "Strategic Determinants of Decisions Not to Settle Patent Litigation." *Strategic Management Journal*, v.24 (2003).

Teece, D. "Profiting From Technological Innovation: Implications for Integration, Collaboration, Licensing and Public Policy." *Research Policy*, v.15/6 (1986).

PERFORMANCE AND LEGITIMACY

New venture performance is often assessed by the successful accomplishment of important milestones such as first sale, breakeven point, or first profitable operating period. Such performance metrics are all linked to the idea of legitimacy in that, once a firm has reached these milestones, the venture has established itself and will maintain successful operations for at least the near term. In essence, the venture has successfully navigated the legitimacy threshold (LT) and is thus able to shift its attention to more traditional performance metrics, such as revenue and profitability targets. Whereas this is clearly a positive development for the entrepreneur, it does pose new issues. It is these issues that will be addressed here.

The Legitimacy Threshold

The LT is the point at which a new venture has acquired a base level of legitimacy that allows the firm access to the resources it needs to survive and grow. Successful navigation of the LT has been accomplished when the firm has been granted initial legitimacy, which is a judgment of appropriateness and viability, by at least one key stakeholder. The granting of initial legitimacy to a new venture is signaled to the market by the provision of tangible resources, such as cash, by the stakeholder to the

For new ventures to survive and to prove legitimacy, the focus must reach beyond the issue of cash flow to include actions like attaining patents, completing market research, and making sales, and their achievements must be communicated to potential investors. (Photos.com)

firm. Therefore, a new venture cannot take or claim legitimacy. Rather, successful navigation of the LT is only accomplished when the venture is granted legitimacy by resource-providing stakeholders.

New ventures can be broadly classified as either pre-threshold or post-threshold. Since pre-threshold ventures have not yet reached the business milestones necessary to convince potential stakeholders of their market viability, such ventures will be in a daily fight for survival. Conversely, given that post-threshold firms have been granted a social judgment of acceptance by stakeholders, such ventures will be able to shift their focus from survival to the accomplishment of long-term strategic objectives.

Performance Metrics and the LT

Firm performance is a multidimensional construct that can be measured according to various criteria, including survival, profitability, growth, customer satisfaction, and achievement of important business milestones. Whether or not a firm has successfully navigated the LT will significantly alter which of these metrics are utilized to assess firm performance. As noted, successfully navigating the LT requires a new firm to be judged as viable by at least one significant stakeholder. Such stakeholders will grant legitimacy based on an assessment of both the entrepreneur operating the venture and the market offering that the venture intends to provide. Therefore, assessing the performance of pre-threshold ventures will focus primarily on verifying the business milestones that the venture has accomplished. Whereas business milestones that may convince a stakeholder to grant legitimacy will vary by firm, examples may include attaining patent protection, developing a prototype, acquiring needed licenses, conducting test-marketing, and achieving a first sale. Stakeholders will assess performance in pre-threshold ventures via the accomplishment of business milestones because financial performance metrics will be of little value, given the limited resource base of such ventures.

Conversely, a post-threshold venture has accomplished enough business milestones that at least one stakeholder has provided the firm with tangible resources. Given that stakeholders desire a return on their investment, financial performance metrics such as revenue growth, sales targets, and profitability will likely be the main tool used to evaluate the performance of post-threshold firms.

Implications for Entrepreneurs

The notion that the LT will likely determine the metrics used to evaluate the performance of newly established firms suggests that entrepreneurs both must be aware of the LT and must act in accordance with their firm's LT status. Since pre-threshold ventures will be judged by accomplishment of business milestones, entrepreneurs operating such ventures must work diligently to accomplish market milestones and signal such accomplishments to potential stakeholders. First and foremost, of course, new ventures must survive, so a focus on cash flow is paramount. However, actions such as attaining a patent, completion of market research, and a first sale have to be accomplished, and their achievement must become known to interested investors. Furthermore, successful navigation of the LT will likely also require entrepreneurs to isomorph (mimic) certain aspects of post-legitimate ventures. Thus, entrepreneurs will want to communicate a sense of appropriateness to the stakeholder by appearing professional, designing effective brochures, securing suitable office space, establishing a legal entity, and completing a business plan. It is significant that many of these can be accomplished pre-start-up.

Two caveats should be addressed. First, when mimicking established ventures, entrepreneurs must also maintain distinctiveness in their core competencies. Second, they must be aware of the temptation to be dishonest. It is likely that potential stakeholders would both discover any dishonesty through their due diligence and spread the word about such practices.

Alternatively, entrepreneurs operating post-threshold ventures must shift their concerns from resource acquisition to effectively managing the firm's resource base. Accordingly, such entrepreneurs will need to focus on the concerns of all significant stakeholder groups in an effort to increase growth and profitability. Actions such as personnel management, customer service, internal controls, and contingency planning will become crucial for post-threshold ventures. Finally, entrepreneurs operating legitimate ventures also need to realize that they have significantly more power than entrepreneurs operating pre-threshold firms. The provision of resources by a stakeholder to a venture indicates that the stakeholder believes the firm possesses a valuable market offering. This fact provides the entrepreneur increased power.

This brief discussion of the LT's influence on use of performance metrics clearly articulates the critical actions that entrepreneurs should take as their young firms develop. Prior to being granted legitimacy, entrepreneurs must focus nearly all their attention on accomplishing market milestones that will convince customers and financiers of their firm's legitimacy. However, once the firm is legitimized, entrepreneurs must quickly shift their attention to the accomplishment of long-term strategic and financial objectives. Therefore, entrepreneurs' ability to modify their managerial styles across the LT will enhance their chances to operate thriving ventures.

Neil Tocher
Idaho State University
Matthew W. Rutherford
Virginia Commonwealth University

See also Gender and Performance; Human Capital Theory; Learning Theory; Measures of Performance; Psychological Views

Further Readings

Aldrich, H. E. and M. A. Martinez. "Many Are Called, but Few Are Chosen: An Evolutionary Perspective for the Study of Entrepreneurship." *Entrepreneurship Theory and Practice*, v.25/4 (2001).

Delmar, F. and S. Shane. "Legitimating First: Organizing Activities and the Survival of New Ventures." *Journal of Business Venturing*, v.19/3 (2004).

Rutherford, M. W. and P. F. Buller. "Searching for the Legitimacy Threshold." *Journal of Management Inquiry*, v.16/1 (2007).

Tornikoski, E. T. and S. L. Newbert. "Exploring the Determinants of Organizational Emergence: A Legitimacy Perspective." *Journal of Business Venturing*, v.22/2 (2007).

Zimmerman, M. A. and G. J. Zeitz. "Beyond Survival: Achieving New Venture Growth by Building Legitimacy." *Academy of Management Review*, v.27/3 (2002).

PLANNING FALLACY

The planning fallacy is a cognitive bias that may lead entrepreneurs to underestimate the time or resources needed to complete tasks, resulting in overly optimistic predictions. This bias was first discussed by Daniel Kahneman and Amos Tversky, who argued that decision makers often focus on internal or controllable factors when making these predictions. A key component of this bias is that, in spite of knowing that predicted completion times tend to be overly optimistic, individuals focus on specific elements of the task, discounting the likelihood of external or unexpected delays. Entrepreneurs might be more susceptible to this bias, given their optimistic perceptions of risk as well as situational pressures commonly found with new ventures. Although strategies such as breaking projects into smaller pieces when making estimates may improve accuracy, it is difficult to completely avoid this bias. Inaccurate or overly optimistic estimates may have costly consequences, including goal conflict or even the failure of a new venture. It is therefore important that entrepreneurs realistically evaluate new opportunities.

The planning fallacy is commonly found to apply to a wide range of tasks, ranging from extremely short and simple tasks, such as buying groceries, to complex and novel tasks, such as the Boston's Central Artery/Tunnel Project (the "Big Dig") or the construction of the Sydney Opera House. Ambiguous, dynamic, and high-risk projects, such as new ventures, may be more likely to result in unrealistic predictions. In a series of experiments, Roger Buehler, Dale Griffin, and Michael Ross argued that, even though individuals may repeatedly underestimate completion times, in part the planning fallacy can be conceptualized as the belief that *this* time it will be different. Their research demonstrated that even "worst case" predictions for completion time were still overly optimistic. However, they also acknowledged that individuals were less likely to miss external deadlines than to miss their predicted completion times.

There is no clear consensus on the cognitive mechanism driving the planning fallacy. Kahneman and Tversky suggested that an internal focus on specific task elements under the individual's control

The planning fallacy, or the tendency to underestimate time or resources needed to complete tasks, can occur when predicting the time to complete anything from simple tasks to complex and novel projects like the Sydney Opera House. The Sydney structure cost almost $100 million more than estimated in 1953 (when a competition for designs of the opera house was launched) and ended up taking 10 years longer than the projected finish date of 1963. (Wikimedia/Anthony Winning)

(ignoring external or unexpected factors) could help explain the planning fallacy. Another possible cause might involve the uncertainty related to unseen pitfalls or abstract tasks. Robert Baron argued that factors like the high pressure, novelty, risk, and uncertainty inherent in starting an innovative new business might make entrepreneurs more likely to show the planning fallacy. Additionally, starting new ventures involves a future-oriented focus that might lead entrepreneurs to discount the relevance of past experiences.

However, other explanations have been proposed. An optimistic prediction could be a tool for favorable self-presentation or a self-serving bias similar to the overconfidence effect. Entrepreneurs are argued to be more optimistic than others and may perceive opportunities as having more potential benefit and less risk; this could increase the planning fallacy. Additionally, time-perception research shows that we anticipate more slack time in the distant future and that we are willing to commit to projects based on this assumed free time. This might lead the entrepreneur to overcommit or fail to prioritize which tasks can be completed in the available time.

Even when the bias emerges, there may be some instances when it has positive consequences. Roger

Buehler and his colleagues demonstrated that, at least under some circumstances, the optimistic predictions that emerge might serve as goals and actually reduce completion times. Although there are clear costs associated with inaccurate estimates for completing projects, in some cases this cognitive bias may be helpful in initiating work on projects, much as goals or deadlines can motivate task-related behaviors. Furthermore, the differences in how entrepreneurs and nonentrepreneurs evaluate opportunities may be fundamental in explaining who starts new ventures. Much as self-serving biases may protect the ego, it may be that a rosy view of potential opportunities might be needed for entrepreneurs to launch new endeavors.

However, unrealistic optimism is also linked to many negative business outcomes, including potential failures of new ventures. Several strategies might help entrepreneurs avoid the planning fallacy and improve the accuracy of predictions. Justin Kruger and Matt Evans asked individuals to "unpack" a larger task by listing the requisite subtasks prior to making their predictions for how long the task would take. Unpacking and other strategies of breaking tasks into required subcomponents seem to increase accuracy of overall completion rates, but these approaches do not appear to come naturally to individuals. These strategies may require extensive cognitive effort that is unlikely to occur without explicit prompting. However, time management research and systems do rely on elements such as breaking up tasks to increase productivity and meet deadlines; such systems may help entrepreneurs implement this de-biasing tactic.

Other promising de-biasing approaches involve a concrete focus on the actual completion time of similar projects, whether completed by the individual or by others. Unfortunately, individuals appear to minimize the possibility of external distractions or delays. Entrepreneurs may not see the relevance of prior efforts or may feel there are no comparable situations on which to draw, especially with innovative projects. If there is no related project on which to base estimates, the entrepreneur might try drawing references from other industries or focus on commonly required project components (such as securing permits or funding) when making estimates. Another strategy to focus on concrete elements of the task involves asking entrepreneurs to focus on when and how the subtasks will actually be implemented and identify which aspects of the time line might be outside the entrepreneur's control.

Entrepreneurs need to recognize the likelihood that they will make overly optimistic predictions for project completion and realize that their focus on the upside and uniqueness of an opportunity might blind them to past experiences that could improve their planning. Deliberately unpacking the project, discovering relevant past experiences, and tempering optimism with realism can help individuals avoid the costs associated with the planning fallacy as they launch new ventures.

Amy C. Lewis
Drury University

See also Cognition; Goal Setting; Time Management

Further Readings

Baron, Robert. "Cognitive Mechanisms in Entrepreneurship: Why and When Entrepreneurs Think Differently Than Other People." *Journal of Business Venturing*, v.13 (1998).

Buehler, Roger, Dale Griffin, and Michael Ross. "Exploring the 'Planning Fallacy': Why People Underestimate Their Task Completion Times." *Journal of Personality and Social Psychology*, v.67/3 (1994).

Kahneman, Daniel and Dan Lovallo. "Timid Choices and Bold Forecasts: A Cognitive Perspective on Risk Taking." In *Fundamental Issues in Strategy: A Research Agenda*, R. P. Rumelt, D. E. Schendel, and D. J. Teece, eds. Boston: Harvard Business School Press, 1994.

Kahneman, Daniel and Amos Tversky. "Intuitive Prediction: Biases and Corrective Procedures." *TIMS Studies in Management Science*, v.12 (1979).

Keh, Hean Tat, Maw Der Foo, and Boon Chong Lim. "Opportunity Evaluation Under Risky Conditions: The Cognitive Processes of Entrepreneurs." *Entrepreneurship Theory and Practice*, v. 27/2 (Winter 2002).

Kruger, Justin and Matt Evans. "If You Don't Want to Be Late, Enumerate: Unpacking Reduces the Planning Fallacy." *Journal of Experimental Social Psychology*, v.40 (2004).

POLITICAL ECONOMY AND ENTREPRENEURSHIP

Understanding entrepreneurship is much more complicated than a domestic business approach because countries differ in many ways. Each country has varying political, economic, and legal systems, just as cultural practices may vary. Hence, political economy has been at the heart of entrepreneurship since its outset, as political economy offers a rewarding approach to entrepreneurship. The political economy approach is indeed necessary in order to understand how the political system shapes the institutional setup.

A significant number of development economists, including Ricardo Hausmann and Dani Rodrik, have proposed the idea that the key obstacle to economic growth in less developed countries (LDCs) stems from the very insufficient level of entrepreneurship. This problem supposedly arises because markets do not generate adequate incentives to reward entrepreneurship. Thus, entrepreneurship is seen as having some "public good" characteristics. Hausmann and Rodrik have focused in particular on a new type of entrepreneurship-related externality that prevents the market from working efficiently, which is the "information externality."

It has been asserted that exploiting new business opportunities has had considerable positive externalities for other entrepreneurs, who can learn about the profitability of certain ventures and can hence act accordingly. This means that entrepreneurship will be undersupplied and that government should correct market failure, through providing proper incentives in order to reach the optimal level of entrepreneurship.

However, according to economist Bogdan Glavan, the information externality in entrepreneurship theory justly argues that the social benefits arising from entrepreneurial actions are greater than the private gains. Consequently, entrepreneurs who discover profit opportunities signal to other entrepreneurs an efficient path of investments, and the latter can imitate the former acting upon this information. Moreover, market failure to internalize this information externality creates a very useful role for the state, which can then provide adequate incentives, such as subsidizing investment in new projects.

However, Glavan criticizes the claim that entrepreneurship presents positive externalities that prevent the optimal allocation of resources. He stipulates that despite the supposed discovery of new market failures, the case for government intervention is no better at the present than it was decades ago. He also contends that Austrian economists Hausmann and Rodrik have addressed the issues regarding the relation between entrepreneurship and development, and successfully answered the argument that government policy can improve market outcomes.

Magnus Henrekson and Robin Douhan identified three key aspects of entrepreneurship as it relates to political economy. First, entrepreneurship is dynamic in the sense that it adapts to the politically determined institutional framework within which it acts. Under propitious circumstances, it can be a powerful engine of growth, but it can also be channeled in unproductive and destructive directions. Second, entrepreneurship enters directly into the political system. The close connection to property rights constitutes a link between entrepreneurship and private versus public ownership and redistribution. Under unfavorable institutional circumstances, rent-seeking and predatory entrepreneurship, via the political system, offer greater profit opportunities than the market. Third, a political economy approach is necessary in order to understand how the political system shapes the institutional setup. Here, it is emphasized that the distribution of political power is partly determined by economic wealth. Hence, it is relevant to broaden the analysis to the effects on wealth creation and wealth redistribution stemming from entrepreneurial activity.

However, according to Alberto Alesina and Rodrik, the distribution of political power is in fact partly determined by economic wealth. Hence, entrepreneurship is likewise associated with all profit-driven business, that is, wealth creation activities. However, even if the entrepreneur has been frequently regarded as the key figure in the capitalist system, economic sciences have for a long time overlooked the entrepreneur in their analyses of growth.

Other authors, such as economists Peter Boettke and Christopher Coyne, have argued that entrepreneurship is essentially the consequence of economic growth, while institutions are the sole cause. However, entrepreneurial actions very often sway politically determined institutions. Simply said, commercial entrepreneurship can be largely hampered or facilitated by institutions.

Entrepreneurial talent can also be redirected through institutions and can even be unproductive or destructive. However, and according to the public choice school, the reason is that entrepreneurs do not always respond passively to institutions and can directly or indirectly work to alter them. Economists such as Rafael La Porta and colleagues have noted that when faced, for instance, with a prospect of differentially unfavorable tax treatment by government, a person or a group may engage in lobbying efforts, may engage directly in politics to secure access to decision-making power, or may make plans to shift into or out of the affected activity.

There is also a strong association between entrepreneurship and the production system assumed in the small business literature. Moreover, economist Douglass North features the entrepreneur as an agent of institutional change. However, the notion becomes increasingly broad when the entrepreneur is no longer regarded primarily as an agent with unique productive capacities, but rather as an agent of change in general. Consequently, the entrepreneur becomes the key agent in any economic system governed by political institutions.

Moreover, we move away from standard equilibrium analysis by positing that the existence of economic rents is an inherent trait of a dynamic economy. Entrepreneurs are the agents who create rents but who can also find ways to appropriate rents from others. In order to appropriate, rather than create, rents, entrepreneurs must interact with institutions, according to Alberto Chong and César Calderon.

These kinds of entrepreneurship involve some innovative ways of influencing the institutions or an innovation that substitutes for malfunctioning institutions, such as a new contractual form. Furthermore, in the context of institutions, a welfare analysis must be related to an optimal institutional arrangement. A proper analysis of institutions and entrepreneurship cannot focus only on how institutions channel entrepreneurs into more or less productive activities. It must also account for how the more unproductive activities change institutions, with an optimal institutional arrangement as the relevant benchmark.

David Daokui Li and colleagues defined an entrepreneur according to a set of talents. However, there is no consensus about the exact nature of these talents, with some scholars emphasizing cognitive abilities and others pointing to motivational characteristics. In fact, entrepreneurial talent makes an individual more perceptive and more dynamic; it therefore includes both motivation and ability. The entrepreneur is apt to recognize opportunities and prone to take action in response. These actions yield an expected return that exceeds the risk-adjusted market rate of return—that is, an economic rent.

While there will always be a broad definition of the entrepreneur, there will also always be an emphasis on the distinction between actually being an entrepreneur and simply engaging in entrepreneurial activities.

Djamel Eddine Laouisset
Alhosn University, Abu Dhabi

See also Capitalism; Change; Community/Government Buy-Ins; Entrepreneurial Support Systems

Further Readings

Acemoglu, Daron, Simon Johnson, and Robinson James. "Institutions as the Fundamental Cause of Long-Run Growth." In *Handbook of Economic Growth*, Philippe Aghion and Steven Durlauf, eds. Amsterdam: North-Holland, 2005.

Alesina, Alberto and Dani Rodrik. "Distributive Politics and Economic Growth." *Quarterly Journal of Economics*, v.109/2 (1994).

Boettke, Peter and Christopher Coyne. "Entrepreneurship and Development: Cause or Consequence?" *Advances in Austrian Economics*, v.6 (2003).

Chong, Alberto and César Calderon. "Causality and Feedback Between Institutional Measures and Economic Growth." *Economics and Politics*, v.12/1 (2000).

Daokui Li, David, Junxin Feng, and Hongping Jiang. "Institutional Entrepreneurs." *American Economic Review*, v.96/2 (2006).

Glavan, Bogdan. "Entrepreneurship, Externalities and Development: An Austrian Critique of the Hausmann-Rodrik New Argument for Industrial Policy." *New Perspectives on Political Economy*, v.3/1 (2007).

Hausmann, Ricardo and Dani Rodrik. "Economic Development as Self-Discovery." *Journal of Development Economics* v. 72/2 (2003).

Henrekson, Magnus and Robin Douhan. *The Political Economy of Entrepreneurship*. Northampton, MA: Edward Elgar, 2007.

Hill, Charles W. L. *Global Business Today*, 7th ed. New York: McGraw-Hill/Irwin, 2010.

La Porta, Rafael, Florencio Lopez-De-Silanes, Andrei Shleifer, and Robert Vishny. "The Quality of Government." *Journal of Law, Economics and Organizations*, v.15/1 (1999).

North, Douglass C. *Institutions, Institutional Change and Economic Performance*. Cambridge, UK: Cambridge University Press, 1990.

Ricardo, David. *Principles of Political Economy and Taxation*. Reprint, New York: Cosimo, 2006.

Stigler, George J. "The Theory of Economic Regulation." *Bell Journal of Economics and Management Science*, v.2/1 (1971).

Wennekers, Sander and Roy Thurik. "Linking Entrepreneurship and Economic Growth." *Small Business Economics*, v.13/1 (1999).

Yu, Tony Fu-Lai. "An Entrepreneurial Perspective of Institutional Change." *Constitutional Political Economy*, v.12/3 (2001).

POSITIONING A NEW PRODUCT OR SERVICE

Effective product positioning deals with product or service differentiation that is intended to win customers' hearts and minds in times of marketing new products or services. Moreover, positioning products or services starts, first of all, with defining marketing segmentation and then understanding target market values.

In essence, a positioning strategy should focus on and align with the product differentiation strategy. The product or service should be somehow unique, better, economical, profitable for the market, or else have some distinctive criteria that will differentiate it from the other available products and services. However, these points of differentiation must be important and valued by the customers themselves; it is said that "beauty lies in the eyes of the beholder."

Indeed, whenever the entrepreneur introduces a new product, the new product plan needs to be focused on differentiation and positioning strategies and tactics. Moreover, positioning products needs to be focused on delivering a valued and distinctive product to a specific market and delivering it in a way that customers can accept. Hence, good product positioning will make it easy for the intended customers to define why, exactly, they want to buy that product.

Customers have an image of brands based on their experience, their perception of the brand, and their understanding of the product benefits. That positive or negative image will determine whether or not they will buy the product and how much they will be ready to pay for it. Therefore, we can appreciate why pricing strategy is an important part of positioning.

In summary, product positioning involves tailoring a whole marketing program, which needs to include product attributes, image, and price, as well as packaging, distribution, and service, so as to best meet the needs of consumers within a particular market segment. Hence, product positioning is a component of the broad process of market segmentation but obviously entails a narrowing of focus. According to Glen L. Urban and Steven H. Star, "Product positioning takes place within a target market segment and tells us how we can compete most effectively in that market segment. Segmentation analysis tells us how the market is defined and allows us to target one or more opportunities."

Six steps that companies should take in the market segmentation process were identified by Alexander Hiam and Charles Schewe in their book *The Portable MBA in Marketing*. The first step is to determine the boundaries of the market. In completing this step, a marketer should use a formal business plan to develop a broad definition of the business and then consider the offerings of both direct and indirect competitors to gain information about the basic needs of consumers in the market. The second step is to decide which variables to use in segmenting the market. Many companies collect data on many variables and then attempt to draw meaningful conclusions. Instead, Hiam and Schewe recommend that marketers use their market knowledge to select only relevant variables. The third step is actually collecting and analyzing data, which involves applying market research tools. The goal in analyzing the data is to identify market segments that are internally homogeneous but distinctly heterogeneous with respect to other segments. The fourth step is to develop a detailed profile of each market segment, which involves selecting those variables that are most closely related to consumers' actual buying behavior. The fifth step is to decide which segment or segments to serve. In targeting a particular segment, marketers should look for opportunities (that is, customers with unsatisfied wants and needs) that provide a good match for the organization and its resources. It is important that the marketer consider not only the size and potential profitability of a market segment but also whether the venture's skills, technologies, and objectives would enable it to meet the needs of that segment better than its competitors. Product positioning, which is the sixth and final step in the market segmentation process, involves developing a product and marketing plan that will appeal to the selected market segment.

In order to position a product effectively, a venture must identify the attributes that are most important to consumers in the segment and then develop an overall marketing strategy that will attract consumers' attention. Positioning should be applied during the earliest stages of product design, when a venture first identifies who its target customer will be in terms of demographic, geographic, and behavioral characteristics.

Marketers have several different positioning options available to them. One positioning option is quality emphasis, a zero-defect product with a product design and customer service that meet or exceed customer expectations. Another positioning option available to marketers involves offering unique features or benefits that consumers are unable to find in competing products. Ideally, such features and benefits grow out of the venture's unique sources of competitive advantage in the marketplace. This will make it difficult for competitors to match the features and benefits without incurring high costs. According to Urban and Star, "If we develop a unique competitive advantage on a dimension of importance to a significant portion of the market, we can enjoy a substantial share and high margins."

Above all, it is important to remember that continued market research and innovation are necessary to maintain such a competitive advantage.

Djamel Eddine Laouisset
Alhosn University, Abu Dhabi

See also Advertising; Branding; Change Management: Corporate; Innovation Management; Market Evaluation; New Product Development; Selling Products and Services

Further Readings

Gruenwald, George. *New Product Development: Responding to Market Demand*. Lincolnwood, IL: NTC Publishing, 1992.

Hiam, Alexander and Charles Schewe. *The Portable MBA in Marketing*. New York: Wiley, 1992.

McCarthy, Jerome and William Perreault. *Basic Marketing*. New York: Irwin McGraw-Hill, 1990.

Ries, Al and Jack Trout. *Positioning: The Battle for Your Mind*. New York: McGraw-Hill, 1981.

Trout, Jack. "Positioning." *Industrial Marketing*, v.54/6 (June 1969).

Trout, Jack and Steve Rivkin. *The New Positioning*. New York: McGraw-Hill, 1996.

Urban, Glen and Steven Star. *Advanced Marketing Strategy*. Englewood Cliffs, NJ: Prentice Hall, 1991.

PRODUCT INNOVATION

Product innovation is defined, according to the *Oslo Manual* by the Organisation for Economic Co-operation and Development (OECD) and Eurostat, as "the introduction of a good or service that is new or significantly improved with respect to its characteristics or intended uses," including "significant improvements in technical specifications, components and materials, incorporated software, user friendliness or other functional characteristics." Certain changes are excluded from the notion of product innovation, namely, very minor changes or improvements, routine upgrades, regular seasonal changes, and customizations for a single client that are nevertheless similar to products made for other clients. The definition appears overall to be self-evident; however, the multifaceted nature of innovation in products has become a major concern for theorists, policy makers, managers, and employees within organizations. The many facets of product innovation include its relationship to other kinds of innovation and its overall placement within a taxonomy of innovation, the question of the extent and scope of a particular innovation, and the question of whether a product innovation is major (or "radical") versus minor (or "incremental").

Within the current taxonomy of innovations, there is a differentiation between product innovation and process innovation. Process innovation can be related to production in the case of manufacturing or to delivery or operations within both manufacturing and other sectors. Production-related process innovation includes, for example, the installation of new or improved manufacturing technologies, whereas the introduction of bar coding is an example of delivery or operations process innovation. In contrast, product innovations may be goods such as textiles with different characteristics compared to previous ones. In recent years, for example, we have seen the advent of textiles that are able to "breathe" as well as textiles that are simultaneously very light and very strong. Other examples of product innovations are biodegradable plastics and equally environmentally friendly printing inks made from biological materials rather than synthetic chemicals. Within

consumer electronics, product innovation has been dramatic, with the introduction of such products as global positioning systems (GPS) in transport equipment, mobile phones with integrated cameras and other functions, energy-saving functions integrated into products such as refrigerators and other household appliances, laptops with inbuilt wireless networking, and Internet protocol telephones. Other sectors that have recently produced a high number of product innovations include the food industry, with foodstuffs containing different ingredients targeted at health benefits, and improved pharmaceuticals addressing conditions from depression to high cholesterol.

Whereas these examples appear relatively clear-cut, it is not always easy to draw such distinctions in practice. Services constitute a prime example in this regard, since an innovation in a service industry, such as the automated teller machine (ATM), can constitute a product or a process innovation, depending on the perspective one takes. The *Oslo Manual* attempts to provide the following guidelines for distinguishing between different types of innovations: A process innovation involves improved methods, equipment, and/or skills used when performing or delivering an existing service, whereas product innovation for services involves new or significantly improved characteristics of the service itself. If the innovation involves both of these aspects at the same time, then it is both a product and a process innovation. Within new ventures, such as biotechnology ventures, one may also find the line between product and process innovations to be blurry. The product under development may, at the same time as it is a product innovation, constitute a process innovation when the product is, for example, a method or equipment intended for further application within the production process.

Nevertheless, within management theory the main point and practical implication of drawing the distinction between product and process innovation is the assumption that the management of the processes leading toward each type of innovation has to be handled differently. Kathryn Cormican and David O'Sullivan note that the complex management challenges leading toward successful product innovation involve a continuous and cross-functional process that involves and even integrates a growing number of different competencies. Management of the process necessitates successful adoption and adaptation of a "sociotechnical systems approach" to all aspects of the organization, including people and processes as well as technology-related issues. Managers, in other words, must consider tools and procedures as well as individuals and teams when managing product innovation.

Another issue that has been the focus of much attention is the question of how one may determine the extent or scope of a product innovation. There are certain techniques for checking on a global scale whether something is genuinely new or not; however, these methods rely on patenting and trademark information. If one confines the concept of innovation to tangible and intangible things that are introduced into and subsequently in circulation within the economy, the measurement method based on the mentioned sources may cover cases that do not proceed past the patent or trademark stage and subsequently do not result in an actual innovation. On the other hand, if one wants to determine whether the prospective or actual innovation is genuinely new, the data collection and assessment work implied would be overwhelming. Researchers such as Elko J. Kleinschmidt and Robert G. Cooper have pointed to the phenomenon of human cognitive processes and the possible difference between innovativeness according to objective criteria and innovation based on subjective criteria. The *Oslo Manual* has also acknowledged the problem and proposes three types of innovation, irrespective of whether they are products or processes. Apart from an innovation new to the form, one type of innovation is an innovation that is new to the market. The market is in this context simply defined as the firm and its competitors, and it can include either a geographic region or a product line. The notion of the market is thus according to the firm's own view and can be of a regional, domestic, or international character. However, an innovation is new to the world when the firm is the first to introduce the innovation for all markets and industries, domestic and international. A "new to the world" innovation is an innovation that has, qualitatively speaking, a greater degree of novelty than a "new to the firm" or a "new to the market" innovation.

This way of classifying innovation is by no means any solution to the problem. There is still no technique to verify that the innovation is indeed new to the world. In the international and comparative measurement of actual innovations, there has

thus been a need for circumventing the subjective-versus-objective dilemma, if one does not want to rely on the patent or trademark information as a proxy for innovativeness. The method that has been applied within survey research (such as the European Community Innovation Survey) is to follow the distinctions described above and actually ask firm representatives whether the innovative output can be classified as new to the firm, new to the market, or new to the world innovation. The *Oslo Manual* contends that many such surveys find that questions on "new to the market" are sufficient in order to examine the degree of novelty for innovations, and that "new to the world" questions alternatively provide an option when one wishes to examine novelty in greater detail. Indeed, these methods still leave much room for interpretation, but they constitute a means of distinguishing between local innovations that are not innovations in the real sense and innovations that at least the firms themselves think are new to the market.

A final aspect that has been the focus of considerable debate relates to the somewhat vague formulation concerning "significant improvement" within the cited as well as within other and similar definitions of product innovation. At one level, the formulation allows for instinctive understanding of the need for a product to include some kind of fundamental change in order to classify it as a product innovation, and (as mentioned above) there have also been formulated some exceptions to the product innovation definition consisting of minuscule improvements or adaptations. At another level, however, the vague formulation makes it possible to discuss a further differentiation between different types of product innovation. The predominant way of formulating this distinction is based on Joseph Schumpeter's work. He distinguished between major, or "radical," product innovations, on one hand, and minor, or "incremental," innovations, on the other hand. The former type is "an innovation that has a significant impact on a market and on the economic activity of firms in that market" as defined in the *Oslo Manual*, whereas the latter continuously advances the process of change. The concept thus focuses on the impact of the innovation rather than its inherent degree of novelty. The product innovation may be minor but have a great impact as the result of either foreseen or unforeseen circumstances. The impact can, for example, change the structure of the market, create new markets, or even make existing products obsolete. However, sometimes it is not possible to decide whether an innovation was disruptive or not until long after it has been introduced.

Again the distinction may have severe management implications. There is at one level always a strong imperative for fostering innovation, but the fostering of radical innovations entails a very risky development for a firm, since it involves entering into a market that is more insecure than usual. This strategy also may entail the destruction of existing competencies within the firm and the need for new ones. On the other hand, the successive launch of incremental innovations enhances the existing competencies. This "safe" strategy does, however, entail the risk of becoming too set in well-known patterns of operation. Clayton M. Christensen has illuminated the mechanism whereby the incumbent organization pursuing a strategy of incremental (or "sustaining," as he calls it) product innovations sometimes will be ambushed by a disruptive innovation that completely wipes out the existing business niche. Examples from the past include disruptors and "disruptees," such as cellular phones versus fixed-line telephony, discount retailers versus full-service department stores, and retail medical clinics versus traditional doctors' offices.

Terje Grønning
University of Oslo

See also Geography of Innovation; Innovation Diffusion; Innovation Management: Corporate; Innovation Processes; New Product Development; Radical and Incremental Innovation

Further Readings

Christensen, Clayton M. *The Innovator's Dilemma*. Cambridge, MA: Harvard Business School Press, 1997.

Cormican, Kathryn and David O'Sullivan. "Auditing Best Practice for Effective Product Innovation Management." *Technovation*, v.24 (2004).

Kleinschmidt, Elko J. and Robert G. Cooper. "The Relative Importance of New Product Success Determinants: Perception Versus Reality." *R&D Management*, v.25/3 (1995).

Organisation for Economic Co-operation and Development and Eurostat. *Oslo Manual: Guidelines for Collecting and Interpreting Innovation Data*, 3rd ed. Paris: Author, 2005.

Utterback, James. *Mastering the Dynamics of Innovation*. Cambridge, MA: Harvard Business School Press, 1996.

PSYCHOLOGICAL VIEWS

The field of psychology is diverse, with possible specializations including clinical, child, and educational psychology, to name just a few. Many of the fields of psychology have limited relevance to new ventures. However, there is one division of this varied science that can be a particularly valuable resource for individuals starting new businesses. Industrial-organizational (I-O) psychology is a business-oriented field of psychology that submits the various aspects of organizational life to scientific scrutiny to better understand the behavior of individuals in organizations. An understanding of I-O psychology can be a powerful tool for building a successful business. Its findings are represented under many names, including personnel psychology, organizational psychology, human resources, organizational behavior, organizational science, and work psychology. It is a data-driven, researched-based field concerned with the science of people in organizations. The science-based foundation of I-O psychology makes it a valuable asset, as research is conducted to answer many questions about successful organizations that would take a great deal of time and expense for individual organizations to explore.

I-O psychologists study all aspects of human attitudes and behavior as they relate to work, including concepts like the characteristics of people that make them good employees, the interactions between people of differing power levels, and ways to identify good leaders. I-O psychology covers every facet of organizational life as it relates to employees, including selection, training, leadership, motivation, and executive coaching.

All organizations can benefit from I-O psychology. Setting human resource policies according to psychological principles can lead to reduced costs and improved efficiency across organizational departments. For example, hiring practices based on systematic assessments of both the job and the applicant can lead to reduced training costs and less turnover. I-O psychology has demonstrated that hunches and gut feelings of hiring managers generally do not predict future job performance well. Poor hiring practices, such as hiring an individual based on feelings about applicants, will result in an idiosyncratic decision-making process that is no better at predicting performance than random chance. This means that in many organizations, managers make hiring decisions that are as valuable for the company's bottom line as flipping a coin. Individuals hired in this manner will most likely require extensive training to perform adequately, which will mean more money spent on trainers, fewer manhours devoted to actually doing the job, and costly mistakes by underqualified employees. Hiring individuals based on whims instead of empirically tested concepts means that these individuals will be put into positions they are not qualified for and are likely to quit or be terminated. This wastes the organization's time and money. Conversely, using scientifically proven techniques means hiring individuals whose skills and experience match the job, resulting in less training time and a better chance of success for the applicant. I-O psychology describes methods and techniques by which job performance can be modeled, such that the knowledge, skills, abilities, and other characteristics (KSAOs) vital to success can be systematically identified and targeted in the selection process.

This value-added effect, facilitated by the use of psychology, can be applied to almost every facet of organizational life. Training can be more efficient. Systematically targeting individuals who need training and targeting the KSAOs that are directly relevant to job performance will increase employees' productivity efficiently and enhance the bottom line at the least expense. Furthermore, collecting applicants' perceptions of the value of training as well as objectively measuring the impact of training will ensure that training programs are maximizing their impact on learning. Organizational leaders can utilize psychological principles by understanding when to use certain behaviors. For example, participative management, where employees participate in management decisions, leads to increased employee buy-in for company change initiatives. Often, implementing organizational change is hindered by a lack of employee support. The bigger the changes, the more employees are fearful and reluctant to get behind them, even when it is obvious that changes are necessary. Without the full thrust of everyone's effort, these initiatives are likely to fail. Employees may even say that they are behind the changes but in fact either actively or passively act against

them. Getting employees' input and including them in the planning makes them more likely to want the new initiatives to succeed. Their participation in the change process can allay their anxieties and make meaningful changes more likely.

One of the most popular concepts in I-O psychology that can improve the day-to-day functioning of a new venture is justice theory. This theory describes the optimal method by which fairness is understood by employees, which can have many applications for manager-employee relationships. Justice is broken down into three categories. Distributive justice refers to employee perceptions of the fairness of the size or value of rewards or punishments they receive. For example, an employee might have a negative feeling of distributive justice if he finds out that he makes less money than one of his coworkers. Procedural justice refers to employee perceptions about how rewards and punishments are determined. Interactional justice refers to the degree to which reward and punishment decisions are communicated accurately and with compassion to employees. Studies in justice have revealed that procedural and interactional justice is critical to how employees react as a result of changes in distributive justice. For example, management might institute a new policy to treat employees more fairly, but if they do not communicate that fact accurately to the employees, employee retention and performance are unlikely to improve. Conversely, if management must make temporary pay cuts in response to a poor economy, employees are more likely to reduce their day-to-day efforts on the job and also to engage in petty theft, because they feel they are being treated unfairly. However, evidence from studies of justice theory indicate that this effect can be reduced by making a concentrated effort at improving interactional justice by explaining the reason for the pay cuts clearly and with compassion. Simply assuming employees will understand the reason for treatment that seems unfair to them is not sufficient. This is just one example of the specific recommendations that I-O psychology provides for the good of organizations.

In addition to informing human resource strategy, I-O psychology has investigated the characteristics that make entrepreneurs successful. The entrepreneur is perhaps the most important person in a new venture because she is responsible for initial creation of the policies, direction, and culture of the business. It is leadership more than anything else that can determine whether the venture succeeds or fails. In short, superior leaders can be the competitive advantage that sets a business apart. Conscientiousness is likely to be one important psychological attribute for entrepreneurs. Individuals who are conscientious may be described as consistent, reliable, ambitious, and achievement-oriented. The leader of a new venture is likely to be forming new relationships with a number of stakeholders, including clients, vendors, and customers. Whereas these relationships are still developing, these groups will be making a number of judgments about the competency of the new business and its leader to determine whether or not they provide a quality product and are worth doing business with. If a new company misses promised deadlines or makes a product of inconsistent quality, these new relationships are not likely to last. It is also important for new entrepreneurs to possess a great deal of ambition and be oriented toward achievement. Whereas this trait might be assumed of anyone who starts a new business, it is important to make explicit. The owner or leader of a new business must seek out ways to succeed, not simply wait for opportunities to present themselves. When opportunities do arise, achievement-oriented individuals set goals and pursue them relentlessly.

Openness to experience is another important psychological attribute possessed by successful entrepreneurs. This psychological attribute is defined as being intellectually curious; individuals high in openness may be described as imaginative, curious, cultured, and intelligent. Being a curious and critical thinker is essential for an individual who is creating organizational processes, deciding organizational strategy, negotiating employee compensation, and finding new areas of opportunity. Individuals who think in terms of black and white or who fail to recognize the pros and cons of different hypothetical courses of action in different situations will be inflexible and fail to recognize opportunities when they arise. Conversely, individuals who are open to new concepts and view them without preconceived notions will be able to see the value in new or untested ideas, leading to organizational growth and success.

Successful entrepreneurs are likely to have good interpersonal skills; they will be adept at understanding and adapting to the moods and social cues of others. Being able to "read" customers and employees and thus relate to and speak with them on their terms is likely to facilitate the development and maintenance of relationships. Good interpersonal skills also means being perceived as warm and friendly, which helps make others feel at ease and comfortable starting a business relationship. However, there is a risk of being overly friendly and appearing fake, which may have negative consequences. Individuals with good interpersonal skills know when to turn the charm on and when to turn it off, but perhaps most important, they always seem sincere. The leaders of new ventures also need to demonstrate high levels of emotional stability, the ability to react calmly to the inevitable ups and downs of day-to-day stresses in a new venture. There can be a great deal of stress and pressure associated with opening a new business; owners or leaders who succumb to this pressure, who become moody or have outbursts of emotion, will subvert their ability to influence and lead employees.

Yet another important attribute of a successful entrepreneur is customer service orientation. Ultimately, a company exists to serve its customers, and when customers are unhappy, business is likely to suffer. Being customer service oriented means doing whatever it takes to make customers happy, including issuing refunds, replacing defective products, seeking out new ways to enhance a customer's experience, and suggesting products that they might like. Good customer service can save a relationship with a customer. For example, consider a company that sells expensive, proprietary machines through retail channels, a portion of which are defective and do not work as intended. To the customer, the retailer has failed, even if the problem was one of manufacturing. Fortunately, a company with outstanding customer service can keep that client. This means having outstanding service recovery, which could include issuing immediate refunds, overnighting new units, and providing technical support. Service recovery means demonstrating to a customer that their business is valued, their concerns are being heard, and any problem they have will be dealt with as painlessly as possible. Entrepreneurs with customer service orientation understand the value of these services. To someone with a customer service orientation, a customer problem is a company problem.

Motivating employees to carry out a leader's plans is vital to success. Whereas power is always the tool by which employees are directed toward activity, the underlying reason that a leader utilizes power is important. Some individuals have a need for personal power—a need to command others and dominate them. This sort of power, while it may be effective, tends to serve the ego of the leader. A leader who values personal power seeks power for power's sake. Socialized power is another power motive. Individuals who wield socialized power do so not necessarily for their own gratification but to rouse people to greater things. For a new business, creating a sense of mutual destiny and achievement (the ideals a leader with a socialized power motive might inspire) is likely to retain employees longer and gain their respect and cooperation. Whereas employees may listen to and follow a leader with a personal power motive, they may be resentful at feeling like a pawn for someone else's success, as opposed to a partner in that success.

To summarize, I-O psychology can benefit businesses in many ways, from helping entrepreneurs and managers to understand the psychology of employee behavior to identifying the psychological characteristics of successful entrepreneurs. The preceding is not an exhaustive list of the attributes of successful entrepreneurs, nor does this entry include an exhaustive list of the ways that I-O psychology can be used to help new ventures; there are certainly many more. However, new ventures, given their precarious financial position and limited capabilities to test their own human resource strategies, can seek out the science-based knowledge that I-O psychology possesses to stabilize them and put them in the best position to grow and prosper.

Richard N. Landers
Craig M. Reddock
Old Dominion University

See also Human Resource Strategy; Human Resources; Leadership; Learning; Learning Theory

Further Readings

Barrick, M. and M. Mount. "The Big Five Personality Dimensions and Job Performance: A Meta-Analysis." *Personnel Psychology*, v.44 (1991).

Borman, W. C., D. R. Ilgen, R. J. Klimoski, and I. B. Weiner. *Handbook of Psychology*. Vol. 12, *Industrial and Organizational Psychology*. Hoboken, NJ: John Wiley and Sons, 2004.

Cascio, W. F. *Applied Psychology in Human Resource Management*, 7th ed. Upper Saddle River, NJ: Prentice Hall, 2010.

Pinder, C. C. *Work Motivation in Organizational Behavior*, 2nd ed. New York: Psychology Press, 2008.

Yukl, G. *Leadership in Organizations*, 7th ed. Upper Saddle River, NJ: Prentice Hall, 2010.

PUBLIC POLICY: GOVERNMENT STIMULATION OF START-UPS

Successful economies require a strong small business and new start-up sector, which in turn creates an entrepreneurial climate. This sector and the resultant entrepreneurial activity create numerous positive impacts on the economy, notably new starts, job creation, firm growth, and innovation. For the majority of small businesses and the relatively unique and high-growth entrepreneurial firms to survive and flourish, public policy must contain rules and regulations that neither inhibit nor interfere with this sector but instead provide a level playing field, generate competition, and proactively support a sustainable entrepreneurial climate. Public policy can shape the economy in which new ventures operate. It establishes regulations and laws to guide behavior, determines infrastructure and taxes, and even contributes to creating a positive (or negative) entrepreneurial culture. Thus, public policies directly impact start-up venturing in most developed nations and stimulating new business venturing is a focal issue for policy makers at all levels of government. This entry focuses primarily on government systems within the United States, but many of the concepts are replicable and applicable to most of the developed nations around the globe.

Role of the Federal Government

It is widely accepted that the U.S. government plays a role in shaping the overall small business environment in which new ventures operate by establishing rules (such as federal labor laws), tax structures, and other guidelines and regulations. Despite the critical nature of this infrastructure, the most influential and largest-scale policy effort affecting start-ups arguably is that resulting from Congress's passage of the Small Business Act of 1953. This act called for the formation of the Small Business Administration, a government agency under the direction of the president that is tasked with supporting small businesses, small-business owners, and those individuals wishing to start new ventures.

The SBA's statutory authority rests in Title 15, Chapter 14A, Section 633 of the U.S. Code. The agency serves four fundamental functions: access to capital, entrepreneurial development, government contracting, and advocacy.

Access to start-up capital has long been a barrier to many start-up ventures, and the SBA helps mitigate this challenge. Capital refers to the SBA's mission to ensure that new and growing small businesses have the financial resources necessary to start, manage, and grow their businesses. Capital programs consist of one of four types: loans, venture capital, surety bonds, and export financing. The SBA loan programs provide a variety of loan types via a network of more than 5,000 partner banks. Depending on their experience with the SBA or the loan programs, banks are categorized as regular, certified, or preferred. Regular banks send the client's loan package to the SBA for processing and approval of the SBA guarantee, which may take up to 90 days. Preferred banks also send the client's loan package to the SBA, but the SBA must make a decision on guaranteeing the loan package within 15 days. Finally, certified banks are empowered to apply the SBA guarantee on the spot. These loans are typically secured by the SBA and come in a wide variety of sizes.

SBA venture capital efforts take two forms: the Program for Investment in Micro-Entrepreneurs (PRIME), program aimed at ensuring that low-income entrepreneurs can secure capital, and the Small Business Investment Company (SBIC) program, which offers access to debt capital with a 10-year maturity. Many of the United States' well-known entrepreneurial firms (Nike, Buffalo Wild Wings, Staples, and Apple, for example) have received SBIC funding. The SBIC program was designed to assist high-growth entrepreneurial firms requiring larger amounts of capital than were available through the SBA's other loan programs in order to secure equity financing to grow their businesses.

Another SBA program targeted to high-growth entrepreneurs is the Small Business Innovation Research (SBIR) program. Established in 1982 in response to the need of small business to support innovation and research and development, SBIR was created to provide financial support through a multiphase funding model that has

The Small Business Investment Company (SBIC) program was created in 1958 to fill the gap between the availability of venture capital and the needs of small businesses in start-up and growth situations. Many well known entrepreneurial firms—like Staples, Nike, Buffalo Wild Wings, and Apple—have received SBIC funding. (Wikimedia)

provided almost $2 billion annually to stimulate technological innovation and increase private-sector commercialization of innovations derived from federal research and development. Every federal agency with external budgets over $100 million must reserve 2.5 percent for small business through the SBIR program.

SBA surety bonds are forms of insurance that guarantee contract completion, come in a variety of forms, and are primarily used by ventures entering into federal construction contracts.

Finally, SBA export financing seeks to help ventures stay competitive in a global market by providing specialized loan guarantee programs for export financing, working capital, and credit to close a sale. Currently, the SBA loan portfolio guarantees more than $90 billion in loans to both start-up and existing small business ventures—that is direct stimulation of start-ups by public policy.

SBA entrepreneurial development programs have a profound impact on both the number of start-up ventures launched annually and the success of these ventures. As of 2010, the SBA operated more than 1800 field locations, including Small Business Development Centers (SBDCs), SCORE chapters, Women's Business Centers (WBCs), Veterans Business Outreach Centers, U.S. Export Assistance

Centers, Procurement Technical Assistance Centers, and the SBA field offices providing free one-on-one counseling (online and face-to-face), mentoring, technical assistance, and low-cost training (online and face-to-face) to individuals who are starting or currently operating their own small businesses. Annually, the SBA management and technical assistance efforts provide services to more than 1.2 million individuals, many of whom go on to launch new ventures with the support and advice received from the agency. These development programs are implemented by several organizations funded and cofunded by the SBA. As of 2010, there were more than 14,000 SBA-affiliated counselors spread throughout the country to assist start-ups at every stage of the venturing process.

Part of the SBA policy mandate is for the agency to serve as a resource and conduit to individuals and businesses looking to do business with the federal government. More specifically, the SBA works to ensure that a minimum of 23 percent of all federal contract dollars go to small businesses. Two of the most commonly targeted contracting programs are the 8(a) business development program and the HUBZone program. The 8(a) program was designed to aid small, disadvantaged ventures compete in the marketplace by providing sole-source contracts of up to $4 million for goods and services and $6.5 million for manufacturing contacts. The HUBZone program, enacted into law as part of the Small Business Reauthorization Act of 1997, establishes preferential treatment for ventures operating within defined underutilized economic develop zones. HUBZone companies receive competitive and sole source contracting and a 10 percent price evaluation preference in open government contracts. The SBA strives to award at least 3 percent of all dollars for federal prime contracts to HUBZone-certified ventures. However, a majority of small businesses are involved in the Small Business Set Aside Program, where most of the SBA's effort is directed to ensure that all federal contracting officials make every effort to see that small businesses get their fair share of the available federal contracting dollars.

The SBA serves as the "voice" of small business. This function is instrumental in the policy formation and development process, and it most certainly affects start-ups. The SBA advocacy professionals assess the burden of regulation on small business, continually research small businesses and the business environment, and make formal policy recommendations to the president.

Role of State and Local Governments

State and local governments also enact public policies that impact start-ups. One popular way they do this is through the use of subsidies. Subsidies are financial incentives governments pay to a business or economic sector, typically to foster its growth or prevent its decline. These incentives come in many forms, including job creation tax credits, discretionary grants, and enterprise zone credits. Many studies have found that governments recover $1.50 for every $1.00 invested, so at face value subsidies appear to be a wise policy mechanism and have been widely adopted at various state and local levels. For example, in 2010 more than 40 U.S. states committed in excess of $1.5 billion to subsidizing film and television production in the hope that these subsidies would generate new ventures and create new jobs.

Despite the argued success of subsidy programs, many recent studies have called into question whether subsidies actually are positive mechanisms to stimulate venture founding and economic activity. These recent studies, conducted by organizations that do not have a vested interest in promoting subsidies, argue that subsidies are high-cost, low-reward programs with several unavoidable drawbacks. Critics of subsidy programs argue that they incentivize venturing that would have occurred anyway; that the best jobs created typically go to residents outside the state; that many of tax credits go unused by the industries they were intended to target, ultimately getting sold to other for-profit industries for pennies on the dollar; and that the studies that find subsidy programs to be beneficial are flawed. Critics believe that states end up using valuable resources to compete fiercely against one another for start-ups. On one hand, this is bad for the collective good and does little to generate economic vitality; on the other hand, some start-ups may find a real deal in a state they would never have considered otherwise. Some states come out ahead (Louisiana has reaped the benefits of venture formation and job creation by subsidizing the film production industry, receiving an estimated $6.00 return on every $1.00 invested), but the majority may be better able to spend their limited cash resources on other means of stimulating new venture formation.

Certainly, subsidies are not the only policy means by which state and local governments impact start-ups. State and local laws, including tax structures, impact the business environment in the same way that federal laws do at the national level. Often, states mimic federal efforts, and local governments mimic state efforts. For example, it is not uncommon to see local governments provide additional funding to bolster the Small Business Development Centers in their regions. Florida, for instance, has its own minority certification program for government contracting at the state level.

Eric W. Liguori
California State University, Fresno
Dean A. Koutroumanis
University of Tampa
George T. Solomon
George Washington University

See also Barriers to Entry; Infrastructure; Job Creation; Political Economy and Entrepreneurship

Further Readings

Bhide, Amar. *The Origin and Evolution of New Business.* New York: Oxford University Press, 2000.

Birch, David. *Job Creation in America: How Our Smallest Companies Put the Most People to Work.* New York: Free Press, 1987.

Dennis, William. "Entrepreneurship, Small Business, and Public Policy Levers." *Journal of Small Business Management*, v.49/1 (2011).

Dennis, William. "Entrepreneurship, Small Business, and Public Policy Levers—Part 2." *Journal of Small Business Management*, v.49/2 (2011).

Gartner, William, Kelly Shaver, Nancy Carter, and Paul Reynolds, eds. *Handbook of Entrepreneurial Dynamics.* Thousand Oaks, CA: Sage, 2004.

Lyons, Thomas and Roger Hamlin. *Creating an Economic Development Action Plan.* Westport, CT: Praeger, 2001.

Reynolds, Paul. "New Firm Creation: A Global Assessment of National, Contextual, and Individual Factors." *Foundations and Trends in Entrepreneurship*, v.6/5–6 (2010).

Storey, David. *Understanding the Small Business Sector.* London: Routledge, 1994.

Tannenwald, Robert. *State Film Subsidies: Not Much Bang for Too Many Bucks.* Washington, DC: Center on Budget and Policy Priorities, 2010.

Waltzer, Norman, ed. *Entrepreneurship and Local Economic Development.* Lanham, MD: Lexington Books, 2007.

QUALITY

Quality is a critical aspect for large corporations and new ventures alike, although many aspects of quality have been found to be crucial in the entrepreneurial context, such as entrepreneurial quality, quality of relationships with business partners, the correlation between relationship beliefs and quality, quality and the choice of organizational form, and the quality of the entrepreneurial administration.

Entrepreneurial quality refers to adoption of venture initiatives such as innovative activities, the expansion of the business, collaboration with other companies and public or private institutions, and even the setting for practicing basic activities concerning the entrepreneur's managerial and financial spheres. Entrepreneurial requirements can vary by cultural background and experiences. In addition to having the managerial ability to run a business, the entrepreneur must sometimes cope with complex situations in risky or uncertainty environments, needing to build and maintain relationships with partners, officials, employees, and even opponents; the ability to "work with people" is highly valued.

Usually, there are four components developed to configure the quality of entrepreneurs and the factors that determine it. The first is the preference for self-employment, which is a necessary but not sufficient condition. The entrepreneur sometimes shows resistance to authority, has a strong desire and need for independence, and hopes to do something new.

The second component concerns several qualitative components, such as motivation, ambition, and innovativeness. Motivation can be intrinsic or extrinsic, intrinsic motivation belonging to the internal sphere of the individual, while extrinsic motivation is explained as the achievement of goals and belongs to the external sphere of the individual. Entrepreneurs with intrinsic motivations are more likely to carry out the challenging work of starting a new venture and therefore to achieve higher entrepreneurial success. Ambition is very much related to the concept of achievement motivation, and the innovation feature has been analyzed by Schumpeter and other researchers over many years.

The third component concerns the factors that make up the personal environment of the entrepreneur, which are those that create the entrepreneur's attitudes and abilities and, therefore, influence the entrepreneur's psychological processes and thinking.

Finally, cooperation with others is key. Collaboration is undertaken with the objective of cooperating with other companies, organizations, and individuals, so that the enterprise can reach a higher level of growth and development in terms of establishing formal agreements.

Entrepreneurs do not come from out of the blue but build their human intellectual capital through work experience in established firms. Usually, large firms produce entrepreneurs of higher quality than smaller firms, because small firms implement a wage policy that is attuned to workers' outside options, and workers leave a small firm to become entrepreneurs only to the extent that their private benefits, such as more flexible work hours or a sense of freedom and pride, are enhanced, while the large firm has a more rigid wage policy and as a consequence loses the best workers and ideas. Entrepreneurs emerging from large firms will have higher quality than those from small firms. Concerning the value of information and property rights protection, the improved property rights make a larger firm more likely to be optimal and hence increase the quality of entrepreneurs.

As for the correlation between relationship beliefs and quality, it has rarely considered the impact of culture. Researchers have indicated a significant pancultural correlation between dysfunctional beliefs and relationship quality, but a moderating effect for country, with dysfunctional beliefs in some countries explaining more than several times the variance in other countries. These findings are interpreted in the light of major differences between the countries' values, such as their approaches to environmental concerns. Sometimes dysfunctional beliefs relate to poor relationship quality and negative problem-solving behaviors.

How can we manage the nascent firm? That concerns the quality of entrepreneurial administration, which is defined as the directive activities that entrepreneurs carry out within their managerial sphere, which depends fundamentally on their technical knowledge. It is an aspect that would be considered within the managerial sphere of the entrepreneur's performance. Entrepreneurial behaviors are affected by different factors, sometimes stressing psychological processes and at other times stressing environmental factors of the personal and global context of the entrepreneur. On account of managerial complexity, entrepreneurial management depends not only on the business but also on the climate of business, such as networks and relationships with others.

Some firms are for-profit firms and the others are nonprofit firms. The question is, under what circumstance can we set up the for-profit firm? Some scholars apply the Hart et al.'s "incomplete contracts" framework to study the entrepreneur's choice of whether to set up a for-profit firm or a nonprofit organization. When the entrepreneur is sufficiently patient, then for-profit status is the optimal choice, and firms have an incentive to supply high-quality services. In addition, there is an intermediate range for the discount factor of the entrepreneur, where reputation for quality among those consumers valuing quality highly can be sustained only under nonprofit incorporation.

Shuyi Zhang
Shanghai Finance University

See also Innovation Management; Measures of Performance; Performance and Legitimacy

Further Readings

Goodwin, Robin and Stanley O. Gaines Jr. "Relationships Beliefs and Relationship Quality Across Cultures: Country as a Moderator of Dysfunctional Beliefs and Relationship Quality in Three Former Communist Societies." *Personal Relationships*, v.11/3 (2004).

Guzmán, Joaquín and F. Javier Santos. "The Booster Function and the Entrepreneurial Quality: An Application to the Province of Seville." *Entrepreneurship and Regional Development*, v.13 (2001).

Hvide, Hans K. "Quality of Entrepreneurs." *Economic Journal*, v.119 (2009).

Kuznetsov, Andrei, Frank McDonald, and Olga Kuznetsova. "Entrepreneurial Qualities: A Case From Russia." *Journal of Small Business Management*, v.38/1 (2000).

Vlassopoulos, Michael. "Quality, Reputation and the Choice of Organizational Form." *Journal of Economic Behavior and Organization*, v.71/2 (2009).

RADICAL AND INCREMENTAL INNOVATION

A radical innovation refers to a groundbreaking product that offers customers unprecedented performance or a massive reduction in cost and has the potential to restructure the relationship between customers and suppliers, displace current product leaders, create entirely new product categories, or transform an existing industry. Radical innovations are the gale-force wind popularized by Joseph Schumpeter's "creative destruction."

In contrast, an incremental innovation is at the other end of the spectrum, in that it offers customers only modest improvements to existing products. Whereas incremental innovations typically utilize existing production methods and incorporate minimal technological changes, radical innovations often depart considerably from existing practices and include significantly new technology, thereby allowing them to outperform existing products, deliver significantly enhanced customer benefits, and drive fundamental changes in consumer behavior.

While radical innovations can jeopardize the market position of those companies that continue to concentrate on incremental innovations, developing and commercializing such innovations is fraught with risk. Developing a product with substantially new technology (oftentimes based on recent scientific discoveries) is a highly uncertain endeavor that involves developing specifications from the ground up and using unproven technologies whose long-term reliability is untested. Such uncertainty may lead to revisiting earlier stages in the product development cycle, including redefining the original product concept.

Given the uncertainty associated with radical innovation, product development managers often balance standard development processes with flexibility and improvisation. The degree to which development teams are able to learn and act from prior efforts—often in unpredictable ways—is the key to developing radical innovation in rapidly changing and uncertain market conditions. Conversely, incremental innovation demonstrates lower levels of uncertainty all along the new product development cycle. Accordingly, managers often follow a structured development process for incremental innovation. Under this approach, a set of discrete product development phases are completed sequentially, with each phase separated by a decision point. However, while this type of development process may be successful in stable markets, it may be inappropriate under circumstances of rapid change.

Products based on radical innovations face additional uncertainties that incremental innovations do not, in that they may be so innovative that their utility may not be clear to customers. Such products may satisfy latent and currently undefined customer needs. Defining and reaching target customers for products based on radical innovations may be a challenge requiring that new sales and distribution methods be defined. Educating prospective consumers may also be necessary. All this uncertainty leads to higher levels of risk when developing radical innovations than when developing their incremental counterparts.

By establishing a short-term, results-oriented perspective that bears operationally efficient competencies, large organizations have been able to develop reliably profitable products for existing customers. These competencies have generally enabled large organizations to maintain an advantage in developing incremental innovation. Radical innovations' performance, cost, and customer adoption rates, on the other hand, often follow an "S curve." When first introduced in the market, the performance of a radical innovation may lag behind that of existing products. However, while an existing product's performance improvements are slowing, a radical innovation's performance is increasing. A similar pattern may be true for costs and customer adoption rates. Consequently, at some point a radical innovation overcomes the existing product's advantages. However, the point at which a radical innovation will overtake that of existing products cannot be determined precisely.

The uncertainty associated with developing radical innovations calls for overcoming this near-term, results-oriented perspective to developing products and requires the establishment of largely different competencies. Here, research indicates that new venture entrepreneurs may have an advantage in developing radical innovation over their larger counterparts. Individuals with a depth and breadth of technical experience in a problem area, who operate without the constraints of developing products for current customers, appear best able to develop radical innovations. Indeed, experience and freedom from constraints may help to explain why entrepreneurs are responsible for the development of a disproportional number of radical innovations.

For established organizations, investments and skills that once led to success may have to be abandoned, lest they hinder the development of the pioneering technologies necessary for radical innovation. If the development of a radical innovation is to be pursued, management and employees must often first set aside large portions of their accumulated knowledge and experience and be willing to acquire new skills and develop new processes. Relationships with the rest of the organization must be managed, including conflicts with existing product groups that are likely to erupt as competing parties defend their vested interests in the current business model. Funding also has to be established, which may mean cannibalizing larger, more entrenched, and more politically powerful adversaries for resources.

Despite the difficulties, firms have good reason to focus their efforts on the development of such far-reaching, seemingly risky innovations. Products based on radical innovations provide vast benefits to society in the form of lower costs, increased performance, and superior convenience. For individual firms, evidence indicates that radical innovations can help establish a competitive advantage in the marketplace and hasten the creation of considerable and enduring profits. Radical innovations have also been found to be significantly related to a company's innovation performance based on first-mover advantages. Overall, radical innovation is important to firms concerned with long-term growth and renewal. For firms interested in developing a steady stream of new products, radical innovations are critical to creating new markets and business opportunities, even as they act as a catalyst for subsequent, renewed rounds of incremental innovations.

Enrique Nuñez
Ramapo College of New Jersey

See also Innovation Management; Innovation Management: Corporate; Innovation Processes; Product Innovation; Service Innovation

Further Readings

Baumol, W. J. *The Microtheory of Innovative Entrepreneurship*. Princeton, NJ: Princeton University Press, 2010.

Dewar, R. D. and J. E. Dutton. "The Adoption of Radical and Incremental Innovations: An Empirical Analysis." *Management Science*, v.32/11 (November 1986).

Ettlie, J. E., W. P. Bridges, and R. D. O'Keefe. "Organization Strategy and Structural Differences for Radical Versus Incremental Innovation." *Management Science*, v.30/6 (June 1984).

Marvel, M. R. and G. T. Lumpkin. "Technology Entrepreneurs' Human Capital and Its Effects on Innovation Radicalness." *Entrepreneurship Theory and Practice*, v.31 (2007).

Schumpeter, J. A. *Capitalism, Socialism, and Democracy*. New York: Harper and Brothers, 1942.

RESEARCH AND DEVELOPMENT

Research and development (R&D) is important for new ventures as well as for established firms. The ability to generate new knowledge by R&D can serve as a key driver for firms with strong R&D needs. Strong R&D investment and subsequent findings can result in superior products or significant increases in production efficiency. However, R&D can be very resource-consuming and risk-bearing, and the availability of resources for firms located in developed as opposed to developing countries varies significantly. Therefore, firms' motivations to use these resources for R&D are based on their locations as well as their strategic motivations.

R&D Investment and Nations' Stages of Economic Development

Empirical literature has established the relationship between the R&D activity and economic development. Porter (1990) and Porter et al. (2002) identified that countries pass through three stages of the development process: a factor-driven stage, an efficiency-driven stage, and an innovation stage. These transitional periods give each of these countries its comparative advantage. A majority of developing countries are in the efficiency-driven stage, when the agricultural sector contributes to the economy, so there is limited opportunity for the evolution of large numbers of new ventures with significant R&D-intensive activities. Rather, most new ventures in developing nations are small manufacturing and service firms. These ventures also have limited access to human capital. Human capital can have information, technology, or tacit knowledge. Tacit knowledge is difficult to communicate or imitate; therefore, even if developing countries have an ample supply of these, the shortage of formal knowledge makes it difficult to take advantage of these resources.

Countries in the efficiency-driven stage have an educated workforce and consequently are able to adapt well during the subsequent period of technological development. Countries in the innovation-driven stage are marked by an increase in knowledge-intensive activities and rely on new ventures for creating jobs. Therefore, these countries need to have significant access to human capital and to have the ability to use these resources in order to continue to progress. The R&D process helps with the knowledge spillover effect in countries both in the efficiency-driven stage and in the innovation-driven stage. As the countries in the innovation-driven stage make progress toward more efficient processes and new products, countries in the efficiency-driven stage can learn from them, since they are better able to absorb the knowledge spillover.

R&D Investment, Institutions, and Public Policy

Internal institutions and public policy influence entrepreneurs' decisions to invest in R&D. For example, the tax structure of a country influences the R&D investment made by firms. If governments have created incentives for firms to invest in R&D, some firms will be likely to take advantage of these incentives. Generally in developing countries, poor tax structures and/or a lack of their implementation make R&D an unlikely option. Corruption makes implementation of policies a major problem for developing countries. Established firms located in developing countries have an unfair advantage, since their strong financial position enables them to pay bribes.

Investment in R&D by both established firms and new ventures also depends on corporations' confidence in local governments. In corporations located in countries with limited enforcement of intellectual property rights, the incentive to invest in R&D is minimal to none, whereas in locales with strong intellectual property protection policies, incentives are high. Additionally, specific policies influence firms' decisions to undertake R&D activities—for instance (in the United States), the Bayh-Dole Act of 1980, which allowed federally funded researchers (from universities, nonprofits, and small businesses) to file for patents, giving them control over intellectual property rights funded by the federal government. Traditionally, public universities have collaborated with industry. Universities' contributions to U.S. R&D have grown over the years. Massachusetts Institute of Technology (MIT) and Stanford University are prime examples of academic institutions that contribute to the local community.

The United States spends about 2.5 percent of its gross domestic product (GDP) for R&D, and the amount has remained relatively stable over the past three decades, although, according to data from the National Science Foundation, investment by the private sector has increased over the years. U.S. academic institutions are not unique in generating new ventures from universities, however. In Sweden, Chalmers University also produces quite a few new ventures that contribute to the economic prosperity of the local economy. Some emerging countries, such as China and India, have increased their R&D investment over the years.

R&D in Different Types of Ventures

The size and life of the firm also play a role when it comes to decision-making regarding R&D. New start-ups might not have the resources to invest in R&D, even if tax and other incentives are available. Investment in R&D can mean significant risk taking for new ventures, since they have limited ability to diversify their R&D activity in order to minimize risk. When a new venture wants to invest in R&D, it might have to take on only one project. On the other hand, large corporations may have multiple R&D projects, so in case one fails another that is successful can offset that failure and be profitable for the firm.

R&D activity can also contribute to the generation of spin-off entrepreneurship through knowledge spillover. Knowledge spillover can take various forms. Established literature has presented two forms of knowledge spillover: one associated with the exchange of goods (rent spillover) and the other associated with knowledge arising from the research and development (R&D) process. Knowledge spillover entrepreneurship is characterized by the start-up of a new firm based on knowledge or ideas generated but not completely or exhaustively commercialized in an incumbent firm. The new spin-off firm is started in an effort to bring ideas that are perceived to be of value to the entrepreneurs but not necessarily to the incumbent firms or organizations that created that knowledge. The new spin-off eventually leads to new employment opportunities for the region.

R&D investment can have a significant impact on firms' growth as well as on the economy. However, complex interdependencies exist between the national environmental and the condition or type of institution, as well as firms' own internal trajectories for the future. For new ventures to make significant investments in the R&D, both need to be aligned.

Farzana Chowdhury
Indiana University

See also Corporate Entrepreneurship and Innovation; Innovation in Low-Tech Industries; Innovation Processes; International New Ventures; Knowledge; Territorial Strategy and Regions; University Start-Ups

Further Readings

Anderson, Neal. *Practical Process Research and Development*. San Diego, CA: Academic Press, 2000.

Audretsch, David B. and Max Keilback. "The Theory of Knowledge Spillover Entrepreneurship." *Journal of Management Studies*, v.44/7 (2007).

Griliches, Zvi. "Issues in Assessing the Contribution of Research and Development to Productivity Growth." *Bell Journal of Economics, The RAND Corporation*, v.10/1 (Spring 1979).

Porter, Michael E. *The Competitive Advantage of Nations*. New York: Free Press, 1990.

Porter, Michael E., J. Sachs, and J. McArthur. "Executive Summary: Competitiveness and Stages of Economic Development." In *The Global Competitiveness Report 2001-2002*, Michael E. Porter et al., eds. New York: Oxford University Press, 2002.

Ravik, Jain, Harry C. Triandis, and Cynthia W. Weick. *Managing Research, Development, and Innovation*. New York: Wiley, 2010.

Wiethaus, Lars. *Research and Development: Business Strategies Towards the Creation, Absorption and Dissemination of New Technologies*. Saarbrücken, Germany: VDM, 2005.

RESOURCE-BASED VIEW

The term *resource-based view* (RBV) refers to a strategic management approach that has deep theoretical roots based in part on sociology and Ricardian and Penrosian economic theories according to which firms can earn sustainable supranormal returns if, and only if, they have superior resources and those resources are protected by some form of isolating mechanism precluding their diffusion throughout the industry.

Resources, as defined in the context of the RBV, are the tangible and intangible assets firms use to conceive of and implement their strategies. Resources include physical, financial, individual, and organizational capital as well as managerial teams, senior management groups, entrepreneurial skills, proprietary technologies, relationships, and the collective learning in the organization.

Firms that have the ability to capitalize on and exploit such valuable resources can, by doing so, achieve a competitive advantage, with the ultimate goal of transforming a short-run competitive advantage into a sustained competitive advantage. A sustained competitive advantage is defined as the firm's ability to implement valuable product market strategies that are not currently being implemented by its competition and where efforts to imitate those strategies by the competition have ceased. The transformation of a short-run competitive advantage into a sustained competitive advantage requires that the resources available to the firm be diverse in nature, inimitable, not substitutable without extreme effort, and not perfectly mobile. This approach presupposes that the theory of competitive advantage a firm achieves in its portfolio of product market positions is directly reflected in the portfolio of resources it controls.

The fundamental principles of the RBV within the field of strategic management were introduced in 1984 by Berger Wernerfelt in his seminal article "A Resource-Based View of the Firm," in which he posits that firms in control of valuable, scarce, and nonsubstitutable resources that are inelastic in supply can gain persistent competitive advantages by using them to develop and implement strategies. When strategic factor markets are in parity, the cost of acquiring or developing a resource will equal the value of that resource in enabling a firm to conceive of and implement a strategy. Given that the cost of acquiring or developing a resource is equal to the value of the resource, these resources will not be a source of economic rent. However, an economic rent can be achieved if the strategic factor markets are subjected to conditions of competitive imbalance.

In 1986, Jay Barney's article "Strategic Factor Markets: Expectations, Luck and Business Strategy" suggested that strategic factor markets can be competitively imperfect when two conditions exist: (1) when the expectations about the future value of the resources required by a firm to develop and implement its strategy are underestimated, and (2) when some firms have a more accurate assessment of the future value of the resources required than other firms.

Historically, research on the value of resources having a direct affect on firm performance is found in elements of works by Alfred Chandler, Ronald Coase, Edith Penrose, and Oliver Williamson. The firm's bundle of resources can be evaluated using the VRIN criteria, which characterize resources as follows:

- *Valuable:* Resources are valuable to the extent that they must enable a firm to employ a value-creating strategy, by either outperforming its competition or reducing its own weaknesses—or, expressed differently, if they enable a firm "to conceive of or implement strategies that improve its efficiency and effectiveness." Firms that continue to acquire or develop valuable resources in consistently uncertain settings can gain persistent economic rents.
- *Rare:* Resources are rare to the extent that demand for them outstrips supply. One simple approach in determining rarity of a resource is to count them; a resource must, by definition, be rare. In a perfectly competitive strategic factor market, when only one competing firm controls a resource, that resource is rare. Resources are also considered rare when the number of firms that possess a resource is lower than the number required to generate competitive strategic parity.
- *Inimitable:* Resources are inimitable to the extent that they are unique and unmatched by competitors; thus, by extension, an inimitable resource is a source of a competitive advantage if it is controlled only by one firm. The superior performance generated does not lead to competitive parity, since the firms without the resources necessary to conceive and implement a strategy efficiently and effectively will find it costly to acquire and develop them. The paradox of inimitable resources is that, as soon as they show clear promise of a sustained advantage, they risk being competed away; their strength becomes their weakness.
- *Nonsubstitutable:* Resources are nonsubstitutable to the extent that they can be uniquely used to help conceive of and implement a strategy. If a resource can be easily substituted by another resource that delivers the same effect, then it cannot remain a source of a competitive

advantage. Hence, a strategy is nonsubstitutable when such a one-to-one nexus exists between a given resource and a strategy. Nonsubstitutability is not confined to a single resource that enables a firm to develop and implement a strategy; rather, it may consist of a bundle of resources.

The RBV has been criticized for ignoring the existence of the factors surrounding the resources that are the fundamental determinants of firm performance and, as such, does not attempt to explain the nature of the isolating mechanisms that enable entrepreneurial rents and competitive advantage to be sustained.

David Teece, Jay Barney, and Kathleen Eisenhardt have introduced the theory of "dynamic capability" (DC), which extends the RBV to include the firm's evolving capabilities and how they are developed and integrated within the firm. Dynamic capabilities are defined as the firm's ability to integrate, build, and reconfigure internal and external competencies to address rapidly changing environments. Whereas the RBV emphasizes resource choice, or selecting the appropriate resource, the concept of DC emphasizes developing and renewing resources based on sequences of path-dependent learning.

Alfred Lewis
Hamline University
Dan Kipley
Azusa Pacific University

See also Competition; Family Business: Theory; Human Capital Theory; Human Resource Strategy; Knowledge-Based View; Obstacle Identification; Resource-Based View; Strategy

Further Readings

Barney, J. B. "The Resource Based View of Strategy: Origins, Implications, and Prospects." *Journal of Management*, v.17 (1991).

Barney, J. B. "Strategic Factor Markets: Expectations, Luck and Business Strategy." *Management Science*, v.32/10 (October 1986).

Chandler, Alfred D. *Strategy and Structure: Chapters in the History of the American Industrial Enterprise.* Cambridge, MA: MIT Press, 1962.

Chandler, Alfred D. Jr. *The Visible Hand.* Cambridge, MA: Harvard University Press, 1977.

Coase, Ronald H. "The Nature of the Firm." *Economica*, v.4/16 (November 1937).

Penrose, Edith T. *The Theory of the Growth of the Firm.* New York: Wiley, 1959.

Teece, David, Gary Pisano, and Amy Shuen. "Dynamic Capabilities and Strategic Management." *Strategic Management Journal*, v.18/7 (August 1997).

Wernerfelt, Berger. "A Resource-Based View of the Firm." *Strategic Management Journal*, v.5/2 (1984).

Williamson, Oliver E. *Markets and Hierarchy: Analysis and Antitrust Implications.* New York: Free Press, 1975.

RETAILING

In today's free-market economy, there are two markets in which products are sold; retail markets and wholesale markets. In each, the products are the same but their prices, amounts, and to whom they are sold differ. For example, a book can be sold in both the retail and the wholesale market. The price is different in the two markets (lower and based on volume in bundles of multiple units for wholesalers, higher and based on individual units for retailers), the quantities are different (with wholesalers typically purchasing multiple units), and the customers are also different (businesses versus individual end users). The reason resides in the definition of retailing.

Basically, retailing consists of the sale of products or services to the purchaser or the end user. The activity of sales is direct between the seller and the purchaser. Products that are sold are in small quantities, and services are offered one at a time, directly to consumers from fixed locations ranging from department stores to boutiques and kiosks. Other options are ordering online, by telephone, or through postal or courier services. Retailing includes all the activities involved in selling products or services for personal use (to individuals, families, and households); it typically is a nonbusiness use.

Philip Kotler defined a "retailer" as an individual or company that purchases products in large quantities from manufacturers or importers, either directly or through a wholesaler, and then sells smaller quantities to the end user. In retail markets, purchasers are end users who can be individual customers or companies and institutions as well. The daily purchasing is from retail markets. Many institutions—manufacturers, wholesalers, and retailers—do retailing. However, most retailing is done by retailers; businesses' wholesales come primarily from retailing.

Products sold as retail are defined as goods that are sold in small quantities or directly to consumers or from locations like department stores. Larger retail chains position their stores in both shopping malls and urban settings. (Photos.com)

There are different types of retailers. As Kotler noted, the most well known types of retailers are department stores, supermarkets, and convenience stores. Department stores carry a wide variety of product lines and sell many different brands in one place, from apparel (clothing, accessories, and shoes) and perfumes and cosmetics for all segments (men, women, and children) to household appliances and other goods. For example, the company Debenhams is the United Kingdom's most popular department store.

Another type of retailer is the supermarket, the most frequently shopped type retail store. There are many well-known supermarket chains in the world. For example, ALDI is a discount supermarket chain based in Germany, and Tesco and Sainsbury's are the United Kingdom's most popular supermarkets. Today, there has been a positive change in the food retailing sector, and growth can be seen in nearly all countries in the world, especially in Latin America, Southeast Asia, China, and South Africa.

Convenience stores are a third type of retailer, consisting of small stores or shops that carry a limited line of high-turnover convenience goods, such as soft drinks, cigarettes and other tobacco products, cookies, ice creams, newspapers, and magazines. Sometimes convenience stores can be established as part of gas stations, so they may also sell auto-related products. Some of these stores—such as 7–Eleven, the world's largest convenience store chain—are open 24 hours a day.

Retailer shops can be physically located in city centers, especially on shopping streets that people can easily reach, as well as suburbs. Well-known chain retailers position their shops in both shopping malls and on shopping streets. In the late 20th and early 21st centuries, shopping malls have become very popular, especially in highly populated cities such as New York, London, Tokyo, Shanghai, and Istanbul. Retailers in shopping malls are an example of businesses that have adapted themselves to the changing buying and selling habits of their customers. Customers may prefer a shopping mall over a shopping street for many reasons. First, malls tend to collect every kind of retail shop, as well as eateries and entertainment, in one compact location. People can shop, take a break to drink coffee, eat and drink in a restaurant, and see a movie in a cinema, all within in a secure place near where they have parked the car. Second, people can avoid adverse weather conditions, as shopping malls are generally indoor environments protected from the elements and air-conditioned.

In the 21st century, "big-box" retailers have become increasingly successful. These include U.S. companies such as Walmart, Target, Home Depot, Lowe's, and Costco. In 2010, Euromonitor International's *World Retail Data and Statistics* reported that the world's largest retailer was Walmart, followed by France's Carrefour, Germany's Metro AG, and the United Kingdom's Tesco chain.

Although most retailing is done in retail stores, in recent years nonstore retailing has been growing much faster than has store retailing. Nonstore retailing includes selling to end users through direct mail, catalogs, telephone, televised home-shopping shows, home and office parties, door-to-door contact, vending machines, the Internet, and other direct-selling approaches. Generally the products sold through nonstore retailing are relatively cheaper than those sold in brick-and-mortar retail stores.

Mail order was a very common sales technique in the late 19th century. People ordered from huge printed catalogs. As telephones became common, customers could order by telephone, either from a catalog or from contact information placed in magazine and newspaper advertisements. Today, catalog retailing remains a popular technique to sell dozens of different types of products, from gardening supplies to toys, and the prices are relatively lower than those in normal retail stores.

As the world has become more digital, online e-catalogs have come into use. For example, Argos, the United Kingdom's most popular catalog retail company, uses both traditional and online catalogs. Argos has typically located retail shops in the shopping streets of every city in the United Kingdom; people can look at the Argos catalogs, find a product they need or like, and purchase the product in a nearby physical Argos store. If they do not want to go to the shop, they can order via telephone, mail order, or the Internet by looking at Argos's online catalogs.

Since the late 1999s, online retailing has boomed in business-to-consumer (B2C) transactions. It offers exceptional convenience and time savings and is outstripping mail and telephone orders in the 21st century. Some retailers are present only online, the most famous of which is Amazon.com, which began by selling books but now sells all types of products. In 2010, online U.S. retail sales totaled approximately $173 billion. Today, both new venture and traditional retailers must maintain not only an online presence but also online shopping sites in order to compete.

Much research on the retail industry concentrates on customers' buying behavior. As Dhruv Grewal and colleagues have noted, price is one of the most important factors affecting the sales of a product. The higher the price, the less it is sold. There is a difference between retail and wholesale markets in terms of price; in retail markets, prices are higher than in wholesale markets. According to retail researchers, the second most important factor that affects the sales in retail markets is location; proximity to customers and proximity to other stores are key.

Retailing is one of the most important means of bringing products to end-user customers, and it undergoes tremendous development year by year. For new ventures in the retail sector, it is not easy to succeed unless the firm has a brilliant idea or application, because of the dominance of the large, successful retail chains. New venture retailers are most likely to be successful if they concentrate on niche markets, where many opportunities may exist.

Asli Tuncay-Celikel
Isik University and University of Sussex

See also Customer Orientation; E-Commerce; Sales; Selling Products and Services; Venture Capital; Wholesale Markets

Further Readings

Ailawadi, Kusum L. and Kevin Lane Keller. "Understanding Retail Branding: Conceptual Insights and Research Priorities." *Journal of Retailing*, v.80 (2004).

Arnold, Mark J. and Kristy E. Reynolds. "Hedonic Shopping Motivations." *Journal of Retailing*, v.79 (2003).

Farfan, Barbara. "2010 World's Largest Retailers by Country." http://retailindustry.about.com/od/famousretailers/a/retailercountry.htm (Accessed December 2010).

Grewal, Dhruv et al. "Customer Experience Management in Retailing: An Organizing Framework." *Journal of Retailing*, v.85 (2009).

Kotler, Philip. *Marketing Management: International Edition*. Upper Saddle River, NJ: Prentice Hall, 1997.

Krafft, Manfred and Murali K. Mantrala, eds. *Retailing in the 21st Century: Current and Future Trends*. New York: Springer, 2006.

Peres, Renana et al. "Innovation Diffusion and New Product Growth Models: A Critical Review and Research Directions." *International Journal of Research in Marketing*, v.27/2 (2010).

Peterson, Robert A. and Sridhar Balasubramanian. "Retailing in the 21st Century: Reflections and Prologue to Research." *Journal of Retailing*, v.78 (2002).

Puccinelli, Nancy M. et al. "Customer Experience Management in Retailing: Understanding the Buying Process." *Journal of Retailing*, v.85 (2009).

REVENUE: CURRENT VERSUS DEFERRED

This article's title is likely to conjure up images in the reader's mind. How could there be "a contest" between these current and deferred revenues in the eye of the new venture owner? Clearly, any new business would rather experience revenue generation currently than having to defer that revenue. From an accounting perspective, however, it is imperative to define each term, as the connotation generally associated with the latter term is not consistent with the way in which accountants have defined it.

Current revenues are exactly that: revenues earned for delivery of a service at the present time. Any restaurant patron is familiar with the process. One enjoys the meal, and once the delivery and consumption of that meal have been completed, one pays the bill (albeit often with a credit card). If the restaurant patron were to pay with cash, then the payment (settlement) is "current" as well. However, as mentioned, often patrons offer a credit card, which the restaurant then seeks to verify is "good" for the amount of the bill. *Good* is the colloquial term used here to indicate the credit card company has approved the patron's taking on that obligation, and it really means that upon approval of that credit card, the restaurant is entitled to payment from the credit card company in the very near term.

To the restaurant patron it appears as though the restaurant is giving credit terms, but in fact the credit card company effectively lends the restaurant the proceeds (less their fee of, typically, a few percent points) and takes on the risk of nonpayment from the patron. Whereas restaurants prefer not to give discounts, this credit card arrangement gives the restaurant the ability to pay its purveyors and suppliers. Restaurants are often termed a "cash business," cash being synonymous with current revenues, as most of a restaurant's day-to-day financial aspects involve minimal granting of (and/or receiving) credit. Moreover, to our point here, we defined current revenues from the restaurant's perspective and tied it back to the actual cash transactions but also showed the mechanisms going on "behind the scenes" that make the cash settlement items appear current from some parties' perspectives (the restaurant receiving cash, and the credit card paying cash) and deferred to others. Hence, the appearance of the transaction as "current" is somewhat deceptive, with deferred payment by patrons and deferred collections by credit card companies.

Deferred revenue can be also misunderstood or misinterpreted. From an accounting perspective, revenues are recorded as such when they are deemed to have been earned. "Earned" and "paid for" are not always the same thing (hence our discussion of the cash settlement aspects earlier). When the product or service is delivered in advance of the cash payment, the transaction is recorded as revenue earned, and in the language of accounting, the corresponding balancing entry is of a debt due to the selling merchant. However, when the product or service is paid for in advance of delivery, the accountants correctly recognize the cash payment receipt (a debit entry, corresponding to an increase of cash), but they must also show an equal (and opposite) credit entry in order to maintain the balance in the accounting books. In this circumstance, accountants properly recognize that the firm has a liability to the customer, owing the service or product, and that the firm is at risk of having the order canceled and having to refund the payment received.

The term deferred revenue is used to enumerate those situations in which the recognition of the revenue is in fact deferred, *not* the payment receipt. Depending on the business, this can represent a sizable current liability figure, even though there ordinarily is a small probability that the firm in question would need to refund a purchase thus far paid for. In many introductory financial accounting texts, this topic is covered in a section explaining the rationale behind accrual accounting methods, and in those discussions deferred revenue is often used interchangeably with the term *unearned revenue*.

The key point here is that Generally Accepted Accounting Principles (GAAPs) dictate that a company report as revenue only those transactions that have been earned as of the closing of the accounts. This also means that items that previously have been recorded as unearned have likely become earned income in subsequent time periods. Hence, adjusting entries are undertaken at the end of each accounting period to recognize that portion of (previously) unearned (deferred) revenue that is now earned (current).

Let us take a moment to ponder and explore why this approach gives a more accurate picture of a firm's performance than simply recognizing any (advance) payments as revenues. First, let us consider a new venture that initiated a program of advance sales on a product whose costs (direct costs of goods sold) constitute a significant percentage of the sales list price. If a modest discount were offered at year end to induce advance orders and payment, the revenue numbers recorded would quite possibly balloon, but at the same time the firm would not necessarily (or likely) be incurring the significant expenses associated with making those goods they ultimately need to deliver.

The "end accounting result" would be, in the near term (the accounting period just ending), recorded revenues would be increasing/increased, while direct expenses would remain at, or close to, zero. This would have the effect of making profitability appear to be growing, but at the expense of longer-term profitability, since the latter was traded (via the discount for early orders) for near-term orders (and the "appearance" of profits). Without any adjustments for the deferred revenues embedded in this example (and no or little corresponding ultimate expenses), investors could be presented with a financial statement that includes two very meaningful distortions (to say the least).

Three questions remain to be addressed here: What "type" of businesses naturally incur deferred revenues? Are these (deferred revenues) necessarily good or bad? Are these impacts (of deferred revenues) significant?

To the first question, many businesses producing custom products or services (such as clothing, automobiles, home remodeling and construction) will require (sometimes significant) advance deposits before proceeding with any work. Similarly, businesses in the performing arts, intermediaries (loosely defined), and sports management will conduct advance ticket sales efforts, partially to determine if there is demand for the product/service being offered, and if so how much. In that regard, there is a risk management aspect associated with any firm incurring deferred revenues as well.

To the second question posed above, the "beauty" of advance sales is that the cash generated from advance sales can be utilized to pay for the up-front expenses incurred in the production of those custom products or spectator-based events. This serves to keep the investment exposure of the owners of the custom products company (or entertainment-based firm) lower, reducing the risk to said owners, and simultaneously allows for greater returns on invested capital, if profits are in fact forthcoming. In many/most instances, moreover, since the product or service being offered is ultimately delivered to the intended buyer, there is minimal risk to the seller that a (cash) refund will be required.

Last, addressing the third question—Are these impacts (of deferred revenues) significant?—the answer is a robust "It depends," but for some businesses this is a significant (virtually permanent) source of cash with which said business can be run. In the publicly traded company arena, Expedia is a good example of a business benefiting from the incurrence of deferred revenues. Expedia's annual revenue was $3 billion in 2009 and 2010, with deferred revenues averaging $700 million over the same time period. These prepayments have effectively allowed Expedia to finance its investments in accounts receivable and prepaid expenses (averaging $500 million per year) at a cost of zero to the firm's shareholders, leaving an additional $200 million in Expedia's coffers to earn interest for Expedia (and those shareholders) in a marketable securities account.

Similarly, not-for-profit firms leverage their capital through advance ticket sales. The New York Philharmonic, for example, generates annual ticket sales of roughly $28 million and reported deferred revenues (prepurchased/prepaid tickets) averaging $12 million in a recently reported calendar year. This helped to offset the significant cash flow lag experienced in the collection of pledges to the Philharmonic (where pledges made are considered revenues to the Philharmonic when pledged). This "pledges receivable" effect renders cash available to the Philharmonic significantly less than the number shown on the annual revenue line. The net effect is that, for the "right kind of firm," deferred revenues can be a significant source of costless capital, which is a welcome find for any business.

Robert J. Moreland
Columbia College, Chicago

See also Accounting; Business Plans; Cash Flow; Credit; Debt; Debt-Based Financing; Equity- and Debt-Based Financing

Further Readings

Financial Accounting Standards Board. "Statement of Financial Accounting Standards No. 48: Revenue Recognition When Right of Return Exists." June 1981. http://www.fasb.org/pdf/fas48.pdf (Accessed February 2011).

Kimmel, Paul D., Jerry J. Weygandt, and Donald E. Keiso. *Accounting: Tools for Decision Making*. New York: Wiley, 2008.

Rashty, J. and J. O. Shaughnessy. "Accounting for Deferred Revenue Liabilities in Post-Business Combination Statements." *CPA Journal*, v.81/4 (2011).

RISK MANAGEMENT

This article discusses the crucial part that risk management plays in new venture management. Effective risk management is a series of stages joined by feedforward and feedback loops. The stages cover the context of the new venture, communication and consultation with stakeholders, risk assessment, risk treatment, and monitoring and review. To be most effective, risk management in a new venture must include planned and organized activities to manage risks.

Many of the key concepts here are described more fully in an international standard, ISO 31000:2009, *Risk management: Principles and Guidelines*.

Risk and New Ventures

The early stages of a new venture are often characterized by high uncertainty about events, including changes in specific circumstances, such as income and expense timing, phasing and readiness of procedures, equipment, technology, product or services. Effective risk management helps reduce uncertainty about the achievement of objectives to an acceptable level. We therefore can define risk as *the effect of uncertainty on objectives*.

Risks can have one or many consequences that have an impact on objectives positively or negatively. Organizational objectives can include financial, health and safety, and environmental goals; can apply at different levels, such as strategic, organization-wide, project, product, and process; and can be short-, medium-, or long-term.

Risk is often described as a combination of the consequences of an event or a change in circumstances and the associated likelihood of occurrence. This helps us analyze risks by asking what consequences an event might cause and how likely such consequences are.

Uncertainty about an event, its consequences, or the likelihood of each consequence means we are lacking some information. Full or perfect information is a rarity, and it is normal to work with the best-available information. However, the more that is at stake, the more should be done to get better information.

If an event has occurred, there is no uncertainty about timing, but some consequences may have yet to eventuate; nonetheless, a risk may have become an issue that needs management.

Effective risk management should therefore be an integral part of the day-to-day management of any new venture. It helps create value and contributes to decision making.

Context of the Venture

When carrying out a risk assessment, it is necessary to consider the business environment in which the new venture is or will be operating. A context statement (perhaps as part of the business plan) will help with risk assessment (risk identification, analysis, and evaluation) but should also be part of every business case.

For example, in the external environment, what legislation or other regulatory controls will the new venture be subject to, and will these be subject to particular social or political pressures, perceptions, or values? Who are likely competitors, and how will competition be felt? Current and anticipated trends need to be considered and realistic information gathered about how these may affect the new venture. It will also be necessary to consider financial and economic pressures and the availability of required technology—and the people to program and control the technology.

The internal environment will include the venture's capabilities (resources, knowledge, capital, time, people, processes, information and other systems, and technologies), and these will be influenced by the perceptions and values of internal stakeholders and the organization's culture.

Typically, a new venture will start with relatively little formal structure but will progressively adopt standards, guidelines, and models to aid decision making and management. The current and likely governance and organizational structure, roles, and accountabilities and management systems must be understood. Depending on the financial backing for the venture, these may be a source of risk now or in the future.

The form and extent of contractual relationships must be understood, as they may contain legal obligations. Effective communication and consultation with stakeholders will be crucial, not only when developing the context statement but also throughout the whole risk-management process.

Based on an understanding of the business environment, criteria will be needed to aid evaluation of risks by decision makers in determining whether a risk should be accepted, tolerated, or treated. Criteria are developed at this stage as part of understanding the context of the venture. Initially, they should reflect the key issues (financial, start-up lead times, and so on) but fairly quickly need to evolve to reflect more mature matters (customer expectations, safety, environmental issues, reliability, and the like).

Risk Assessment

The risk assessment stage covers risk identification, analysis and evaluation. Some risks will have become evident while considering the business environment, whereas others will be known from previous experience. That experience can help with identifying risks, but it is often advisable to seek advice from an independent person to help ensure that all significant causes and consequences have been considered.

Identified risks are best named in terms of probable cause, consequences, and impacts on objectives.

Risk analysis seeks out information about the potential event, the consequences that might flow from such an event and how they will impact on objectives. The likelihood of each consequence also needs to be estimated. A good analysis results in clear characterization of the risk.

There are many risk analysis techniques, and it is important to select techniques that will give useful information about uncertainties, consequences and their likelihood, factors influencing each, and how they might combine to impact on objectives. The level of detail required will depend on the nature of the risk. For example, a new product that may provide great health benefits but that could also cause considerable harm to people will require quite different analysis from a new fashion design.

One common risk analysis tool is a consequence/likelihood matrix, often having a five-by-five structure with cells labeled or colored to indicate risk severity. A matrix needs to reflect the risk profile of the venture, as a poorly designed matrix may give misleading results. David Hillson has described one way of using a matrix to analyze both positive and negative impacts (opportunities and threats). This technique is useful, as the areas of greatest opportunities and threats form an inverted triangle showing which of these the new venture should pay greatest attention to.

Each risk analysis should be carried out twice: first, taking no account of any internal controls; then repeated, with current controls to show venture management how much effect controls have on the level of risk. The results can be plotted onto a matrix to show graphically where the greatest opportunities and threats lie and how risks compare.

Risk evaluation compares the risk analysis outcomes with the risk criteria developed earlier to decide if the level of risk is acceptable or tolerable. For example, a new consumer product might have been analyzed as carrying a trivial but real level of risk. How much risk consumers and regulatory agencies will accept may be quite different from the risk acceptance of the new venture owners.

At this point, it is not uncommon to find criteria are not relevant or have not been developed and that it is necessary to return to the criteria development stage. This may, in turn, show the need to partly or completely amend the risk assessment.

Risk Management

There is a range of generic options if the current level of a risk has been evaluated as requiring management action. These are to avoid the risk (do not start, or halt or defer an activity), to start an activity that creates opportunity, to remove the source of the risk, to alter the likelihood or the consequences or both, to share the risk with a third party, or (from a position of knowledge) to retain the risk.

Some options may, of course, create new risks or modify other risks. Selected treatment options must be managed to implementation unless discarded by a conscious decision (for example, in the case of a change in risk level or risk evaluation).

Effective risk management also requires monitoring of the whole process by venture management. This helps ensure that agreed or required activities are completed and facilitates the continual improvement of the venture. Risk management must be part of day-to-day management if it is to be effective and aid achievement of the objectives of a new venture.

Chris Peace
Massey University

See also Accounting; Contracts and Trust; Credit; Crisis Management: Corporate; Entrepreneurial Orientation; Insurance; Negotiating Strategies; Overconfidence;

Revenue: Current vs. Deferred; Test Markets; Tolerance for Failure; Venture Capital

Further Readings

Crouhy, Michel et al. *The Essentials of Risk Management.* New York: McGraw-Hill, 2005.

Hillson, D. "Extending the Risk Process to Manage Opportunities." *International Journal of Project Management*, v.20/3 (2009).

International Standards Organisation. *Risk Management: Principles and Guidelines.* Geneva: Author, 2002.

Kazemek, E. A. and A. Epstein. "Poor Risk Assessment Can Doom New Ventures." *Healthcare Financial Management*, v.44/2 (February 1990).

Kemshall, Hazel. *Good Practice in Risk Assessment and Risk Management.* London: Jessica Kingsley, 1999.

Vose, David. *Risk Analysis.* New York: Wiley, 2009.

S

SALES

Sales in business can refer to the passage of ownership from one owner to another, a reseller agreement in which one agrees to operate as the seller of another's goods or services, or other technical types of agreements in which ownership is being transferred. *Sale* is a widely used term in business. Sales figures and trends are used to assess risk, create internal controls, benchmark, and determine rewards. Accountants study taxable and nontaxable sales. Business leaders use sales figures to measure success.

Provision of services, legally speaking, is governed by common law. Common law is law made by courts. There exists a large body of cases, from precolonial English law to interpretation and rules set by modern courts that can guide in structuring sales for services and realty. Sales of goods are predominantly governed by the Uniform Commercial Code (UCC), specifically Article 2 of the UCC. Parties do, however, have the ability to opt out of UCC application to their transaction by making any rules for transfer that they wish. General contract law mandates that parties bargain legally and with good intentions. The UCC has been adopted by all states within the United States except for Louisiana. The UCC provides largely common rules regarding sale of goods, which aids in the seamless movement of goods across state borders. Article 2 applies to all sales of goods, regardless of whether the intended use is for a commercial or a consumer purpose.

If parties do allow the UCC rules to control their agreement, specific sections define how and when things happen in the contract to avoid lack of certainty. Also, there are warranties implied in transactions which common law does not imply—for example, warranty of title. There is in a contract for sale a warranty by the seller that the title conveyed shall be good and its transfer rightful. This warranty would not exist in a common-law transaction. In common law, the principle of *caveat emptor* ("buyer beware") largely applies, meaning that the buyer must examine the title for himself. For example, it is very common in a real estate transaction for the buyer to examine title (ownership) back in time 40 years or more in order to determine whether the present seller has clear ownership and ability to convey title. This examination takes time, and days or even months can pass while title examinations are made.

This type of time cannot be invested in a sale of goods transaction. The UCC is extremely helpful in bringing great efficiency to the typical business transaction. When a customer comes to a store or a car dealer, she simply takes or identifies the good she desires, bargains a price, pays for the item, and becomes its owner. There is no process whereby the buyer undertakes to discover how the seller came to have the right to sell the item. Title in the seller is implied by the seller's possession and advertisement of the good. This speeds the transaction so that the contract can be executed and the sale made in less than a minute, in many cases, as when one purchases a candy bar or soda from a vending machine. With sales made efficiently, taxes can be collected, manufacturing can take place, goods can be shipped, workers can be employed, and taxes can be collected. It is necessary for economic reasons that sales be voluminous and frequent.

Sales can be accomplished by the use of money or by barter. Barter involves the exchange of goods or services for other goods or services. UCC Article 2 walks parties through the contract process. Contract negotiation is governed by specific rules. These rules apply most dramatically when two merchants bargain, but also when there are two nonmerchants or one merchant and one nonmerchant. There is a section of Article 2 governing firm offers. A firm offer is an offer made by a merchant that must be left open for the buyer's consideration for the time stated in the offer.

Warranties are expressed and implied and can be modified or removed from a contract under Article 2. The moment of acceptance, rejection, and revocation are all spelled out in detail in Article 2. Article 2 has its own statute of limitations for bringing a claim of breach of contract. The statute of limitations is shorter than that provided by most states for breach of other types of contracts.

UCC Article 2 is designed to provide speed, efficiency, and preservation of relationships between contracting parties by providing rules that tell contracting parties in advance what will happen and how a conflict will be resolved.

Article 2 defines a *good* as any thing (including a specially manufactured good) that is not movable at the time of identification to the contract for sale other than by the money or price to be paid, investment securities, and things in action. Goods also include the unborn young of animals, growing crops, and other identified things attached to realty, as described in the section on goods to be severed from realty. Goods must both exist and be identified before any interest in them can pass.

Some sales of goods cross international borders, and for those the United Nations Convention on Contracts for the International Sale of Goods (CISG) may govern the contract. The CISG was drafted by the UN Commission on International Trade Law (UNCITRAL) and adopted and opened for signature and ratification by a UN-sponsored diplomatic conference held at Vienna in 1980. The CISG does apply to and govern a contract if the transaction is between parties whose places of business are in different states (nations) and the transaction is for commercial rather than consumer goods. However, the CISG is not so tight in its governance that there is no room left for negotiation. In the context of an international agreement, the CISG allows enough flexibility for negotiation of terms; at the same time, however, it provides a helpful frame for the contract. The CISG is helpful in overcoming the complications inherent in an international contract. These complications are occasioned by the great geographic distance between the parties, different currencies necessitating a choice of currency, language barriers necessitating a choice of bargaining language, traffics, taxes, government regulations on imports and exports, risks of loss, choices of law, and cultural differences, to name a few. There are 76 nations that have adopted the CISG (there are 192 member states in the United Nations). The CISG governs contracts for the international sales of goods between private businesses, excluding sales to consumer facilities, unless the parties have specifically opted out of the CISG governance of their contract.

From a business and law perspective, considerations to be taken into account in the sale of goods include inventory control, reliability of supply, quality, taxation, assembly, and insurable interest. Sales are addressed in a section on the examination for certified public accountants because the taxation and structure of contracts is so extremely important in business.

In the context of new ventures, the ability for a new enterprise to sell goods or services is paramount, given that no income can accrue without the exchange or sale activity. In some instances, a new venture can sell to another party and then sell the accounts receivable to a third party in order to help its cash flow position. This is known as "factoring," whereby the third party discounts the face value of the accounts receivable to cover costs and allow for some profit.

Dominic DePersis
Broome Community College
Alfred Lewis
Hamline University

See also Advertising; Contextual Marketing; Focus Groups; Market Evaluation; Market Orientation; Selling Products and Services; Target Markets; Test Markets; Wholesale Markets

Further Readings

American Law Institute. *Uniform Commercial Code 2010-2011 Edition*. Philadelphia: Author, 2011.

Cravens, David W., Kenneth Le Meunier-FitzHugh, and Nigel Piercy. *The Oxford Handbook of Strategic Sales and Sales Management.* New York: Oxford University Press, 2011.

Gitomer, Jeffrey H. *Jeffrey Gitomer's Sales Bible.* New York: Collins, 2008.

Sales Educators. *Strategic Sales Leadership: Breakthrough Thinking for Breakthrough Results.* Mason, OH: Thomson, 2006.

United Nations Convention on Contracts for the International Sale of Goods. http://www.uncitral.org/uncitral/en/uncitral_texts/sale_goods/1980CISG.html (Accessed February 2011).

SEARCH-BASED DISCOVERY

Entrepreneurial opportunity is a fascinating topic and central to the field of new venture management, but what have we learned about how to find an opportunity? The dominant theories reflect an assumption that entrepreneurs either search and discover opportunities or create opportunities without a deliberate search. Sharon Alvarez and Jay Barney describe these views as "discovery theory" and "creation theory."

Creation theory indicates that opportunities do not necessarily develop from existing industries or markets and it is the entrepreneur's actions that result in opportunities. According to this view, entrepreneurs do not seek to find opportunities but instead act and observe how consumers and markets respond to their actions as opportunities that are social constructions and cannot exist independent of the entrepreneur.

Discovery theory differs fundamentally from creation theory in that discovery theory assumes that competitive imperfections result in opportunities that come about exogenously from changes in technology, society, and the regulatory or the political environment. Since opportunities come about by exogenous changes to an industry or market and since these opportunities are observable, all individuals associated with an industry or market can be aware of the opportunities brought about from these changes. However, if everyone within a particular industry or market knew about the opportunities, they could all try to exploit them. Therefore, entrepreneurs who effectively search and discover opportunities may be different from others in their abilities to either see or exploit opportunities. Previous research shows that the most important factors for effective search-based discovery are an individual's alertness and his or her idiosyncratic knowledge.

Israel Kirzner first discussed the importance of alertness, which he referred to as a motivated propensity to formulate an image of the future. Whereas the alertness perspective is extremely well known within the field, it has been widely criticized because it offers very little guidance to aspiring entrepreneurs other than to *stay alert*. Jim Fiet put forward an alternative perspective that emphasizes alertness while also restricting and maximizing search outcomes based on entrepreneurs who had been repeatedly successful. He describes a process whereby successful entrepreneurs conduct targeted systematic searches based on their alertness to promising information channels that reflect their specific knowledge.

Information about industries or markets cannot be completely known by any one individual, as every individual's accumulation of knowledge and experience is different. Therefore, to discover an opportunity, it is important that the entrepreneur have specific knowledge associated with an opportunity. Some types of specific knowledge have been shown to be especially germane to discovery and venture creation. For example, Scott Shane examined the commercialization of a single patented technology by different entrepreneurs and showed that specific knowledge of markets, knowledge about ways to serve markets, and knowledge about customer problems were important to entrepreneurial discovery. However, few studies examine specific types of knowledge and whether they are of equal importance to search-based discovery versus other modes, such as opportunity creation.

A key challenge in entrepreneurship education is how best to prepare students who have the desire to be entrepreneurs to discover and exploit an opportunity. Can we better prepare individuals to effectively search and discover opportunities? Research suggests that the answer is yes, we can. For example, in a study of undergraduate business students, Dawn DeTienne and Gaylen Chandler showed that creativity training was related to a greater number of ideas as well as more innovative ideas.

Other research shows that the ability to search and discover an opportunity can be facilitated through individual knowledge and educational initiatives. In a study of high-tech entrepreneurs, Matt Marvel found that varying dimensions of knowledge and experience affected search-based discovery. Among the key findings were that individuals with more years of experience and education are less likely to search for an entrepreneurial opportunity. The wage and risk considerations of owning a venture may be considered unattractive, given their alternatives. However, three specific types of knowledge and experience were found to enhance search-based discovery and include (1) knowledge of ways to serve markets, (2) knowledge of customer problems, and (3) experience within start-ups. These specific types of knowledge and experience are described next as well as how they may be integrated into education initiatives.

First, knowledge of ways to serve markets concerns how a technology can be developed as a product or service offering that satisfies market needs. A number of studies have shown that the products or services entrepreneurs introduce are related to where they were once previously employed. An individual who has knowledge of how to create a particular type of product or service is more likely to create similar products again and again. For example, individuals with experience in designing machines are more likely to package a technology as a product rather than a service. Academic discipline, as well as experience, plays a role in developing this knowledge. For example, business school students tend to create more service-based ventures compared to engineering students, who tend to create product-oriented ventures.

Second, prior knowledge of customer problems also has been shown to enhance effective search-based discovery. Integrated projects with the business community, where students learn about specific customer problems and develop proactive solutions, may enhance entrepreneurship education efforts.

Third, the experience acquired from working within other new ventures appears to enhance the likelihood of searching and exploiting future opportunities and provides support for education programs with integrated learning opportunities within start-ups. As universities continue to invest in venture incubators to spur economic development and technology transfer, these may also provide an opportunity for a broader approach to entrepreneurship education with experiential components.

Without question, search-based discovery is a fundamental research question and a topic of great practical value. This brief review has highlighted some of the most salient research within the entrepreneurship literature. Given the inherent need to enable those individuals who have the desire to start a venture, this topic is certain to receive increasing attention.

Matthew R. Marvel
Western Kentucky University

See also Creativity; Creativity and Opportunities; Discovery and Exploitation; Opportunity Development; Opportunity Identification and Structural Alignment

Further Readings

Alvarez, S. A. and J. B. Barney. "Discovery and Creation: Alternative Theories of Entrepreneurial Action." *Strategic Entrepreneurship Journal*, v.1/1 (2007).

DeTienne, D. and G. Chandler. "Opportunity Identification and Its Role in the Entrepreneurial Classroom: A Pedagogical Approach and Empirical Test." *Academy of Management Learning and Education*, v.3/3 (2004).

Fiet, J. O. "A Prescriptive Analysis of Search and Discovery." *Journal of Management Studies*, v.44/4 (2007).

Fiet, J. O. *The Systematic Search for Entrepreneurial Discoveries*. Westport, CT: Quorum Books, 2002.

Kirzner, I. *Discovery and the Capitalist Process*. Chicago: University of Chicago Press, 1985.

Marvel, M. R. "Human Capital and Search-Based Discovery: A Study of High-Tech Entrepreneurship." *Entrepreneurship Theory and Practice* (May 25, 2011).

Shane, S. "Prior Knowledge and the Discovery of Entrepreneurial Opportunities." *Organization Science*, v.11/4 (2000).

SELLING PRODUCTS AND SERVICES

Selling is one of the principal activities of any business, an indispensable core activity; without sales, there is no business. In its simplest terms, selling is the offer of the business's product for cash or barter, a value of which the seller sees as being equal to or greater than the product's value. Some process of negotiation occurs between the buyer and seller sides of the transaction. In the modern West, haggling is rare in retail sales, but negotiations over price, terms, and other considerations often occur at the business level between businesses and suppliers or wholesalers and retailers. Other aspects of the negotiation process have essentially been sublimated into market research to determine the best price for a product or are performed by market forces, like supply and demand. The law of supply and demand dictates that, when a product sells out too quickly at a given price, that price may go up; when it sells too slowly, the price may come down. Eventually equilibrium is achieved, just as it would be if the buyer and seller were negotiating face to face.

Part of negotiating, whether explicit or made implicit in the product's promotional materials and advertising, may lie in stressing that the cash cost of a product does not represent its real value. If two refrigerators are priced the same but one of them uses less electricity, it will cost the buyer less money over time. The cost of the product may be mitigated by its benefits; it may be something that will save the business money in operating expenses by accomplishing a current task more efficiently or making another product unnecessary; it may help increase the business's customer base and sales; or there may be benefits to which it is difficult to assign a cost. Purchasing higher-quality computers and office chairs for employees may have no obvious impact on a business's profits, for example, but if such small expenditures make employees happier and contribute to attracting and retaining a better class of employee (or obviating a potential legal action associated with workers' compensation), then the company will function better and more efficiently. In other cases, a cost may be justified because of the potential cost of not having it—an argument everyone accepts when paying for insurance and one that can apply to numerous products with emergency applications.

In the sales profession itself, methods are called selling techniques and vary wildly according to the product, the industry, and the preferences of the salesperson. Techniques include prospecting and seeking referrals to potential buyers, as well as sales presentations to interested parties at industry events such as conventions. Selling requires a degree of empathy and the ability to read buyers, as well as thick enough skin to handle the inevitably high level of rejections. Selling strategies focus on quick action to take advantage of opportunities, especially important with new ventures that may be filling a recently

In Western society, excessive bargaining over price is rare in retail sales, but negotiations over price, terms, and other aspects can and will occur at the business level. A buyer may be able to negotiate on a sale when they believe that the cash cost of a product does not represent its real value. (Photos.com)

created niche. The effective salesperson knows how to cultivate relationships with customers, understands when to allow those relationships to become interdependent, and can use the venture's product or service as a symbol of a change in the marketplace—informing customers of that change as part of the sales "pitch," through the age-old traditional selling technique of identifying a need in the customer's life and presenting the product as a remedy to that need. However, communication needs to be two-way. The salesperson or entrepreneur must understand what customers and potential customers are communicating, whether they purchase the product or not—that is, what they really are saying, and what those statements say about the venture and its marketing strategies. Presenting customers with choices in such a way as to influence their decisions has been called choice architecture, or permission marketing.

With a new venture, sales strategies are key because customers must be courted and created, not simply retained. They may need to be actively courted away from a competing product. Business-to-business sales will require creating a relationship with business customers and selling them the solution to their needs. An entrepreneur is often both manager and salesman, especially in the early days of the venture and perhaps through its lifespan; the benefit there, though, is that the entrepreneur knows the product best and can answer any questions about it and its niche.

While selling shares the same goal as marketing, they are different activities. Marketing impacts the environment in which selling takes place. Marketing attracts customers, informs customers, and creates a brand identity for the venture, while sales creates the specific relationship between the business and each customer. The field of sales process engineering treats selling as one part of a larger system rather than a dedicated and autonomous department, and new ventures, particularly those with small staffs, can benefit from perceiving sales in that fashion. Sales process engineers view sales, marketing, and customer service as all elements of the interaction between customers and the firm.

Bill Kte'pi
Independent Scholar

See also Advertising; Barter; Cash Flow; E-Commerce; Sales

Further Readings

Godin, Seth. *Purple Cow*. New York: Portfolio, 2009.
Jones, Eli, James A. Roberts, and Lawrence B. Chonko. "Motivating Sales Entrepreneurs to Change: A Conceptual Framework of Factors Leading to Successful Change Management Initiatives in Sales Organizations." *Journal of Marketing Theory and Practice*, v.8/2 (Spring 2000).
Lopes, Miguel Pereira, Miguel Pina E. Cunha, and Patricia Jardim da Palma. "Case Studies on What Entrepreneurs Actually Do to Attract Resources: A Two-Route Framework." *Journal of Enterprising Culture*, v.17/3 (September 2009).
Stack, Jack. *The Great Game of Business*. New York: Doubleday, 1994.
Stephenson, Harriet Buckman. "The Most Critical Problem for the Fledgling Small Business: Getting Sales." *American Journal of Small Business*, v.9/1 (Summer 1984).

Selling Successful Businesses

Business owners have many reasons for selling a successful business. Regardless of their reasons for exiting, owners want to see a return on their investments, and a sale is a good way to convert their equity in the business into cash. This sale can be a complicated process, but there are some common issues in all sales of successful businesses. These issues include the underlying motivations for buyers when purchasing, the methods for valuation of the business enterprise preparing the organization for sale, and identifying types of buyers.

Just as marketers strive to understand why their customers buy their products to better position themselves in the marketplace, it is important for companies to understand why potential buyers are interested in the purchase of the firm. There are two primary motivations that drive buyers to acquire a business: financial and strategic. Financial motivations consider future economic gain to be had from purchasing the business. Firms that buy for financial reasons are considering future profits from the acquisition discounted by estimated risks, and they rely on traditional valuation methods to evaluate and set selling prices. Business valuation considers the processes and procedures used to apply an economic value to a company and become the basis of what a buyer is willing to pay in a sale of a business. Most business valuations models take into consideration both internal financial aspects of the firm and external economic conditions facing the firm.

There are three basic approaches to these evaluations: the income approach, the asset-based approach, and the market approach. Income valuation considers current or expected profits for cash flows, then applies a discount rate to reflect the risk involved in future earnings to determine the value of the company. Asset-based approaches to valuation consider the value of company assets minus company liabilities to determine the business value. Finally, market approaches to valuation consider the selling price of similar businesses to determine pricing multiples for financial performance measures to arrive at the proper selling price.

While financial transactions tend to view the purchased company as a stand-alone or a loosely integrated entity, strategic purchases consider the synergistic benefits that can come from the deal. Strategic sales occur because the buyer recognizes that there are opportunities for integrating the operations that allow for leveraging its assets and capabilities with those of the acquired firm. Some such opportunities include gaining market share, expanding into new markets, reducing competition in industry, expanding a customer base, expanding product and service offerings, reducing the cost of servicing the customer, or improving the service provided to the customer. As the seller, an organization can improve the chances of a sale if it can position itself favorably in relation to the motives that are driving the buyer, since valuation will be based on the value generated by the combined entity, not solely on the basis of the acquired firm's value.

With both types of acquisitions, there are additional steps sellers can take to improve their valuations. Some of these are similar to building "curb appeal" when selling a home, while others reflect serious business improvement. To improve valuation it is important that the business keep good records, including financial records, inventory records, human resources records, and customer records. More substantial moves will improve the business while improving valuation, making the company more attractive overall. It becomes vital to invest in activities to grow earnings, including marketing and sales force initiatives and facility improvements. Marketing and sales force expenditures should increase earnings, driving up the financials used to calculate valuations. Facilities should be in good repair and should be able to handle anticipated growth to ensure that they do not counter these gains.

Another necessary improvement to enable high valuations is that proper management and staff be put in place. A company that is dependent on the founder to work has little value in the market. This can especially be a problem in service companies in which the owner's expertise is often the delivered service. This problem can be alleviated if the company creates a standard service offering that can be duplicated and taught to others. Before the sale, management duties must be standardized and delegated to others. Once a strong management team is in place, the company should create incentive plans that encourage the team to stay on after the sale.

After all these steps have been implemented, the final step, before identifying a buyer, is to develop a strong company narrative. This narrative is the story of the company that tells others what the business is all about. It is important that this narrative explain who the customer is, what customer needs the business fulfills for the customer, how the company differentiates itself from competitors, and how the enterprise can make a profit in meeting these needs.

This narrative must be tailored to the purchaser's goals but can help potential buyers see the value in the company.

Different types of buyers tend to have different goals for purchase. For example, wealthy individuals are likely buyers for companies valued under $2 million and are financial buyers who view the purchase as an alternative to another large investment. Similarly, investment trusts are usually financial buyers, who typically are not interested in owning all the equity in the business and are not interested in running the business but rather view it as a way to diversify investment portfolios. Private equity groups can be either financial or strategic partners, depending on whether their motives are to create synergies between portfolio companies or are purely financial. Private equity groups are different from investment trusts in that they typically desire a controlling or substantial minority stake in the transaction. Finally, other companies are potential buyers, and can be either financially or strategically motivated, depending on the goals for the purchase and the level of integration expected. Business brokers can be used to identify potential buyers and will have an understanding of the motivations behind the purchase.

Carolyn Popp Garrity
Louisiana State University

See also Exit Strategies; Initial Public Offering; Venture Valuation

Further Readings

Denning, Stephen. *The Leader's Guide to Storytelling: Mastering the Art and Discipline of Business Narrative.* San Francisco: Jossey-Bass, 2005.

Margretta, Joan. "Why Business Models Matter." *Harvard Business Review* (May 2002).

Storey, D. J., ed. *Small Business: Critical Perspectives on Business and Management.* London: Routledge, 2000.

Warrillow, John. *Built to Sell.* Toronto, ON: Flip Jet Media, 2010.

Service Innovation

Innovation in services, or service innovation, is defined in the *Oslo Manual* by the Organisation for Economic Co-operation and Development (OECD) and Eurostat as "new services that significantly improve customers' access to goods or services." The *Oslo Manual* strives to highlight some general characteristics that apply to most services, although at the same time acknowledging that services include a wide range of different types of business models and activities. Here it will be worthwhile to review the general characteristics first and then discuss classifications focusing on intraservices' similarities and differences, as well as some of the findings and controversies within research on service innovation.

The *Oslo Manual* notes that the distinction between products and processes is often blurred. The distinction that is being referred to here is between product innovation and process innovation, and as reviewed below the distinction is more complicated than it is, for example, in manufacturing. Compared to manufacturing, the development of innovative processes can be more informal within services. It is sometimes more difficult to identify single innovations in services, because they might be immersed in a more complex whole. However, there have also been examples of highly acclaimed and large-scale innovations in services. For example, increasing the capacity of airport runways has been achieved at some major airports without building additional runways. This has been accomplished through improved efficiency in ground operations, better coordination, and developments in technology that have facilitated safer spacing of landing times. In retail services, bar-code scanners required retailers to go through several nontechnological changes, such as changes to distribution networks and improved delivery procedures.

Although it is sometimes difficult to draw the line between product and process innovation in services, the following constitute examples of product innovations. Some new services conform to the overall definition of innovation in services above, such as pick-up and drop-off service at home for rental cars. Another fairly recent service is subscription service for DVDs, video on demand via broadband, and Internet-based banking or payment systems. We have also seen a proliferation of new forms of warranty, such as extended warranties or warranties bundled with other services. The *Oslo Manual* gives additional examples, such as variable-rate loans with fixed-rate ceilings and other new types of loans. Compared to the single-purpose customer cards of the past, there has been an influx of smart cards and multipurpose plastic cards. Various

Service innovations can occur when a service concept, system, or technology is new or considerably changed. For example, increasing the capacity of airport runways has been achieved at some major airports by improving operations, enhancing coordination, and implementing safer spacing of landing times. (Photos.com)

services are increasingly being bundled together with goods, such as subscriptions to audio file services purchased together with an MP3 player, or software updating or hardware maintenance services purchased together with computer hardware.

Businessweek reported in 2007 on the establishment of a Service Research and Innovation Initiative, where large corporations such as IBM, Oracle, Hewlett-Packard, Microsoft, and Cisco have come together in order to learn more about the service function itself as well as about innovation in services. More recently, entirely new business models, such as carbon trading, have emerged in the wake of increasing awareness about global warming. Companies that have carbon dioxide emission permits can trade these if they have cut their emissions and have permits to spare—for example, through the European Emissions Trading Scheme. The thinking is that polluters who can cut their emissions most cheaply will more than meet their legally binding targets and end up with extra permits. In many cases these companies are very small (for example, small farmers) and do not have the energy or time to invest in trading issues. This makes room for a whole new group of professional services falling under the category of carbon brokering.

The new service in question may be of one type. In the case of a pure product innovation, for example, a company can offer a new service or a traditional service with new characteristics without significantly changing the way the service is provided. Also, service innovation may involve cost-reducing measures that significantly change the way the service is provided—in other words, process innovation—while the service itself remains unchanged. For example, retail sales of books and medicines, which in many countries have undergone deregulation processes, have changed because these products are now sold through grocery stores and the Internet in addition to traditional bookshops and drugstores. The service—delivery and distribution of the product—has not changed, but the process for accomplishing that service has undergone innovation.

Distinguishing between product and process innovations is not simply a matter of academic interest. The basic assumption here is that activities aiming at product and process innovations respectively necessitate somewhat different efforts. When the distinction between the two is blurred, as often is the case within service innovations, the challenges when it comes to innovation management are considerable. One development in this regard, in addition to distinguishing between different types of forms within services, is to distinguish between product innovations within services and marketing innovations. Making this distinction makes the field a little more manageable by way of exclusion. The difference between service innovations and marketing innovations is that the innovation involves a marketing method only in the case of the latter, whereas the innovation has to do with the product itself in the case of service innovations. The distinction depends on the nature of the firm's business, although firms in general are able to distinguish between the two. For a manufacturing firm introducing Internet-based sales of its goods, the innovation is within marketing. For a firm that is in the business of electronic commerce (for example, an auction firm), a significant change in the characteristics or electronic capabilities would be a service innovation.

The field of service innovation is large and difficult to grasp, first and foremost because the services sector itself is diverse. There are several classifications dividing different services and service firms into categories. A basic classification scheme is offered by Jeremy Howells and Bruce Tether, who classify services into four groups. The first is services dealing mainly with goods, such as transport and logistics. The second deals with information, such as call centers. The third is a group of knowledge-based services, such as consultancy and accountancy. The fourth is a group of services dealing with people, such as healthcare. Ian Miles, noting that a more detailed subdivision is necessary in order to understand the mechanisms of service innovation more fully, identifies a kind of continuum, with personal services (such as hairdressing) at one end of the continuum, which involve basic technologies and often are organized on a small-scale basis. At the other end of the continuum is a group of services often referred to as FIRE (finance, insurance, and real estate) services, which use advanced information technologies intensively. In other subsectors are groups such as "distributive services" (transportation in all its varieties, retail and wholesale trade, and, in some classifications, telecommunications and broadcasting), HORECA services (hotels, restaurants, and catering), social and collective services, and business services. Miles also notes that, in addition to these intrasector variations, the markets for services are very heterogeneous as well, ranging from end consumers to businesses and the public sector. Some services are indeed similar to manufacturing in terms of structure and organization, whereas others are vastly different.

Certain countries have progressed on the path of transition from a predominantly industrial economy toward a service economy. In *50 Years of Figures on Europe*, published in 2003, Eurostat shows that already during the 1970s more than half of the value added was contributed by services within the then European Union countries as a whole. By 2000 it was more than two thirds. There are, however, vast differences among countries. Ireland grew from 44.5 to 49 percent during the 1973–2001 period; the Netherlands, from 52.2 percent to 65.5 percent; Denmark, from 58.8 percent to 64 percent; Germany, from 48.1 percent to 64.9 percent; France, from 50.8 percent to 66.8 percent; Spain, from 47.8 percent to 64.2 percent; and Luxembourg, from 46.9 percent to 83.8 percent. According to Miles, the differences in growth reflect the composition of the service sectors in the different countries. Again, the term *service sector* comprises a huge range of different activities with very different characteristics.

Despite all these differences, a common denominator is that most services (and hence, service innovations) are intangible. In addition, services are most often interactive, where a huge amount of contact between the service provider and the customer is frequent. This allows for a particular form of innovation processes, where there may be input from the customer regarding, for example, the design, production, or delivery of the service activity. In addition, many services are information-intensive. These three factors in combination refute the claim held within some camps of research, stating that innovation services predominantly consisted in adopting or implementing innovations originating in other sectors. As Tether and Howells have pointed out, innovation in services is more complex than earlier perspectives that emphasize technology adoption would suggest. This also implies that greater attention should be paid to issues like skills, organizational structure, and their interaction with technologies.

One can ask whether increased innovation intensity within services will lead to more diversification or more standardization in clients' lives. Indeed, an answer to such a question is likely to be that both trends appear to be happening at the same time. On one hand, there have been major service innovations resulting in the possibility for individualization, such as supplies delivered to or services performed at one's home or business. On the other hand, the standardization consequences of many innovations in services are sometimes questioned, including the proliferation of global templates for Internet and television entertainment, a seemingly lessened scope of diversity within fast-food choices, and depersonalization of telephone-based services such as call-center-based services.

Terje Grønning
University of Oslo

See also Innovation Diffusion; Innovation Processes; Product Innovation; Radical and Incremental Innovation

Further Readings

Barras, Richard. "Interactive Innovation in Financial and Business Services: The Vanguard of the Service Revolution." *Research Policy*, v.19 (1990).

Barras, Richard. "Towards a Theory of Innovation in Services." *Research Policy*, v.15/4 (1986).

Castellacci, Fulvio. "Technological Paradigms, Regimes and Trajectories: Manufacturing and Service Industries in a New Taxonomy of Sectoral Patterns of Innovation." *Research Policy*, v.37/6–7 (2008).

Department of Trade and Industry. *Innovation in Services.* DTI Occasional Paper 9. London: Author, 2007.

Eurostat. *50 Years of Figures on Europe.* Luxembourg: Author, 2003.

Howells, Jeremy and Bruce Tether. *Innovation in Services: Issues at Stake and Trends.* Luxembourg: Office for Official Publications of the European Communities, 2006.

Jana, Reena. "Service Innovation: The Next Big Thing." *Businessweek* (March 29, 2007).

Miles, Ian. "Innovation in Services." In *The Oxford Handbook of Innovation*, Jan Fagerberg, David Mowery, and Richard Nelson, eds. Oxford, UK: Oxford University Press, 2005.

Pearce, Fred. "Carbon Trading: Dirty, Sexy Money." *New Scientist* (April 19, 2008).

Sundbo, Jon and Faiz Gallouj. "Innovation as a Loosely Coupled System in Services." *International Journal of Services Technology and Management*, v.1/1 (2000).

Social Capital

Social capital has been loosely defined as benefits accrued as a result of social relationships. Whereas social capital has been a topic of interest across numerous disciplines for many years, it has only recently gained traction in entrepreneurship literature. Empirical research related to social capital in entrepreneurship has accumulated over the past 20 years. The vast majority of theoretical contributions related to social capital in entrepreneurship have come since the beginning of the 21st century. Several traditional theoretical views of social capital have been the most prevalent in the entrepreneurial context. Those seeing the widest application include the embeddedness, network closure, structural holes, and strong/weak ties perspectives.

The embeddedness perspective has been the most commonly utilized theoretical base in entrepreneurship research and comes in two forms: structural and relational. Structural embeddedness focuses on the configuration of the relationships in a social network, whereas relational embeddedness focuses on the quality of the relationships within the network. The underlying suggestion by Mark Granovetter in the embeddedness view is that exchange is based on social relationships. This view, however, has usually been combined with other theoretical views in studies of entrepreneurial situations.

The network closure perspective is often seen as complementary to the embeddedness view. This view emphasizes the value created by having a network of individuals and firms that are well connected and established. In such a setting, risk is reduced as confidence in actors' actions is high and trust is established. In addition, operating within a closed network allows for increased transfer of information, depth of knowledge, and the ability to accrue favors from other actors over time that can be acted upon at a later date.

Specific to entrepreneurship research, studies in the area of family business have often used both the network closure and embeddedness perspectives. These types of firms often emphasize relationships between organizations within the family business network (such as those with a high level of interlocking directorates). In this setting, network members, while in competition, enhance long-term survival through coordinated effort. In addition, research building on embeddedness and network membership has shown a link between corporate governance and social capital utilization in family businesses. Across other areas of entrepreneurship, entrepreneurs have been found to increase social capital via membership in various groups, clubs, or organizations, enabling them to overcome resource constraints and disadvantages.

R. S. Burt's theory of structural holes is another common theoretical base used for social capital research in entrepreneurship. Structural holes theory argues that there are particular advantages that can be realized by being properly placed structurally in a relationship. In this way, firms seek to bridge the gap between two parties, thus filling a relational hole and providing the connection. As a result, the social capital developed is based on positioning of the firm, rather than the relationship present between two parties—both parties are now dependent on the bridging relationship. From a practical view, this approach closely follows the ideas of opportunity recognition and exploitation—finding a market asymmetry and acting proactively to capitalize by providing a connection. This can be seen in practice with firms connecting two parties, or even in situations such as disintermediation and reintermediation. Similar to the weak ties view, the structural holes view seeks to maximize the number and variety of ties in the network.

A third view of social capital that has been widely applied in entrepreneurship literature is that of strong and weak ties. Strong ties are those social relationships that are direct associations between parties. Emphasis is placed on developing deep relationships, providing trust and confidence in a partner. This view has been commonly used in venture capital research. Entrepreneurs seeking funding can benefit from the continued development of a trusting and mutually beneficial relationship with their investors. Past research has shown the importance of not only a market idea or business proposition but also the reputation of an entrepreneur and the depth of the venture capitalist-entrepreneur relationship when looking at the likelihood of venture funding. The social capital built over time, leading to a depth of a network relationship, is often the primary determinant of the funding decision.

Weak ties, on the other hand, are indirect, network-based relationships. Complemented by the structural holes perspective, the weak ties view prescribes minimal redundancy of ties, with emphasis placed on developing network breadth, as opposed to depth. Thus, the number of ties is emphasized, providing the ability to draw upon a wide range of relationships and/or social links. This enables increased access to a variety of information and/or resources. Weak ties usually lead to more timely or useful information, as they usually bridge a connection between otherwise unconnected groups. The benefits of weak ties to entrepreneurs include access to ideas, access to social resources, enhanced social connections leading to financing, and access to potential customers.

Other social capital theories used in entrepreneurship research include, but are not limited to, social resource theory, network membership, community level social capital, and trust/norms.

Future research in the area of social capital in entrepreneurship will likely span across issues such as social capital as a antecedent to social entrepreneurship, social capital in emerging economies, social capital as a transferable resource, and social capital's use in ventures owned by women and minorities. It seems the next steps for social capital research in the field of entrepreneurship will be to specifically examine the influence of the various types and levels of social capital in differing settings to identify its optimal structure and utilization in varying situations.

Justin L. Davis
Jason Stoner
Ohio University

See also Human Capital Theory; Human Resource Strategy; Human Resources; Managing Human and Social Capital; Measures of Performance; Microfinance; Social Entrepreneurship; Social Intelligence; Social Networks; Sustainable Development

Further Readings

Batjargal, B. and M. Liu. "Entrepreneurs' Access to Private Equity in China: The Role of Social Capital." *Organization Science*, v.15/2 (2004).

Burt, R. S. *Toward a Structural Theory of Action.* New York: Academic Press, 1982.

Carney, M. "Corporate Governance and Competitive Advantage in Family-Controlled Firms." *Entrepreneurship Theory and Practice*, v.29/3 (2005).

Coleman, J. S. *Foundations of Social Theory.* Cambridge, MA: Harvard University Press, 1990.

Granovetter, M. S. "Economic Action and Social Structure: The Problem of Embeddedness." *American Journal of Sociology*, v.91 (1985).

Molina-Morales, Francesc Xavier, and María Teresa Martínez-Fernández. "Social Networks: Effects of Social Capital on Firm Innovation." *Journal of Small Business Management*, v.48/2 (April 2010).

Stam, W. and T. Elfring. "Entrepreneurial Orientation and New Venture Performance: The Moderating Role of Intra- and Extra-Industry Social Capital." *Academy of Management Journal*, v.51/1 (2008).

Social Entrepreneurship

Social entrepreneurship refers to the use of entrepreneurial skills and practices to achieve social missions and goals. Social entrepreneurship involves pursuing opportunities to create social value by developing innovative solutions to meet social needs, deploying resources in novel ways to stimulate social change, or launching new enterprises aimed at generating positive returns to society. Such efforts result in social value creation, that is, positive social impacts and outcomes that can be assessed in economic terms. Examples of value creation with a social dimension include improvements related to education, poverty, healthcare, race relations, gender relations, and empowering people with disabilities.

Beyond basic definitions of social entrepreneurship, there is a plethora of idiosyncratic definitions about which there is little agreement. To wit, S. Bacq and J. Frank have identified 12 published definitions of the term *social entrepreneurship* and 17 definitions of the term *social entrepreneur*. Such a proliferation of definitions is indicative of how young social entrepreneurship is as a field of research. At this stage in the development of the field, significant definitional consistency seems limited to the presence of both social and economic goals. To address different aspects of social entrepreneurship, some researchers distinguish between three types of entities: nonprofit organizations endeavoring to act entrepreneurially, for-profit organizations with social missions, and hybrid organizations that combine elements of for-profit and nonprofit activity.

In practice, social entrepreneurship is a relatively small yet prevalent and growing phenomenon. Whereas reliable global statistics on social entrepreneurship are currently unavailable, indicators from individual countries attest to its size. For example, a 2006 survey estimated that there were approximately 55,000 social enterprises in the United Kingdom, with a combined turnover of £27 billion each year; this constituted approximately 5 percent of all businesses with employees in the United Kingdom. The most cited, most recognized, and arguably the most successful social entrepreneur to date is Muhammad Yunus. Yunus is the founder of Grameen Bank, a microfinance institution that generates both financial wealth from loan interest and social value by helping borrowers rise out of poverty. Notably, Yunus argues that social entrepreneurship not only is a new type of business but also may be the foundation of a "new kind of capitalism that serves humanity's most pressing needs."

Beyond the rise of social entrepreneurs, the last two decades have produced supporting organizations and institutions to foster social entrepreneurship. Noteworthy organizations of this sort include Ashoka, a fellowship program that provides venture capital to social entrepreneurs, and the Skoll Foundation, whose mission according to its Website is to drive "large-scale change by investing in, connecting, and celebrating social entrepreneurs and other innovators dedicated to solving the world's most pressing problems." With regard to institutions, governments around the world are implementing legislation specifically tailored to the formation of social enterprises. Examples of current legal forms of incorporation include the Community Interest Company (CIC) in the United Kingdom and the Low-Profit Limited Liability Company (L3C) in the United States.

Although it is considerably outpaced by practice, research on social entrepreneurship has also thrived over the last two decades. In a quantitative analysis of social entrepreneurship research, T. W. Moss and colleagues found six published articles on the topic between 1991 and 1996, 56 published articles between 1997 and 2002, and 267 published articles between 2003 and 2008. Further evidence of the growth and relevance of social entrepreneurship research is provided by three recent developments. The first is the establishment of academic conferences devoted to social entrepreneurship research. Two of the most prominent examples of such conferences are the Satter Conference on Social Entrepreneurship, held annually at New York University, and the Social Enterprise Research Conference (SERC), held annually by Oxford University. The second development is the establishment of research centers devoted to social entrepreneurship. The Center for the Advancement of Social Entrepreneurship (CASE) at Duke University's Fuqua School of Business and the Wilson Center for Social Entrepreneurship at Pace University are examples of these types of centers. The third development is the recent creation of a scholarly journal devoted solely to social entrepreneurship research: the *Journal of Social Entrepreneurship*, published by Routledge.

In general, social entrepreneurship research supports the notion that social entrepreneurship is qualitatively and significantly different from commercial entrepreneurship (although notable counterarguments have been put forth by P. A. Dacin and colleagues). Whereas arguments for unique processes have been purported, the majority of published studies comparing social and commercial entrepreneurship have focused on the unique antecedents and outcomes of social entrepreneurship. A study by G. T. Lumpkin and colleagues offers a useful framework for explicating salient differences in antecedents and outcomes between social and commercial entrepreneurs. This study identified four

antecedents and three outcomes distinct to social entrepreneurship. The antecedents are social motivation/mission, opportunity identification, access to resources/funding, and multiple stakeholders. The outcomes are social value creation, sustainability of solutions, and satisfying multiple stakeholders. We briefly address each in turn.

A mission comprises both the motivations and the overall purpose of a venture. The fundamental difference in missions between commercial and social entrepreneurs is that the former are generally directed toward private financial gain, whereas the latter are directed toward public value generation, which may or may not be financially oriented. Opportunity identification in social entrepreneurship is distinct in that these types of opportunities lie in solving social problems. As such, the opportunity identification process may require an entirely new paradigm. For instance, many social entrepreneurs may need to recognize that the extremely poor can be valuable customers. Social entrepreneurs also have access to different types of resources as compared with commercial entrepreneurs. For example, many of them may be eligible for government grants or may have the ability to solicit public donations. Contrarily, social entrepreneurs may have difficulty securing traditional venture capital funding, because they are less focused on maximizing internal wealth. Finally, social entrepreneurs tend to have a broader collection of stakeholders as compared to their commercial counterparts. For instance, they likely include the local community, donors, and beneficiaries among their important stakeholders.

Regarding outcomes, social value creation is frequently cited as a defining facet of social entrepreneurship. Social value creation, which can be defined generally as advancement of the common welfare, is often generated by commercial firms through job creation, tax revenue, or otherwise, yet it is rarely an intended outcome. However, social entrepreneurs focus on social value creation, and in many cases it is their raison d'être. Another salient focus for social entrepreneurs is the satisfaction of multiple stakeholders. Satisfying the demands of not just owners but also employees, donors, communities, beneficiaries, governments, and others is a challenge that many social entrepreneurs must both endure and take pride in accomplishing. The third outcome concerns the sustainability of the social initiatives. Social entrepreneurs place a premium on solutions to social ills which are self-sufficient and enduring.

This framework of antecedents and outcomes in social entrepreneurship is by no means exhaustive; it is a parsimonious representation of some of the more distinguishing dimensions. Importantly, each of the antecedents and outcomes has tremendous implications for social entrepreneurs. For instance, the goal of social value creation may render competition with other social entrepreneurs counterproductive, which limits the applicability of existing strategy research. Lumpkin and colleagues have conducted an extensive investigation of how these antecedents and outcomes influence the entrepreneurial orientation of a firm.

Taken together, the foregoing arguments support the notion that social entrepreneurship is a unique and interesting domain of scholarly inquiry. Scholars have uncovered critical differences between social and commercial entrepreneurs, yet there is still much to do. Owing to its nascency, its widespread use in practice, and its continual development, the domain of social entrepreneurship is ripe with future research needs. On an abstract level, the domain is in great need of research that (1) is quantitative and (2) makes a theoretical contribution. With regard to the former, the vast majority of extant social entrepreneurship research is purely theoretical, and those that include data are most often case studies. Whereas useful findings have resulted from such research, producing large-sample quantitative studies is crucial in extracting generalizable, rigorous, and valid findings useful for a wide range of practitioners. With regard to the need for making theoretical contributions, most social entrepreneurship research that involves theory applies established management or entrepreneurship theoretical frameworks to a social context. Whereas this practice is also useful, the future of the domain will be greatly limited in its scholarly and practical impact if it cannot contribute to established theoretical frameworks.

David Gras

G. T. Lumpkin

Syracuse University

See also Measures of Performance; Microfinance; Social Capital; Social Intelligence; Social Networks; Sustainable Development

Further Readings

Austin, J., M. Stevenson, and J. Wei-Skillern. "Social and Commercial Entrepreneurship: Same, Different, or Both?" *Entrepreneurship Theory and Practice*, v.30/1 (2006).

Bacq, S. and F. Janssen. "The Multiple Faces of Social Entrepreneurship: A Review of Definitional Issues Based on Geographical and Thematic Criteria." *Entrepreneurship and Regional Development*, v.23/5–6 (2011).

Bornstein, D. *How to Change the World: Social Entrepreneurs and the Power of New Ideas*. New York: Oxford University Press, 2004.

Bornstein, D. *The Price of a Dream: The Story of the Grameen Bank*. Chicago: University of Chicago Press, 1997.

Bornstein, D. and S. Davis. *Social Entrepreneurship: What Everyone Needs to Know*. New York: Oxford University Press, 2010.

Dacin, P. A., M. T. Dacin, and M. Matear. "Social Entrepreneurship: Why We Don't Need a New Theory and How We Move Forward From Here." *Academy of Management Perspectives*, v.24/3 (2010).

Dees, J. G. "Enterprising Nonprofits." *Harvard Business Review*, v.76 (1998).

Dees, J. G. "Taking Social Entrepreneurship Seriously." *Society*, v.44/3 (2007).

Dees, J. G. and B. Anderson. "For-Profit Social Ventures." In *Social Entrepreneurship*, M. L. Kourilsky and W. B. Walstad, eds. Birmingham, UK: Senate Hall Academic, 2003.

Dewey, J. *Theory of Valuation*. Chicago: University of Chicago Press, 1939.

Lumpkin, G. T. et al. "Entrepreneurial Processes in Social Contexts: How Are They Different, If at All?" *Small Business Economics*, forthcoming.

Mair, J. and I. Martí. "Social Entrepreneurship Research: A Source of Explanation, Prediction, and Delight." *Journal of World Business*, v.41/1 (2006).

Moss, T. W., G. T. Lumpkin, and J. C. Short. "Social Entrepreneurship: A Historical Review and Research Agenda." In *Historical Foundations of Entrepreneurship Research*, F. T. Lohrke and H. Landström, eds. Northampton, UK: Edward Elgar, 2010.

Short, J. C., T. W. Moss, and G. T. Lumpkin. "Research in Social Entrepreneurship: Recent Challenges and Future Opportunities." *Strategic Entrepreneurship Journal*, v.3 (2009).

Skoll Foundation. "Mission Statement." http://www.skollfoundation.org (Accessed February 2011).

Small Business Service. *Annual Survey of Small Businesses*. London: Author, 2006.

Spear, R., C. Cornforth, and M. Aiken. "The Governance Challenges of Social Enterprises: Evidence From a UK Empirical Study." *Annals of Public and Cooperative Economics*, v.80/2 (2009).

Weerawardena, J. and G. S. Mort. "Investigating Social Entrepreneurship: A Multidimensional Model." *Journal of World Business*, v.41/1 (2006).

Yunus, M. *Building Social Business: The New Kind of Capitalism That Serves Humanity's Most Pressing Needs.* New York: Public Affairs, 2010.

SOCIAL INTELLIGENCE

Adjustment to the cognitive processes of innovation, creativity, and risk taking that entrepreneurship entails requires a high level of intelligence. As an aspect of generalized ability, intelligence is considered to be a basic driving force for successful management of new ventures. General intelligence had been emphasized over time as the foundation for effective performance in leadership and management of resources. In almost every venture, a degree of intelligence is required to perform effectively. A focus on entrepreneurship as a new venture creation activity requires some measure of intelligence in order to be successful. Individuals who are higher in intelligence and engage in entrepreneurship, either individually or as a group, are able to identify entrepreneurial opportunities where other people do not recognize possibilities. Apart from opportunity recognition, a highly intelligent entrepreneur is able to identify, attract, develop, and retain critical talents for organizational effectiveness. People who are highly intelligent are able to gain greater cognitive understanding of where to engage in certain ventures and when and how to engage in those ventures. Hence, the fostering and development of entrepreneurship are tied to intelligence.

As a psychological concept, intelligence comprises different facets. Whereas many aspects of intelligence enhance an individual's abilities to function effectively, social intelligence specifically enhances an individual's social capabilities. Entrepreneurship involves human actions and interactions in the social dimension of new venture creation. Many entrepreneurial activities involve people as either internal or external customers. Consequently, it is desirable for entrepreneurs and others involved in new ventures to develop social skills. Such skills constitute a human resource that can be used to transform other resources and thus achieve the twin goals of survival and sustainability. Hence, it is obvious that successful entrepreneurship depends not only on a high level of general intelligence but also on social intelligence, which enables the entrepreneur to handle relationships while coping effectively with the pressures of new venture creation.

A successful leader will have the ability to influence others in an organization in such a way that they are able to contribute to the attainment of the goals and objectives of the enterprise with little or no resistance. (Photos.com)

People differ significantly on the dimensions of intelligence. These differences can help to explain variations in entrepreneurship outcomes. Whereas all the aspects of intelligence are desirable, social intelligence is considered to be central for entrepreneurship. It is a measure of an individual's social capability, the ability to handle relations with others and adjust to demands that center on human factors. In discussions of new venture creation and management, social intelligence refers to being able to understand and relate to people as key stakeholders who carry out core tasks that define the entrepreneurial focus. There is growing attention to the need to understand the social aspect of intelligence as it relates to entrepreneurship and effective management of new ventures.

Social intelligence relates directly to leadership skills. Entrepreneurial development through new venture creation requires effective leadership for success. In entrepreneurship, leadership occurs as a social process in a social context. A successful individual will have the ability to influence others in the organization in such a way that they are able to contribute to the attainment of the goals and objectives of the enterprise with little or no resistance. An entrepreneur or new venture manager with good social intelligence can position a team to work toward task accomplishment and the mission of the venture. The responsibility of influencing members of an organization to ensure effectiveness and success can sometimes try the emotions of the leader. Thus, effective leadership practice requires sufficient understanding and regulation of emotions as an important aspect of leadership skills. This explains the association of social intelligence with organizational behavior. Hence, social intelligence becomes essential to successful leadership and entrepreneurship.

Although social intelligence has enjoyed increased attention as a contemporary social skill, Edward Thorndike proposed multiple forms of intelligence, including abstract, mechanical, and social intelligence, as early as 1920. As a social relational aspect, social intelligence has enjoyed increased emphasis as an important skill, especially in organizational dynamics. Irrespective of the differences in emphasis from one organization to another, social intelligence has helped to ensure success across cultures in situations that require people to work together and interact globally. Social intelligence has been identified by Robert House and R. Aditya as a required trait in leadership. This is based on the assertion that leadership is rooted in a social context. When a new venture is created through entrepreneurship, leadership shapes the direction of its effectiveness.

Apart from leadership, the role of social intelligence is well documented in human interactions across situations and settings. Using the term *emotional intelligence*, Daniel Goleman noted that it allows leaders to use social skills to get work done through people. Goleman explained that social skill persuades others to respond to leadership through influence. People are required to produce the goods or services guided by the entrepreneurship focus. Therefore, social intelligence is an important social skill for everyone, especially those interested in entrepreneurship.

Since it enables individuals to understand and regulate their emotions, R. Hooijberg et al. described social intelligence in 1997 as a significant aspect of social skills that anyone involved in management requires. Perhaps it is salient to note that the association between social intelligence and leadership has made it imperative for anyone considering entrepreneurship to develop it as a critical trait for effectiveness and success.

Contemporary organizational experiences in both developed and less developed countries have shown that people issues are quite challenging in new venture management. This is further aggravated by increasing diversities that characterize the modern workplace, where people are hired based on their skills rather than their geographic or biological backgrounds. Yet, they must interact and relate with one another in the process of carrying out job responsibilities that are needed for the organization to be effective and successful. In relating with one another, particularly in the workplace, people have held beliefs and perceptions of others who share certain characteristics different from theirs. Stereotyping and other attitudinal postures create challenges in social relationships. Preventing and controlling the challenges of attitudinal and behavioral biases in organizations necessitates social skills that are shaped by social intelligence, particularly in managers. Hence, entrepreneurs and their ventures' managers need social intelligence in social context to effectively handle the people issues of new venture creation and sustainability.

In a conversation reported in the *Harvard Business Review*, John Baldoni identified three traits associated with successful entrepreneurs. They include being practical, purposeful, and impatient. Those who work for themselves, he notes, exhibit low levels of disagreement with colleagues while cohering around a common opinion. These traits are important for successful entrepreneurship. However, they are not known to be effective in enhancing warm social relationships in the organizational setting. Having a practical outlook and being focused and impatient for success do not provide popular and sufficient strategies for promoting cordiality in social relations at work. They help the entrepreneur to be comfortable with uncertainties and be resilient. Much scholarship on entrepreneurship, as reported by Howard Aldrich and C. Zimmer, rarely focuses attention on cognitive understanding. However, as people who work for themselves, entrepreneurs need to combine several traits with social intelligence to be effective and successful in both new venture creation and development.

During the last decade, much attention has been directed at economic capabilities in entrepreneurship. Sourcing, deploying, and monitoring finance have been regarded as core. Less consideration has been given to psychosocial competencies that play equally important roles in entrepreneurial success. The psychosocial aspects of entrepreneurship are usually accompanied by challenges that require psychosocial competencies, including social intelligence for effective management. The experience of conflicts in human relations, coupled with attitudinal and behavioral deficiencies, makes social intelligence imperative in entrepreneurship.

John Oselenbalu Ekore
University of Ibadan

See also Communication Styles; Emotions; Leadership; Leadership: Training and Development; Leadership: Transformational; Measures of Performance; Microfinance; Negotiating Strategies; Networks; Social Capital; Social Entrepreneurship; Social Networks; Sustainable Development

Further Readings

Aldrich, Howard and C. Zimmer. "Entrepreneurship Through Social Networks." In *The Art and Science of Entrepreneurship*, D. Sexton and R. Smilor, eds. New York: Ballinger, 1986.

Baldoni, John. "Three Traits of Successful Entrepreneurs." *Harvard Business Review* (June 14, 2011).

Goleman, Daniel. *Working With Emotional Intelligence.* New York: Bantam, 1998.

Hooijberg, R., J. G. Hunt, and G. E. Dodge. "Leadership Complexity and Development of the Leaderplex Model." *Journal of Management*, v.23/3 (1997).

House, Robert and R. Aditya. "The Social Scientific Study of Leadership: Quo Vadis?" *Journal of Management*, v.23/3 (1997).

Thorndike, Edward. "Intelligence and Its Uses." *Harper's Magazine*, v.140 (1920).

Social Networks

Social networks, broadly defined, are tools used in organizations to connect employees, customers, and partners, providing new opportunities to conduct business. Social network theory comes from sociology and is used to describe the relationships between people and organizations. In this theory, each individual is represented by a "node," and each node is connected by "ties" that represent the relationships between the individuals or organizations in the social network. When social network theory is used to illustrate all of the individuals and relationships between them, a map is created with all of the nodes and ties, revealing all of the direct and indirect links between the individuals. These ties can represent not only social relationships but also the information,

commerce, and similar resources and activities that the nodes share.

A map of this sort can be very useful for an organization looking to leverage its connections in order to improve business by finding new opportunities or consumer needs not yet met by the market. For example, an entrepreneur who has ties to many different industries may be able to branch out more easily by utilizing these connections in a new venture. One can imagine that, much like the network connecting one business to another, this sort of network is most useful for everyone involved if it is open and has many connections outside the direct business-to-customer connections. If those persons any given customer knows are also already customers of the organization, the business has no new connections to make in the network. For this reason, a company may seek to expand its network to include more customers outside its current customer base in order to make new connections at a later time. Recent research has indicated that larger social networks and networks with more weak ties are related to increased opportunities and ideas recognized by entrepreneurs. These opportunities and ideas can be put to use to start up a new area of business or support an existing venture, strengthening an entrepreneur's overall portfolio.

It is important to remember that a social network does not need to be thought of as simply a business-to-business or business-to-customer network. Social networks can be quite complex, incorporating any number of other interpersonal relationships. Specific personnel are nested within organizations, and relationships may be between specific personnel. For example, a supplier with a good relationship with a business might refer specific customers. Just as before, the most useful social networks in this case are open, with many connections outside the current customers and partners providing many potential customers and partners.

Three advantages to social networks have been defined by researchers: information, influence, and solidarity. First, social networks allow entrepreneurs to transfer information to resource holders, directly or indirectly, which can improve confidence and understanding in the new venture. Second, social networks allow entrepreneurs to influence these resource owners either by the entrepreneur's good reputation spreading through the network or by connecting resource holders. Such connections increase competition, giving the entrepreneur greater price control when acquiring new resources. Finally, the social network promotes solidarity by uniting its members and developing norms of reciprocity, which in turn can result in lower costs and smoother transactions in the future.

Unfortunately, social networks can underperform for a number of reasons. One issue that can plague a social network is relying too heavily on the same individuals again and again, which can retard growth. Although it is important to find trusted advisers and partners, if an organization never seeks out new ways to accomplish tasks, the network will become closed, with few connections to the outside. Without those outside connections to bring in new customers or new business partners, an organization can quickly become stagnant. In particular, research has shown that during the growth stage of a new venture, social networks may have insufficient resources to meet the needs of a growing firm. For continued growth, an entrepreneur must expand his or her network as business needs change. This concept can be illustrated as follows: If a person always circulates among the same social group year after year and those individuals generally associate only with one another, that person will not make new social connections and as a result will miss the opportunity to meet new people and expand his or her network. If this person instead maintains this social group and actively meets new people, this person will expand their social network, creating new connections that would not have been possible before. Entrepreneurs can capitalize on social networks in the same way to bring in new clients, find new partners, and help their organization run more smoothly.

Entrepreneurs often rely upon a very close-knit social network, especially if the venture is a family business. Although relying upon such close connections has many advantages, it can also pose some important problems worth special consideration. For example, close members in the social network may expect to be placed in certain positions in a business. The entrepreneur may give in to these demands particularly if the members are family members. This can result in a selection of decision makers that is ultimately harmful to the business's success. Furthermore, even if close network members are qualified for positions, they may not provide enough diversity for a growing firm that aims to be innovative. Larger social networks are related to innovation, which provides further incentives for entrepreneurs to increase the size of their social networks and to diversify in order to remain competitive.

Social networks often rely upon word of mouth. This mode of communication is perceived as a strength because it allows information to be spread quickly and instills trust in others better than many other avenues. Unfortunately, word of mouth is not always positive. Negative ties in a social network may have a stronger impact on the success of a new venture than do positive ties. For example, if a potential investor learns that a colleague had a bad experience with an entrepreneur, he or she may choose not to invest, regardless of other positive information, because the colleague is a trusted member of the investor's social network. This means that entrepreneurs must focus not only on what can be gained from an existing social network but also on the active management of the network to increase positive ties and reduce negative ties.

Social networks in the foregoing sense are distinct from online social networks, although there are many similarities. Some familiar examples of online social networks include Facebook and LinkedIn, both of which have millions of members from all over the world and as a result have a lot of potential to help a new venture expand rapidly. Online social networks, much like traditional social networks, link individuals and groups through relationships and the sharing of information. This creates a web of all of the social ties in the network. Just as traditional social networks can be leveraged to meet a business's needs, online social networks are increasingly being used for the same purpose. These services are also increasingly used to find prospective employees and business partners; although business-oriented online social networks (like LinkedIn) have built-in features to allow users to perform these kinds of activities, it is important to note that other services can be used this way as well. Aside from quick network expansion, online social networks are especially useful because they can bring together individuals and organizations from nearly anywhere in the world. A new venture could utilize this capability to form alliances with businesses or customers across the country or across the world to quickly establish a national or international presence. Thus, what previously would have taken years can now be accomplished in a matter of months if this is a priority for the organization.

It is important for the leaders of new ventures to understand social networks in order to take advantage of the opportunities they provide both in the traditional sense and in the Internet age. Social networks allow managers of new ventures to reach out to clients and peers to whom they would not otherwise be connected, which can provide real competitive advantage.

Rachel C. Callan
Richard N. Landers
Old Dominion University

See also Entrepreneurial Support Systems; Human Resources; Knowledge; Social Entrepreneurship

Further Readings

Bargh, J. A. and K. Y. A. McKenna. "The Internet and Social Life." *Annual Review of Psychology*, v.55 (2004).

Batjargal, B., M. Hitt, J. Webb, J. L. Arregle, and T. Miller. "Women and Men Entrepreneurs' Social Networks and New Venture Performance Across Cultures." *Academy of Management Annual Meeting Proceedings* (2009).

Cross, R., A. Parker, and R. Cross. *The Hidden Power of Social Networks: Understanding How Work Really Gets Done in Organizations*. Boston: Harvard Business School Press, 2004.

Greve, A. and J. W. Salaff. "Social Networks and Entrepreneurship." *Entrepreneurship Theory and Practice*, v.28 (2003).

Jones, O. and D. Jayawarna. "Resourcing New Businesses: Social Networks, Bootstrapping and Firm Performance." *Venture Capital*, v.12 (2010).

Lux, S. "Entrepreneur Social Competence and Capital: The Social Networks of Politically Skilled Entrepreneurs." *Academy of Management Annual Meeting Proceedings* (2005).

Molina-Morales, F. X. and M. T. Martínez-Fernández. "Social Networks: Effects of Social Capital on Firm Innovation." *Journal of Small Business Management*, v.48 (2010).

Singh, R. P., G. E. Hills, G. T. Lumpkin, and R. C. Hybels. "The Entrepreneurial Opportunity Recognition Process: Examining the Role of Self-Perceived Alertness and Social Networks." *Academy of Management Proceedings and Membership Directory* (1999).

Zhang, J. "The Problems of Using Social Networks in Entrepreneurial Resource Acquisition." *International Small Business Journal*, v.28 (2010).

STAKEHOLDERS

A management term, a *stakeholder* is any entity (individual, group, or organization) that can affect or be affected by, or that can have a direct or indirect interest (stake) in, an organization's actions, objectives, resources, outputs, and policies. Researchers argue that this definition of the stakeholder should also include the latent or potential relationship with the firm, to include groups and organizations that may be affected by the firm's activities without necessarily interacting with the firm on a social level, as well as stakeholders that may affect the firm's activities without having a direct relationship with the firm.

In 1932, Edwin Dodd cited General Electric's first use of the term *stakeholder* to identify employees, customers, and the general public as key constituent groups. R. Edward Freeman, in his book *Strategic Management: A Stakeholder Approach*, asserts that the term stakeholder is actually derived from the Stanford Research Institute's term for *stockholder*, defined as any groups without whose support the organization would cease to exist.

The influences of stakeholders on the performance of an organization are critical factors. Management must know how to identify stakeholders accurately, how to assess their current and future impact on the organization's performance, and subsequently how to manage the various stakeholder group interests in order to develop their organization's best strategic future.

Although there is the assumption that new ventures and entrepreneurial endeavors cannot afford the time or resources needed to effectively manage competing claims in addition to growing the enterprise, management of stakeholders is as important to new ventures as it is to established firms, allowing them to achieve success and sustained growth. The organization's overall performance is ultimately determined by identifying who the stakeholder is and the stakeholder's knowledge, interests, power, influence, positions, alliances, and criteria for judging the new venture's performance.

Researchers commonly agree that stakeholders are driven by a "goal-seeking" agenda, each with varying loci of power, and that management's awareness of the primacy of stakeholders' agenda is essential to the organization's success. It becomes important for management to understand that stakeholder goal seeking is only central to the loci of power determining their strategies for achieving their goal. This understanding allows key decision makers and managers to interact with stakeholders more effectively to increase support for a given program, position, or policy.

Determining the locus of power and interest within any stakeholder group is vital, but this information alone is insufficient. Management must also comprehend the potential influence of each group in order to "strategically manage" the stakeholders. The importance of this interaction is further evidenced by management's publication of the firm's annual report, which communicates the firm's overall position in relation to its stakeholders.

In 2004, in an article published in the influential journal *Public Management Review*, John Bryson stated that a firm is more likely to meet its mandates, fulfill its mission, and create public value when the strategic management process employs a reasonable number of competently conducted stakeholder analyses.

Stakeholders most commonly fall into one of the following three categories: primary stakeholders, those who are ultimately affected either positively or negatively by the actions of the organization; secondary stakeholders, those affected "indirectly" by the actions of the organization; and key stakeholders, those who have significant influence on or who are part of the organization, such as creditors, customers, directors, employees, owners, suppliers, unions, and the community. Examples of other types of stakeholders include national or political stakeholders (local, state, federal, and international governmental agencies), interest groups (associations, foundations, and clubs), and not-for-profit organizations, among others.

All stakeholders are not equal and different stakeholders are allowed varying levels of consideration. As an example, customers are entitled to fair treatment but not entitled to the same considerations as the firm's employees.

Considerable research has been conducted on how to identify which stakeholders or groups have legitimate interests in the behavior of a company. In their seminal 1997 *Academy of Management Review* article, Ron Mitchell, Bradley Agle, and Donna J. Wood used a Venn diagram to illustrate the levels of stakeholder salience with the nexus of three variables—power (P), legitimacy (L), and urgency (U)—and showed that certain groups of stakeholders will possess varying levels of each, thus determining eight types of stakeholders. The typologies used in the research to describe the eight types of stakeholders are as follows:

1. *Dormant stakeholders (P):* These stakeholders have the power to affect the standardization process, but their participation is not considered legitimate.

2. *Discretionary stakeholders (L):* These stakeholders do not have the resources to affect the standardization process, and they feel no need to participate.

3. *Demanding stakeholders (U):* These stakeholders do not have power or legitimacy, but they have urgency toward the issue.

4. *Dominant stakeholders (P, L):* These stakeholders do not see the immediate interest in participating, even though participation is considered desirable.

5. *Dangerous stakeholders (P, U):* These stakeholders have power and urgency but no legitimacy; they sometimes will take violent, unlawful actions to achieve their objectives.

6. *Dependent stakeholders (L, U):* These stakeholders lack the resources to participate properly in the organizational process; definitive stakeholders are important to this group, as they add the support necessary to the dependent stakeholders for the standardization process to take place.

7. *Definitive stakeholders (P, L, U):* Little effort is required to involve this group; their involvement in the process is indisputable and they have the power to effect change. Definitive stakeholders in general have a long-lasting commitment to the standardization process. Management is cautioned to prevent this group from gaining too much power.

8. *Nonstakeholders:* Anyone falling outside the Venn diagram is by definition a nonstakeholder, with no power, legitimacy, or urgency.

The Mitchell typology enables managers with a list of identifiable characteristics to aid in stakeholder prioritization. The challenge for management is the tendency for a group, once classified, to be considered static. It should be noted that the variables of power, legitimacy, and urgency are all dynamic variables that are highly reactive to the environment.

Firms rarely exist in an environment with dyadic stakeholder ties; rather, several direct and indirect stakeholder groups or networks influence them. Networks, and by extension stakeholder networks, are defined as a group of three or more individuals, groups, or organizations connected in ways that are believed to facilitate achievement of a common goal. Network relationships are primarily nonhierarchical, have considerable operating autonomy, and can be linked by several types of connections and flows, such as information, materials, economic resources, services, and social support. Network theory relies on social network constructs and attempts to consider the interactions between the firm and the multiple interactions comprised by the stakeholder network. Networks are complex structures, and an explanation of the actions and structures of network members and the network as a whole cannot be easily confined to one theory; also, scholars in various disciplines, including management, psychology, political science, anthropology, and sociology, have used numerous theories over the years to explain the network structure. Hence, no single comprehensive theory of network exists. Stakeholder networks are critical to the functionality of an organization. However, attempts to apply what scholars know about networks to improve organizational effectiveness in complex areas such as change management have been extremely limited.

Several studies have established that networks are exceptionally important to organizations and can improve both their efficiency and the effectiveness of the services and programs that they offer. Potential benefits of networks include less duplication of effort, improved communication, and improved access to information and innovation.

Alfred Lewis
Hamline University
Dan Kipley
Azusa Pacific University

See also Boards of Directors; Change Management: Corporate; Communication Styles; Contracts and Trust; Ethics; Exit Strategies; Family Business: Stewardship; Family Business: Theory; Leadership; Negotiating Strategies; Performance and Legitimacy; Psychological Views; Risk Management; Social Entrepreneurship; Social Intelligence; Succession Planning

Further Readings

Bryson, John M. "What to Do When Stakeholders Matter." *Public Management Review*, v.6/1 (2004).

Coombs, Joseph E. and Jeffrey S. Harrison. "Stakeholder Treatment Amongst IPOs and the Acquisition of Resources for Entrepreneurial Ventures." *Journal of Enterprising Culture*, v.18/1 (March 2010).

Dew, Nicholas and Saras Sarasvathy. "Innovations, Stakeholders and Entrepreneurship." *Journal of Business Ethics*, v.74/3 (September 2007).

Freeman, R. Edward and William M. Evans. "Corporate Governance: A Stakeholder Interpretation." *Journal of Behavioral Economics*, v.19 (1990).

Mitchell, Ron K., Bradley R. Agle, and Donna J. Wood. "Toward a Theory of Stakeholder Identification and Salience: Defining the Principle of Who and What Really Counts." *Academy of Management Review*, v.22/4 (1997).

Oliver, Christine. "Strategic Responses to Institutional Processes." *Academy of Management Review*, v.16 (1991).

Schlange, Lutz E. "Stakeholder Identification in Sustainability Entrepreneurship." *Greener Management International*, v.55 (Winter 2009).

Stouder, Michael D. and Scott L. Newbert. "Treating Stakeholders Fairly: The Golden Rule as a Moral Guiding Principle for Entrepreneurs." *Business and Professional Ethics Journal*, v.26/1–4 (2007).

Vandekerckhove, Wim and Nikolay A. Dentchev. "A Network Perspective on Stakeholder Management: Facilitating Entrepreneurs in the Discovery of Opportunities." *Journal of Business Ethics*, v.60/3 (September 2005).

START-UP TEAMS

Start-up teams are groups of two or more individuals who establish and manage new ventures. By working together they enhance the knowledge in the venture and share risks. Teamwork is more effective when interaction processes are of high quality, which allows start-up teams to cope with a wide range of challenges.

In the history of research on new ventures, starting with Joseph Schumpeter in the 1930s, start-ups were characterized by one champion entrepreneur who puts effort into his ideas. That person implements innovations in such a proactive manner that he or she has the motivation to persevere until market penetration. Team entrepreneurship as an area of study is a more recent phenomenon. In 1987, Robert Reich reconsidered entrepreneurship, elevating the start-up team to the status of hero. He posited that people need to work together as a collective to resist global competition.

Organizational science substantially dealt with the term *team* but could not find a consistent definition. J. R. Hackman, for example, described teams as a subtype of groups, with two or more people who interact with one another, perceive themselves as members, are perceived as such by others, and finally pursue common goals. Supported by those ideas, several definitions for start-up teams came up. Most definitions go back to Judith Kamm and her colleagues, who in 1990 suggested that at least two founders "jointly establish a business in which they have equal financial interest." They also postulated the presence of the team members already in the pre-start-up phase, before the start-up actually begins making products or services available to the market. However, the focus on the incubation stage needs to be amplified, because an individual could become a

Robert Reich, who served under the Bill Clinton administration as the U.S. secretary of labor, made a statement that entrepreneurial start-up teams should be regarded as heroes. (U.S. Department of Labor)

team member at subsequent phases in the maturation of the start-up. All team members are in responsible positions because of their financial charges but also because of their active role in establishing and managing the start-up.

The fusion of several founders brings either a high diversity of skills and competencies or additional knowledge to the founding process, which improves the specialization of start-ups. This influences venture capitalists to favor start-up management teams over individual entrepreneurs, since there is no possibility to exhibit prior entrepreneurial performance as measurement. William Bygrave formed the latter idea by positing that venture capitalists would rather invest in a great start-up team with a mediocre idea than in a mediocre start-up team with a great idea. The enhanced organizational knowledge in start-up teams leads to better problem solving, a broad horizon of experiences, and finally, through the exchange of thoughts and ideas, creation of new knowledge. Furthermore, founders' widespread sensation of loneliness or uncertainty decreases and they receive mental support. In the end, the exit of a member can be coped with.

The literature also suggests various negative consequences of working together in a team. Conflicts within the team can arise and inhibit people's performance; merely the presence of other team members can serve as distraction or block creativity processes. Teams run the risk of engaging enthusiastically in favor of an innovative idea rather than evaluating its worthiness clearly. There are several explanations of why start-up teams often lack in critical decision making ability, such as a susceptibility to groupthink, or the ambition for high consensus within the group, as well as susceptibility to polarization, the tendency that people in a group make more extreme decisions than they do as individuals, so that risk tolerance increases.

How effective start-up teams can be depends strongly on, first, the input, such as team structure or context factors, and, second, the interaction processes within the team. In the team creation stage, the formation of the group can be influenced by size, knowledge in terms of human capital, or members' cross-linkages, contributing to a start-up's social capital. As the complexity of problems and quantity of tasks increases, the relevance of teamwork increases. Teamwork within start-ups leads to reasonable workload sharing only when the collaboration is of high quality. Martin Hoegl and Hans Georg Gemünden discuss six facets of internal interaction quality: sufficient communication between the members, well-structured coordination of activities, balanced contribution of members' task-relevant knowledge, mutual support instead of competition, shared norms on members' potential efforts, and finally an adequate level of cohesion, meaning that the members desire to stick with the team. When all six facets are of high value, so is the team's performance on the innovative projects that characterize start-up companies.

Typically start-up teams self-manage their development, meaning that the team has the full responsibility to manage how the team advances. Start-up teams are often formed by friends, family members, and other equal relationships, so no designated authority is necessarily provided. Sometimes one person in the team emerges to take a dominant position and is the major source of influence for both task processes and teamwork quality. Commonly, a collective sense of leadership is cultivated whereby the traditional responsibilities of the leader are distributed among the team members with mutual influence. Next to high-quality team work, which enhances the start-up's innovativeness, (shared) leadership skills are required to bring start-up teams to business success.

Maura Kessel
Jan Kratzer
Hans Georg Gemünden
Technical University of Berlin

See also Human Resources; Knowledge; Leadership; Team Composition

Further Readings

Bygrave, William D. and Jeffry A. Timmons. *Venture Capital at the Crossroads.* Boston: Harvard Business School Press, 1992.

Ensley, Michael et al. "Top Management Team Process, Shared Leadership, and New Venture Performance: A Theoretical Model and Research Agenda." *Human Research Management Review*, v.13 (2003).

Franke, Nikolaus et al. "Venture Capitalists' Evaluations of Start-Up Teams: Trade-Off, Knock-Out Criteria, and the Impact of VC Experience." *Entrepreneurship Theory and Practice*, v.32/3 (2008).

Hackman, J. R., ed. *Groups That Work and Those That Don't.* San Francisco: Jossey-Bass, 1990.

Hoegl, Martin and Hans Georg Gemünden. "Teamwork Quality and the Success of Innovative Projects: A Theoretical Concept and Empirical Evidence." *Organization Science*, v.12/4 (2001).

Kamm, Judith et al. "Entrepreneurial Teams in New Venture Creation: A Research Agenda." *Entrepreneurship Theory and Practice*, v.14/4 (1990).

Reich, Robert. "Entrepreneurship Reconsidered: The Team as Hero." *Harvard Business Review*, v.87/3 (1987).

Wheelan, S. A. *Creating Effective Teams: A Guide for Members and Leaders*, 2nd ed. Thousand Oaks, CA: Sage, 2005.

STRATEGY

Strategy is a management action plan whose etymological foundation is derived from the Greek military term *strategos*, meaning a general set of maneuvers carried out to overcome an enemy and the actions that can be taken in the light of actions taken by opposite parties. Particular attention must be paid to the term *general set of maneuvers*, as opposed to specific sets of maneuvers. The latter are those that are carried out by lower levels of management when translating the strategy into operational tactics.

More than 2,500 years ago, the famous sixth-century military strategist Sun Tzu wrote about the value of understanding strategy in his classic *The Art of War* when he stated that "strategy is the great works of the organization. In situations of life or death, it is the Tao of survival or extinction. Its study cannot be neglected."

In business, strategy is defined as management's coordinated action plan for pursuing the organizations mission to achieve its targeted long-term goals and objectives by positioning the firm and allocating its resources in such a way that it sells more products or services than the competition, to improve the company's financial and market performance. Most strategic theorists agree that strategy is a plan or course of action and a set of decision rules, forming a pattern or creating a common thread that is related to the organization's activities, which are derived from policies, objectives, and goals that move that organization from its current position to a desired future position.

Considerable as well as varied contributions to the definition of strategy have been written in management literature by leading strategic theorists. The following are definitions provided by the leading strategist of the 20th century.

One of the earliest contributions to the analysis of strategy was by Alfred D. Chandler in 1962, who based his conclusions on a study of 70 manufacturing firms in the United States. Chandler defined strategy as "the determination of the basic long-term goals and objectives of an enterprise and the adoption of the courses of action and the allocation of resources necessary for carrying out these goals." His definition specifically highlights three key aspects of strategy: First, a firm must have a determination of its basic long-term goals and objectives. Second, the firm must adopt a course of action to achieve those goals and objectives. Finally, the firm must allocate the necessary resources to pursue the course of action.

A prolific author, acknowledged in the field of strategic management as the father of strategic planning and strategic management, Igor Ansoff defined strategy in 1965 as "the common thread among the organization's activities and product markets that defines the essential nature of the business that the organization was or planned to be in the future." Ansoff emphasized the unity of actions that exists in diverse organizational activities that direct the present and planned actions of the business.

George Steiner, also considered to be the father of strategic planning in the business world, defined strategy in 1979 as the amalgamation of the following five points. First, strategy is that which top management does that is of great importance to the organization. Second, strategy refers to basic directional decisions as to purpose and missions. Third, strategy consists of the important actions necessary to realize these directions. Fourth, strategy answers the question, What should the organization be doing? Fifth, strategy answers the question, What are the ends we seek and how should we achieve them?

William Glueck, a well-known author and distinguished professor of management at the University of Georgia, defined strategy quite succinctly as "a unified, comprehensive, and integrated plan designed to assure that the basic objectives of the enterprise are achieved." Glueck's definition illuminates three key elements of the strategy definition. First, it is unified; the strategy must join all parts of the organization together. Second, it is comprehensive; the strategy must cover all of the major aspects of the organization. Third, it is integrated; all elements of the strategy must be compatible with one another.

In 1992, Henry Mintzberg added a holistic view to the definition of strategy, stating not only that strategy has an explicit meaning but also that there are other implicit meanings for the term. Mintzberg listed the five Ps of strategy and defined them as follows: Strategy is a *plan*, defined as a conscious, intended course of action that is developed purposefully, a means of getting "from here to there." Second, strategy is a *ploy*, defined as a specific maneuver intended to outwit an opponent or competitor. Third, strategy is a *pattern*, defined as a continuous flow or stream of actions in which a consistency of behavior can appear without preconception. Fourth, strategy is a *position*, defined as the means of locating the firm relative to its industry "environment"; through this definition, strategy then becomes a mediating force between its internal and external forces. Fifth, strategy is a *perspective*, defined as the organization's mantra, or personality; it is an ingrained way of perceiving the world that is a collective thought shared by all members of the organization. Hence, a firm may start with a perspective that warrants a certain position that can be achieved by formulating a strategic plan, with the results reflecting a strategic pattern supported by the decisions and actions of the firm over time.

A strategic management approach that has deep theoretical roots—based in part on sociology and Ricardian and Penrosian economic theories in which the firm can earn sustainable supranormal returns if and only if it has superior resources and those resources are protected by some form of isolating mechanism precluding their diffusion throughout industry—is recognized as the resource-based view (RBV). The fundamental principles of the field of strategic management were first introduced in 1984 by Berger Wernerfelt in his seminal article "A Resource-Based View of the Firm," in which he posits that firms in control of valuable, scarce, and nonsubstitutable resources that are inelastic in supply can gain persistent competitive advantages by using them to develop and implement strategies.

Michael Porter's competitive position, based on the "five forces," provides an accessible model for assessing and analyzing the competitive strength/position of an enterprise. The model describes the competitive environment in terms of five basic competitive forces that shape every industry and every market: the threat of a *new entrant* into the market, the bargaining power of *buyers* bargaining, the bargaining power of *sellers* bargaining, the threat of *substitutes* into the market, and the degree of rivalry between competitors.

Strategy concentrates on how to achieve the organizational performance targets, how to outcompete the firm's rivals, how to achieve a sustainable competitive advantage, how to strengthen the organization's long-term competitive position, how to grow the business, how to satisfy customers, and how to respond to changing market conditions. Basically, the central thrust of business strategy is how to build and strengthen the company's long-term competitive position in the marketplace. It should be noted that the field of strategic management is not restricted to large organizations or firms that have been in existence for several years. New ventures and entrepreneurs need to be strategic in order to survive, given that they do not have the financial staying power of larger firms and long timers.

An article by J. Starr and I. Macmillan in 1990 discussed the acquisition of needed resources by independent entrepreneurs and corporate entrepreneurs through social transactions. The transactions may include prior working relationships, intentional connections, and community connections, especially for independent entrepreneurs. The authors introduced the label of *cooptation*, defined as a mechanism for obtaining resources which aligns with the RBV.

Strategy is dynamic. It can be both intended and emergent; an intended strategy is one that is planned and deliberate and comprises a set of intentional acts that have been contemplated and planned to achieve a stated goal or objective. Intended strategy may also be referred to as deliberate strategy. Emergent strategy also referred to as realized strategy or organic adaptation is that which is developed over a period of time in the absence of specific goals and objectives and, as such, implies that the organization is learning what works best by adapting to those events in a changing environment. Strategy therefore is a bridge as well as the general framework that provides guidance for actions to be taken and is shaped by actions taken; it is a bridge between the organizational goal and objectives and the actions or tactics to achieve them. Although both strategy and tactics are defined in relation to some broader goal, strategy yields to tactics when the actual implementation begins and has no existence apart from the goals and objectives sought.

The responsibility of strategic formulation and implementation in business is defined on three levels; corporate, business, and functional. Corporate strategy involves top management and concentrates its plans on the entire organization and changes when industry and market conditions shift. It is the "magnus opus" view of the organization and includes such decisions as the scope of the geographic area in which to operate, in which product or service markets to compete, how the firm should allocate its resources among its existing business units, how diversified the business should become, how the firm should be structured, and whether the firm should enter into strategic alliances, mergers, or acquisitions. Thus, corporate-level strategy represents the long-term direction of the firm.

Similar to corporate-level strategies are business-level strategies, in that they focus on the firm's overall performance. However, business-level strategies are more granular, as they may focus on one business unit of the firm and on a particular product, its product life cycle, the competitive environment, and the firm's competitive advantages of its products or service lines. In a single product firm, business-level strategies and corporate-level strategies are the same.

A business unit represents those individual entities that are specific to a particular industry, product, or market. Business-level strategies are focused primarily on the coordination and integration of unit activities to create congruence or synergy with the overall organizational strategy; development of competitive advantages and distinctive competencies within each unit; identifying and developing product or market niche areas and formulating strategies with which to compete; and conducting environmental scanning of the evolution of markets for the products and services, so that the unit strategy meets the needs at the current stage.

The relationship between corporate-level strategy and business-level strategy is critical. Business-level strategy must support corporate-level strategy by matching its functions with the overall goals and objectives of the corporate-level strategy while congruently maintaining a competitive posture in the markets in which the business competes, in such a way that the business has a financial or marketing competitive advantage relative to the other businesses in the industry.

Functional-level strategies have a shorter time orientation that involves the coordination of the organization's various functional areas (production, research and development, marketing, finance, human resources, and so on) with operations to design, manufacture, deliver, and support the products or services of each business unit within the corporate portfolio. Functional strategies are concerned mainly with increasing the efficiencies within the functional area; coordinating activities (such as advertising and promotion, marketing research and marketing, purchasing and inventory control, and shipping and production) within the functional areas. With functional strategies, lower-level managers are most likely involved and accountability is easier to establish.

Tactics, like strategy, has its etymological foundation in a Greek military term: *taktika*, defined as the "purposeful procedure" achieved by exercising "the science or art of maneuvering in presence of the enemy." Strategy and tactics are closely linked, as both are about deciding the means by which a goal is reached. However, strategy focuses on the long-term future, whereas tactics look ahead just far enough to secure the objectives set by the strategy. The Prussian military theorist Karl von Clausewitz described tactics as "the planning of a single battle" and strategy as "the planning of the whole campaign."

Multiple and diverse definitions of tactics can be found in literature having either a military focus or a focus toward business. The business definition of tactics is "the specific maneuvering or adroit management sequence of actions for affecting and fulfilling your strategic goals and objectives." Typical questions that are asked at the tactical level are "What do we need to do to reach our growth, size, profitability goal?" "What is our competition doing?" and "What equipment is required to achieve our goals?"

Other definitions offer a perspective of tactics and its scope relative to strategy. "Tactics are the actionable, granular-level messages and activities designed to achieve a desired result. Tactics have an immediate or short time frame (usually one year or less) and are the specific techniques and actions that are narrowly focused on the management of activities and the deployment of resources required to achieve a particular single goal." This definition provides specificity to tactics (granular) as well as a temporal limit (short-time frame).

Tactics are also defined as having an interrelationship with the firm's functional departmental strategies. "Tactics are how the strategies are to be performed linking strategy and operations." Without tactics there would be no effective implementation, operations, or systems development.

Senior leadership often formulates the strategy, and tactics are what department heads, line managers, and employees do to implement the formulated strategy. Therefore, the differences between strategy and tactics can be defined simply: Strategy is what you plan to do; tactics are how you plan to do it.

Alfred Lewis
Hamline University
Dan Kipley
Azusa Pacific University

See also Advertising; Branding; Business Models; Business Plans; Exit Strategies; Feasibility Studies; Geographic Location; Growth; Initial Public Offering; Research and Development; Selling Successful Businesses; Venture Capital; Venture Management Firms; Venture Valuation

Further Readings

Ansoff, H. Igor. *Corporate Strategy*. New York: McGraw-Hill, 1965.

Chandler, Alfred D. *Strategy and Structure: Chapters in the History of the American Industrial Enterprise*. Cambridge, MA: MIT Press, 1962.

Glueck, William F. *Business Policy: Strategy Formation and Management Action*. New York: McGraw-Hill, 1976.

Hanzhang, Tao. *Sun Tzu: The Art of War*. Ware, UK: Wordsworth, 1993.

Lee, I. and M. Marvel. "The Moderating Effects of Home Region Orientation on R&D Investment and International SME Performance: Lessons From Korea." *European Management Journal*, v.27/5 (October 2009).

Majumdar, Satyajit. "How Do They Plan for Growth in the Auto Component Business? A Study on Small Foundries of Western India." *Journal of Business Venturing*, v.25/3 (May 2010).

Manning, Kingsley, Sue Birley, and David Norburn. "Developing a New Ventures Strategy." *Entrepreneurship Theory and Practice*, v. 14/1 (Fall 1989).

Mintzberg, Henry and J. B. Quinn. *The Strategy Process*. Englewood Cliffs, NJ: Prentice-Hall, 1992.

Park, Sangmoon and Zong-Tae Bae. "New Venture Strategies in a Developing Country: Identifying a Typology and Examining Growth Patterns Through Case Studies." *Journal of Business Venturing*, v.19/1 (January 2004).

Porter, M. *Competitive Advantage*. New York: Free Press, 1985.

Starr, J. and I. MacMillan. "Resource Cooptation via Social Contracting: Resource Acquisition Strategies for New Ventures." *Strategic Management Journal*, v.79 (1990).

Steiner, George. *Strategic Planning*. New York: Free Press, 1979.

Wernerfelt, Berger. "A Resource-Based View of the Firm." *Strategic Management Journal*, v.5/2 (1984).

SUCCESSION PLANNING

Succession planning refers to the process whereby an organization recruits, identifies, and develops high-potential individuals for specific positions in order to ensure the continuity of an organization's leadership. It is a critical element in building the "bench strength" of an organization, which refers to the competencies and employees who are prepared to fill vacant leadership positions. The main goal of succession planning is to provide a talent pool and leadership pipeline throughout the organization. This entry reviews the main elements of succession planning, associated concepts, and best practices related to implementing this process in a new venture.

Two related processes to succession planning are replacement planning and succession management. Replacement planning most often refers to a contingency plan for emergency situations that is focused on an organization identifying individuals who can take over roles for both short and long terms and is typically utilized for top-tier positions. Succession management refers to a comprehensive program that combines succession planning with leadership development in order to cultivate the competencies of high-potential employees for a range of critical positions.

Although succession management and planning are often used interchangeably, *succession planning* usually refers to a more static reactive process involving the top levels of an organization whereas *succession management* customarily refers to a proactive process involving the entire organization. Given that the most successful succession processes are comprehensive and proactive, the term *succession management* is used throughout this entry. In fact, increasing bench strength is best achieved when one combines succession planning with leadership development in a comprehensive program.

Given the increase in global competition for talent in today's business environment, coupled with the positive outcomes associated with investment in succession management (such as increasing the financial performance of an organization, aligning leaders with their organizations' goals, and assisting companies in retaining top talent, which in turn decreases recruitment and training costs), this process has become a necessity for any new venture. Succession management is, at its core, a plan for the future and, as such, is essential for the success and development of any new venture in that it ensures that an organization has the talent pool needed during reorganizations, expansions, and the loss and redeployment of critical employees.

The succession management process has become more systematic over time, involving a broad range of activities, including recruiting top talent, comprehensively developing competencies, placing designated employees in increasingly challenging and demanding leadership positions, measuring performance, and analyzing the overall program fit with the organization's strategy and bench strength.

Most research that examines the interface of new ventures and succession management focuses on family-owned business. Family firms are notorious for their difficulty with succession; in fact, only 30 percent of these businesses survive into the second generation. Their high failure rate is most often attributed to their inability to implement succession management and attract a talent pool.

Preferably, succession management happens at the planning stage of a new venture, thus allowing the venture to couple its human resource strategy with the vision and goals of the company. Ideally, the process is implemented at all stages of an organization, whereby a company builds feeder groups throughout the entire leadership pipeline and is integrated closely with leadership development and training programs and owned by everyone in the organization. As a result, upper management plans for possible leader replacement, board members identify and develop high-potential employees, and line managers share their top performers with other units. In a new venture, a succession strategy also must focus on the new roles that will develop as the company grows.

For a succession management strategy to be owned by everyone in a company, an organization must work to create a value-driven culture that adopts a talent mind-set. A talent mind-set, according to Jay Conger and Robert Fulmer, is the deep-seated belief that talent is critical to competitive advantage and key to better performance. This mind-set ensures that a dependable source of leadership competencies throughout the firm is a critical goal.

In Conger and Fulmer's seminal 2003 research study, they identify five best practices for implementing a successful succession management system within an organization. First, companies must integrate their succession planning with leadership training and development. It is imperative that any plan determines what competencies high-potential employees need in their potential new positions; also, one must determine the best process to ensure the development of these skill sets. Therefore, programs must incorporate a mixture of development practices, including learning from work experience (job rotation and project management), learning from others (such as mentors and coaches), and course work (class-based training and ropes courses). State-of-the-art programs now utilize a blended development approach that includes on-the-job, classroom, and e-learning experiences.

Second, an organization must continually identify key jobs that are essential to the stability of their business and at the same time identify high-potential employees who will be able to fill these positions in the future, train these employees through integrated programs, and continually evaluate their performance to determine their eligibility for these roles and their ability to take on more challenging positions.

To guard against cloning, a broad range of individuals throughout the organization should be utilized when identifying high-potential employees for specific positions. Organizations that utilize just the current incumbent often find that bosses select candidates very similar to themselves and thus that other department members have a greater propensity to feel disaffected and experience diminished motivation.

Third, organizations must make their succession management process transparent. Employees must be provided feedback on their performance and their potential to advance. Web-based tools allow employees and their managers the ability to access information concerning their performance on demand and in real time.

Fourth, organizations need to monitor their succession management program continually in order to make sure that their high-potential employees are moving into critical leadership positions. Specifically, it is recommended that an organization examine the number of vital positions that have been filled with internal candidates and the number of essential positions that have internal candidates ready to fill them.

A final point is that organizations must continually evaluate and update their succession management process and evaluate its link to the organization's strategic business plan. A successful succession management strategy is not static; it is constantly evolving through a thorough review process. For optimal success, reviews should be conducted quarterly; the company should conduct an external audit of succession management best practices coupled with an internal audit whereby employee feedback is solicited and used to adjust the program so that it remains state-of-the art and responsive to employees' needs.

Lisa Rosh
Yeshiva University

See also Human Resource Strategy; Human Resources; Leadership; Leadership: Training and Development; Start-Up Teams

Further Readings

Berke, David. *Succession Planning and Management: A Guide to Organizational Systems and Practices.* Greensboro, NC: Center for Creative Leadership, 2005.

Charan, Ran, Stephen Drotter, and James Noel. *The Leadership Pipeline: How to Build the Leadership Powered Company.* San Francisco: Jossey-Bass, 2001.

Cohn, Jeffry M., Rakesh Khuranam, and Laura Reeves. "Growing Talent as if Your Business Depended on It." *Harvard Business Review* (October 2005).

Conger, Jay A. and Robert M. Fulmer. "Developing Your Leadership Pipeline." *Harvard Business Review* (December 2003).

Goldsmith, Marshall and Louis L. Carter. *Best Practices in Talent Management: How the World's Leading Corporations Manage, Develop and Retain Top Talent.* San Francisco: Pfeiffer, 2010.

Guenther, Robert L. "Is It Time to Replace Your Replacement-Planning Strategy?" *Harvard Management Update*, v.9/4 (2004).

McCall, Morgan W. *High Flyers: Developing the Next Generation of Leaders.* Boston: Harvard Business School Press, 1998.

Michaels, E., Helen Handfield-Jones, and Beth Axelrod. *The War for Talent.* Boston: Harvard Business School Press, 2001.

SUSTAINABLE DEVELOPMENT

In the midst of the economic downturn that began in 2008, existing companies struggled for survival, making many difficult decisions concerning how to leverage financial, physical, and human capital for competitive advantage. One of the interesting megatrends is the business-driven advancement of sustainable development activities within organizations. For entrepreneurs, sustainable development offers fresh areas of opportunity for value creation in new ventures.

In defining what sustainability is, it is important to understand what it is not. Conservation is one of the related concepts with which sustainability is often confused. Also known as "nature conservation," this political and social movement was placed on the national agenda in the early 20th century by the Teddy Roosevelt administration with the passage of the Newlands Reclamation Act, and it was later advanced by Richard Nixon with the creation of the Environmental Protection Agency (EPA). A second closely related concept is environmentalism. This social movement is rooted in the work of John Muir and is directed at lobbying, activism, and education activities to protect natural resources and ecosystems.

While sustainability integrates some philosophical elements of conservation and environmentalism in approach, research indicates that sustainability takes a broader view of the protection of resources. Rather than simply protecting resources for resources' sake, sustainability seeks to balance social, environmental, and economic factors for benefits in the present as well as the future. This broader concept has important implications for business practices and serves as a catalyst for the investigation of sustainable development activities as part of the organization design process. Sustainable development is development that meets the needs of the present without compromising the ability of future generations to meet their own needs.

While regulatory efforts to dictate business practices largely fell flat with the denial of passage of the measures and cap-and-trade policies put forth at the 2009 Copenhagen Summit, the amount of business activity and the number of innovative business programs in the area of sustainable development at the organization level is promising. From SAP to Coca-Cola, organizations are designing new systems and processes to harness new green technologies.

As sustainable development grows in prominence, it follows that entrepreneurial opportunities in the area will also increase. Sustainable entrepreneurship (SE) combines sustainability and entrepreneurship and is the process of creating value through enterprises that promote resource conservation, now and into the future. Many advocates suggest that sustainable entrepreneurship activities will serve as the primary force toward achieving sustainability on a global scale.

One of the features that make new ventures attractive places for sustainable development is that sustainability challenges existing organizations to engage in culture change, which is often a difficult

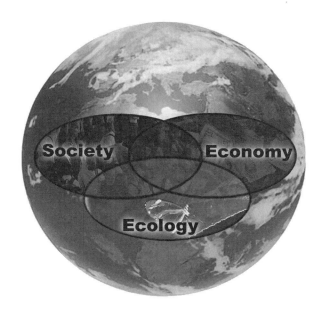

A sustainability diagram depicts ecology, economy, and society as interconnected and bound by the environment, represented by the Earth. Sustainability seeks to balance social, environmental, and economic factors for benefits in the present, as well as the future. Sustainable development meets the needs of the present population without compromising the well-being of future generations. (Wikimedia)

proposition. New ventures do not face that hurdle because they are in the position to create value around products and services building their foundation from the beginning of the business.

As sustainable entrepreneurs consider entry into these new markets, there are a number of lessons to learn from common characteristics of successful existing sustainable development-focused industries. First of all, organizations successful in the market have deeply engrained values about the importance of the work they do. These businesses engage in strategic positioning for products and services throughout the organization design process. In some cases, a product or service promoting sustainability is the ultimate goal, while in others the goal is to advance sustainable practices as part of their organizational fiber. Furthermore, top management supports the overall direction of the organization and provides leadership for some of the difficult choices that may result in sacrificing short-term gains for long-term results. Toward this end, systems throughout the organization are aligned around sustainability processes and support this direction. Metrics are designed to measure performance at all levels of the organization.

In organizations adopting sustainability as a focus, best practices show integration across functions from human resources to information technology to purchasing. In other words, the focus on sustainability is not just an ad hoc process; rather it becomes part of the organization. There are tools and processes, including communication systems, that facilitate this through the organizational culture. Finally, there is stakeholder integration to promote understanding of the need for and results of sustainability as a core competency of the organization.

Dana Cosby-Simmons
Western Kentucky University

See also Agility and Rapid Response; Change; Change Management: Corporate; Corporate Entrepreneurship and Innovation; Family Business: Defining; Measures of Performance; Microfinance; Partnerships; Social Capital; Social Entrepreneurship; Social Intelligence; Social Networks; Stakeholders

Further Readings

Brundtland, Gro Harlem and the World Commission on Environment and Development. *"Our Common Future" Annex.* New York: United Nations, 1987.

Drayton, Bill and Valerie Budinich. "New Alliance for Global Change." *Harvard Business Review* (September 2010).

Gibbs, David. "Sustainability Entrepreneurs, Ecopreneurs and the Development of a Sustainable Economy." *Greener Management International*, v.55 (2006).

Hitchcock, Darcy and Marcia Willard. *The Business Guide to Sustainability: Practical Strategies and Tools for Organizations.* London: Earthscan, 2006.

Kuckertz, Andreas and Marcus Wagner. "The Influence of Sustainability Orientation on Entrepreneurial Intentions: Investigating the Role of Business Experience." *Journal of Business Venturing*, v.25/5 (September 2010).

Lubin, David and Daniel Esty. "Lessons for Leaders From Previous Game-Changing Megatrends." *Harvard Business Review* (May 2010).

Meyer, Christopher and Julia Kirby. "Leadership in the Age of Transparency." *Harvard Business Review* (April 2010).

National Research Council. *Our Common Journey: A Transition Toward Sustainability.* Washington, DC: National Academy Press, 1999.

O'Neill, Gerald D., Jr., James C. Hershauer, and Jay S. Golden. "The Cultural Context of Sustainability Entrepreneurship." *Greener Management International*, v.55 (Winter 2009).

Parrish, Bradley. "Designing the Sustainable Enterprise." *Futures*, v.39/7 (2007).

Parrish, Bradley. "Sustainability-Driven Entrepreneurship: Principles of Organization Design." *Journal of Business Venturing*, v.25/5 (September 2010).

Schaper, M. *Making Ecopreneurs: Developing Sustainable Entrepreneurship.* Burlington, VT: Ashgate, 2005.

Schick, Hildegard, Sandra Marxen, and Jurgen Freimann. "Sustainability Issues for Start-Up Entrepreneurs." *Greener Management International*, v.38 (Summer 2002).

Shepherd, Dean and Holger Patzelt. "The New Field of Sustainable Entrepreneurship: Studying Entrepreneurial Action Linking What Is to Be Sustained With What Is to Be Developed." *Entrepreneurship Theory and Practice* (January 2011).

Society for Human Resource Management. *Green Workplace Survey.* http://www.shrm.org/Research/SurveyFindings/Articles/Documents/SHRM%20Green%20Workplace%20Survey%20Brief.pdf (Accessed February 2011).

Spence, Martine et al. "Sustainable Entrepreneurship: Is Entrepreneurial Will Enough? A North-South Comparison." *Journal of Business Ethics*, v.99/3 (April 2011).

Wirtenberg, Jeana, Joel Harmon, and Kent Fairfield. "HRs in Building a Sustainable Enterprise: Insights for Some of the World's Best Companies." *Human Resource Planning*, v.30/1 (2010).

World Business Council for Sustainable Development, University of Cambridge Programme for Industry. *Driving Success: Human Resources and Sustainable Development*. 2005. http://www.wbcsd.org/plugins/ DocSearch/details.asp?type=DocDet&ObjectId=MTcx MDQ (Accessed February 2011).

SYSTEMATIC SEARCH

Systematic search is the organized and methodical attempt to find information related to a clear set of criteria. It assumes ordered patterns of information within relatively ordered environments and relies on analytic, rule-based modes of thinking. Systematic search is important in the creation and growth of new ventures, as entrepreneurs must often solve defined problems in the recognition and validation of opportunities and the gathering of resources needed to exploit new opportunities.

In contrast, nonsystematic or random search gathers information through opportunistic scanning, luck, and serendipity, typically without defined search criteria. It assumes that information signals are very difficult to predict in uncertain and chaotic environments, and therefore general alertness is the key to productive search, not prescribed search criteria. Such nonsystematic search relies heavily on intuition and associative modes of thinking.

The general interest in search reflects the widely held view that rational intelligence is bounded, or inherently limited, and therefore complex problems often defy full analysis and calculative resolution. Rather, in a world of limited or bounded rationality, many problems are solved and decisions made by searching for solutions rather than by deducing them axiomatically. The following questions then arise for new ventures: What is the appropriate search process and to what degree can it be systematic?

Studies suggest that venturing environments are often sufficiently ordered and thus suited to systematic search. A range of systematic search behaviors are therefore employed. First, entrepreneurs can draw on prior experience to select appropriate search criteria. For example, if an entrepreneur previously worked in the pharmaceutical industry, he or she will be better equipped to search for relevant information based on industry-specific criteria,

such as conditions in the regulatory environment. Second, entrepreneurs may possess relevant contacts and networks in their target industry. If so, they can systematically search their contacts for relevant information. Third, search can exploit existing knowledge through learning. For example, an entrepreneur may be interested in the automotive sector and can therefore consult with existing producers and distributors to learn about opportunities. Finally, entrepreneurs can set clear boundaries to search. For example, when exploring opportunities in the pharmaceutical industry, the entrepreneur will probably avoid seeking information from automotive manufacturers.

These forms of systematic search can be employed in all major phases of the new venture process: opportunity identification and validation, resourcing, and execution. To begin with, when seeking venturing opportunities, entrepreneurs can search based on their prior experience, established networks, and existing knowledge sources, all within specific boundaries. In this way, opportunities can be discovered or created. If most features of a venturing opportunity already exist, then systematic search may be sufficient to discover the opportunity. Alternatively, if significant features of an opportunity are not yet clear, search may require creative input by the entrepreneur. In this context, systematic search will be used to gather additional relevant information from relevant sources.

In the second major phase of new ventures, the entrepreneur needs to validate the feasibility of a potential opportunity. This will often require systematic search for information about specific markets, potential customers, competitors, and technologies. In fact, search must often be systematic in these contexts. Otherwise, relevant information may not be incorporated into the analysis.

In the third and fourth major phases of the new venture process, entrepreneurs must access resources and then exploit the opportunity. These required resources may be financial, technological, material, informational, and human, while operational problems may relate to production, marketing, and logistics. Once again, the entrepreneur will need to gather relevant information to solve specific problems. Hence, systematic search will be required. For example, when exploiting opportunities in the pharmaceutical sector, an entrepreneur would systematically search for relevant scientific and patent information.

In summary, there are numerous contexts in which systematic search is important for new venture creation and development. This implies that entrepreneurs, as the founders of new ventures, must focus on the information to be gained through leveraging prior experience, networks, and existing knowledge sources and then search systematically within appropriate boundaries. At the same time, it is likely that nonsystematic search processes will also be important, especially in the earlier stages of opportunity identification and validation. Yet, once an opportunity is identified and validated, increasingly systematic search processes will be required to access and exploit resources. Moreover, as ventures develop, entrepreneurs tend to acquire greater knowledge and experience and hence adapt search behavior. Such adaptation is normal, but it carries risks. For example, if search is too routine and prescriptive, it tends to become myopic and fails to detect information about new trends and opportunities.

In order to perform systematic search, the founders of new ventures need skills in defining appropriate search criteria and leveraging experience, networks, and knowledge sources to gather information. In large part, these skills can be developed, whether formally through education or informally through experience. Consequently, both educational institutions and potential entrepreneurs should aim to develop these skills as an important factor in new venture success. At the same time, they must be skilled at nonsystematic search within more uncertain and dynamic environments and know when and why to employ different search methods. In fact, all organizations that seek to identify and exploit opportunities need to perform systematic search, while also combining it with being alert and open to fresh ideas.

Peter T. Bryant
IE Business School, Madrid

See also Creativity and Opportunities; Discovery and Exploitation; Information; Opportunity Development; Opportunity Identification and Structural Alignment; Opportunity Recognition; Search-Based Discovery

Further Readings

Cooper, Arnold, Timothy Folta, and Carolyn Woo. "Entrepreneurial Information Search." *Journal of Business Venturing*, v.10/2 (1995).

Levinthal, Daniel and James G. March. "A Model of Adaptive Organizational Search." *Journal of Economic Behavior and Organization*, v.2 (1981).

Patel, Pankaj C. and James O. Fiet. "Systematic Search and Its Relationship to Firm Founding." *Entrepreneurship Theory and Practice*, v.33/2 (2009).

TARGET MARKETS

Understanding potential clients, where they come from, and what characteristics they share helps companies both to develop services that will meet their clients' needs and to communicate with them effectively. Although each potential client is distinct, it is infeasible to custom-tailor promotional materials and marketing communications to each individual. On the other hand, a mass-marketing approach, whereby a marketer uses a single marketing strategy for all potential clients, can be equally ineffective, since it fails to address how products or services can meet individual customers' needs. A more effective approach is market segmentation, which entails dividing the market into distinct groups of potential clients having common characteristics. Targeting markets in this way allows the entrepreneur to focus marketing efforts on the segments that are most likely to respond to marketing communications. Using market segmentation and focusing communication efforts on key groups do not require restricting clients to these groups. Rather, this approach simply helps the company focus its marketing efforts and communication to make effective use of resources and reach the customers who would benefit from the firm's products or services.

Since issues, preferences, and usage patterns vary along an array of personal characteristics, identifying factors such as age, gender, and ethnicity can help marketers specifically address the needs of the target market. A potential client's or customer's family characteristics, such as marital status, family size, structure, and stage in the family life cycle, are also important to understand, since they can affect the customer's needs, issues, priorities, preferences, and usage patterns. Household income and related variables, such as level of education, social status, and occupation, can also influence potential customers' decisions about seeking and utilizing services, types of information they want, and how they evaluate their options. Socioeconomic factors can also shape whether people select a provider based on cost, value, or quality and whether they can afford the offered service or product.

Knowing where potential clients live, work, shop, attend school, and engage in recreational activities can help identify effective ways to reach them. Defining the geographic area allows the marketer to identify the marketing opportunities and communication channels available and focus promotional efforts in those specific areas. Knowing whether people are relatively settled, whether or not they relocate and change jobs frequently, can also shape the company's marketing approach.

Hence, how potential clients see the company, the services it offers, and the people who seek those services have an important bearing on how to market the business. In fact, target clientele values, such as positive relationships, achievement, independence, personal growth and development, and status, will influence the type of communications they attend to and the way they respond to the company's marketing efforts. Understanding the subgroups that potential clients identify with and their general lifestyle—the way they allocate time and money and the types of activities they value—will also help in communicating effectively with them and providing services that meet their needs.

Understanding when and under what circumstances prospective clients access services, how ready they are to make changes in their lives, and their most likely usage patterns will inform the company's marketing efforts. Similarly, factors such as how target clients find out about available services, how well informed they are, who influences their decisions and choices, and who the typical referral sources are also have important implications for how the company communicates with them.

If the company wants to internationalize or export its products, market research can be the most important contributor to its international success. There are more than 190 countries in the world, and the company obviously wants to pick the right ones for its products or services. To do this, the company needs information that will provide a clear picture of the political, economic, and cultural factors affecting operations in a given market. Market research is the key to understanding these opportunities. It can confirm that an opportunity actually exists in a particular market and can help the company understand the market's characteristics. It can give insight into how a new market can be developed. Most important, it helps businesses discover what is important to potential customers and what may influence their buying decisions.

Exploring foreign markets can take longer and cost more than expected. Although there is usually a lot of detail involved, the three basic steps of international market research are not particularly complex. They are, first, screening potential markets, second, assessing target markets, and third, drawing conclusions.

Generally speaking, markets are often categorized into three broad types. When a company is at the screening stage of its research, understanding these broad classifications can help focus on one or several markets. The types of markets are therefore, first, fast-paced markets; second, competitive economies' markets; third, relationship-based markets; fourth, relatively affluent economies' markets; and finally, markets in economies that are funded by international financial institutions.

The second step of international market research may take different forms, because there are many ways to study a market. Companies' leaders sometimes rely on intuition, but they still use very sophisticated statistical techniques as well. The more detailed the research, however, the less likely the company is to overlook something important. There are two main types of market research: secondary and primary research.

Of the utmost importance is knowing exactly what the company is selling. This will help identify the target market. It is vital to understand the target market, not only to decrease unsuccessful advertising expenses but also to ensure that the market is being reached appropriately. This is why understanding what the company is selling is so important. By understanding what it is that the company actually provides for the customer, marketers can better help the company advertise directly toward its market.

Marketing demographics, which include age, race, sex, income, employment status, and location, as well as any additional physical features that can describe the company's customer, help immensely in the advertising industry because they allow the marketing department to isolate the exact customer base and determine the best way to reach them. Understanding these demographics will eliminate trial-and-error campaigns and avoid tying up cash flow. Along with demographics, it is important to know and understand the psychographics of the target market. Psychographics are any influential traits that can be traced to spending habits, such as religion, lifestyle, attitudes, values, and morals. Both demographics and psychographics can increase the company's customer base by increasing its marketing reach.

Hence, understanding exactly who the customers are will keep the company in business. The customer, quite simply put, is the person who spends the money, the person who gives the cash or writes the check to the company. Obviously, it is important to reach customers in order to generate some cash flow in the business, but the marketing campaign should not always be directed at the customer. It is also important for the marketing campaign to create a want or a need in consumers, along with creating a desire to purchase for the customer. Parents and children are a perfect example of customer-consumer relationships. The customer is obviously the parent, while the consumer would be the child playing with the newly purchased toy. If the child has no desire for the toy, then it will not be purchased. Similarly, if parents see no beneficial gain from the toy, such as occupying the child, then they will not buy it.

To conclude, it is imperative to find a balance in marketing campaigns in order to reach the appropriate avenues to increase profits.

Djamel Eddine Laouisset
Alhosn University, Abu Dhabi

See also Advertising; Branding; Market Evaluation; New Product Development; Selling Products and Services

Further Readings

Gruenwald, George. *New Product Development: Responding to Market Demand.* Lincolnwood, IL: NTC Publishing, 1995.

Hiam, Alexander and Charles Schewe. *The Portable MBA in Marketing.* New York: Wiley, 1992.

McCarthy, Jerome and William Perreault. *Basic Marketing.* Homewood, IL: Irwin, 1990.

Morgan, H. L., A. Kallianpur, and L. M. Lodish. *Entrepreneurial Marketing: Lessons From Wharton's Pioneering MBA Course.* New York: Wiley, 2001.

Ries, Al and Jack Trout. *Positioning: The Battle for Your Mind.* New York: McGraw-Hill, 1981.

Trout, Jack. "Positioning." *Industrial Marketing,* v.54/6 (June 1969).

Trout, Jack and Steve Rivkin. *The New Positioning.* New York: McGraw-Hill, 1996.

Urban, Glen and Steven Star. *Advanced Marketing Strategy.* Upper Saddle River, NJ: Prentice Hall, 1991.

TAXES

Taxes are a fact of life for any (successful) ongoing business. However, this aspect of financial (and cash flow) management is like most others in the new venture environment. It can be managed—and in a manner of speaking—optimized. This article addresses the issues new entrepreneurs need to consider as they formulate their business plans and proceed with the launching of their businesses.

Legal Forms of Businesses

First, and possibly most obvious, the specific "legal form" of business the new venture takes will have a direct and significant impact on the tax liability the new venture incurs, if, in fact, it is profitable. The specific legal forms of business can take many forms, and hybrids of those "tried and true" categories are appearing with greater frequency, which makes the business manager's decision all the more difficult.

Proprietorships and partnerships are often the choice of small business owners because they are less costly and less cumbersome to form and appear in most regards to be an extension of the owners. "Extension" here means that the income from these ventures simply appears as regular income to the owner(s), much as though this income was earned as an employee of someone else's business. Tax-wise, these business owners pay taxes on this business income once, where this business income is considered earned income to the business owner.

Corporations, by comparison, are the typical business form when the management of the entity is not also the majority (or significant) owner of the enterprise. Corporations offer the investors (owners) limited liability (to the extent of their investment)—but at a price. That price is exacted in the form of double taxation on the profits of the business. The corporation pays taxes (up to a 35 percent marginal rate), and when it distributes those profits to investors (as dividends), those distributions received are taxed again (usually) at the investor's marginal tax rate.

That said, many U.S. corporations with non-U.S. operations are able to delay (sometimes indefinitely) the payment of taxes on offshore profits by reinvesting those gains offshore. Additional subsidies, shelters, and special breaks often mean U.S.-based corporations with significant earnings are able to manage their tax rate down as much as 10 percent from the stated maximum of 35 percent cited above.

Also, S Corporations are now an option as a legal form of business, where the corporation's limited liability attribute remains, but the taxation at the corporate level is alleviated. Medium and smaller businesses may select this form, but it does contain the provision that the company can have no more than 75 owners/shareholders. LLCs (limited liability companies) and LLPs (limited liability partnerships) are similar hybrid structures, where the single taxation "event" is a decided advantage to the owners.

Tax Increment Financing (TIFs), as the name implies, clearly involves taxation, but the emphasis therein is somewhat different. Here, redevelopment is the motivating force (for the relevant municipality), while reduced taxes or a tax subsidy is a benefit/lure to the new business.

Any new business owners should believe that their business is going to provide benefits to its constituents. One of those constituents is the municipality in which the business resides, where that municipality will derive incremental tax revenues from additional business activity. These TIF districts can be created in all areas—major cities or small towns. Chicago has been using TIF funding since the mid-1980s as a tool to encourage private enterprise to participate in the redevelopment process, designating over $1.5 billion for these endeavors. The emphasis is on investment in fixed assets, whereby Chicago recognizes this investment as value added and rewards those investors with future (typically, property tax) relief.

After Chicago designates an area as a TIF district, property taxes that the city, county, school districts, and other local governments collect are frozen for 23 years. Clearly, in a rising tax rate environment, this serves as a cost reduction to a new business in the long term. But the municipalities do not simply give up tax revenues; instead, any new tax revenue generated from rising property values on surrounding properties—the tax increment—is collected by the city of Chicago and, per the TIF regulations, must be spent within the district or in a bordering one. Investment from private investors is leveraged and allows infrastructure to be renovated, which, in turn, draws other businesses and customers of existing businesses.

Increased tax revenues resulting from these redeveloped TIF areas have been significant, cited in some sources as being over $500 million in one fiscal year. One can presume these new-found revenues were used in ways such that other tax increases (or service reductions) were not invoked, thereby hindering economic activity.

Taxes and Entrepreneurial Activity

Second—but possibly foremost—the question is: Do taxes drive entrepreneurial activity? Is there a (reliable) cause-and-effect relationship, such that this factor should be factored into discussions of new business formation?

The answer is yes—and, in fact, it is yes twice. Donald Bruce and Tami Gurley examined the impact marginal tax rates have on new business formation and the impact differentials in tax rates between entrepreneurial income and "traditional" wages

had on new business formation, exit, and duration in business. These tax "causalities" were found to be highly significant: "The net effect of across-the-board marginal tax rate reductions is an increase in entrepreneurial entry and a decrease in entrepreneurial exit." And, to the point of long-term benefits to entrepreneurial activity, "Marginal tax rate changes have effects on the duration of entrepreneurship." All of these findings are what we would consider common (business) sense; lower costs drive individuals to those lower-cost activities for whatever period of time those savings benefits exist.

Business Incentive Tax Credits

Numerous states offer tax incentives if companies open offices (or new operations) in said states, and some offer tax credits if companies agree to retain employees. In March 2010, similar provisions were enacted at the federal level, all of which reinforce the idea that, selectively, opportunities exist for new businesses to trim their anticipated costs of operations by strategically deciding where to establish their business through a series of negotiations with all of the relevant taxing bodies.

These tax credits are given as a reduction in the payroll taxes (Social Security contributions) paid by the employing firm. While many will find this disarming at one level, (given Social Security's funding issues), the new business owner will realize a 6.2 percent decrease in the effective cost of employees (earning under $106,800 per year). In summary, taxes are inevitable if a business is a success at most any level. However, the tax bill paid by new businesses is not a "set-in-stone" percentage figure. Instead, it is highly dependent on a number of factors over which the entrepreneur has control and/or can negotiate prior to launching the business.

Robert J. Moreland
Columbia College, Chicago

See also Accounting; Bankruptcy; Business Models; Cash Flow; Debt

Further Readings

Bruce, Donald and Tami Gurley. "Taxes and Entrepreneurial Activity: An Empirical Investigation Using Longitudinal Tax Return Data." U.S. Small Business Administration, Office of Advocacy, March 2005.

City of Chicago, Housing and Economic Development. "TIF Projection Reports." http://www.cityofchicago.org/city/en/depts/dcd/supp_info/tif_projection_reports.html (Accessed December 2011).

Kocieniewski, David. "U.S. Business Has High Tax Rates but Pays Less," *New York Times* (May 2, 2011).

Velez, Juan-Pablo. "Tracking TIF Spending." *Chicago News Cooperative* (August 7, 2011). http://www.chicagonewscoop.org/chicagos-1-7-billion-in-tif-spending-aided-public-and-private-projects-almost-evenly (Accessed December 2011).

TEAM COMPOSITION

Entrepreneurs are critically concerned with innovation and creativity, and particular attention must be given to risk-taking propensity and tolerance for ambiguity. Team creation is the art of matching individual competencies and characteristics to the demands on the team. These demands include goals, tasks, and roles that draw upon the knowledge, skills, and abilities (KSAs) of team members. The proper mix of individual competencies—interrelated sets of KSAs—must be achieved in order to create synergy and value through member behaviors. Effectiveness is determined by the quality and quantity of productive output, through personal satisfaction, and with individual and team growth. For new ventures, this requires selecting members who have a strong need to achieve, a high energy level, an internal locus of control, self-confidence, and a results orientation. Studies show that firms started by teams are more successful than individual start-ups.

Knowing the venture's strategy is the logical first step in team creation. Leaders must understand the limits on team activities that are imposed by organizational resources and environmental conditions. An analysis of internal strengths and weaknesses matched to external opportunities and threats (SWOT) accounts for environmental conditions. This process creates a cascade of plans and goals, from long- to intermediate- to short-term, and establishes the accountability of divisions, departments, and teams for strategy execution and goal achievement.

Strategic plans and goals dictate the quantity and quality of organizational resources—human, financial, information, technological, and input materials—that are available to the team, as well as its potential accomplishments. The strategic process establishes team plans and goals; team activities and processes determine tasks and roles. The team creation challenge is to select individuals who generate synergy and value through behaviors—productive, membership, and adaptive—that advance the tasks and roles necessary to reach team goals. These behaviors include communication and coordination, enactment of team norms, resolution of conflicts, decision making, leadership, adaptation, task completion, and management of team processes.

It is critical that the proper team size be achieved with an appropriate diversity of competencies. The size of the team is important; it must be neither too large nor too small. Whereas small teams may move rapidly through the stages of development to performing, they may lack the competencies needed to resolve complex problems, to complete large quantities of work, or to make optimum decisions under conditions of ambiguity. Teams too large are subject to the inefficiencies of redundant competencies, to "freeloading," and to the inability to make timely and accurate decisions, especially if they fall victim to groupthink. Large teams may place a greater emphasis on social conformity than goal achievement and may splinter into cliques. As the size of the team increases, social costs typically increase; the ability to create synergy is critical to achieve higher levels of productivity. Social or membership costs coupled with the cost of adaptability and change can decrease, even overwhelm, productive benefits in large teams.

A diverse and capable mix of individual competencies and characteristics, as well as knowledge, skills, and abilities (KSAs), should be sought in order to create synergy and value when bringing together a team. (Photos.com)

Team roles are a set of expected behaviors related to social, task, and change activities within a team. Norms are standards of behavior that protect and defend the team's survival, status, and power while they provide behavioral predictability among team members that are important for success. Norms facilitate coordination and cooperation within the team and with other teams, without which conflict could become disruptive. Multiple conflict resolution techniques are available to team leaders to manage internal conflict; these vary with the importance of outcomes and the relationships between the parties. Likewise, there are several approaches that can be used to manage teams in interteam conflict situations.

Cohesiveness reflects the desirability of remaining in the team, the forces of team attraction greater than the inducement to leave. Highly cohesive teams achieve team goals, and teams with low cohesiveness perform hardly better than a collection of individuals. Cohesiveness is increased with team interaction, shared goals, personal attraction, competition with other teams, and success. Team leaders must shape team goals that conform to organizational demands or a highly cohesive team can successfully pursue its goals at the expense of the organization.

Teams typically go through stages of development with distinctive challenges and problems in each stage. The stages include getting acquainted; agreeing on leadership, goals, and tasks; setting norms; becoming efficient and productive; and termination. Whereas teams may progress through each stage in sequence, frequently teams recycle to previous stages, when critical events or disruptions occur, and may fail at any stage.

Provided the potential for team effectiveness is created through strategy and resources, if the required individual competencies are available, and if appropriate systems and processes are utilized during the stages of team development, it can be anticipated that the team will effectively meet its goals. Moreover, for an entrepreneur these goals are survival and growth in a dynamic, complex, and uncertain world. This makes the creation of successful teams a true challenge.

Tom D. McFarland
Tusculum College

See also Goal Setting; Human Resource Strategy; Innovation Management; Leadership

Further Readings

Chen, Ming-Huei. "Entrepreneurial Leadership and New Ventures: Creativity in Entrepreneurial Teams." *Creativity and Innovation Management*, v.16/3 (September 2007).

Chowdhury, Sanjib. "Demographic Diversity for Building an Effective Entrepreneurial Team: Is It Important?" *Journal of Business Venturing*, v.20/6 (November 2005).

Clarysse, Bart and Nathalie Moray. "A Process Study of Entrepreneurial Team Formation: The Case of a Research-Based Spin-Off." *Journal of Business Venturing*, v.19/1 (January 2004).

Ferriani, Simone, Gino Cattani, and Charles Baden-Fuller. "The Relational Antecedents of Project-Entrepreneurship: Network Centrality, Team Composition and Project Performance." *Research Policy*, v.38/10 (December 2009).

Godwin, Lindsey N., Christopher E. Stevens, and Nurete L. Brenner. "Forced to Play by the Rules? Theorizing How Mixed-Sex Founding Teams Benefit Women Entrepreneurs in Male-Dominated Contexts." *Entrepreneurship Theory and Practice*, v.30/5 (September 2006).

Hackman, J. R., ed. *Groups That Work and Those That Don't*. San Francisco: Jossey-Bass, 1990.

Iacobucci, Donato and Peter Rosa. "The Growth of Business Groups by Habitual Entrepreneurs: The Role of Entrepreneurial Teams." *Entrepreneurship Theory and Practice*, v.34/2 (March 2010).

Johnson, Michelle Kirtley, Kendra Reed, Kate Lawrence, and Marina Onken. "The Link Between Communication and Financial Performance in Simulated Organizational Teams." *Journal of Managerial Issues*, v.19/4 (Winter 2007).

Levi, D. *Group Dynamics for Teams*. Thousand Oaks, CA: Sage, 2001.

Steiner, I. D. *Group Processes and Productivity*. New York: Academic Press, 1972.

Tuckman, B. W. and M. A. C. Jensen. "Stages of Small Group Development Revisited." *Group and Organizational Studies*, v.2/4 (December 1977).

Wheelan, S. A. *Creating Effective Teams: A Guide for Members and Leaders*, 2nd ed. Thousand Oaks, CA: Sage, 2005.

TECHNOLOGY TRANSFER

University-based technology transfer has become a significant driver of entrepreneurial activity. The Association of University Technology Managers

(AUTM) estimates that in 2009 U.S. universities generated approximately 600 new companies, 4,300 new licenses, and $2.3 billion of licensing revenues. More than 3,200 start-up companies based on university research are currently active in the United States.

University-specific technology transfer offices (TTOs) manage the commercialization of intellectual property (IP) resulting from university research. Academic researchers disclose innovations to the university's TTO, which determines whether to file for legal protection, usually in the form of patents. TTOs both protect and monetize university IP. Protecting IP usually involves litigation or the threat of litigation against organizations infringing on patents. Commercializing university-owned IP transfers technology from the university to the commercial world via services, royalty-based licensing, and equity-based licensing.

Many academic researchers transfer knowledge to the commercial context via services or consulting arrangements. In most cases there is no transfer of ownership or rights. Commercial entities pay for the specialized knowledge and capabilities of the researcher and the university. At many universities, these arrangements are coordinated by the TTO or another entity within the university structure, both to protect university IP and to ensure ethical standards and good practice.

Licensing patents to large, established corporations represents the primary IP commercialization process for most academic institutions. An existing company licenses the rights to a patented or patent-pending technology, usually in return for a combination of up-front and royalty payments. The license identifies the assets, know-how, and documentation to be transferred. Common contract terms include remuneration, fields and geography of use, rights to improvements, term of use, and contingencies for defaults or forfeits. The right to use a technology for research purposes may be distinct from the right to sell products based on that technology. In addition, a company that licenses a fundamental technology may make improvements to develop a new product and then license that product to other companies. License terms often establish contingencies to cover these downstream events. Milestone payments may also be paid, as is often the case when a licensed therapeutic successfully completes a regulatory trial. These licensing agreements are generally based on so-called good-faith efforts to commercialize the innovation.

A new mode of technology transfer, however, emerged in the 1980s and 1990s. TTOs began licensing technologies to new ventures formed by university researchers or other businesspeople in exchange for equity (stock ownership) in the new venture rather than an up-front cash payment. For example, Larry Page and Sergey Brin licensed their own search and indexing algorithms developed at Stanford University as a critical step in founding Google. This equity-based licensing process alleviates cash requirements for the new venture and encourages early-stage commercialization of unproven technologies. TTOs facilitating equity licensing accept higher risks in the hope of participating in higher returns.

University technology transfer leads to hundreds of new ventures each year, primarily in technology-intensive fields. Utilizing and commercializing assets and skills acquired through technology transfer, however, present challenges to smaller, younger firms. Specialized knowledge, training, and physical assets may be required to exploit novel technologies. Entrepreneurial firms may underestimate the full investment in time and funds needed to use and develop technologies licensed from large research organizations, because additional foundational technologies and skills are already in place at those larger entities. On the other hand, new ventures that license university patents have better survival rates than those that do not. The costs of protecting transferred technologies may also be significant, especially in a global context where legal infrastructures diverge widely, and especially in countries where enforcement of intellectual property law is undeveloped or weak.

Most university-based technology transfer practices are based on the United States' University and Small Business Patent Procedures Act, more commonly known as the Bayh-Dole Act, which regulates commercialization of innovations arising from federally funded research. The Bayh-Dole legislation was set in motion when the University of Wisconsin–Madison lobbied Congress in 1973 to participate in institutional patent agreements. Prior to Bayh-Dole, title for innovations generated from federal funding was presumed to be held by the federal government. Bayh-Dole effectively enabled universities to exercise title rights, including commercialization, with the returns to commercialization accruing to the university. The federal government retains "march-in" rights to use or grant use of such intellectual property, but those rights have, to date, never been exercised. Globally, university technology transfer practices vary based on national legal environments and institution-specific policies, but the Bayh-Dole Act generally serves as a foundation for most TTO activities.

The Bayh-Dole Act appears to have significantly increased university-based patenting and commercialization activities, especially in fields where licensing represents an important knowledge transfer mechanism. Although the majority of university-technology transfer activities generate modest returns, some schools generate significant income from these activities. Nearly $1 billion in total licensing revenue was generated by the 10 American universities with the highest technology transfer income in 2010. In two extraordinary cases, Northwestern University licensed the novel therapeutic Lyrica for $700 million, while New York University received approximately $650 million for the license to Remicade.

Many universities have set up incubators, accelerators, and even early-stage venture funds to support venturing activities driven by researchers. University spinouts are more likely to require and obtain venture funding than the general population of new firms. Imperial College London has successfully floated the IP portfolio of its technology transfer office, Imperial Innovations, on the London AIM stock exchange. Successful technology transfer programs have been linked to local economic development and the creation of technology ecosystems. Some research, however, suggests that the formation of these knowledge clusters is contingent on a variety of local economic characteristics, and universities should not anticipate that technology transfer activities will have significant economic impact in the short term. A university with a small research base may not generate enough high-potential innovations to support such clustering activity.

Adam J. Bock
University of Edinburgh

See also Incubators; Knowledge; Licensing; Patent
    Protection; Research and Development; University
    Start-Ups

Further Readings

Association of University Technology Managers. "University Technology Transfer: Why We Do What We Do." http://www.autm.net (Accessed September 2010).

Fini, Richard et al. "Inside or Outside the IP System? Business Creation in Academia." *Research Policy*, v.39/8 (July 5, 2007).

Gans, Joshua S., David H. Hsu, and Scott Stern. "The Impact of Uncertain Intellectual Property Rights on the Market for Ideas: Evidence From Patent Grant Delays." *Management Science*, v.54/5 (May 2008).

Gerard, George and Adam J. Bock. *Inventing Entrepreneurs: Technology Innovators and Their Entrepreneurial Journey*. Trenton, NJ: Prentice Hall, 2008.

Hoye, Kate and Fred Pries. "'Repeat Commercializers,' the 'Habitual Entrepreneurs' of University–Industry Technology Transfer." *Technovation*, v.29/10 (October 2009).

Knockaert, Mirjam, Bart Clarysse, and Mike Wright. "The Extent and Nature of Heterogeneity of Venture Capital Selection Behaviour in New Technology-Based Firms." *R&D Management*, v.40/4 (September 2010).

Markman, Gideon D. et al. "Entrepreneurship and University-Based Technology Transfer." *Journal of Business Venturing*, v.20/2 (2005).

Miner, A. S. et al. "The Magic Beanstalk Vision of University Venture Formation." In *The Entrepreneurship Dynamic*, Kaye Schoonhoven and Elaine Romanelli, eds. Stanford, CA: Stanford University Press, 2000.

Shane, S. "Encouraging University Entrepreneurship? The Effect of the Bayh-Dole Act on University Patenting in the United States." *Journal of Business Venturing*, v.19/1 (2004).

Siegel, Donald S. et al. "Commercial Knowledge Transfers From Universities to Firms: Improving the Effectiveness of University–Industry Collaboration." *Journal of High Technology Management Research*, v.14 (Spring 2003).

Speser, Phyllis. *The Art and Science of Technology Transfer*. New York: Wiley, 2006.

Wright, Mike, Andy Lockett, Bart Clarysse, and Martin Binks. "University Spin-Out Companies and Venture Capital." *Research Policy*, v.35/4 (2006).

TERRITORIAL STRATEGY
AND REGIONS

The notion of territorial strategy emerged in the 1990s and has become more and more popular since. It refers to that combination of factors purposely assembled by governments, private and public companies, universities, and industrial associations to exploit a specific geographic competitive advantage in order to boost economic growth through the development of entrepreneurial activity and innovation. Three factors are generally considered to be the building blocks of a territorial strategy: natural resources, human capital, and industrial capabilities. Natural resources derive from environmental conditions and represent raw materials or land available in a region. The presence of natural resources characterizes the typology of an industry (related to tourism, oil, wood, fish, and so forth) that exists or could exist in a certain area. Human capital refers to the stock of competences available in a certain region resulting from education and work experience. Industrial capabilities relate to complex constructs of specialized expertise, the confidence to apply knowledge and skills in various contexts and under changing conditions, and an ability repeatedly to improve methods and processes in a specific industry.

Once a territorial strategy is properly defined, the success of its implementation rests on the ability to draft policies that fittingly define the desired level of interplay between localized systems of territorial governance and business innovation dynamics. Through appropriate policies defined to increase knowledge flows, attract and retain the right human capital, and improve internal cooperation and competition, the local government aims at maximizing, in a sustainable manner, its potential so that the territory can become competitive in the global market.

Government-business relations are becoming increasingly structured in regional rather than national contexts, hence positively influencing the amount of political power that small businesses can exert and the extent to which policy is oriented toward the promotion of entrepreneurial activities. The actors, who are generally most likely to influence decisions concerning the path of economic development in regional governance models, include networks of small firms and universities closely engaged with local governments. This situation is quite different compared to national governance models, in which typically large firms and unions have greater voice. National policy initiatives in support of small businesses and entrepreneurship bring a strong emphasis on internal

competition as a driver of economic activity. Such initiatives can take different forms, with some of the most common being provision of grants, investment in education, and programs related to research and development (R&D) linked to the building blocks of the territorial strategy.

If successful in the implementation of its territorial strategy, a region will benefit from attracting successful companies and concurrently will witness an increase in competition as well as collaborative activities among multiple actors, hence facilitating innovation growth. In other words, an industrial cluster will be created, which Michael Porter defined as a geographically close group of interconnected companies and associated institutions in a particular field, linked by commonalities and complementarities. Classic examples of geographic areas that have become world leaders in specific industry sectors and have maintained their status over multiple decades include the Silicon Valley as a hub for high-tech innovation and development, Hollywood as a center of the film industry, Las Vegas as the entertainment capital of the world, northern Italy as the home of fashion shoes, and southern Germany as a leader in high-performance auto companies.

Today's global economy is dominated by clusters, virtually present in any nation, region, or even metropolis. Successful clusters display four characteristics. First there is proximity among firms and institutions, as participants need to be sufficiently close in space to improve communication and allow sharing of common resources to occur. A second observation relates to linkages, as individual firms' activities need to share compatible goals for them to be able to benefit from proximity. Then there is the need for interactions, because being close and having similar objectives are not enough to spark changes. This, of course, can be done quite informally, without forcing vertical integration, formal alliances, or partnerships. Finally, there has to be a critical mass of participants for the interactions to have a meaningful impact on industry performance and therefore regional growth.

Once a cluster has been developed around certain industrial capabilities, there is danger over time for it to become too dependent on that particular path of economic development and therefore suppress innovation. Thus, it is critical for regional clusters to constantly evolve. Functioning clusters provide a high degree of information flows, not simply vertically, between consumers and suppliers, but especially horizontally, between firms in the same industry and across industries; the interactions inside companies are important, but the relations that take place in the immediate business environment outside companies are arguably even more significant. Porter's 1998 article on clusters and the new economics of competition is one of several studies to support the view that regional clusters are an important source of productivity and innovation. More precisely, this body of research asserts that clusters are critical for modern competition and links successful clusters to heightened innovation capacity achieved through learning by interacting across companies.

Consequently, for a territory to remain competitive it must maintain a high degree of innovativeness over time, and the regional level of analysis constitutes an important arena for innovation because of four core ingredients. The first constituent refers to the actors involved in the process of knowledge generation, which include R&D organizations (such as universities, research institutes, and public laboratories), educational bodies (such as universities, technical colleges, and vocational training organizations), and innovation-supporting organizations (such as technology licensing offices, science parks, incubators, and technology centers). The second element is the concept of regional cluster, with its flows of knowledge and skills among local actors (companies, clients, suppliers, competitors, and partners), leading to regional collective learning and systemic innovation. Next is the regional policy subsystem, which plays a crucial role in encouraging the region's development by providing financial support or by implementing favorable innovation and cluster policies. The last constituent influences the learning processes that can be realized and is about socioinstitutional factors, which encompass business behavior, routines, attitudes, and rules prevailing in the area. Of course, the regional economy remains affected by some aspects of the national business environment, such as the tax regime and legal system, but these are generally not as significant, especially in advanced economies.

Summing up, competition in today's global economy is primarily innovation-based and occurs less and less among firms and more often across geographic areas. This is despite the expectation that more open global markets, faster transportation, and more reliable communication should have diminished the role of location in competition. A vast number of cases from around the world confirm that the enduring competitive advantages in a global economy lie increasingly in local things, not limited to geographic features but also including knowledge, relationships, and inspiration.

Marcello Tonelli
Australian Centre for Entrepreneurship Research
Luigi Serio
Catholic University of the Sacred Heart, Milan

See also Competition; Geography of Innovation; Knowledge; Networks; Public Policy: Government Stimulation of Start-Ups

Further Readings

Amin, Ash. "An Institutionalist Perspective of Regional Economic Development." *International Journal of Urban and Regional Research*, v.23/2 (1999).

Braczyk, Hans-Joachim, Philip Cooke, and Martin Heidenreic. *Regional Innovation Systems: The Role of Governance in a Globalized World.* London: UCL Press, 1998.

Etzkowitz, Henry and Magnus Klofsten. "The Innovating Region: Toward a Theory of Knowledge-Based Regional Development." *R&D Management*, v.35/3 (2005).

Florida, Richard. "The Economic Geography of Talent." *Annals of the Association of American Geographers*, v.92/4 (2002).

Koch, Andreas and Thomas Stahlecker. "Regional Innovation Systems and the Foundation of Knowledge Intensive Business Services: A Comparative Study in Bremen, Munich, and Stuttgart, Germany." *European Planning Studies*, v.14/2 (2006).

Porter, Michael. "Clusters and the New Economics of Competition." *Harvard Business Review*, v.76/6 (1998).

Pouder, Richard and St. John Caron. "Hot Spots and Blind Spots: Geographical Clusters of Firms and Innovation." *Academy of Management Review*, v.21/4 (1996).

Test Markets

The fatality rate for new ventures is high. New businesses and even new products from established businesses fail frequently, for one reason or another. Test-marketing new products has become key to the risk management involved in new ventures, because such tests can shed light on the product's potential appeal before the full complement of resources has been committed to rollout. A market test is a key element of market research, in which a new or modified product, good, or service is offered to a limited market in order to observe its response. This is done after initial research—the in-house development, determination of pricing, and so on—and often after the focus group stage, in preparation for introduction to the full market. The process is known both as market-testing and as test-marketing. Some well-known products spent most of their lives in test markets: Crystal Pepsi was test-marketed throughout 1992 in more and more test markets but was discontinued very shortly after its official nationwide launch after the 1993 Super Bowl.

For a company like Pepsi, test-marketing is a nearly constant activity. The new products introduced in Pepsi's case are, usually, new flavors of an existing product. The distribution channels and physical facilities for producing the product already exist, and a good deal of demographic information is known about the potential consumers, their habits, and how much Pepsi they already consume. Slightly varying the product line is one way Pepsi can distinguish itself from Coca-Cola, or refresh the palates of loyal customers who may be feeling fatigued by familiarity. For instance, Crystal Pepsi was just one well-known test-market product in a long line of similar Pepsi variations. It had been preceded the previous year by strawberry, raspberry, and tropical fruit flavored Pepsis, which never made it to nationwide release. Before that, there had been Pepsi AM, a Pepsi with additional caffeine, intended as a morning coffee substitute; one of the factors in its failure to be selected for nationwide distribution was the caffeine limit imposed on soft drinks by the Food and Drug Administration. Elements of the Pepsi AM concept were revisited when Josta was introduced in 1995, two years before Red Bull was introduced to the United States, and it succeeded well enough to be added to the product line for the rest of the 1990s. After its cancellation, Pepsi test-marketed Pepsi Kona, a coffee-flavored cola.

Various criteria inform the selection of a test market. Ideally, the market should duplicate the national market, on a smaller scale; pricing should be the same, distribution and other factors should be the same, and the demographics of the consumers should be the same. For this reason, a product may often be introduced in test markets in several different parts

For companies like beverage manufacturers, test marketing is a nearly constant activity. Such tests can shed light on the product's potential appeal before resources are committed to rollout, whereas some products will be removed from the market following poor test marketing. (Photos.com)

of the country—say, southern California, upstate New York, Kentucky, and Montana—in order to build a total test-market consumer pool that is demographically similar to the entire country. Small markets can introduce large distortions to the results, so test-marketing may have multiple phases, as success in each test justifies a slightly larger test while leading up to the nationwide launch. Some products become market-tested so extensively that consumers remember the end of the market test as a cancellation, having become accustomed to the product's availability. In some rare cases a product may remain permanently available in a limited market even though market testing did not lead to a nationwide permanent adoption; Coke's C2 remained available in Chicago for years, for instance, while McDonald's Cajun McChicken never left the menus in Louisiana franchises after being introduced as part of a limited market test.

Eventually, Pepsi—like many food and beverage companies—changed the nature of its test-marketing by limiting the market not to a specific region but to a specific period of time, adopting limited-edition flavors that, if they prove popular, can be brought back to market at a later date. For new businesses, though, test-marketing in a limited region is still a valuable tool, and by limiting the area in which it is sold, the brand identity can be kept in flux while kinks are worked out in the concept. Further, if the test-marketing goes well, it can double as word-of-mouth advertising. Often firms will give away a new product in order to see what people say about it; events like baseball games and music festivals, if appropriate to the target demographic, are a good opportunity for this.

Bill Kte'pi
Independent Scholar

See also Advertising; Focus Groups; Obstacle
Identification

Further Readings

Adams, Rob. *If You Build It, Will They Come? Three Steps to Test and Validate Any Market Opportunity.* New York: Wiley, 2010.

Clancy, Kevin J., Peter C. Krieg, and Marianne McGarry Wolf. *Market New Products Successfully.* Lanham, MD: Lexington Books, 2006.

Coates, B. J. *A Study of the Ability of Test Markets to Predict New Product Performance.* Manchester: UMIST, 1975.

Longenecker, Justin G., J. William Petty, Leslie E. Palich, and Carlos W. Moore. *Small Business Management.* Stamford, CT: South-Western College, 2008.

Press, Donald. *Simulated Test Markets: A Business Perspective.* Baruch College, 1987.

Time Management

Time management refers to a range of skills, tools, and techniques used to manage time when accomplishing specific tasks, projects, and goals. This skill set encompasses a wide scope of activities, including setting goals, planning, allocating, delegating, analyzing time spent, monitoring, organizing, scheduling, and prioritizing. The aim of time management is to concentrate one's effort on the things that matter the most and help one become aware of how to use time as one resource in organizing, prioritizing, and succeeding in a business in the context of all the competing activities of start-ups and new ventures. Initially time management just focused on business

or work activities, but eventually the term broadened to apply to personal activities as well.

Usually, time management has been considered as a subset of project management; in this case, it is more commonly known as project planning or project scheduling. It is also a subset of attention management, which refers to the management of cognitive resources, particularly the time that humans allocate to thinking and making decisions about a task or other activity. Time management can also be discussed in the context of personal knowledge management, which is identified as a collection of processes that an individual conducts to gather, classify, store, search, retrieve, and share knowledge in his or her daily activities and how these processes support work activities.

There are four approaches to time management. The first aims to alert a person when a task is to be done based on clocks and watches, or computer implementation if possible. The second focuses on setting goals or planning and preparation based on calendars and appointment books. The third pays more attention to spending some time in clarifying values and priorities by planning, prioritizing, and controlling activities on a daily basis using personal organizers and other paper-based tools or systems based on personal digital assistants (PDAs). The fourth sets goals and roles as the controlling element of the system and favors importance over urgency.

In order to determine the tasks for any given moment dynamically, some techniques have been devised. Task lists, for example, identify tasks to be completed, functioning as an inventory tool that serves as an alternative or supplement to memory. Task lists are widely used in self-management and business management. This approach may involve more than one list. When one task is completed, it can be crossed off. Such systems, unlike traditional open to-do lists, are closed to-do lists on which tasks are prioritized. Traditional open to-do lists are never-ending, virtually guaranteeing that some of one's work will be left undone. The use of closed task lists advocates getting all one's work done every day. If one is unable to achieve that workload, then it is important to diagnose where things are going wrong and what needs to change.

There are other time techniques for setting priorities, such as ABC analysis, Pareto analysis, and goal setting. ABC analysis has been used in business management to categorize the large amounts of data into groups marked A, B, and C, based on the following general criteria: A refers to something urgent and important, B means important but not urgent (or urgent but not important), and C includes tasks that are neither urgent nor important. A tasks are done immediately and personally, C tasks are dropped, and B tasks are delegated or get an end date. Pareto analysis is based on the idea that typically 80 percent of unfocused effort generates only 20 percent of results; one can optimize one's effort by concentrating as much time and energy as possible on high-payoff tasks that ensure one will achieve the greatest benefit possible with the limited amount of time available. The entrepreneur can sort tasks into two groups: those that fall into the first category should be assigned a higher priority and should be completed immediately, and others can be postponed accordingly. Based on the notion that one is motivated by clear goals and appropriate feedback, goal setting emphasizes setting SMART goals: that is, goals that are specific, measurable, attainable, relevant, and time-bound.

Entrepreneurs must bear these time management strategies in mind and chose ones that will work for them, including time for study as well as breaks to have a snack or relax. It is important to dedicate a space in the workplace that is free from distractions, where it is possible to maximize concentration. Tasks and assignments should be reviewed and prioritized weekly, beginning with the most difficult subject or task, achieving "stage one" by getting something done, and postponing unnecessary activities.

With the help of the information technology, many software applications have been invented to facilitate time management dynamically, so as to assist the entrepreneur in determining the best tasks for any given moment. Some of these applications support multiple users, allowing the manager to delegate tasks to other users and communicate those assignments through the software.

Shuyi Zhang
Shanghai Finance University

See also Agility and Rapid Response; Change; Labor Costs; Planning Fallacy; Women's Entrepreneurship: Best Practices; Work-Life Balance

Further Readings

Fiore, Neil A. *The Now Habit: A Strategic Program for Overcoming Procrastination and Enjoying Guilt-Free Play.* New York: Penguin Group, 2006.

Grundspenkis, J. "Agent Based Approach for Organization and Personal Knowledge Modeling: Knowledge Management Perspective." *Journal of Intelligent Manufacturing*, v.18/4 (2007).

Le Blanc, Raymond. *Achieving Objectives Made Easy! Practical Goal Setting Tools and Proven Time Management Techniques.* Maarheeze, Netherlands: Cranendonck Coaching, 2008.

Wright, Kirby, "Personal Knowledge Management: Supporting Individual Knowledge Worker Performance." *Knowledge Management Research and Practice*, v.3/3 (2005).

TOLERANCE FOR FAILURE

The creation of new ventures, especially when these involve technological innovations, is widely considered to unleash a wealth of positive effects on the economy, such as higher employment, increased productivity, and enhanced development. By their very nature, new ventures are uncertain. No entrepreneur knows a priori which, out of many possible outcomes, he or she will obtain and with which probability. However, by definition, some of these outcomes involve firm closure or, as it is sometimes called, firm failure.

Firm failure has historically been a cause for concern, with a rate of closure slightly higher than 60 percent six years following creation. However, both the data of U.S. Census Bureau's Business Information Tracking Series (BITS) and the U.S. Census Bureau's Characteristics of Business Owners (CBO) show that between a half and a third of closed businesses are financially successful at closure. To account for these facts, a more recent perspective considers that a venture has failed when its termination is caused by an actual or expected performance falling below a critical threshold. Whereas from the point of view of "firm closure" most firms fail, from the point of view of "financial feasibility" only one third of these closures are failures.

Firm closure has been attributed to irrational behavior, such as failure to assess the amount of expected competition in the market (blind spot), an excessive preference for risk, and cognitive biases such as overconfidence, which occur when an individual overrates his or her chances of success. This last hypothesis is the one that counts, according to empirical evidence in experimental settings, yet it should be acknowledged that in the case of novel products and services, the entrepreneur will most likely lack any information to form rational beliefs as to his or her chances of success.

Population ecologists contend that success rates of organizations are age dependent. Whereas some scholars stress the liability of newness as a factor of firm failure, others argue that there is an early window of survival due to the stock of assets gathered at founding, after which the liability of adolescence reduces the life expectancy of firms. Besides the high probability of infant mortality, the literature indicates that a high probability of failure rises again at old age as firms become highly inertial and misaligned with their environments.

The experience of failure can have a painful impact on entrepreneurs and stakeholders, both financial and emotional. Furthermore, significant psychological barriers, such as fear of stigmatization, can accompany a failure experience. The feelings and the perceptions of individuals are reinforced by social and cultural norms that encourage success over failure. This explains why the natural aversion to failure is linked to its social cost. Furthermore, as the Insolvency Service Consultation Document evidences, the attitude toward failure is, to some extent, rooted in the culture of each country. For example, in the United States the attitude toward failure is mainly positive, whereas in other countries, such as the United Kingdom and Japan, it is negative.

Failure has also been found to have a positive side, as it represents an essential prerequisite for learning. Although learning from failure is not automatic or instantaneous, there is evidence of transformative learning about oneself (one's strengths, weaknesses, skills, attitudes, beliefs, and areas in need of development) and double-loop learning about the venture (strengths and weakness, including reasons for failure).

In line with these previous findings, scholars have distinguished between *firm* failure and *entrepreneurial* failure on the grounds that firms may sometimes constitute instruments through which entrepreneurs accumulate experience to improve the chances of survival of their forthcoming ventures. This argument strongly depends on the existence of learning effects behind repeated founding of ventures and the possibility of transferring experience and knowledge from one venturing context to another. Although results are not conclusive, the general wisdom is

that previous ownership increases survival rates, probably by inducing more calibrated expectations and strengthening the perception of having been successful.

Finally, it is necessary to understand that firm failure is inevitable. Entrepreneurial rents can be earned by those who take out real options on opportunities that are not obvious to others and that, as a consequence, are undervalued. Furthermore, entrepreneurial initiatives that fail may still improve the knowledge of other people, so that in the aggregate, failure can have positive consequences. In uncertain environments, such as the ones in which most ventures are created, miscalculations are bound to occur. For this reason it is important to focus on education as a tool to ameliorate inevitable failures.

Maribel Guerrero
Graciela Kuechle
Basque Institute of Competitiveness,
Deusto Business School

See also Business Failure; Knowledge; Measures of Entrepreneurial Activity Across Countries; Overconfidence; Risk Management

Further Readings

Aldrich, Howard and Marlene Fiol. "Fools Rush In? The Institutional Context of Industry Creation." *Academy of Management Review*, v.19 (1994).

Cope, Jason. "Entrepreneurial Learning From Failure: An Interpretative Phenomenological Analysis." *Journal of Business Venturing* (2010).

Gimeno, Javier, Timothy Folta, Arnold Cooper, and Carolyn Woo. "Survival of the Fittest? Entrepreneurial Human Capital and the Persistence of Underperforming Firms." *Administrative Science Quarterly*, v.42 (1997).

Headd, Brian. "Redefining Business Success: Distinguishing Between Closure and Failure." *Small Business Economics*, v.21/1 (2003).

McGrath, Rita. "Falling Forward: Real Options Reasoning and Entrepreneurial Failure." *Academy of Management Review*, v.24 (1999).

Sarasvathy, Saras, Anil Menon, and Graciela Kuechle. "Failing Firms and Successful Entrepreneurs: Serial Entrepreneurship as a Temporal Portfolio." *Small Business Economics*, forthcoming.

Watson, John and Jim Everett. "Defining Small Business Failure." *International Small Business Journal*, v.11/3 (1993).

TRADEMARKS

Judge Learned Hand, writing on *Yale Electric Corp. v. Robertson* (1928), said of a merchant's trademark, "His mark is his authentic seal; by it he vouches for the goods which bear it; it carries his name for good or ill. If another uses it, he borrows the owner's reputation, whose quality no longer lies within his own control." The U.S. government recognizes and provides mechanisms to protect a trademark, service marks, certification marks, and collective marks. According to the U.S. Patent and Trademark Office, "A trademark includes any word, name, symbol, or device, or any combination, used, or intended to be used, in commerce to identify and distinguish the goods of one manufacturer or seller from goods manufactured or sold by others, and to indicate the source of the goods." The trademark exists for the protection of the consuming public. It allows a consumer to identify a good. The marks that identify a good or service or organization must be intended to be used in commerce in order to qualify for protection. Since at least as early as the 17th century, the common law in England has recognized the right to use a mark as an identifier. Courts have recognized that the mark develops a reputation of its own and that the associated quality or lack thereof, dependability, and status become synonymous with the mark.

According to common law, the exclusive right to a trademark belongs to the one who first uses it. As goods can take on a very similar shape, size, and style, the reason for a trademark is to provide a means for consumers to distinguish one good from another. Thus, marks will be enjoined from use whose similarity is deceptively confusing to the consumer, making it difficult or impossible for the consumer to tell in whose product they are investing. Currently in the United States, there is federal and state legislation relating to registration and recognition of trademarks. The U.S. Patent and Trademark Office has exclusive jurisdiction at the federal level to the review and granting of the right to ownership and use of a mark. Furthermore, international law on the matter of registration and protection of a mark exists in multiple jurisdictions. Trademark law grants rights to the mark of an individual, a business organization, and an association. Once established, a trademark can be licensed, transferred, or sold as an asset.

Trademark rights are maintained by use. Rights can be relinquished through abandonment or dilution. When the mark becomes so strong that it becomes part of popular culture and associated with the product rather than the brand, then the right to the mark can be lost.

Formal registration of a trademark is not necessary, though it has advantages. Some advantages of registration in public records include a general notice to the public of a claim to a right of exclusive use of a mark; registration can provide the basis for international registration and a claim of right and can also serve as a basis for enforcing a bar to the importation of goods from foreign manufacturers who copy or infringe on the mark without license.

As far as enforcement is concerned, once the right to a mark has been established through common-law use or registration, if a party engages in unauthorized infringement of a trademark there can be liability. There may even be personal liability for the corporate agents, depending on the degree of involvement and culpability. The punishment stems from the unlawful infringement on the property rights of another, as well as the need to protect the public from confusion about the origin of the product. The mark prevents the public from being deceived about the authenticity of the good and protects the owner of the good and the reputation developed over time regarding the good and its mark. The public's belief that the mark's owner sponsored or otherwise approved the use of the trademark satisfies the confusion requirement.

A disparagement claim may also come from one who has trademark rights. Disparagement may result where one competitor makes a false statement about a product and causes a loss of market standing for the product. Thus, damage results to the mark and its associated reputation. In this instance, a lawsuit may ensue for damages to offset market loss in sales and/or for funds for a corrective advertising campaign, usually for at least the sum spent in the attack campaign, to correct the damage. There is no federal statute of limitations for trademark infringement.

It is important for entrepreneurs or those engaged in new ventures to have a thorough understanding of trademarks from the point of view of protecting their mark as well as to avoid unintentional infringement. Given increasing globalization, it is also possible to file, register, and enforce trademark rights in multiple jurisdictions on a regional or global basis with the aid of the Community Trademark System (CTM) or the Madrid system. The CTM covers the European Union, whereas the Madrid system provides the possibility of a centrally administered system for trademark registrations in member states by the extension of protection of "international registration" via the auspices of the World Intellectual Property Organization. This international registration is contingent on a duly effected application or registration obtained by a trademark applicant in the home jurisdiction.

As discussed earlier, trademarks help to protect consumers by the proper identification of a good in addition to protecting the provider of said goods so as to avoid confusion. A related area is patent law, which is designed to protect recent and useful inventions, including the visible form and appearance of a manufactured article. Another adjunct to trademark, especially for an entrepreneur or those engaged in new venture, is the law of copyright, which helps to protect original artistic, literary, and creative works.

Dominic DePersis
Broome Community College
Alfred Lewis
Hamline University

See also Branding; Entrepreneurs in Franchising; Franchisee and Franchisor; Franchises: Legal Aspects; Incorporation; Licensing; Patent Protection; Product Innovation; Venture Valuation

Further Readings

Bouchoux, Deborah E. *Intellectual Property: The Law of Trademarks, Copyrights, Patents, and Trade Secrets for the Paralegal.* Clifton Park, NY: Delmar Cengage Learning, 2008.

Conroy, Helen. "Intellectual Property 101—for Entrepreneurs." *Contract Management*, v.41/7 (July 2001).

Gilbert, Jill. *The Entrepreneur's Guide to Patents, Copyrights, Trademarks, Trade Secrets, and Licensing.* New York: Berkley Books, 2004.

Goldstein, Paul. *Copyright, Patent, Trademark and Related State Doctrines, Cases and Materials on the Law of Intellectual Property*, 6th ed. New York: Foundation Press, 2002.

Stim, Richard. *Patent, Copyright and Trademark: An Intellectual Property Desk Reference*, 11th ed. Berkeley, CA: Nolo Press, 2010.

U.S. Patent and Trademark Office. http://www.uspto.gov/trademarks/basics/index.jsp (Accessed February 2011).

U.S. Patent and Trademark Office. *Trademarks, the Fingerprints of Commerce: An Educational Guide to Understanding the Importance of Trademarks.* Washington, DC: Author, 2000.

University Start-Ups

Driven by internal demands to produce new revenue streams and external pressures to help generate economic development, universities have become more entrepreneurial. Leading up to the 1980s, officials in the federal government were worried that the nation was not getting the full benefit of university research. At the time, a good deal of research was theoretical, whereas other promising research went undeveloped and often remained virtually unknown to all but a handful of other faculty.

To address these concerns, the Bayh-Dole Act of 1980 was passed to establish incentives to induce organizations to orient work along commercially viable paths and allow universities to keep the rights to patents from federally funded research. As a result of this and subsequent legislation, universities began encouraging faculty to consider commercial applications for their research and let them share in any resulting revenue.

The Bayh-Dole Act has had its intended effect: Larger numbers of faculty have pursued research agendas with more near-term, practical outcomes. In the eight years following the introduction of the legislation, the patenting of university-developed technology increased nearly sevenfold, and a sample of top research universities reported that their licensing of those patents to industry had more than doubled.

The media are awash with licensing success stories. In 1967, medical researchers at the University of Florida developed the formulation for what would become Gatorade, resulting in more than $30 million in royalties. In recent years, the University of Wisconsin has received nearly $100 million in royalties from licensing vitamin D technologies, while Michigan State University has received more than $85 million in royalties by licensing a cancer treatment drug.

Whether it is through the founding of firms based on university research, developing proprietary technology and obtaining patents, pursuing consulting engagements with business, establishing joint venture or knowledge transfer arrangements with industry, or creating externally funded applied

Universities can contribute to the private sector through licensing formulations to manufacturers. For example, researchers at the University of Florida developed the formulation for the product now known as Gatorade in 1967, resulting in more than $30 million in royalties. (Photos.com)

research centers, universities are becoming more entrepreneurial. Whereas this surge in academic entrepreneurship may take many forms, the university start-up in particular has received much attention because of the economic benefits arising from the commercialization of research.

A university start-up is a firm founded for the purpose of commercializing university-developed intellectual property. Universities may decide to pursue a university start-up strategy when the research produces proprietary technology that has broad-based applications and can be developed into a commercial product that has the potential to transform an industry or, at least, outdo an existing product. Whereas universities may prefer to license such technology, under these circumstances the technology is sufficiently transformational that existing companies may be unwilling to manage its development.

As university start-ups typically lack the resources needed to fully develop the commercial potential of their research as a free-standing company, a joint venture with an industry partner may be utilized. Under these circumstances, commercial development of the technology is handed over to an external partner.

Many newly formed firms recruit experienced professional managers from outside the university while barring academics from executive positions. This allows the start-up to be independent of the university and helps avoid the hazards of conflicting missions. This way, universities can focus on the objectives on which they are judged within academia, which is teaching students and conducting research, not developing commercial products. Even so, maintaining a connection to the institution that spawned the research is important. Universities have responded by creating institutional structures that allow faculty to remain employed by the university while maintaining an advisory role in the start-up.

Research suggests that university start-ups help to create new industries and stimulate economies by helping to create wealth and generate significant employment. According to one source, university start-ups contributed nearly 300,000 jobs to the U.S. economy and more than $30 billion in economic value-added activity between 1980 and 1999. In fact, studies suggest that a firm that originates from a university creates more jobs than the average start-up in the United States.

Another study found that university start-ups originating from the Massachusetts Institute of Technology since the 1940s helped to establish the Route 128 high-technology corridor. Another study explained how graduates from the institute had founded thousands of companies by the late 1990s, creating more than a million jobs worldwide and generating hundreds of billions of dollars in annual sales. Similar results have been found in Canada. One study in the province of Alberta found that nearly 100 new ventures were created by faculty, generating more than 100 new jobs.

In addition, the benefits of university start-up activity are not limited to job creation. Studies suggest that university start-ups are more than 100 times more likely than the average start-up to go public. Furthermore, the survival rate of university start-ups is exceptionally high. U.S.-based university start-ups also outdo their nonuniversity counterparts' survival rates. One study of more than 3000 university start-ups, founded over a 20-year period beginning in 1980, determined that 68 percent remained operational in 2001. Moreover, university start-up survival rates are not an American phenomenon. One study discovered that only 13 percent of the start-ups from a university in Sweden founded over a 33-year period had failed. Another investigation of French university start-ups found that only 16 percent had failed over the six-year period of the study.

The reason for these astonishing survival rates may lie in the types of technologies these start-ups exploit, how well those technologies are protected, and the status of the university relationship after the start-up is established. In a study investigating the commercialization of inventions owned by the Massachusetts Institute of Technology, researchers found that start-ups are more likely to survive if they seek to develop far-reaching technologies that are extensively protected by patents. Another study of university start-ups found that the transfer of researchers' tacit knowledge and their relationships with the research community helped to increase survival of these firms.

The results of university start-up activity would seem to be decidedly positive. Universities generate new revenue streams and help to alleviate the pressures to generate economic development. Faculty gain funding for research as well as an opportunity to generate substantial wealth from commercializing their research. The results, however, have been mixed, as only a relatively low number of institutions have experienced the remarkable economic success described above.

Faculty may have reason to be distrustful of the trend in commercializing university research and the expansion of the university mission beyond teaching and research. Studies suggest that as universities have strengthened relationships with industry, threats to academic freedom have appeared. Universities have moved more toward applied research to benefit their industry partners, thus causing delays and outright restrictions on the publication of new knowledge. In fact, studies demonstrate that faculty share knowledge much more readily when no commercialization is involved. In addition, uncertainty concerning the ownership of the resulting knowledge remains.

Critics point to a self-reinforcing cycle, as demands to identify new sources of revenue to sustain ever costlier research activities quell internal resistance to industry influence on academic inquiry. As a consequence, conflicts over institutional equity arise, as budgets tilt toward the more commercially viable fields, thus restarting the cycle. Such maneuvers can cause deep divisions within academe, as those departments that have suffered severe funding cuts but have no commercial opportunities are left behind.

While faculty entrepreneurs are generally more productive researchers than their nonentrepreneurial peers, and their productivity does not decrease following the formation of a firm, others within academe may still justifiably criticize the misallocation of time and energy away from their primary responsibilities as teachers and researchers. Evidence suggests that faculty may be distracted as they struggle to balance their start-up responsibilities with their professorial duties to the university.

Enrique Nuñez
Ramapo College of New Jersey

See also Entrepreneurs in Technology; Incubators; Public Policy: Government Stimulation of Start-Ups; Research and Development; Technology Transfer

Further Readings

Clarysse, B., M. Wright, A. Lockett, P. Mustar, and M. Knockaert. "Academic Spin-Offs, Formal Technology Transfer and Capital Raising." *Industrial and Corporate Change*, v.16/4 (2007).

Meyer, Martin. "Academic Entrepreneurs or Entrepreneurial Academics? Research-Based Ventures and Public Support Mechanisms." *R&D Management*, v.33/2 (2003).

Siegel, D. S., M. Wright, and A. Lockett. "The Rise of Entrepreneurial Activity at Universities: Organizational and Societal Implications." *Industrial and Corporate Change*, v.16/4 (2007).

Vohora, A., M. Wright, and A. Lockett. "Critical Junctures in the Development of University High-Tech Spinout Companies." *Research Policy*, v.33/1 (2004).

Wright, M., S. Birley, and S. Mosey. "Entrepreneurship and University Technology Transfer." *Journal of Technology Transfer*, v.29/3–4 (2004).

V

VENTURE CAPITAL

Venture capital is a form of investment money provided in return for a share of equity in an enterprise that has significant growth potential. Typically it is injected into a venture before it has returned a profit. This may be given in the form of seed, start-up, or expansion funding. Seed finance is provided to help an inventor or entrepreneur prove that a concept has business potential, whereas start-up funding supports a move from pilot-testing a concept to implementing it commercially for the first time. Expansion funding provides working capital for the initial expansion of the enterprise. Venture capital might also refer to funding provided to finance acquisitions, including funding for management buy-outs as well as funding for a second or even later expansion phase. Uniting these various applications of venture capital is the association with supporting critical stages in the development of either wholly new or substantially transformed ventures.

Venture capitalists aim to invest early in the life cycle of an enterprise and to disinvest when the value of the firm's equity has grown sufficiently to yield a substantial capital gain over the sum that was invested originally. Periods of from three to eight years to realize investments have been typical, but according to data from the National Venture Capital Association (NVCA)—an industry association representing venture capital providers in the United States—venture capitalists are tending to hold investments for longer periods. At the height of the dot-com boom in 1999, the average period between first receiving venture capital and the enterprise becoming a public company was just under six years. In 2009, the equivalent period had stretched to 11 years, but the comparison may be misleading, as the number of investments involved fell from 271 in 1999 to 12 in 2009.

With a focus on investing in new ventures and recognizing that previously untested business opportunities frequently fail to realize their initial expectations, investment returns are expected to be concentrated on a few highly successful ventures. To cater to this, venture capitalists seek to support a portfolio of ventures at any point in time, selling out of individual investments as their valuations increase and perhaps at a point when substantial further investment is needed to execute a second stage of growth.

The NVCA identified 794 venture capital firms as existing in the United States in 2009. This is around double the number of providers existing in 1989, but over the same period the value of funds under management grew from $28.4 billion to $179.4 billion. Much of this expansion took place in the late 1990s with a peak of $203.7 billion in venture capital invested in 2006. Almost two thirds of the funding was allocated to expansion and later-stage funding in roughly equal amounts, with the balance predominantly early-stage funding. Seed and start-up funding accounted for 9 percent of the total funds allocated.

Venture capital has attracted attention through its role in supporting new technology-based enterprise, but as the researcher Martin Kenny points out, venture capitalists themselves are agnostic as to the types of activity in which they invest. Rather than being attached to any particular sector, Kenny suggests that venture capital seeks out any type of firm that shows a prospect of opening a "new economic space." This term comes from the writing of Joseph Schumpeter and was used to identify the swarming of new enterprises around the business opportunities created in the wake of technological breakthroughs. The development of the Internet space illustrates the kind of transformation targeted by venture capital. Companies such as Netscape allowed more people to make use of the World Wide Web, in turn increasing demand for software to build Websites. As the number of Websites and users increased, so did the possibilities of establishing ventures based on online sales and subsequently other types of enterprises linked to the burgeoning new forms of communication media. Venture capitalists aim to fund the pioneers that shape and underpin this type of entrepreneurial upwelling.

New economic spaces offer prospects for the kind of "supersized" investment returns targeted by venture capitalists. This fits with what has been viewed as the particular skill of venture capitalists: the ability to look just over the horizon to see what the next step in the technology and business evolution might be and to support a firm in occupying that space before incumbents or other aspiring entrants seize the opportunity. This explains why venture capital is especially associated with the electronics information processing (EIP) and biotechnology sectors. Other industries are not overlooked, but they typically provide fewer of the high-growth propositions that venture capital targets. For example, the NVCA identifies Home Depot and Starbucks as recipients of venture capital, but hardware retailing and coffee shops as a whole have not attracted venture capital. Overall in the United States, non-high-tech ventures accounted for slightly more than a fifth of the new venture capital deals executed in 2009.

One reported estimate is that one in 15 investments made by venture capitalists may earn returns of more than 10 times the original investment, while around a third of investments result in an absolute loss. With this type of outcome, risk control measures are important and a further source of the distinctiveness of venture capital funding. This links to an agency theory interpretation of venture capital as a form of funding that resolves impediments to

supporting new ventures. According to this framework, the relationship between the entrepreneur and funder is asymmetrical because the entrepreneur has much greater insight into the venture's true prospects and an incentive to withhold information that might limit their ability to attract funding. Venture capital funding mechanisms can partly be understood as responses to these problems.

A screening process in which only a low percentage of proposals receive funding is a first step in risk control. The NVCA suggests that for every 100 business plans taken to a venture capital firm, usually around 10 might be given any consideration and only one given any funding. As well as having a credible management team, venture capitalists prioritize innovative ventures that ideally address world markets and offer potential for scalability over a comparatively short period of time. Other risk management measures are applied at the individual (micro) and portfolio (macro) investment levels.

The structuring of investment and ongoing influence over the strategic management of the enterprise receiving venture capital are two micro forms of risk control exercised by the funding provider. Rather than giving the entrepreneur a large sum "up front," venture capitalists may allocate funding over time according to an agreed performance schedule. This gives the venture capitalist an early exit route and a mechanism to focus the entrepreneurial team on activities that are of most commercial significance. Venture capitalists typically nominate a person as their representative on the boards of the companies in which they invest and may use this position to maintain involvement in the enterprise's strategy development. Directing that the entrepreneurial team's compensation be weighted in favor of stock options rather than cash salary can be used as a further mechanism for aligning the interests of both parties.

At the macro level, venture capitalists may seek to manage risk through either a specialization or a diversification approach to their portfolio of investments. Investment in a diversity of projects can guard against the failure of a technology or business model that is common to a group of similar new ventures. Equally, specialization can be used as a risk-control measure where this results in deep insight into a particular area of activity or stage of funding and the venture capitalist can transfer insight gained from close involvement with one venture to other ventures in the portfolio and can use industry-specific insight to evaluate new proposals. Of course, large venture capital providers may be able to employ both strategies alongside the full range of micro measures.

Venture capital is generally thought to make a substantial contribution to economic development through its assistance to enterprises at the early stages of creating new economic spaces. This has led to efforts to understand the conditions needed for a flourishing venture capital industry. Research published by the Berkeley Roundtable on the International Economy based on experience in the United States and Israel has developed an evolutionary perspective on how venture capital industries emerge, overcome challenges, and restructure around a more sustainable form of organization. The Berkeley Roundtable's life cycle model of the evolution of venture capital industries distinguishes five phases.

1. *Background conditions phase:* This denotes the context in which an incipient industry forms and evolves. These conditions are not necessarily consciously recognized or acted upon, but they have a key influence on shaping how the industry develops.

2. *Pre-emergence:* This phase begins with the earliest venture capital investments and results in venture capital being an identifiable segment of the financial market.

3. *Emergence:* During this phase, the industry takes a coherent form. There may be experimentation with organizational forms alongside rapid expansion.

4. *Crisis:* A period of instability has characterized the development of venture capital industries, partly as successful growth depends on balancing the development of a sufficient volume of high-quality start-ups, addressing organizational issues, and attracting suitable professionals.

5. *Restructuring and consolidation:* In this stage, the venture capital industry becomes a sustainable part of the "national system of innovation."

Such an evolutionary perspective raises doubts about the value of efforts to promote the availability of venture capital in places where it is not already well developed. According to this perspective, the establishment and growth of a venture capital industry occurs interdependently with other business environment conditions. Critically, a flow of investment opportunities that meet the attributes looked for by venture capitalists must exist. Efforts to promote the supply of venture capital are unlikely to be effective without incipient demand from innovative entrepreneurs already being present. Consequently, an evolutionary perspective argues that venture capital develops alongside the emergence of new economic spaces rather than being an independent causal agent.

Innovative capabilities and research-and-development activity are the source of new technology-based ventures and the opening up of new technological trajectories rather than the existence of funding. Venture capital has become associated with the ingredients of an innovative economy because the availability of venture capital becomes one of the influences helping to draw commercial ventures out of research-and-development activity. The presence of venture capital reshapes the business environment to make it more conducive to new ventures than it otherwise would be. As the potential targets of investment respond to the availability of funding, the stage is set for venture capital to become embedded into the innovation environment. In the Berkeley Roundtable model, important forms of entrepreneurial adaptation that facilitate the development of a vibrant venture capital industry include entrepreneurial acceptance of some degree of outside control and the emergence of a supporting sector of lawyers, accountants, and intellectual property experts.

The development of mechanisms to assist venture capitalists exit their investments further consolidates the place of venture capital in a national innovation system. An initial public offering (IPO) is often a favored exit route for a venture capitalist, as it can maximize the value of their equity offered for sale. Private sales of some or all of the venture capitalist's equity are possible but unlikely to yield the same return as when members of the public are invited to compete for a share of the equity. A barrier to a company's making its first offering of stock to the public is that this requires the company to list on a stock exchange. As the scale of the venture on IPO is likely to be small relative to the majority of public companies, this can be a problem if available stock exchanges are geared to the interests of big, established companies. A response by stock markets has been to open so-called second-tier markets, which place less onerous demands on the companies they list than do main boards.

According to estimates of the NVCA, the total value of venture capital funding outside the United States is worth only around a fifth of that invested in the United States. The NVCA puts this down to the entrepreneurial spirit pervasive in the American culture, including the acceptance of financial recognition for success and the access to good science. As well as the extent of funding, venture capital in other countries tends to have a larger focus on funding buyouts of existing ventures than on supporting new ventures.

While national culture affects the availability of venture capital, geographic concentration is a feature of the distribution of venture capital funding in the United States, as it is in other economies. Three states—California, Massachusetts, and New York—accounted for two thirds of the value of venture capital invested in the United States in 2009. A recent trend has seen some leading U.S.-based venture capital firms make increasing numbers of investments outside the United States in fast-growing Asian economies, especially that of China. The stock of venture capital invested in China is now worth half that invested in the United Kingdom, which is the second largest venture capital market after the United States. The shift to Asia has been noted in the IPOs brought to market by some of the United States' venture capital companies. For example, Sequoia Capital, a Silicon Valley–based financier that was an early backer of companies such as Apple, Cisco Systems, and Google, brought 12 IPOs to market during the period between 2009 and October 2010. Of these, only two were U.S. ventures, but this is affected by depressed market conditions following the global financial crisis, which is encouraging venture capitalists to rely on sales to bigger companies rather than taking the IPO exit route. From 1991 to 2000, typically 150 venture-capital-backed companies went public every year in the United States. Between then and 2010, the average was fewer than 50 per year. This trend is creating uncertainty about the future of venture capital funding. Venture capital funds are finding it hard to raise money with the decline in demand for IPOs, but with technologies such as biotech, medical devices, and clean energy needing finance, it remains unclear whether the industry is undergoing a temporary lull in activity or the importance of venture capital has peaked.

Martin Perry
Massey University

See also Agency Theory; Business Angels; Equity- and Debt-Based Financing; Initial Public Offering

Further Readings

Avnimelech, G., M. Kenney, and M. Teubal. "Building Venture Capital Industries: Understanding the U.S. and Israeli Experiences." Paper 160, Berkeley Roundtable on the International Economy, 2004.

National Venture Capital Association. *2010 National Venture Capital Association Annual Yearbook.* Washington, DC: Author, 2010.

Wright, M. and K. Robbie. "Venture Capital and Private Equity: A Review and Synthesis." *Journal of Business Finance and Accounting*, v.25/5–6 (1998).

VENTURE MANAGEMENT FIRMS

Venture management firms provide their venture clients with the necessary capital, interim management support, and relevant resources to achieve business tractions for the company's product or service. Donald King and Robert Thornton define *venture* as an abbreviated word for "entrepreneurial adventure" and a venture management firm as "an organization initiated to capitalize on new products and markets. The objective of venture management is to launch *new* businesses. If ventures are related in some way to existing businesses they must be dissimilar from, and not direct extensions of, existing operations." By way of example, if Coca-Cola introduces a new soft drink, this is not a venture. When DynaShot Corporation, an emerging entity, comes out with a new process for more rapid printing of three-dimensional photographs, this is a venture. However, if Eastman Kodak Company developed a similar process, it would not be a venture.

Venture management builds on the entrepreneurial function, and it involves the inherent risk and speculative nature of new products and markets. Ventures are distinguished from other businesses by the uniqueness of their product or market: The higher the degree of innovation for a company's product or service and the more risk it takes on, the greater is the identification of the company as a venture. Basically, ventures have no direct competition. If successful, they attract competition, but this occurs later in their life cycle, when they are no longer classified as ventures.

All businesses rely on financial resources to begin activity. However, venture capital as a distinct form of U.S. business financing did not begin until after World War II. In his book *The New Ventures: Inside the High Stakes World of Venture Capital*, John Wilson cites 1946 as the year the venture capital industry originated in the United States. The first venture capital fund started when John Hay Whitney and colleagues contributed an initial capitalization of $10 million. The structure of this first venture fund served as the model for others as the industry grew.

The American Research and Development Corporation followed as an early venture capital fund based in Boston and headed by George Doriot. In *The Arthur Young Guide to Raising Venture Capital*, authors Steven Burrill and Craig Norback state that Doriot's leadership set the course for future venture capital organizations. Through early success with their client, Digital Equipment Corporation, the American Research and Development Corporation's initial investment of $67,000 grew to more than $600 million.

In 1958, the Small Business Investment Act was passed by the U.S. Congress, and it served as a key incentive for potential venture capital (VC) organizations. The act provided privately managed VC firms organized as small business investment companies (SBICs) with an opportunity to increase the amount of funds available to entrepreneurs. Through the Small Business Administration, SBICs were granted access to federal money that could then be leveraged four-to-one against privately raised funds. The SBICs then made the financial resources available to new ventures and local entrepreneurs.

Over time, as increasing capital has stepped onto the VC platform, the focus of VC firms has grown more conservative. Whereas early venture capitalists provided funding to companies for initial start-up activities, the industry increasingly seeks out ventures more advanced in their development. As a result, there is a tendency for VC firms to provide funds for products and services with proven markets and a higher chance of success in the marketplace rather than support early-stage and start-up financing.

Two predominant types of organizations disburse venture capital: leveraged firms and equity firms. The structure of the client venture usually determines how the organization can profit.

Leveraged firms lend to new ventures at a higher rate than the one at which they borrow money from the government, private sources, or other financial institutions. These leveraged firms profit by charging their clients a higher interest rate, and they primarily provide disbursements in the form of loans to new ventures.

Equity firms pool investors' money and then use the proceeds to purchase equity in new ventures by selling stock in the venture capital organization to individual or institutional investors. Equity VC firms build investment portfolios in companies; they profit by reselling the stock of portfolio businesses after five to eight years. Whereas a leveraged firm can expect a relatively steady stream of interest income, an equity firm does not experience a return on its investment for years, and that usually results from the sale of equity in the new venture. Venture capital organizations either can sell their equity back to the company or can sell on a public stock exchange (like the American Stock Exchange) in an initial public offering (IPO).

VC firms have a variety of ownership structures. The vast majority of VC firms are private companies formed by individuals, families, or small groups of investors. Very few firms are publicly traded companies; because of the nature of ownership, these firms tend to be larger than most VC organizations. Some firms are also limited partnerships formed by insurance companies or pension funds; these organizations generally achieve a greater rate of return on VC investments than on most of their other investments. Other firms are organized as bank subsidiaries, allowing banks to own equity in small businesses, though these firms are independent of other bank activities. Some firms are set up by corporations, although these are relatively rare. In other cases, corporations seeking high returns on their funds will invest in existing VC limited partnerships, where risk can be shared and liabilities are limited.

Competition for VC funding is extremely intense and, according to the National Venture Capital Association (NVCA), less than 1 percent of companies that solicit funds actually receive them. Generally, only firms with significant growth potential are considered; venture capital is not an option for small, individual-based businesses with less ambitious plans. The typical VC recipient expects sales in the tens of millions of dollars within the first years of their product or service reaching the market, with increasing long-term potential.

The VC firm must be confident that its investment will pay out according to the plans offered by the entrepreneur. Before making the investment, the VC firm thoroughly investigates the client and the client's business in a process called due diligence. Due diligence means extensive research into the industry, the entrepreneur's background and experience, and the reliability of the client's financial projections. Through the due diligence process, the firm tries to maximize its understanding of the opportunity, as well as its potential risks and rewards, and better prepares itself to make the best possible decision about the investment.

The efforts of most VC firms are focused within a specific investment profile that outlines their industries of interest, the stages of development of companies in which the firm is willing to invest, geographies of interest, and the expected investment range. By targeting investments within certain business types, the VC firm can develop a deep understanding of the industry and thus be better prepared to decide which new or expanding businesses are the superior investments. Some VC firms invest in computer software businesses; other firms selectively work with businesses in the medical devices field. Consequently, VC firms with such specialties turn away businesses that do not fit their area of expertise.

New ventures have been a major source of business innovation and creation, and they are often funded with venture capital. The VC industry has become big business. From 1985 through 2010, there were 1,673 VC firms founded and 4,347 funds raised, totaling $490.1 billion, according to NVCA reports. By the end of 2010, 791 firms managed 1,183 individual funds, and each fund was typically established as a separate limited partnership; capital under management by those funds was $176.7 billion. In 2010, total venture investment increased 20 percent from 2009 levels, from $18.3 billion to $22.0 billion.

In recent years, emerging information technology (IT) has dominated funds of venture management firms. In 2010, the IT industry class outperformed the next-highest-ranked class, medical/health/life sciences, at a better than two-to-one ratio, according to NVCA. Investments by U.S. state demonstrate the power of California, with 1,298 of the VC companies (39 percent of the U.S. total) and investment of $11,054.9 million (equaling 50 percent of the U.S. total for VC investment) in 2010. Massachusetts held second place, with 353 companies (11 percent of the total) and investment of $2,383.4 million (equaling 11 percent of the total), and New York ranked in third place, with 264 companies (8 percent of the total) and investment of $1,312.8 million (equaling 6 percent of the total).

Trends in the venture capital industry show that 2007 saw a post-bubble high, with figures reaching nearly $30 billion. The resizing of the industry's levels to $22 billion in 2010 followed the credit crunch and issues in the world economic market. However, resizing began following the technology bubble burst and was not unexpected. After years of taking on 1000 or more new companies annually, the industry in 2009 funded 772 first-time companies, and that count increased in 2010 to 1001. Regardless of actual numbers, it should be noted that each first funding represents a fresh commitment by venture capital funds to the future.

Monica J. Hagan
University of California, Los Angeles

See also Innovation Management; Innovation Management: Corporate; New Product Development; Venture Capital

Further Readings

Burrill, Steven and Craig Norback. *The Arthur Young Guide to Raising Venture Capital*. Summit, PA: Liberty House, 1988.

Finkel, Robert and David Greising. *The Masters of Private Equity and Venture Capital*. New York: McGraw-Hill, 2009.

Hosmer, LaRue Tone. *A Venture Capital Primer for Small Business*. Washington, DC: U.S. Small Business Administration, 2009. http://permanent.access.gpo.gov/gpo4954/pub_fm5.pdf (Accessed July 2011).

King, Donald C. and Robert L. Thornton. "Venture Management and the Small Businessman." *Journal of Small Business Management*, v.12/4 (1974).

Lloyd, Bruce, ed. *Entrepreneurship Creating and Managing New Ventures*. London: Oxford/Pergamon Press, 1989.

Loch, Christopher H., Michael E. Solt, and Elaine M. Bailey. "Diagnosing Unforeseeable Uncertainty in a New Venture." *Journal of Product Innovation Management*, v.25/1 (2008).

Wilson, John. *The New Venturers: Inside the High Stakes World of Venture Capital*. Reading, MA: Addison-Wesley, 1985.

VENTURE VALUATION

Venture valuation is defined as the act of determining the economic worth of a business, including current or future projected value. Valuation is generally performed in order to assign a price to equity in the company. There are different valuation methods, each of which can result in varying values; hence selection of the appropriate method should be based on where the firm derives its value and the level of uncertainty in the venture. The major valuation methods are discounted cash flow, risk-adjusted net present value, asset-based, market/comparables-based, Chicago venture method, option-based, and venture capital valuation.

In general, there are three main reasons for valuing a venture: raising capital or selling equity, selling the business, and tracking the progress of the venture. The valuation method greatly affects the assessed value. For example, an owner selling a venture prefers a high value, while an investor prefers a reasonable or low-value estimate. Additionally, proposed ventures can be evaluated using a rough form of valuation before any work is performed or investments are made.

Many factors create differences in the valuation of a venture. Owners always expect a higher venture valuation because they have an "ownership bias," and thus their espoused value is rarely accurate or realistic without considerable objective justification. Book value, which is the current value of the business based on the worth of its assets or revenues, may understate value, especially since it does not take into account growth trends. Market value, which is the market's average price, does not reflect the highest or lowest price someone is willing to pay. Finally, intangible assets such as brand trademarks or patents may have highly subjective values that are negotiable. "Goodwill" in a business purchase is the difference between the book value and purchase price and often takes into account the value of these intangible items. Consequently, the right valuation method is needed to uncover the underlying value of the venture in a fair, dependable, and reliable way.

Many valuation methods exist and can be categorized into (1) earning-based approaches, which include discounted cash flow, risk-adjusted net present value, and scenario-based methods; (2) asset-based valuation; (3) real-options-based valuation; and (4) market valuation approaches. Hybrid methods, such as venture capital valuation, use several methods simultaneously.

The earning-based valuation methods seek to value a business using its revenues, profit, or cash flow over a period of time, with the most popular being discounted cash flow (DCF). DCF calculates the sum value of future cash flows (usually at yearly increments of free cash flow) and discounts each year using the net present value calculation (NPV). The discount rate is at minimum the U.S. bond rate (risk-free rate) and may also include other things, such as the company's weighted average cost of capital and inflation. Another method, called risk-adjusted valuation, uses a discount rate (DR) equal to the risk-free rate plus beta times the risk premium (for example, 2009 start-ups in biotech have a RFR of 4 percent, risk premium of 7 percent, and beta of 2.5, resulting in a DR of 21.5 percent). The first downside of all earning-based valuation is their high sensitivity to differences in predicted cash flow or revenues, including projected growth rates. Second, they are highly dependent on accurate prediction of capital expenditures. Finally, they are sensitive to the discount rate used. Consequently, this method often fails to value new ventures that have disruptive or unique business models with unknown cash flows.

Asset-based valuation simply sums the value of the company's assets. Asset-based valuation is important especially if some "assets" of the new ventures are sought in an acquisition or if the company is undergoing liquidation. Asset-based valuation is also useful for companies with high asset values that are divided into tangible and intangible assets. Tangible assets include natural resources (like minerals), real estate, equipment, machinery, vehicles that are valued at their depreciated rate, cash and investments, and accounts receivable with prices based on market value. Intangible assets include intellectual property (IP), knowledge and capabilities, sales relationships, and Web assets. IP consists of patents, copyrights, trademarks, and trade secrets. Valuing patents is difficult and requires a detailed patent analysis, as well as an understanding of the patented area. Copyrights are valued based on the revenue generated. Valuing brands and their trademarks is usually done by estimating the cost to reproduce the brand presence and reputation. Finally, trade secrets are valuable only if they remain a secret, and their values are estimated via their competitive revenue benefits.

Other assets may also have value. Cisco Systems is famous for purchasing small companies for their patents and their talented employees. Sales relationships are also of value, especially when other companies want to enter a new market, and are valued by what the purchaser expects to profit from them.

Finally, Websites, domain names, and other Web assets contain value. Wikipedia contains a 100 percent open license content, yet the domain name is worth millions. E-commerce business Websites are a substantial part of the business's value. Automated valuation of these Web assets is expected to be the next major advance in these areas of valuation.

Scenario-based valuation (SBV) methods define a series of cases, which in combination are used to estimate the most likely value of the venture. The most common methods are the probability tree, the First Chicago Method, and Monte Carlo Simulation. The probability tree method is performed like a decision tree but uses major events and their probability to determine a firm's possible value. The First Chicago Method is the simplest and estimates a low (worst-case) average, and high (best-case) value for the firm, then averages them. Scenario-based valuation works well in biomedical start-ups where the chances of a major event (such as approval of a new drug by the Food and Drug Administration) can make or break the business. Furthermore, scenario-based valuations can use any of the other methods to compute the base value of the firm for each scenario.

The market valuation approach determines worth by comparing the venture and its assets to similar ventures that recently sold (also called valuation by comparables). This is common practice in real estate and automotive sales and works well for standard businesses such as franchises, restaurants, and hotels. Market valuation methods typically compare sales price to company revenues with a price-to-earnings (PE) ratio. For example, real-estate businesses in South Florida sell for between 3.5 and 5 times earnings. Typically the range of values is further refined through comparison to very similar businesses, but the range is open for negotiations. Some variations on the market valuation approach include comparing profits, considering return on assets (especially for asset-heavy businesses), or allowing for market share valuation (where inventors bid on shares of stock in a company, essentially performing a valuation similar to that provided by a stock market). One major downside of the market valuation approach is that it provides poor valuation for unique or atypical businesses, such as technology ventures. Even though market valuation can be the quickest to perform, it can often be affected negatively by market downturns.

Options-based valuation is the least used because of its complexity. Generally, it values the option to delay a business, abandon a business, or launch other ventures in that business's markets. For example, Microsoft favors this technique because it has allowed the company to value the X-Box venture, which lost money for the first three years but gave them the ability to enter and eventually dominate the multibillion-dollar video games market. In other words, how much would an investor pay to have the option to enter a possible billion-dollar market in three years in a market leadership position? This method uses uncertainty to its benefit, where options have great value in uncertain markets.

Venture-capital-based (VC-based) valuation uses a fixed sale date and price to determine the value of the company. It starts by estimating the terminal value of the company at some fixed date when it is acquired, goes public, or buys back the investor's shares. Then it uses the targeted rate of return (usually 30 percent to 50 percent) and the present value calculation to determine the company's current value less the invested amount. Unfortunately, this valuation method does not take into account poor business performance and assumes very high growth rates.

Brian Glassman
International Journal of Innovation Science
Abram Walton
Purdue University
Darrel L. Sandall
Purdue University

See also Bankruptcy; Cash Flow; Exit Strategies; Selling Successful Businesses; Venture Capital

Further Readings

Beaton, Neli J. *Valuing Early Stage and Venture Backed Companies.* Hoboken, NJ: Wiley Finance, 2010.

Holton, Lisa and Jim Bates. *Business Valuation for Dummies.* Hoboken, NJ: Wiley Finance, 2009.

Tim, Koller et al. *Valuation: Measuring and Managing the Value of Companies.* Hoboken, NJ: Wiley Finance, 2010.

WHOLESALE MARKETS

Wholesaling refers to all activities involved in offering goods and services for resale, for the manufacture of other products, and for general business use. A wholesaler is an individual or business that buys mostly from producers and sells mostly to business owners and companies, whether industrial, commercial, or institutional, or to other wholesalers or retailers. In the supply chain, wholesalers have an intermediary role between the manufacturer and the retailer. It is very common for some used products to be resold to retailers in wholesale markets; retailers then buy the products and sell them to end users.

In wholesaling, the amount of buying is generally in large quantities and selling is in smaller amounts. Wholesalers have warehouses where products bought from the manufacturer are stocked. Once a product is ordered, wholesalers manage their inventory in a way that allows them to send orders quickly and easily without delays. Keeping large inventories is risky; that is why good inventory management is essential for wholesalers.

As Philip Kotler stated, many of the nation's largest and most important wholesalers are unknown to final consumers. On the other hand, consumers are generally aware of retailers. According to Kotler, wholesalers fall into three major groups: (1) merchant wholesalers, (2) agents and brokers, and (3) manufacturers' sales branches and offices. Merchant wholesalers are the largest single group of wholesalers, accounting for roughly 50 percent of all wholesaling. Merchant wholesalers include two

Wholesalers buy stock in large quantities and store it in warehouses, where products are stocked and inventoried and then sold in smaller amounts. There are a variety of types of these companies in operation, yet many of the nation's largest and most important wholesalers remain unknown to final consumers. (Photos.com)

broad types: full-service wholesalers and limited-service wholesalers. Full-service wholesalers provide a full set of services, whereas the various limited-service wholesalers offer fewer services to their suppliers and customers. The several different types of limited-service wholesalers perform various specialized functions in the distribution channel. Brokers and agents generally specialize by product line or customer type. A broker brings buyers and sellers together and assists in negotiation. Agents represent buyers or sellers on a more permanent basis. Manufacturers' agents (also known as manufacturers' representatives) are the most common type of agent wholesaler. The wholesaling done in manufacturers' sales branches and offices is performed by sellers or buyers themselves, rather than through independent wholesalers.

In addition to these traditional types of wholesaling, there is another method: selling from online channels and Internet. This type of wholesaling is called business-to-business (B2B) transactions. B2B is used as a commerce transaction in businesses. In terms of new venture firms, venture capitalists work similarly, because venture capitalists bring entrepreneurs who want to fund their firms, which need cash money, to venture capitalists. Basically venture capitalists are the main funding body, inherently entrepreneurs and risk takers with innovative ideas who are looking for companies that need investment. New venture firms that are small and medium-sized are ideal for venture capitalists. Both entrepreneurs and firms want to earn money from the product or the service that they will sell or provide, and that product or service will be an innovation that has never before been developed.

Negative trends in wholesaling figures have been observed since the 1990s, especially during times of recession. Retailers, especially the large chains, prefer to buy directly from manufacturers and want to cut wholesalers from the supply chain, because it is cheaper to buy products directly from manufacturers than it is to use wholesalers. Retailers in general want to perform wholesalers' functions themselves, and in fact ordering and taking delivery directly from manufacturers have become easier than in the past, particularly with the advent of the Internet. Day by day, retailers are succeeding in dealing directly with manufacturers, and it is becoming difficult for wholesalers to compete. Some wholesalers may ultimately lose their customers and disappear from the market.

The North American Free Trade Agreement (NAFTA) encouraged wholesalers to expand their operations to Mexico and Canada, and similar conditions apply for the European Union (EU). As more countries have become involved with the EU, wholesaler markets have expanded their operations within the EU market. As the competition has increased, however, wholesalers have become increasingly eager to access different markets. The wholesaler's role is riskier than the retailer's, which is why wholesalers perform more competitively. Especially now that retailers and manufacturers are more powerful in economies, wholesalers no doubt will decline. New markets, new countries, and new systems present a

difficult environment for wholesalers. Although it is less risky for wholesalers operating in domestic markets, to succeed in today's economy new venture wholesalers will inevitably take on high risks if they are to have a chance of seeing high rewards.

As new ventures, wholesalers face growing competitive pressures, more demanding customers, new technologies, and competition from the direct buying programs in which large industrial, institutional, and retail buyers engage. As mentioned before, in the supply chain, the wholesalers are caught in the middle, with producers (manufacturers) on one side and retailers on the other. In this competitive environment, new venture wholesalers need new strategies, adaptations, and ideas, such as high-quality customer service, more customer-driven products, and other ways of adding value to their existing services. Like retailers, wholesalers must define their target markets and position themselves effectively. Some considerations include size of the customer (for example, only large retailers), type of customer (such as convenience stores only), and need for service (such as customers who need credit). Within the target group, new ventures can identify the more profitable customers, design stronger offers, and build better relationships with them. For example, they can propose automatic reordering systems, setup management training and advising systems, or even sponsor a voluntary chain.

Asli Tuncay-Celikel
Isik University and University of Sussex

See also Business-to-Business Marketing; Distribution; Retailing; Selling Products and Services

Further Readings

Boeker, Warren and Robert Wiltbank. "New Venture Evolution and Managerial Capabilities." *Organization Science*, v.16/2 (2005).
Bowersox, Donald J. and M. Bixby Cooper. *Strategic Marketing Channel Management*. New York: McGraw-Hill, 1992.
Carter, Nancy M. et al. "New Venture Strategies: Theory Development With an Empirical Base." *Strategic Management Journal*, v.15 (1994).
Kotler, Philip. *Marketing Management: International Edition*. Englewood Cliffs, NJ: Prentice Hall, 1997.
Kuratko, Donald F. and Jeffrey S. Hornsby. *New Venture Management: The Entrepreneur's Roadmap*. Englewood Cliffs, NJ: Prentice Hall, 2009.
Lambert, Douglas and James R. Stock. *Strategic Logistic Management*. Homewood, IL: Irwin Press, 1993.

Pride, William and O. C. Ferrell. *Marketing Concepts and Strategies*. Boston: Houghton Mifflin, 2000.

Ward, Getahn. "Firms Tell Suppliers to Trash Paper, Take Orders by Computer." *Commercial Appeal*, v.16 (1995).

WOMEN'S ENTREPRENEURSHIP

Gender is often the first feature a person notices in another person during face-to-face interaction, but researchers debate its relevance to entrepreneurship. On one side, the environmental selection pressures that new businesses face in competitive environments are unconcerned with whether founders are men or women. On the other, women are a powerful economic and creative force: Better understanding their entrepreneurial experiences can create increased prosperity and innovation if women entrepreneurs are currently underutilized or performing below their capabilities.

The research conducted thus far on men and women entrepreneurs has produced several noteworthy empirical findings. First, most entrepreneurs are men, but the number of women entering entrepreneurship has grown considerably in recent decades. Second, women's businesses are concentrated in service and retail industries, with few ventures in construction and manufacturing started by women. Third, women's businesses have smaller annual revenues than men's businesses and employ fewer workers than men's businesses. Women-owned businesses capture only a small fraction of equity financing in the form of angel capital, venture capital, or initial public offerings. Fourth, men and women have different types of human capital, albeit comparable levels of formal education. Human capital refers to the value acquired through education and experience that can be used to obtain financial resources through paid employment or entrepreneurship. Fifth, men and women exhibit marked similarity with regard to entrepreneurial motivations and behaviors.

Explaining Gender Differences

Candida G. Brush and her colleagues on the Diana Project identified four primary explanations found in the literature for why women entrepreneurs receive such a small amount of venture capital and are underrepresented among the most successful entrepreneurial firms. The first explanation is that the women's own preferences, human capital, and business acumen are incompatible with building high-growth businesses. Women are more likely than men to place an upper bound on the desirable size of their business and want to control the growth of their business. Women more often desire flexibility and the ability to balance their work and family life through entrepreneurship than do men. Further, the type of human capital that women bring to entrepreneurship may be less attractive to equity investors when compared to the education and experience typical of men entrepreneurs. Women more often have educational backgrounds in the arts and natural sciences rather than in engineering or business. They often have less managerial experience compared to men entrepreneurs. The second explanation is that women start businesses that have limited growth potential and scalability. In other words, women disproportionately start businesses that are unattractive to investors. The third explanation is that women are relatively excluded from networks that provide access to financial resources. The fourth explanation is that venture capitalists are overwhelmingly male and prefer to work with male entrepreneurs. The researchers of the Diana Project found through their interviews with women entrepreneurs of high-growth ventures that women must first decide to pursue high-growth enterprises and then acquire the resources they need to pursue them.

The Embeddedness Perspective

Entrepreneurs, both women and men, are not isolated but rather embedded in relationships with others. Entrepreneurs' networks are an important part of their businesses, whether they form entrepreneurial teams and partnerships or simply receive assistance and support from people they know. Two types of networks receive special attention in the field of women's entrepreneurship: families and professional relationships.

Building expressive relationships, such as those with family and friends, can either facilitate or hinder entrepreneurial efforts. Family and friends can provide material resources, advice, and support but can also create demands that interfere with the demands of the venture. For women entrepreneurs, being married to an employed person will provide income to support themselves while they start the venture. Family members sometimes also provide labor at free or reduced wages. In these ways, family formation can provide advantages to women entrepreneurs.

However, marriage and parenthood have traditionally been associated with decreased labor force attachment for women. Therefore, women who leave the labor force for a period of time because of marriage or parenthood before they become entrepreneurs may find themselves in a disadvantageous position when they seek to start or grow their businesses. They have less human capital in the form of experience, less financial capital from accumulated wages, and less social capital from making and building social contacts through employment. Social capital refers to the value acquired through connections with other persons. Further, some mothers who are entrepreneurs start home-based lifestyle businesses to supplement the household's income as a means of achieving flexibility unavailable in many wage and salary positions. Although these businesses tend to generate low revenues, many women entrepreneurs work more hours than full-time employees. Therefore, home-based businesses do not always deliver flexibility to their founders. Families can also be important for women (and men) entrepreneurs because the family may be the basis for the founding team. In fact, many ventures cannot be classified as male- or female-owned because they are owned by members of a family of both sexes.

Building instrumental relationships with professionals in certain industries can provide entrepreneurs with access to helpful advice, inside information, and funding opportunities. Although women entrepreneurs exhibit similar behaviors to men entrepreneurs when building their professional networks, women can find themselves in a disadvantageous network position for securing resources for their ventures. Women are underrepresented in high-growth industries and in venture capital firms. Because of homophily, or the preference to interact with similar others, underrepresented women may be excluded from key networks.

Fostering Women's Entrepreneurship

The efforts to increase women's participation in high-growth entrepreneurship are varied. For example, many institutions have launched educational efforts to attract girls and young women to study entrepreneurship, engineering, and finance in the hope of increasing their entrepreneurial awareness and self-efficacy to fill the pipeline with future women entrepreneurs. Educational programs are also aimed at attracting adults of varied occupations to entrepreneurship. Some training programs help adults already pursuing entrepreneurship to acquire skills in areas of deficiency. Beyond education, many organizations direct efforts toward the development of women's social capital by providing opportunities for women to meet potential investors, lenders, suppliers, vendors, or other potential business partners. Mentoring programs link successful women entrepreneurs with novices and provide them with guidance and support. Springboard Enterprises offers training, networking programs, and forums to link women entrepreneurs to equity finance. In addition to programs aimed at individual women, some programs attempt to address institutional factors that may inhibit women's participation in entrepreneurship, such as child care provisions or tax and labor policy.

Although venture performance is typically measured by revenues, profits, and employment levels, researchers, policy makers, and social activists have also turned their attention to the value of women's participation in micro-enterprises that may only generate a few thousand dollars in revenue each year. In recent years, in both Western and non-Western contexts, fostering women's entrepreneurship has been pursued as an approach to address poverty. The reasoning is that the opportunity for poor women to generate income for themselves and their children will lead to improved health and educational outcomes necessary to escape intergenerational poverty. In the United States, entrepreneurial training has been offered to women leaving welfare (TANF, or Temporary Assistance to Needy Families) to start businesses including day-care services and salons. An example of one such program is the Edge Connection, housed at Kennesaw State University. Micro-lending programs, which offer loans with low principals but sometimes high interest rates, launched by organizations such as the Grameen Bank, Kiva, and BRAC, have become a popular way to finance the businesses of women, especially poor women.

A Critique on Studies of Women Entrepreneurs

As noted at the beginning of the entry, women and men entrepreneurs behave quite similarly: Their businesses have similar structures and predictors of success, they share similar career motivations, and they have similar personalities. Helene J. Ahl noted that researchers sometimes make "mountains out of molehills" by devoting so much attention to what are actually small differences among men and women entrepreneurs. For example, although women entrepreneurs' low desire for growth is often seen as a problem, most men entrepreneurs also do not desire high growth. In fact, most men and women entrepreneurs start small ventures that remain small. Because the small minority of entrepreneurs that do run fast-growing businesses are disproportionately men, the average for all men increases. Therefore, theorizing as to how gender explains why more women do not grow their businesses does not enhance our understanding of why so few men grow their businesses as well. In addition, more can be revealed by investigating differences among women entrepreneurs. Not only do individual factors such as the women's human capital, wealth, social networks, age, and family background affect entrepreneurial behaviors and outcomes; contextual factors such as institutional environment, historical conditions, and cultural norms affect entrepreneurial behavior as well.

Amy E. Davis
College of Charleston

See also Family Business; Gender and Acquiring Resources; Gender and Industry Preferences; Gender and Performance; Home-Based Businesses; Microfinance; Minorities in New Business Ventures; Motivation and Gender; Social Networks; Women's Entrepreneurship: Best Practices; Work-Life Balance

Further Readings

Ahl, Helene J. *The Scientific Reproduction of Gender Inequality: A Discourse Analysis of Research Texts on Women's Entrepreneurship*. Copenhagen, Denmark: Copenhagen Business School Press, 2004.

Aldrich, Howard E. and Jennifer E. Cliff. "The Pervasive Effects of Family on Entrepreneurship: Toward a Family Embeddedness Perspective." *Journal of Business Venturing*, v.18 (2003).

Brush, Candida G., Nancy M. Carter, Elizabeth Gatewood, Patricia G. Greene, and Myra M. Hart. *Clearing the Hurdles: Women Building High-Growth Businesses*. Upper Saddle River, NJ: Financial Times Prentice Hall, 2004.

Ruef, M. *The Entrepreneurial Group: Social Identities, Relations, and Collective Action*. Princeton, NJ: Princeton University Press, 2010.

Shirk, Martha and Anna S. Wadia. *Kitchen Table Entrepreneurs: How Eleven Women Escaped Poverty and Became Their Own Bosses*. Boulder, CO: Westview, 2004.

Wilson, Fiona, Jill Kickul, and Deborah Marlino. "Gender, Entrepreneurial Self-Efficacy, and Entrepreneurial Career Intentions: Implications for Entrepreneurship Education." *Entrepreneurship Theory and Practice*, v.31 (2007).

WOMEN'S ENTREPRENEURSHIP: BEST PRACTICES

Women face the same challenges as their male counterparts in their entrepreneurial endeavors; in addition, they often must address gender-specific issues, most notably, limited access to capital and other resources. Commonly, they also must factor into their business practices greater demands in their personal lives, as they typically shoulder most childcare and household responsibilities. In light of this, female entrepreneurs have developed a number of highly effective managerial practices to enhance their competitive effectiveness and guide their business growth.

The management foundation for female entrepreneurs is laid in self-knowledge. They are aware of what drives them to succeed; they know their core competencies, as well as areas of weakness; and they fully understand their financial expectations and their level of risk tolerance. More so than men, many female entrepreneurs rely, at least in part, on their intuition to guide them in their business growth. They pay attention to their personal preferences, motivations, and expectations, and bring them to bear on new venture creation.

The forces motivating female entrepreneurs to launch a new venture are just as powerful as those of men but take a somewhat different focus, resulting in a leadership style that tends to be more collaborative. Entrepreneurial businesswomen know the value of leveraging empathy and listening skills to forge cooperative bonds with employees, customers, suppliers, and other entities critical to the success of their firms. Rather than adhering to the traditional top-down managerial hierarchy, women prefer a wheel model, with the business owner as the hub and subordinates and colleagues as the spokes. This approach assures more reciprocal interaction and enhances communication and teamwork. Many also form strategic alliances based on mutual benefit, as opposed to those geared solely to raise the standing of their own firms.

Female entrepreneurs look to both informal and structured networks to secure informational, material, and human resources for their firms. They recognize that early venture success, as well as long-term growth, is linked closely to the breadth and depth of their contacts. Informal peer advisory networks (often known as mastermind groups) complement national organizational networks such as the National Association of Women Business Owners (NAWBO). Many female entrepreneurs also engage in building robust virtual organizations, a networking approach that enables them to expand the scale or scope of their firms without extensive financial investment.

Financial matters, particularly access to capital, are critical issues for emerging women-owned ventures, as women still face cultural stereotypes in the world of finance. Female entrepreneurs overcome this obstacle by hand-picking a team of professional advisers (bankers, accountants, and attorneys) to guide them and to help them increase their knowledge base in this vital area. Some formalize this structure by holding regular business meetings of all their advisers, to ensure their efforts are consonant with the overriding goals of the venture; others prefer to communicate more informally, and on a one-on-one basis. Whichever form this collaboration takes, female entrepreneurs incorporate management of their advisory team as a regularly scheduled event.

Attending to such administrative matters means that female entrepreneurs make time management a central focus of their daily work. This is crucial, for typically women are striving to balance their long-term business goals with personal objectives to establish a better work-family balance. To achieve this dynamic, they institute processes and systems to handle repeated tasks, often incorporating state-of-the art technological means. They establish clear metrics for assessing managerial efficiency and effectiveness, and they evaluate performance on an ongoing basis.

Similarly, businesswomen conduct evaluations of their own personal development as entrepreneurs. A commitment to professional growth is crucial for female entrepreneurs, for many bring less business knowledge and management experience than men to their new ventures, a consequence of the historical concentration of women at lower levels of most organizations. Female entrepreneurs conduct skills assessments, often in conjunction with their advisers and peer networks. Based on what they learn, they set about updating their skills, particularly in technology, operations, and marketing, in a variety of ways, from reading to taking relevant courses (online and off) to seeking mentor advice.

Female entrepreneurs likewise regularly reexamine and refine their business practices, in order to keep up with the fluid and fast-paced economy of the 21st century. Because their businesses tend to be concentrated in competitive sectors such as retailing, personal care services, catering, and restaurants, these efforts involve attentive tracking of shifting consumer needs and tastes. Even as they embrace the risks inherent to these environments, female entrepreneurs often choose to introduce iterative modifications to their companies, such as adjusting a marketing program or tweaking a business model, rather than make wholesale, companywide changes.

Women make up one of the fastest-growing entrepreneurial populations in the world, and as such they are an undeniable economic, cultural, and social influence. However, there remains a paucity of research on women-owned businesses. According to Diana Project International, a global collaborative effort of scholars researching women's entrepreneurship, less than 10 percent of all research in the field focuses on women entrepreneurs. Since 1999, this group has been working to identify and learn more about female business owners and the growth of their ventures.

Terri Lonier
Columbia College, Chicago

See also Family Business; Gender and Acquiring Resources; Gender and Industry Preferences; Gender and Performance; Home-Based Businesses; Microfinance; Minorities in New Business Ventures; Motivation and Gender; Social Networks; Women's Entrepreneurship; Work-Life Balance

Further Readings

Brush, Candida G., Anne De Bruin, Elizabeth J. Gatewood, and Colette Henry. "Introduction: Women Entrepreneurs and Growth." In *Women Entrepreneurs and the Global Environment for Growth: A Research Perspective*, Candida G. Brush, Anne De Bruin, Elizabeth J. Gatewood, and Colette Henry, eds. Northampton, MA: Edward Elgar, 2011.

Coughlin, Jeanne Halladay and Andrew R. Thomas. *The Rise of Women Entrepreneurs: People, Processes, and Global Trends.* Westport, CT: Quorum Books, 2002.

Diana Project International. http://www.dianaproject.org (Accessed February 2011).

Kepler, Erin and Scott Shane. "Are Male and Female Entrepreneurs Really That Different?" Office of Advocacy, U.S. Small Business Administration, Washington, DC, September 2007. http://www.sba.gov/advo/research/rs309tot.pdf (Accessed December 2010).

Moore, Dorothy P. and E. Holly Buttner. *Women Entrepreneurs: Moving Beyond the Glass Ceiling.* Thousand Oaks, CA: Sage, 1997.

U.S. Senate, Committee on Small Business and Entrepreneurship. "Opportunities and Challenges for Women Entrepreneurs on the 20th Anniversary of the Women's Business Ownership Act." 110th Congress, Second Session, September 9, 2008. http://purl.access.gpo.gov/GPO/LPS110062 (Accessed December 2010).

WORK-LIFE BALANCE

Work-life balance involves employee prioritization of work and home life. The achievement of a work-life balance is a fundamental skill to be cultivated by employees (Greenblatt, 2002). This balance is not necessarily 50–50 for work versus home, nor does it remain constant across an employee's career.

Failure to achieve balance may result in the development of personal problems, including high stress and its psychological impact (such as depression) and physical effects (including fatigue, burnout, and a depressed immune system). The effects also may translate into organizational-level problems, including higher absenteeism and turnover, rising workers' compensation claims, and decreased worker productivity.

Historically, the achievement of work-life balance in U.S. organizations has become more difficult as workplaces have struggled to become more competitive, technologically advanced, and efficient. At the same time, more and more families either are led by a single person or have both spouses working outside the home. Thus, pressures are being exerted from outside the organization, within the organization, and within individuals as they tend to the demands of both work and home. Females in particular may experience heightened pressure, as they are more likely than males to be either a single head of a household or predominantly responsible for the household and childcare requirements. Still, more and more males are reporting the same struggle over work-life balance that females experience.

One consequence has been the choice of entrepreneurship by some as a means to better control the work-life balance. Women entrepreneurs, still taking on the lion's share of the childcare duties and domestic tasks, may in fact find that they have an advantage over other business owners because the many skills acquired through caregiving and managing a household can translate into valuable business practices.

More and more organizations are focusing on programs and practices that can serve to ease organizational pressure on employees and facilitate easier balance of work and home life. Several of these organizational initiatives have shown some promise.

Telecommuting is a program that permits certain employees to work all or part of their workweek from home. This arrangement can facilitate work-life balance, particularly helping to simplify life for those who care for family who are dependent upon them. Telecommuting can be especially helpful for employees who live long distances from the workplace. In fact, some research has indicated that employees who work all or part of their workweek from home are actually more productive than those who do not.

Because the telecommute can be such a dramatically different experience from the daily physical commute to work, it is recommended that organizations train and follow up with their telecommuting employees to be sure that they develop effective work habits designed to optimize their work and use of the program for work-life balance. For example, training programs can focus on the development of certain functional daily routines, such as taking a walk around the block at the start of the workday and then entering the home as if it were now the workplace, creating signal for the home-based employee to switch his or her mind-set to one focused on work. Home-based employees who do not learn functional skills or allocate a specific space that is for work only may feel that they now work 24 hours a day, seven days a week, with home inextricably linked to work. As a result, their experience of stress may actually amplify.

Another program that is designed to support employee work-life balance is job sharing, in which two people perform the same job, each working half time; one works certain hours of each day or certain days of the week, while the other works in a complementary fashion during nonoverlapping hours or days.

Still other organizational initiatives include employee assistance programs that offer psychological support to employees during times of crisis; workplace wellness programs that emphasize proper diet, weight maintenance, and exercise as means to heartier, more stress-tolerant individuals; and on-site childcare and eldercare programs, including provision of vans that pick older children up from school. Flextime permits the employee to work a certain core set of hours but have flexible start and stop times and is especially useful for those raising small children or caring for elderly parents. Finally, mentorship programs yoke accomplished senior personnel with early-career juniors.

Although it is recommended that employees utilize the resources provided by employers, it is essential that employees also take independent measures in the individualized management of their work-life balance. Various balance experts offer the following recommendations:

- Set clear priorities. List priorities and then make work and home choices that support these priorities. This serves to reduce ambivalence, guilt, and overcommitment. Achievement of a work-life balance itself should be a high priority. Priorities also make it easier for the employee to drop unnecessary activities.
- Be proactive in support of a private life. Make sure that schedules always include ample time for a personal life.
- Recognize that balance is not perfection.
- Be attuned to body and mind as signals regarding strain, stress, and overwork are sent.
- Organize. This is among the best ways to use time more effectively.

Work-life balance for the entrepreneur is especially problematic in the early days of start-up, when it may be challenging to give sufficient attention to home when work demands constantly present themselves. For the family-run entrepreneurial venture, experts highlight the need for flexibility and the importance of communication.

Maria L. Nathan
Lynchburg College

See also Family Business; Gender and Acquiring Resources; Gender and Industry Preferences; Gender and Performance; Home-Based Businesses; Labor Costs; Labor-Management Relations in Start-Ups; Motivation and Gender; Social Networks; Women's Entrepreneurship; Women's Entrepreneurship: Best Practices

Further Readings

BlueSuitMom.com. "Work-Life Balance for Executive Mothers." http://www.bluesuitmom.com (Accessed, December 2010).

Davenport, T. H. and K. Pearlson. "Two Cheers for the Virtual Office." *Sloan Management Review*, v.39/4 (1998).

Dempsey, Sarah E. and Matthew L. Sanders. "Meaningful Work? Nonprofit Marketization and Work/Life Imbalance in Popular Autobiographies of Social Entrepreneurship." *Organization*, v.17/4 (July 2010).

Fisk, D. M. "American Labor in the 20th Century." http://www.bls.gov/opub.cwc (Accessed December 2010).

Greenblatt, E. "Work-Life Balance: Wisdom or Whining?" *Organizational Dynamics*, v.31/2 (2002).

Griffin, M. A. and S. Clarke. "Stress and Well-Being at Work." In *American Psychological Association Handbook of Industrial/Organizational Psychology*, Vol. 3. Washington, DC: American Psychological Association, 2011.

Hammer, L. B. and K. L. Zimmerman. "Quality of Work Life." In *American Psychological Association Handbook of Industrial/Organizational Psychology*, Vol. 3. Washington, DC: American Psychological Association, 2011.

Martin, M. "College Tells Women Healthy Balance Is Key." National Public Radio (April 14, 2009). http://www.npr.org/templates/story/story.php?storyId=103073298 (Accessed February 2011).

Milligan, A. L. "Work-Life Balance Still a Juggling Act." *Crain's Chicago Business*, v.25/42 (2002).

Orser, B. and L. Dyke. "The Influence of Gender and Occupational-Role on Entrepreneurs' and Corporate Managers' Success Criteria." *Journal of Small Business and Entrepreneurship*, v.22/3 (2009).

Slate, B. G. "Insights for Working With Woman-Owned Family-Run Firms." *Solutions* (July/August 2007). http://www.fpanet.org (Accessed February 2011).

Sturges, J. and D. Guest. "Work/Life Balance Early in the Career." *Human Resource Management Journal*, v.14/4 (2004).

Work Life Balance Foundation. http://www.worklifebalancefoundation.com (Accessed December 2010).

Glossary

Adjective test list: A psychological test developed by Harrison G. Gough and Alfred B. Heilbrun intended to identify the personality traits of an individual; as the name suggests, the test is administered by having subjects select adjectives from a list of traits they believe describe themselves.

Agency theory: Part of contract theory, agency theory uses asymmetric informative game theory to analyze the relationships that arise when principals (one or more individuals) hire agents (other individuals) to perform a service and give the agents decision-making authority, with the principal rewarding the agents based on the quality and quantity of services. In such situations, all individuals may not have access to the same information, and it may be assumed that they have different interests that will come into conflict: for instance, the principal wants to maximize his wealth, whereas the agent wants to maximize his compensation.

American factfinder: A Website, http://factfinder.census.gov, maintained by the U.S. Census Bureau which provides demographic and economic data by geographic area.

Barriers to entry: Obstacles that prevent or impede the entry of competitors into a market; examples include capital requirements, government regulation, high demands for education or skills, and economies of scale that favor large, established firms.

Brainstorming: A method of creative problem solving developed by Alex Faickney Osborn. Brainstorming, often used in groups, focuses on generating a large number of ideas while withholding critical judgment of them, and combining and improving ideas before evaluating whether they will work for the problem at hand.

Compatibility: One of the characteristics that influence how quickly an innovation is adopted; it has two aspects, compatibility in terms of technical features (for instance, does software work with existing computer operating systems?) and social norms (for instance, a food product containing pork would be unlikely to achieve widespread adoption in a region where the population is predominantly Muslim).

Complexity: One of the characteristics that influence how quickly an innovation is adopted: generally, innovations that are perceived as easy to implement and integrate with existing structures and products will be accepted more quickly, whereas those perceived as difficult or complex will be adopted more slowly.

Cooperative growth: A hybrid type of growth of an enterprise through the use of networks and individual relationships to acquire and employ complementary resources.

Corporation: A formal business entity, governed by corporate law, that has some rights and responsibilities analogous to those of human persons (for instance, they can be convicted of criminal offenses) and that offers shareholders the protection of limited liability, meaning that if the corporation goes bankrupt the shareholders cannot be held liable (beyond their investment in the corporation) for the corporation's debt.

Creative class: A term developed by the economist Richard Florida to designate creative professionals in a variety of occupations, including marketing, scientific research, engineering, and accounting and finance, as well as art and music. Florida argues that creativity should be fostered because it leads to continuing economic growth.

Doing Business: A program of the World Bank Group, founded in 2002, that analyzes the regulatory environments applicable to domestic small- and medium-sized businesses in 183 economies around the world.

Employee life cycle: The path of an employee through an organization from initial contact (for instance, when the employee inquires about a job opportunity) to departure (for instance, to go to another job).

Entrepreneurial orientation: A construct, developed by Danny Miller and refined by Jeffrey Covin and Dennis Slevin, that characterizes the degree to which an organization is entrepreneurial or conservative. Dimensions of entrepreneurial orientation include innovativeness (a tendency toward new ideas and experimentation), proactiveness (a tendency to anticipate and act on future needs or wants), and risk taking (the willingness to commit resources to projects whose outcome is unknown and whose cost of failure may be high). G. T. Lumpkin and Gregory Dess add two more dimensions: competitive aggressiveness (the willingness and capability to engage in intense, head-to-head posturing) and autonomy (the ability and desire to act independently and with self-direction).

Evolutionary economics: An economic perspective that considers a firm as analogous to a biological organism, which can grow and adapt, with varying abilities to make the changes necessary to survive in changing environments. This theory also identifies stages of firm growth similar to stages of human development; moving through each requires dealing with a specific type of crisis.

Executive summary: A brief summary (from less than a page to a few pages) written in plain English that summarizes the main points of some document, such as a business plan or technical report.

Expectancy theory: A psychological theory stating that behavior is at least partly governed by expected outcomes; for instance, if an employee feels that hard work will lead to results, which in turn will lead to rewards (such as a raise), that employee is more likely to put forth effort on a project.

Expertise: A combination of knowledge, skill, and experience appropriate to a given domain that facilitates high performance in that domain.

External growth: Growth of an enterprise by non-organic means, most often mergers and acquisitions.

Family business: A business in which the founding family owns at least 50 percent of equity and members of the founding family (related through blood, marriage, or adoption) hold management positions in the company or sit on its board of directors. In the United States, family businesses generate about 78 percent of all new job creation and 60 percent of total employment.

Focus group: A research technique in which a group of people are asked to give their opinions about or reactions to a product or other subject of interest.

Franchise: A type of business in which the owner pays a fee for the right to replicate a business model, benefiting from name recognition of the business and a proven business model; examples of franchises in the United States include McDonald's (fast food), Great Clips (hair salons), and 7-Eleven (convenience stores).

Geographic information systems (GIS): A set of technologies that aid in the analysis and display of information linked to specific geographic locations.

Global Entrepreneurship Monitor (GEM): A research program, founded as a collaboration between Babson College and the London Business School, that evaluates the national level of entrepreneurial activity in (as of 2009) 56 countries.

Human capital theory: A theory formulated by Gary Becker that argues that investment in human capital, such as education and experience, may lead to an increase in productivity.

Import/export: A type of business that specializes in purchasing goods in one market for distribution in another, buying the goods from manufacturers (foreign or domestic), and reselling them on the import/export firm's own account.

Incoterms: Standing for "international commercial terms," terms of sale widely used in international commercial transactions. Examples include free on board (FOB), cost, insurance and freight (CIF), and delivered at frontier (DAF).

Industrial-organizational psychology: Also known as I-O psychology, a branch of psychology concerned with behavior in organizations and workplaces.

Initial public offering (IPO): The first time a company issues common stock to the general public.

Innovation diffusion: The process by which an innovation (such as a new product or service) is communicated to and adopted by potential users. The pattern of diffusion of innovation has been formally studied since at least the 1960s and tends to follow an S-curve (in terms of cumulative percentage of adoption) and a normal distribution (in terms of the numbers of users who take up the innovation over time).

KSAOs: An abbreviation for "knowledge, skills, abilities, and other characteristics," categories used to aid in specifying the qualifications required to do a particular job.

Locus of control: A concept in social psychology that classifies people according to how much control they feel they have over their lives, including their success or failure at specific tasks. People with a high internal locus of control believe that outcomes are based primarily on their own behavior; those with a high external locus of control believe that outside factors are more responsible for outcomes.

Management information system (MIS): A system for collecting, storing, and using information to support the goals of a company.

Market creation: Creating a new market for a product or service, a process that often coincides with technical innovations. Examples of successful new market creation include cell phones and applications for them, video games, and online auctions.

Mentalist theory: A type of cognition theory that argues that people have mental representations of themselves that help guide their behavior; for instance, a person with a mental image of herself as an innovative person would be predicted to be more likely to act on a new business opportunity.

National Association of Women Business Owners (NAWBO): An organization founded in Washington, D.C., in 1975 to further the interests of women business owners. As of 2009, it had more than 80 chapters and 7,000 members and was affiliated with the international organization the World Association of Women Entrepreneurs (Les Femmes Chefs d'Enterprises Mondiales).

New capabilities creation: A type of business opportunity in which a new capability offers a competitive advantage. Examples include the assembly line system of manufacturing adopted by the Ford Motor Company and the just-in-time manufacturing process, which Dell brought to the computer industry.

Novice: Someone who lacks the skill, knowledge, and experience that constitute expertise in a field or domain.

Observability: One of the characteristics that influence how quickly an innovation is adopted; products whose use or results are more visible are more likely to be adopted.

On-boarding: A process intended to help a new employee acclimate to an organization; this may include an orientation process to communicate company policies and values and the use of a mentor to help the employee learn about formal and informal structures in an organization.

Organic growth: Also known as "internal growth," the growth of an enterprise based on its own strength and using its own internal resources.

Patent thicket: Also known as a patent flood or patent cluster, a group of numerous related patents obtained deliberately to create a web of patents that serves as a protective barrier around a new technology; a patent thicket forces competitors to "hack through the thicket" in order to create competing new technology.

Planning fallacy: A cognitive bias, first discussed by Daniel Kahneman and Amos Tversky, which leads individuals to make overly optimistic predictions about the time and resources required to complete a project.

Primary data: Data gathered by the person who will use them—for instance, data collected from one's own business for use in a business plan or research data collected by the person who will also analyze the data.

Process theory: A type of cognition theory that argues that people perceive and transform information differently, and that some styles of processing may predict better success in, for instance, new ventures.

Product lifestyle management: An approach to product management which looks at the entire lifestyle of a product, from conception to disposal.

Product/service market creation: Creating new products to market, often by creating unique functionality. Examples include sports utility vehicles (SUVs), energy drinks, and smart phones.

Relative advantage: One of the characteristics that influence the rate of adoption of an innovation; it refers to the degree to which an innovation is perceived as better (on any dimension, including quality, price, and convenience) than other available competing products or services.

Resource-based view (RBV): An approach to strategic management that states that a firm's competitive advantage rests on the ability to capitalize on resources, including both tangible and intangible assets.

Retail markets: Markets in which products are sold directly to the consumer or end user, usually singly or in small quantities.

Rural Policy Research Institute (RUPRI): A joint program of the University of Missouri, Iowa State University, and the University of Nebraska to collect and disseminate information and conduct research to inform public policy relating to rural areas.

Secondary data: Data collected by someone other than the person who will use it—for instance, data collected by the federal government that may be cited in a business plan or analyzed for research purposes.

Self-efficacy: A concept within social cognitive theory in psychology: if a person has high self-efficacy about a task, that person is more likely to attempt it, believing that he or she can accomplish it satisfactorily.

Silicon Valley: A geographical area of California including the Santa Clara Valley south of San Francisco, which is home to many technology companies, including Apple, Oracle, Google, and Cisco; it was originally home to many silicon chip manufacturers and is often used to refer to the high-technology industry in general.

SMART: An acronym describing characteristics of effective goals: specific, measurable, attainable, realistic/relevant, and time-based.

Social entrepreneurship: The application of entrepreneurial principles in order to achieve social change.

Stage-gate process: A method of product development in which the process is divided into a number of stages, each bounded by a gate; when a stage is complete, the decision is made whether to move on to the next stage or not.

Stakeholders: A management term referring to all individuals and groups that have an interest in an organization's actions or policies and may be directly or indirectly affected by them.

Technology opportunity creation: A type of business opportunity based on a product that can do tasks in a revolutionary manner. This type of innovation is often the focus of venture capital. Examples include Velcro and Super Glue.

Time management: A set of techniques used to manage time in order to accomplish particular tasks or goals more efficiently.

Torrance Test of Creative Thinking: A series of tests developed by Ellis Paul Torrance, based in part on the work of Joy Paul Gilford, which are used to assess different aspects of creativity, including fluency, elaboration, and originality.

Triability: One of the characteristics that influence how quickly an innovation is adopted. A product that can be tried at low risk and low cost (as in the free trial periods that some software products offer) is more likely to be rapidly adopted.

TRIZ: A collection of problem-solving tools developed in 1946 by the Russian engineer Genrich Altshuller and colleagues; in English, the method is sometimes called TIPS, for Theory of Inventive Problem Solving. The TRIZ technique focuses on solving technical contradictions, focusing on the desired result rather than the current situation, functionality rather than solutions, and maximizing the use of all elements of the project.

Value proposition creation: A type of business opportunity in which a new value proposition is applied to existing services or products. An example is Southwest Airlines, which offered efficient and friendly airline travel at low cost for a market that did not value services (such as the right to have a reserved seat) that were built into other airlines' cost structures.

Virtual prototyping: A technique used in product development in which a virtual model of the product is created and tested using computer software before an actual physical prototype is created.

Wholesale markets: Markets in which goods are sold, usually in large quantities, to retailers or business users rather than directly to consumers.

Sarah E. Boslaugh
Kennesaw State University

Resource Guide

Books

Anderson, John. *Language, Memory and Thought.* Hillsdale, NJ: Erlbaum, 1976.

Becker, Gary. *Human Capital: A Theoretical and Empirical Analysis, With Special Reference to Education.* Chicago: University of Chicago Press, 1964.

Bennis, W. and B. Nanus. *Leaders: Strategies for Taking Charge,* 2nd ed. New York: HarperCollins, 2003.

Birkeland, Peter M. *Franchising Dreams: The Lure of Entrepreneurship in America.* Chicago: University of Chicago Press, 2002.

Braczyk, Hans-Joachim, Philip Cooke, and Martin Heidenreic. *Regional Innovation Systems: The Role of Governance in a Globalized World.* London: UCL Press, 1998.

Carsrud, Alan and Malin Brännback, eds. *Understanding the Entrepreneurial Mind: Opening the Black Box.* New York: Springer-Verlag, 2009.

Christensen, Clayton M. *The Innovator's Dilemma: When New Technologies Cause Great Firms to Fall.* Boston: Harvard Business School Press, 1997.

Csíkszentmihályi, Mihály. *Flow: The Psychology of Optimal Experience.* New York: Harper & Row, 1990.

Davenport, Thomas and Lawrence Prusak. *Working Knowledge: How Organizations Manage What They Know.* Cambridge, MA: Harvard Business School Press, 1998.

Drucker, Peter F. *Innovation and Entrepreneurship.* New York: Harper and Row, 1985.

Dugan, Ann. *Franchising 101: The Complete Guide to Evaluating, Buying, and Growing Your Franchised Business.* Chicago: Dearborn Financial, 1998.

Dyche, Jill. *The CRM Handbook: A Business Guide to Customer Relationship Management.* Boston: Pearson Education, 2002.

Fiore, Neil A. *The Now Habit: A Strategic Program for Overcoming Procrastination and Enjoying Guilt-Free Play.* New York: Penguin Group, 2006.

Florida, Richard. *Cities and the Creative Class.* London: Routledge, 2005.

Florida, Richard. *The Rise of the Creative Class: And How It's Transforming Work, Leisure, Community and Everyday Life.* New York: Perseus Book Group, 2002.

Friedman, Milton. *Capitalism and Freedom.* Chicago: University of Chicago Press, 1962.

Gerard, George and Adam J. Bock. *Inventing Entrepreneurs: Technology Innovators and Their Entrepreneurial Journey.* Trenton, NJ: Prentice Hall, 2008.

Gray, Douglas. *The Entrepreneur's Complete Self-Assessment Guide.* London: International Self-Counsel Press, 1987.

Hackman, J. R., ed. *Groups That Work and Those That Don't.* San Francisco: Jossey-Bass, 1990.

Hayek, Friedrich A. *The Road to Serfdom.* Chicago: University of Chicago Press, 1944.

Heilbroner, Robert L. *Between Capitalism and Socialism.* New York: Vintage, 1970.

Judd, Richard and Robert Justis. *Franchising: An Entrepreneur's Guide.* Mason, OH: Thompson, 2008.

Katz, Jerome and R. Green. *Entrepreneurial Small Business.* Burr Ridge, IL: McGraw-Hill, 2007.

Kotter, John P. *Leading Change.* Cambridge, MA: Harvard Business School Press, 1996.

Kouzes, J. M. and B. Posner. *Leadership: The Challenge,* 3rd ed. San Francisco: Jossey-Bass, 2002.

Le Blanc, Raymond. *Achieving Objectives Made Easy! Practical Goal Setting Tools and Proven Time Management Techniques.* Maarheeze, Netherlands: Cranendonck Coaching, 2008.

Levi, D. *Group Dynamics for Teams.* Thousand Oaks, CA: Sage, 2001.

MacBride, Peter. *Living Ethically.* Blacklick, OH: McGraw-Hill, 2008.

Maslow, A. H. *The Farther Reaches of Human Nature.* New York: Viking Press, 1971.

Moore, Dorothy P. and E. Holly Buttner. *Women Entrepreneurs: Moving Beyond the Glass Ceiling.* Thousand Oaks, CA: Sage, 1997.

Penrose, Edith T. *The Theory of the Growth of the Firm.* New York: Wiley, 1959.

Poutzioris, Panikkos, Kosmas Smyrnios, and Sabine Klein. *Handbook of Research on Family Business.* Northampton, MA: Edward Elgar, 2006.

Rand, Ayn. *Capitalism: The Unknown Ideal.* New York: Signet, 1967.

Reich, R. B. *The Work of Nations: Preparing Ourselves for 21st Century Capitalism.* New York: Alfred A. Knopf, 1991.

Robson, C. *Real World Research.* Oxford, UK: Blackwell, 2002.

Romano, R. and M. Leiman. *Views on Capitalism,* 2nd ed. Beverly Hills, CA: Glencoe, 1975.

Ruane, J. *Essentials of Research Methods: A Guide to Social Science Research.* Malden, MA: Blackwell, 2005.

Sayers, Janet and Nanette Monin, eds. *The Global Garage: Home-Based Business in New Zealand.* Melbourne, Australia: Dunmore Press, 2005.

Schumpeter, Joseph A. *Capitalism, Socialism, and Democracy.* New York: Harper & Brothers, 1942

Shannon, Claude E. and Warren Weaver. *The Mathematical Theory of Communication.* Chicago: University of Illinois Press, 1949.

Speser, Phyllis. *The Art and Science of Technology Transfer.* New York: John Wiley and Sons, 2006.

Steiner, I. D. *Group Processes and Productivity.* New York: Academic Press, 1972.

Sternberg, Robert, ed. *Handbook of Creativity.* Cambridge, UK: Cambridge University Press, 1999.

Suzuki, D. and H. Dressel. *Good News for a Change: Hope for a Troubled Planet.* Sydney, Australia: Allen and Unwin, 2002.

Thurow, Lester C. *The Future of Capitalism: How Today's Economic Forces Shape Tomorrow's World.* New York: William Morrow, 1996.

Utterback, James. *Mastering the Dynamics of Innovation.* Cambridge, MA: Harvard Business School Press, 1996.

Volkmann, Christine K., Kim Oliver Tokarski, and Marc Gruenhagen. *Entrepreneurship in a European Perspective: Concepts for the Creation and Growth of New Ventures.* Wiesbaden, Germany: Gabler, 2010.

Von Mises, Ludwig. *The Anti-Capitalist Mentality.* Princeton, NJ: D. Van Nostrand, 1956.

Ward, John L. *Perpetuating the Family Business: 50 Lessons Learned From Long-Lasting, Successful Families in Business.* New York: Palgrave Macmillan, 2004.

Weber, Max. *The Theory of Social and Economic Organization.* New York: Free Press, 1947.

Wheelan, S. A. *Creating Effective Teams: A Guide for Members and Leaders,* 2nd ed. Thousand Oaks, CA: Sage, 2005.

Zuboff, S. and J. Maxmin. *The Support Economy.* New York: Viking Penguin, 2002.

Journals

Academy of Management Journal
Administrative Science Quarterly
American Economic Review
American Psychologist
Annual Review of Psychology
Atlanta Business Chronicle
Business Horizons
California Management Review
Cambridge Journal of Economics
Education + Training
Entrepreneur
Entrepreneurship Theory and Practice
Environment and Planning A
European Journal of Information Systems
European Planning Studies
Family Business Review
Franchising World
Harvard Business Review
Human Communication Research
International Journal of Auditing
International Journal of Gender and Entrepreneurship
Journal of American Academy of Business
Journal of Applied Psychology
Journal of Business Research
Journal of Business Venturing
Journal of Finance
Journal of Financial Economics
Journal of Information Science
Journal of Law and Economics
Journal of Management
Journal of Marketing Channels
Journal of Personality and Social Psychology
Journal of Small Business and Enterprise Development
Journal of Technology Transfer
Management Communication Quarterly
Management Research News
Organization Science
Organization Studies
Organizational Behavior and Human Decision Processes
Pacific-Basin Finance Journal
Psychology and Marketing
Qualitative Health Research
Review of Quantitative Finance and Accounting
Small Business Economics
Small Enterprise Research
Social Psychology Quarterly
Strategic Management Journal
Technology Analysis and Strategic Management
Technovation
Venture Capital

Internet

American Association of Franchisees and Dealers: http://www.aafd.org

Angel Capital Education Foundation: http://www.angelcapitaleducation.org

Better Business Bureau: http://us.bbb.org

BizBuySell: http://www.bizbuysell.com

Bizwomen: http://www.bizwomen.com

Brandweek: http://www.brandweek.com

Diana Project International: http://www.dianaproject.org

Direct Marketing Association: http://www.the-dma.org

Entrepreneur.com: http://www.entrepreneur.com

Entrepreneur Connect: http://econnect.entrepreneur.com

Fambiz.com: http://www.fambiz.com

Franchise Expo: http://www.franchiseexpo.com

Franchise.com: http://www.franchise.com

Hoover's: http://www.hoovers.com

Kauffman Foundation: http://www.kauffman.org

Small Business Administration: http://www.sba.gov

Survey of Current Business: http://www.bea.gov/scb

TradePub.com: http://www.tradepub.com

U.S. Department of Labor, Office of Small Business Programs: http://www.dol.gov/osbp

VentureDeal: http://www.venturedeal.com

WomenEntrepreneur.com: http://www.womenentrepreneur.com

World Business Angel Association: http://www.wbaa.biz

Appendix

The following selected Websites, along with editorial commentary, are provided for further research in new venture management.

Center for the Advancement of Social Entrepreneurship, Duke University Fuqua School of Business

www.caseatduke.org

The Center for the Advancement of Social Entrepreneurship (CASE), based at the Fuqua School of Business of Duke University, is a research and education center focused on social entrepreneurship, defined (on the CASE Website) as "the process of recognizing and resourcefully pursuing opportunities to create social value." CASE was cofounded by J. Gregory Dees and Paul N. Bloom and seeks "to bridge the gap between business and the social sector, and between theory and practice, so that knowledge will be translated effective for use by front-line social entrepreneurs, nonprofit leaders, and philanthropists. CASE is also committed to building credibility for this field in academia."

Information available on the CASE Website falls into the following categories: information about CASE and related programs at Duke University, information and resources related to social entrepreneurship in general, and archives of previous CASE events (including video presentations by social entrepreneurs such as Martin Eakes, Jordan Kassalow, and Jacqueline Novogratz). The Website also aggregates news about CASE and related topics and provides a list of upcoming events, and the CASE blog "CASE Notes" (blogs.fuqua.duke.edu/casenotes) provides more informal notes about CASE and about social entrepreneurship in general.

The "Knowledge & Resources" section of the Website will be the most useful for those with a general interest in social entrepreneurship. Most of the resources in this section are related to CASE projects, knowledge development, and knowledge dissemination, and they are organized into six categories: the concept and process of social entrepreneurship, economic strategies for social impact, scaling social impact, social entrepreneurship case studies, Fuqua faculty research projects, and CASE working papers. Within each category, the Website provides a variety of information, from topic overviews intended for the novice to links to articles, book chapters, bibliographies, and other resources for scholars; many of the documents are available for free download. The case study section includes links to case studies, which can be downloaded for free in PDF format, on social entrepreneurship projects (31 as of 2011) authored or coauthored by CASE faculty. Two additional sections provide information about general social entrepreneurship resources (e.g., links to other organizations involved in social entrepreneurship, and publications relating to social entrepreneurship), and community resources (information for the general public who are interested in social entrepreneurship and/or the CASE program).

The Website also includes information about educational opportunities available in social entrepreneurship at Duke, through the CASE and other parts of the university. Some of this information will also be useful to those with a more general interest in social entrepreneurship or who teach or study at other universities; for instance, syllabi for many courses related to social entrepreneurship, links to information about volunteer and internship opportunities, and information about careers in social entrepreneurship.

European Private Equity and Venture Capital Association

www.evca.eu

The European Private Equity and Venture Capital Association (EVCA), founded in 1983, is a nonprofit trade association that, according to its Website, "represents, promotes and protects the interest of the European private equity and venture capital industry" and whose goal is "to create a more favorable environment for equity investment and entrepreneurship." Based in Brussels, Belgium, the EVCA has over 1,200 European members and works in five main areas: representing the European private equity and venture capital industry, including engaging in dialogue with regulatory bodies and policy institutions; raising professional standards; providing networking opportunities through various events and workshops; enhancing professional development through training courses; and conducting and commissioning research, publishing quarterly and annual statistics on industry activity and performance, and maintaining a library of industry data and information.

Basic information about many issues of interest to those involved with venture capital (particularly in a European context) is available on the EVCA Website, and often this introductory information also includes links to white papers and other, more in-depth, treatments of the same issues. EVCA position statements for the years 2002–11 are available for free download; many of these are responses to current events, such as the European Union's 2003 Pension Funds Directive, or comments on the European Union's 2009 recommendations regarding SME (micro, small, or medium-sized enterprises) and how they would affect venture-backed companies. The EVCA updates (published three times per year) on tax and legal issues affecting the European private and venture capital industry are available for free download. Links to executive summaries and the full text of many research papers are also provided. Information about EVCA surveys is also available on the Website, as are issues of the *EVCA Barometer*, a monthly publication that presents information about an industry sector (e.g., life sciences, energy, and environment) based on EVCA surveys.

The EVCA "Toolbox" also provides both elementary and more advanced information about venture capital issues. This includes a glossary of terms, information about industry standards (including a downloadable copy of the June 2011 *EVCA Handbook: The Professional Standards for Private Equity and Venture Capital*), and a tutorial introduction to private equity, including downloadable copies of the EVCA special paper "Guide on Private Equity and Venture Capital for Entrepreneurs" and the European Commission's "Report of the Alternative Investment Expert Group: Developing European Private Equity."

New Ventures: Entrepreneurship. Environment. Emerging Media.

www.new-ventures.org

New Ventures, founded in 1999, is a center for environmental entrepreneurship within the World Resources Institute, a global environmental think tank based in Washington, D.C. The mission of New Ventures, according to its Website, is "to empower environmental entrepreneurs in emerging markets to develop market-based solutions that protect Earth's environment and its capacity to provide for current and future generations." New Ventures accomplishes these goals by "providing business development services to environmentally focused small and medium enterprises (SMEs) in emerging markets" and "addresses the key barriers to 'green' entrepreneurial growth by building in-country support networks for environmental enterprises and increasing their access to finance."

New Ventures has five key areas of interest: people and ecosystems (concerned with reversing environmental degradation and ensuring the environment's capacity to support life in the future); climate change (concerned with preventing further damage to the global climate system and helping people and the natural world adapt to climate change); markets and enterprise (concerned with using enterprise and markets to expand economic opportunity while also protecting the environment); access (concerned with guaranteeing public access to information about the environment); and institutional excellence (supporting the World Resources Institute's ventures). New Ventures has local centers in Brazil, China, India, Colombia, Indonesia, and Mexico (each of which partners with a local organization) and has worked with 346 enterprises since 1999 and facilitated over $225 million in investment. Funding for New Ventures is provided by a variety of private and public donors, including the Alcoa Foundation, Morgan Stanley, the Rockefeller Foundation, the U.S. Department of State, and the Dutch Ministry of Foreign Affairs.

The New Ventures Website provides basic information about environmental entrepreneurship but is mainly devoted to describing its own efforts in this field. Most useful is a searchable (by company, sector, environmental intent, and keyword) database of 80 of New Ventures' portfolio companies that provides basic and sometimes more detailed information about each enterprise. Examples of the types of companies listed in this database include Accura Bikes, an Indian company that manufactures and sells electric bikes (scooters); Beijing Kingbo Biotech, a Chinese company that produces herbal pesticides, insecticides, fertilizers, and herbicides (the herbal extracts are drawn from plants grown on the company's sustainable plantation in the Mongolian desert); Garper Energy Solutions, a Colombian company that measures and analyzes energy consumption to determine which energy-efficiency measures and equipment will be most useful; and T-Files Indonesia, an Indonesian company that develops turbines to generate energy from ocean and river currents.

World Entrepreneurship Forum

www.world-entrepreneurship-forum.com

The World Entrepreneurship Forum (WEF) is a global think tank that includes entrepreneurs working in economics, politics, academia, and the social sciences. The WEF was founded by the EMLYON Business School (a European business school with branches in France and China) and KPMG, a Netherlands-based international professional services firm. In 2010, two additional founding members joined the WEF: Nanyang Technological University and the Action Community for Leadership, both located in Singapore. The WEF describes itself, according to its Website, as "a global community of entrepreneurs who aim at shaping the world of 2050 with an entrepreneurial vision, creating wealth and social justice." The WEF has three aspects: a global think tank, an international network of entrepreneurs, and a center of expertise on entrepreneurship; it is currently (as of 2011) active in 55 countries.

The WEF Website includes information about its activities as well as news and information of general interest to those involved in or studying entrepreneurship. The WEF's major activities are its annual meeting (the most recent was held in Singapore in November 2011); the junior forums (forums organized by students, which have been held in a number of countries, including France, China, India, Pakistan, Indonesia, Argentina, and Kenya); and forums held by local chapters of the WEF (two such forums were held in 2011, in Argentina and in Chile). Some materials from these forums are available online, including a video from the 2010 forum and the program of the 2011 Singapore forum, a downloadable PDF document that includes general information about entrepreneurship and the WEF as well as the specific program and speakers. WEF white papers from 2009, 2010, and 2011 are also available from the Website.

The news section of the WEF Website aggregates information about entrepreneurial activity, including videos, news, professional articles, photographs, white papers, and press releases. The WEF also has a Twitter feed and a Facebook site that provide more information about its activities.

Sarah E. Boslaugh
Kennesaw State University

Index

Entry titles and their page numbers are in bold. Page numbers referring to figures or photographs are followed by (figure) or (photo).